[redacted]

Allan Buitendag
Jackson's
4A-Fe

HEARTLAND AND HINTERLAND

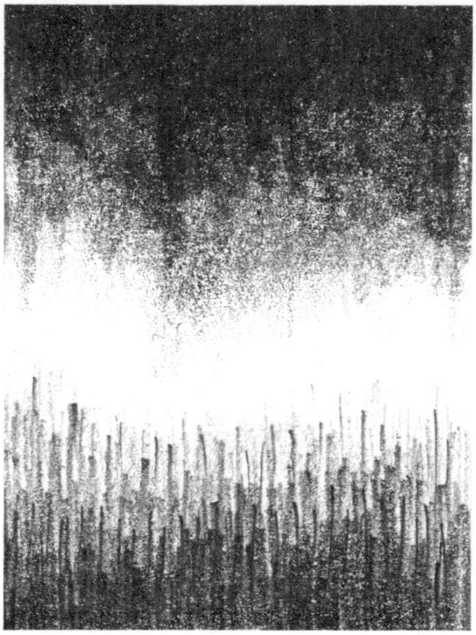

HEARTLAND AND HINTERLAND

A Geography of Canada

Second Edition

edited by L.D. McCann

Prentice-Hall Canada Inc., Scarborough, Ontario

Canadian Cataloguing in Publication Data

Main entry under title:
Heartland and hinterland : a geography of Canada

Includes bibliographical references and index.
ISBN 0-13-385154-0

1. Canada – Economic conditions – regional disparities. I. McCann, L. D. (Lawrence Douglas), 1945- .

HC113.H42 1987 330.971 C86-093836-0

Prentice-Hall, Inc., Englewood Cliffs, *New Jersey*
Prentice-Hall International, Inc., *London*
Prentice-Hall of Australia, Pty., Ltd., *Sydney*
Prentice-Hall of India Pvt., Ltd., *New Delhi*
Prentice-Hall of Japan, Inc., *Tokyo*
Prentice-Hall of Southeast Asia (Pte.) Ltd., *Singapore*
Editora Prentice-Hall do Brasil Ltda., *Rio de Janeiro*
Prentice-Hall Hispanoamericana, S.A., *Mexico*
Whitehall Books Limited, Wellington, *New Zealand*

ISBN 0-13-385154-0

Cover Design: Marcela Poblete-Gougain
Production Editor: Monica Schwalbe
Production: Matt Lumsdon
Cartography: Geoffrey Lester, Michael Fisher,
Stephanie Kucharyshyn, Inge Wilson,
University of Alberta, Edmonton

1 2 3 4 5 6 THB 92 91 90 89 88 87

Typesetting by Computer Composition of Canada, Inc.
Printed and bound in Canada by T.H. Best Printing Company Ltd.

Contents

Foreword to the Second Edition

It is fair to say that the first edition of *Heartland and Hinterland: A Geography of Canada* has received general acclaim as a book that extended traditional regional geography beyond the normal bounds of descriptive analysis. The first edition, in offering a broad synthesis of Canada's evolving regional geography from the heartland-hinterland perspective, placed interpretation high on its agenda. The intention was to make a unified and integrated statement about the structure of Canada's geography and the forces that shaped the various regional landscapes. The widespread acceptance of this approach has been gratifying, but in their assessments of the book, colleagues and students alike have also offered critical comments and suggested ways of improving our interpretation. Could we say more about the role of the physical environment in shaping the heartland-hinterland process? What about adding more descriptive passages to give a stronger sense of place to Canada's regions? Would provinces be more meaningful units for regional analysis? This second edition aims to improve upon the first by responding not only to questions like these, but also by up-dating material, adding new maps, refining the analyses, and of course, by seeking better ways of expressing the basic ideas of our arguments.

In this edition, too, contributors were guided by the heartland-hinterland framework in their assessment of a region's geographic character. Each contributor examines the economic and social development of the region to explain economic growth and change, the peopling and settlement of a region, and urbanization and the rise of cities. Essential in any analysis of the heartland-hinterland process is a discussion of the ways regions interact with each other — economically (e.g. capital flows and the movement of staple commodities and manufactured goods), socially and culturally (e.g. the diffusion of social values and cultural traditions), and politically (e.g. the organization and use of power). Each contributor has considered how these and other relevant relationships have shaped regional character. A region, of course, is a homogeneous segment of the earth's surface with physical and human characteristics distinct from those of neighbouring areas. As such, a region is sufficiently unified for its people to be conscious of its geographic character, that is, to possess a sense of identity distinct from those of other regions. The term regionalism refers to the collective distinctiveness of a region's characteristics and to a society's identification with a territorial unit. Regionalism is therefore shaped by the interplay of land, economy, and society; by the emergence of a group consciousness that voices regional grievances and demands; and by the behaviour of society as expressed most commonly through political actions. The fact that in Canada the heartland-hinterland process bears so heavily on the shaping of regional character means that many problems of regionalism must be analyzed from this perspective. Indeed, each author discusses significant problems of regionalism and assesses the effect of the heartland-hinterland process, relative to other factors, in determining the nature of these problems. Of course, there are other processes in addition to those associated with the heartland-hinterland mode that influence a region's geography, and all contributors have weighed these accordingly. But unifying all considerations is the heartland-hinterland theme.

All editors, I am sure, vow at one time or another, that they will never again become the steward of a collective enterprise. But such promises usually fade, and when Marta Tomins and Cliff Newman of Prentice-Hall suggested the need for a second edition, I found my enthusiasm rekindled to undertake the task. This, apparently, was also the case for the various contributors. All reassessed their chapters and offered revised essays. Several chapters, in fact, are newly conceived. To each and all, I again express my sincere thanks for a job well done. Many friends and colleagues, in ways often unknown to them, have offered the kind of on-going support that makes possible a book such as this. Particular thanks are extended to Alan Artibise, Stephen Bell, Paul Bogaard, Phil Buckner, Jack Bumstead, Peter Ennals, Ernie Forbes, David Frank, Bill Godfrey, Greg Kealey, Donald Meinig, Richard Preston, J. Lewis Robinson, Eric Ross, Jim Simmons, Peter Smith, Michael Staveley, Gil Stelter, John Warkentin, and Graeme Wynn. A grant from Mount Allison University's Research Committee facilitated the hiring of Stephen Maynard as a research assistant to compile data for several tables and maps. The manuscript was again read in its entirety by Alan Macpherson, whose many suggestions of substance and style have improved the quality of the text.

One of the greatest pleasures in preparing this new edition has been my further association with Geoff Lester and his "cartographic family" at the University of Alberta — Michael Fisher, Stephanie Kucharyshyn, and Inge Wilson. Their skills received deservedly high praise in reviews of the first edition, and many of the new maps have taxed their ingenuity even further. To each of you, for both your craftsmanship and friendship, thank you. Mary Ann Lorette, who helped type the first edition, mastered the nuances of word processing to take full charge of preparing the manuscript for the publisher. She will be missed as she moves on to her new job. At Prentice-Hall, Monica Schwalbe, through her superb editorial skills, did a masterful job of improving all aspects of the book. I now fully understand what it means when a writer states how invaluable an editor can be.

Since the first appearance of the book, the "little ones," Meaghan and Hugh John, have grown to the point where they now understand the meaning of the word metropolis. With my wife, Susan, they provide the warmth of family life that sustains my teaching and research. Our shared field trips have helped me in many ways to understand the meaning of the Canadian landscape.

This book is dedicated to two former teachers, Charlie Forward and Peter Smith, who have helped immeasureably in my education as a geographer and hence in my stewardship of this book. Charlie Forward was my undergraduate thesis advisor at the University of Victoria. He has continued to take an interest in my career, but I will always appreciate his efforts to improve my research and writing skills. My graduate training was guided by Peter Smith. For those of us who studied under him at the University of Alberta, the rewards have been many and lasting: we shared his depth of knowledge, strived to meet his high standards of scholarship, and gained from his firm but understanding guidance. For me personally, our association is now that of colleagues, albeit separated by a great distance, but his friendship over the years is one of the richest rewards of my academic career.

L.D. McCann
Sackville, New Brunswick
1986

CONTRIBUTORS

BRENTON M. BARR is a Professor of Geography at the University of Calgary. He holds a Ph.D. from the University of Toronto, where he wrote a thesis on the Soviet wood products industry. He has since diversified his research interests considerably, and has recently published extensively on the economic development of the Western Interior. He is a past President of the Canadian Association of Geographers.

JOHN H. BRADBURY received his Ph.D. from Simon Fraser University. He is now an Associate Professor at McGill University. An expert on the economy of resource towns, he is presently engaged in a major study of Canada's iron and steel industry.

ROBERT M. GALOIS has done research for the Historical Atlas of Canada Project and has taught at the University of British Columbia. His research interests focus upon resource developments and the restructuring of regional and international economies. He holds a doctorate from Simon Fraser University.

R. COLE HARRIS, Professor of Geography at the University of British Columbia, is the author of several books on Canada's historical geography including *Canada Before Confederation* (with John Warkentin) and *The Seigneurial System in Early Canada.* He is the Editor of Volume I of the *Historical Atlas of Canada* and is currently (1986-87) President of the Canadian Association of Geographers.

DONALD KERR, recently retired from the University of Toronto where he taught for many years in the Department of Geography, remains actively involved in the research of Canada's geography as Editor of Volume III of the *Historical Atlas of Canada.*

JOHN C. LEHR, Associate Professor of Geography at the University of Winnipeg, is a graduate of the University of Alberta where he wrote his dissertation on Ukrainian settlement in the Western Interior. His present research focuses on ethnic settlement patterns and vernacular architecture and he has published many articles on these subjects.

ALAN MABIN, who received his Ph.D. from Simon Fraser University, teaches geography in South Africa. His present research is concerned with the implications of apartheid for the peoples of South Africa.

LARRY McCANN studied geography at the University of Victoria and the University of Alberta and is now a professor at Mount Allison University. He has written widely on Canadian urban and regional development in the post-Confederation era, and is at work on a book about the nineteenth century Canadian city for Cambridge University Press.

PETER J. SMITH teaches in the Geography Department at the University of Alberta. He has served as Chairman of that department, is a past-President of the Canadian Association of Geographers, and edited *The Canadian Geographer* for many years. He is the author and editor of several books and writes extensively on planning history and urban development.

MICHAEL STAVELEY is Dean of Arts at Memorial University. He holds a Ph.D. in Geography from the University of Alberta and has published articles on the population and settlement geography of Newfoundland.

PETER J. USHER, whose main vocation is doing consultant work on northern affairs, has recently taught in the Department of Political Economy at the University of

Toronto. Since earning his Ph.D. from the University of British Columbia, he has published studies on the Canadian North. He is a contributor to the Historical Atlas of Canada Project.

ERIC WADDELL is a professeur titulaire at Laval University. His research interests range widely across cultural matters and he has published articles on the place of Québécois in the United States and Canada.

IAIN WALLACE, a graduate of Oxford University, is Chairman of Carleton University's Geography Department. He is the author of several monographs including *The Transportation Impact of the Canadian Mining Industry* and a soon-to-be-published text in the field of economic geography.

GRAEME WYNN earned his Ph.D. in Geography at the University of Toronto. An Associate Professor and member of the University of British Columbia's Geography Department, he is the author of the widely acclaimed *Timber Colony: A Historical Geography of Early Nineteenth Century New Brunswick* and many articles on Canada's evolving regional landscapes.

MAURICE YEATES is the author of many articles and books on the urban and regional geography of Canada and the United States. A former Dean of Graduate Studies and Chairman of the Department of Geography at Queen's University, he is now involved with aspects of post-secondary education for the government of Ontario.

For Charles N. Forward and Peter J. Smith

Teachers, Scholars, Friends

PART I
Introduction

1

Heartland and Hinterland: A Framework for Regional Analysis

L.D. McCann

Canada, like most countries, is continuously undergoing change. Since the mid-nineteenth century, the economy has expanded and diversified; society has urbanized; and political tensions have forged stronger regional identities. Throughout this metamorphosis, however, many features of Canada have proven to be remarkably durable. The production of natural resources continues to stimulate regional economies across the country, particularly in Alberta and British Columbia, but most secondary manufacturing industries and financial institutions remain firmly rooted in the towns and cities of southern Ontario and southern Québec. Such features mark Canada with the unmistakable, and enduring, pattern of heartland and hinterland.

The notion of a metropolis or heartland holding sway over a vast resource hinterland is germane to a discussion of Canadian life and letters, as exemplified in the writings of historians such as Maurice Careless,[1] and in the richly detailed studies of political economist Harold Innis.[2] It is in the Canadian tradition to speak of metropolis and hinterland. Geographers have not been averse to interpreting Canada in this context either, as Michael Ray has done on several occasions.[3] But until the first edition of this book, published in 1982, geographers had not offered a comprehensive interpretation of Canada's regional geography from this particular perspective.[4] Now, as before, there is considerable merit in using the heartland–hinterland approach. It accurately defines Canada's position in the world-system at large; it assigns geographical roles to the regions of Canada; it accounts for significant shaping forces of regional growth and development; and it focusses attention on the issues of regionalism — to cite several of its explanatory and interpretive advantages. Here, then, is ample justification for employing the heartland–hinterland approach to interpret Canada's regional geography. Not only have Canadian scholars long recognized the pervasiveness of the metropolitan influence over Canada's economy and society, and its role in the spatial ordering of the country's landscape, but the approach also readily lends itself to regional analysis.

By blending theory and empiricism, this introductory chapter outlines the heartland–hinterland approach as a framework for regional analysis and introduces important themes which are expanded more fully throughout the book. The chapter also emphasizes that to understand Canada's regional geography, an approach stressing change and development over time is essential, for regional character is the accumulation of both past and present geographies. By focussing on change and development since the late nineteenth century, we are able to identify the full impact of the heartland–hinterland process in shaping the regional geography of Canada.

HEARTLAND AND HINTERLAND: LANDSCAPES OF CONTRAST

As expressed in the literature on the subject, the heartland–hinterland dichotomy is also referred to as the metropolis–hinterland, core–periphery, centre–periphery, or centre–margin model,[5] and all are used synonymously throughout this book. Regardless of the pairing of terms, their meaning can be clearly defined by reference to certain economic, social, settlement, and political processes, as well as to geographic factors. Heartlands usually develop in areas which possess favourable physical qualities and grant good accessibility to markets; they display a diversified profile of secondary, tertiary, and quaternary industries; they are characterized by a highly urbanized and concentrated population which participates in a well-integrated urban system; they are well advanced along the development path and possess the capacity for "innovative change";[6] and they are able to influence and usually control — through the metropolis — economic, social, and political decisions of national importance. Hinterlands are characterized by the obverse: an emphasis on primary resource production; scattered population and weakly integrated urban systems; limited innovative capacity; and restricted political prowess. Hinterlands, therefore, are all the regions lying beyond the heartland whose growth and change is determined by their dependency relationships with the heartland. The heartland–hinterland model has been defined by John Friedmann as a "general theory of polarized growth" which is applicable at all geographic scales: international, national, or (in the case of Canada) provincial.[7] Just as the trading areas of central places overlap in a hierarchical fashion, so also do the spheres of influence of heartlands and hinterlands.

In their various ways, as recounted in the chapters of this book, factors of soil quality, vegetation cover, climatic condition, and physiography have all shaped patterns of human occupance, forming the physical milieu for heartland and hinterland development in Canada (Figs. 1.1 to 1.3). Canada's heartland in southern Ontario and Québec coincides with favourable physical characteristics. It occupies the Great Lakes–St. Lawrence Lowlands physiographic unit, which is endowed with rich grey-brown podzolic soils and a humid continental climate. Climatic conditions, particularly the number of growing days above 6°C (some 2000), warm summer temperatures, and frost-free days (more than 140) place Canada's heartland at a distinct advantage over hinterland regions in terms of supporting diversified agricultural production. The St. Lawrence and Great Lakes water system also affords the heartland the advantage of accessibility.

The hinterland regions generally display harsher or more limiting physical characteristics. The Cordillera, Interior Plains, Canadian Shield, and Appalachian regions yield tremendous resource wealth, but their soils, vegetation, and climatic patterns do not favour wide distributions of population and concentrated development. In the southern Interior Plains region, the vast flat landscape with its brown–black soils and dry continental climate is limited largely to grain and cattle production. Variability of precipitation creates seasons of drought, and early frosts and summer hail can spell disaster. In the Shield, the rugged terrain, severe climate, and vast wooded areas have made settlement difficult. Maritime resource production is also affected by the physical environment. Unless ocean water temperatures are near 5°C, cod will not spawn in inshore waters. Offshore storms and icebergs are a threat to the oil industry.

Population patterns across the country reflect the heartland–hinterland scheme. A little more than 25 000 000 people inhabit Canada's 9 970 000 square kilometres. Some three–quarters of them live in towns and cities, and nearly one of every three resides in metropolitan Toronto, Montréal, or Vancouver; but only one–eighth of the country is effectively occupied, and there are still large areas where no human has yet set foot. Agricultural societies emerged early in the Lowlands fringing the lower Great Lakes and parallelling the St. Lawrence River, and later appeared across the prairies and parklands of the Great Plains; but still, only about four percent of Canada is now cultivated, and it is estimated that little more will ever be useful agricultural land. In the Cordilleran region and across the massive Canadian Shield, population is scattered, hugging valley bottoms or staying close to transportation routes. Settlements appear in isolation — logging camps, lumbering towns, mining communities — fixed in space by the availability of forest and mineral resources.

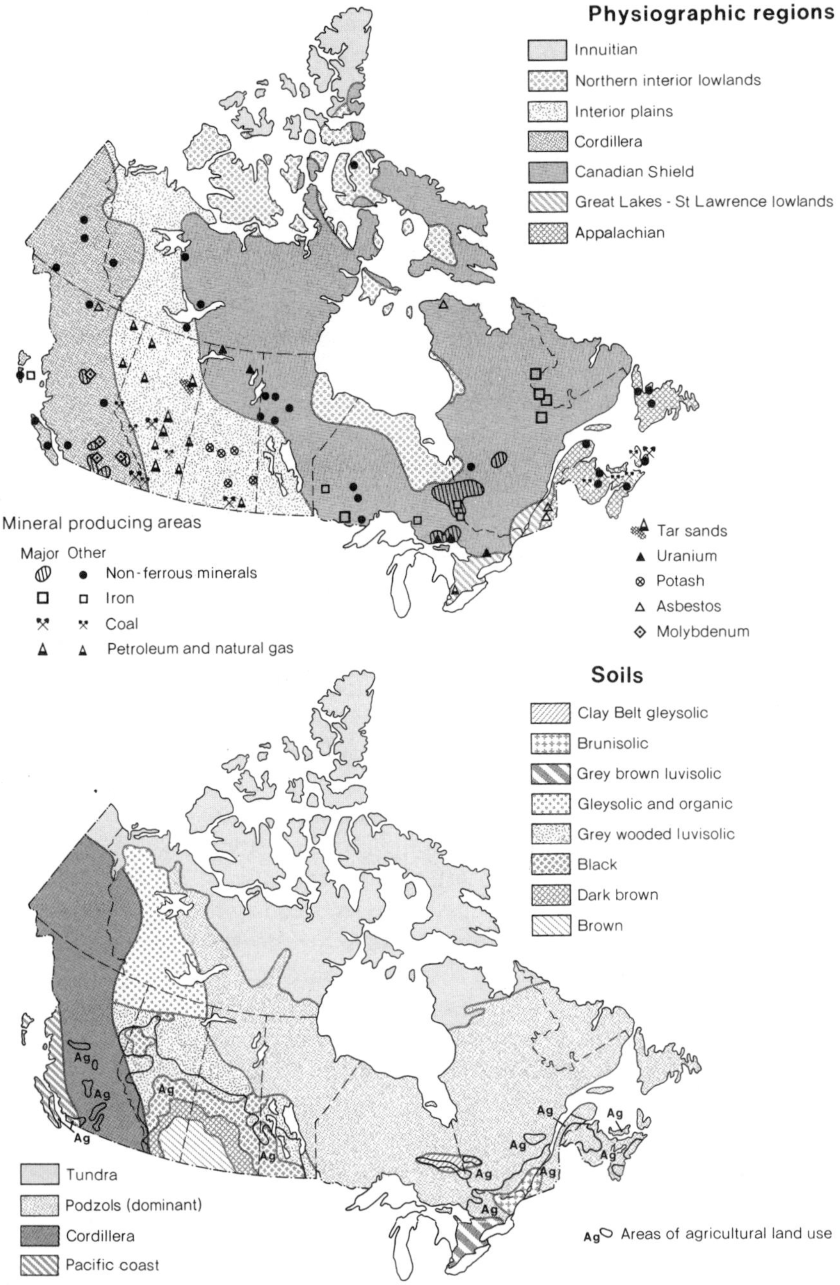

Figure 1.1 Physiographic and soil regions of Canada.

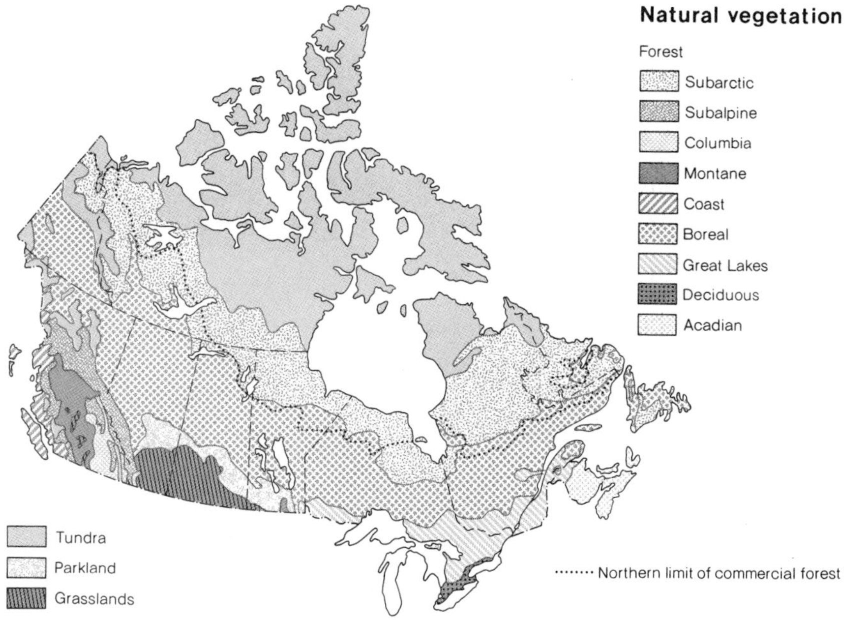

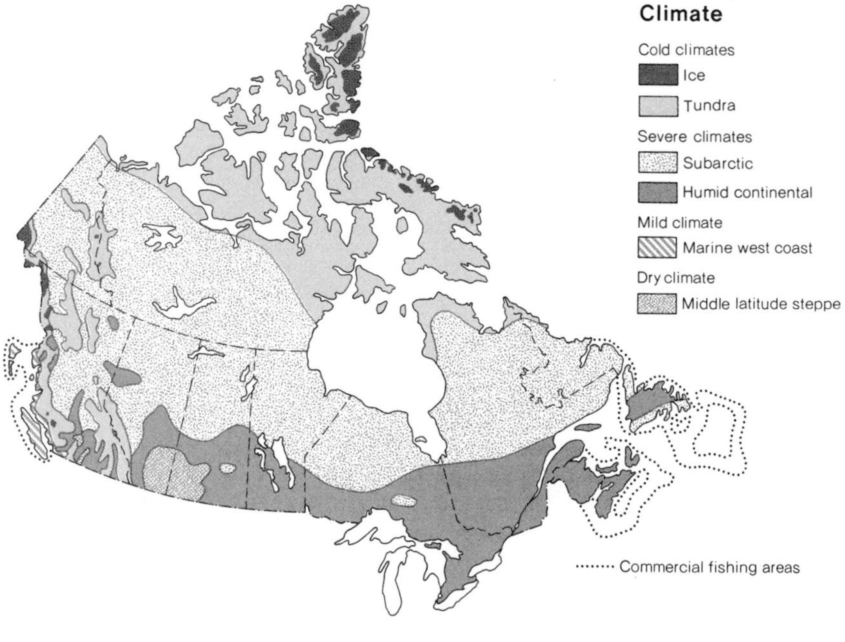

Figure 1.2 Vegetation and climatic regions of Canada.

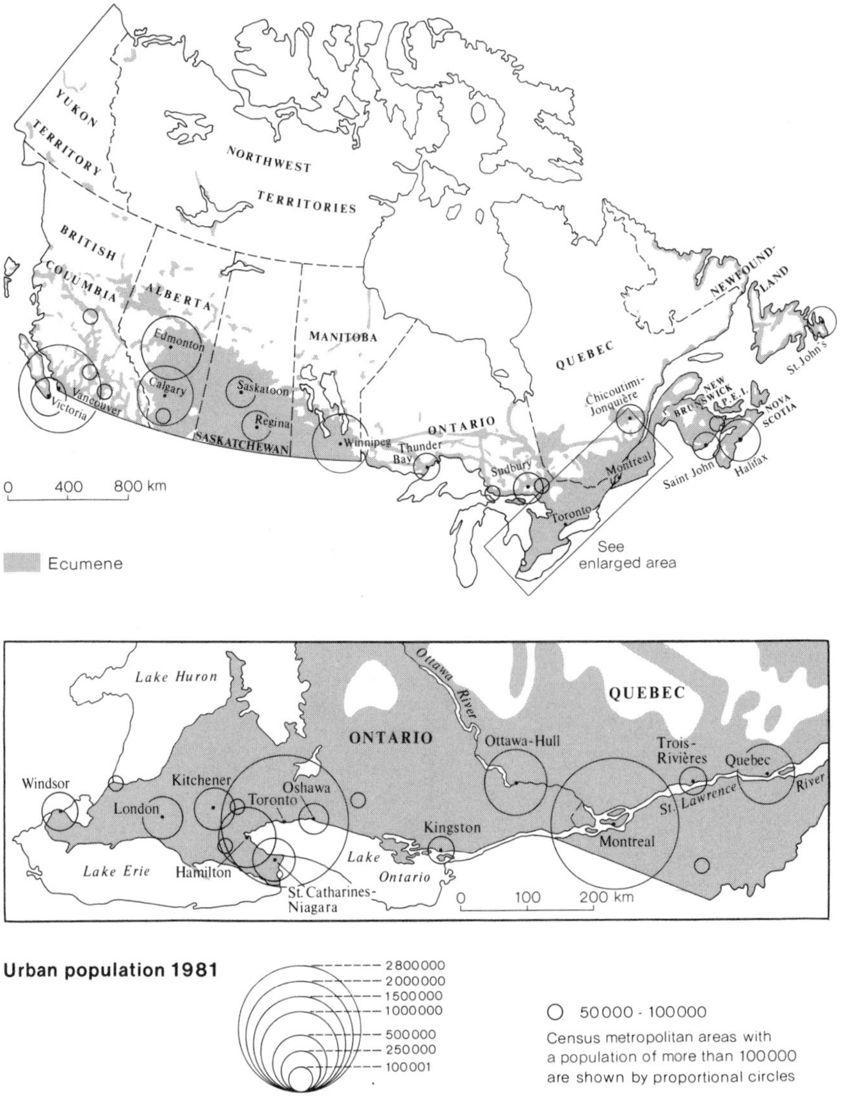

Figure 1.3 The Canadian ecumene and the distribution of urban population, 1981.

These settlement patterns are characteristic of the great resource-producing hinterlands of the country. Thus, the physical environments of Canada — the immense physiographic divisions, the broad sweeps of climatic variations, the diversity of vegetation types — influence population patterns and set the stage for distinguishing between heartland and hinterland.

Standing in sharp contrast to the bulk of the Canadian landscape, several densely populated regions have emerged as core areas where people have concentrated in large cities to manufacture goods and provide tertiary services for the surrounding countryside. These are the pivot points of Canada's regional geography. In the west, Victoria and Vancouver centre the Georgia Strait region of British Columbia; Calgary and Edmonton anchor a burgeoning development corridor in the heart of Alberta; and Winnipeg, which once controlled entry to the Western Interior, is Manitoba's primate city. On the east coast, a string of towns and cities, stretching from Saint John through Moncton to Halifax,

Resource production in the hinterland: Canada's regional geography is distinguished by staple production in single-enterprise communities such as this pulp mill at Dalhousie, New Brunswick. (*Larry McCann*)

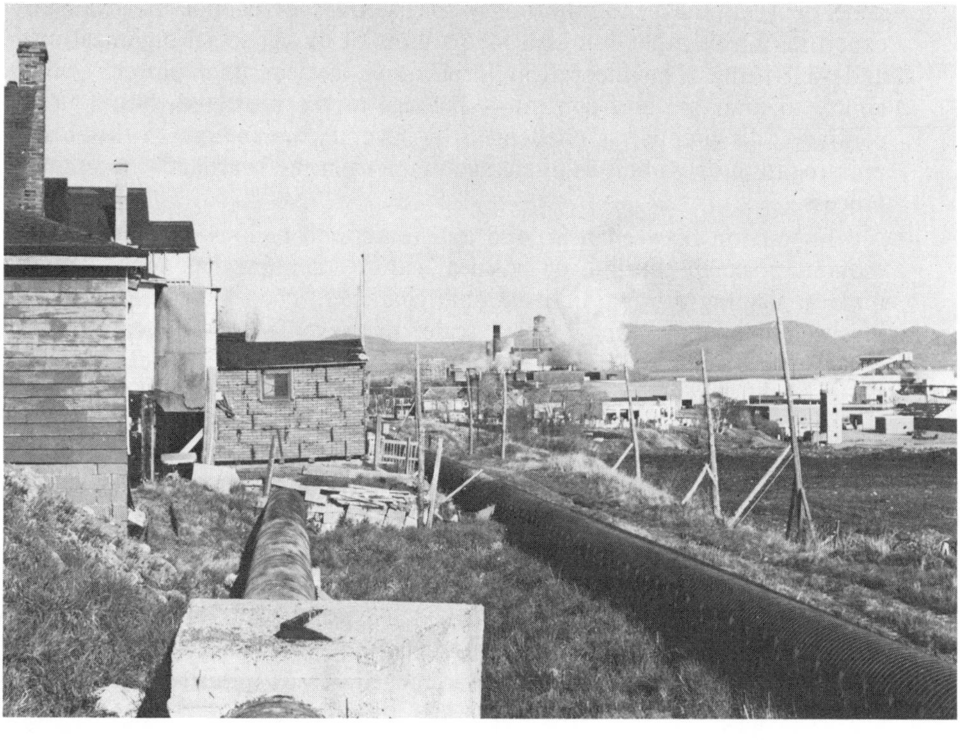

supports the development aspirations of the Maritimes; and in Newfoundland, St. John's alone plays the pivotal role. But standing above all others in national importance is the highly urbanized Windsor to Québec City corridor, the core of the Canadian ecumene, where the economy is diversified, population concentrated, and settlements interconnected. The regional structure of heartland and hinterland is a notable feature of the Canadian landscape.

THE HEARTLAND–HINTERLAND PROCESS

The basic forms of the heartland–hinterland relationship are indicated graphically in Fig. 1.4, which distinguishes staple-producing hinterlands from an industrial heartland.[8] It is the heartland that creates the demand for staple commodities, supplying the hinterland, in turn, with capital, labour, technology, and entrepreneurship, those factors of production which are so essential for the initial growth and sustained development of the hinterland. The heartland–hinterland model thus offers a framework for examining, at various geographic scales, the movement of people, goods and services, investment capital, and technology from one region to another, and of internal and external change over time. It also suggests that because the source of demand rests at the centre, the periphery is dependent on the centre not only for supplies of capital or technical expertise, for example, but also for patterns of living, social organization, and well-being. The theoretical implication is clear, that power — the ability to innovate and control — belongs to the heartland; but, to the contrary, this premise is challenged by several contributors to this text, pointing to the possibilities of change inherent in the heartland–hinterland process.

Interaction between heartland and hinterland regions, whether of an economic, social, cultural, or political nature, therefore has considerable force in shaping regional and national character. The following examples illustrate this point. On a world scale, the seventeenth and eighteenth century migrations of French and British peoples from European hearth areas established settlement patterns across eastern Canada that have persisted to the present; and the nineteenth century emigration of Maritimers to the "Boston States" records not only the powerful attraction of the American heartland, but also a declining regional economy. Even today, Canada exports billions of dollars worth of staple commodities (those raw materials or resource–intensive goods such as grains or wood pulp) to world markets — wheat to China and Russia, copper and coal to Japan, pulp and paper to the United States, asbestos to Australia — but comparatively few manufactured products or specialized services. Canada is therefore characterized as a hinterland source of industrial materials.

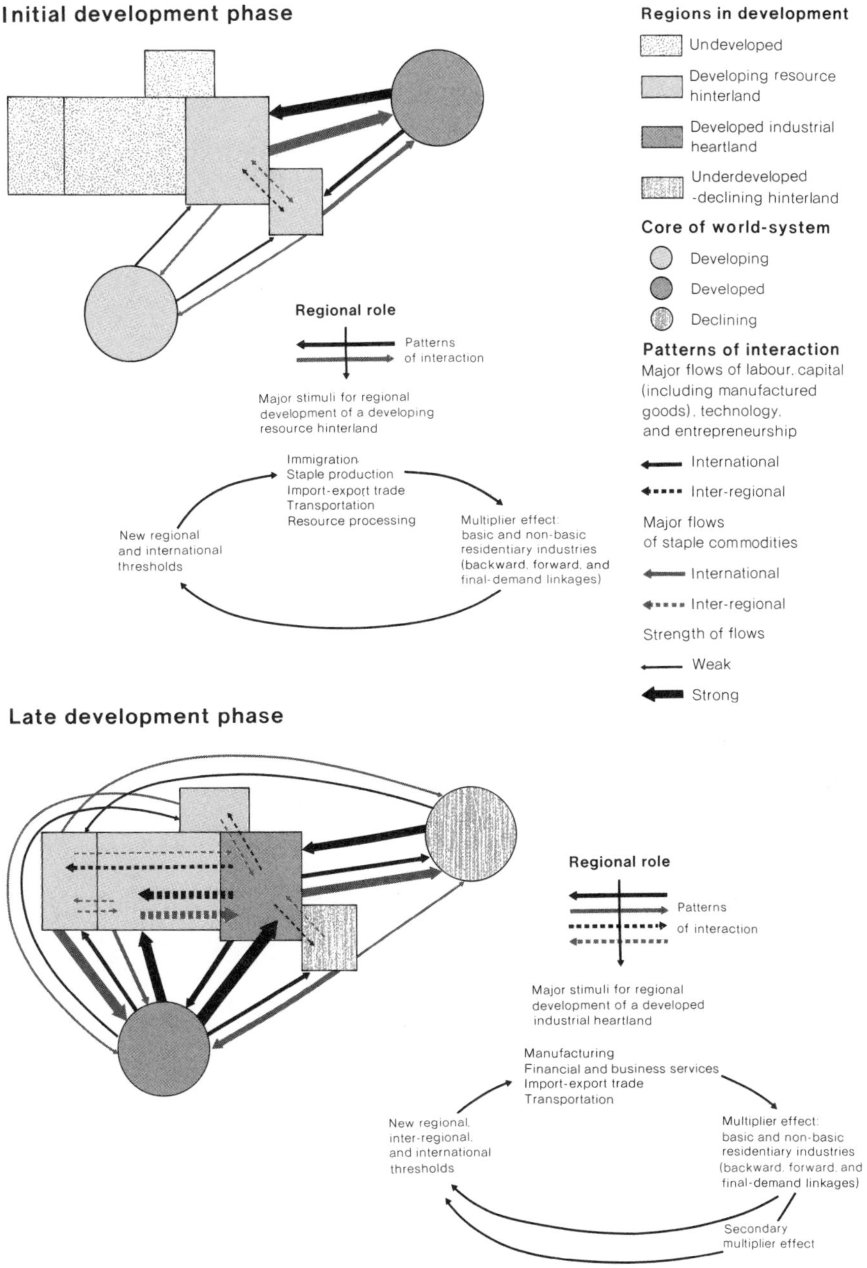

Figure 1.4 The process of regional development in a heartland and hinterland economic system.

But Canada's position in the world–economy is paradoxical, for it does send abroad a limited range of manufactured products, and it does invest directly in many foreign economies (see Figs. 2.4 and 2.5).

Indeed, heartland–hinterland interaction is, at times, a complex matter. Canada's hinterland areas, for example, ship many of their staple commodities directly to foreign customers, so that the goods neither pass through the national core nor use its business organizations. It can thus be argued that, to a degree, the Canadian heartland depends on the development of the periphery, not the other way around. Without the hinterland's demand for the core's goods and services, would central Canada be as prosperous or as important as it is today?[9] On the other hand, when the shipment of manufactured goods is considered, industrially important central Canada stands in marked contrast to the resource–oriented hinterlands — the heartland is the country's chief source of manufactured goods. In addition, the internal movement of goods within the heartland (including semi–finished, producer goods such as steel which are destined for further up–grading) is an indication of regional integration, giving added character to the Windsor–Québec City corridor as a highly specialized functional region.[10]

Regional structure, then, is the product of the interaction between heartland and hinterland areas at various geographic scales, and of the processes giving definition to each type of area. Locational forces and even policy decisions of a political nature draw secondary manufacturing and service activities, as well as a skilled labour force, to core areas. The further concentration of corporate headquarters and financial institutions there also causes a flow of profits from the hinterland to the heartland, making it difficult to raise development capital within the periphery. Such occurrences lie at the root of the hinterland underdevelopment problem, and are difficult to overcome without state intervention. But even then, government assistance through transfer payments, development projects, and other incentives is no guarantee that disparities between core and peripheral regions will narrow, let alone disappear.

If the disparities are to be diminished, it seems more likely that hinterland areas must develop generally according to the ways in which heartland areas have developed, although the specific growth factors need not, nor would they likely, be the same. For a region to achieve heartland status and therefore be capable of innovating change and wielding power, it must advance beyond the phase of merely supplying staples to an industrial core, generating, instead, through the multiplier process, a diversified industrial profile in most economic sectors (Fig. 1.4). By this process, linked industries emerge as spin–offs from the principal staple exports. The region must also become highly urbanized and develop an integrated city system. These developments will only come about when capital, derived from the export sector, is re–invested directly into a programme of regional economic diversification, providing, of course, that local or external markets warrant such a programme. At this point, the emerging heartland will begin to attract additional supplies of labour, investment, and technical expertise, not just to the export sector, but also to residentiary industries serving an internal market. As the regional market expands and region-serving activities proliferate, conditions may develop for self-reinforcing growth, and new internal factors — a decisive entrepreneurial group, for example — may become more important in determining the rates of regional growth. Internal growth will be reinforced as more industries are attracted by the external economies associated with overhead capital and the agglomeration or clustering of industries.[11]

The effect of such economic and population growth is to create new settlement patterns within the developing region. The structure of the settlement system will increasingly display visible signs of regional integration. Highway construction, rail and air networks, even communication flows, will show features of an internal core–periphery design. As the Alberta chapter vividly shows, such changes, built within the framework of provincial autonomy, can and do occur.

In Canada generally, the course of regional economic development and population growth has largely depended on the exploitation of a number of staple products and their export to world markets.[12] After Confederation, over half the country's labour force was still engaged in agriculture, lumbering, fishing, and mining activities, mostly in eastern Canada. These activities supplied a growing demand for lumber, fish, coal, and foodstuffs in Europe, the United States, the West Indies, and elsewhere (Table 1.1). Since the late nineteenth century, there has been a steady east-to-west progression of resource production because foreign demand has continued to increase, a transportation system has been put in place, and new staples have replaced exhausted supplies. This spatial progression across Canada has affected immigration, population shifts, manufacturing location, the build-up of cities, and social well-being.

In the context of our theoretical discussion of regional development, staple exports stimulated the development of the Canadian economy through spread effects. Income from the staple-based economy was used to manufacture consumer and producer goods and for specialized tertiary services, creating the basis for the emergence of a national industrial and financial core. Merchants invested heavily in a variety of manufacturing activities and founded banking and insurance companies throughout Ontario and Québec. Transport and route developments, the accumulation of agglomeration economies, entrepreneurial behaviour (particularly combination and merger practices and oligopolistic competition), factor immobility, and initial advantages in the guise of situation, relative accessibility, labour and capital availability, and tariff protection, have placed central Canada at a distinct advantage over peripheral regions. By the mid–1980s, as the labour force data in Table 1.1 show, Canada's traditional pattern of heartland and hinterland is still in place.

Canada's industrial core continues to attract the majority of foreign investment funds in secondary manufacturing and the business operations of multinational corporations, but its relative share of population and certain sectors of the economy has been slipping, particularly since the early 1970s. Since 1961, Ontario and Québec's share of census value added in Canada's goods–producing industries declined almost 10 percentage points, from about 70 to 60 percent; at the same time, Alberta's share almost doubled to over 17 percent, gaining 8 points since 1971.[13] Within the Heartland, Ontario has maintained its 50 percent share of manufacturing, but Québec has fallen back slightly from 33 percent to about one–quarter, a loss taken up by British Columbia's secondary forest industry. In fact, British Columbia now produces over half of Canada's total output of lumber, plywood, and pulp and paper. Like its other prosperous hinterland counterpart, Alberta, whose control of the mining sector has risen dramatically from less than one–third to almost two–thirds since 1961 as a result of oil and natural gas development, British Columbia is developing rapidly. Resource–generated wealth is transforming the hinterland structure of Canada's western provinces. Increasingly, immigrants and Canadians alike are heading west to live, ignoring the once magnetic pull of central Canada. The force of the flow may slow in response to world market conditions, as it has done in the mid-1980s, but the long–term trend is apparent. More importantly, these western provinces are using their new–found wealth not only to diversify the regional economy where that is feasible, but also to invest outside the region, as a core area would, through the formation of broadly–based corporations, a Heritage Fund, and government agencies.[14]

Regions vary widely in their capacity to achieve full development, and certainly in their ability to attain heartland status. Few regions ever achieve a position of dominance in an economic system. Not only is it difficult to overcome the cumulative advantages of an existing heartland, but a rationalized and diversified profile of economic functions, which might serve as a basis for heartland power, is unlikely to develop in a region which does not have good access to large external markets. Few regions are so blessed. All of those functions, such as manufacturing and wholesaling, dominated by important internal and external scale economies would be denied to such a region. The region would have to continue its growth and expansion through more limited but specialized activities and remain a hinterland. Its people might enjoy a high standard of living, but fully diversified development would be unlikely. With our concern in this book for regional development, this is an important point to keep in mind, particularly when we interpret the evolving geography of the Canadian hinterland.

TABLE 1.1 ECONOMIC DEVELOPMENT AND URBANIZATION IN CANADA, BY REGIONS, 1891–1978

	Gainfully Occupied by Sectors, 1891							*Population, 1891*		
	Percentage of Regional Total			*Total Regional Labour Force (000s)*	*Percentage of Canadian Total*					
Region	*Primary*	*Secondary*	*Tertiary*		*Primary*	*Secondary*	*Tertiary*	*Total Regional Population*	*Percentage of Canadian Total*	*Percentage of Regional Population Urban*
HEARTLAND										
Ontario	48.0	26.9	25.1	724.7	43.7	48.4	46.2	2 114 321	43.8	38.7
Québec	48.6	26.8	24.6	449.6	27.5	29.9	27.9	1 488 535	30.9	33.6
HINTERLAND										
Nova Scotia	54.2	20.3	25.5	156.5	10.6	10.1	10.1	450 396	9.3	17.1
New Brunswick	52.2	24.3	23.5	107.2	7.0	6.5	6.4	321 263	6.6	15.2
Prince Edward Is.	65.1	17.7	17.2	35.0	2.8	1.6	1.5	109 078	2.3	12.8
Maritimes	*54.8*	*21.4*	*23.8*	*298.7*	*20.4*	*15.6*	*18.0*	*880 737*	*18.2*	*16.5*
Manitoba	64.6	13.4	22.0	53.7	4.3	1.9	3.0	152 506	3.1	26.8
Saskatchewan	64.0	10.9	25.1	21.1	1.7	.7	1.3	—	—	—
Alberta	—	—	—	—	—	—	—	—	—	—
Western Interior	*64.4*	*12.7*	*22.9*	*74.8*	*6.0*	*2.6*	*4.3*	*98 967*	*2.0*	*.0*
British Columbia	40.7	29.6	29.7	47.2	2.4	3.5	3.6	98 173	2.0	39.9
Canada	50.0	25.3	24.7	1 595.5	797.7	403.2	394.6	4 833 239	—	31.8

TABLE 1.1 (continued)

	Gainfully Occupied by Sectors, 1929							*Population, 1931*		
	Percentage of Regional Total			*Total Regional Labour Force*	*Percentage of Canadian Total*					
Region	*Primary*	*Secondary*	*Tertiary*	*(000s)*	*Primary*	*Secondary*	*Tertiary*	*Total Regional Population*	*Percentage of Canadian Total*	*Percentage of Regional Population Urban*
HEARTLAND										
Ontario	25.2	32.2	42.6	1 423.8	25.6	44.2	36.3	3 431 683	33.1	58.7
Québec	26.5	31.4	42.1	1 082.0	20.5	32.6	27.2	2 874 662	27.7	58.6
HINTERLAND										
Nova Scotia	47.4	17.4	35.2	197.9	6.7	3.3	4.2	512 846	4.9	43.5
New Brunswick	44.9	18.3	36.8	142.3	4.6	2.5	3.1	408 219	3.9	31.1
Prince Edward Is.	63.9	9.0	27.1	33.2	1.5	.3	.5	88 038	.9	19.5
Maritimes	*47.9*	*17.0*	*35.1*	*373.4*	*9.4*	*6.1*	*7.8*	*1 009 103*	*9.7*	*36.3*
Manitoba	37.7	17.4	44.9	276.8	7.5	4.6	7.4	700 139	6.8	42.0
Saskatchewan	61.0	6.9	32.1	335.5	14.6	2.2	6.4	921 785	8.9	20.3
Alberta	55.0	9.6	35.4	286.6	11.2	2.7	6.0	731 605	7.1	31.1
Western Interior	*53.3*	*9.5*	*37.1*	*898.9*	*33.3*	*9.5*	*19.8*	*2 353 529*	*22.8*	*30.1*
British Columbia	51.8	10.9	44.3	337.9	7.8	7.6	8.9	694 263	6.7	55.4
Canada	34.0	25.3	40.7	4 116.0	1 398.7	1 039.7	1 677.6	10 376 786	—	49.7

TABLE 1.1 (continued)

Region	*Gainfully Occupied by Sectors, 1956*							*Population, 1956*		
	Percentage of Regional Total			*Total Regional Labour Force*	*Percentage of Canadian Total*					
Region	*Primary*	*Secondary*	*Tertiary*	*(000s)*	*Primary*	*Secondary*	*Tertiary*	*Total Regional Population*	*Percentage of Canadian Total*	*Percentage of Regional Population Urban*
HEARTLAND										
Ontario	11.2	38.8	49.0	2 148.2	24.6	44.8	37.6	5 404 933	33.6	75.9
Québec	16.1	37.9	46.0	1 598.2	24.3	32.5	26.3	4 628 378	28.8	70.0
HINTERLAND										
Nova Scotia	22.6	24.3	53.1	242.8	5.1	3.1	4.6	694 717	4.3	57.4
New Brunswick	25.3	25.1	49.6	180.4	4.3	2.4	3.2	554 616	3.5	45.8
Prince Edward Is.	40.4	16.4	43.2	36.6	1.4	.3	.6	99 285	.6	30.3
Maritimes	*25.1*	*24.0*	*50.9*	*459.8*	*10.8*	*5.8*	*8.4*	*1 348 618*	*8.4*	*50.6*
Manitoba	24.5	22.1	53.4	328.4	7.5	3.9	6.3	850 040	5.3	60.1
Saskatchewan	46.6	10.4	43.0	323.7	14.1	1.8	4.9	880 665	5.5	36.6
Alberta	34.6	17.7	47.7	387.4	12.6	3.7	6.6	1 123 116	7.0	56.6
Western Interior	*35.2*	*16.8*	*48.0*	*1 039.5*	*34.2*	*9.4*	*17.8*	*2 853 821*	*17.8*	*51.5*
British Columbia	13.6	29.0	57.4	483.0	6.1	7.5	9.9	1 398 464	8.7	73.3
Canada	18.6	32.6	48.8	5 728.7	1 066.9	864.7	2 797.1	16 080 791	—	66.6

TABLE 1.1 (continued)

Region	Labour Force by Sector, 1981							Population, 1981		
	Percentage of Regional Total[a]			*Total Regional Labour Force*	*Percentage of Canadian Total*					
	Primary	*Secondary*	*Tertiary*	*(000s)*	*Primary*	*Secondary*	*Tertiary*	*Total Regional Population*	*Percentage of Canadian Total*	*Percentage of Regional Population Urban*
HEARTLAND										
Ontario	4.4	28.1	62.8	4 548	24.2	43.0	36.0	8 625 110	35.4	81.7
Québec	4.3	25.5	62.8	3 100	16.1	26.6	25.0	6 438 400	26.4	77.6
HINTERLAND										
Newfoundland	9.4	22.6	60.1	232	2.6	1.8	1.8	567 680	2.3	58.6
Nova Scotia	7.0	20.3	67.0	388	3.3	2.7	3.3	847 445	3.5	55.1
New Brunswick	7.7	22.5	63.1	308	2.9	2.3	2.5	696 405	2.9	50.7
Prince Edward Is.	15.6	17.7	61.3	57	1.1	.3	.5	122 510	.5	36.3
Maritimes	*12.6*	*20.9*	*64.9*	*753*	*7.3*	*5.3*	*6.3*	*1 666 360*	*6.9*	*142.1*
Manitoba	10.0	18.6	67.2	510	6.2	3.2	4.4	1 026 245	4.2	71.2
Saskatchewan	21.7	12.6	61.3	461	12.1	2.0	3.6	968 310	4.0	58.2
Alberta	13.2	19.1	64.0	1 213	19.3	7.8	10.0	2 237 725	9.2	77.2
Western Interior	*14.2*	*17.6*	*64.1*	*2 184*	*37.6*	*13.0*	*18.0*	*4 232 280*	*17.4*	*206.6*
British Columbia	6.9	21.5	66.5	1 412	11.8	10.2	12.0	2 744 470	11.3	78.0
Yukon	11.5	9.1	71.1	13	.2	.04	.12	23 150	.1	64.0
N.W.T.	12.6	7.1	74.1	19	.3	.05	.19	45 740	.2	48.1
Canada	6.8	24.2	63.6	12 267	–	–	–	24 343 180	–	75.7

[a]These data do not add up to 100 percent because they exclude the share of the unspecified labour force.

Sources: Labour force data have been derived from information published in Alan G. Green, *Regional Aspects of Canada's Economic Growth* (Toronto: University of Toronto Press, 1971), Appendix C, pp. 102-7; Statistics Canada, *Labour Force Annual Averages 1975-78* (Ottawa: 1979), Table 10, p. 54; and Statistics Canada, *Census of Canada, 1981.* Green's analysis for 1891, 1929, and 1956 excludes Newfoundland. Population data have been compiled from information in *Census of Canada, 1891-1981.*

HEARTLAND AND HINTERLAND CITIES

Cities play a fundamental role in shaping heartland and hinterland development by integrating a region and giving it character. Let us turn then to a discussion of the distinctiveness of heartland and hinterland cities and the special roles of metropolitan centres. From a heartland–hinterland perspective, it is useful to think of cities as intermediaries, whose economic bases and functional roles stem from their handling of the factors of production as these move between core and periphery. Such interaction creates cities whose livelihoods depend on trade, transportation, manufacturing, or financial and business activities (Fig. 1.5).[15] Although both heartland and hinterland cities will perform these functions, the degree of specialization and the composition of economic sectors in each type of city will differ.

Consider these differences. It is unlikely that a hinterland city will have a fully diversified economic base, for depending upon the type and

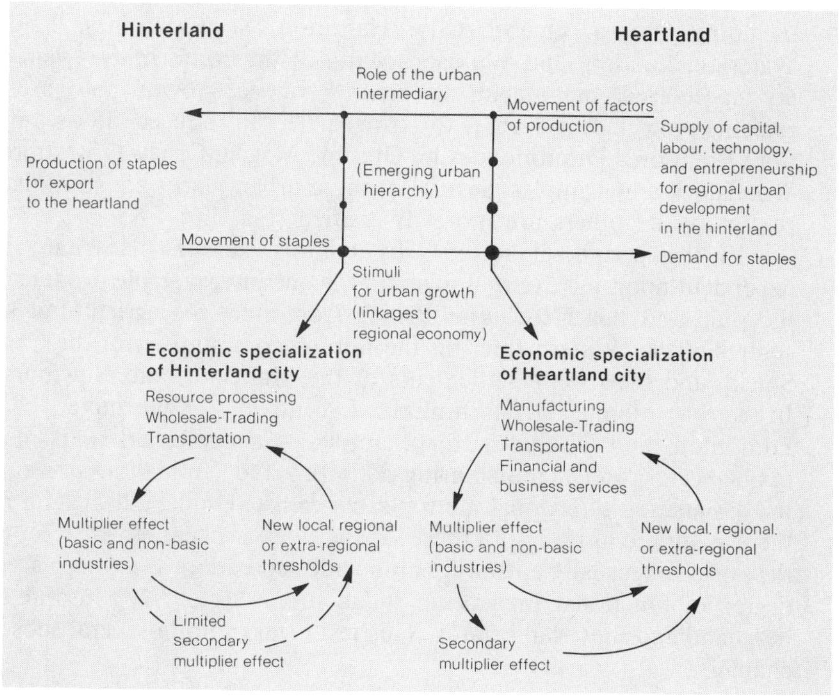

Figure 1.5 The process of urban growth in a heartland and hinterland economic system.

distribution of resources found within the periphery, cities there will function primarily as resource towns (forest products, mining, fishing, hydroelectricity), as central places (agriculture), as break-in-bulk or trans-shipment points, or in those exceptional situations where location or circumstance favours diversification, as multi-functional settlements. In most heartland cities, manufacturing is emphasized because the core's accessibility to national markets creates an initial advantage, making possible the manufacture of a wide range of primary, consumer, and producer goods. Such production in turn stimulates considerable regional employment and population growth. Manufacturing is supplemented in these primate centres by highly specialized financial and management activities. Manufacturers of consumer and producer goods are generally lacking in hinterland cities, just as they are in peripheral regions, because cities of the heartland can supply national markets more efficiently and economically.

Clearly, the attributes of cities — their size, functions, and regional settlement patterns — tell us a great deal about the geographic character of heartland and hinterland regions.[16] Without doubt, Canada's largest and most economically diverse cities are located in Ontario and Québec. Toronto and Montréal lead the way, but there are other important centres, including Ottawa, Québec City, Hamilton, St. Catharines, Kitchener, Waterloo, London, and Windsor. Many of the core's other urban places are specialized manufacturing centres whose growth and prosperity remains protected by a series of tariff barriers introduced after Confederation. Brantford, Drummondville, Granby, Magog, Oshawa, Stratford, and Woodstock are examples. Several of these urban places are administrative centres, while others are more diversified (Fig. 1.6).

In the peripheral regions, by contrast, urban places are largely dependent upon the external demand for one or two staple products, as in the pulp and paper towns of British Columbia, the agricultural service centres of the Western Interior, the mining communities of the Canadian Shield, and the fishing settlements of the Maritimes and Newfoundland. In a few of the larger hinterland centres — Vancouver, Calgary, Edmonton, and Winnipeg, for example — a combination of resource, public sector, and manufacturing activities and population size supports the designation of regional metropolitan centre. Unlike a heartland region, there is little clustering of cities, for the dispersed pattern of resources in the periphery usually encourages the wide separation of urban places. The degree of functional integration in an urban system is a useful test of heartland and hinterland status. This test is taken up in several subsequent chapters.

Central Place → is a key center (Edmonton → oil and grain)
Break in Bulk → change in method of transportation (Thunder Bay - change from boat to trains and trucks)

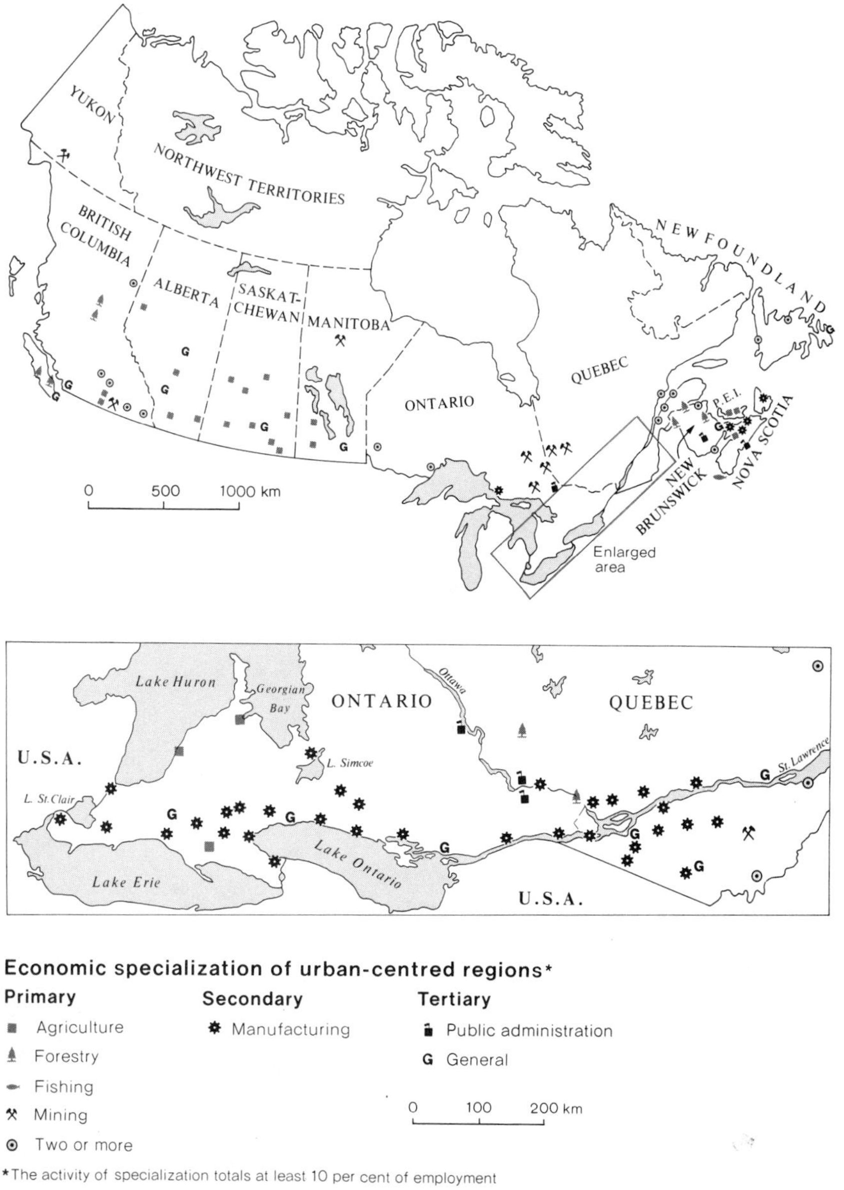

Figure 1.6 Economic specialization of urban-centred regions. (Adapted from James W. Simmons, "The Canadian Urban System," in L.S. Bourne, K. Dziewonski, and R. Sinclair eds., *Urbanization and Settlement Systems – International Perspectives,* London: Oxford University Press, 1984.)

THE ROLE OF THE METROPOLIS

Of Canada's many cities, there are several which, by the sheer weight of their importance, invoke use of the concept of metropolitanism. Maurice Careless, who has outlined the relevance of the concept for understanding Canada's historical development, has written that

> metropolitanism is at root a socio–economic concept . . . . [implying] the emergence of a city of outstanding size to dominate not only its surrounding countryside but [also] other cities and their countrysides, the whole area being organized by the metropolis, through control of communication, trade, finance, into one economic and social unit that is focussed on the metropolitan 'centre of dominance' and through it trades with the world. Political activity, too, may often become centred on the metropolis.[17]

The twentieth century financial metropolis: The Central Business District of Toronto, the major control point of Canada's heartland-hinterland system (*The Globe and Mail*)

In Canada, this definition of metropolitanism certainly applies to both Toronto and Montréal, and possibly describes the emerging power of Vancouver, Edmonton, and Calgary. Metropolitan centres have considerable bearing on the functioning of a heartland–hinterland system. They organize and give definition to a region. A metropolis operates from a position of acquired strength, achieved gradually through the successive attainment of trading, manufacturing, transportation, and financial roles. Because of its concentration of people, wealth, and economic activity, a metropolis takes a leading role in influencing the economy, society, and culture of a nation; but it is particularly through economic power that it binds a heartland–hinterland system together.

If the power of the metropolis is as all-pervasive as we suggest, it should be possible to measure the social and economic features of its strength, demonstrating that in such areas as manufacturing, financial, and corporate concentration, the metropolis dominates its competitors. From the evidence offered in Table 1.2, it is apparent that economic strength remains in the domain of the urban–industrial core of Ontario and Québec. Toronto is the main control point of the heartland–hinterland system, commanding nearly 50 percent of the non-financial sector of the Canadian economy, and far out-distancing Montréal (26 percent), Vancouver (5.5), Calgary (5.3), and Winnipeg (4). Not only is Toronto the overall leader, but it also ranks first in revenues earned by manufacturing, service, and resource industries. Montréal's only remaining concession to its one-time leadership lies in the realm of assets held by Canada's major banks and holding companies. In this sector, Montréal holds a very slight edge over Toronto; but in overall assets, the financial corporations of Toronto outperform Montréal by a ratio of 7:5.[18] As we enter the so-called "post-industrial age," Toronto's prominence will continue to gain momentum. The growing importance of access to skilled technical personnel and information will give Toronto the advantage over Montréal. The economic benefits of urbanization (e.g. more business contacts and better services) which favour only large metropolitan centres in post-industrial societies, have given Toronto the upper hand.[19]

This evidence raises two questions important for an understanding of the changing roles of heartlands and hinterlands. First, how do cities grow in size and economic status to become metropolitan centres? Second, are we justified in asserting that Vancouver, Calgary, and Edmonton deserve the status of metropolitan centre? Both questions are significant because the emergence of a metropolitan centre leads to the formation of a regional core–periphery system capable of innovating change on a broad geographic scale, and to the restructuring of longstanding dependency relationships between heartland and hinterland regions. Cities grow in size and prominence through natural population growth and immigration or by attracting new investment and employment opportunities. Over time, growth can become self-perpetuating and expansionary, particularly when

TABLE 1.2 LEADING CANADIAN CITIES CONTROLLING THE FINANCIAL AND NON-FINANCIAL SECTORS OF THE CANADIAN ECONOMY, 1977 (ranked by control of non-financial sector)

		Non-Financial Sectors[a]					*Financial Sectors*[b]	
Rank	*City*[c]	*Manufacturing*	*Service*	*Resource*	*Total*	*Percentage of Total*	*Total*	*Percentage of Total*
1	Toronto (H)	39 484	24 450	19 334	83 268	48.2	140 783	47.1
2	Montréal (H)	19 892	22 205	2 409	44 506	25.8	104 032	34.8
3	Vancouver (WP)	4 787	2 796	1 927	9 510	5.5	12 202	4.1
4	Calgary (WP)	897	1 267	6 968	9 132	5.3	6 887	2.3
5	Winnipeg (WP)	527	6 456	—	6 983	4.0	7 431	2.5
6	Windsor (H)	4 910	—	—	4 910	2.9	—	—
7	Hamilton (H)	3 113	524	—	3 637	2.1	545	.2
8	Ottawa (H)	524	1 571	—	2 095	1.2	2 270	.8
9	London (H)	1 276	660	—	1 936	1.1	8 276	2.8
10	Edmonton (WP)	131	1 144	32	1 307	.8	4 062	1.4
11	Sarnia (H)	1 029	—	—	1 029	.6	172	.1
12	Kitchener (H)	898	—	—	898	.5	2 388	.8
13	Sault Ste. Marie (NP)	687	92	—	779	.5	—	—
14	St. Catharines (H)	488	17	—	505	.3	—	—
15	Halifax (EP)	294	153	—	447	.3	1 064	.4
16	Cambridge (H)	288	—	132	420	.2	—	—
17	Saskatoon (WP)	304	—	109	413	.2	—	—
18	Thunder Bay (NP)	299	104	—	403	.2	—	—
19	Brockville (H)	363	—	—	363	.2	—	—
20	Saint John (EP)	—	110	210	320	.2	—	—
	Total	80 191	61 549	31 121	172 861	100.0	298 970	97.3[d]
	Percentage of Total	46.4	35.6	18.0	100.0			

[a]Controlled domestic and foreign revenues in millions of dollars.
[b]Controlled domestic and foreign assets in millions of dollars.
[c]H = heartland; WP = western periphery; EP = eastern periphery; NP = northern periphery.
[d]2.7 percent of financial assets are controlled by several other places.

Source: R. Keith Semple and W. Randy Smith, "Metropolitan Dominance and Foreign Ownership in the Canadian Urban System," *The Canadian Geographer*, 25 (1981), pp. 9 and 22.

income earned by local entrepreneurs from export activities is reinvested in the urban economy, spawning a more diverse profile of specialized manufacturing, tertiary, and quaternary services which supply and control external markets. But it is only when the emerging metropolitan centre becomes innovative, transmitting social values, political prowess, and economic control well beyond its traditional hinterland into a larger arena — in effect, challenging and recasting traditional dependency relationships in its favour — that it is clearly recognizable as a metropolitan centre.

Such a proposition surely applies to Vancouver, Edmonton, and Calgary, for each is increasingly drawing financial and corporate power away from central Canada. During the 1970s, Calgary's growth rates in financial transactions — for example, cheques cleared, stocks sold, business offices attained — out-stripped those of Toronto and Montréal. As seats of national corporate power, Vancouver headquarters many of the country's largest forest industry companies, and Calgary today houses over 85 percent of the Canadian-based exploration and production companies in the oil-and-gas sector. In this national context, Edmonton's political role has enhanced its metropolitan prominence, for government decisions are as crucial to regional development as the decisions made by large corporations. If there is validity in the popular notion that Canada's centre of gravity has shifted somewhat westward, the shift is bipolar — economic power towards Calgary, political power towards Edmonton. In the mid-1980s, the capital, technology, and corporate strategies of Calgary, Edmonton, and Vancouver — all fueled by newly acquired resource wealth — are being implemented well beyond the cities' traditional hinterlands in an innovative and controlling manner. These urban centres are recasting the traditional roles of heartland and hinterland regions in Canada.[20]

The metropolis is a powerful agent of change, and an examination of its deleterious actions may help in understanding Canada's regional geography, particularly the notion of regionalism. Regionalism is the expression, by the people or institutions of an area, of the values, interests, and concerns which are shared by the region's population. From an urban perspective, regionalism can be, on the one hand, an internal behavioural response to forces emanating from an external metropolis and, on the other hand, the use of internal metropolitan power to express regional character outside of the region.[21] At one level, then, the metropolis can cause underdevelopment or at least deindustrialization in the hinterland by restricting economic expansion there or by stealing away industries through what can be viewed as either rational economic processes or seemingly unjust policy decisions. Conversely, the metropolis is capable of adjusting levels of inequality through its support of various regional development programmes.

Several examples illustrate these different metropolitan actions. Some would argue that one policy decision in particular — the withdrawal of freight rate concessions immediately after World War I — was critical in creating the subsequent and longstanding depressed condition of the economy in the Maritimes. The explanation of the woeful state of Maritime well-being is much more complex, of course, but the regional expression of anger and distrust voiced against metropolitan interests in central Canada as a consequence of that railway policy, despite considerable federal assistance to the regional economy, illustrates that regionalism is a powerful and enduring element in shaping regional consciousness — in short, in forging a collective identity or creating a unified regional character.[22] Similar expressions by Québec separatists and Newfoundland fishermen, or Alberta's stand on the energy issue, have also forged strong regional identities. On an international level, the critics of American penetration of the Canadian economy by giant multinationals — of the actions of an external core or metropolis — are responding from the same emotional base. The only difference is that the term "nationalism" rather than "regionalism" is used when questioning issues of an international dimension. Often these responses are bounded by political space, and although the use of provincial boundaries for regionalization purposes can be questioned, it has been argued that "for all practical purposes 'province' and 'region' [in Canada] are now synonymous."[23] If this is so, one reason is that the provinces have become increasingly unified over time in their expression of regionalism.

At another level, the metropolis diffuses social and cultural processes, but with conflicting effects on regional character and regionalism. With today's use of the mass media and computer technologies, metropolitan-based values and norms spread rapidly. The corporate operations of Hollis Street in Halifax or Portage and Main in Winnipeg differ in scale but not in purpose from those of Bay Street in Toronto or St. James Street in Montréal. Even in suburbia, there is little to differentiate the regional cities of Canada, for the ubiquitous bungalow conforms to national housing standards. Notwithstanding Canada's ethnic pluralism, nor the tensions between English and French, the cities of Canada have, in a sense, coalesced in their social character. There is little evidence of regional protest against the social and cultural values of the metropolis, at least not at the urban level. Regionalism based on social and cultural issues tends to be more strongly rural in origin, and in these circumstances the protest can be directed as much against the regional city as it can against a national or international metropolis.

The overall effect has two possible consequences for an interpretation of the regional character of Canada: the rural and urban components of a region are either drawn together or pushed apart. Throughout its development, Cape Breton Island has at times displayed an uneasy tension with mainland Nova Scotia, but shared problems of economic disparity on a national scale now override past issues and pull the region together. The differences between northern Ontario, a resource hinterland for both national and international markets, and southern Ontario, a mature, post-

The nineteenth century industrial metropolis: With the completion of the Canadian Pacific's transcontinental railroad system in the mid-1880s, Montréal sealed its metropolitan role as Canada's leading commercial-industrial centre. (*Notman Photographic Archives*)

industrial society, run deeper and amplify the physical differences presented by the Shield–Lowlands interface that separates the areas.[24] At this level, therefore, the force of the national metropolis is replaced by rural–urban differences on a provincial scale.

THE EVOLVING PATTERN OF HEARTLAND AND HINTERLAND

One of the striking features of Canada's regional geography is that the roles of major regions have, at times, been significantly altered, and the heartland–hinterland approach provides a meaningful framework for analyzing regions in evolution. For this analysis, we will incorporate some of the themes discussed to this point in an overview of the changing pattern of heartland and hinterland in Canada, and thereby establish a context of regional development for the chapters that follow.

The first sign of an industrial heartland in Canada, with a national metropolis, integrated industrial complex, concentrated population, and political strength, appeared following the federation of some of the British

North American colonies in 1867. The pre–Confederation colonies, characterized by staple economies and a settlement system of rural farmsteads and scattered and loosely integrated staple entrepôts, garrison outposts, and commercial towns, were essentially hinterlands of a European core based in London. The urban settlements were chiefly the intermediaries of an Atlantic economy, because through them, and on to the frontier, flowed the immigrants, investment capital, and goods and services sent in exchange for commodities of the sea, forest, mine, and land. There were some important cities — Halifax, Saint John, Québec City, Montréal, and Toronto — but only Montréal had a substantial influence beyond its immediate hinterland. Moreover, because most people lived on farms or in small villages, rural localism and ties to the Atlantic economy were the most characteristic patterns. Although there were significant regional differences in the pre–Confederation period, these were basically between the land–based economies of the Canadas and the maritime orientation of Newfoundland, New Brunswick, Nova Scotia, and Prince Edward Island. No region had advanced to the stage in its development where it could stand alone as a heartland.[25]

With Confederation came increased social and economic interaction between regions, forming the basis for regional integration — railroad construction, interregional trade, a uniform legal structure — and with integration, in turn, came the centring force of a metropolitan presence (Fig. 1.7). The localism of communities tied to a trans–Atlantic hearth was partly undone and replaced by linkages to central Canadian leadership and innovation. New and successive political and resource frontiers were developed across Canada — Manitoba (1870), British Columbia (1871), Prince Edward Island (1873), and Saskatchewan and Alberta (1905). Mining and lumbering thrust into both British Columbia and the Canadian Shield and agriculture expanded into the Western Interior. Following these developments, the hinterland regions became attached primarily to Montréal and Toronto.

Within the world–economy at large, however, even central Canada remained peripheral. Nevertheless, the Canadian pattern of heartland and hinterland continued to intensify. Building on income derived from a relatively rich agricultural base and the staple trades, Ontario and Québec entrepreneurs used the National Policy of industrial incentives, first introduced in the late 1870s, to establish further strength in their manufacturing, transportation, and financial sectors. As Canada entered the twentieth century, factors of cumulative advantage — geographic situation, large local markets, the nexus of transportation routes, and political power — continued to reinforce the heartland status of central Canada. The expanding urban places of southern Ontario and southern Québec, the result of an intensive period of industrial–led urbanization, acted in unison as a core system to wield substantial control over the developing resource hinterlands of the Shield and the West, and to bring

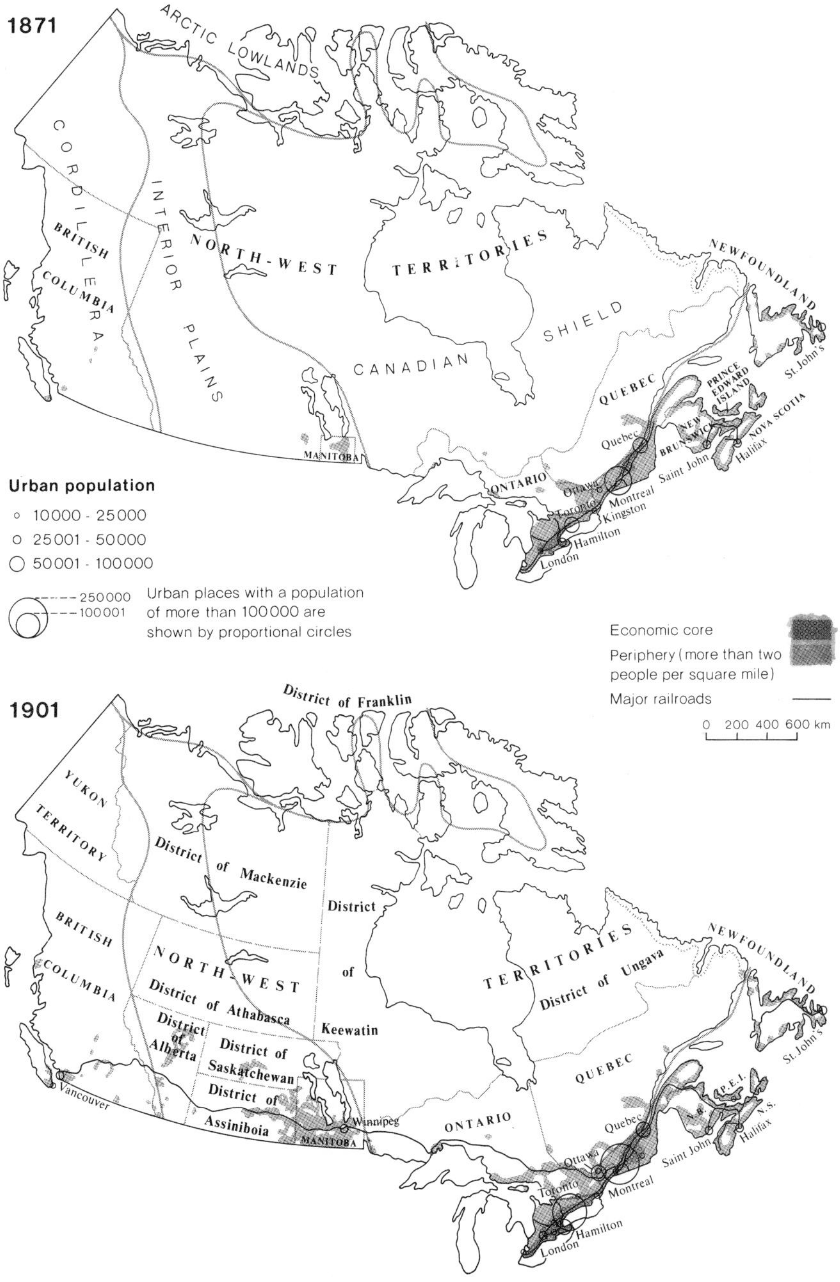

Figure 1.7 The changing pattern of heartland and hinterland, 1871 and 1901.

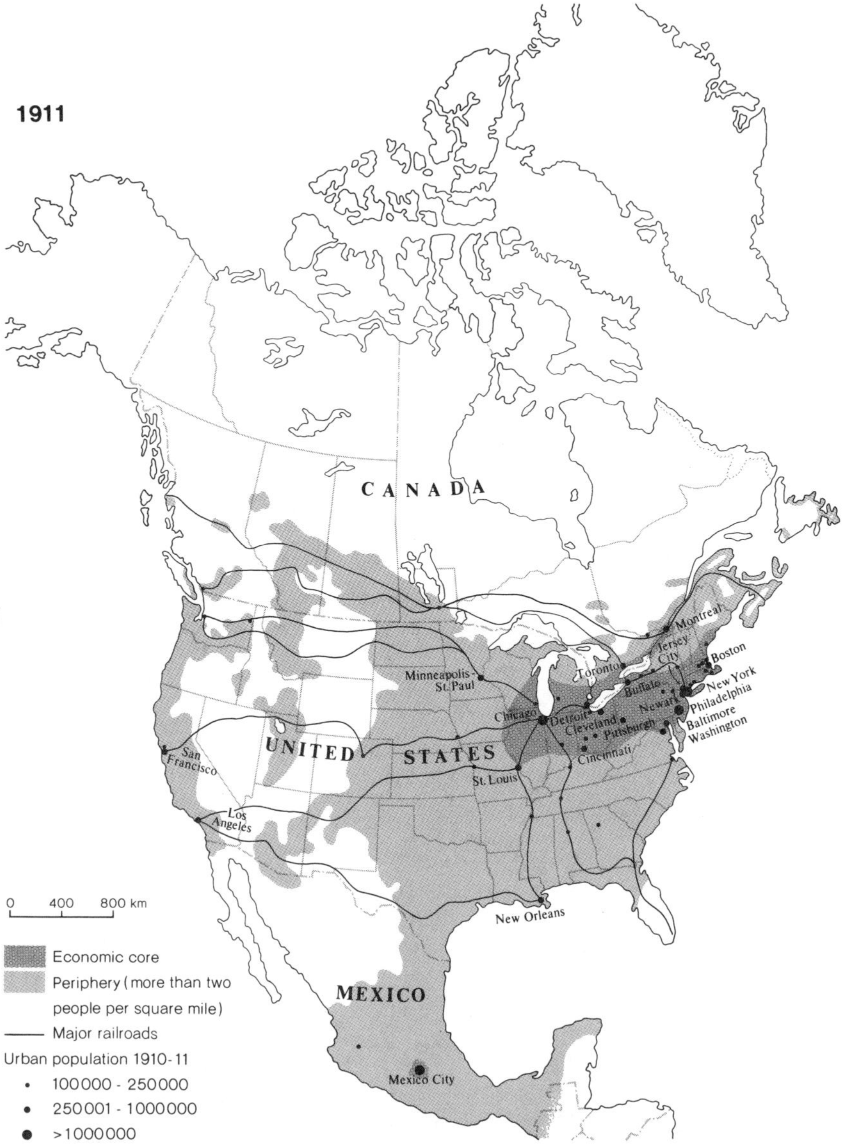

Figure 1.8 The pattern of heartland and hinterland in North America, 1911.

about, in part, the demise of a short-lived industrial revolution in the Maritimes. Although a national heartland was therefore firmly in place by the eve of World War I, the lines of ultimate control still extended beyond Canada to reach an international metropolis, including London and New York, a pattern which has remained remarkably stable over time (Fig. 1.8).[26]

As subsequent chapters will show, this pattern of heartland and hinterland remained little changed during years of war and depression and even during the expansionary era of the 1950s and 1960s (Fig. 1.9). Central Canada consolidated its position of leadership through the increased participation of American branch plants in its manufacturing sector, by controlling the wartime economy, and through financial and corporate management of the rush for a new generation of staples. The Maritimes remained entrenched in difficult times, its population earning incomes well below the national average, and none of the western provinces showed signs of diversification around traditional export sectors. On the other hand, the external and internal features of the pattern had become more complex. Canada's links to the United States were more diverse and stronger than ever before, and new ties with Japan and other nations had been forged; internally, as resource exploration and the limits of settlement expanded, cities of heartland and hinterland grew in size and intensified their characteristic functions.

There were, nonetheless, portents of change in the evolving pattern of heartland and hinterland, and the precursors of change were chiefly political and economic in nature. The expansion of federal administrative responsibilities into the Yukon and the Northwest Territories, particularly after 1912 and during the 1920s, and the joining of Newfoundland to Canada in 1949 bolstered the political make-up of the hinterland, giving Ottawa a heightened status. More recently, the thrust of the *Parti Québécois* onto the political stage in Québec in the 1970s was a warning of the possible fracture of Canadian unity. On an economic level, new resource potentials were being realized that would alter the traditional metropolis-hinterland relationship. Increased world demand for lumber and pulp and paper and new calls for metallic ores, coal, and hydroelectricity have enriched British Columbia's economy. The province now sends over 90 percent of its extra-regional exports to foreign countries, making it increasingly independent of other Canadian regions and thus generating its own pattern of metropolis and hinterland in microcosm. For Alberta, the international energy crisis of the early 1970s generated windfall profits from oil and natural gas development, creating for that province an unprecedented position of economic strength. Economic development also consolidated an integrated settlement system characteristic of a core area, making Alberta all the more distinguishable from Saskatchewan and Manitoba. Saskatchewan can now also claim a

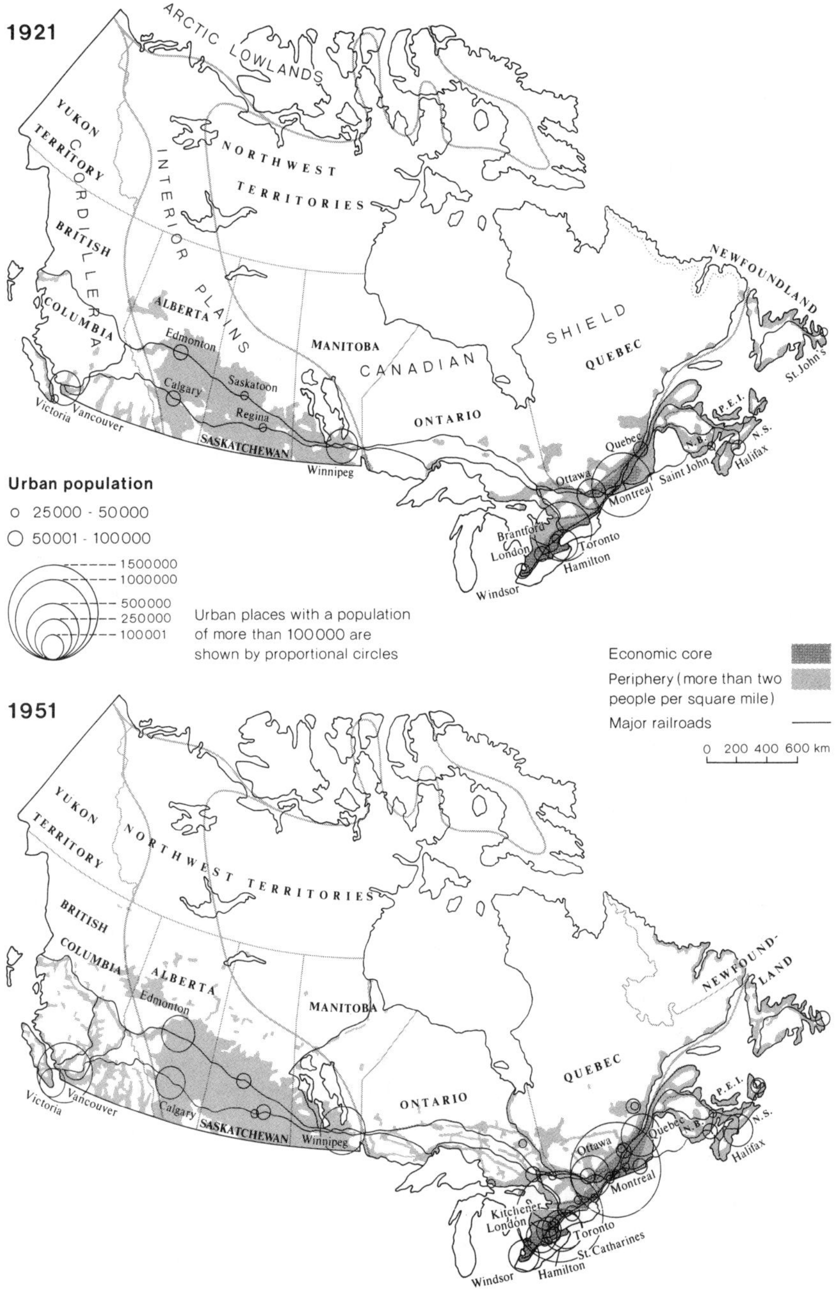

Figure 1.9 The changing pattern of heartland and hinterland, 1921 and 1951.

more diversified economy and improved well-being as a result of potash and uranium development and rising profits from grain and livestock production. Increasingly, new specialized financial services, corporate officers, and a wide range of lesser businesses are being established in the "New West," including some which have left the heartland. More alarming for the heartland, however, is the withdrawal of American branch plants from Ontario, as the United States consolidates its industrial empire.

Elsewhere in the hinterland, traditional dependency relationships are being challenged. The potential for massive resource development in the territorial North has drawn that region closer to the industrial core and in the process has nurtured a strong sense of unity among the region's Native peoples, causing the imposition of a ten-year moratorium on oil and natural gas pipeline construction. In eastern Canada, notably in Newfoundland and Nova Scotia, where income levels have been converging slowly on the national average, the prospects for further and quickened advance have been buoyed by recent discoveries of offshore oil and natural gas. With world oil and natural gas prices falling in the mid-1980s, the potential short-term impact of these discoveries remains limited. Still, federal-provincial negotiations to resolve jurisdictional conflicts over these reserves show just how significant heartland-hinterland relationships can be for directing regional development in Canada. As the 1980s come to a close, Canada's pattern of heartland and hinterland continues to evolve and change (see Fig. 1.3). The structure of core and periphery remains, but the country's regions are developing new roles.

ORGANIZATION OF THIS BOOK

The chapters of this book have been written to capture the essence of the evolving pattern of heartland and hinterland in Canada and the factors which have shaped regional character. A regional schema is offered, not as a definitive statement on Canada's regional structure, but as a hypothesis of what seems realistic in light of our understanding of how the heartland-hinterland process has shaped the Canadian landscape (Fig. 1.10). In the context of Canada, two types of regions come immediately to the fore — heartlands and hinterlands. We have already defined these regions using various criteria, including the physical environment, types of economic activity, population and settlement features, the ability to innovate and organize power, and sentiments of regionalism. On these bases, Canada can be divided into a number of distinct regions: (1) the national core — the Industrial Heartland — centred in southern Ontario and southern Québec; (2) the provincial hinterland regions — Newfoundland, the Maritimes, the Western Interior, Alberta, and British Columbia — each possessing its own core-periphery system; and (3) the resource and

Figure 1.10 A heartland and hinterland scheme of Canadian regions.

political hinterlands — the Canadian Shield and the territorial North — which lack core areas, but stand alone because physical differentiation from southern Canada, economic specialization, or political dependency mark them as distinctive regions.

The heartland–hinterland approach stresses the importance of economic processes in shaping regional structure; and some would argue, justifiably, that this emphasis downplays (although it does not dismiss) the importance of culture and society in defining meaningful regions. Is not

Québec, they would argue, culturally and socially unique within Canada? For these people, even Québec's economic role within the Industrial Heartland is characterized by dependency relationships. The point is well taken, and a separate chapter on Québec has been conceived to stimulate further consideration of this important question. Similarly, because Alberta is being separated increasingly from the traditional perception of a "prairie" region, united by common agricultural economies and hinterland status, it is accorded distinction as a singular region. Atlantic Canada, like the Western Interior, is too diverse a region to be treated holistically. Instead, we focus separate consideration on the Maritimes and Newfoundland. The North, too, draws distinction from the resource-oriented Canadian Shield. All of these adjustments to traditional regionalization schemes of Canada emphasize how political and functional forces are giving more identity to the provinces as the regional building blocks of Canada.

The economic emphasis of the heartland–hinterland approach would also tend to downplay the effect of environmental factors — climate, landforms, and soil resources — on the country's regional structure. The role of physical factors in shaping Canada's regions is nonetheless considered in this edition. The treatment of environmental factors provides a fundamental definition of the country's regions and contributes to our understanding of Canada's human geography. Indeed, there is much to consider and debate in any interpretation of Canada's geography. Inevitably, some points are stressed more than others. Nevertheless, the primary objective of this book is to offer a stimulating — hopefully provocative — interpretation of Canada's evolving regional geography.

NOTES

1. J.M.S. Careless, "Frontierism, Metropolitanism, and Canadian History," *Canadian Historical Review,* 35 (1954), 1–21.
2. Harold Innis, *The Fur Trade in Canada: An Introduction to Canadian Economic History* (New Haven: Yale University Press, 1930); and *idem, The Cod Fisheries: The History of an International Economy* (New Haven: Yale University Press, 1946).
3. See, for example, D. Michael Ray, *Dimensions of Canadian Regionalism,* Geographical Paper No. 49 (Ottawa: Canada, Department of Energy, Mines and Resources, 1971); *idem,* "The Spatial Structure of Economic and Cultural Differences: A Factorial Ecology of Canada," *Papers of the Regional Science Association,* 23 (1972), 7–23; *idem, The Urban Challenge of Growth and Change* (Ottawa: Ministry of State for Urban Affairs, 1974); *idem,* "Canadian Regions: A Hierarchy of Heartlands and Hinterlands," in *Our Geographic Mosaic,* ed. David Knight (Ottawa: Carleton University Press, 1985), pp. 49-58; and D. Michael Ray and T.N. Brewis, "The Geography of Income and its Correlates," *The Canadian Geographer,* 20 (1976), 41–71.

4. There are several books on the geography of Canada which are rich in detail but lack an interpretive framework, including John Warkentin, ed., *Canada: A Geographical Interpretation* (Toronto: Methuen, 1968); and D.F. Putnam and R.G. Putnam, *Canada: A Regional Analysis,* 2nd edition (Toronto: Dent, 1979).
5. The literature on heartland and hinterland is vast, but several of the more important writers who treat the subject are Samir Amin, *Unequal Development* (Hassocks: Harvester Press, 1966); Fernand Braudel, *The Perspective of the World,* trans. S. Reynolds (New York: Harper and Row, 1984); André Gundre Frank, *Capitalism and Underdevelopment in Latin America* (New York: Monthly Review Press, 1967); John Friedmann, *Urbanization, Planning, and National Development* (Beverly Hills: Sage, 1973); and Immanuel Wallerstein, *The Modern World-System, I* and *II* (New York: Academic Press, 1974 and 1978).
6. John Friedmann defines innovation as the introduction of ideas or artifacts perceived as new into a social system and argues that it is the ability to innovate, above all else, that distinguishes core from peripheral areas — "Major centres of innovative change will be called core regions." John Friedmann, *Urbanization, Planning, and National Development,* pp. 45 and 51.
7. *Ibid.*
8. For a theoretical discussion of regional economic development relevant to the Canadian context, see R.E. Caves, "Vent for Surplus Models of Trade and Growth," in *Trade, Growth and the Balance of Payments,* eds. R.E. Baldwin *et al.* (Chicago: Rand McNally, 1965), pp. 95–115; James M. Gilmour, *Spatial Evolution of Manufacturing in Southern Ontario, 1851–1891,* Research Publication No. 10 (Toronto: Department of Geography, University of Toronto Press, 1972); and M.H. Watkins, "A Staple Theory of Economic Growth," *The Canadian Journal of Economics and Political Science,* 28 (1963), 141–58. These and other models are summarized in O.F.G. Sitwell and N.R.M. Seifried, *The Regional Structure of the Canadian Economy* (Toronto: Methuen, 1984).
9. This point is argued in J. Tait Davis, "Some Implications of Recent Trends in the Provincial Distribution of Income and Industrial Product in Canada," *The Canadian Geographer,* 24 (1980), 221–36.
10. Maurice Yeates, *Main Street: Windsor to Québec City* (Toronto: Macmillan, 1975).
11. Harvey S. Perloff, *How a Region Grows: Area Development in the U.S. Economy,* Supplementary Paper No. 17 (New York: Committee for Economic Development, 1963), pp. 21–36.
12. This position is argued in the major books in Canada's pattern of economic development: R.E. Caves and R.H. Holton, *The Canadian Economy: Prospect and Retrospect* (Cambridge, Mass.: Harvard University Press, 1959); W.T. Easterbrook and Hugh G.J. Aitken, *Canadian Economic History* (Toronto: Macmillan, 1956); and William L. Marr and Donald G. Paterson, *Canada: An Economic History* (Toronto: Macmillan, 1980).
13. Data in this paragraph are derived from Statistics Canada, *Provincial Gross Domestic Product by Industry, 1983* (Ottawa: 1985).
14. Larry Pratt and John Richards, *Prairie Capitalism: Power and Influence in the New West* (Toronto: McClelland and Stewart, 1979).
15. Theoretical perspectives on the character of the Canadian city can be found in L.D. McCann, "Urban Growth in a Staple Economy: The Emergence of Vancouver as a Regional Metropolis, 1886–1914," in *Vancouver: Western Metropolis,* ed. L.J. Evenden, Western Geographical Series, Vol. 16 (Victoria: Department of Geography, University of Victoria, 1978), pp. 17–41; and *idem* "Staples and the New Industrialism in the Growth of Post-Confederation Halifax," *Acadiensis,* 8 (1979), 47–79.
16. See, for example, Shin-Neu Li, "Labour Force Statistics and a Functional Classification of Canadian Cities," in *Canadian Urban Trends: National Perspective,* Vol. 1, ed. D.M. Ray (Toronto: Copp Clark, 1976), pp. 57–102; J.W. Maxwell *et al.,* "The Functional Structure of Canadian Cities: A Classification of Cities," in *Readings in Canadian Geography,* 2nd. ed., ed. R.M. Irving (Toronto: Holt, Rinehart, and Winston, 1972), pp.

146–67; Richard E. Preston, "Notes on the Development of the Canadian Urban Pattern," in *Essays on Canadian Urban Process and Form II,* eds. Richard E. Preston and Lorne H. Russwurm, Department of Geography Publication Series, No. 15 (Waterloo: University of Waterloo, 1980), pp. 1–149; and J.W. Simmons, "The Evolution of the Canadian Urban System," in *The Usable Urban Past,* eds. Alan F.J. Artibise and Gilbert A. Stelter (Toronto: Macmillan, 1979), pp. 9–33.

17. Careless, "Frontierism Metropolitanism, and Canadian History," p. 17. See also Don Davis, "The 'Metropolitan Thesis' and the Writing of Canadian Urban History," *Urban History Review,* 14 (1985), 95–114; N.S.B. Gras, *An Introduction to Economic History* (New York: Harper, 1922), pp. 186–240; and Donald P. Kerr, "Metropolitan Dominance in Canada," in *Canada: A Geographical Interpretation,* ed. J. Warkentin, pp. 531–55 for discussions of metropolitan development.
18. Data in this paragraph have been drawn from R. Keith Semple and W. Randy Smith, "Metropolitan Dominance and Foreign Ownership in the Canadian Urban System," *The Canadian Geographer,* 25 (1981), 4–26.
19. For a useful discussion of the geography of post-industrialism see: David Clark, *Post-Industrial America: A Geographical Perspective* (New York: Methuen, 1984).
20. Calgary, Edmonton, and Vancouver are the subjects of three recent monographs: B.M. Barr, ed., *Calgary: Metropolitan Structure and Influence,* Western Geographical Series, Vol. 12 (Victoria: Department of Geography, University of Victoria, 1975); P.J. Smith, ed., *Edmonton: The Emerging Metropolitan Pattern,* Western Geographical Series, Vol. 15 (Victoria: Department of Geography, University of Victoria, 1978); and Evenden, *Vancouver: Western Metropolis, op. cit.* See also the essays in A.W. Rasporich, ed., *The Making of the Modern West: Western Canada Since 1945* (Calgary: University of Calgary Press, 1984).
21. L.D. McCann, "The Myth of the Metropolis: The Role of the City in Canadian Regionalism," *Urban History Review,* 9 (1981), 52–8.
22. Ernest R. Forbes, *The Maritimes Rights Movement, 1919–1927: A Study in Canadian Regionalism* (Montréal: McGill-Queen's University Press, 1979).
23. Garth Stevenson, "Canadian Regionalism in Continental Perspective," *Journal of Canadian Studies,* 15 (1980), p. 18.
24. A most persuasive argument for distinguishing these two regions of Ontario on economic and political grounds is authored by G.R. Wellar, "Hinterland Politics: The Case of Northwestern Ontario," *The Canadian Journal of Political Science,* 10 (1977), 727–54.
25. R.C. Harris and J. Warkentin, *Canada Before Confederation* (Toronto: Oxford University Press, 1974).
26. The development of a core-periphery pattern in the United States is best described by David Ward, *Cities and Immigrants: A Geography of Change in Nineteenth Century America* (New York: Oxford University Press, 1971), pp. 11–49.

2

Canada, the United States, and the World-System: The Metropolis-Hinterland Paradox

R.M. Galois and Alan Mabin

> *No man is an island, entire of itself . . . Each is a piece of the continent, a part of the main . . . .*
>
> John Donne

Before focussing on the metropolis–hinterland structure of Canada's internal geography, it is important to consider Canada's position in the world–system because Canada's economy and society are strongly influenced by external relationships of global significance. Our concerns are twofold. First, we are interested in Canada's role within the capitalist world–system. We begin by examining the system itself; Canada's external relationships are conditioned by the ways in which the system functions. Second, we approach the topic historically. As the international community has evolved, Canada's position in the world–system has shifted from that of a British colony to, paradoxically, both "an economic hinterland" of the United States and a "quasi-metropolitan state." Our intent is to examine the development of this paradox.

The world–system is, put simply, a unit with a single but integrated division of labour, and multiple cultures. There are two varieties of world–systems, one with a common political system and one without. These are designated respectively as world–empires and world–economies. A world–economy is therefore a single, integrated division of labour with multiple politics and cultures, forming an economic whole.[1] Our concern here is primarily with the world–economy.

There are two basic types of world–economies, the capitalist and the communist or centrally-planned economic system. According to Braudel, the world–economy which is the product of capitalism has three facets: it occupies a given geographic space; it always has a pole or centre — a metropolis; and it is divided into successive zones.

> There is the heart, that is, the region about the centre .... Then come intermediate zones about this central pivot. Finally, there are the very wide peripheral areas, which, in the division of labour characteristic of the world–economy, are subordinates rather than true participants. Within these peripheral zones, life often resembles purgatory or even hell. Their mere geographical location provides sufficient explanation of this.[2]

Thus for countries such as Ethiopia, which is experiencing the ravages of drought and the exploitation of meagre land resources, and for many other Third World countries suffering from economic marginality, there is little prospect of immediate advance.

Capitalism is the full development and economic predominance of market trade, that is, the financial exchange of raw materials for manufactured goods. Within this context, underdevelopment is the failure of a society to achieve political maturity or industrial diversification within the international division of labour. It is the result of being involved in the world–economy as a peripheral, raw material producing area. As some would argue, it is the necessary product of capitalism itself.

EVOLUTION OF THE WORLD–SYSTEM: A SYNOPSIS

Some writers, of whom W.W. Rostow is the most widely known, have interpreted economic and social differences between countries in the world–system by reference to stages of development. In this particular view, each country passes through a number of stages — traditional society, pre–conditions for take–off, take–off, and drive to technological maturity — as it progresses towards the most advanced level of high mass consumption (Fig. 2.1).[3] Accordingly, the process of development for any country is deemed linear and cumulative. World development is a continuum — from "developing" to "developed," "industrializing" to "industrialized," and "traditional" to "modern" — along which all countries will eventually progress. From this perspective, underdevelopment is reduced to a mere temporal lag or delay, which the passage of time will supposedly rectify.

Because the gap between the developed and developing countries persists, this comfortable view of the capitalist world–system has been greeted, not surprisingly, with less than universal acclaim. Indeed, there is now a considerable body of literature which interprets the world–system in quite a different manner. The theories of Amin, Frank, and Mandel stand in contrast as examples of a critical approach to the issue of world development.[4] Their approach recognizes that development and underdevelopment are different facets of the same process. In other words, the

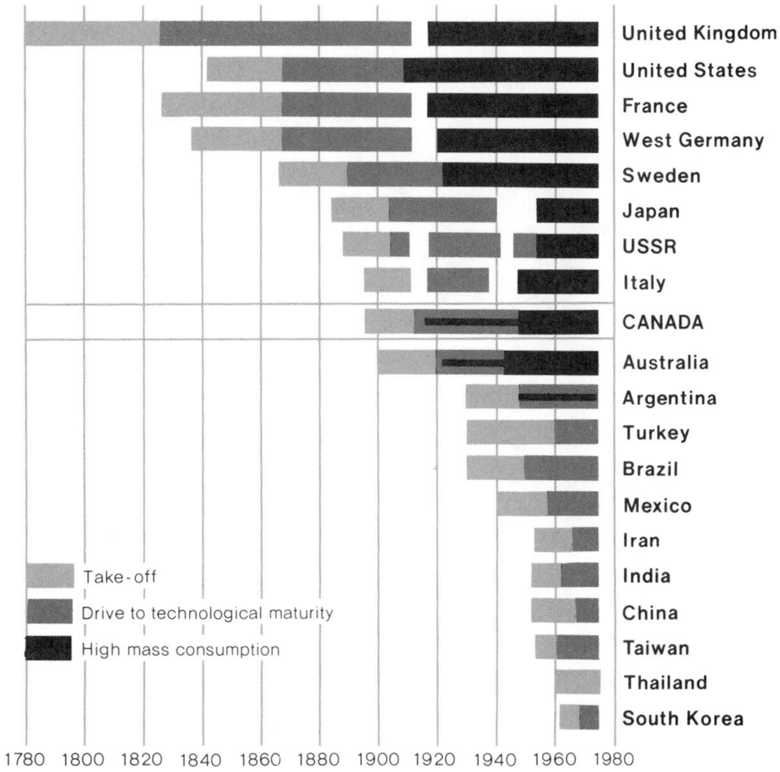

Figure 2.1 Stages of economic growth: twenty countries. (Adapted from W. W. Rostow, *The World Economy: History and Prospect*, by permission of The University of Texas Press.)

development of one group of countries can create the relative underdevelopment of other countries. As Frank has written, "economic development and underdevelopment are the opposite faces of the same coin."[5] Underdeveloped countries of the periphery, facing a very different global context, are unable to repeat the course of the developed countries. On the world scale, then, the international economic order is characterized by a unified process, but one which is expressed in terms of spatially uneven or unequal development. As Fig. 2.2 shows, there are wide divisions in world economic development, whether in centrally planned economies or in the capitalist world–system.

The meaning of this point will become clearer through a brief review of the world–system's development since the late nineteenth century. Particularly useful for such an analysis is the work on periodization by a number of scholars, particularly Kondratieff, Kuznets, Mandel, and

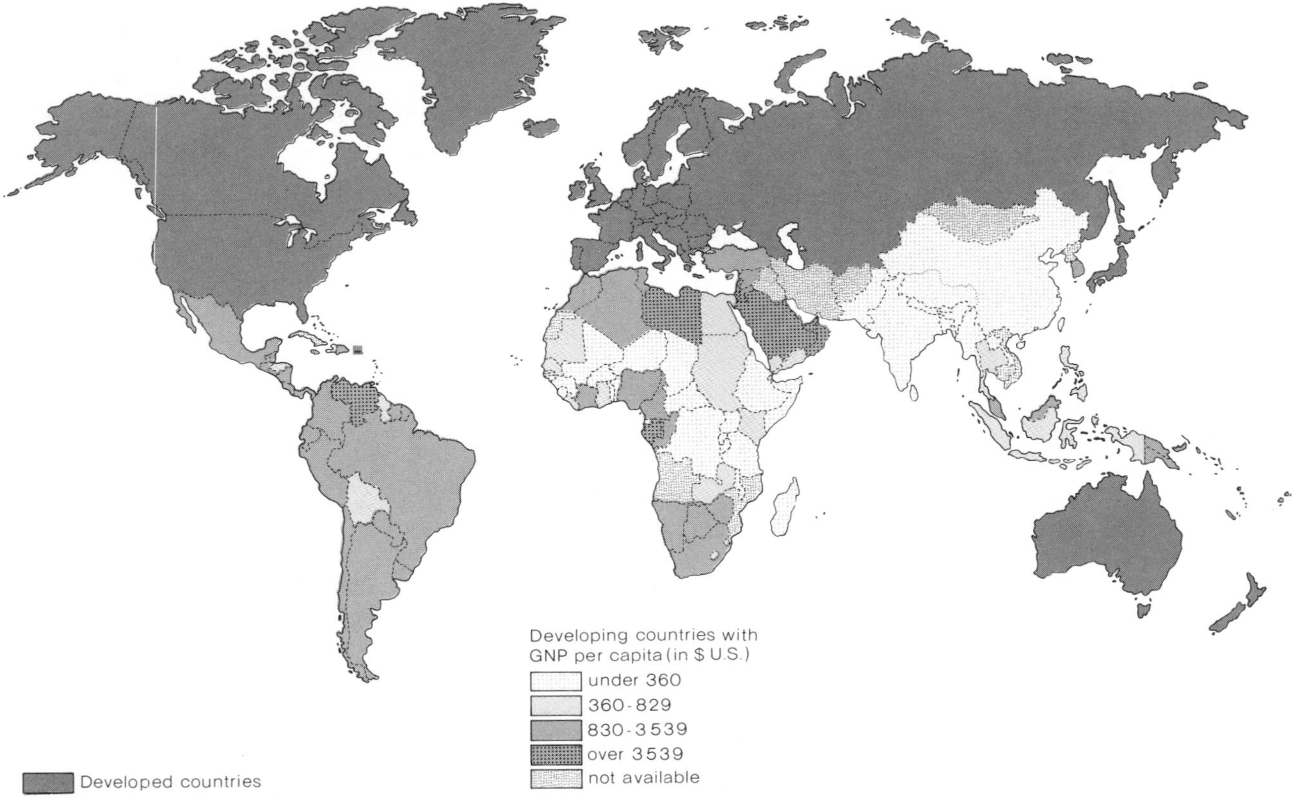

Figure 2.2 The World in Development. (Adapted from *A Developing World* produced by the Canadian International Development Agency, 1984).

The world metropolis: New York, the centre of the capitalist world-economy. (*Larry McCann*)

Schumpeter, who have discerned a series of long-term movements (cycles or waves) in the evolution of the world-economy. They have identified a succession of periods of expansion and stagnation — of accelerating and decelerating growth — which have lasted for as long as twenty-five or more years: 1873–1895; 1896–1913; 1914–1939; 1940–1970; and beyond 1970.[6]

The Great Depression, 1873–1895

The "Great Depression," as the period between 1873 and 1895 is commonly described, was characterized by deceleration in the world-economy: prices generally declined; profits were lower; and unemployment increased. The initial thrust of the first industrial revolution, based on steam-driven machinery, had passed; and Britain's dominant position in the world-economy was challenged by the economic development of a number of other nations, including the United States. One response to these changes was the growth of protectionism. Another, of broader significance, was the competition for colonies and spheres of influence to capture markets, secure raw materials, and obtain outlets for profitable and secure investment. Hence, a central feature of the process of colonialism, especially after 1880, was the growth in the export of capital, which reinforced the dominance of the metropolitan countries. The conditions of this period also facilitated the growth of large corporations with monopolistic powers, such as Standard Oil of New Jersey in the United States and the Canadian Pacific Railway in Canada.

Expansion and Consolidation, 1896–1913

The world-economy recovered by the late 1890s when a series of new technological innovations, including electrical machinery and automobiles, provided new investment opportunities in the home markets of industrialized countries, as well as overseas. At the same time, the renewed demand for raw materials stimulated a marked advance in international trade. Further expansion occurred as people from Europe migrated to independent countries, including the United States, Brazil, Argentina, Canada, Australia, and South Africa, and to the colonies of the world powers located throughout the Third World. This migration was accompanied by the continued and considerable export of capital, chiefly from Great Britain, but also from France, Germany, and elsewhere. Much of the capital was of the portfolio type (bonds), the deployment of which was determined in the periphery by resident elites, although interest and profits were transferred abroad to metropolitan centres. This capital was frequently used in the exploitation of raw materials, such as wheat, wool, and gold, and in the transportation facilities needed to move commodities to industrial markets.

The World-System in Transition, 1914–1939

In retrospect, it is clear that the character of the world-system changed fundamentally after World War I. This change was nowhere more apparent than in the dramatic reversal of the relative prominence of Great Britain and the United States. A re-centring in the world-system had taken effect. Indeed, the United States had emerged by the 1920s as the world's foremost industrial and financial economy.

Economic stress and change in the international order also took the form of post-war slumps, growing unemployment, and numerous large-scale strikes, including those in Canada, South Africa, and Britain. Revolution in Russia also altered the structure of the capitalist world-economy. Economic expansion did occur in the mid- and late twenties, but was accompanied by the inflationary force of speculation in commodities, land, and stocks. The subsequent collapse of the speculative boom in 1929 signalled the onset of depression — of massive unemployment and reduced production — which was resolved only by increased state involvement in economic planning, and by war.

The 1930s were indeed years of depression, but change in the organization and scale of the world–economy did not cease. Although production fell back in the short term, forcing many businesses the world over to close, the long–term consequences included the consolidation of corporations and the creation of new conglomerates through mergers and acquisitions. This trend was particularly apparent in the United States where, for example, Anaconda Copper, Du Pont, Ford, General Electric, General Motors, Standard Oil of New Jersey (later to become Exxon Corporation), and United States Steel all expanded during the 1930s. These corporations, along with others headquartered in Europe, gained new markets and developed alternative production facilities in foreign countries, earning the appellation "multinational corporations."

United States Hegemony and the Long Boom, 1940–1970

World War II, in part the product of the stresses of the 1920s and '30s, initiated a further revolution in the structure of the world–system. Three major events characterize the change in this period. First, there was a "long boom" of fairly sustained economic expansion led by the United States. Second, the formal decolonization of much of the world took place: independence was gained, for example, by India, Pakistan, and Indonesia; the political map of Africa lost its European colours; China underwent a revolution; and anti–colonial wars were staged in French Indo–China and British Malaya. Third, the United States consolidated its role as the undoubted centre of the capitalist world–system. American direct foreign investment grew from $7.2 to $25.1 billion between 1946 and 1957, and then tripled again by 1970 to total some $78 billion.[7] No other country approached the extent of this investment abroad.

Thus this period saw change in the international order and, above all, American hegemony over the capitalist world–system. Despite newly won political independence, the hinterland countries (with a few exceptions such as China) did not experience any fundamental change in their economic status. Most of south and southeast Asia, a major portion of Africa, and much of Latin America remained subordinate to external metropolises. Although the Third World was no longer partitioned by formal empires and exclusive spheres of influence, it was penetrated by the economic neo–colonialism of various countries. Of these, Britain had become, except in certain of its highly specialized financial activities, merely a sub–centre of the world–system. France, Germany, and Japan rose to positions of prominence in industries such as electronics and automobile manufacturing. Among these metropolitan nations, the United States expressed its pre–eminence in a number of ways: American corporate control reached into European economies because Europe depended, to a degree, on American military protection, and because European countries lagged behind in technological development.

In the new international division of labour produced by these developments, the activities which controlled the world–economy, such as finance, management, and research, continued to concentrate in the metropolitan countries. The hinterland, by contrast, remained oriented chiefly to resource-based activities. Between these two extremes were countries that defied precise classification because their paths of development stood separate, being neither of the metropolis nor of the hinterland. Several, including Argentina, experienced stagnation and increasing external domination after World War II. Others, such as Canada, Australia, and New Zealand, and to a lesser degree Brazil and South Africa, experienced rapid economic expansion and were marked by generally higher standards of living than the countries of the world's hinterland. Moreover, the corporations of these countries increasingly invested abroad. Yet, these countries still received a high inflow of foreign capital which maintained and, in some cases, even increased the extent of external control over domestic production and trade. Neither metropolises nor hinterlands, these semi-peripheral countries pose special problems for the basic metropolis–hinterland dichotomy. In the subsequent analysis we see that the evolution of Canada's position in the world–system constitutes just such an ambiguous case.

Restructuring of the World–System: Beyond 1970

It is inherently difficult to assess any development phase while it is still in progress. Nevertheless, in the 1970s the world–system was marked once again by stress and restructuring. Rapid inflation and increased unemployment swept through most capitalist economies. Competition was intense among the major corporations throughout the world for scarce capital and raw materials, cheap labour, and secure markets. At the centre of the capitalist world–economy, the expanded production of some European economies and of Japan challenged United States hegemony. In the periphery, several countries, most notably Taiwan, South Korea, and Mexico, experienced rapid economic growth and so became distinguishable from the mass of other peripheral states (see Fig. 2.1). Meanwhile Canada, Australia, and South Africa remained dependent on raw material exports and faced problems of competition with foreign manufactures. Of broader significance, two of the most widely discussed events of the 1970s were the marked increase in certain commodity prices, notably of oil, and the rising financial strength of the oil-exporting countries. Certainly the Middle East oil states acquired some of the characteristics of a metropolis. In the mid-1980s, the decline in oil prices has weakened the financial strength of some OPEC countries, notably Mexico and Nigeria, but Saudi Arabia, through its worldwide investment practices, is now a financial power.

Since so much world economic activity is now undertaken by corporate enterprises global in scale, these so-called multinationals are increasingly characterized by a global division of labour. IBM, for example, one of the truly giant multinationals, actually has no single plant outside the United States in which a complete product is manufactured. Each phase of the production process — ranging from management control and raw material production, through simple and more complex component manufacture, to research, design, and final assembly — is usually located in a different place, with the market perhaps in still another country. Such global production processes have changed the international division of labour, and continue to do so.

The availability of labour and the political stability of a host country have become important determinants of industrial location. If instability or other detrimental conditions prevail, branch plant operations in one country can be phased out and replaced by production elsewhere in the international market. Most multinationals are now also involved in a wide variety of production processes. International Telephone and Telegraph of the United States, for example, produces through its many subsidiaries such diverse goods as minerals, coffee, electrical equipment, and paper. The company also has interests in transport and financial services. These various activities are scattered throughout the world, including Canada.

CANADA IN THE WORLD–SYSTEM

Canada developed as a nation while being part of the North Atlantic Triangle, a trade framework dominated by Great Britain and the United States. Within this triangle, Canada occupied a minor position as a supplier of raw materials (fur, fish, wheat, and timber) and as a market for manufactured goods. In the difficult depression years which followed Confederation in 1867, two important steps were taken to improve this position. The first was the creation of a national system of railroads essential for an integrated economy. The second was the attempt, through the National Policy, to promote indigenous manufacturing. The potential benefits of these policies, however, were limited by the exigencies of the general economic climate; they failed at the time to alter Canada's peripheral position in the world-economy.

Dependence in the World–Economy, 1896–1913

With the upturn in the world-economy by the late 1890s, Canada's potential for development was widely recognized. The new century was hailed by Laurier and others as "Canada's century," and such optimism was not without foundation. Renewed economic expansion was signalled by a series of mining booms, of which the Klondike gold rush was the most spectacular. Facilitated by technological developments, mining reinforced Canada's role as a supplier of staples and restructured the hinterland within the country — the frontier was pushed across the Canadian Shield and into the Kootenays of British Columbia.

Mining development was followed and soon overshadowed by massive expansion in wheat production, brought about in part by Great Britain's increased demand for foodstuffs. The wheat boom encouraged settlement and cultivation of the Western Interior, and for the first time since Confederation there was a positive net migration to Canada, amounting to more than 700 000 people in the first decade of the century (Table 2.1). Access to free or inexpensive land and relatively high wage rates created a society markedly different from colonies elsewhere, particularly in Asia, Africa, and areas of South America, where surplus labour drove wages down and land was inaccessible to most. The influx of population was accompanied by an inflow of foreign capital (Table 2.2). Most was British portfolio investment, used to build the railroads and industries of the expanding national economy. Concomitantly, manufacturing expanded in both quantity and diversity of products. Canada also reached outwards, exporting not only staples but some capital too. Small amounts were invested in Europe, the United States, and in several developing countries in the Caribbean and South America.

TABLE 2.1 COMPONENTS OF POPULATION GROWTH FOR CANADA, 1871–1981 (thousands of persons)

Decade	*Population Start of Decade*	*Births*	*Deaths*	*Natural Increase*	*Immigration*	*Emigration*[a]	*Net Migration*
1871–81	3 689	1 477	754	723	353	440	−87
1881–91	4 325	1 538	824	714	903	1 109	−206
1891–1901	4 833	1 546	828	718	326	506	−180
1901–11	5 371	1 931	811	1 120	1 759	1 043	716
1911–21	7 207	2 338	988[b]	1 350	1 612	1 381	231
1921–31	8 788	2 415	1 055	1 360	1 203	974	229
1931–41	10 377	2 294	1 072	1 222	150	242	−92
1941–51	11 507	3 186	1 214[b]	1 972	548	379	169
1951–61	14 009[c]	4 468	1 320	3 148	1 543	462	1 081
1961–71	18 238	4 063	1 360	2 703	1 429	802	627
1971–81	21 568	3 578	1 665	1 913	1 446	585	862

[a]A residual, calculated by adding natural increase and immigration to the population count at the start of the decade and subtracting the population count at the end of the decade.
[b]Includes deaths resulting from the two World Wars, numbering 120 000 and 36 000 respectively.
[c]Includes Newfoundland.

Sources: Canada, Department of Manpower and Immigration, *Immigration and Population Statistics* (Ottawa: 1974), p. 8; and Jean Dumas, *Current Demographic Analysis: Report on the Demographic Situation in Canada, 1983* (Ottawa: 1984), pp. 21 and 115.

Economic progress was accompanied by initial but halting steps towards achieving autonomy in external affairs. Despite Confederation, Great Britain continued to determine the pattern of Canada's foreign relations. But the spirit of future actions was captured by John A. Macdonald in 1884 when he refused to send troops to the Sudan in support of Britain, remarking that "the Suez Canal is nothing to us."[8] Subsequent events heightened Canada's growing independent political identity. In 1910, Wilfrid Laurier insisted, over Imperial objections, on the establishment of a Canadian Navy. American acceptance of Canada as a distinct political entity — distinct, that is, from Great Britain — also developed rapidly in the years prior to World War I. As one example, Canada was represented by its own officials, and not by the British Ambassador, in Washington on the International Joint Commission which regulated those waterways shared jointly by Canada and the United States.

It could be argued that Canada was in the process of becoming a mature industrial society on the eve of World War I. The attainment of internal political autonomy through Confederation was complemented by growing economic strength and control over external affairs. Yet such an argument ignores the fact that the seeds of a new dependency were also being nurtured. The protective tariff schemes of the National Policy of 1879 had stimulated some domestic industry, but these measures also facilitated the development of a branch plant economy within Canada.[9] Indeed, the long boom that started in the late 1890s was characterized by substantial American direct investment in the Canadian economy. This important investment tended to concentrate in those dynamic sectors of

TABLE 2.2 ESTIMATES OF NET CAPITAL FLOWS INTO CANADA, 1871–1983 (in millions of dollars)

Decade	*Net Capital Flows*	*Decade*	*Net Capital Flows*
1871–80	259	1931–40	-688
1881–90	409	1941–50	-1 159
1891–1900	326	1951–60	8 701
1901–10	1 085	1961–70	8 120
1911–20	1 777	1971–80	21 383
1921–30	190	1981–83	2 484

Note: The 1871–1900 data are estimates by Hartland reported in Bloomfield; the 1901–1930 data are estimates by Buckley; and from 1931 onwards the data are official government estimates.

Sources: A.I. Bloomfield, *Patterns of Infrastructure in International Investment Before 1914* (Princeton: Princeton University Press, 1968), pp. 42–4; K. Buckley, *Capital Formation in Canada, 1896–1930* (Toronto: McClelland and Stewart, 1974), p. 99; Statistics Canada, *Canadian Statistical Review: Historical Summary, 1970*, Cat. No. 11-505 (Ottawa: 1972); *idem, Canadian Statistical Review*, Cat. No. 11-003 (Ottawa: 1984); M.C. Urquhart and K.A.H. Buckley, eds., *Historical Statistics of Canada* (Toronto: Macmillan, 1965), pp. 142-72; and M.C. Urquhart *et al.*, eds., *Historical Statistics of Canada*, 2nd ed. (Toronto: Macmillan, 1984), pp. G-84-243.

The metropolis-hinterland paradox: Despite growing dependency in the world-system following Confederation, Canada exported capital to developing countries. This 1922 photograph of the Royal Bank in Kingston, Jamaica, is a symbol of Canada's outward reach. (*Royal Bank of Canada Archives*)

the economy (for example, resources, electrical machinery, and automobiles) whose expansion played an important role in the accelerated growth of the period. The weakness or absence of domestic control in these sectors and Canadian patent laws, which encouraged the borrowing of technology rather than its innovation, promoted an acute technological dependence. A high proportion of this American investment was concentrated in central Canada, particularly in Ontario. In a sense, Canada's own industrial core was merely peripheral to the American manufacturing belt. Integration among Canadian regions was weakened as a consequence of these intensified north–south links. In this way, American influence in Canadian production was advanced, establishing a pattern that would continue in later decades.

Canada's Growing Dependency, 1914–1939

After 1918, Canada's formal external autonomy grew substantially. Until World War I, Canada was a junior partner in the affairs of the British Empire, a status indicated by its automatic entry into war along with Britain. But with an enhanced sense of its own independence and of the importance of its role in the war, Canada delayed Britain's ratification of the ensuing Peace Treaties until the Canadian Parliament had debated the matter. More significantly, Canada and the other British dominions — Australia, Newfoundland, New Zealand, and South Africa — pressed for *de facto* recognition of their constitutional equality with Britain as independent states. In 1926, the Balfour Declaration gave formal acceptance of this principle:

> They are autonomous communities within the British Empire, equal in status, in no way subordinate to one another in any aspect of their domestic or external affairs, though united by a common allegiance to the Crown, and freely associated as members of the British Commonwealth of Nations.[10]

With continued pressure, principally from Canada and South Africa, this declaration became law in 1931 as the Statute of Westminster.

The attainment of autonomy in external relations accompanied the less visible, but equally significant, reduction in Canada's economic dependence on Britain. As the British Imperial influence on Canada's economy and society declined, it might be anticipated that Canada would make further strides in its progression from colony to independent nation. Unfortunately, such expectations were only partially realized. Newly acquired political autonomy failed to generate economic independence because American involvement in Canada's economic and cultural affairs made further and significant inroads.

The recentring of the core of the world-system from Europe to the United States in the inter-war period established a new metropolis-hinterland relationship for Canada. High wheat prices and tremendous growth in wheat exports, as well as increased exports of other primary products and some manufactures, had produced a surge in Canadian external trade before and during World War I. But at the end of the war, an economic slump set in, lasting until 1922; not until 1926 did imports and exports regain their wartime levels. As wheat prices fell during the 1920s and the inflow of British capital declined, the Canadian economy became tied much more closely to the United States. Between 1910 and 1925, American investment increased from 19 to 56 percent of all foreign capital invested in Canada. Much of this remained in the form of portfolio rather than direct investment, which reveals that Canadian governments and companies increased their borrowing and raising of capital in the United States. Conversely, the British share of total foreign capital in Canada declined over the same period, from 77 to 41 percent (Table 2.3).

Further developments hastened the reorientation of the Canadian economy towards the United States. When Britain returned to the Gold Standard in 1925, the cost of British goods increased enormously, prompting importers all over the world to search for alternatives. One obvious result was that Canadian importers turned to American suppliers. In addition, with the encouragement of successive Canadian governments,

TABLE 2.3 ESTIMATED DISTRIBUTION OF FOREIGN CAPITAL INVESTED IN CANADA, SELECTED YEARS, 1900-1980

	Percentage by Country of Origin			
Year	*Great Britain*	*United States*	*Other Countries*	*Total ($ millions)*
1900	85	14	1	1 232
1905	79	19	2	1 540
1910	77	19	3	2 529
1915	69	27	4	4 017
1920	53	44	3	4 870
1925	41	56	3	5 714
1930	36	61	3	7 614
1933	36	61	3	7 365
1939	36	60	4	6 913
1945	25	70	5	7 092
1950	20	76	4	8 664
1955	18	76	6	13 527
1960	15	75	10	22 214
1965	12	79	9	29 603
1970	9	79	12	44 037
1975	8	77	15	68 649
1980	7	69	24	129 000

Sources: Canada, Foreign Investment Review Agency, *Compendium of Statistics on Foreign Investment* (Ottawa: 1978), Table 2; Statistics Canada, *Canada's International Investment Position, 1979 and 1980* (Ottawa: 1982), Table 17.

American companies increased their productive operations in Canada. This pattern of American direct investment was evident elsewhere in the world, but Canada remained the single most important locus for surplus American capital. Here, American corporations could combine both market and supply oriented investments. By the late 1920s, the largest automobile companies, the leading aircraft manufacturers, the major mining concerns, and other important industrial corporations had either established or consolidated branch operations in Canada.

One prominent example of this interaction with the United States was in the pulp and paper industry.[11] Canadian exports of newsprint made up 65 percent of the world total at the close of the 1920s; 85 percent of this total went to the United States. The pulp and paper trade thus reflected some past patterns, but showed signs of future change as well. It remained under the control of all–Canadian companies, but far more foreign capital was directly involved than ever before. International Paper, one of the three largest companies in the industry, was American controlled. Perhaps of most significance, the industry was growing increasingly dependent on new technologies and techniques developed in the United States.

Aided by several political events, most notably by the renewal of the Imperial preferential tariff system and by severe depression in the world-economy, the Americanization of the Canadian economy continued to gain momentum through the 1930s. Imperial preference, in part a response to the schemes of tariff protection established by the United States in the 1920s, meant differential duties on trade with members of the Commonwealth and the British colonies, on the one hand, and with foreign countries, on the other. American businesses seized this opportunity to use their branch plants in Canada to gain access to British-controlled markets. Thus, the Ottawa trade agreements of 1932, although designed to strengthen the British and Commonwealth position in a world besieged by increasingly protectionist trade policies, ironically had the effect of stimulating further American direct investment in Canada. For example, to circumvent restrictive Imperial tariffs, the Detroit-based Ford Motor Company expanded its Canadian operations and even established plants in Australia, South Africa, and Malaya as branches of its wholly-owned subsidiary, Ford of Canada.

The Imperial preferences nevertheless provided the incentive for Canadian companies to penetrate markets outside Canada. Some Canadian industries, financed by Canadian banks, even imported raw materials from the developing world. The harshness of the Great Depression, however, deepened the degree of Canadian dependency: the expanding staple industries — pulp and paper, mining, oil and gas, even hydroelectricity — all required huge infusions of capital and technology which Canada alone could not supply. In each region where new natural resource industries were established, the continued strengthening of north-south links was frequently at odds with the expressed desire for the east-west integration of the Canadian economy. More than ever before, Canada had been incorporated into a continental economy centred in the United States.

Canada and the Metropolis–Hinterland Paradox, 1940–1980

Despite well-established links with the United States, in 1939 Canada's allegiance to Great Britain remained strong. Canada repeated, within one week, Britain's declaration of war against Germany, and rushed troops and supplies in support of the war effort. Nevertheless, World War II and its immediate aftermath revealed the extent of Canadian dependence on the United States and ushered in a new period — a long boom — of growing affluence under American-dominated development. From 1940 onwards, Canadian trade and production grew almost every year. During the war, the Canadian government invested almost one billion dollars in industry; and after the war, when a recession might have been expected, the boom in production continued as unprecedented amounts of American direct investment capital, in search of a stable supply of materials and markets, poured into Canada. Not only did production increase dramatically, but unemployment fell and the wages of Canadian workers actually rose at more rapid rates than those of their American counterparts.

The expanding Canadian economy required an expanding labour force. In the 1950s and '60s, even allowing for emigration, immigrants accounted for up to one-quarter of the increase in Canada's population. While most post-war immigrants continued to come from Europe, far more than ever before arrived from southern European countries, especially Italy. Many were refugees from the war-shattered areas of central Europe. In the sixties, as restrictions which had effectively encouraged only European immigration were relaxed, more immigrants began to arrive from the hinterland areas of the world: Africa, Asia, and Latin America. Previously, less than 5 percent of Canada's immigrants came from Third World countries; in the 1970s and early 1980s over 40 percent came from these regions, more than from Europe (Table 2.4). Changes in Canada's immigration programme stemmed not only from pressure to eliminate all features of racial discrimination, but also from external demands to erase the economic disparity between Canada and Third World countries. Thus, Canada sought to reduce the population pressure in developing countries by accepting more immigrants from the Third World. This policy has not always produced the desired effect, for

TABLE 2.4 IMMIGRATION TO CANADA FROM MAJOR WORLD AREAS, SELECTED INTERVALS, 1946-1981

	1946-1957		*1958-1969*		*1970-1981*	
Major World Areas	*No.*	*%*	*No.*	*%*	*No.*	*%*
Europe	1 467 202	87.9	1 031 922	73.0	640 574	37.3
North and Central America	123 050	7.4	197 068	13.9	356 595	20.8
South America	11 829	0.7	24 504	1.7	91 056	5.3
Asia	33 771	2.0	99 094	7.0	508 184	29.6
Africa	8 240	0.5	30 013	2.1	85 937	5.0
Australasia	14 266	0.9	28 798	2.0	19 446	1.1
Oceania	10 972	0.7	1 557	0.1(a)	10 372(c)	0.6
Not Classified	-	-	874	0.1(b)	4 392(d)	0.3
Totals	1 669 340	100.0	1 413 830	100.0	1 716 556	100.0

(a) 1958-68 only (b) 1969 only (c) 1974-81 only (d) 1970-3 only

Sources: Canada, Department of Manpower and Immigration, *Canada Immigration and Population Study: Immigration and Population Statistics* (Ottawa: 1974), pp. 32-7; and J. Dumas, *Current Demographic Analysis: Report on the Demographic Situation in Canada, 1983* (Ottawa: 1984), p. 115.

too often Canada has accepted highly-skilled immigrants from Third World countries, thus draining these countries of a badly needed resource.

Canada's ties with the Third World go beyond the bonds of immigration. Of the world's industrial countries, Canada has developed a unique diplomatic relationship with the Third World because it is perceived as a relatively friendly country by many hinterland nations. As a result, Canada was a participant in United Nations peacekeeping forces in the Middle East, at a time when none of the major metropolitan states would have been accepted for this role. Ghana turned to Canada when a military training scheme was needed after independence in 1957. Moreover, good relations with Latin American countries have assisted the growth of Canadian-based companies such as Distillers Corporation and the major Canadian banks. When foreign banks in Cuba were nationalized in 1960, Canadian banks were exempted initially and later compensated at full book value when finally bought by the Cuban government. Such developments are a reflection of Canada's semi-peripheral status. It is able, in certain spheres of international affairs, to chart an independent course.

Yet, despite close and friendly relations with many hinterland countries, by the 1970s Canadian corporations and even government officials were experiencing difficulties in their business and diplomatic dealings with other countries. The change was not merely the result of Canadian diplomats adopting positions like those of the United States. It was also due to the provocative actions taken by some Canadian companies.

The connection between Canada and the Caribbean illustrates these changing relations. After World War II, Canadian direct investment in the Caribbean grew rapidly, as did indirect investment through Canadian subsidiaries of American multinationals. For example, Alcan, a Canadian-owned corporation with American ties, channels large sums of Canadian and American money into the Caribbean. Like other aluminum producers, Alcan grew rapidly during World War II by using bauxite mined in Guyana. After the war, Alcan pioneered similar resource development in Jamaica, where it reaped considerable profits throughout the long boom by paying low wages, negligible taxes, and minimal royalties. As a result of protests in the 1970s, Alcan no longer pays minimal royalties to the Jamaican government, but while the company's holdings have not been nationalized, the Jamaican economy now receives more benefits through higher taxation of Alcan's industrial activities. Thus, the actions of some Canadian-based multinational companies differed little from those of their American or European counterparts, and at times received the scorn of the host country.

Actions by Canadian banks in the Caribbean provide another example. The Royal Bank, the Bank of Nova Scotia, and the Canadian

Imperial Bank of Commerce rank among the four largest banks of the region. Active here for more than 80 years, all expanded their Caribbean activities rapidly in the 1950s and '60s. Pressure for local participation in their management mounted in the 1970s, but redirection has proceeded slowly, and control remains firmly in the hands of head offices in Montréal and Toronto. Moreover, the banks continue to favour large-scale traders and businesses, avoiding the risk of financing small farmers or independent traders. If banks were to reconsider this policy, relationships would probably be less strained.

Thus, after World War II it became clear that Canada was charting a paradoxical course in the world–system. On the one hand, Canada has one of the highest average levels of wages and living standards in the world; it is not inaccurately described as an industrial country; it has served as a political "buffer" in international disputes; and it is the domicile for a number of global corporations which have participated in creating conditions of dependency in the world hinterland. On the other hand, Canada remains economically dependent on the United States. The ultimate control of significant segments of the Canadian economy still rests with American corporations, and the continental pattern of core and periphery places Canada in a distinctive position (Fig. 2.3). Canada's industrial heartland is an extension of the United States heartland; the rest of Canada is periphery. Branch manufacturing plants of American multinationals and American demands for minerals and forest products exemplify this pattern.

To complete this portrayal of Canada's paradoxical position in the world–system, it is essential to examine the unfolding American and Canadian relationship during the long boom. Under the prosperous conditions fostered by the influx of American capital and technology, most sectors of the Canadian economy expanded appreciably in the post–war era. But so, too, did the overall influence of American corporations. By the early 1970s, for example, almost 60 percent of all financial assets in the mining and smelting industry were controlled by American companies (Table 2.5). Some, such as Hanna Mining and Kennecott Copper, were oriented primarily to the resource sector; these companies frequently participated in joint ventures with other American and even Canadian manufacturing corporations to export unprocessed staples south of the border. Thus, an externally–controlled conglomerate such as the Iron Ore Company of Canada extracts iron ore in Québec and Newfoundland–Labrador for export to the American industrial core. The same pattern prevailed in the oil and natural gas sector, where American corporations maintained their level of approximately two–thirds ownership established in the pre–war period. Finally, Canadian manufacturing industries expanded rapidly after the war, but American interests dominated this sector too, achieving nearly 50 percent control by 1970.

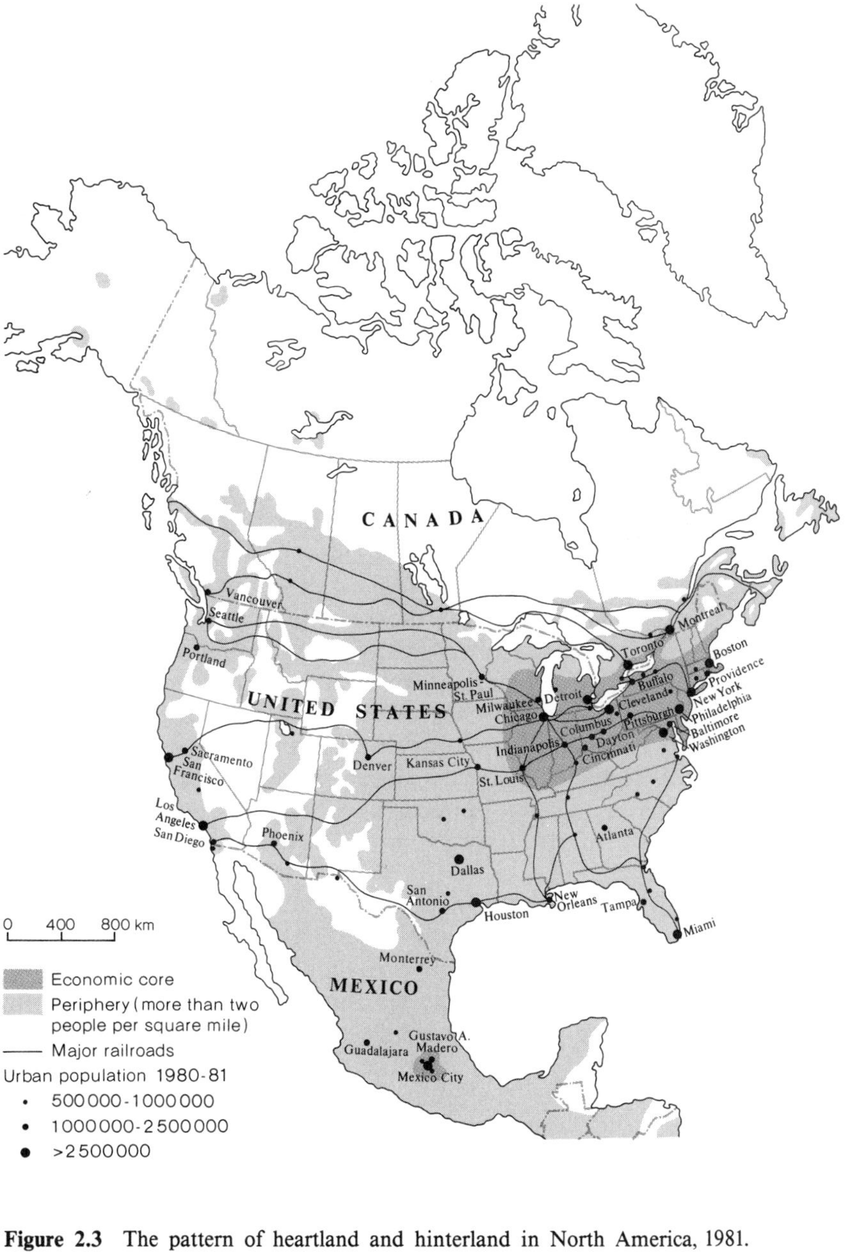

Figure 2.3 The pattern of heartland and hinterland in North America, 1981.

A revealing example of Canada's weak position in manufacturing is the automotive industry.[12] By the mid–1960s, the automotive industry employed at least 100 000 Canadians, and indirectly maintained the jobs of at least another 200 000. Endeavouring to reduce prices relative to those prevailing in the United States, while simultaneously expanding domestic production and employment, the Canadian government negotiated the Canada–United States Automobile Products Agreement (the Auto Pact), which was signed in January of 1965. The Auto Pact was unique because it eliminated duties on most automotive products, including new vehicles and parts, traded between the two countries. It was, arguably, the clearest admission by the federal government that the developments of the post–war period were creating a single North American market.

Both before and after the signing of the Auto Pact, the Canadian automotive industry was almost completely owned and controlled by the three largest American corporations in the field: General Motors, Ford, and Chrysler. These same companies also controlled, either directly or through market dominance, the new–parts industry, which itself is almost 80 percent American–owned. In the long run, these simple facts would spell difficulty for Canada. The first effect of the Auto Pact was to allow these large auto companies to rationalize their corporate organizations on a continental scale. They integrated production and marketing across both Canada and the United States, thereby achieving economies of scale which allowed, simultaneously, both lower prices and higher profits. From a trade deficit in automotive products, which approached nearly one billion dollars in 1964, the first seven years of the agreement created a Canadian trade surplus with the United States. The surplus occurred because Canadian–made parts were exported more extensively than American parts were imported.

Thereafter Canada fell back, as Canadian parts manufacturers failed to adapt to the new technical requirements and the more stringent environmental standards required by the American market. Furthermore, the factors which had originally encouraged American parent companies to establish branch plants in Canada, such as the comparative advantage of lower wages, had diminished. These same corporations instead sought locations in the American South, as well as in some countries of the hinterland, such as Mexico and Brazil. With control exercised by headquarters in Detroit and New York, and with little technological development occurring in Canada, the results were hardly surprising. From a pre–Auto Pact ratio of $1.13 of imported parts per $1.00 of Canadian–made parts used in auto assembly in Canada, by 1973 each dollar of Canadian parts was matched by $102.00 of imported parts![13] By 1982 Canada's accumulated deficit in Auto Pact trade had reached $14 billion, nearly half of which was built up over the three years from 1979–1982.[14] Yet, the impact of the Auto Pact was not simply financial: it

TABLE 2.5 UNITED STATES INVESTMENT IN CANADA AND CONTROL OF CANADIAN NON-FINANCIAL INDUSTRIES, SELECTED YEARS, 1914-1979*
(in millions of dollars and percentage share of control)

	1914		*1929*		*1950*		*1970*		*1979*	
Sector	*$*	*%*	*$*	*%*	*$*	*%*	*$*	*%*	*$*	*%*
Manufacturing	221	n.a.	819	31	1 897	39	10 050	47	24 400	39
Petroleum and natural gas	25	n.a.	55	n.a.	418	n.a.	4 809	61	14 700	40
Mining and smelting	159	n.a.	400	32	334	37	3 014	59	5 100	37
Others (including agriculture, railroads, trade, and utilities)	205	n.a.	737	n.a.	929	n.a.	4 927	n.a.	5 800	0.5
Total investment	618		2 010		3 579		22 801		50 000	

*latest available figures

Sources: Mira Wilkins, *The Emergence of Multinational Enterprise: American Investment Abroad from the Colonial Era to 1914* (Cambridge: Harvard University Press, 1970), p. 110; United States, Commerce Department, *United States Business Investments in Foreign Countries* (Washington, D.C.: 1960); *Survey of Current Business,* October 1971; W. Clement, *Continental Corporate Power* (Toronto: McClelland and Stewart, 1977), p. 91; and Statistics Canada, *Canada's International Investment Position, 1979 and 1980* (Ottawa: 1982), p. 98.

represented the comprehensive incorporation of the Canadian auto industry into a continental economy.

As the 1960s closed, relatively little new American investment was entering Canada. Most of the increase in American-controlled capital, which was nevertheless substantial, came from reinvested profits generated by Canadian-based operations. At the same time, there was a considerable outflow of capital, sent not only by American companies, but also by some wholly-owned Canadian corporations. Apart from the banks, the major participants in this process were Canadian manufacturers, such as Alcan and Massey-Ferguson, and the land development companies,

The American penetration of the Canadian economy: The Ford Motor Co. of Canada's Oakville, Ontario, auto assembly complex. Since the late nineteenth century, many American multinationals have established branch plants in Canada, particularly in southern Ontario. (*Ford Motor Co. of Canada*)

including Marathon Realty (The Canadian Pacific Railway's property arm), Cadillac Fairview, Daon Development, and Trizec. These multinationals have contributed another facet to the metropolis–hinterland paradox: Canada is the recipient of considerable foreign investment, yet it also sends abroad vast sums of capital. Most capital comes from and goes to the United States, of course; but the global scale of Canadian foreign investment is indicative of Canada's paradoxical position within the capitalist world–economy (Fig. 2.4).

Patterns of foreign trade also demonstrate the direction Canada is taking in the world–economy (Fig. 2.5). The United States is Canada's most prominent trading partner. By the early 1980s, exports comprised nearly one–quarter of Canada's Gross National Product (compared to less than 5 percent for the United States). Almost three–quarters were shipped south to American markets, and nearly three–quarters of this total were raw materials destined for American manufacturing industries. By contrast, less than one–quarter of United States exports were shipped to Canada, and most were finished manufactured products. Canada retains strong ties with its traditional European trading nations and with the European Economic Community. The demand for staple products - grains, pulp and paper, base metals - by countries such as the U.S.S.R., Britain, West Germany, and the Netherlands continues to expand; in return Canada buys automobiles, precision machinery, books, and clothes, but few raw materials. This is not the case with OPEC–centred trade. Canada needs large quantities of crude oil, and although it runs a trading deficit with Middle Eastern and other oil exporting nations, it tends to supply manufactured products — not raw materials — to these countries. For example, Canadian pre–fabricated housing is used extensively in Saudi Arabia, as is Canadian technical expertise in new–town building.

There are other, newly–emerging trade patterns which demonstrate Canada's increasing interaction with other states in the world–economy and its decreasing dependency on the United States. Foremost is Canada's strong position as a member of the Pacific Rim trading community. Two brief examples illustrate the importance of this trade. First, the growing Japanese market has significantly increased the volume of Canadian trade. During the 1970s, Japan replaced Britain as the second largest market for Canadian exports. For Japan, Canada is a secure source of raw materials. It is politically stable and there is therefore little threat that trade will be curtailed or that Japanese investments will be nationalized. A second, more symbolic development was Canada's recognition of the People's Republic of China in 1970. This step, taken well in advance of a similar move by the United States, paved the way for the emergence of China as an important trading partner in foodstuffs, particularly wheat. Moreover, it stressed Canada's determination to strike an independent course in international affairs.

Foreign direct investment in Canada, 1980

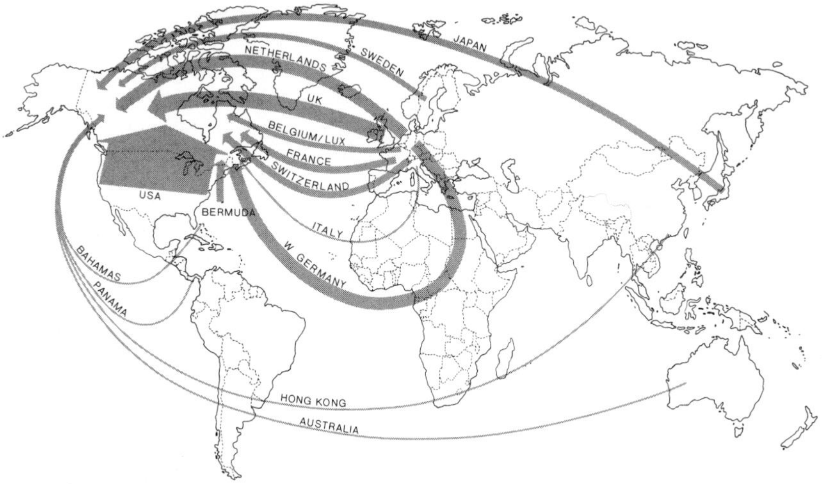

	$ '000000	Percent
USA	48684	79.0
UK	5333	8.7
Total	61637	

Capital flow in $ '000000

500 | 5000 | 15000 | 30000 | 60000

Note: Only countries with capital flows >$ 50000000 are shown

Canadian direct investment abroad, 1980

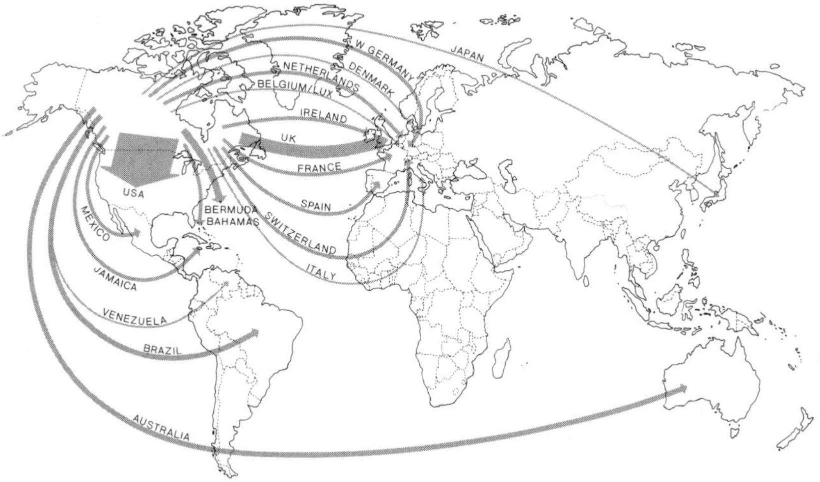

	$ '000000	Percent
USA	13603	63.2
Developed countries	18013	83.7
Developing countries	3518	16.3
Total	21531	

Figure 2.4 Canada in the world-economy: spatial patterns of investment, 1980.

Destination of Canadian exports, 1983

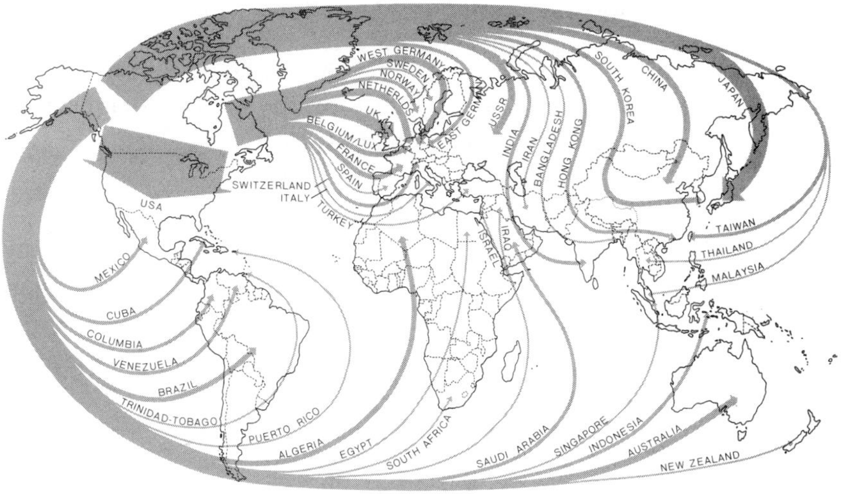

	$ '000000	Percent
USA	66333	72.9
UK	2509	2.8
Japan	4762	5.2
Total	90964	

Value of commodities in $ '000000
500 | 5000
15000
30000
60000

Note: Only countries trading >$ 100000000 in commodities are shown

Source of Canadian imports, 1983

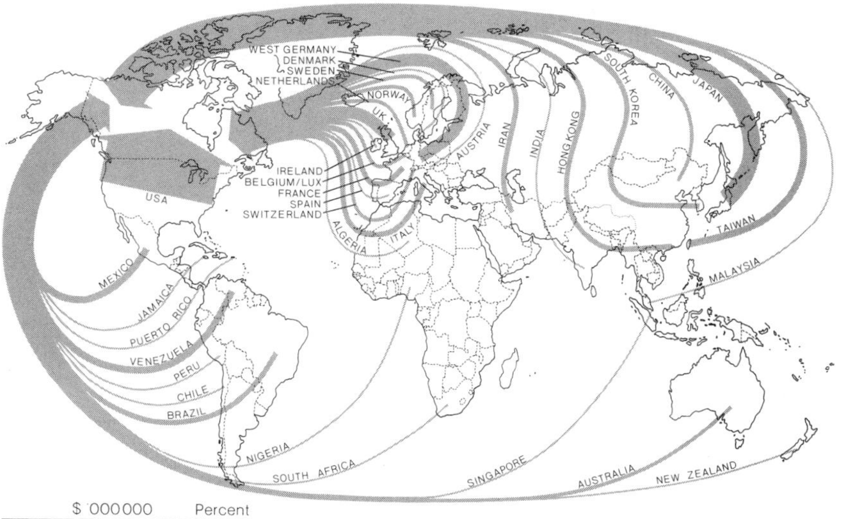

	$ '000000	Percent
USA	54103	71.6
UK	1810	2.4
Japan	4409	5.8
Total	75587	

Figure 2.5 Canada in the world-economy: spatial patterns of trade, 1983.

Despite increased diversification of spatial trade patterns, Canadian trade is still largely based on the export of staples and the import of manufactured goods. While this imbalance is well-recognized, it is the lack of those comparative advantages such as cheaper labour costs, market accessibility, or industrial linkages accompanying industrial development, especially manufacturing, that keeps Canada at a disadvantage in the global division of labour.

Regional Implications

Canada's dependency on the U.S. and on raw material exports has had important consequences for its internal spatial economy. Canada's internal economy is explored in detail in subsequent chapters, but some general comments are appropriate here. The single most important point is that the imbalance of Canada's position within the global economy has contributed to an internal pattern of regional inequalities, that is, to a metropolis–hinterland structure. Already well established by the beginning of the twentieth century, this structure has proven very resistant to change.

Since Canada's economy centres on the export of raw materials, the staple–producing hinterland regions have played a crucial role in the country's economic development. Yet the benefits of staples production have, to a considerable extent, gone to the heartland region. Why? To begin with, the infrastructure (such as transportation) and financial institutions necessary for the export of staple commodities have largely been controlled in Ontario and Québec. This infrastructure, in turn, contributed towards the industrialization of the heartland region. The latter process, extended via tariff barriers and import substitution, could rely upon a captive market in the hinterland. The staple–producing hinterland, in contrast, was in the position of selling cheap (on the open world market) and buying dear (on the protected home market). The implications of this structure became dramatically evident during periods of global depression such as the 1930s. In the case of the Maritimes, which had experienced a short–lived industrial revolution in the late nineteenth century but fell victim to the economic power of central Canada, periods of world depression like the 1930s made economic development even more precarious. For the western hinterland regions, whose natural resources (wheat, lumber, minerals, and oil) have been in greater demand, the situation has been less severe.

The pattern of foreign investment also contributed to the establishment of a metropolis–hinterland structure within Canada. Studies undertaken in the 1930s indicated that American investment had contributed towards the concentration of manufacturing in central Canada.[15] This pattern was subsequently confirmed in the work of D. Michael Ray[16] and, more graphically, in the *Gray Report.* The latter, using data from the late 1960s on twenty–one specific manufacturing industries, argued that,

> the concentration of foreign–owned manufacturing activity in Ontario reflects both the fact that Ontario is Canada's manufacturing centre and that foreign investors are investing relatively more in Ontario than in other regions, as compared to domestic investors.[17]

More recent information provided by the Federal Investment Review Agency (now Investment Canada), although lacking a sectoral breakdown, indicates that the predilection of foreign corporations for investment in Ontario has continued. Over 50 percent of total assets are targeted for Ontario, about three times the amount proposed to each of British Columbia and the Western Interior.[18]

CONCLUSION

Since Confederation, Canada has successfully escaped from the political orbit of its colonial origins. Yet, in the process, a new pattern of dependency has taken root through economic association with the United States. The clearest expression of this relationship is the control of significant segments of the Canadian economy by American corporations. Some Canadians view this continental integration as beneficial, or at least unavoidable. Indeed, as wages and the standard of living rose in the post–war decades, there was much support for this position, at least on economic grounds.

Nevertheless, those who wished to maintain a separate Canadian identity, and those who foresaw the problems an increasingly dependent status might bring, actively opposed continentalism.[19] Just as a new sense of Canadian identity fed the movement for increased independence from Great Britain, so too a sense of Canadian nationalism has arisen to challenge American involvement in Canada.

The information in Table 2.5 indicates that the pressure of economic nationalism achieved some concrete results during the 1970s. The United States' share of control in non–financial industries decreased to below 50 per cent by 1979. The "Canadianization" of the economy, including measures such as the establishment of Petro–Canada, the Federal Investment Review Agency (now Investment Canada), and the National Energy Policy (NEP), was largely the product of an interventionist stance by the federal government. The quest for autonomy was also reflected in the ranks of labour. Canadian unions such as the Canadian Association of Industrial, Mechanical, and Allied Workers have taken root and in 1986 the Canadian section of the United Auto Workers of America separated from its parent organization in the United States.

Yet these manifestations of economic nationalism, particularly the NEP, have not proved universally popular. In Alberta primarily, the NEP was viewed as an attempt to maintain regional inequalities. More recently, following the election of a Conservative government in 1984, there are signs that government policy is undergoing a shift in orientation. The NEP has been dismantled, granting greater provincial autonomy over the oil industry, and the government's rhetoric indicates that it is adopting a continentalist stance, to the extent of advocating free trade.

Whatever the outcome in this regard, it needs to be noted that nationalism embodies dimensions other than the purely economic. On the cultural plane, there have been both successes and failures in recent years. While Canadian literature, vital to our national identity, has been revitalized, the Americanization of the broadcast media has continued.

In light of such contradictory developments, we cannot view Canada as simply a "colony" of the United States. Nor is Canada comparable to the poorer and obviously peripheral nations of the world's hinterland. Canada's position in the world-system is paradoxical. It is neither just a part of the global metropolis, nor just a part of the periphery. It should be described as a part of both. According to some indices, Canada is marked by hinterland traits: foreign control of investment and technology; a high proportion of foreign trade within its Gross National Product; and the predominance of raw materials in the composition of exports. By other standards, Canada has many characteristics of a metropolitan economy: relative affluence; an international outreach in political matters; diversified industries; multinational corporations; and one of the highest standards of living in the world. To view Canada solely as a dependent country, especially during the long boom leading up to 1970, would be misleading. Canada presents a paradox — no other country combines such a high degree of dependency with an ability to exploit external connections.

NOTES

1. For elaboration on the meaning and interpretation of the world-system, see Immanuel Wallerstein, "The Rise and Future Demise of the World Capitalist System: Concepts for Comparative Analysis," *Comparative Studies in Society and History,* 16 (1974), 387–415; and *idem, The Modern World-System* (New York: Academic Press, 1974).
2. Fernand Braudel, *Afterthoughts on Material Civilization and Capitalism,* trans. P.M. Ranum (Baltimore: The Johns Hopkins University Press, 1977), p. 82.
3. Rostow discusses the stages of world economic development in his book, *The World Economy: History and Prospect* (Austin: University of Texas Press, 1978). His original statement appears in *The Stages of Economic Growth* (Cambridge: The University Press, 1960).
4. Samir Amin, *Accumulation at the World Scale* (New York: Monthly Review Press, 1974); *idem, Unequal Development* (Hassocks: Harvester Press, 1976); Andre Gundre Frank, *Capitalism and Underdevelopment in Latin America* (New York: Monthly Review Press,

1967); C. Furtado, *Economic Development of Latin America* (Cambridge: Cambridge University Press, 1977); and Ernest Mandel, *Late Capitalism* (London: New Left Books, 1975).

5. Frank, *Capitalism and Underdevelopment,* p. 9; Raul Prebisch, *The Economic Development of Latin America* (New York: 1950).
6. N.D. Kondratieff, "The Long Waves in Economic Life," *The Review of Economic Statistics,* 17 (1935), 105–15; Simon Kuznets, "Long Swings in the Growth of Population and in Related Economic Variables," *Proceedings of the American Philosophical Society,* 102 (1958), 25–53; Mandel, *Late Capitalism,* chap. 4; and J. Schumpeter, *Business Cycles* (New York: McGraw–Hill, 1964).
7. W. Woodruff, *America's Impact on the World* (Toronto: Halsted Press, 1975), pp. 236–43.
8. J.B. Brebner, *North Atlantic Triangle* (Toronto: Ryerson Press, 1945), p. 270n.
9. Glen Williams, "The National Policy Tariffs: Industrial Underdevelopment through Import Substitution," *Canadian Journal of Political Science,* 12 (1979), 333–68.
10. Brebner, *North Atlantic Triangle,* p. 269n.
11. H. Marshall, *et al., Canadian–American Industry* (Toronto: McClelland and Stewart, 1971), pp. 36–52.
12. John N.H. Britton and James M. Gilmour, *The Weakest Link,* Science Council of Canada, Background Study 43 (Ottawa: 1978), pp. 37–8; and Ontario Ministry of Treasury, Economics and Intergovernmental Affairs, *Canada's Share of the North American Automotive Industry: An Ontario Perspective* (Toronto: 1978).
13. R. Starks, *Industry in Decline* (Toronto: Lorimer, 1978), p. 84.
14. See G. Williams, *Not For Export* (Toronto: McClelland and Stewart, 1983), p. 136.
15. H. Marshall *et al., Canadian–American Industry: A Study in International Investment* (Toronto: McClelland and Stewart, 1976).
16. D. Michael Ray, "The Location of United States Subsidiaries in Southern Ontario," in R.L. Gentilcore, ed., *Geographical Approaches to Canadian Problems* (Toronto: Prentice–Hall, 1971), pp. 59–68.
17. Canada, Government of Canada, *Foreign Direct Investment in Canada* (Ottawa: 1972), popularly known as the *Gray Report.*
18. Foreign Investment Review Agency, *Annual Report, 1983–84* (Ottawa: 1984), pp. 13–27.
19. See the collection of essays on this theme in Ian Lumsden, ed., *Close the 49th Parallel etc.: The Americanization of Canada* (Toronto: University of Toronto Press, 1970).

PART II
The Heartland Regions

VIEW OF MONTREAL.

From Saint Helens Island.

Published by A. Bourne, Montreal. 1830.

3

The Emergence of the Industrial Heartland, c. 1750-1950

Donald Kerr

The remarkable paradox of central Canada is that, although it can claim status as Canada's heartland, it has been and continues to be sharply divided along the Ottawa River into two distinctly different linguistic and cultural regions. At Confederation there was a marked contrast between the deeply-rooted, French-speaking Catholics living in Canada East and the strongly British, English-speaking Protestants of Canada West. These two contrasting jurisdictions, joined in an uneasy political alliance, have persisted over two centuries.

If central Canada has little or no cultural or social unity, what justification is there for demarcating a region beyond some vague historical identity? The answer lies in the economic realm. Squeezed between the Shield and the American border on a relatively small lowland, central Canada has attracted innumerable factories, trading enterprises, and financial institutions, both foreign and domestically owned. As the centre of industry, trade, and finance, it controls the Canadian economy. Although there is little social connection between individuals or communities in Québec and those in Ontario, there is a strong and deeply-rooted economic interaction and interdependence.

The purpose of this chapter, then, is to provide a geographical study of the Industrial Heartland's changing economic structure and its dominant position in the Canadian space economy. The chapter emphasizes historical economic geography and aims to interpret geographic change through the examination of four interrelated themes: resources and economic development; inter-regional trade and growing interdependence between Ontario and Québec; the Industrial Heartland's role in economic development and control *vis-à-vis* the rest of Canada;

and the impact of growth on the spatial organization of central Canada's economy.

Although the relationship between resource endowment and economic growth is complex, staple theory provides an appropriate framework for analysis.[1] Put simply, the export of first furs and later timber products provided revenue to support the beginnings of a domestic economic system. In the nineteenth century the agricultural resources of the region proved to be the critical catalyst to growth. In fact, it might be argued that had the direction of geological events been somewhat different, causing the ancient boundary of the Canadian Shield to lie anywhere from 100 to 150 kilometres further south of its present position, the course of Canadian history might have changed. If the lowland had been compressed more tightly between the Pre-Cambrian mass to the north and the Appalachians to the south, thereby reducing the amount of arable land significantly, a viable agricultural society could not have been supported and Canada as we know it may not have survived. Be that as it may, there is no question that in the nineteenth century wheat became the main staple of the agricultural lowland. Producers found overseas markets and the rising optimism stimulated land clearing and immigration and subsequently encouraged domestic manufacturing, railway building, and an expanding urban network.[2]

A succession of staples — furs, timber, and then wheat — were shipped through the Great Lakes–St. Lawrence system across the North Atlantic to markets in western Europe. From an early date the merchants of Montréal took charge, directing the flow of goods in and out of the "Commercial Empire of the St. Lawrence" by exchanging foreign manufactured goods for staples. They thus developed the infrastructure of transportation systems, commercial contacts, and financial mechanisms necessary for the flow of goods and information between Upper and Lower Canada. Although closed by ice to ships during the winter and interrupted by rapids and waterfalls, the St. Lawrence–Great Lakes system played a decisive role in the pattern of trade, and not surprisingly the most progressive of the early towns were ports. Later, canals, railways, highways, and telegraph and telephone lines were built to facilitate trade, and new manufacturing towns sprang up away from the St. Lawrence. The roots of modern inter-regional trade had been established.

By the middle of the nineteenth century, changes in the economic structure of the emerging core *vis-à-vis* the rest of Canada could be detected — the region was showing signs of national importance. The growth of manufacturing industries and financial institutions and the strengthening of wholesale and retail trading houses all coincided with the development of railways and gave strength and diversity to the region's economic base.

Thus, at the time of Confederation, the central Canadian economy had reached a level of maturity that allowed it to take an active role in the development of the hinterland. Aided by the protectionist policies of the federal government, especially those embodied in the National Policy of the late 1870s, centrally-based companies expanded into the periphery; and through corporate policies of centralization, they reduced or eliminated the ability of many hinterland firms to compete. The imposition of high tariffs on most agricultural machinery made it almost impossible for farmers in western Canada to buy machinery from anywhere else but southern Ontario. The Bank Act of 1871 fostered the rise of national banks which, by 1920, through merger and financial acquisition, made the financial houses of Montréal and Toronto the undisputed masters of accounts from the Atlantic to the Pacific. Low postal rates created opportunities for large catalogue distributors, such as Eaton's of Toronto, to challenge local retailers and regional wholesalers. In similar fashion, the weak corporate trust laws of the pre–1929 era encouraged central Canadian institutions to take over sectors of the economy in the Maritimes.

Despite their consequences, such measures integrated the growing national economy. The Industrial Heartland controlled wholesale and retail prices, interest and insurance rates, and trading and investment policies, and in doing so, it created a system of dominance which has persisted to the present. It would be incorrect, however, to conclude that control was absolute, because some sectors of regional economies, such as the British Columbia forest industry and the Alberta oil industry, have prospered independently of central Canada. Ironically, with the increasing penetration of direct American investment in Canada in the twentieth century, many critical decisions have been made in New York, Detroit, and other American cities, bypassing the Industrial Heartland completely. Nonetheless, the extraordinary geographical concentration of economic power in the central region is a distinct characteristic of Canada.

What impact, then, has this economic growth had on the internal geographical organization of the Heartland? While some towns have grown into large, multi–functional centres, others have remained unchanged, part of a stagnating local economy. The group of towns and cities stretching from Québec City to Windsor has come to form the economic core of central Canada, often described as "Main Street." Railways and highways integrate this bustling corridor, which stands in sharp contrast to the stable rural economies of eastern Ontario, the Chaudière Valley of Québec, and the Huron Uplands of Ontario. Yet, within the corridor itself, growth has been differential. Some once prosperous old ports such as Cobourg, and industrial towns such as Valleyfield, have declined.

In contrast, the two metropolitan centres of Montréal and Toronto, including towns and cities within a radius of about 100 kilometres, have grown rapidly and account for over 40 percent of the population in

Canada, 55 percent of the manufacturing, and most of the critical corporate and financial decision making. The result is a strikingly bi-polar spatial pattern. In fact, while these prosperous metropolitan centres have given the Heartland national pre-eminence, they have also created, at the regional-provincial scale, a strong internal core-periphery structure: Montréal within Québec and, to a lesser degree, Toronto within Ontario.

All of these geographical changes have taken place gradually but consistently over the course of almost two hundred years, beginning in the mid-eighteenth century and reaching maturity by the 1950s. During this *longue durée*[3] — the historical geography of a long time span — strong economic and political forces made the Industrial Heartland the dominant region of Canada. The strength of the Heartland is now being challenged by other regions, particularly Alberta, breaking the pattern of dominance. Furthermore, the spatial patterns of metropolitan growth, reflecting strong provincial core-periphery structures, combined with the growing cultural distinctiveness and vigorous nationalism in Québec, have challenged the Heartland's ability to act as an integrating national force. A new era of core-periphery development is unfolding.

STAPLES AND EARLY DEVELOPMENT

In 1760, the area north of the Great Lakes was taken over by Britain and the basis of modern Canada was formed. Thirty years later, in 1791, this territory was divided into two jurisdictions: Lower Canada, the well-established French colony in the St. Lawrence Valley; and Upper Canada, the vast and almost empty forest beyond.

Understandably, the geographic framework of Lower Canada was well in place at the time of the Conquest, the product of a settlement history of at least 150 years. Québec and Montréal, which by 1760 had grown to house populations of 8000 and 5200 respectively, dominated the economic and social life of the colony. Standing guard over the estuary of the St. Lawrence, Québec City maintained a superb location where the French had centred their military operations and administered the colony. Deep water, without significant currents or tidal variations, provided an ideal harbour for sailing ships, and Québec functioned as the terminus for virtually all Atlantic shipping. Montréal, situated at the Lachine Rapids and commanding the Ottawa, St. Lawrence, and Richelieu valleys, existed primarily as a trans-shipment centre and controlled much of the fur trade. Although farming provided the livelihood for the bulk of the population, the fur trade created some wealth for the colony, encouraged exploration of the back country, and brought the French into contact with the Indians. At the time of the Conquest, the British acquired an established colony of some 60 000 French-speaking Catholics who had cleared considerable land for agriculture within a few kilometres of the St. Lawrence River, and

A seigneurial landscape in Québec: Long lots stretch into the Canadian Shield, revealing a system of land tenure and settlement that has characterized the region for four centuries. (*Larry McCann*)

who had built two cities in which virtually all commercial, political, and religious activities were centred.[4]

In the period immediately following the British Conquest, the economic geography of Lower Canada changed very little. The fur trade not only persisted but expanded, as it was increasingly controlled by British traders who eventually merged many small operations into the continent-wide North West Company. Although French Canadians lost control of much of the fur trade, they continued to provide most of the work force. Important, too, was the immediate movement of French-Canadian farmers onto empty seigneurial lands, where they produced a modest surplus of wheat for export. Linear villages ran through the countryside, but most remained commercially insignificant. In contrast, Loyalist immigrants took up land in the Eastern Townships within the framework of a rectangular survey. In Montréal and Québec City, the number of Scottish and American entrepreneurs and poor English and

Irish immigrants increased markedly, thus reducing the native French population to less than half.[5]

Around the turn of the nineteenth century, the rich pine, spruce, and maple resources of the central lowlands and neighbouring Shield began to be exploited. Newly formed companies appropriated large tracts of land and exploited timber along the Ottawa, Saguenay, and other valleys of central Canada. Squared timber and lumber were exported to Britain when, during the Napoleonic Wars, traditional Baltic supplies were cut off and, subsequently, when tariff legislation gave preference to Canadian suppliers. For the most part, the timber trade was organized by merchants in Montréal and Québec City, and not by those in Upper Canada.[6]

The territory to the west, when partitioned off as Upper Canada and opened for European settlement late in the eighteenth century, was only

Lumber ships at Québec City, 1872: The staple timber trade was vital to the economies of Upper and Lower Canada in the pre-Confederation era. Its significance waned when accessible forests were exploited and international demand declined. (*Notman Photographic Archives*)

sparsely populated by Native peoples. United Empire Loyalists and Americans accounted for most of the early settlement, to be joined in the decades after the War of 1812 by large numbers of immigrants from the British Isles. The population of Upper Canada grew rapidly, and in a period of nine years — from 1842 to 1851 — it more than doubled from 450 000 to 952 000 people.[7] Nearly all of these settlers took up farming. From the outset they grew wheat, most of which was sold to Britain, and increasingly after 1840, these sales provided the necessary support for an expanding agrarian economy.[8]

That most of the wheat came from Upper Canada may be explained, at least in part, by the region's superior physical resources. In terms of present climatic conditions, southwestern Ontario has a growing season that is longer, warmer, and less susceptible to unseasonable frost than southern Québec. Windsor, which has an energy supply of almost 2 400 growing degree days (Celsius) and an average frost-free period of 170 days (and thus is similar to areas of the American Midwest), stands in contrast to Québec City, which maintains an average of just less than 1 600 growing degree days (Celsius) and a frost-free period of 132 days (conditions resemble those of northern New England). For the most part, the soils of southern Ontario were more productive than those of Québec, and although the soils of both regions deteriorated in the nineteenth century because of improper cultivation, the acid soils of Québec suffered more. Wheat grown there also became susceptible to insect infestation and disease at an earlier date than in Ontario, reducing yields accordingly. Spring wheat continued to be grown in Lower Canada through the nineteenth century, but acreages remained small.

The traditional literature on farming in central Canada in the nineteenth century has stressed regional farming distinctions, emphasizing the development of a more prosperous agriculture in Upper Canada, based on the export of wheat, and the persistence of a stagnant rural economy in Lower Canada. The conservative cultural traditions of French–Canadian farmers are cited as the main reason for this distinction. By subdividing their land so that most sons could enter farming, French Canadians created uneconomical farm units. Soil exhaustion and the difficulty of securing local and external markets further depressed the economy. The British Canadians, by contrast, usually passed on land only to the eldest son and used new technologies to their economic advantage.[9] More recent investigations have challenged this interpretation, however, and emphasize that until the late nineteenth century, both groups were slow to adopt new farming techniques and were for the most part inefficient farmers.[10] By inheriting a superior climate and richer soils, it was inevitable that farmers in Upper Canada would enjoy greater commercial success than those in Lower Canada.

The "failure" of the wheat economy in Lower Canada, combined with rapid population growth in relation to a shortage of land, initiated an out–

migration of French Canadians to the United States in the 1830s. At the same time, emigration to the American Midwest continued apace from neighbouring and supposedly more prosperous areas of Upper Canada. From both areas, out-migration seemed to occur in pulsations more closely related to economic conditions in the United States than to any other factor. The expanding industrial economy of the United States drew migrants particularly after mid-century. Thus, as arable land in Québec fell in short supply and the high birth rate persisted, many French-Canadian families pushed into the textile towns of New England and in many areas established large French Catholic parishes.[11]

The differential impact of the wheat trade on the early economic landscape can be explained in a number of ways.[12] In Canada West, a varied trading network — composed of lake ports, inland towns, villages, and rudimentary roads — took shape and facilitated the export of wheat. There was no comparable development in Canada East where, apart from Montréal and Québec City, the urban hierarchy remained poorly developed. For example, by 1850, some 38 urban centres housing over 1000 people could be identified in Canada West. The populations of Kingston, Hamilton, London, and Ottawa ranged between 5000 and 25 000, and Toronto stood at 30 800. In contrast, there were only 16 centres in Canada East which exceeded the urban threshold, and 14 of these had fewer than 5000 people. The two largest centres — Montréal (57 700) and Québec City (42 000) — were exceptional indeed (Fig. 3.1). In short, these different urban hierarchies, whose basic form still exists, have their origins early in the nineteenth century and are apparently related to commercial agriculture more than to any other factor.

Capital accumulated from the sale of wheat and timber, and the injection of funds by the British for defence and administration supported the rise of manufacturing in urban centres early in the nineteenth century. Invariably, small manufacturers — including grist and saw mills, tanneries, and distilleries — grew up at settlements with access to water power, and these activities were soon augmented in some places by industries producing consumer goods such as farm implements and furniture. In the parlance of staple theory, the sale of resource commodities abroad created capital to purchase necessities and even luxuries, an increasing number of which were produced locally. Later, on a larger and urban scale, first in the 1840s in Montréal and then in the 1850s in Toronto, manufacturing expanded significantly in response to the growing rural market of Canada West.[13]

The economy of Montréal continued to prosper in the face of a depressed local agriculture. This juxtaposition of rural depression and urban buoyancy can be explained by the stimuli of immigration and the wheat trade. The merchants of Montréal organized the wheat trade by pressing the Legislature of Lower Canada for funds to build, widen, and deepen canals for the improvement of transportation along the St.

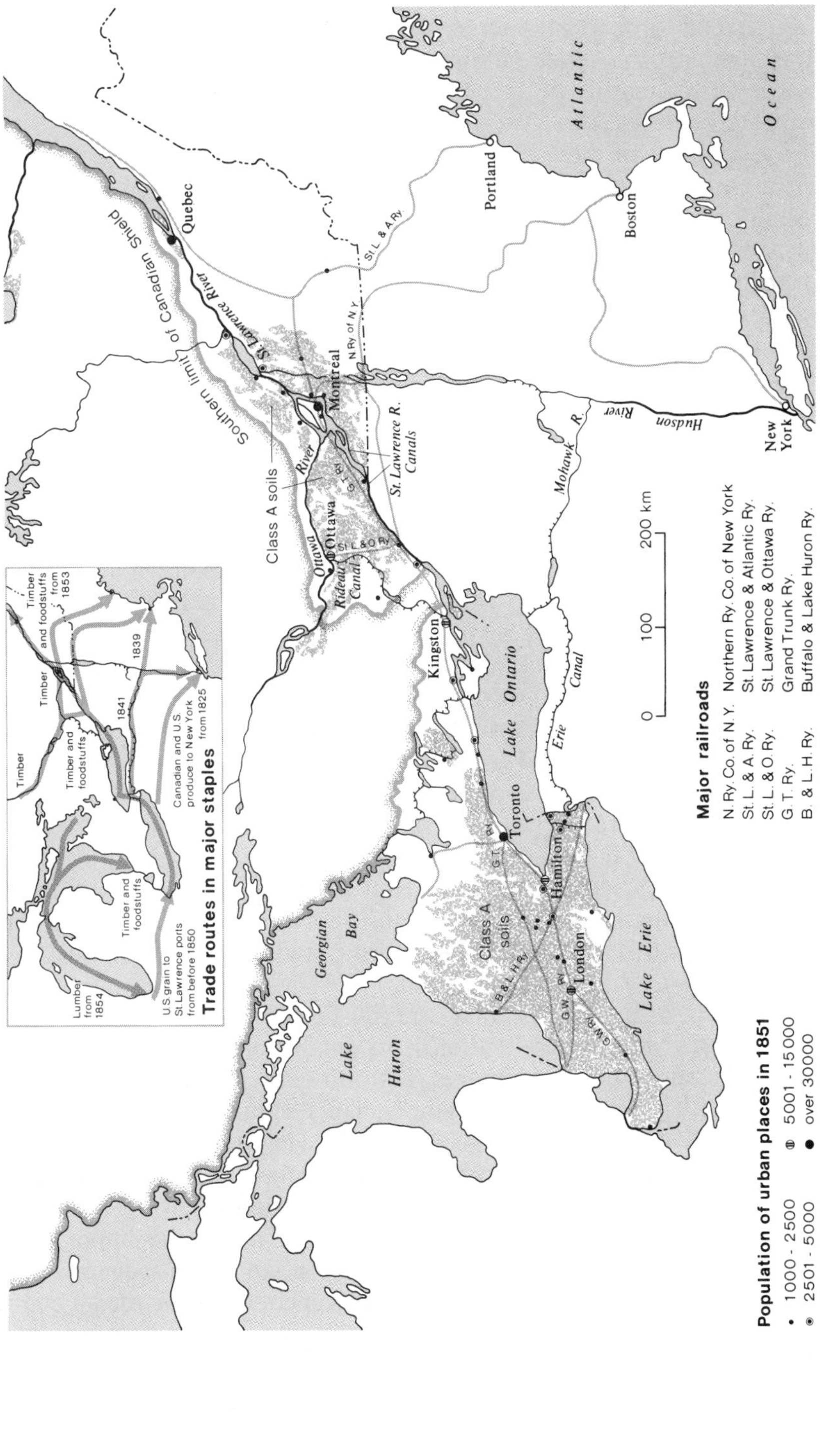

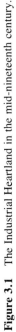

Figure 3.1 The Industrial Heartland in the mid-nineteenth century.

Lawrence system. The most serious impediment to ocean-going vessels, apart from the ice of winter, was the shallow and treacherous water at the western end of Lac St. Pierre. Through the deepening, widening, and straightening of channels, unimpeded access to Montréal was gained in 1848. An increasing number of vessels then sailed directly inland, bypassing Québec.

As a result of these developments, between 1850 and 1899, the value of the import and export trade at Montréal increased from $8.9 to $129 million, while over the same period at Quebéc City it remained virtually unchanged ($7.2 to $9.9 million). Even as canal building increased upstream from Montréal, plans for railroad construction were well under way, and Montréal businessmen pursued this activity as well. In fact, a short line had been built to bypass the rapids on the Richelieu River along the water route from Montréal to New York as early as 1836 and in 1847, the Champlain Railway was opened around the Lachine Rapids. Of far more importance was the completion, in 1853, of a railroad from Montréal to Portland on Maine's Atlantic coast. This line was further extended as the Grand Trunk to Toronto in 1856 and on to Sarnia by 1859 (Fig. 3.1).[14]

Complementing the canal and rail developments of the 1840s, the flow of information also improved. In 1848 telegraphic communications were opened between Montréal and Toronto and in 1856, following the regular scheduling of rail services, the time required to deliver a letter between the two cities had dropped from about 10 days to less than 24 hours.

As transportation and communication improved, and as the economy became more concentrated geographically, some cities grew at the expense of others. Québec City found itself in an increasingly marginal position as new rail routes converged on Montréal. At Confederation, when its population of 50 000 was only one half the size of Montréal, it was still engaged in a desperate struggle to gain access to Montréal and Toronto through the building of the North Shore Railway.[15] The eventual bankruptcy and sale of this railway further reduced the economic role of Québec City as a rival to Montréal.

In Upper Canada a similar struggle for urban leadership eventually gave primacy to Toronto. Although its small but well-sheltered harbour provided some natural advantages, Toronto's rise must be explained by its role as political capital and by its merchants' staunch belief that it would gain control over the rich Northwest. In fact, the notion of Toronto exerting control over trade in the Northwest began early in the writings and policies of Governor Simcoe. By the late 1840s, George Brown was writing frequently in the newly-formed *Globe* about the importance of western trade and the need to acquire western lands. Subsequently, in the late 1850s, a consortium of Toronto entrepreneurs was awarded a contract by the Canadian government to develop roads and railways in the Thunder Bay district through the new Northwest Transport Company.

At the same time, increasing amounts of wheat were being shipped through the port of Toronto and although the merchants of Hamilton and London were aggressive rivals, those in Toronto dominated. The extension of the Great Western Railway in the mid-1850s diverted substantial trade from Hamilton, previously the foremost wholesaling centre. Kingston, equal in size and importance to Toronto in the early nineteenth century, possessed a restricted agricultural hinterland and failed to keep pace. Thus, the increasing concentration of merchants, financiers, and some manufacturers in Toronto provided the basis for regional control and eventually Toronto mounted a sustained challenge against the hegemony of Montréal. In fact, through the 1850s and '60s, Toronto entrepreneurs partially freed themselves from Montréal's grasp, strengthening ties with New York via the Hudson–Mohawk route and developing a stronger industrial base.[16]

By Confederation, then, the Industrial Heartland had emerged as an integrated and distinctive economic region, bound together by a network of transportation and communication facilities. The region's principal sources of capital were derived from the sale abroad of wheat and timber, from the expenditures of the British government on local defence and administration, and increasingly from the transfer to Canada of undetermined amounts of capital by British immigrants. The large-scale benefits of the staple trade in wheat and timber accrued not only to the merchants of Montréal, but also to their rivals in Toronto. There is little doubt that at the time of Confederation, many merchants, manufacturers, and financiers of these two cities were ready to participate in the exploitation of both the new western territories and the provinces of Nova Scotia, New Brunswick, and Prince Edward Island.

THE INDUSTRIAL HEARTLAND A CENTURY AGO

By the 1880s, the spatial arrangement of settlement and transportation facilities in the Industrial Heartland had crystallized to the extent that the outline of today's patterns of regional differentiation were well in place (Figs. 3.2 and 3.3). Agricultural settlement had reached its outer limits in southern Ontario where, in fact, some rural depopulation had already occurred. Québec farmers, occupying all but the poorly drained parts of the St. Lawrence Lowlands, had invaded, with varying degrees of success, portions of the Appalachian roughlands and even the terrain of the Shield. Some 3360 kilometres of railroads integrated the region. Urbanization proceeded apace with approximately one of every four people living in towns or cities in 1881. The agricultural economy was giving way to industrialization.

Within Québec, regional patterns distinguished the St. Lawrence Lowlands from both the Eastern Townships and the fringe of the Shield,

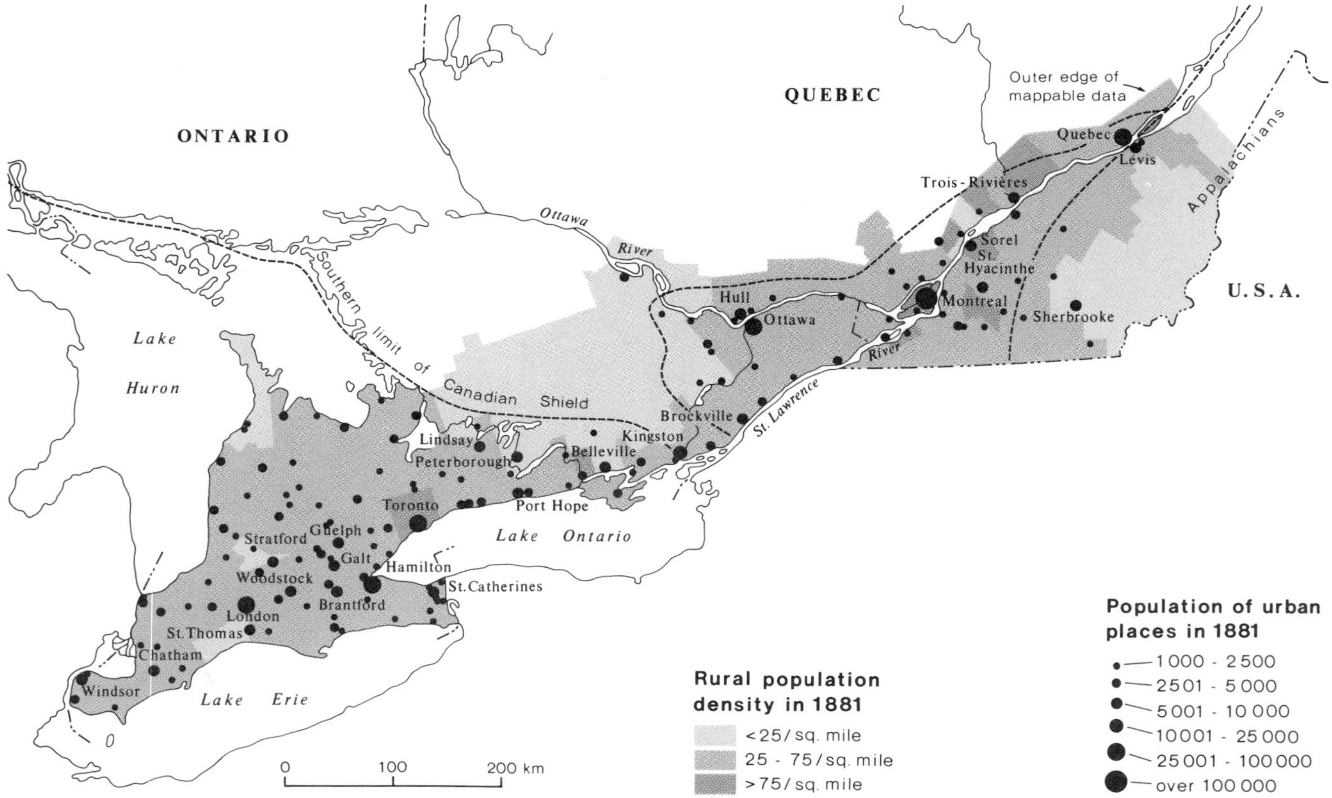

Figure 3.2 The distribution of population in the Industrial Heartland, 1881.

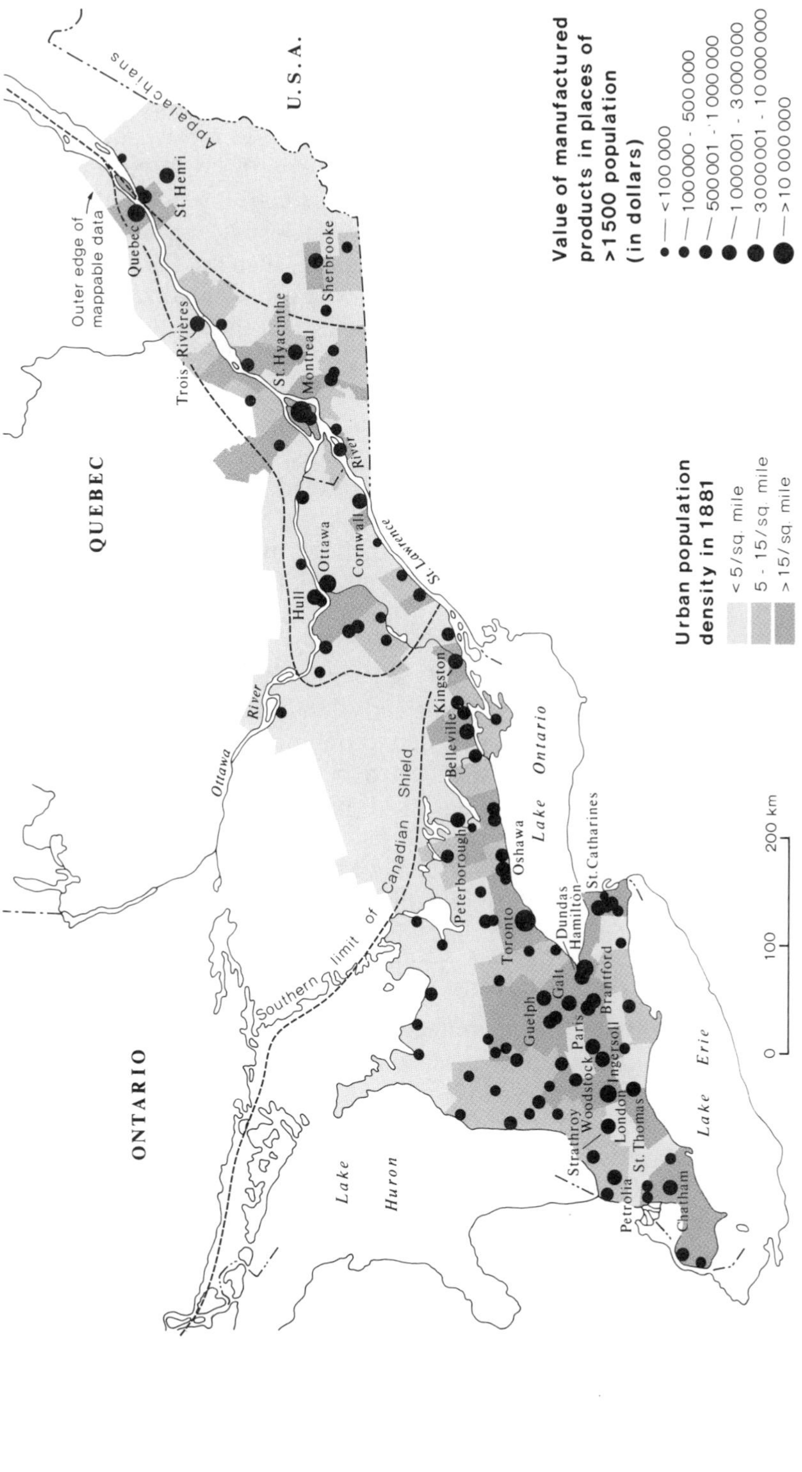

Figure 3.3 Urban-centered manufacturing in the Industrial Heartland, 1881.

and further emphasized the importance of Montréal and, to a lesser extent, Québec City. Rural French–Canadian society was strongly entrenched in the Lowlands where mixed–farming was prominent. Although modest progress had been made in commercial farming in Québec, especially in the production of dairy products, population pressure on agricultural lands had increased. For this above all other reasons, out–migration from the Lowlands continued to New England, to the crowded tenements of Montréal, to the clay lowlands of the Lac St. Jean area, along the south shore toward Gaspé, and into the Eastern Townships. A few towns of the Lowlands, such as St. Hyacinthe, had expanded in response to both the increasing commercialization of farming and the expansion of railways, and provided another outlet for the surplus rural population.

In the more rolling country of the Eastern Townships, French and British were interspersed in almost equal numbers. The French were late arrivals, pre–empting poorer lands bypassed earlier by the British and purchasing farms the British had since vacated. Sherbrooke, with good rail connections, functioned as the regional capital with a population of about 7200. In addition to basic service functions, it housed several industrial establishments employing approximately 1350 workers. To the north of the St. Lawrence, on the fringes of the Shield, attempts at settlement had proven to be difficult.[17]

Standing in sharp contrast to rural Québec was Montréal, the Canadian metropolis, which in the early 1880s had a population of almost 200 000. Its strong and diversified economy was based on trade and related manufacturing, a fact reflected in the large number of wholesale establishments, commission agents, financial institutions, and entrepôt manufacturers. Water–borne traffic had increased quickly in the second half of the nineteenth century to make Montréal Canada's most important seaport. By the early 1880s manufacturing already boasted over 32 000 workers employed in a variety of enterprises making ships, foundry products, marine engines, railway engines and equipment, shoes, tobacco, sugar, and flour. Led by the energies of Scottish, English, and some American entrepreneurs, manufacturing in Montréal thus accounted for approximately half the provincial total, a ratio which has remained fairly constant to the present.

Fronting the north side of the St. Lawrence River, Montréal a century ago extended west beyond Atwater Avenue and well into St. Henri, east beyond rue d'Iberville into Hochelaga, and north beyond Mount Royal Avenue into St. Louis Du Mile End (Fig. 3.4). French Canadians, increasing in number, comprised nearly 60 percent of the population and were found mainly to the east and northeast of the business core. In the core, British institutions dominated the economic life of the city. Their

Figure 3.4 H. W. Hopkins' map of Montréal in 1879. (*AT/340/Public Archives Canada.*) ▶

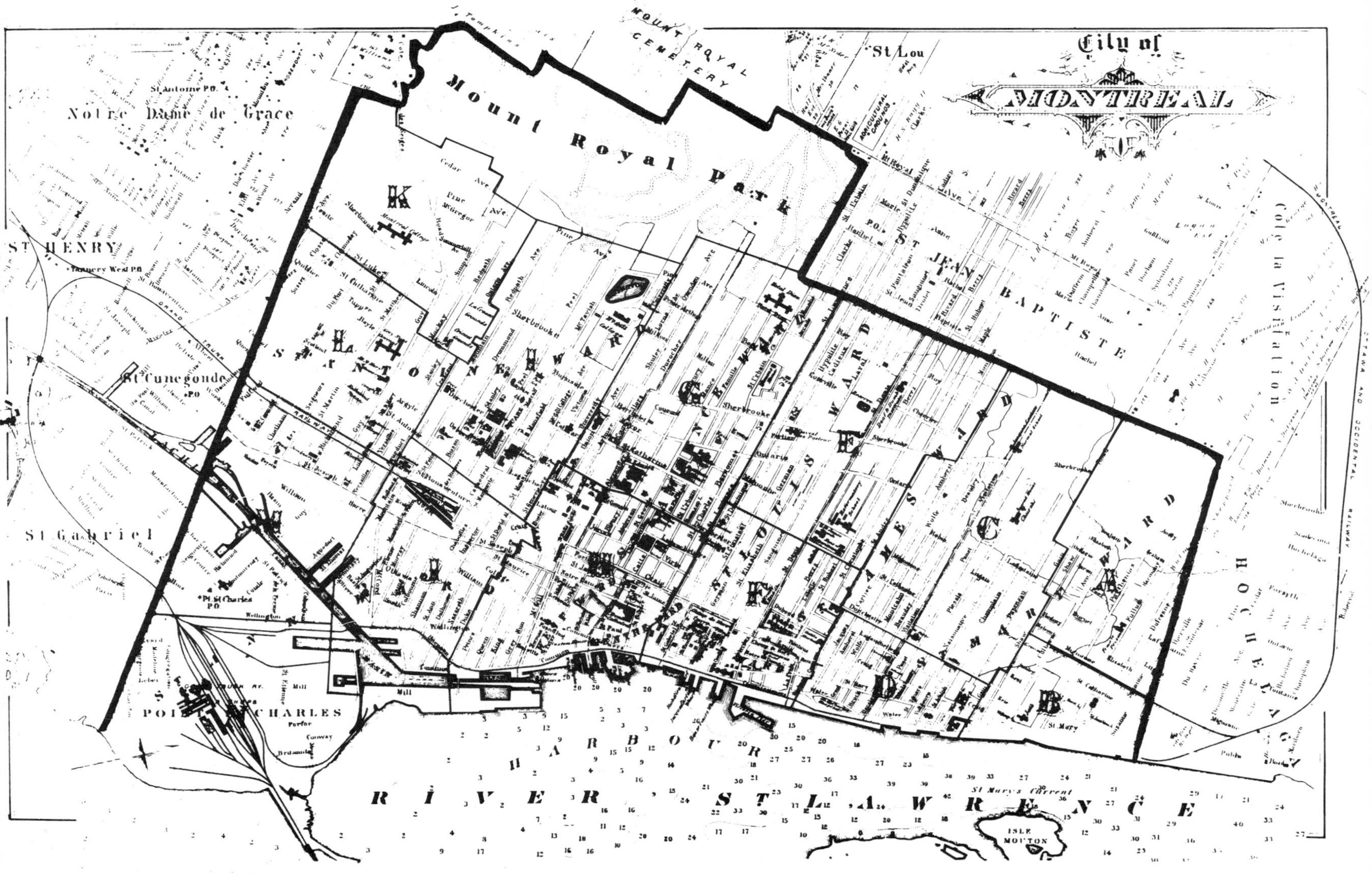
City of
MONTREAL
Mount Royal Park
Mount Royal Cemetery
St Jean Baptiste
Cote la Visitation
Hochelaga
Notre Dame de Grace
St Henry
St Cunegonde
St Gabriel
Point St Charles
Harbour
River St Lawrence
St Mary's Current
Isle Mouton
Ottawa and Occidental Railway
Grand Trunk
Lachine Canal
Sherbrooke

control stretched from the docks and wharves along the river, through the nearby wholesaling districts, to the financial district on St. James Street, and on to the new retail district of Notre Dame Street built in the 1860s. Along Dorchester, St. Catherine, and Sherbrooke Streets, middle- and upper-class housing extended to Westmount, where a new street plan had just been drawn and a few houses built. French-Canadian economic institutions, fewer in number but by no means insignificant, had taken up positions mainly within and just to the northeast of the downtown area.

The growing industrialization of the nineteenth century had created distinctive landscapes of its own, especially in the suburbs around the Lachine Canal. The development of hydraulic power at the Mill Street and St. Gabriel Locks in the late 1840s gave rise by the 1870s to rolling mills, foundries, a sugar refinery, flour mills, and sash and door, tool, and textile factories. In response, working-class houses were built close by, creating distinctive Irish and French-Canadian neighbourhoods. Further west, the old village of St. Henri was being integrated into the industrial fabric of the city, with the building of the Montréal Street Railway car barns, a large sewing machine plant, an abattoir in the 1860s and '70s, and a spate of industrial development in the later decades. Further south, closer to the river, the Grand Trunk Railway had built a complex of shops in the 1850s which provided employment for hundreds of workers, many of whom had been brought directly from England. Point St. Charles, located close by, had become a distinctive English working-class district. A similar pattern of industrialization extended to the northeast of the downtown area, from Molson's Brewery, built in 1790 at the foot of avenue Papineau, to include, by the 1870s, sugar, tobacco, and rubber factories, a gas works, a cotton mill, and the shops of the Montréal Street Railway Company and of the Québec, Montréal, Ottawa, and Occidental Railway. Houses were built for French-Canadians at St. Jacques and Ste. Marie in the East end. These were the forerunners of the innumerable francophone districts, such as Hochelaga and Maisonneuve, which were constructed in the late nineteenth and early twentieth centuries.[18]

Downriver at Québec City, where the lumber trade had previously stagnated, ship building was in decline; and the exodus of the English, which began at mid-century, had accelerated. As a result, the city was growing very slowly, if at all. Nevertheless, by emphasizing its role as provincial capital, by maintaining important functions in church administration, by supporting a few labour-intensive industries (such as shoemaking), and by serving a moderately prosperous but rather small agricultural area, Québec City was able to withstand serious economic decline. The die had been cast, however, and Québec would thereafter remain less than one-quarter the size of Montréal.

By 1880 in southern Ontario, the general aura was one of well-being. Wheat still accounted for much of the improved farm acreage, but its decline had already set in, and the change to more modern specialized

Landscapes in contrast: The French influence and simplicity of design distinguish a seventeenth century farm house on Ile d'Orléans, Québec from Ringwood Farm, Whitby Township, Ontario (1877). Farm size and railroad symbolize prosperity and progress in the agricultural economy of Ontario. (*Top: Larry McCann; Bottom: A/420/Public Archives of Canada*)

farming was well underway. A combination of low wheat prices, increasing incidences of blight, and declining soil productivity forced farmers to seek new options, but fortuitously, important structural changes in agriculture made possible both alternative strategies and the maintenance of attained living standards. New drainage techniques encouraged the use of rich lands otherwise too wet for cultivation, including, in particular, areas of level land in southwestern Ontario. A relatively long and warm growing season facilitated the successful cultivation of corn and related crops.

Other sectors of the agricultural industry prospered as well. Improved strains of dairy cattle, mechanical inventions such as the cream separator, and expanding markets for butter and especially cheese in Britain all supported a remarkable expansion of dairy production. Although the dairy industry was widespread, concentration was apparent even in the 1880s in Oxford County in the southwest, and in Dundas County in the east. Elsewhere, the urban market for fruits and vegetables was expanding, and because of general improvements in farming methods, horticulture was becoming increasingly specialized in the Niagara Peninsula and along the shores of the Great Lakes. Here risks of unreasonable spring and late summer frosts and winter kill were minimal.

Throughout these rural areas of Victorian Ontario, the landscape reflected a mix of British and American influences and a striking uniformity. Only the French–Canadian settlements in eastern Ontario and the Mennonite settlements in Waterloo County provided a modicum of diversity. True, there were areas of Irish, Scottish, and English settlement, but their field patterns, houses, barns, and villages were more alike than dissimilar.

Standing out sharply from this rural countryside were the industrial cities of southwestern Ontario, including Toronto, Hamilton, Brantford, Galt, and Guelph (Figs. 3.2 and 3.3). By the early 1880s, Toronto possessed a population of almost 90 000, making it twice the size of Hamilton, its nearest rival. Building on its advantageous location as a focal point of rail and road routes, Toronto had steadily increased its share of the production and distribution of goods in southern Ontario and had contributed significant capital to its own activities and to those of other parts of Ontario and western Canada. In fact, Toronto exhibited, on a somewhat more modest scale, the same multi–functional characteristics as Montréal. The city housed various types of wholesaling, including dry goods, food products, and medicines; manufacturing, particularly industries producing food and beverages, clothing, boots and shoes, machinery, furniture, and metal products; and financial institutions, which varied from insurance and trust companies to banks and a stock exchange.[19]

These activities brought change to the city. By the early 1880s, Toronto had spread across much of the level terrain of the old Lake Ontario Plain. It ran a northward course along Yonge Street and showed more growth to the northwest than to the northeast. To the regret of many, the railways had pre–empted the lakeshore area, thereby reducing access to what were once attractive recreational grounds. Industries followed the railways and wholesalers strengthened their concentration nearby, especially on Front Street. Predominantly British and Protestant and divided into distinctive classes, the Toronto townscape revealed the stately mansions of the wealthy on Jarvis Street, the tenements of the poor to the east and west of the business core, and everywhere red brick Presbyterian and Methodist churches.

Urban change also prevailed elsewhere. Hamilton was in a state of transition — manufacturing had expanded to offset declines in wholesaling and financial activity. Strong entrepreneurial and municipal leadership partially explain the rise of textile and metal fabricating to augment well-established clothing and hardware industries. Much the same kind of development characterized Brantford, where the manufacture of farm machinery and engines dominated, and also Guelph, which produced sewing machines and musical instruments. The growth of manufacturing in these and other nearby places fostered the growth of population in the Toronto–centred region, creating a legacy of concentration which has continued to influence the geographical structure of southern Ontario well into the present century (compare Figs. 3.3 and 3.5).

But urban and industrial growth were by no means insignificant in other parts of Ontario. The discovery of petroleum in the extreme southwest, at Petrolia, provided the basis for modest industrial development there and paved the way for significant growth at nearby Sarnia a half–century later. In anticipation of the western Canadian grain trade, flour milling was established at the Georgian Bay port of Collingwood. Along the Grand Trunk corridor, on the north shore of Lake Ontario, at least 2000 railway cars were built at the Cobourg Car Works in 1880 alone; and just over 150 kilometres to the east, at Kingston, a short–lived industrial revival produced textiles, locomotives, and biscuits. Ottawa, despite its status as the capital of Canada, was dominated by the lumber industry which employed many and provided the financial basis for a local bank. In some other communities in eastern Ontario, such as Cornwall and Almonte, Montréal interests had built textile mills.

THE DRIVE TO INDUSTRIAL MATURITY

Toward the end of the nineteenth century, the Canadian economy began to expand considerably. The Gross National Product, one measure of this growth, quadrupled from $581 million to $2.2 billion between 1880 and 1910. Leading this surge was central Canada, where the population increased from just over 3 million in 1881, to 5 million in 1921, and then to approximately 8 million in 1951. Employment in all sectors except agriculture experienced a similar upward spiral. In fact, by 1913 Canada ranked third in the world after the United States and Britain in the output of manufactured goods per capita.[20] The extent to which this expansion was due to the acquisition of new markets in western and eastern Canada, and just how much was the result of continued regional growth, is, of course, impossible to measure. But it is clear that many manufacturing firms, trading companies, and financial institutions of the Heartland — aided by federal policies of high tariffs and favourable rail rates, and employing considerable entrepreneurial initiative to reduce and eliminate competitors in the quest for markets — soon came to control much of the Canadian economy.

The increasing number of mergers in the banking industry illustrates this geographical and economic concentration.[21] By the early 1880s, there were at least 44 chartered banks in Canada operating a small network of about 300 branches. The largest maintained head offices in either Montréal or Toronto and accounted for 71 percent of all assets, but there were also at least 28 others scattered in 16 centres, including Hamilton, Ottawa, Winnipeg, Halifax, Québec City, and Victoria. Through merger and acquisition, or simply because of insolvency, the number of banks had shrunk to 11 by the mid–1920s, but the banking network itself totalled over 4000 branches from coast to coast. National control from either Montréal or Toronto had eliminated all the regional banks but one, a small enterprise based in Weyburn, Saskatchewan. Particularly serious for hinterland interests was the disappearance of the Winnipeg banks, which on the eve of World War I managed almost 300 branches scattered throughout western Canada. The decline of Halifax banks was also a blow because they supported local industry.

This take–over pattern, reflecting the merger movement so characteristic of Canada in the early twentieth century, had its root in the policies of The Bank Act of 1871. Unlike its American counterpart, the Act did not restrict the establishment of branches beyond political (provincial) boundaries. Furthermore, by setting special requirements for the establishment of any new bank, it made entry into the system difficult for both domestic aspirants and foreign banks alike. Whether the large national banks such as the Royal and the Commerce were as sensitive to the needs of peripheral areas as regional banks might have been is debatable, but what is important is that the image of metropolitan control of banking — in fact, of most aspects of finance — was strengthened in the minds of all Canadians, particularly those in the peripheral regions. Indeed, the intrusion of metropolitan financial institutions into the economy of the Maritimes in the late nineteenth and early twentieth centuries was widespread and has long been a source of regional protest and discontent. Regional banking was eliminated when the Bank of Nova Scotia transferred its major management facilities to Toronto (1900), when the Merchants Bank of Halifax was transformed into the Royal Bank based in Montréal (1904), and when the Halifax Banking Company was absorbed by the Bank of Commerce (1903), the People's Bank by the Bank of Montréal (1905), and the Union Bank by the Royal Bank (1910).

Although all sectors of the Canadian economy grew rapidly, the most apparent trend was the transformation of the Heartland into an integrated, strong, but internally differentiated industrial region. By the 1920s, all segments of a diversified industrial economy were well in place, including primary iron and steel, automobiles, electrical goods, industrial machinery, chemicals, food and beverages, textiles, clothing, and shoes. Not only did employment in manufacturing double from about 200 000 in 1880 to 400 000 by 1920, and then double again to 900 000 by 1950, but manufacturing's share of the total labour force rose to just over 25 percent by the end of World War II. Because manufacturing was largely urban-oriented, it became the catalyst of growth for many towns and cities. Peterborough, an old industrial centre, grew in population from 6800 in 1881 to 38 000 in 1951 when 55 percent of its labour force was employed in manufacturing. By contrast, the hinterland city of Saskatoon, with a population of 53 000 in 1951, placed only 14 percent of its labour force in that sector.

Despite Montréal's early industrial revolution, the towns and cities of southern Ontario matched its pace of development. By 1880, manufacturing employment in Ontario exceeded that in Québec by a ratio of 4:3. Since then the gap between the two provinces has continued to widen in Ontario's favour. Significant, too, are differences in the structure of provincial manufacturing.[22] In 1880, Québec led in the production of leather and tobacco products; Ontario's strength rested on foods, beverages, and metalworking. Beyond these differences, considerable structural similarity prevailed, but by the early 1900s Québec supported a slightly higher share of clothing, shoes, and textiles. The rise first of the electrical apparatus industry and later of primary iron and steel and automobiles gave Ontario undisputed leadership in these important categories by the 1920s. Other changes gradually took hold by 1951. The major differences and similarities in structure at that time are outlined in Table 3.1.

At this point, we need to raise two interrelated questions. First, what factors explain the concentration of manufacturing in the Industrial Heartland? Second, why did manufacturing have a differential impact on the industrial structures of Ontario and Québec? Several factors provide the basis for at least a partial explanation: the character of the resource and energy base; human initiative and entrepreneurship; the role of government policy; foreign direct investment; and corporate mergers and monopolistic control. Differences in industrial structure do not negate the principle of a unified economic region; rather, they have fostered complementary activities and functional integration.

Any discussion of the relationship of resources and energy to industrial development emphasizes the complexity of the issue. In the nineteenth century, energy for the industrial economy was provided initially by wood and water power and later by coal. Because wood was

TABLE 3.1 OVER REPRESENTATION AND UNDER REPRESENTATION IN MANUFACTURING IN QUEBEC, 1951

Type[a]	*Group*	*Value Added in Québec as Percentage of the Same Group in Ontario*	*Employment in Québec as Percentage of the Same Group in Ontario*	*Percentage of Overall Under Representation in Employment*[b]
A	Tobacco	602	414	+495
	Clothing	173	171	+146
	Textiles	137	156	+123
	Leather	110	123	+77
	Paper	109	102	+46
B	Petroleum and coal	96	43	−39
	Wood products	79	90	+29
C	Foods and beverages	59	61	−12
	Chemicals	58	81	+16
	Non-metallic minerals	53	56	−26
D	Printing	49	52	−26
	Miscellaneous	40	46	−34
	Iron and steel and non-ferrous	37	40	−42
	Electrical operators	36	39	−44
	Transportation equipment	22	44	−37
	Rubber	22	45	−39
All Manufacturing		58	70	

[a]Type A: absolutely greater than in Ontario, and relatively more important in Québec; type B: absolutely less than in Ontario, but relatively more important in Québec; type C: absolutely less than in Ontario, but of approximately same relative importance as in Ontario; type D: absolutely less than in Ontario, and relatively less important than in Ontario.

[b]Employment in Québec was 70 percent of employment in Ontario. This was used as a base level in expressing over or under representation in industrial groups. Employment more or less than the employment required to make Québec employment equivalent to 70 percent of employment in Ontario was expressed as a percentage above (over representation) or below (under representation) the employment required to produce 70 percent.

Source: See footnote 22.

plentiful everywhere, it had little impact on the regional variation of economic growth. Coal was imported in increasing amounts after 1860 from the American Appalachians, giving the lake ports of western Ontario — particularly Hamilton and Toronto — a definite advantage of accessibility.[23] Even when coal shipped from Nova Scotia became available in the last quarter of the nineteenth century, centres in Québec and eastern Ontario still had to pay a higher price than their competitors to the west. Industrial progress in southwestern Ontario's metalmaking and metalworking sectors was due at least in part to the accessibility of cheaper American coal, made even cheaper early in the 1900s by subsidies from the Ontario government.

Industries along the Lachine Canal, 1896: Many of Canada's earliest and most important manufacturing industries located along the canal, where hydraulic power and ease of transportation were locational advantages. Lumber yards, Ogilvie's flour mill, and the smoke stacks of several large-scale foundries are visible in this picture. (*Notman Photographic Archives*)

In the pre-industrial economy, many industrial entrepreneurs explored the possibilities of using water power. Streams were harnessed by building small dams at waterfalls or rapids, creating reservoirs which channelled water to turn the wheels that powered grist and sawmills. On a larger and more elaborate scale, the hydraulic power scheme associated with the development of the Lachine Canal in Montréal in the 1840s attracted moderately large industries such as machinists, shoe factories, and engine works.

Toward the end of the century new technological developments harnessed large flows of water to generate electricity, and the huge reserve of central Canada's "white coal" became the catalyst for considerable industrialization. The modern electrical age in Canada was born in the late 1890s, when a hydroelectric station with a small generating capacity was opened at Niagara Falls. At first there was widespread apprehension that any locally produced electricity would be exported to the United States or monopolized by Toronto, but the government of Ontario responded to these fears by establishing an industrial inquiry in 1905.[24] As a direct outcome the Ontario Hydro Electric Power Commission was established to regulate the production and transmission of electricity by private utilities. Under the aggressive leadership of Adam Beck, Hydro, as it became known, expanded its role not only in regulating the private utilities but in producing power to compete with other firms. So extensive was its growth that by the 1920s, most of the private segment had been expropriated, and Ontario Hydro was in firm control. It was the policy of the Commission to disperse electricity as widely as the technology of transmission allowed. Thus factories at Guelph, London, and other towns and cities within the transmission radius of Niagara Falls were assured a supply. The Commission also equalized rates whenever feasible, regardless of distance from the generating site. This policy enhanced the industrial development of towns and cities throughout southern Ontario. Furthermore, Beck offered domestic customers relatively low rates, thus encouraging the consumption of electricity for all sorts of household appliances and stimulating the electrical appliance industry in southern Ontario.

In Québec, by contrast, private utilities, fully supported by the provincial government, gained control of the development and distribution of hydroelectric power.[25] One of the most important was the Shawinigan Water and Power Company, which was comprised of a consortium of American and English–Canadian entrepreneurs. In 1899 these entrepreneurs harnessed Shawinigan Falls, located about 40 kilometres north of Trois–Rivières on the St. Maurice River. The company immediately adopted a policy of selling low-cost electricity on a long–term basis to heavy industries. This policy led to the emergence, as early as 1900, of both an aluminum plant and a pulp mill at the site of the first generating station. In 1903, the company acquired another large market and an international reputation for long distance transmission by selling power to the Montréal Light and Power Company, some 145 kilometres away. Successive developments along the St. Maurice River (obtained through leases from the provincial government) and the acquisition of other facilities at Grand Mère and La Tuque gave the company control of *La Mauricie* by 1931. At each stage of development, surplus power was created which led the company to maintain and expand its policy of persuading industries in need of cheap electric power to locate in the Valley. As a result, important electro–chemical and electro–metallurgical industries appeared at Shawinigan, and pulp and paper and other resource industries were established at Trois–Rivières, Grand Mère, and La Tuque. Similar developments soon took place on the Saguenay River, where a large aluminum mill was built at Arvida in 1926. Other power–consuming industries located at Chicoutimi.

In contrast, the much smaller Southern Canada Power Company of the Eastern Townships inaugurated a policy of industrialization and market expansion through the acquisition of light industries. The Montréal Light and Power Company formulated no industrial policy whatsoever and launched no campaigns to persuade industry to locate in the Montréal area, even though it held a firm monopoly on the distribution of power. The provision of hydroelectric power in Québec thus had the same effect on the spatial distribution of manufacturing as it did in southern Ontario — dispersion — but for entirely different reasons.

The extent to which industrial growth in central Canada may be explained by the rise of commercial agriculture is debatable.[26] It can be argued that in the nineteenth century Ontario farmers consistently produced a surplus of agricultural products for sale to local food processors and foreign markets, using profits from this trade to purchase a variety of products including new and technically-improved farm machinery. Clearly, their demand for farm equipment stimulated industrialization, but it cannot be said, for example, that Hamilton's iron and steel complex owes its expansion to the material needs of farm implement manufacturers.

In Québec, commercial agriculture was less developed. Although commercial farming, especially dairying, had become moderately widespread by the 1880s, the sale of products was confined mainly to the Québec market and returns were correspondingly low. As a result, the purchasing power of Québec farmers was weak, and incentives for industrialization stemming from agriculture were minimal. Québec agriculture did, however, create an indirect impact on industrial development. The combination of a shortage of agricultural land and rapid rural population growth, especially in the last quarter of the nineteenth century, created a situation of serious population pressure, forcing many people off the land and into the growing industrial centres of Québec and the United States. Because of their large numbers, these migrants provided cheap labour for labour-intensive industries such as tobacco, shoe, clothing, and textile manufacturing. Women and children formed a relatively large segment of the work force and working conditions were often deplorable. Although conditions had improved somewhat by World War II, wages remained low.

Initiative and entrepreneurship also played a vital role in industrialization. Much of the Heartland's industrialization can be traced to entrepreneurs of Scottish and American origin who were prepared to experiment with new techniques, work hard, pay low wages, and re-invest their profits in expansion. In Montréal, and throughout Upper Canada, craftsmen, artisans, engineers, inventors, and entrepreneurs of American and British origin teamed up with merchants to build shipyards, foundries, flour mills, and chemical plants.

The role of French-Canadian entrepreneurs is more controversial. It has long been held that their participation in the industrial process was minimal, explained by the *mentalité* that placed a higher value on careers in the professions and the Church than on those in industry. Evidence now shows that the participation of Québécois businessmen in shipbuilding, shoe manufacturing, textiles, transportation, trade, and banking was greater than previously acknowledged.[27] The fact that their contribution was not more impressive must be explained by capital shortages, limited access to English-controlled industrial and financial institutions, and strong language and social barriers, rather than by any absence of capitalistic values or lack of entrepreneurial skills. In fact, entrepreneurial behaviour *per se* has little, if any, relevance in explaining the differences in the industrial structures of Québec and Ontario.

Nor should traditional views of the conservative role of the Catholic Church remain unchallenged, for the Church was not entirely opposed to industrialization. At times, it acted boldly as an entrepreneur. In the 1870s, for example, the Grey Nuns financed the building of a large warehouse in downtown Montréal for lease to commercial enterprises. During the period of feverish railway promotion in the nineteenth century, the Church participated by investing directly or by giving tacit approval to projects. Later, as *La Mauricie* became a development focus, the Church supported and in fact encouraged industrialization by working with managers and investors.[28]

What role did government policy play in industrialization? It has long been stated that the real basis of industrialization in the Heartland is tariff protection from foreign competition. The roots of industrial protection can be found in scattered policies of the mid-nineteenth century, but the most important and all-embracing legislation was enacted in 1879 as a prime element of the National Policy.[29] Although the debate on the precise effects of these tariffs continues, it is apparent that manufacturers in Ontario and Québec used this protective shield to build a nation-wide market. Thus, loggers in British Columbia and fishermen in Nova Scotia wore boots made in Montréal; farmers in Saskatchewan and Prince Edward Island purchased the agricultural machinery of Toronto; and lawyers in Edmonton and Halifax drove automobiles made in Windsor. Manufacturing in the Industrial Heartland was given protected access to a captive national market. The largest part of this market was in Ontario and Québec, of course, but the peripheral regions were nevertheless critical for maintaining the economic viability of most companies.

The National Policy also encouraged the branch plant character of manufacturing in the Heartland.[30] To win Canadian markets, American direct investment jumped the tariff barrier and was used to build plants throughout Canada, especially in Ontario. Westinghouse, Gillette, and Singer Sewing Machine, to name some well-known American firms, were among the approximately 100 companies operating in Canada at the turn of the century. They were soon joined by hundreds more and, by 1950, American corporations accounted for at least half of central Canada's manufacturing activity. American industry favoured Ontario over Québec largely because of Ontario's higher market potential and the proximity of southwestern Ontario to the head offices of parent organizations in the United States manufacturing belt.

Closely related to the expansion of American branch plants was the increasing dependence of Canadian industry on foreign technology.[31] Much of the machinery which provided the infrastructure for Canadian industry was either being imported from the United States or made in Canada under licence from American enterprises. Throughout the early and mid-twentieth century, the rapidly changing technology of American

Open hearth furnaces, Steel Co. of Canada, Hamilton, Ontario, c. 1918: By World War I, the steel industry of Ontario had surpassed that of Nova Scotia. As a leading sector of the region's industrial revolution, it provided necessary and competitively priced materials for manufacturing diversification within the Industrial Heartland. (*PA-24646/Public Archives of Canada*)

industries became irresistible to most Canadian manufacturers, who eventually succumbed to its accessibility. All of the promising Canadian automobile manufacturers of the early 1900s had disappeared by the late 1920s, swallowed up in the rapidly changing and increasingly concentrated American industry.

As American control increased, the status of Canada as a world industrial nation declined. American investment created jobs and stimulated some sectors of the economy, but the present weakness of Canada's industrial structure, the relative insignificance of its export trade (except resource–based industries such as newsprint), and the general lack of research and development facilities have their origins in increasing American participation in the first half of the twentieth century. One notable exception is the steel industry of Hamilton which fortuitously remained under Canadian ownership. As industry expanded, both the Steel Company of Canada (STELCO) and Dominion Foundries (DOFASCO) grew significantly by diversifying their products and developing research facilities. With high quality production, they eventually won a few foreign markets.

As the pace of manufacturing growth accelerated at the turn of the century, so did the move towards larger corporations. Large size often meant cheaper production costs, and savings in production could be applied to the costs of transporting goods to distant markets. In the increasingly competitive national market, small companies located across Canada were frequently absorbed by Heartland interests. The textile industry of the Maritimes is but one example of an industry that all but disappeared because of industrial concentration. Geographically, the main effects of the merger movement were to centralize operations in southern Ontario and Québec, especially in the vicinity of Toronto and Montréal, and to close down peripherally situated plants. Thus, central Canadian corporations came to control many sectors of Canada's manufacturing structure, particularly those industries producing consumer goods.

THE INDUSTRIAL HEARTLAND IN THE 1950s

How did sustained economic development during the course of the *longue durée* affect the spatial organization of the Heartland? The main effect was urban concentration (Fig. 3.5). Between 1881 and 1951, while the region's population increased from just over 3 million to some 8 million people, the proportion living in towns and cities rose from 25 to 70 percent. Montréal (1.5 million) and Toronto (1.1 million) dominated all other urban places. Although most cities in the Windsor–Québec City corridor grew at rates exceeding the national average, the populations of some hamlets, villages, and even towns, especially those located off the beaten track, actually decreased.

By the 1950s, Montréal and Toronto together exerted a profound influence on Canadian society. From 1871 to 1951, Montréal's share of Québec's population rose from 9 to almost 40 percent; Toronto's share of Ontario's increased from 3.5 to just over 25 percent. Together, they housed one of every four Canadians in 1951, and their 430 000 manufacturing workers comprised about one–third of the Canadian total. Of equal importance was the striking concentration of corporate and financial power, as the tertiary sector added its force to urban growth. Mergers had reduced the number of Canadian banks to nine, all of which had head offices in either Toronto or Montréal. Based on corporate assets, 75 percent of all insurance companies and 80 percent of all trust and loan companies had head offices in these two cities. Fully 95 percent of all stock market transactions and practically all dealings in bonds were made on the Toronto and Montréal markets. Of all the cheques written in Canada in the post–war decade, approximately 35 percent passed through Toronto clearing houses; Montréal cleared another 25 percent. Finally, at least three out of every four Canadian corporations were based in Toronto and Montréal.[32] The internal organization of both cities reflected the ascendancy of metropolitan functions — corporate and financial districts emerged in their downtown cores and the demand for industrial and residential land created significant suburban expansion.

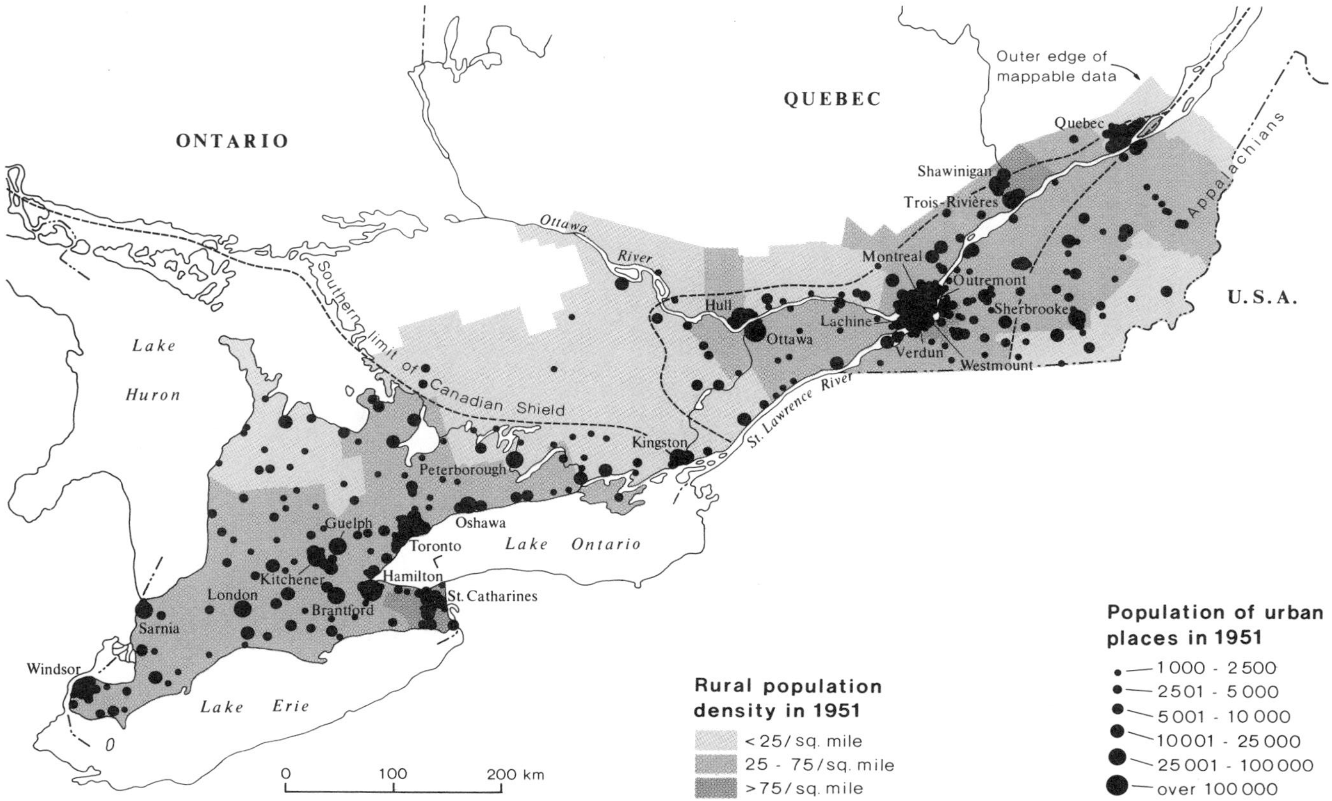

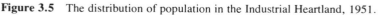

Figure 3.5 The distribution of population in the Industrial Heartland, 1951.

Other regional changes occurred to the southwest of Toronto in peninsular Ontario, where industrialization continued to have a strong urban impact. The output of automobiles and chemicals in Windsor and Sarnia, of farm machinery in Brantford, of food and beverage products in London, and of electrical appliances and steel in Kitchener and Hamilton continued to increase, though over half of this output was produced by American branch plants. Agriculture changed in response to technological and industrial change, as people left farms for cities and new specializations developed. Based on a warm and long growing season (by Canadian standards), cash crops such as corn, soya beans, and sugar beets prospered in the extreme southwest. Tobacco became concentrated in Norfolk County and soft fruits as well as hard were grown in the Niagara Peninsula below the escarpment. Dairying remained widespread, easily meeting the increased urban demand for fluid milk and other dairy products. Southwestern Ontario's primary, secondary, and tertiary sectors had built a strong and diverse economic base, whose influence extended across Canada, and whose geographic pattern has remained stable in the post-war decades.

Manufacturing industry at mid-century: General Motors Co. of Canada's newly constructed South Plant Complex at Oshawa in 1950 stands as a symbol of the ascendency of manufacturing within the Industrial Heartland's drive to industrial maturity. (*General Motors Co. of Canada*)

Those areas embracing the Huron Uplands, fringing the Shield, and running eastward through central and eastern Ontario experienced limited, even stagnating urban and industrial growth. They created a hinterland within a heartland. Two of the more promising centres of the late nineteenth century, Collingwood and Brockville, stagnated. Peterborough, using hydroelectric power to build an industrial base, and Ottawa, the national capital, were exceptions. Agriculture in the area was based on cattle production in the Huron Uplands and mixed farming and dairying elsewhere. In rural Ontario as a whole, farm depopulation was endemic by the early 1950s, but society remained strongly conservative and firmly British and Protestant.

The St. Lawrence Lowlands between Montréal and Québec City remained much as it had since the Conquest — the rural heartland of French-Canadian society. Although spotted by urban and industrial activity, this area retained a high man/land ratio; dramatic rural depopulation did not come until the 1970s. Farmers of the Lowlands practiced mixed farming with an emphasis on dairying for the urban market. There were several small to medium-sized cities, such as St. Hyacinthe, which built labour-intensive textile, shoe, and furniture factories, but they were fewer in number than in Ontario. Québec City, housing a population of 275 000 in 1951, was sustained by its historic roles in government and religious affairs, but functioned increasingly as a focal point for the lower St. Lawrence Valley and as a pulp and paper centre. During the 1960s and '70s, Québec City became the focus of powerful economic and social changes in Québécois society, and more than doubled its population.

Flanking the Lowlands on the south, the Eastern Townships retained a mixed English and French population, although the proportion of the latter had increased in some districts to over 80 percent by World War II. Sherbrooke continued to thrive as a regional and industrial centre, reaching a population of some 50 000 people. To the north, on the edge of the Shield, engineers, entrepreneurs, and industrialists succeeded where farmers failed, and the harnessing of the St. Maurice, Saguenay, and Gatineau Rivers by large-scale hydroelectric projects continued to stimulate industrialization and urban growth. The combined population of Shawinigan Falls and Grand Mère, which stood at 6300 in 1901, reached 19 500 in 1921, and then more than doubled to 45 000 in 1951. Over 8000 people were employed in chemical, textile, pulp and paper, and several other minor industries. In the Lac St. Jean district, the Chicoutimi-Jonquière-Arvida complex, which took shape after the mid-1920s, counted almost 70 000 people just after World War II. Many were associated with the aluminum industry which dominated the industrial structure. In retrospect, energy-based developments like these proved to be the forerunners of Québec's industrial expansion of the 1970s and '80s, led by the Manicouagan and giant James Bay projects.

SHIFTS IN METROPOLITAN POWER

Montréal and Toronto have exerted a powerful metropolitan influence on the development of regionalism in Canada. To understand the extent of their influence, we need to review their changing relationships, particularly the shifts in power between them. Historically, Montréal has been the more dominant, counting twice the population of Toronto at Confederation. Since then, however, the gap has narrowed and the two are now approximately the same size. Montréal's economic base has eroded, especially in the spheres of corporate and financial decision-making. Today Toronto claims primacy and is challenged more by Calgary and Vancouver than by its historic rival. Since the tertiary and quaternary sectors are central to an explanation of differential metropolitan growth, we now turn to an analysis of major events related to changes in the geographical concentration of financial power to the 1950s.

As Montréal's wholesale trade expanded early in the nineteenth century, so, too, did the banks, insurance companies, and other financial institutions which served trans-Atlantic and intra-regional trade. Although Montréal merchants were in control of most of the economy, Toronto traders formed local financial institutions to facilitate the rapid growth of the regional wheat economy. By the late 1840s, Toronto interests had also achieved some success in breaking Montréal's monopoly by exporting goods over the Erie Canal system and through New York. Toronto thus developed a trading and financial infrastructure which was remarkably similar to that of Montréal. Both cities were headquarters for chartered banks and insurance and trust companies; both housed small but active stock and bond markets; and both supported numerous wholesale establishments. Although small compared to world cities such as London and New York, they operated within separate but interrelated decision-making systems, and soon rivalled each other for the control of investment and trading in the new Dominion.

By controlling the national rail network and expanding much of its industrial trading and financial structure, Montréal maintained its lead over Toronto immediately after Confederation. Toronto, in response, expanded its trading interests with western Canada and made gains in the Maritimes.[33] Its wholesalers won a larger share of western and Maritime trade than their Montréal counterparts, and Toronto banks led in the establishment of branches in the west. Toward the end of the century, Toronto financiers, unlike those in Montréal, responded enthusiastically to the exploration and development of mineral deposits across the Canadian Shield in northern Ontario and Québec, and in the Kootenays of British Columbia. By establishing two mining exchanges in the 1890s (merged in 1899) and by setting up other facilities to promote mining, Toronto strengthened its financial activity. Despite this vibrancy, Toronto was still overshadowed by Montréal. Not only was Montréal's volume of banking activity larger, but its image in international financial circles had more lustre.

On the other hand, there is at least fragmentary evidence to support the assertion that Toronto investment houses surpassed their Montréal rivals in the trade and sale of bonds. By examining the volume and nature of transactions on the stock exchanges of the two cities, it is possible to monitor their changing status. Although these data have serious limitations, their use can be justified in the absence of any other continuous statistical series.[34] In the early 1900s, when between 2 and 5 million shares were traded annually in Canada, Montréal dealers accounted for at least 55 to 60 percent of this total. Industrial stocks were more frequently traded on the Montréal exchange; but, surprisingly, bank shares were not, favouring Toronto instead. Transactions of high quality mining shares were about equal. As the volume of trading in industrials, utilities, and banks climbed in the 1920s (reaching almost 10 million shares by 1926 and peaking at 36.5 million shares in 1929), Montréal's control of total transactions increased to an average of 70 percent and reached an all-time high of 77 percent in 1928. With the onset of the Depression, trade diminished, dropping to about 5 million shares in 1932, but recovering to nearly 17 million in 1933. For the first time, in 1932, the Toronto market achieved a slight lead in the trade of industrials, and in 1933, it won 55 percent of the total market volume (excluding the Standard Mining Exchange). Thereafter, Toronto continuously increased its share of trade (as measured by value) from almost 60 percent in the late 1930s, to more than two-thirds by the mid-1950s, and to 80 percent in the early 1980s.

Why did this shift in power take place? Present research can offer only tentative explanations. There is little question, however, that the Depression affected the stability of the Canadian financial community. In terms of the stock exchange, Montréal suffered more than Toronto. Before the crash of 1929, the Toronto Stock Exchange had inaugurated, under the direct supervision of the Commissioner of the Ontario Securities Board, a very thorough audit of its members. Although the evidence is fragmentary, it appears that marginal and potentially dishonest companies were weeded out, for there were no insolvencies of Toronto-based brokerage and investment houses during the Depression. By contrast, several well-established but over-extended Montréal firms did declare bankruptcy. Furthermore, during the depth of the Depression, the Toronto exchange resisted pegging prices at artificial levels for prolonged periods in order to maintain a free market. Montréal's policy of providing artificial support for the market for unusually long periods, on the other hand, led to considerable resentment and loss of business.

In the 1930s Toronto emerged as a more important mining centre than Montréal. Gold, unlike most other commodities, was particularly buoyant during the Depression and its trade was centred mainly on the Toronto Exchange. Just what the connection was between a strengthening mining market and the increasing market in industrials on the Toronto Exchange is impossible to state. But it is significant that in the post–war period when Canada's mining frontier was expanding dramatically with the discovery and development of all sorts of metallic minerals and fuels, the financing was being manipulated to a large extent by investment bankers on Bay Street. Furthermore, American participants were increasingly channelling their funds through Toronto rather than Montréal. All of this led the *Financial Post* to claim in the late 1930s that "evidence is not lacking to show that Toronto has passed Montréal as a centre of finance" and that "several head offices have left Montréal to locate in Toronto."[35] Of all explanations, however, the most cogent concerns the gradual but persistent industrial and economic growth of southwestern Ontario as compared to southern Québec. Given the instability of traditional money markets during the depression years, the Toronto Exchange, by enlarging its trade in industrials, simply reflected what in fact had already been accomplished.[36]

In summary, Montréal's financial activity exceeded that of Toronto until the 1930s, though there was little difference in their infrastructure or functions expecially after the 1850s. After the 1930s, the two cities reversed positions and, at present, Toronto is clearly ahead in all categories of Canada's corporate–financial structure. Although only tentative explanations can be offered, it is clear that this differential growth is not a recent phenomenon, tied solely to the Québec Crisis or other contemporary issues. It is deeply rooted in the basic structure of the two cities.

A PERSPECTIVE ON THE *LONGUE DURÉE*

Over the course of the *longue durée* — as the Heartland developed from a frontier region to become an industrialized, urbanized, and integrated economic centre — it functioned as the centre of Canadian development. A moderately rich resource base fostered initial growth, and the production and export of wheat and timber were critical in generating revenue for re–investment and economic diversification. Indeed, the early staple economy and the linkages it spawned explain much nineteenth century growth.

There is, however, another advantage associated with the resource base. After the partitioning of North American territories in the late eighteenth century, Britain retained a relatively small and narrow lowland along the southern flank of the Shield. In Lower Canada, the rich soils in the St. Lawrence Lowlands proved to be crucial to the survival of the densely settled and rural population; in Upper Canada, almost four times as much arable land, combined with a more favourable climate, supported a much stronger agricultural economy. Good land is important to the market economies of all societies, and it was crucial to the development of central Canada. At a critical stage in industrial development, hydroelectric power also played a role in shaping the region's economic character.

Although Ontario and Québec are sharply divided on cultural and linguistic grounds, they continue to function as a single economic region. The close integration of their economies matured during the *longue durée.* From the late eighteenth century, important trading lines grew up along the St. Lawrence–Great Lakes waterway. Staple products were exchanged for British manufactured goods at Montréal, thus establishing the basis of an evergrowing exchange system. The early infrastructure of canals, waterways, telegraph lines, and rudimentary roads eventually gave way to modern systems of transportation (rail, road, air) and communication (telephone, telex, computer). These, in turn, carried an increasingly large and more diverse volume of goods, messages, and information. Each change created greater economic interaction and hence economic unity. By the 1980s, the daily flow of freight along the Heartland's transportation facilities exceeded the inter-provincial trade of all other regions in Canada. Surveys in the late 1970s have emphasized the large volume of inter-regional trade between Ontario and Québec, especially of manufacturing materials and products: each is the best customer of the other.[37]

Using aggressive strategies of acquisition and merger, facilitated by government policies, central Canadian institutions reduced or eliminated considerable competition in the periphery. The rise to prominence, fuelled by industrialization and tertiary activity, has not been without consequence. Hinterland regions continue to protest over many issues, particularly the uneven distribution of economic power. Paradoxically, however, most national organizations — including banks, insurance and trust companies, chain retailers, and centrally-based manufacturers — are dependent on a trans-Canada market. The total or even partial loss of this market would force many to make drastic structural adjustments and may lead some to bankruptcy.

Evidence is mounting, however, to suggest that for the first time since Confederation, the traditional pattern of dominance is weakening. The rise of an increasingly strong western economy, for example, has forced a re-examination of heartland-hinterland relationships. By the close of the *longue durée* in the early 1950s, however, the Industrial Heartland, and in particular Montréal and Toronto, remained the unchallenged base of metropolitan power in Canada.

NOTES

1. Staple theory was developed by the distinguished Canadian scholar, Harold Innis, in his studies of the fur trade and cod fisheries in Canada. For a succinct summary, see Richard Pomfret, *The Economic Development of Canada* (Toronto: Methuen, 1981), pp. 33–38.
2. John McCallum, *Unequal Beginnings: Agriculture and Economic Development in Québec and Ontario until 1870* (Toronto: University of Toronto Press, 1980).

3. On the nature and meaning of the *longue durée* in historical analysis, see Fernand Braudel, *On History,* trans. Sarah Matthews (Chicago: University of Chicago Press, 1980), pp. 27–34.
4. Society and economy in pre-Conquest Québec are well described in Cole Harris and John Warkentin, *Canada Before Confederation* (Toronto: Oxford University Press, 1972), chap. 2.
5. Fernand Ouellet, *Economic and Social History of Québec, 1760–1850,* trans. ed. (Toronto: Macmillan, 1980), pp. 33–231.
6. The timber trade is discussed in William Marr and Donald Paterson, *Canada: An Economic History* (Toronto: Macmillan, 1980), pp. 61–73.
7. Louis Gentilcore, "Settlement," in *Ontario,* ed. Louis Trotier, Studies in Canadian Geography (Toronto: University of Toronto Press, 1972), pp. 23–44.
8. Douglas McCalla, "The Wheat Staple and Upper Canadian Development," *Historical Papers of the Canadian Historical Association,* 1978, pp. 34–46; and Ouellet, *Economic and Social History of Québec,* pp. 255–392.
9. John Isbister, "Agriculture, Balanced Growth and Social Change in Central Canada since 1850: An Interpretation," *Economic Development and Cultural Change,* 25 (1977), pp. 673–97; R.L. Jones, *History of Agriculture in Ontario, 1613–1880* (Toronto: 1946); R.L. Jones, "Agriculture in Lower Canada, 1792–1815," *Canadian Historical Review,* 27 (1946); and Maurice Séguin, *La nation 'canadienne' et l'agriculture* (Trois Rivières: 1970).
10. R.M. McInnis, "Reconsideration of the State of Agriculture in Lower Canada in the First Half of the Nineteenth Century," *Canadian Papers on Rural History,* 3 (1981).
11. On the theme of out-migration, see "Le Québec et l'Amérique Française: Le Canada, La Nouvelle-Angleterre et le Midwest," Numéro Spécial, *Cahiers de Géographie du Québec,* 23 (1979).
12. The best summary of this relationship is McCallum, *Unequal Beginnings.*
13. This pattern of development is discussed fully in James G. Gilmour, *Spatial Evolution of Manufacturing of South Ontario, 1851–1891,* Department of Geography Publication Series, No. 10 (Toronto: University of Toronto Press, 1972).
14. Much of the information in this paragraph comes from Gerald Tulchinsky, *The River Barons* (Toronto: University of Toronto Press, 1977).
15. Brian Young, *Promoters and Politicians: North Shore Railways in the History of Québec, 1854–1885* (Toronto: University of Toronto Press, 1978).
16. On the economic growth of Toronto, Hamilton, and Kingston, see Jacob Spelt, *Urban Development in South Central Ontario,* Carleton Library Series, No. 57 (Toronto: McClelland and Stewart, 1972); Douglas McCalla, "The Decline of Hamilton as a Wholesale Centre," *Ontario History,* 65 (1973), 247–54; and Brian S. Osborne, "Kingston in the Nineteenth Century: A Study in Urban Decline," in *Perspectives on Landscape and Settlement in Nineteenth Century Ontario,* ed. D. Wood, Carleton Library Series, No. 91 (Toronto: McClelland and Stewart, 1975), pp. 159–81.
17. Cole Harris, "Of Poverty and Helplessness in Petite-Nation," *Canadian Historical Review,* 52 (1971), 23–50.
18. The discussion of the Montréal landscape in the early 1880s draws upon personal communication with David Hanna and the work of David B. Hanna and Frank W. Remiggi, *Les Quartiers de Montréal: Un Guide d'Excursion* (Montréal: L'Association Canadienne des Géographes, 1980).
19. Gregory S. Kealey, *Toronto Workers Respond to Industrial Capitalism, 1867–1892* (Toronto: University of Toronto Press, 1980), chap. 2; and Jacob Spelt, *Toronto* (Dons Mills: Collier-Macmillan, 1973), chaps. 2 and 5.
20. W. Arthur Lewis, *Growth and Fluctuations, 1870–1913* (London: George Allen and Unwin, 1978), p. 163.
21. The trends in banking in Canada at this time are discussed in Marr and Paterson, *Canada: An Economic History,* pp. 243–58.

22. James Gilmour and Kenneth Murricane, "Structural Divergence in Canada's Manufacturing Belt," *The Canadian Geographer,* 17 (1973), 1–18.
23. David Walker, "Energy and Industrial Location in Southern Ontario, 1871–1921," in *Industrial Development in Southern Ontario,* eds. David Walker and James H. Bater, Department of Geography Publication Series, No. 3 (Waterloo: University of Waterloo, 1974), pp. 41–68.
24. Viv Nelles, *Politics of Development* (Toronto: Macmillan, 1974).
25. John Dales, *Hydro-Electricity and Industrialization in Québec, 1898–1940* (Cambridge, Mass.: Harvard University Press, 1957).
26. McCallum, *Unequal Beginnings,* pp. 83–114.
27. Paul-André Linteau, René Durocher and Jean-Claude Robert, *Histoire du Québec contemporain* (Montréal: Boréal Express, 1979), and Paul-André Linteau, *Maisonneuve, Comment des Promoteurs Fabriquent Une Ville* (Montréal: Boréal Express, 1981); and Ronald Rudin, *Banking en français: The French Banks of Québec, 1855-1925* (Toronto: University of Toronto Press, 1985).
28. William Ryan, *The Clergy and Economic Growth in Québec, 1896–1914* (Québec: Laval University Press, 1966); and Brian Young, *In Its Corporate Capacity: The Seminary of Montréal as a Business Institution, 1816–1876* (Montréal: McGill-Queen's University Press, 1986).
29. The National Policy is the focus of a special issue of *The Journal of Canadian Studies,* 14 (1979).
30. Glen Williams, "The National Policy Tariffs: Industrial Underdevelopment through Import Substitution," *Canadian Journal of Political Science,* 12 (1979), 333–68.
31. Glenn Williams, *Not for Export* (Toronto: McLelland and Stewart, 1983).
32. Donald Kerr, "Metropolitan Dominance in Canada," in *Canada: A Geographical Interpretation,* ed. John Warkentin (Toronto: Methuen, 1968), pp. 531–55.
33. Donald Kerr, "Wholesale Trade on the Canadian Plains in the Late Nineteenth Century: Winnipeg and its Competition," in *The Settlement of the West,* ed. Howard Palmer (Calgary: University of Calgary Press, 1977), pp. 130–52; and L.D. McCann, "Metropolitanism and Branch Businesses in the Maritimes, 1881–1931," *Acadiensis,* 12 (1983), 111–125.
34. Because there was a large volume of low-value mining shares traded on the Standard Mining Exchange which would distort a meaningful discussion of these transactions, they have been excluded from all analyses. It should be noted that stock market transactions provide only one measure of the transition, but, unfortunately, data on other types of financial transactions are not available in a comprehensive form.
35. *Financial Post* (Toronto), January 7, 1939, p. 1.
36. See the seminal paper by Albert Faucher and Maurice LaMontagne, "History of Industrial Development," in *French Canadian Society,* eds. Marcel Rioux and Yves Martin, Carleton Library Series, No. 18 (Toronto: McClelland and Stewart, 1964), pp. 257–71.
37. Government of Ontario, *Inter-provincial Trade Flows, Employment, and the Tariff in Canada* (Toronto: 1977).

481-5244
Yellow

4

The Industrial Heartland: Its Changing Role and Internal Structure

Maurice Yeates

By the 1950s, the Industrial Heartland functioned as the undisputed core of Canadian economic development. In all spheres of economic activity — trade, transportation, manufacturing, and finance — the Heartland predominated. This position was consolidated in the immediate post-war years, but thereafter, particularly since the early 1970s, portents of change appeared. The energy crisis of the 1970s thrust Alberta into the vanguard of a new phase of national economic development.[1] The issue of Québec sovereignty threatened the complementary roles of Montréal and Toronto, and the issue of repatriating the Constitution revealed the growing strength of the hinterland provinces. In the early 1980s the country experienced a major cyclical downturn in the economy which slowed the growth of the Heartland. Equally, the rapid switch from "baby boom" in the 1950s and '60s to "baby bust" in the 1970s and '80s has had a profound effect not only on the rate of urban growth, but also on the general orientation of society.

Like its counterpart in the northeastern United States, the traditional core of Canadian power and innovation is now showing features of post-industrial decline. Its economy is growing with new jobs and new industries, but its share in the national economy is decreasing as other regions grow more rapidly. Its society, so attuned to the accoutrements accompanying high mass consumption, is now being forced to contend with serious urban problems — loss of jobs, spiralling land costs, and ethnic tensions. In short, the Industrial Heartland is in a state of transition. Its external relations with the national and international economy are experiencing stress. Internally, the regional landscape is being modified, as Toronto supersedes Montréal, as loss of industry becomes reality, and as the high costs of urbanization prevail. Our purpose in this chapter is to assess the changing social and economic character of this urban–industrial region — the "Main Street" of Canada — in the post–World War II period.

Before we turn to major indicators of change, however, it is important to establish a clear definition of the Heartland as it stood after the *longue durée.* The region's physical, economic, and social characteristics are integral to understanding the forces of change and the Heartland's emerging role in the country as a whole.

THE HEARTLAND: PHYSICAL DEFINITION

The geographical extent of the Industrial Heartland after the *longue durée* is indicated in Fig. 4.1a.[2] The Heartland extends some 1000 kilometres from Windsor to Québec City and averages about 300 kilometres in width. Although it is but a small part of the country as a whole, and also a small part of the two provinces that comprise the region, it is large when compared with other political and geographical entities in the world. It is larger than England and Wales combined, for example, and is about two–thirds the size of France. If the Canadian Heartland were transported to Europe as an independent political entity, it would be one of the largest countries in that part of the world.

The area has been defined on the basis of population densities, major spheres of urban influence, and physical features.[3] In general, the Heartland is highly urbanized, so that population densities are much higher than elsewhere in the country. More than half of Canada's metropolitan areas and urban agglomerations are concentrated in this area, and together they comprise an urban system that integrates and defines the region.

The Heartland is not, however, a uniform physiographic region. It encompasses two sections of the St. Lawrence Lowlands (termed the West and the Central St. Lawrence Lowlands by the *National Atlas of Canada*) in which most of the population and cities are located; and part of two upland and generally barren physiographic units (the Canadian Shield and the Appalachians).

The West St. Lawrence Lowland has been affected by several physical processes, most recently (some 15 000 years ago) by retreating glacial action (Fig. 4.1b). In some areas, deposits have produced fertile soils (Fig. 4.1c), but in others the surface debris, including drumlin fields, makes for poor farmland. A major feature of this Lowland region is the Niagara Escarpment, which extends from the Bruce Peninsula to the Niagara Peninsula and then into New York state. It is noted for recreation (hiking and downhill skiing) and spectacular scenery.

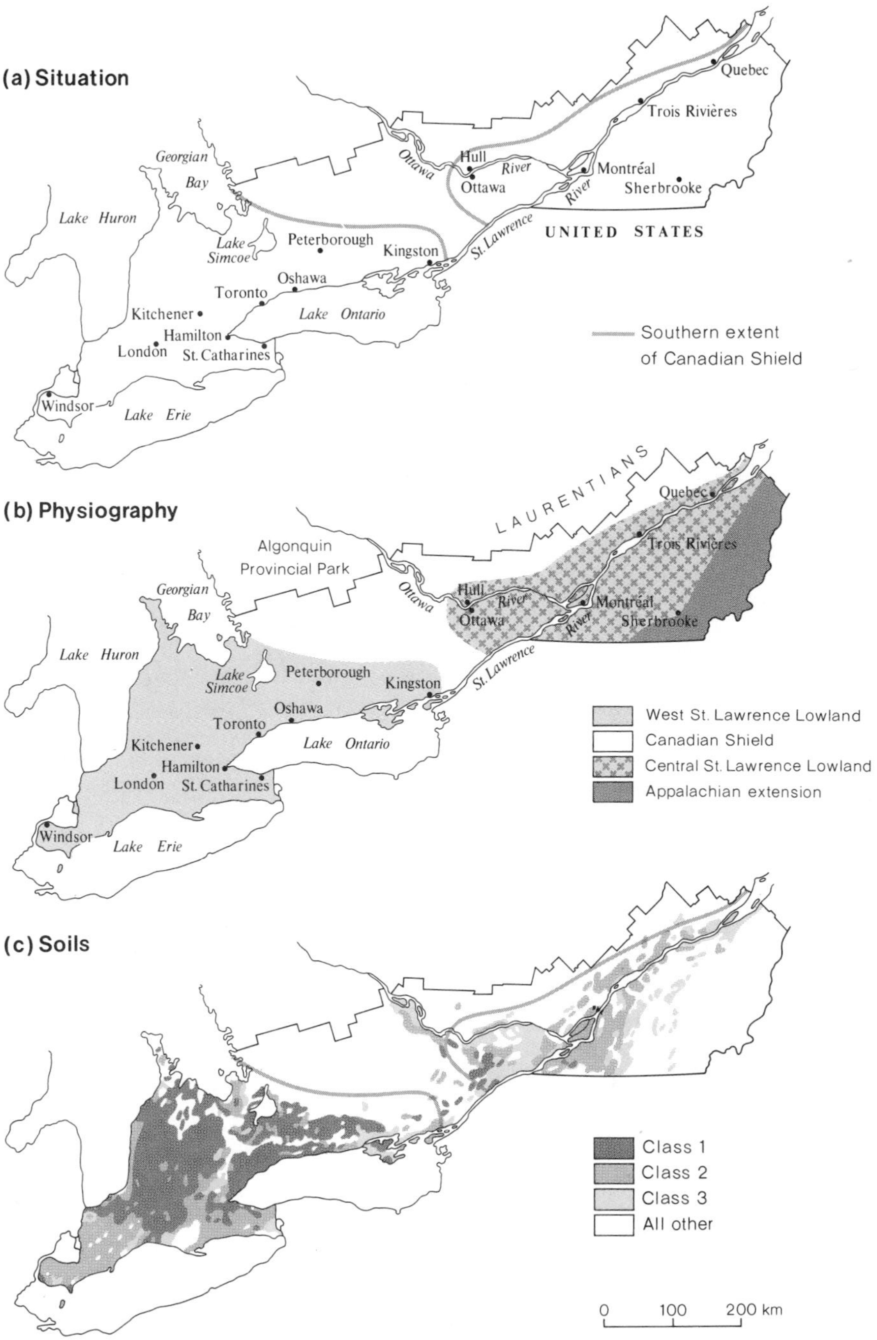

Figure 4.1 The geographical extent, and physiographic and soil regions of the Industrial Heartland.

A large-scale dairy operation near Waterloo, Ontario: Rich soils and a warm climate combine to create the prosperous agricultural base of southwestern Ontario. (*Larry McCann*)

The small portion of the Canadian Shield within the Heartland has the appearance of a dissected plateau, varying in height from 945 metres at Mont Tremblant to only a few hundred metres in eastern Ontario. Although this area has little good topsoil and is basically inimical to settlement, it is the location of much recreational development including ski resorts (in the Laurentians and Gatineau Hills) and second homes (such as in Muskoka) for the urban population. The prong of the Shield that leads into the Thousand Islands separates the West and Central Lowlands.

The area of the St. Lawrence Lowlands extending east of the Thousand Islands to near Québec City consists of broad areas of clay interspersed with pockets of sandy soil. The flat plain, which is excellent for agriculture (Fig. 4.1c), is relieved of its monotony by the eleven Monteregion Hills, three of which are outliers of the Canadian Shield. The other eight are made of hard volcanic rocks, remnants from the erosion of the softer material around them. One of these, Mount Royal in Montréal, is a prized site for recreational and residential use.

The southeastern portion of the Heartland is part of the Appalachian physiographic region which extends from the United States, through southern Québec, and into the Maritimes and Newfoundland. In the Heartland, this well–worn mountainous system is not particularly high, most peaks being between 600 and 1200 metres above sea level. The upland areas are covered with forests or rough scrub. They support forest activity, but abandoned farms are evidence of the poor soils and difficult slopes. The river valleys, full of deposits and glacial infil, have attracted considerable farm settlement. By comparison to the Lowlands, the area is sparsely populated.

The most favourable climatic (and soil) conditions for agriculture and settlement are found in southern Ontario. Although the whole Heartland is located in a humid continental, short summer climatic zone, the warmest summer climate, greatest heat accumulation, and shortest winters are in Essex County around Windsor, on the Niagara Peninsula, and along the coastal regions of Lakes Erie and Ontario. Elsewhere, beyond southwestern Ontario, the winters are longer and colder, the summers shorter and cooler.

The Appalachian region of the Industrial Heartland: Poor upland soils contribute to the marginal farming near Ste. Praxide and Disraeli in the Eastern Townships of Québec. (*Larry McCann*)

THE HEARTLAND: ECONOMIC DEFINITION

The role of southern Ontario and southern Québec as the core of the Canadian economy can be illustrated in two ways. First, with particular indicators comparing heartland and hinterland, we can demonstrate recent changes in the importance of the core *vis à vis* the rest of the nation. Second, we can compare heartland and hinterland with respect to international trade. The first approach describes the heartland and hinterland system; the second indicates the general pattern of trade that results from this system.

Heartland–Hinterland Indicators

Table 4.1 lists specific indicators that describe the heartland–hinterland system. Although there are some fluctuations, the information emphasizes the dominant role of the Heartland. The area of the Heartland is small compared to the hinterland, even when the comparison is restricted to that of the "occupied" territory or "ecumene." But, over 54 percent of Canada's population is located in the Heartland, a concentration greater than that in any other nation of comparable economic wealth.

In economic terms, the major distinguishing feature of the Heartland is its dominance in manufacturing. This position is apparently strengthening relative to the hinterland, even though the rate of growth in manufacturing employment between 1971 and 1980 was comparatively low. The greatest single source of employment, and the fastest growing in terms of jobs created, is, however, the tertiary or service sector (excluding construction). Since tertiary employment is distributed roughly in accordance with the population, the Heartland does not dominate in this sector of economic activity. Nevertheless, the concentration of corporate headquarters makes the Heartland the dominant control point of the Canadian space economy.

Farm cash receipts and hectares in farmland provide indicators of the relative importance of agricultural staples in the economy of the hinterland as compared with the core. Only 12 percent of the farmland in the country is located in the Heartland, and this proportion has been declining rapidly in recent years. Nevertheless, on this limited amount of farmland is generated production which yields over one–third of the total cash receipts received by the nation's farmers. Clearly, the agricultural activities in the area are generally intensive, involving high revenue per hectare of economic activities. The high levels of productivity are due to two main factors: the excellent nature of much of the farmland; and the accessibility of urban markets which generate a large local demand for perishable but high value agricultural commodities such as dairy products, meat, vegetables, and fruit.

TABLE 4.1 SOME INDICATORS OF THE CHANGING IMPORTANCE OF CANADA'S HEARTLAND AND HINTERLAND REGIONS

Indicators	*Heartland*	*Hinterland*	*Percentage in Heartland*
Area (in thousands of sq. kms)			
Total area	175	9 800	1.8
Occupied area	175	1 099	14.0
Population (in thousands)			
1951	7 275	6 734	51.9
1961	9 745	8 583	53.2
1971	11 920	9 648	55.3
1981	13 194	11 154	54.2
Per capital income			
1961	1 315	1 010	
1970	2 600	2 300	
1981	9 550	9 685	
Manufacturing employment			
1971 (in thousands)	1 173	464	71.7
1980	1 355	495	73.2
Tertiary labour force			
1971 (in thousands)	2 821	2 159	56.6
1981	4 393	3 407	56.3
Hectares in farmland			
1971 (in thousands)	8 950	59 714	13.0
1981	8 075	57 815	12.0
Farm cash receipts			
1971 ($ millions)	1 747	2 766	38.7
1981	6 356	12 325	34.0

Source: Calculated from data in the *Census of Canada.*

Heartland–Hinterland Patterns of Trade

The external trade patterns of the core and the periphery reflect the different economic characteristics of the two regions. Unfortunately, as external trade information is not available for parts of provinces, the heartland in this section will be regarded as Ontario and Québec, and the periphery as the rest of Canada. This division means that the primary-producing areas of northern Ontario and Québec — involving mainly mining and partial refining (Sudbury, Chicoutimi–Jonquière, Rouyn–Noranda), forestry, and hydroelectric power — are included within the core. The data are therefore weighted more to primary production than is actually the case.

During the early 1980s, Canada's balance of trade has been positive (Table 4.2). This favourable balance is, however, somewhat misleading because the balance of payments — which includes financial transfers relating to loans, interest and dividend payments on foreign capital, international capital transfers, and foreign travel — has been negative. However, the trade data in Table 4.2 indicate that Canada basically imports manufactured products and pays for these with the export of crude materials, food products, partially fabricated materials, and some manufactured end products.

The different roles of heartland and hinterland in trade are illustrated in Fig. 4.2. The periphery dominates the export trade (79 percent) in crude materials (particularly oil, natural gas, and forest products), most of which go to the United States (70 percent) and the rest to other foreign areas (30 percent). Moving down the diagram to groups of products involving higher levels of fabrication, the contribution of the hinterland becomes smaller and that of the core larger. Crude materials are often partially fabricated; usually in the core, and then exported to the United States. On the other hand, food products involve both heartland and hinterland almost equally (53 percent and 47 percent), and three–quarters of the exports go to the rest of the world. Manufactured end products are produced virtually only in Ontario and Québec and exported almost exclusively to the United States (84 percent).

TABLE 4.2 CANADA'S IMPORTS AND EXPORTS, BY COMMODITY GROUPING, 1982

Commodity Group	*Percentage of Imports*	*Percentage of Exports*
Live animals	.2	
Crude materials, inedible	12.9	18.1
Food, feed, beverages, tobacco	7.1	12.1
Fabricated materials, inedible	17.5	34.2
Manufactured end products, inedible	60.8	34.8
Special transactions	1.5	.3
Total volume ($ 000)	67 355 341	81 463 975

Source: Statistics Canada, *Summary of External Trade, December, 1982* (Ottawa: 1983), pp. 36 and 12; and Ontario Ministry of Industry and Trade, *Ontario Exports and Imports, 1982* (Toronto: 1983).

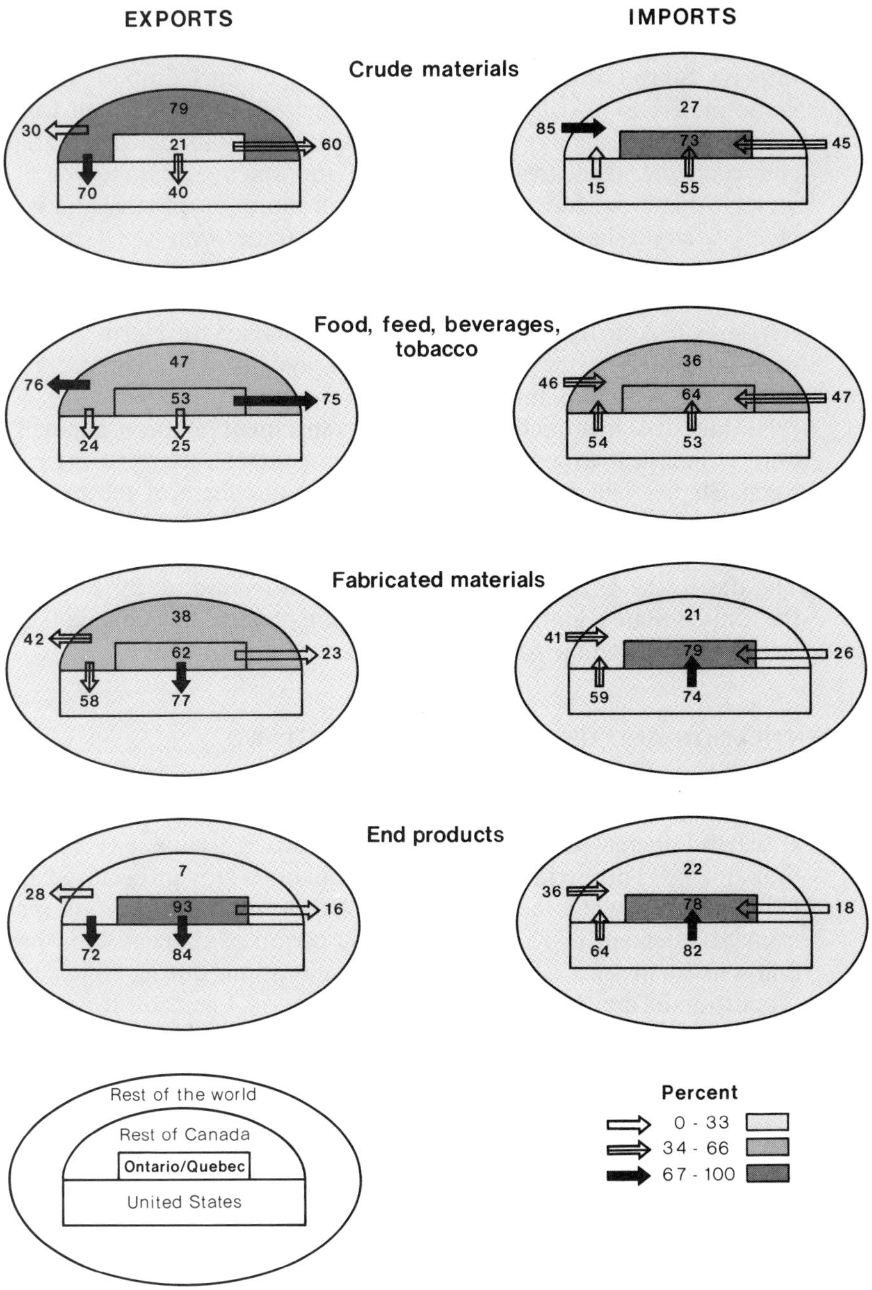

Figure 4.2 The import-export trade of Canada's heartland-hinterland space economy.

This overwhelming link with the economy of the United States, and the role that the core plays in this link, is emphasized with respect to imports. Since Canada is a staple-producing country, imports of food and crude materials (usually sub-tropical and fresh vegetables and fruits, and oil to Eastern Canada) are few compared with fabricated materials and end products. The greatest value of imports by far involves a whole variety of end products which come from the United States and go to the core. A large share of the end product trade with the United States (imports and exports) involves automobiles and parts, for since the institution of the Canada-United States Automotive Trade Products Agreement (Auto Pact) in 1965, the auto industry in North America has been integrated by the major companies, and there is a considerable flow across the border of these high-value products.[4]

Thus, the heartland-hinterland arrangement of the Canadian economy is manifest to a large extent in the general pattern of international trade. Staples and food products form a large share of the exports, and these emanate to a large extent from the periphery. The Industrial Heartland dominates both the export and import of fabricated products. The ties to the United States are strong and reciprocal, for not only does the United States dominate Canada's trade pattern, but Canada is also the largest single trading partner of its southern neighbour.

CONCENTRATION AND CHANGE IN THE HEARTLAND

Although the proportion of Canada's population residing in the Heartland increased steadily to 1971, relative decline has since set in (Table 4.1).[5] The period of greatest population growth occurred between 1951 and 1971, when the area's share of the nation's population increased from 51.7 percent to 55.3 percent. This period of concentration has been followed by at least a decade of deconcentration, during which time the proportion in the Heartland dropped back to 54.2 percent. It now appears, however, that during the recession and recovery of the early 1980s, the deconcentration trend halted and has perhaps even been reversed. At the provincial scale, Ontario and Québec's share of Canada's population in 1981 was 61.8 percent; the 1985 proportion stood at 61.7 percent.

A more noticeable decline has occurred in the accumulation of wealth. The Heartland, as the focus of manufacturing employment, has tended to be the wealthiest part of the country. In 1961 the average income of each person in central Canada was 30 percent greater than that of the average person living in the hinterland regions. This gap slowly diminished between 1961 and 1976, and with the surge in energy-related capital investments in the west during the latter part of the 1970s, per capita incomes in hinterland regions actually began to exceed those in the Heartland — hence the deconcentration of population. Since 1981 this income difference has once again diminished, and the two regions are now about equal in this regard.

There are several factors, however, that maintain the comparative strength of the Heartland: its proximity to markets and capital in the United States, its relatively large local domestic market, the agglomeration economies derived from a relatively well-educated and large urban population, the productivity of agriculture, and the highly integrated urban system of southern Ontario and southern Québec. Although investment in large resource-based projects has and will continue periodically to attract capital away from the Heartland, the long-run effects of such developments are to boost economic activity in the Heartland because most of the manufacturing and organization of industry in Canada is focussed in this part of the nation.

Urban and Cultural Concentration

The concentration of the nation's manufacturing into the industrial core is matched by a concentration of the population into a few large urban areas. About 73 percent of the Heartland population is located in seventeen metropolitan areas and large cities (Table 4.3 and Fig. 4.3).

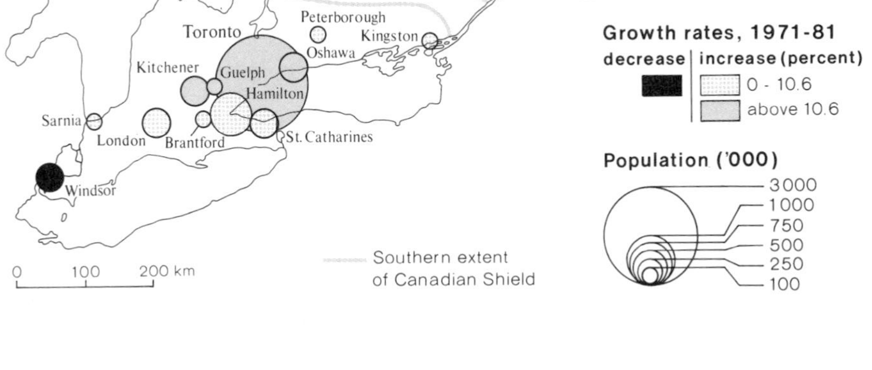

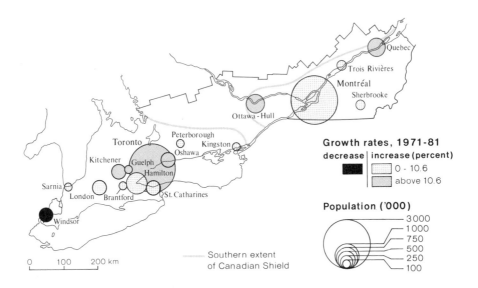

Figure 4.3 The growth of major urban centres in the Industrial Heartland, 1971–1981.

TABLE 4.3 POPULATION OF CENSUS METROPOLITAN AREAS (CMAs) AND LARGE CENSUS AGGLOMERATIONS (CAs), 1971-1981[a]

Urban Area	*1971*	*1981*	*Percentage Change 1971-1981*
Toronto	2 605 253	2 998 947	15.11
Montréal	2 715 428	2 828 349	4.16
Ottawa-Hull	619 845	717 978	15.83
Québec City	500 714	576 075	15.05
Hamilton	503 154	542 095	7.73
St. Catharines-Niagara	285 800	304 353	6.49
Kitchener-Waterloo	238 570	287 801	20.64
London	253 910	283 668	11.72
Windsor	248 715	246 110	- 1.05
Oshawa-Whitby	120 320	154 217	28.17
Sherbrooke	106 244	117 324	10.43
Trois Rivières	103 703	111 453	7.47
Kingston	105 915	114 982	8.56
Brantford	80 285	88 330	10.02
Peterborough	79 160	84 701	8.26
Sarnia	78 411	83 951	7.07
Guelph	66 386	78 456	18.18
	8 711 813	9 619 790	10.42

[a] 1981 boundaries are used for both dates

Source: Calculated from data in the *Census of Canada.*

Three general features of this urban distribution should be emphasized: (1) the Census Metropolitan Areas (CMAs) of Toronto and Montréal, with a population of about 3 million each, clearly dominate over all other urban areas; (2) there are many more large urban places in southwestern Ontario than there are in the Québec portion of the Heartland; and (3) there has been a wide variation in urban growth rates. Toronto and the urban areas around it, as well as the administrative centres of Ottawa–Hull and Quebéc City, have rates of increase greater than that for the Heartland as a whole (10.6 percent). One metropolitan area, Windsor, actually experienced a decrease in population between 1971 and 1981 when the automobile industry suffered setbacks. Thus, though the Heartland's basic urban structure remains stable, social and economic trends can cause internal fluctuations.

In addition to this urban concentration, the Heartland is pivotal because it is the crucible around which the multi–cultural nation has been forged. The Heartland consists of the densely populated areas of two provinces in which the two linguistic groups which founded the nation are concentrated. But these linguistic groups are focussed in distinct parts of the Heartland, reflecting a cultural polarity which on the one hand has sparked social and political conflict, but on the other has encouraged a dynamic complementarity of social and economic values.

Nearly 80 percent of the population in the Québec portion of the Heartland is French-speaking, and the only two parts of the province in which the proportion drops below 80 percent are along the Ontario and United States borders, and on the Ile de Montréal (Fig. 4.4a). A small part of Ontario, along the Québec border around Hawkesbury, is also predominantly French-speaking. The location of the English-speaking population is virtually a mirror image of the French (Fig. 4.4b). Almost the whole portion of Ontario located in the Heartland is English-speaking, with the only exceptions being along the Québec border. Of particular note is the English language concentration in the western part of Ile de Montréal.

The Italian-speaking population has been included because it forms the largest of the "minority" language groups. It is the product of a particular recent period of immigration (1951–71), and is highly localized in the major metropolises of Toronto and Montréal (Fig. 4.4c). The number of Italian-speaking people, along with people from other southern European countries, has now reached sufficient magnitude in certain locations that they have become a major political force in both provinces.

The proportion of the Heartland population located in Québec that is French-speaking has increased steadily from 78 percent in 1961 to almost 80 percent in 1981. The proportion that is originally English-speaking has declined from 15.3 percent in 1961 to 12.4 percent in 1981. In Ontario, the proportion that is originally English-speaking has declined slightly, presumably as a result of recent immigration from non-English-speaking countries, and the proportion that is French-speaking is small and becoming smaller. There is, therefore, an increase in the level of polarization as the Québec portion of the Heartland has become more French, and the Ontario portion even less French.

The Location of Manufacturing Industries

As noted earlier, the Heartland is the manufacturing centre of the nation. Manufacturing industries are found in a large number of Heartland cities, but the bulk of the employment is in major metropolitan areas large enough to generate local industrial complexes.[6] The seventeen cities demarcated in Fig. 4.3 account for about three-quarters of the labour force in Heartland manufacturing, with the metropolitan areas of Toronto and Montréal providing one-half of the total in 1981. Hamilton

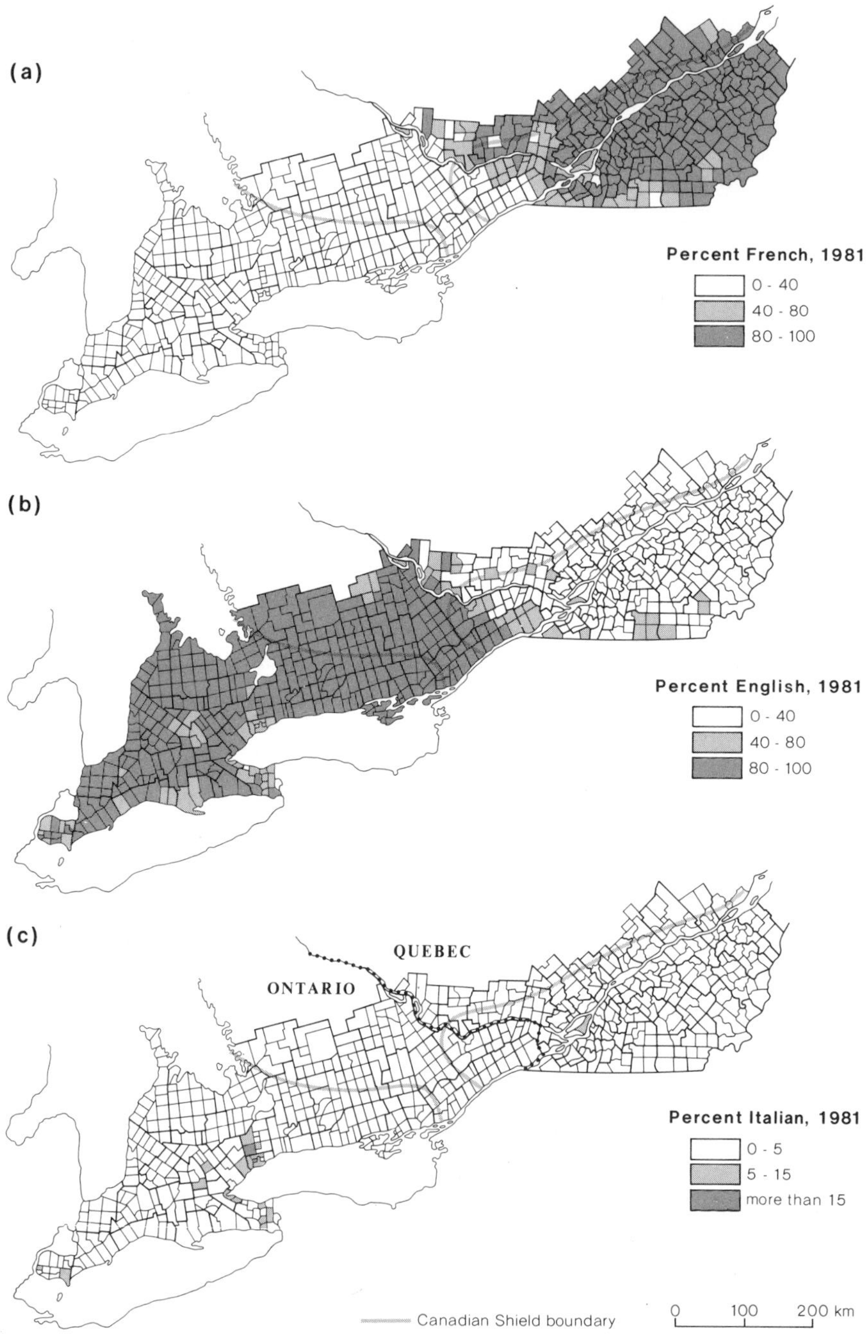

Figure 4.4 The distribution of French, English, and Italian linguistic groups in the Industrial Heartland, 1981.

Manufacturing in the Industrial Heartland: This aerial view of Stelco's 900-acre Hilton Works site shows the rolling mills at the far left, the steel-making shops at centre, and the blast furnaces and coke ovens on the far side. The site is on Hamilton Harbour, to the southwest of downtown Hamilton. (*Steel Company of Canada*)

has about 6 percent of all the core manufacturing jobs; Kitchener–Waterloo 3.5 percent; St. Catharines–Niagara, Windsor, London, Québec City, Oshawa–Whitby, and Ottawa–Hull between 2 and 3 percent of the total; and the remaining places about one percent each.

All types of manufacturing are represented in the core (Table 4.4), but over 50 percent of the labour force is concentrated in transport equipment, food and beverage processing, metal fabricating, electrical products, and different aspects of the clothing and textile industries. The various industrial types can be divided into two groups on the basis of industry-wide estimates of value-added per worker in the manufacturing process. Low value-added industries tend to have low capital/labour ratios and pay relatively low wage rates, whereas high value-added industries tend to have high capital/labour ratios and pay relatively high wage rates.

The contrasting distributions of these two types of industry are illustrated in Fig. 4.5. The high value-added industries (Fig. 4.5a) tend to be clustered in the largest metropolitan areas: Toronto and Montréal. But, the concentration is particularly evident in the "Golden Horseshoe" around eastern Ontario from Oshawa–Whitby to Hamilton, and extending westwards along the major limited access highway (401) and rail routes to Kitchener–Waterloo, London, and Windsor–Chatham.

TABLE 4.4 THE DISTRIBUTION OF EMPLOYMENT AMONG, AND RELATIVE CONCENTRATION OF EMPLOYMENT IN, THE MAJOR MANUFACTURING GROUPS WITHIN THE HEARTLAND, 1981, AND PERCENTAGE CHANGE IN LABOUR FORCE 1971-1981

Major Group	*Percentage of Heartland Manufacturing Labour Force*	*Percentage in Heartland*	*Percentage Change 1971-81*
Food and beverages	10.4	53.9	18.4
Tobacco products	0.5	94.4	- 8.3
Rubber and plastics	3.7	83.8	41.0
Leather industries	1.9	94.1	13.1
Textile industries	4.7	89.3	13.6
Knitting mills	1.3	88.8	21.6
Clothing industries	7.0	86.3	31.6
Wood industries	2.7	27.4	61.5
Furniture and fixtures	3.5	77.6	51.5
Paper and allied industries	4.7	49.7	16.6
Printing and publishing	6.3	71.1	30.4
Primary metals	5.6	63.1	20.1
Metal fabricating	9.3	76.0	36.0
Machinery industries	6.0	76.3	41.4
Transport equipment	10.6	79.9	24.2
Electrical products	7.8	89.9	13.6
Non-metallics	3.0	67.0	15.6
Petroleum and coal	1.2	67.5	36.7
Chemicals	5.2	81.0	23.8
Miscellaneous	4.6	84.0	32.9
Total or average	100.0	70.0	26.1

Source: Calculated from data in the *Census of Canada.*

The low value–added industries (Fig. 4.5b), on the other hand, appear to be quite dispersed. Some (such as clothing and furniture and fixtures) are present in the two largest metropolises, but most are found in the smaller towns beyond the major urban centres. There is a particular pattern to these industries in Québec, with the textile industry being concentrated in the townships immediately to the east of Montréal, an area defined somewhat more broadly than usual in Fig. 4.5b as Cantons–de–l'est. Wood and paper industries are centred in the small towns and in Québec City somewhat farther from Montréal in a territory described as "zone mixte"[7] because it supports a variety of economic activities.

This emergence of high and low value–added geographic concentrations of industry may be related to the differing availabilities of two factors of production, capital and labour, in the two provinces over the

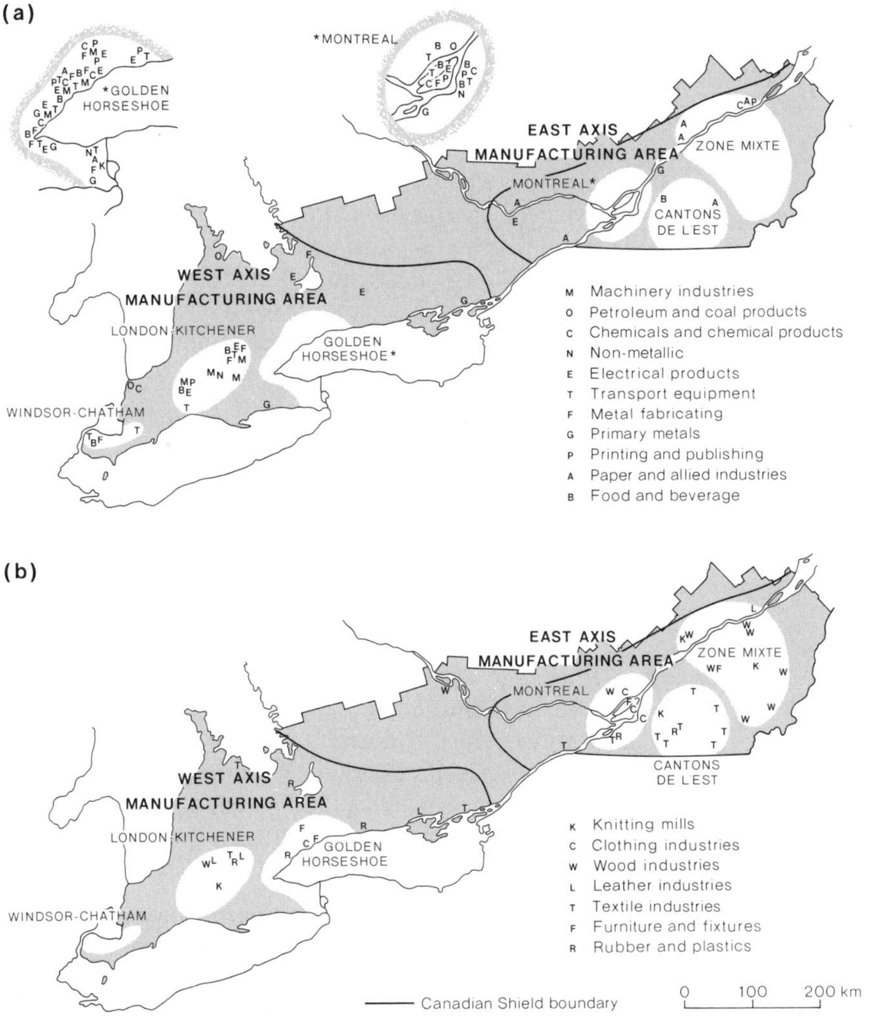

Figure 4.5 The distribution of high value-added and low value-added industries in the Industrial Heartland.

past few decades. As capital has been relatively more abundant than labour in southern Ontario, capital–intensive (and hence high value–added) industries have tended to concentrate in that part of the Heartland. In Québec labour has been relatively more abundant than capital, leading to more labour–intensive (and hence low value–added) industries.[8]

Thus, in summary, the major regions of industrial specialization are:

I. The East Axis Manufacturing Area consisting of
   (a) *The Montréal Region*: with mainly high value-added industries (transport equipment, electrical products, chemical products, printing, publishing) and clothing.
   (b) *Cantons-de-l'est:* which has been expanded to include the textile towns of Magog, Sherbrooke, Drummondville, and Cowansville. This region is interlinked with the clothing industry of Montréal.
   (c) *"Zone mixte"*: in which are found mainly industries based on wood in cities and towns such as Trois Rivières, Shawinigan, and Arthabaska. Québec City stands out as an anomoly with a slightly wider manufacturing base.

II. The West Axis Manufacturing Area consisting of
   (a) *The Golden Horseshoe:* focussing primarily on Toronto, Mississauga, and Hamilton. This is the largest concentration of manufacturing employment in Canada and involves mainly high value-added manufacturing industries. The dominant industrial types are transport equipment (particularly automobile assembly, trucks, farm equipment), metal fabricating, primary metals, and electrical products.
   (b) *London-Kitchener corridor:* involving newer high value-added industries such as automobile manufacture in St. Thomas; and older high value-added industries such as electrical products and machinery industries in London, Waterloo, and Brantford, and metal fabricating in Kitchener and Guelph.
   (c) *Windsor-Chatham:* focussing almost entirely on high value-added automobile and metal fabricating industries.

There are also two areas of minor concentration that should be mentioned. One is the limited, but growing, area of manufacturing employment in Ottawa-Hull. The chief industry was once pulp and paper manufacturing, but the more rapidly growing modern industry involves computer and communications hardware and software production, which is subsumed partly under the "electrical products" heading.[9] The second area of minor concentration is the petro-chemical industry in Sarnia, which is based largely on the resources of Alberta and reflects the locational requirements of chemical and plastic manufacturers for accessibility to the central Canadian market.

Office and Service Activities

Though central Canada is known as the "industrial" Heartland of the country, it is the service (or tertiary) activities that provide most employment. The service activities listed in Table 4.5 involve almost three

Capital-intensive and high technology manufacturing: Sarnia is Canada's leading petrochemical centre. This manufacturing complex ships a vast array of industrial products to forwardly-linked Heartland manufacturing industries. (*Imperial Oil Limited*)

times as many people in the regional labour force as manufacturing, and the recent rate of increase in jobs in this large sector has been more than twice that in secondary industry. This shift of the labour force to service activities mirrors changes that have occurred in other wealthy countries over the past few decades, and is often referred to in the context of an emerging "post–industrial" society.[10]

Employment in most service activities is usually directly related to the distribution of population. The concentration indices in Table 4.5 describe whether the Heartland has more (greater than 1.0) or less (less than 1.0) than expected of the labour force in a particular type of employment. For the Heartland, with 54.2 percent of the total population of the country and, for example, 70.5 percent of the total national employment in wholesale trade, the index is 70.5/54.2 = 1.30. In other words, there is more employment in wholesale trade than expected based on the Heartland's share of the national population.

The tertiary activities in which the Heartland has a greater share of the national employment than expected are: wholesale trade; services to business management; and finance, insurance, and real estate. These are precisely the tertiary activities that would be concentrated in an economic/business core of a country. What is surprising, however, is that the region

TABLE 4.5 THE TERTIARY SECTOR OF THE INDUSTRIAL HEARTLAND, 1971-1981

Type of Tertiary Employment	*Percentage of Heartland Tertiary Employment*	*Concentration Index*	*Percentage Increase 1971-81*
Transportation, communications, etc.	10.97	0.95	39.9
Wholesale trade	8.96	1.30	97.4
Retail trade	17.40	1.01	46.9
Finance, insurance, real estate	8.59	1.12	59.4
Education	9.63	1.02	31.1
Health and welfare services	10.65	1.01	61.1
Services to business management	6.71	1.13	113.6
Personal and miscellaneous services	8.43	1.08	51.8
Accommodation and food services	8.05	0.98	101.9
Federal administration	4.81	1.01	23.0
Provincial and local administration	5.77	0.94	43.6
Other government employment	0.03	1.43	21.3
Total or average	100.0	1.04	55.7

Source: Compiled from data in the *Census of Canada.*

has only an expected share of the national employment in federal government activities. Though federal government facilities are concentrated in the Ottawa–Hull area, the various hinterland regions share in government functions. The Maritimes and coastal British Columbia, for example, have many armed forces personnel, and elsewhere federal government employees contribute significantly to local economies. The major decision-making apparatus, however, is still located in the Heartland.

Places that have more of the labour force in a particular type of tertiary activity than expected (concentration index greater than 1.15) include Ottawa–Hull and Québec City, both of which are especially dependent upon service and governmental activities (Fig. 4.6). The metropolitan area of Toronto has a particular concentration of the tertiary labour force in finance, services and business management, and wholesale trade. Montréal focusses on the same activities, except for finance.[11] Two smaller urban agglomerations, Kingston and London, are particularly dependent upon health and education-related activities. It is evident that the places having greater than expected numbers of the labour force in

The political metropolis of Canada: The Ottawa-Hull urban region houses the Parliament Buildings and most of the federal government's administrative offices. The tertiary sector is the leading stimulus for urban growth and development. (*NFB Phototheque*)

particular service activities are the largest metropolises. There are, in effect, four major service centres in the entire area — Toronto, Montréal, Ottawa–Hull, and Québec City. The other places that have some concentrations of the tertiary labour force are local regional centres (such as London, Kingston, and Sherbrooke), university towns, and recreational centres. As mentioned earlier, however, the Heartland does not dominate in the tertiary sector of the economy.

Agriculture in the Heartland

Although the Heartland has only 12 percent of all the farmland in the country (which includes the extensive range lands and summer ranch lands in the west), it has 91 percent of land devoted to tender fruit and tobacco; 76 percent of land in vegetables, nursery products, and greenhouses; 63 percent of dairy cattle; 61 percent of land in apples and pears; 57 percent of hens, chickens, turkeys, ducks, and geese; 42 percent of beef cattle, pigs, and horses; 37 percent of sheep; 29 percent of land in potatoes, sugar beets, beans, peas, etc.; and 15 percent of land in grains (principally corn, oats, and wheat) in the country. This list emphasizes the high production–per–hectare nature of the agriculture in the area. Some of this agricultural production competes directly with sprawling urban areas for land.[12]

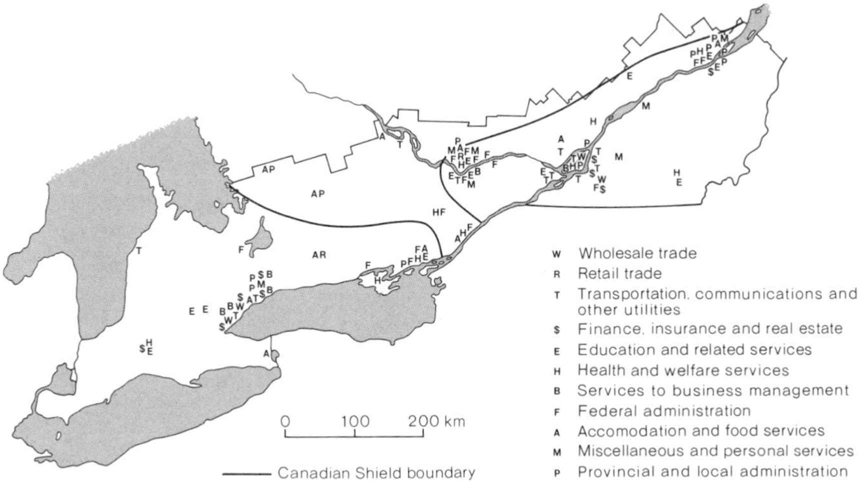

Figure 4.6 The distribution of tertiary or service activities in the Industrial Heartland.

Competition with expanding cities is greatest in the areas of tender fruit, tobacco, and apple production (Fig. 4.7a). Tender fruit and tobacco are grown on the rich, well-drained soils and in the most equable climatic area between Lakes Erie and Ontario. Apple orchards occur in the same areas as tender fruit, and also on other south-facing slopes around Lake Ontario, between Lake Erie and Lake St. Clair, in the western townships of Québec, and in Prince Edward County in eastern Ontario.

The distribution of vegetables, nursery products, and field crops (potatoes, sugar beets, peas, beans) emphasizes the impact of local demand on agricultural land use (Fig. 4.7b). The large urban areas of southern Ontario and Québec provide a big market for these crops, which are produced particularly around Montréal and Toronto and the other urban areas of southern Ontario. The good soils and the modifying effect of the Great Lakes make southwestern Ontario and the St. Lawrence Lowland in Québec especially favourable for this type of crop production.

Local urban markets are also the main reason for the intensity and location of dairying in the Heartland (Fig. 4.7c). Dairying is concentrated in eastern Ontario and along the St. Lawrence River valley. It requires not only markets but the particular dedication of the farmer, since the care of dairy herds and the preparation of dairy products (e.g. butter and cheese) is not only capital-intensive, but extremely time consuming. Tradition and dedication have fostered the persistence of this type of agriculture in Québec, and particularly in the Cantons-de-l'est and the Chaudière River Valley.[13] Beef cattle, pigs, and some dairying are found in other parts of Québec and extensively in southwestern Ontario in the counties bordering Lake Huron.

Figure 4.7 The concentration of agricultural production in the Industrial Heartland.

The presence and location of particular types of agriculture within the area is, therefore, influenced by physical factors and the distribution of urban markets. Although production fails to meet all food requirements of the regional population, it does go a long way toward meeting domestic needs with respect to some types of commodities such as summer vegetables and fruit products, and provides some surplus for export. Although Fig. 4.2 indicates that more than half Canada's exports of food, feed, beverages, and tobacco come from the Heartland, it is estimated that only about 28 percent of the nation's total food exports comes from farms within the area.

Internal Structure and Interaction

It is, therefore, evident that the role of the Heartland is reflected in the concentration of the population into urban areas, in patterns of trade, and in the intensity of agricultural production, manufacturing, and certain tertiary activities. The location of all these activities in the major urban areas gives rise to a particular pattern of flows that characterizes the organization of the urban system within the Heartland. As the largest share of the intercity movement of people and goods (by value) occurs by road transport, flows along highways can be used (1) to demonstrate the internal structure of the Heartland in terms of interaction, and (2) to provide some clues as to its changing geography.

The maps in Fig. 4.8 depict the daily volume of road traffic within the Heartland during the early 1970s (Fig. 4.8a) and early 1980s (Fig. 4.8b). There are, quite clearly, two large metropolitan nodes — Montréal and Toronto — which serve as the generator or destination of most flows. Two secondary nodes, Québec City and Ottawa–Hull, serve as secondary organizing foci. The main direction of traffic is along the corridor from Windsor to Québec City, hence the appelation "Main Street."

The major changes within the Heartland's pattern of flows are three-fold. First, the volume of traffic across the entire area increased considerably during the 1970s, suggesting that the gross level of economic (and social) integration also increased. Second, the increase in traffic has been largest in southwestern Ontario, from Toronto west to Kitchener and London, north to Barrie, and south to the United States via the Niagara Peninsula. Third, the metropolitan areas of Ottawa–Hull and Québec City are now more conspicuous hubs than they were in the early 1970s. The essential binodal nature of the flows has not, however, been diminished. If anything, the basic pattern has been strengthened.

ISSUES FACING THE HEARTLAND

The changing role of the Heartland in the Canadian economy, and the particular geographic locations of various economic activities, raise a

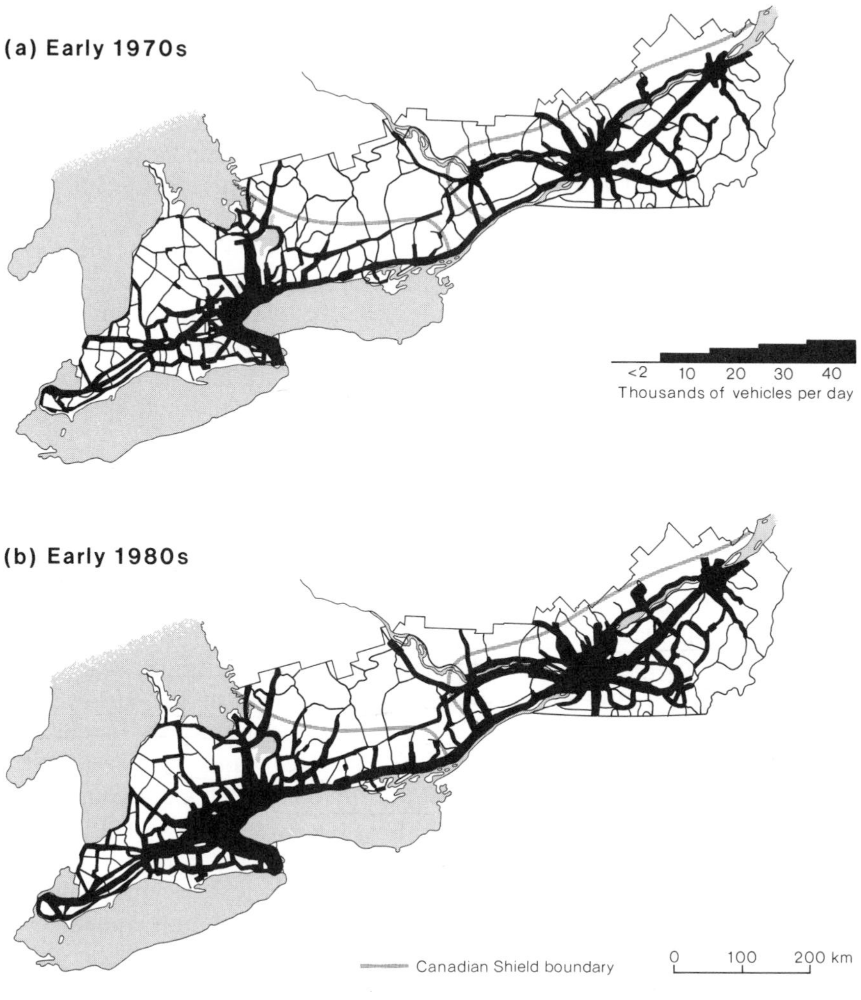

Figure 4.8 Flows of road traffic within the Industrial Heartland, 1970 and 1980.

number of issues relating to both national trends and shifts within the Heartland itself. Will the deconcentration of population and economic activities away from the core to the periphery continue? What are the general patterns of differential growth within the Heartland and the factors underlying them? What are the long-term trends in the spread of urban development and population, and how might these trends affect agriculture? Finally, given the significant restructuring of industry throughout the world, how healthy is the Heartland's manufacturing base?

Population Deconcentration

Is the deconcentration of population away from the Heartland that occurred between 1971 and 1981 likely to continue into the future? We can examine this question in demographic terms, particularly with respect to within–Canada migration, because changes in the location of population occur for three main reasons: as a result of changes in economic conditions, as a result of social trends (such as the aging of the population) and, occasionally as with foreign immigration, as a result of political events. To define the demographic changes, we focus on three factors: net natural increase (births minus deaths), net domestic migration (inflows minus outflows, all originating within Canada), and net foreign immigration (inflows minus outflows, with the origin or destination being outside Canada) (Fig. 4.9).

The differences in net natural increase between regions (Fig. 4.9a) are based on differences in birth rates, which in turn are affected by the age profile of the population and cultural factors. Though there used to be considerable differences between provinces in birth rates, these differences have diminished, and there is now little regional variation. The large net natural increase that occurred in Alberta and British Columbia in the 1976–81 period is related to net domestic migration, because migrants were often in the early family formation stage of the life–cycle.

The main regional differences occur with respect to net domestic migration (Fig. 4.9b). Prior to 1966, the Heartland tended to grow at the expense of population in the rest of Canada. British Columbia and Alberta have invariably gained from internal migration.[14] Between 1966 and 1971, the Heartland incurred a small loss to peripheral regions as a whole, particularly Alberta, and in the 1970s this net loss became almost 30 000 per year. In other words, the Heartland lost population equivalent to that of a city the size of Drummondville or Cobourg every year during the decade of the 1970s. While this loss has diminished in the early 1980s, it remains on the average at about the level of the early '70s.

Population loss in the Heartland as a result of net domestic migration has generally been balanced by a large net foreign immigration (Fig. 4.9c), particularly to the major metropolises of Toronto and Montréal. About one–quarter of Canada's population growth since 1945 is attributable to immigration, and this immigration has undoubtedly helped stimulate the growth of the Heartland. In the latter half of the 1970s, however, both the total number of immigrants and the number concentrating in the Heartland decreased.

What immigration trends can we expect in the latter 1980s and the 1990s? Immigration is influenced to a considerable extent by federal government policies, which in turn are related to domestic labour requirements and unemployment. As high rates of unemployment are likely to continue through the 1980s, the immigration levels of the late

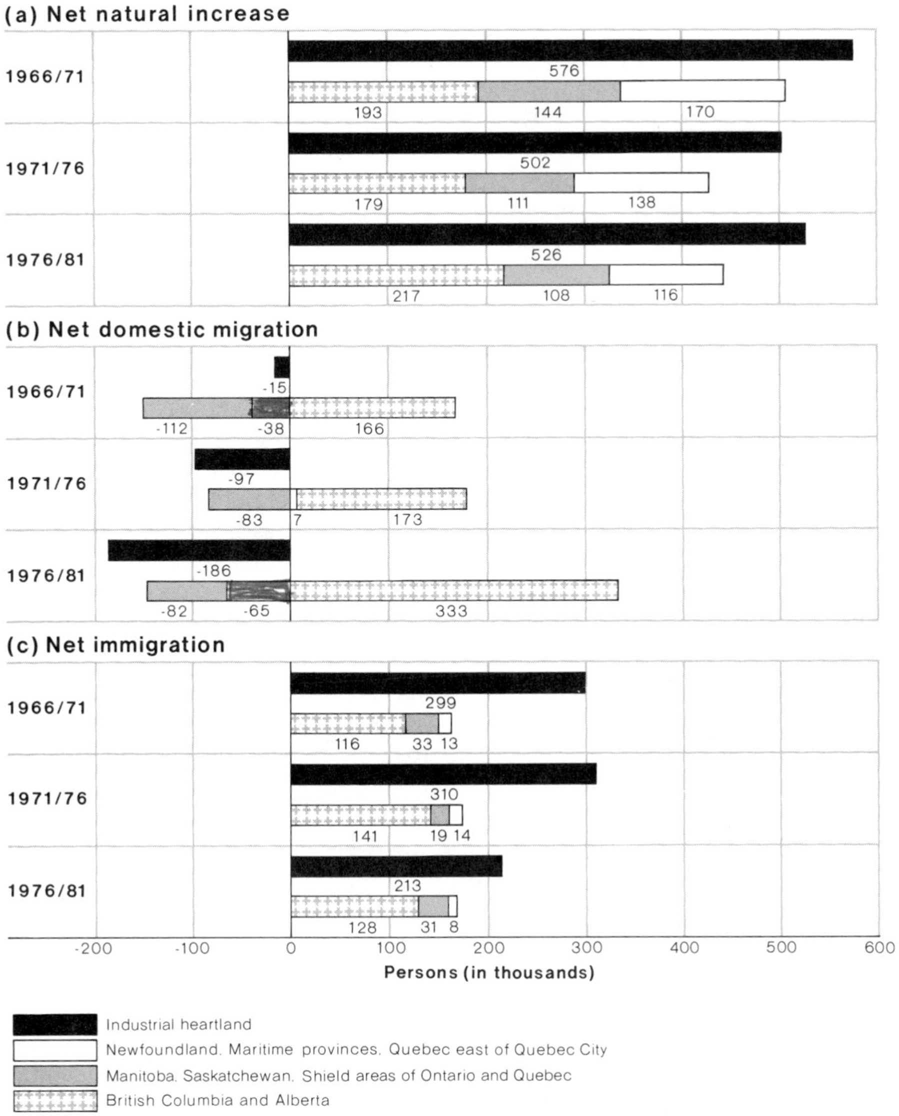

Figure 4.9 Components of demographic change, 1966–1971, 1971–1976, and 1976–1981.

1970s (with the Heartland orientation of destinations) are also likely to continue. The volumes may, however, increase once again in the 1990s when there are fewer young people competing for jobs and as federal limitations on immigration are eased.

Thus population deconcentration away from the Heartland to the western provinces will continue, but at a much slower rate than that experienced during the latter part of the 1970s. The magnitude of deconcentration will probably be equivalent to that of a small town (10 000–20 000 per year). At the same time, the overall growth rates of both the Heartland and the peripheral regions will diminish as well. There will, therefore, be a continuation of the situation within the core in which some urban places will actually lose people, while others may be burgeoning.

Urban Concentration and Differential Growth

Population in the Heartland has generally concentrated into a number of urban regions. The four largest are compared in Table 4.6. In order to make the information comparable, the metropolises of Ottawa and Québec City are defined by a 25-kilometre radius, the distance defined as urban around these cities in 1981. The urban regions of Montréal and Toronto extended to a radius of 65 kilometres from the Central Business District (CBD) of each, for it is within this area that most of the commuting to the major municipalities located within the two regions occurs. The areas included within Ottawa and Québec City differ slightly because census subdivisions (or townships) are not partitioned.

The information indicates significant population shifts. In the period between 1921 and 1951, when the core population increased at the same rate as that for the hinterland regions, population concentrated in these four extended urban areas. Montréal and Toronto grew at almost exactly the same rate, whereas the population of the extended Québec City area more than doubled as a result of the war effort. In the period between 1951 and 1971, when the population of the country grew at a high rate and economic activities and people concentrated into the Heartland, these four extended urban areas grew more rapidly than the core as a whole. But, the extended urban area around Toronto grew at a faster rate than that around Montréal, and Ottawa–Hull grew much faster than Québec City. This comparatively greater growth in Toronto and Ottawa is related to the diversification and expansion of manufacturing, and to both public and private sector office activities in these cities.

In the most recent period of heartland–hinterland deconcentration, the population of the core has continued to concentrate within these four extended urban regions. Montréal's share, however, has declined, while that of Toronto and Ottawa has continued to increase. Québec City's population has remained constant. Thus, the extended Toronto urban area has been gaining in dominance over Montréal since the 1950s, and in the most recent period has continued to grow at a rate well above the national average.

A number of factors have contributed to these differential urban growth patterns. First, as a result of both national and international

TABLE 4.6 THE CONCENTRATION OF THE URBAN POPULATION WITHIN FOUR MAJOR URBAN REGIONS, 1921-1981 (Population in thousands)

Urban Region	*1921* *Pop.*	*1921* *Percentage of Heartland*	*1951* *Pop.*	*1951* *Percentage of Heartland*	*1971* *Pop.*	*1971* *Percentage of Heartland*	*1981* *Pop.*	*1981* *Percentage of Heartland*	*km²*
Montréal (within 65 km)	1 013	22.0	1 840	25.3	3 174	26.6	3 350	25.4	11 938
Toronto (within 65 km)	929	20.2	1 696	23.3	3 413	28.6	3 935	29.8	7 563
Ottawa-Hull (within 25 km)	177	3.9	305	4.2	588	4.9	780	5.2	1 965
Québec City (within 25 km)	157	3.4	321	4.4	507	4.3	580	4.4	1 847
Total share of Heartland population		49.5		57.2		64.4		64.8	

Source: Calculated from data in the *Census of Canada.*

trends, Toronto has emerged as the financial and office headquarter capital of Canada. Since the 1930s, a number of leading financial institutions and capital markets within Canada have shifted to Toronto. Sun Life, for example, moved its corporate headquarters from Montréal to Toronto in 1978. On an international level, Toronto has become one of a number of "world cities." Together, these world cities form a high-level world capital and headquarter conduit, with each major city serving as the economic (and often political) focal point of a country or region.[15] Second, those urban centres that serve as foci for national and provincial governments have also continued to grow rapidly as a result of the increasing involvement of the state in social and economic matters. Finally, while the acceleration of the drive for French-language dominance in Québec during the 1970s definitely encouraged the exodus of many young English-speaking Québecers, this political, social, and cultural pressure may have only accelerated a decline in the position of Montréal that was already well in evidence.

Thus, it may be that the Heartland is contracting into an area focussing on Toronto and extending politically to Ottawa-Hull. If this is so, the division of powers in the country will change. Up to 1971 the Heartland was organized around two nodes, Montréal and Toronto, each of which served regional and national purposes. Regionally, each was the focal point and driving force for a number of cities that depended upon it. Nationally, each played a role that appeared to be relatively equal in the economic organization of the country, and Montréal served as the main link between the two major language groups within the nation. With the apparent collapse of the core to southern Ontario, Montréal is left with a diminished role — it may become a city of only regional importance. From the point of view of Canada as a multi-cultural and bilingual nation, the decline of Montréal could be detrimental. A southern Ontario heartland, while being efficient for both internal and external economic interactions, will not by itself be able to serve the long-term interests of a nation with such a large and geographically concentrated linguistic minority.

Metropolitan Decentralization

Although the total population of the Heartland increased between 1971 and 1981 at a rate considerably less than that for the country as a whole, about one-third of the core actually increased in population at a rate greater than the national average (Fig. 4.10). In addition, the types of population change have been diverse. Some rural and central city decline, for example, has been counterbalanced by suburban and exurban growth.

However, reasonably large portions of the rural Heartland, particularly in the Appalachians of southwestern Québec and parts of the Shield, are experiencing population decline. Farm abandonment and out-

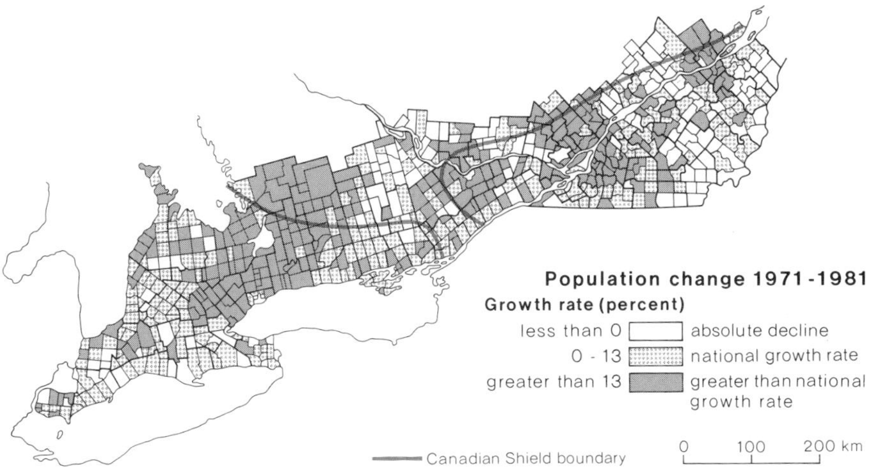

Figure 4.10 Population change in the Industrial Heartland, 1971–1981.

migration have occurred in these areas for decades, but the rate of decrease has accelerated with a decline in the rate of natural increase. Many small communities in eastern Ontario, the Chaudière Valley, and the Megantic–Arthabaska district are experiencing severe population losses, particularly when a major economic activity, such as a mine, lumber mill, or manufacturing plant closes down. There is considerable debate over what can be done to alleviate losses of employment in small settlements. The debate focuses on the advantages of maintaining small-town economies and lifestyles versus the costs of public action that would be required for their economic support beyond that of unemployment insurance. Ameliorative action is usually only possible and successful in times of fairly rapid economic expansion, for in times of slow national growth, investment is often not self-sustaining.

Population decline is also evident in the centres of the large metropolises including Montréal, Toronto, Hamilton, Ottawa, Windsor, and Québec City (Fig. 4.8). People and economic activities are continually moving out to the suburbs and beyond. Such decentralization can significantly alter the commercial structure of central cities, for a loss of central city population invariably means a decrease in purchasing power for the support of inner-city economic activities.[16] The location of a new shopping centre in an outer suburban housing development, for example, often draws inhabitants and consumers away from the city core and leaves the inner city with older facilities and a limited range of establishments.

Some large metropolises, such as Toronto, Ottawa, and Montréal, have fought back by adapting the idea of the enclosed, climate-controlled shopping centre to the downtown by creating interlinked underground and enclosed multi–functional facilities (e.g. office and shopping facilities), or new facilities (e.g. Eaton Centre in Toronto and the Rideau Centre in Ottawa). There has also been considerable redevelopment of the older parts of some central cities through the upgrading of residential districts (such as Cabbage Town in Toronto), or complete redevelopment and renovation (such as Little Burgundy in Montréal). These changes have brought back (or retained) a relatively wealthy population (professionals, and upwardly mobile single or two–person household units) to central cities and have led to changes in the commercial structure of their local service areas as fashionable boutiques, computer stores, and other specialty shops became established.

Suburban developments immediately adjacent to the built–up city area have been joined in the 1970s and 1980s by exurban developments on a fairly large scale.[17] Exurban developments have grown as people who work in the cities relocate to live in small towns and villages or on small farms some distance from the contiguous built–up metropolitan area. Exurbanites are often searching for an environment that offers a different way of life from that which can be experienced in the city. This trend has created extensive areas of population increase around the major metropolises of southern Ontario and Montréal, and has caused considerable urban encroachment on quality agricultural land.

A comparison of the rapid growth areas in Fig. 4.10 with the best soil areas in Fig. 4.1c shows that much of the suburban and exurban population growth is encroaching on the best agricultural areas. Although a large part of the agricultural land lost between 1971 and 1981 resulted from farm abandonment, it is estimated that about 10 percent was the result of direct suburban expansion, and as much as another one–third may have been lost due to indirect urban effects such as exurban developments, the creation of energy corridors, and the establishment of recreational facilities, amusement parks, severance housing, and so forth.[18]

The important issue is the loss of prime land (class 1 in Fig. 4.1c), for there are less than 5 million hectares of such land in Canada, and slightly more than half is found in the Industrial Heartland. An example of a particularly important area of prime land subject to considerable urban encroachment is the Niagara Fruit Belt (Fig. 4.11).[19] The amount of land with soil and climatic conditions suitable for the production of tender fruit crops (peaches, cherries, pears, plums, grapes) in Canada is limited to the lower Fraser Valley, the southern Okanagan Valley, and a small part of the Niagara Peninsula. As the Niagara Peninsula is in the heart of Canada's most populated area, the fruitlands are particularly important because they are directly accessible to the bulk of the market. The largest acreage of tender fruit production on the Niagara Peninsula was achieved in 1951 (21 530 hectares). Since that time the expansion of urban areas has resulted in the loss of some 20 percent of this maximum average.

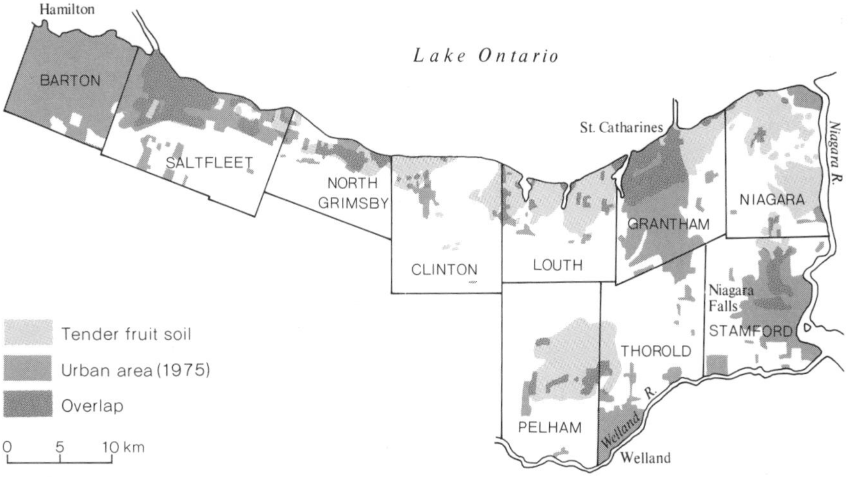

Figure 4.11 Urban encroachment on agricultural land in the Niagara Peninsula.

Responsibility for the preservation of prime land has been allocated to regional and local governments. In Ontario, these governments must act in accordance with a *Foodland Guidelines* position paper which establishes standards for agricultural land use and urban development patterns.[20] In Québec, the *Loi sur le zonage agricol* stipulates policies of preservation and self-sufficiency, but again there are numerous loopholes that allow developers to hold the property. As a result, though conservation of prime land is a major public issue, there has been no sound planning to preserve the most productive farmland in the country.

De–industrialization in the Heartland

As described earlier, manufacturing in the Heartland has expanded considerably since the 1950s, but the comparative contribution of this economic sector to the Gross Domestic Product (GDP) has actually decreased (Fig. 4.12). In the early 1950s, Canada was among the top ten industrial countries in the world; now it does not rank among the top thirty in terms of value of output. Since 1951, manufacturing has provided a smaller share of the GDP and created relatively fewer jobs. In 1971 over 26 percent of the labour force in the Heartland was involved in manufacturing; in 1981 it was less than 24 percent. Such a phenomenon can be described as "de–industrialization." The decline of manufacturing in the Heartland can be attributed to: (1) the restructuring of manufacturing throughout the world–system; (2) the stagnation of industries in those regions of the United States with which manufacturing firms in the Heartland are linked; and (3) the slow growth of industries in the high technology sector.

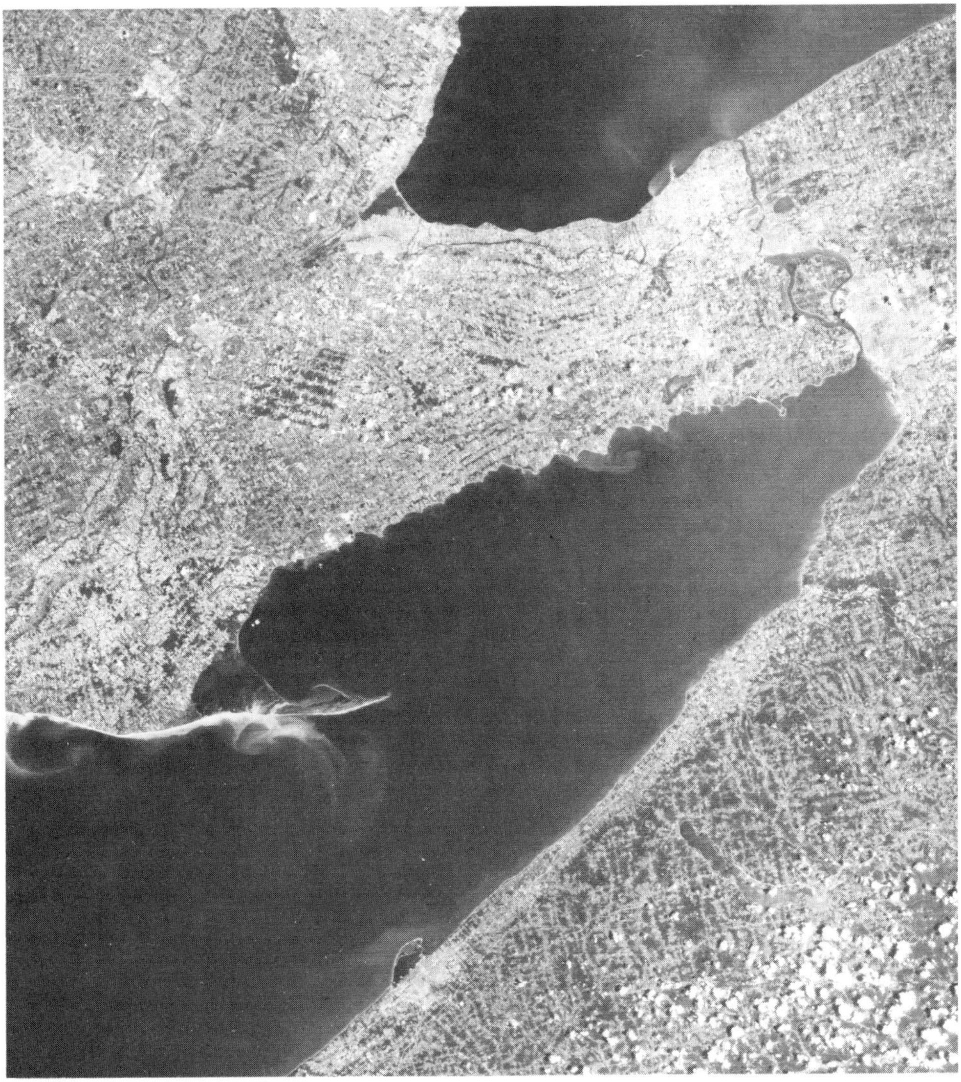

The Niagara Fruit Belt: This satellite view shows the geographical context of the map area of Fig. 4.11. Hamilton appears adjacent to the southwestern corner of Lake Ontario; Buffalo, New York, lies at the northeastern edge of Lake Erie. (*Canada Centre for Remote Sensing, Energy, Mines and Resources Canada*)

Given the desperate state of the economies of many countries in Western Europe and Asia following World War II, it is not surprising that Canadian manufacturing was, by comparison, in a healthy state in 1951. The apparent industrial strength of the industry as a whole in the 1960s and 1970s was in large part a result of the Auto Pact. In 1983–84 the auto

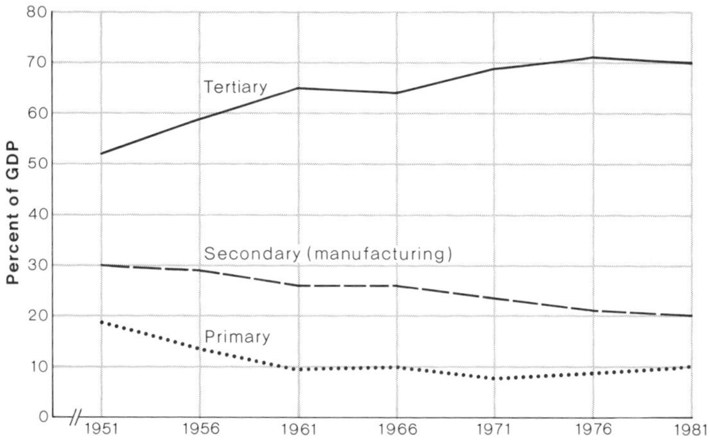

Figure 4.12 Economic activities as a percentage of Canada's Gross Domestic Product, 1951–1981.

industry contributed over one–quarter (by value) of all exports to the United States. But, apart from the automobile industry and some firms in communications, iron and steel, and alcoholic beverages, Canadian manufacturing has shown little growth in the late 1970s and early 1980s.

This comparative decline is due in part to the growth of national industrial economies such as Japan and West Germany, in which the national governments and large manufacturing concerns develop cohesive and integrated approaches to research, development, and marketing that surpass those in Canada. In addition, many multinational firms have restructured their organizations so that branch plants can easily be relocated from one country to another. In this way, firms can take advantage of less restrictive environmental standards and low wage rates around the world.

This process of international restructuring has had a negative effect on the general complex of industrial activities in the Northeast and Mid–West of the United States, with which manufacturing in the Heartland is strongly linked. The basis of manufacturing in this large area is iron and steel, automobiles, heavy transport equipment, petro–chemical industries, and textiles. During the past two decades the growth performance of these industries has been desultory, and, as a consequence, the manufacturing base of the major cities of central Canada has been eroded. For example, the difficulties experienced by the large auto companies in Detroit in coming to terms with the competition from Japan and West Germany have been reflected in huge lay–offs in Ontario as well as in Michigan and other parts of the United States. Moreover, the expansion of auto production in the mid–1980s has not restored all the jobs lost during the recession of the early 1980s.

The one sector of manufacturing in the United States that remained relatively buoyant during the 1970s, and which will undoubtedly continue to expand at a rapid pace during the 1980s, is the high technology industry located primarily in the "sun–belt" states (eg. California and Texas) and in Massachusetts. These industries are characterized by a high rate of technical innovation and change, and large expenditures on research and development. They embrace firms ranging from electronics and computer hardware–software to bio–engineering. Although there are a few examples of successful innovation and development by Canadian–owned companies (such as Northern Telecom), the structure of Canadian manufacturing is still largely composed of firms in the traditional sector. The reasons for the failure of the Canadian manufacturing industry to create new activities in the high technology sector are: (1) the low volume of research and development expenditures in the country; and (2) the branch–plant nature of the manufacturing economy.[21]

Canada devotes only about one percent of its GDP to research and development, as compared with the 3 to 4 percent of GDP spent in such countries as Japan, West Germany, and the United States. It is thought that a major reason for this low expenditure is that Canadian manufacturing is largely foreign–owned (about 60 percent), and that the foreign companies prefer to undertake research and development activities at their home base. If this hypothesis is correct, re–industrialization, led by growth in the wide variety of firms embracing new technologies, will not occur unless domestic research and development is stimulated, and this may not take place unless the proportion of foreign–owned manufacturing companies operating in Canada is reduced. Otherwise, even the Industrial Heartland will continue to be primarily a branch–plant economy dependent for its production and jobs on decisions made by foreign–owned organizations. De–industrialization would then undoubtedly continue.

CONCLUSION

The Industrial Heartland remains the pivot of the Canadian economy and is the most heavily urbanized part of the nation. More than 80 percent of the 13.2 million people living in the region reside in urban areas, and the trend towards urban concentration continues. A major change has occurred since 1971, however. The population of the core is growing more slowly than that of the rest of Canada, and for the first time in recent history, the region has been losing population as a result of migration. This loss of population, primarily in the younger age and lower salary–earner groups, is occurring as a result of declining job opportunities.

The basis for urban growth has always been manufacturing, service, financial, and governmental activities. Manufacturing, however, is not

The nineteenth century headquarters of the Bank of Montreal. (*Larry McCann*)

growing as rapidly as it did in the past. Although the tertiary employment activities remain highly concentrated in Ottawa–Hull, Montréal, and Toronto, this sector of the economy is also in transition. The slowdown in the growth of governmental activities has diminished the growth of Ottawa–Hull, and the shift of financial and head office activities from Montréal to Toronto has reduced the growth of Montréal. Only Toronto has grown in population at about the national average, mainly because of its strong position as the financial and corporate centre of the country, though Calgary and Vancouver have been cutting into this base.[22]

Without doubt, the most significant factor affecting urban growth has been the poor performance of the manufacturing industries. It is apparent that the boom in manufacturing employment opportunities in the late 1950s and 1960s occurred as a result of the rapid growth of branch plants (many auto related), the health of which depends upon the dynamism and creativity of the parent companies. When the parent companies do not perform as well as other competitors, their foreign branch plants in Canada are the first to reduce output, and regions experience decreases in investment. Furthermore, the branch-plant economy has not provided the creative environment for research and development vital for technological innovation and a healthy creative core.

Thus the role of the Industrial Heartland *vis à vis* the hinterland regions of Canada is changing. Resource development in regions such as Alberta and British Columbia has in the past, and will in the future, attract population away from central Canada. The Heartland itself is also changing, contracting and concentrating its national economic functions into southern Ontario. As a result, Montréal's status as a national business capital has been reduced. This concentration will undoubtedly continue as the post-industrial age gains momentum and it may contribute toward a re-emergence of regional issues and factionalism. French-Canadian businessmen are increasingly taking a leading role in the Montréal and Québec economy, and in the world-economy as well. Their progress over the next few decades will have considerable bearing on the future internal cohesiveness of the Industrial Heartland.

Acknowledgement

The research upon which much of this chapter is based was undertaken with support from the Social Science Research Council of Canada and the Lands Directorate (Environment Canada).

NOTES

1. For a discussion of this see: The Economic Council of Canada, *Western Transition* (Ottawa: Ministry of Supply and Services, 1984) and O.F.G. Sitwell and N.R.M. Seifried, *The Regional Structure of the Canadian Economy* (Toronto: Methuen, 1984).
2. It should be noted that, unless otherwise indicated, all figures and tables in this chapter are taken from: M. Yeates, *Land in Canada's Urban Heartland* (Ottawa: The Lands Directorate, Environment Canada, 1985); and *idem,* "The Windsor-Québec City Axis: Basic Characteristics," *Journal of Geography,* 83 (1984), 240–249.
3. A more detailed discussion of the definition of the Heartland is contained in: M. Yeates, *Mainstreet: Windsor to Québec City* (Toronto: Macmillan of Canada, 1975), pp. 4–25.
4. The origins and "political economy" of the Auto Pact agreement are detailed in: N.B. MacDonald, *The Future of the Canadian Automotive Industry in the Context of the North American Industry,* Working Paper No. 2 (Ottawa: Science Council, 1980); and J. Holmes, "Industrial Reorganization, Capital Restructuring and Locational Change: An Analysis of the Canadian Automobile Industry in the 1960s," *Economic Geography,* 59 (1983), 251–271.
5. A discussion of the three major periods of consolidation, concentration, and deconcentration with respect to the heartland and periphery is contained in: M. Yeates, "Urbanization in the Windsor-Québec City Axis, 1921–81," *Urban Geography,* 5 (1984), 2–24. A more detailed analysis of the period of concentration relating to southern Ontario is presented in: J.U. Marshall and W.R. Smith, "The Dynamics of Growth in a Regional Urban System: Southern Ontario, 1951–1971," *The Canadian Geographer,* 22 (1978), 22–40.
6. G.B. Norcliffe and L. Ekotseff, "Local Industrial Complexes in Ontario," *Annals* of the Association of American Geographers, 70 (1980), 68–79.
7. This, and the other manufacturing regions of Québec, are defined in: J.C. Thibodeau and T-M Holz, "Etude spatiale de la structure l'industrie manufacturière au Québec, 1961–1971," *Annuaire du Québec 1977–78,* (1978), 988–998.

8. A theoretical discussion, and empirical test, of the effects of varying availabilities of capital and labour in Ontario and Québec on manufacturing location is in: G.B. Norcliffe and J.H. Stevens, "The Heckscher-Ohlin Hypothesis and Structural Divergence in Québec and Ontario, 1967–1969," *The Canadian Geographer,* 23 (1979), 239–254.
9. G.P.F. Steed and D. DeGenova, "Ottawa's Technology-Oriented Complex," *The Canadian Geographer,* 27 (1983), 263–278.
10. The classic reference concerning the manufacturing service transition is: D. Bell, *The Coming of Post-Industrial Society* (New York: Basic Books, 1976). A brief history of the emergence of a service society in Ontario is outlined in V. Lang, *The Service State Emerges in Ontario 1945–1973* (Toronto: Ontario Economic Council, 1976).
11. There is abundant literature on the change in the location of headquarter and office activities in Canada. Recent examples include: R.K. Semple and M.B. Green, "Interurban Corporate Headquarters Location in Canada," *Cahiers de Géographie du Québec,* 27 (1983), 389–406; and E.S. Szplett, "The Current State of Office Location and Office Functions in Canada: I. Managerial Aspects of the Firm, and II. Office Location and Linkage," *The Operational Geographer,* 1 (1983, 1984), 35–39 and 27–31.
12. C.R. Bryant, L.H. Russwurm, and S-Y Wong, "Agriculture in the Urban Field: An Appreciation," in M.F. Bunce and M.J. Troughton, eds., *The Pressures of Change in Rural Canada* (Toronto: York University Press, Geographical Monographs, 1984), pp. 12–33.
13. W. Smith, "The Changing Geography of Québec Agriculture," in M.F. Bunce and M.J. Troughton, eds., *The Pressures of Change in Rural Canada.*
14. Discussions of the various demographic components of regional population change in Canada are contained in: M.G. Termote, *Migration and Settlement: Canada* (Laxenberg, Austria: IIASA, 1978); W.E. Kalback and W.W. McVey, *The Demographic Basis of Canadian Society* (Toronto: McGraw-Hill Ryerson Ltd., 1979); J.W. Simmons, "Forecasting Future Geographies: Provincial Populations," *The Operational Geographer,* 1 (1983), 7–12; and L.S. Bourne, "Urbanization in Canada: Recent Trends and Research Questions," in L. Gentlecore, ed., *China in Canada: A Dialogue on Resources and Development* (Hamilton: Department of Geography, McMaster University, 1984).
15. J. Friedmann and G. Wolff, "World City Formation: An Agenda for Research and Action," *International Journal of Urban and Regional Research,* 6 (1982), 309–343.
16. For a discussion of this issue as it relates to Toronto in particular see: K.G. Jones, *Specialty Retailing in the Inner City: A Geographic Perspective* (Toronto: York University Press, 1984).
17. Exurban developments are not new, but have certainly become more evident in the heartland over the past decade. See: Y. Brunet, "L'Exode Urbain, Essai de classification de la Population Exurbaine des cantons de l'Est," *The Canadian Geographer,* 24 (1980), 385–405; and C.R. Bryant, L.H. Russwurm, and A.G. McLellan, *The City's Countryside: Land and Its Management in the Rural-Urban Fringe* (London: Longmans, 1982).
18. Yeates, *Land in Mainstreet.*
19. The most detailed research, covering a number of years, on the urbanization of land in the Niagara Peninsula (and also in the Okanagan Valley of British Columbia) has been undertaken by: R.R. Krueger, "Urbanization in the Niagara Fruit Belt," *The Canadian Geographer,* 12 (1978), 179–194.
20. R.R. Krueger, "The Struggle to Preserve Specialty Crop Land in the Rural-Urban Fringe of the Niagara Peninsula of Ontario," *Environments,* 14 (1982), 1–10.
21. This argument is developed in some detail in: J.N.H. Britton and J.M. Gilmour, *The Weakest Link* (Ottawa: The Science Council of Canada, 1978); and a response is provided by K.S. Palda, *The Science Council's Weakest Link* (Vancouver: The Fraser Institute, 1979).
22. R.K. Semple and W.R. Smith, "Metropolitan Dominance and Foreign Ownership in the Canadian Urban System," *The Canadian Geographer,* 25 (1981), 4–26.

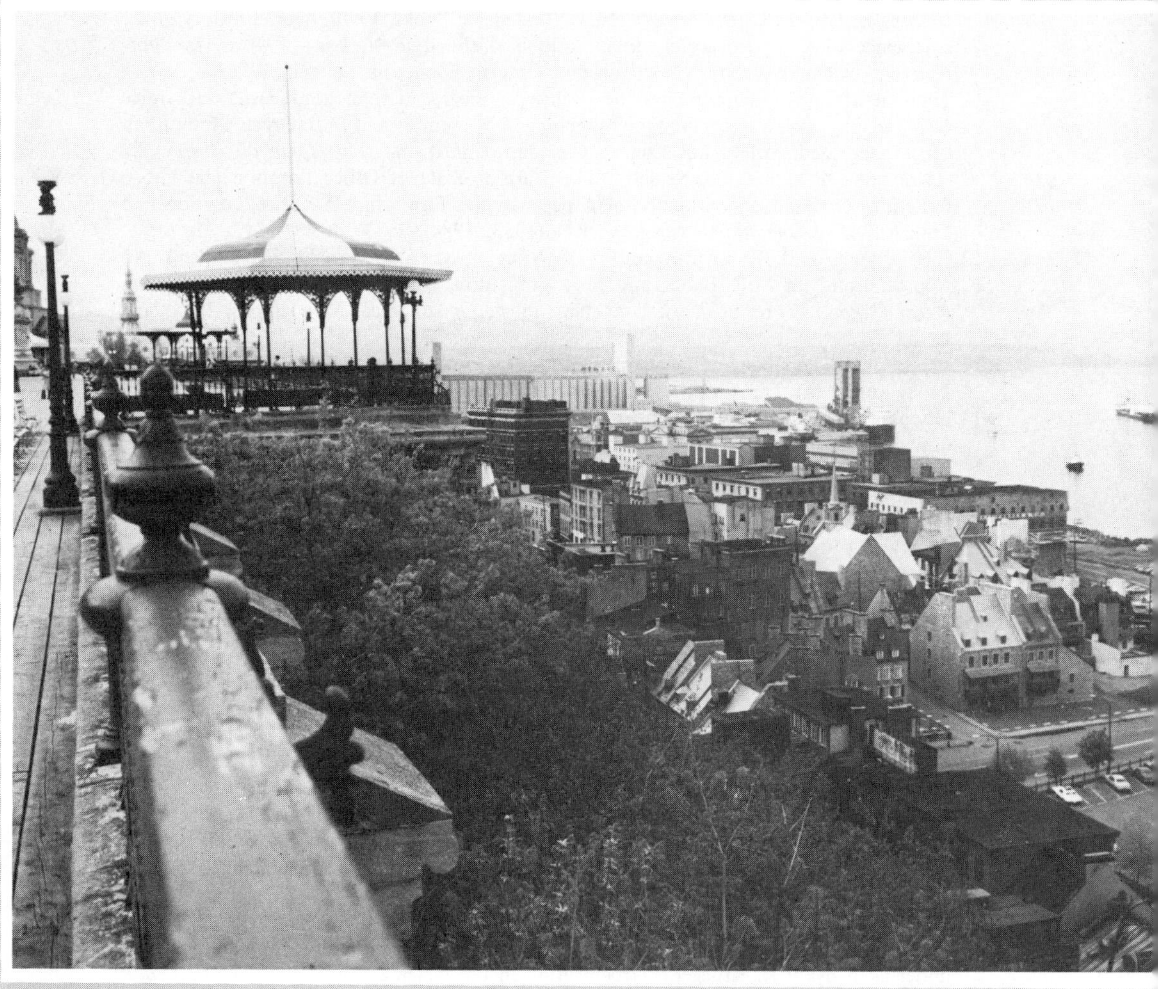

5

Cultural Hearth, Continental Diaspora: The Place of Québec in North America

Eric Waddell

> *Les Québécois ne sont pas peuple de l'espace. Ils ne l'occupent pas, ils le parcourent. Ils sont peuple de passage et non de l'enracinement.*
>
> C. Morissonneau

Even a cursory review of the major geographical statements on Québec gives the impression of a province distinct from the rest of North America, of a place and a people all too easy to describe and characterize.[1] It was a mixture of Frenchness, and hence sentimental considerations, and a readily manageable settlement history that attracted the spiritual father of Québec geographers, Raoul Blanchard, to the Saint Lawrence Valley.[2] Not surprisingly, he was to affirm at the end of his research that: "C'est une belle histoire, qui fait grand honneur *au rameau français établi en terre américaine.*"[3] (emphasis added)

Notably, for Blanchard, Québec was synonymous with French Canada; a province in which a distinctive people had settled, survived, and prospered in spite of immeasurable odds dictated by a difficult environment and British rule. More recently, Paul Claval has provided much the same characterization: Frenchness, Catholicism, and a unique historical experience — hence a distinctive culture — demarcate, if not isolate, the province from the rest of North America.[4] Pierre Biays, too, highlights Frenchness, plus language, and the creation of a distinctive rural society dominated by the *seigneurie* and the *rang,* a society that was nevertheless transformed through industrialization and urbanization commencing at the turn of the twentieth century.[5]

These interpretations are those of metropolitan French geographers, but it would be erroneous to assume that nationality accounts for their sometimes charged views of Québec, for the same themes recur in the writings of the province's own geographers. Thus, for Louis-Edmond Hamelin: "Le Québec de langue française est une expérience politique originale, mettant en cause une écologie américaine, une formule anglaise et une âme française."[6] Marcel Bélanger is more explicit in his analysis of the originality of modern Québec: "... la population de cette grande région d'urbanisation de l'Amérique du Nord est issue, pour les quatre cinquièmes, du peuplement des terres seigneuriales. ..."[7] In other words, although newly integrated into the continental economic system, the people of Québec remain politically and culturally bound to their ancestral land in the St. Lawrence Valley.

Time and again, therefore, scholars invoke the cultural specificity of Québec — the interweaving of a European past, or history, with a North American present, or geography — to create a region characterized by a distinctive landscape and society in which the long-lot and rurality figure prominently. The land has shaped the actions and decisions of generations of French Canadians. The availability or lack of land has determined whether they have remained in the rural areas, migrated to the cities, or left for other parts of North America. The fact that for generations rural fathers tried to give many of their sons at least some agricultural land has reinforced the importance of rural tradition. The subdividing of land into smaller and smaller strips has also preserved the traditional seigneurial landscape of long lots.

The region's symbols, or markers, almost assume the dimensions of a litany: "langue, foi, charrue" in the Church of one epoch, and "seigneurie, paroisse, manoir, église, village, rang, ferme" in the Academy of another. It is little wonder that the poetic visionaries of the 1960s and '70s frequently spoke of Québec as "Presqu'amérique" or "une autre Amérique." From this perspective, also, it is easy to understand why the major contributions to the geographical literature inspired by Québec lie within the realm of historical geography.[8]

Although this literature generally succeeds in furnishing an adequate description of Québec, it does not always help us understand the province. Most descriptions, in considering the region to be unique, treat it in isolation and fail to address questions about the manner in which the province interacts with, and is inserted into, the larger, continental, core–periphery design. In addition, their analyses occasionally lead to the somewhat dangerous conclusion that Québec is an anachronism, a society trapped by the irony of history on the wrong side of the Atlantic. Consider, for instance, Claval's suggestion that the mission of Québec geography may well be "... à faire découvrir aux Québécois la raison pour laquelle ils ont été exilés sur les rives du Saint-Laurent."[9]

Yet, if Québec is indeed different, it is precisely because of its role within the broad North American context. For there to be a French Canada, there must be an English Canada; for there to be an *Amérique française,* there must be an *Amérique anglaise.* This chapter, then, seeks to place Québec society in a continental perspective to determine the kinds of relationships Québec — the cultural hearth — entertains with the rest of North America — the continental diaspora. The cultural hearth is the core region of a society's traditions (e.g. language, architecture, religion); the diaspora is the hinterland to which the people and its traditions have spread.

A number of questions thus establish our focus in this chapter: Are Québec and French Canada or French America synonymous? Is Québec society homogeneous or heterogeneous? Should the province be considered a part of the Canadian heartland or of the hinterland? Since Québec's economic development has already been examined in the preceding chapters, we focus here on the social and cultural facets of Québec's character.

SITUATING QUÉBEC IN NORTH AMERICA

Our analysis of the central question of this chapter — "Are Québec and French Canada or French America synonymous?" — begins with the premise that there exists a French–Canadian nation, that is, a society with a marked degree of internal cohesion and solidarity based on such considerations as language, religion, a common historical experience, a referential universe set in the St. Lawrence Valley, and a plethora of "national" institutions.

Yet, if consensus as to such a nation exists, there is disagreement about the roots and ultimate geographical expression of Québec's national or ethnic identity. The classic view, articulated first by the ideologues of the Catholic Church and subsequently by nationalist historians, expresses notions of race and racial purity, of French people separated from their metropolitan hearth, and of the integrating forces of language and religion.[10] Grafted onto these notions are others, of Latin–ness, and of the idea of French Canadians being bearers of a rich cultural tradition, or civilization. In the eyes of the Church these qualities rendered the French Canadians a "chosen people" endowed with a "providential mission" in North America, first to civilize and to christianize the Native people and later to win Protestants to the Catholic faith. Loyalty was linked with rurality and attachment to the land, evoking the image of a peasantry bound to the soil. For the peasantry, the Church and the parish were enduring institutions.

These ideas are most clearly articulated by Abbé Lionel Groulx,[11] but also by other nationalist scholars writing about Québec between the mid–nineteenth and mid–twentieth centuries.[12] For these intellectuals, there is a vision of empire, but of an empire lost. For them, the British Conquest of 1763 is a critical watershed in the history of French America; a turning point that assumed dramatic proportions in the collective imagination:

"... je regrette cette brisure atroce dans notre histoire qui fut la conquête anglaise; sans elle, que n'aurait donc pas donné notre génie? Depuis notre histoire est celle d'une lente et implacable dégradation de l'âme française. ..."[13]

Given such a premise, it was inevitable that the regional context of many subsequent analyses of French-Canadian society would be limited to a clearly defined geopolitical realm conceived as a stronghold into which a defeated people withdrew to reconstruct its future, inspired by institutions and a rural experience derived from the *ancien régime.* Conceived in this manner, Québec and French America are necessarily synonymous — Québec alone is French America. But a number of social scientists, including geographers, are now expressing dissatisfaction with a vision of a people that is so truncated in time and space. With regard to race, some insist that as much Amerindian-French intermingling occurred in the St. Lawrence Valley during the French Regime as took place later in the Western Interior.[14] The only difference was that the situation in Québec did not give birth to a "New (or Métis) Nation." For others, close contact with the Amerindians created a distinctive ethnic configuration for French-Canadian society — "un homme nouveau naissait en terre d'Amérique."[15] It gave birth to an anti-authoritarian element and a tradition of mobility of continental dimensions, both of which continue to pervade French-Canadian society.

On the surface, at least, there is a profound contradiction in these two visions of Québec society. One presents French-Canadian society as rooted firmly in the past, tightly circumscribed, almost hermetic, and hence profoundly *québécois.* The other views the people of Québec as fluid, nomadic, responding to opportunities across the continent, and hence resolutely *franco-américain.* Yet, on closer reflection, these visions can be seen as two powerful and distinctive forces generating a basic dialectic that has pervaded French-Canadian society since its inception. The result is the simultaneous existence of the *habitant* — the sedentary peasant, and the *coureur de bois* — the nomad, in the history of a people. This vision also leads to the duality, ambivalence, and conflict that is symbolized in such literary classics as *Maria Chapdelaine* and *Le Survenant,* and that is manifest above all in the enigmatic personality of Jack Kerouac, counter-culture hero of the 1960s, and Canuck from Lowell, Mass. *Québécois, canadiens français,* and *franco-américains* — nationalists, federalists, and continentalists — coexist as expressions of a single cultural universe.

In such a universe, where mobility is practised and valued by at least a part of the population, the St. Lawrence Valley emerges less as an ethnic bastion, that is, as a finite or limiting space on an alien continent, and more as a referential hearth — a place to which the migrants may return, or where they have historic roots and distant family connections. Viewed from this perspective, Québec emerges as a cultural hearth having intimate and enduring links with the rest of North America, and particularly with *l'Amérique française.* The framework that assures this French unity is typically one of kin and friendship, a solidarity born of a shared experience that, because of the weakness of institutional arrangements beyond the frontiers of Québec, has an almost clandestine quality about it. Ethnic identity and solidarity, instead of being articulated around institutions whose legitimacy is constantly questioned and whose ability to survive is weak, is based on language, food, and music, all of which gravitate around family and kin — *pépère, mémère,* and an infinity of *mononcles* and *matantes.* Such is the intensity of these ties across the boundaries of Québec that Yolande Lavoie can ask, rhetorically, on the cover of her study of *québécois* emigration to the United States, "Y'a-t-il un Québécois qui n'ait pas de parents en Nouvelle-Angleterre ou ailleurs aux Etats-Unis?"[16]

The "family," of course, is infinitely variable in size. At one extreme it is simply a set of identifiable kin. At another it is the massive «réunions de familles» that the Church or the Province have organized from time to time in Québec City; the Congrès de la langue française of 1912, 1937, and 1952; and the annual Fêtes du Retour aux Sources, first organized in 1978. There are also associations of people bearing the same family name that have a continental membership and are united by a common interest in family history and a recognition of Québec, and more particularly of the Ile d'Orléans and the Côte de Beaupré, as being their cultural hearth.

To map such a space is almost impossible for it is a territory without frontiers occupied by a people constantly on the move. At best it can be conceived as a hearth in Québec and a diaspora that, for one generation, may be represented by the American Midwest, for another, New England, and for a third, Florida. Taken in this perspective, a Québec radically different from the classic view emerges, a Québec no longer defined in terms of legal or political history and the affairs of government, but rather in terms of a collective ethnic experience that assumes a continental trajectory (Fig. 5.1).

The Expansion and Retreat of Québec in North America

Early French colonists forged a new identity in the St. Lawrence Valley, attempting on the one hand to reconstruct their ancestral society based on a loyal peasantry, and turning on the other to the call of the wilderness that opened up invitingly beyond the seigneurial lands. Inhabited by Indians and abundant game, the wilderness offered unlimited opportunities for hunting and trading. It was this mixture of autarchy and mercantilism, and the discovery, in the Indians, of a new and egalitarian society, that precipitated a sense of being "of this continent," of being *Canadien* rather than French. To be Canadien to this group meant to be individualistic, mobile, rebarbative; to seek the company of Indians; to

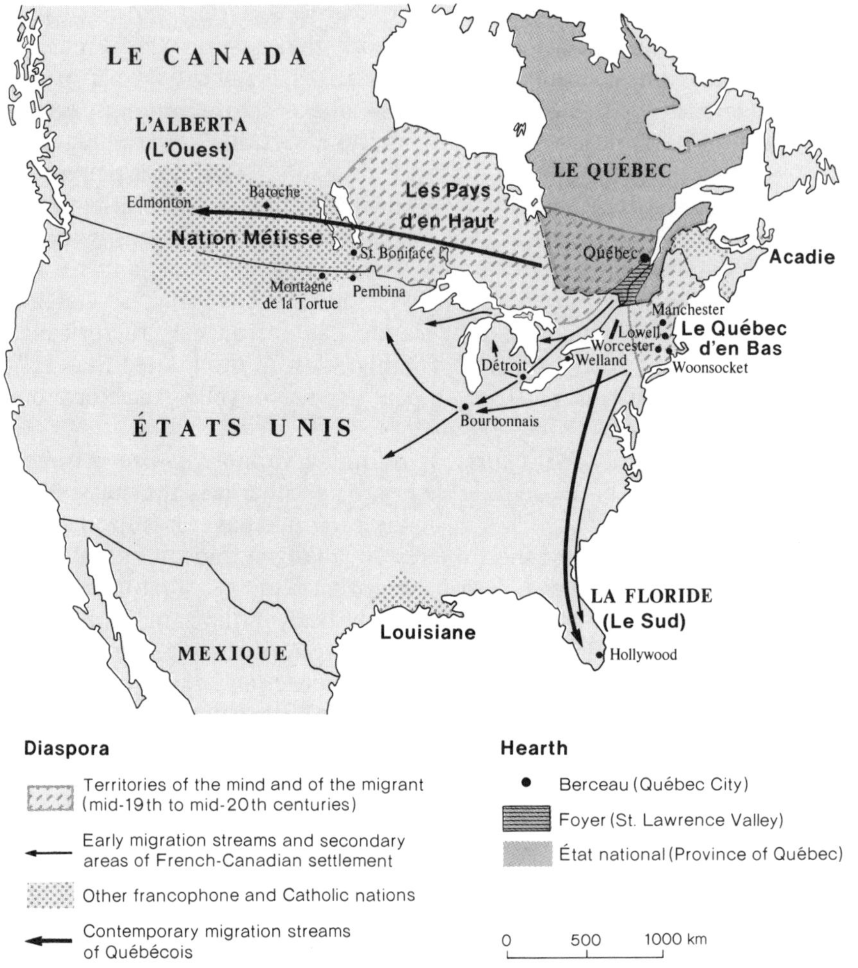

Figure 5.1 Cultural hearth, continental diaspora: the people of Québec in North America.

value leisure and kin; and to fill, gradually, an economic niche as the intermediary between a Europe living in the age of mercantilism and the largely self-sufficient lifestyle of the Indian. Such are the roots of a *peuple d'insoumis* whose indifference to, if not outright rejection of, authority has resurfaced time and again in Québec.

For such a people, little was changed by the Conquest other than the language and the country of origin of the authorities and the bourgeoisie.

If anything, the more aggressive commercial policies of the British and the much less restrictive licensing systems of the fur trade facilitated the diffusion of French Canadians out of Québec and across half a continent. Those who chose to remain in the Great Lakes area after the departure of the French were soon joined by others in the employ of the two major fur trading enterprises, the Hudson's Bay Company and the North West Company. The latter operated out of Montréal and employed, almost exclusively, French Canadians as voyageurs, guides, interpreters, servants, and, to a lesser extent, as clerks and even managers of its trading posts.

Practising aggressive trading policies, the North West Company urged its agents to live among the Indians who supplied the furs. In the process, these fur traders forged a separate ethnic identity based initially on a simple wintering in the country and later on a cultural and then a racial merging with the Indians. The result was a distinctive people, the Métis, who were centred in the west but nevertheless shared a great deal with the people of the St. Lawrence Valley hearth. Although the Métis language was Cree and several other Indian tongues, it was also French. Their religion was Catholic. They valued the liberty of mobility, of being *coureur de bois.* They became, in a sense, the ultimate expression of the mobility so highly valued by the québécois society of the time.[17]

By the early nineteenth century, a Métis "empire" had been created by French Canadians leaving the St. Lawrence Valley either individually or in small groups for the "pays d'en haut" and the "pays des Illinois" (Fig. 5.1). Dozens of small settlements were established around the Great Lakes, along the Red, Assiniboine, and Saskatchewan Rivers, and in the Upper Mississippi and Missouri Valleys. Their names include Sault-Ste-Marie, Rivière Raisin, Fort Wayne, Prairie du Rocher, La Baie, St-Paul, St-Cloud, Pembina, St-Norbert, Batoche, Prince-Albert, Saint-Albert, Fort Benton, Le Havre, and Lewiston.

The notion of migration was strengthened later in the nineteenth century when successive economic frontiers carried other French Canadians westward, imbued by the continuing tradition of mobility and the possibility of material gain. Lumbering attracted migrants to the Saginaw, Sable, and Muskegon Valleys and the towns of Grand Rapids and Bay City in Michigan. Mining in the copper region of the Keweenaw Peninsula and across the iron fields of the Marquette Range in Wisconsin beckoned others. Finally, some were attracted by the farming frontier in such widely scattered places as Georgian Bay (Penetanguishene), Welland, Monroe County near Detroit, and Bourbonnais in Illinois.[18]

As the agricultural frontier moved westward during the nineteenth century, so did some French-Canadian settlers, leaving the Red River Valley to move west across the Western Interior, south into Kansas and Minnesota, and beyond. But these groups never numbered more than a few hundred, and by the second quarter of the nineteenth century the main thrust of migration out of the St. Lawrence Valley had shifted direction, towards the factories and mill towns of New England. Cultural attachment to the hearth in Québec would continue to sustain western settlements, but increasingly the Western Interior became an economic hinterland of Montréal, dependent more on the capital and business organization of the metropolis than on cultural attachment. Hence it slowly became a region distant from and only tributary to Montréal's ethnic élite. The Scots, with the capital and knowledge they had accumulated in the fur trade, became instead the major promoters of western development.

People had been trickling into northern New England from Québec since at least the beginning of the nineteenth century, either to settle as farmers in northern Vermont and the Saint John River Valley of Maine, or to work in the lumbering camps of northern Maine. By mid-century, however, this trickle had become a flood, creating by the end of the century a second national *foyer,* or hearth, in the industrial towns and cities of New England. This *Québec d'en bas* took root above all in the mill towns — Manchester, New Hampshire; Lowell, Fall River, Worcester, Lawrence, and Holyoke, Massachusetts; Lewiston and Biddeford, Maine; and Woonsocket, Rhode Island. By 1930, when Québec had a population of about 3 000 000, New England was home to between 700 000 and 1 000 000 French Canadians who had left Québec to work south of the border.

This massive displacement had far-reaching demographic and sociological effects.[19] A largely illiterate rural peasantry, living on the verge of autarchy, riddled by frequent agricultural crises, indebtedness, and over-population, viewed with enthusiasm the rapid industrialization of New England and, in particular, the development there of a flourishing textile industry. Significantly, the mill towns were readily accessible from rural Québec. One could even walk there, and certainly travel by cart. With the opening of the Northern Railway Company of New York in 1850, linking Montréal with Boston, and of the St. Lawrence and Atlantic Railway in 1853, connecting Montréal and Portland, Maine, these journeys were transformed into a short and cheap train ride across an open and unpoliced international boundary (see Fig. 3.1).

An additional attraction was the availability of work for all members of the family. The manual skills required in the textile mills were more or less familiar, and certainly readily accessible, to a people raised in a social context where carding, spinning, and weaving were common. In the major textile centres of Woonsocket and Lowell, for example, these skills ensured a steady salary and new-found material wealth — the opportunity to dress in a *habit de dimanche* every day of the week. American factory owners were eager to employ what were generally considered to be industrious and docile workers — the "Chinese of the East" — and recruiters regularly travelled to Québec in search of labour. The Depression, the closing of the international boundary, and the erosion of the industrial strength of New England, together with the gradual development of an industrial base in

Coureurs des facteries: At the end of the nineteenth century, the Amoskeag cotton factory in Manchester, New Hampshire, was the largest in the world, with a labour force of some 15 000, of which 40–50 percent were Québécois. (*Manchester Historic Association*)

Québec, ended the massive migration.

In the eyes of the Québécois, the mill towns of New England offered prospects entirely different from the resource frontiers of Western Canada and the American Midwest. To go west was to pose an irrevocable gesture, for distance almost eliminated the possibility of return. Moreover, federal government policies did little to ensure the strengthening of French-Canadian communities in the Western Interior. Newly arrived immigrants from Europe received free rail passage to the frontier from Québec City and Montréal, but no such privileges were offered to those Québécois seeking an alternative to unemployment and rural poverty. Cost and distance forced their attention on New England. Movement between Québec and New England, either to visit or to settle, was entirely feasible and an organic relationship, at the level of family and community, developed between these two *foyers*.

Such was the scale of the out-migration and the intensity of the relations between francophone communities on either side of the border that by the turn of the century Québec society had been radically changed. Its centre of gravity had shifted away from the St. Lawrence Valley to sit astride the international frontier, thereby providing a link between two distinct, but complementary universes: a rural peasantry in Québec and an urban proletariat in New England. Not surprisingly, political, intellectual, and cultural leadership for this single French-Canadian nation came from

Pictures home: Many of the photographers in the New England textile towns at the turn of the century were Québécois. They catered to compatriots who were eager to send photos to their relatives at home, to strengthen ties and bear witness to their new-found prosperity. Often, however, the photographers supplied the clothes. (*Author's collection*)

New England until at least the late 1920s, and lingered on until World War II. At the turn of the century, Woonsocket ranked second only to Québec as the city with the largest proportion of francophones in all of North America. Calixa Lavallee, the author of Canada's national anthem, was a native of Lowell, while Henri Bourassa, founder of *Le Devoir* and an ardent nationalist, frequently crossed the frontier in the course of his career. The internal cohesion of French America was strong.

The integration of the two national foyers into a single ideological realm was facilitated by another critical development, the return of the Catholic Church as a shaping force of society by the mid-nineteenth century. The Catholic Church in Québec suffered as a result of the Conquest, through challenges to its authority, loss of clergy, and damage to property.[20] In 1838, for instance, there were fewer clergy than at the time of the French regime, yet the population had increased from 60 000 to 500 000.

Ironically, this period of isolation encouraged a new, Canadian, identity and hence the emergence of an "Eglise nationale" that determined the actions of the Church for a hundred years or more. It was to this nascent "national church" that many foreign religious orders gravitated from the late 1830s on, bringing with them human resources and a conservative, ultra-montane ideology that wedded well with the sentiments of the Catholic Church in Québec. The Frères des Ecoles chrétiennes appeared in 1837, the Oblats in 1841, the Jésuites in 1842, and the Clercs de St-Viateur and the Ordre de Ste-Croix in 1847, initiating a movement away from revolutionary France that was to continue until the end of the century. The number of priests in Québec multiplied accordingly, rising from 225 in 1830 to 2465 in 1910.

The impact of the Church on the population both inside and outside the boundaries of Québec was far-reaching. By their very presence the various religious communities formed an articulate, indigenous élite. Of more importance, the Church provided the structure for a French presence in North America that this élite could serve and promote. On the one hand, the Church provided an explicit ideology that ascribed a vocation to the French Canadians; on the other, it furnished the institutional framework for the establishment, survival, and development of French-Canadian communities across the continent. For the architects of Catholicism there quite clearly existed a French race or nation in North America whose origins and spiritual hearth lay in the St. Lawrence Valley. The French were, moreover, a chosen people, having a providential (religious and civilizing) mission first among the Amerindians, but subsequently among all the peoples that inhabited the continent.[21] Evidence of this vocation was furnished by the numerical strength of the people and by their continental mobility. They shared a loyalty to religion and language, and a marked sense of ethnic solidarity.

Inevitably, then, the Church sought to cater to the needs of French Canadians wherever they might be, and even to channel and direct their migrations across the continent. What had been a simple parish within Québec became, beyond its frontiers, a *paroisse nationale* that provided the population directly or indirectly with a broad set of social and economic institutions — church, parochial school, convent, orphanage, mutual aid society, credit union, cooperative. Classical colleges were established[22] and national organizations such as the Union Saint-Jean-Baptiste d'Amérique emerged. An individualistic people were thereby provided with an institutional framework that generated not only a collective identity, but also the notions of a *foyer* in Québec and of a fluid diaspora scattered across a continent — in short, of a French America.

By the last quarter of the nineteenth century, French-Canadian civilization (and nationalism) had established continental dimensions. These were expressed in the migration of people out of the St. Lawrence Valley to New England, the American Midwest, and the Western Interior; reinforced by the movement of priests, students, and politicians through the network of institutions; and symbolized in the frequent patriotic rallies in Montréal and in Québec City. All this evoked a sense of euphoria among the francophone élite, expressed in Henri Bourassa's speech on the history of Québec given before the archbishop of Westminster in Montréal in 1910:

> De cette petite province de Québec, de cette minuscule colonie française, . . . sont sortis les trois-quarts du clergé de L'Amérique du Nord. . . .
>
> Eminence, . . . Il vous faudrait rester deux ans en Amérique, franchir cinq mille kilomètres de pays, depuis le Cap Breton jusqu'à la Colombie Anglaise, et visiter la moitié de la glorieuse république américaine — partout où la foi doit s'annoncer, partout où la charité peut s'exercer — pour retracer les fondations de toutes sortes — collèges, couvents, hôpitaux, asiles — filles de ces institutions mères que vous avez visitées ici. Faut-il en conclure que les Canadiens-français ont été plus zélés, plus apostoliques que les autres? Non, mais la Providence a voulu qu'ils soient les apôtres de l'Amérique du Nord.[23]

Yet, at the very time when the idea and expression of a French America reached its apogee, it was also being challenged; and the fact that the francophones outside Québec were generally few in number, scattered, and organized around the Church facilitated the challenge. North America was a secular and not a sacred space by the end of the nineteenth century, and power in the Catholic Church was increasingly shared with another powerful ethnic group, the Irish. The diaspora was progressively weakened and largely assimilated by defeat after defeat: the hanging of Riel in 1885; the elimination of French from the Legislature of Manitoba in 1890; the elimination of French education in Ontario in 1912, Manitoba in 1916, and Saskatchewan in 1929; and the Sentinellist crisis in New England in 1928–29 which led to the elimination of French-language parochial schools. The

Serving the diaspora: The principal institutions of the *paroisses nationales* scattered across the continent were established and staffed by religious communities based in Québec. So, in 1881, it was the Soeurs de Jésus – Marie de Sillery who came to Manchester (N.H.) to assume the direction of the city's first Franco-American parochial school, Académie Notre-Dame. (*Association Canada – Américaine*)

idea of a French America lingered on until the early 1950s: the third, and last, Congrès de la langue française took place in Québec in 1952, and the last Church–sponsored group designed to establish an agricultural community and national parish beyond the boundaries of Québec left Lac St–Jean for St–Isidore in the Peace River Country of Alberta in 1953.

Alternative Visions, New Frontiers

Even as a French America had been taking shape in the late nineteenth century through massive out–migration from Québec and through the creation of an institutional structure comprised of a thousand national parishes, numerous political and religious leaders were voicing their concern.[24] Within Québec voices spoke out increasingly against out–migration for fear that it would irrevocably weaken the demographic, economic, and political viability of the hearth. For almost a century, from 1870 to 1950, the intellectual and clerical élite in Québec promoted a myth of the North, a vision of a promised land where French Canadians were destined to settle, and where spiritual and material regeneration were to be assured through a tactical retreat from Anglo–America. The project was the agricultural colonization of the Laurentian Shield, a virgin territory which for some was limited to Québec, but which for others extended westward to join with the isolated Métis and French–Canadian settlements of the Western Interior (Fig. 5.2).[25] In seeking to focus the energies of a nation within a more clearly circumscribed territory, the leaders of this movement aimed to redefine the collective identity. Nomads had to be sedentarized, or at least carefully oriented in their movements. Hence, an old social type re-emerged, the *habitant,* or peasant, to be glorified by attachment to the land, tenacity, and loyalty.

This dream of salvation and regeneration in the North failed to materialize, but there took root the idea of a people established for generations in the St. Lawrence Valley, impermeable both to history and to the dictates of a new continent — the sentiment of a fortress that was

Retour aux sources: The picture shows the gathering of Franco-Americans at the Monument to Monseigneur de Laval on the occasion of the Third Congrès de la Langue française, Québec City, June 1952. Monseigneur de Laval was the first titular head of the Catholic Church in New France and founder of the Séminaire de Québec. (*Conseil de la vie française en Amerique*)

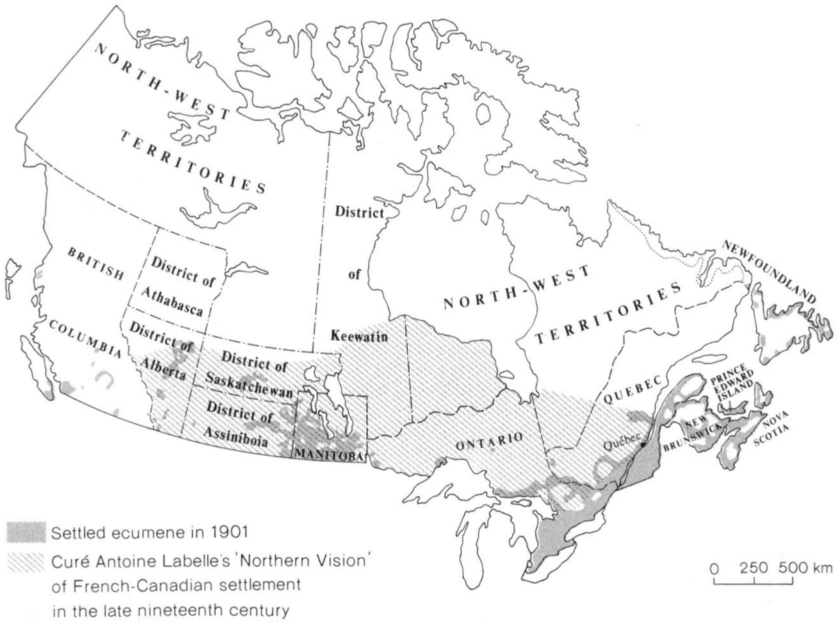

Figure 5.2 The northern vision of Québec in the late nineteenth century.

Québec itself. By mid-century the diaspora, and therefore the vision of Québec on the continent, had virtually disappeared. Changes in migration patterns did much to account for this. The Depression had defined the boundary between the United States and Canada more sharply and a rapidly industrializing and urbanizing Québec generated new and abundant employment opportunities in the mining towns of the Canadian Shield and in the Montréal metropolitan area.

World War II reinforced these trends. There was no longer any need for the people of Québec to migrate beyond the boundaries of the province in search of work. With the virtual collapse of the Catholic Church, the institutional arrangements linking Québec with the diaspora were also eroded. Some 2000 priests were ordained in Québec in 1947, but by the early 1970s the number had fallen to less than 100. Consequently, the Church was less able to play an active role in the education, health, and social welfare of Québec society within the hearth, and to provide tangible aid and direction to the diaspora.

The migrants were also shifting their allegiance. The francophones of the Western Interior were no longer calling themselves French Canadians, but Franco-Manitobains, Franco-Saskois, and Franco-Albertains. Those of New England had become Franco-Américains, if not simply Americans. In Québec, French Canadians were also in the process of redefining their collective identity — as Québécois — to bear witness to the new secular authority, the one North American state in which they constituted the majority of the population. It had become urgent to exercise political power in an aggressive manner 'at home' because doubts were being raised about the long–term survival of the French fact even in the St. Lawrence Valley. The farm, the network of kin, and the parish were no longer the main 'action space' of the French majority; now it was the factory, the office, and the suburb, where the French came into direct confrontation with the English minority. English was commonly the language of work and economic power and was welcomed by most immigrants and even by some French Canadians. Demographers warned that the Montréal metropolitan area, containing almost half of Québec's population, could become predominantly English–speaking by the end of the century.

The movement to redefine the collective identity, however, has produced some concrete results. Within the last two decades demographic trends have been reversed, French is the language of the public domain and, increasingly, of business, and the provincial government has become sufficiently powerful to regulate the private sector. Québec's relation to the diaspora has also undergone changes. In nationalizing Québec's electricity industry in the early 1960s, René Lévesque, as energy minister, turned to the francophone minorities across Canada for some of the necessary expertise to operate Hydro–Québec. In addition, as communities across the continent faced assimilation, many invited the Québec government to "...établir une politique vigoureuse d'incitation au retour au pays non seulement au Canada, mais aussi aux Etats–Unis."[26] At least one minister of immigration in the Parti Québécois government that was in power from 1976 to 1985 talked of introducing a "loi de retour," inspired by Israel, that would open the doors of Québec to any member of the continental diaspora wishing to return to the hearth.

Although the idea of a French America as a tangible expression of a single nation disappeared in the 1960s, an increasingly nationalistic Québec did not deny the existence of the diaspora. For many it evoked memories of a futile adventure, but some Parti Québécois officials gave it considerable significance. They did so as heirs to the Catholic Church in Québec and as principal purveyors of the institutional structures for the French of North America. Guy Frégault, historian and first head of the ministère des Affaires culturelles, believed it essential to develop a Québec foreign policy articulated through the francophone minorities of the continent: "Pour créer le Québec, il faut se reconnaître d'abord chez les autres, tout en leur rendant service et en étant disponsible.[27] A powerful and assertive hearth was deemed essential for the survival of the diaspora, and Frégault established a *Service du Canada français d'outre–frontières.* Hence, official visits by Québec government ministers to such places as St. Boniface, Manitoba and Layfayette, Louisiana and the opening of Québec government offices in New Brunswick and Louisiana serve the diaspora in much the same manner and for many of the same reasons as the Church did before. Notwithstanding the shifts in political power in Québec, the idea of the province being the *foyer national canadien-français* has been reaffirmed, with the hearth and the diaspara now conceived of as separate but interdependent realities. So, in 1986, the Acadians of the Maritime provinces envisage establishing a Maison de l'Acadie in Québec City, and Franco-ontarian intellectuals talk of a "continent Québec."

This relationship with a continental diaspora has played a significant role in shaping the distinct character of Québec. Its government is not simply a provincial government, but rather the government of a linguistic community whose geographical limits are not clearly defined.[28] Recently, during the late 1970s and early 1980s, a new wave of migrants has left the hearth, moving in two main directions — south to Florida and west to Alberta. The migration is in part a search for new economic opportunity and in part a reaction to a Québec that is too tightly circumscribed. Anti-authoritarianism and concern for mobility have been reaffirmed as the marks of a collective identity.

The migrants to Florida stem largely from the affluent francophone middle class that established itself during the Quiet Revolution. Those migrants represent an older generation in search of leisure and others seeking new economic opportunity. The phases leading to this migration resemble those of earlier departures from the St. Lawrence Valley. Starting as tourists spending a week or two in winter in a hotel catering to Québécois, these migrants become *hivernants,* residing from two to six months in a rented or purchased condominium or mobile home. Finally, they take up permanent residence and shift all their assets. The bases of group solidarity are much the same as before: ties of language, kin, and friendship. These ties are further expressed in Catholic masses, mutual aid, and a host of other social activities. This new generation of Québécois migrants is concentrated in distinctive neighbourhoods or mobile home parks in places such as Hollywood, Pompano Beach, Fort Lauderdale, and Miami Beach. The *Soleil de la Floride,* a weekly newspaper published by Québécois interests who claim to have the largest North American circulation of a French-language newspaper of its kind outside Québec, estimates that there are at least 250 000 Québécois permanently residing in Florida. In this new environment, they intermingle with Franco-Americans, many of whom arrived as early as the 1920s from New England, attracted by economic opportunity. This group established hotels, small businesses, and social organizations, catering explicitly to a francophone clientele.

If affluence has drawn an older generation of Québécois to Florida, the economic recession in Québec in the early 1980s pushed a younger one to Alberta. Beginning in the late 1970s, this migration had similarities to the one which took people to New England in the nineteenth century. The combined factors of internal recession and external expansion forced the young and unskilled to migrate. Generally perceived as a temporary solution — to find short-term work, accumulate some savings, and return home within a few months — many migrants moved seasonally between Québec and Alberta. Some, because of the possibilities of rapid promotion and greater material well-being, established themselves permanently in the west. Even though most have since returned to Québec following the collapse of the oil boom in Alberta, the message relayed by the experience is clear: provincial, state, or international boundaries are of little significance as barriers to movement. The migrants have a sense of belonging to a continent, even though they face stronger challenges to their ethnic identity outside the St. Lawrence Valley. In a context of continental mobility based on Québec, it is always possible to return to the hearth if challenges from the anglophone majority or the *mal du pays* become too great.

QUÉBEC: A HOMOGENEOUS OR A PLURAL SOCIETY?

If Québec is at once the *berceau* and the *foyer* of French America, the only province or state in which power is effectively exercised by francophones, it is nevertheless not entirely French. According to the 1981 Census, 82.4 percent of the province's population is of French mother tongue, but there are also some 695 000 anglophones and 426 000 allophones who constitute, respectively, 10.9 and 6.7 percent of the total population. Five years earlier, at the 1976 Census, allophones totalled only 334 000 or 5 percent of the total population. The number of anglophones did not grow between 1976 and 1981, indicating the stabilizing effect of births compared to deaths and out-migration.

Following World War II and until the enactment of the *Chartre de la langue française* in 1978, the majority of allophones gravitated towards the anglophone population in their choice of a second language and of schooling for their children. The effective leverage of the minorities is enhanced by the fact that they are heavily concentrated in the Montréal metropolitan area. About three-quarters (74.9 percent) of the anglophones live there, and they are joined by more than 90 percent of the other language groups. About 60 percent of the population of the Island of Montréal was of French mother tongue in 1981, making Montréal a plural urban society in the heart of a massively francophone province.

The roots of the English and the Scots in Québec can be traced to the immediate post-Conquest period, and those of the Irish to the early nineteenth century. Their pasts are closely interwoven with Québec's past. As seigneurs or settlers, entrepreneurs or labourers, their presence has been felt throughout the province: on the Lower North Shore and The Gaspé, in Charlevoix County and the Beauce, throughout the Eastern Townships, along the Laurentian front and the Ottawa River Valley, and of course in Montréal. The legal system of Québec is based, in part, on English civil law and the parliamentary system is modelled on its British counterpart.

At another level, the folk traditions of the Québécois have been inspired by the music of Ireland and Scotland, while the cultural values of the people are rooted as much in the Anglo–Saxon as the Latin tradition. Moreover, the intellectual élite of the province has been attracted to the universities of Oxford and London as well as to their French counterparts. In other words, the British, by virtue of their historical role, constant intermingling, and intermarriage have contributed significantly to defining the personality of the province.[29]

Despite their numerical strength, economic power, and status in the towns and cities until well into the twentieth century, the British presence did not significantly alter the structure of French–Canadian society. True, in the eyes of the Catholic Church, Protestantism was viewed as an evil force and the cities as places of moral disintegration; but, authority was clearly vested in the Church, the parish furnished the basic institutional and social fabric of French–Canadian society, and a fluid French America facilitated the society's geopolitical expression.

The urbanization of French–Canadian society within Québec from the late nineteenth century onward, however, meant direct confrontation with the English worlds of Montréal, Three Rivers, Québec City, Drummondville, Sherbrooke, Valleyfield and Seven Islands. Secularization followed apace. The transfer of power and leadership from the Church to the provincial government since World War II transformed the social climate within the province. From a situation of tolerance, expressed by indifference, marked social distance, and occupational divergence, Québec has become an arena of ethnic conflict. The main thrust of the Quiet Revolution, culminating in the election of the Parti Québécois in 1976, was the creation of a powerful *Etat national,* heir to the *paroisses nationales* of an earlier era. Thus, within French–Canadian society there is a concern to strengthen and widen the scope of the public domain and to integrate non–francophones into the larger society. The most dramatic expression of this movement has been the succession of language legislation (Laws 63, 22, and 101) establishing French as the province's sole official language and progressively strengthening its presence in the public domain, the work place and the educational system. The *Chartre de la langue française* passed in 1978 is the final manifestation of this transition.

The process of appropriating anglophone "spaces" began, in fact, in the mid–nineteenth century with the expansion of francophones out of the St. Lawrence Valley onto agricultural land vacated by English, Scottish, and Irish settlers in the Eastern Townships and along the Laurentian front. This process also took place in the neighbourhoods of the major cities. Increased educational opportunities and two World Wars accelerated the process. The gradual appropriation of the secondary urban centres (for example, Drummondville and Sherbrooke) followed during the depression years, and again stemmed from demographic change, increased francophone economic initiative, and a rapidly developing provincial bureaucracy. So, Three Rivers became Trois-Rivières, Seven Islands became Sept-Îles, and Arvida was absorbed into the expanded city of Jonquière.

The integration of Montréal into the new Québec constitutes the last phase in the process. Anglophones had established a strong economic and demographic base in Montréal, but since 1941 their proportion of the total population had been declining and by 1976 they had become a minority. Although recognizing the existence of a diversity of cultural minorities, the Québec government has sought to promote among these minorities — through language and educational practices — a tendency that some sociologists describe as "franco-conformity." In other words, the model or norm to which all members of the population tend to gravitate, irrespective of language or culture of origin, is a French-Canadian one. According to this model, Québec is the *patrie,* the territorial expression of collective identity, French is the national language, and it is the history of the québécois people (or nation) that determines the course of present and future actions. Québec exists as the hearth of the French-Canadian nation and as the centre for the continental diaspora.

This trend toward a more homogeneous Québec with a distinct regional identity within North America has been reinforced by a redefinition of Canadian identity. A national identity crisis in the early 1960s led, as a result of the recommendations of the Royal Commission on Bilingualism and Biculturalism, to a reformulation of "Canadianness" that was henceforth to be based on the principle of two founding peoples, two languages, and two cultures. The existence of two official languages was accepted in 1969 and with them, inevitably, the idea of two Canadas, one French and one English, each with a distinct geographical expression and an official language minority. Within such a symmetric arrangement, Québec is viewed as being synonymous with French Canada, hence the destiny of the English minority is linked to that of the province and compared with that of the francophone diaspora scattered through English Canada. While some Anglo-Québecers left the province, including many from the western, English-speaking neighbourhoods of Montréal, others are undergoing a shift in territorial affiliation and collective identity that may lead to their merging with the larger québécois identity.

CONCLUSION: A MATTER OF CENTRES AND PERIPHERIES

In *The Liberal Idea of Canada,* James and Robert Laxer point to the paradoxical position of Québec within Canada.[30] For them, the province has features of both metropolis and hinterland. Montréal is a Canadian metropolis which, in spite of a major loss of economic power to Toronto, continues to assume essential metropolitan functions. It is a leader in transportation, manufacturing, and finance, and is assuming stronger ties with the international business community, particularly with multinationals from France and other European countries. In addition, its resource corporations are linked with markets in the United States, whose demand for hydroelectricity and pulp and paper products remains strong.

The heartland–hinterland paradox within Québec is closely related to the ethnic divisions in the province. Montréal's metropolitan power, for example, has been led primarily by the anglophone commercial élite. In the course of Québec's development and the building of the metropolis, the anglophone society of Montréal espoused a completely different ideology from that of the province's francophones. The leaders of anglophone society were concerned with entrepreneurship, the development of a transcontinental transportation system, and the accumulation of capital. Their institutions were chartered banks and commercial, industrial, shipping, and railway enterprises, as well as the private clubs where one socialized and created business alliances. Montréal, rather than the larger St. Lawrence Valley or Québec itself, was their home. Rather than being primarily a cultural hearth, it was a centre — an economic gateway to a continent. Because of the sophistication of the English educational system, its Protestant values, and the evident material successes of the anglophone bourgeoisie, this ideology was readily espoused by the anglophone population in general. There was not the cleavage that marked the francophone community. Divisions between urban and rural francophones, between the Church and businessmen, between businessmen and professionals, were not as prominent in anglophone society.

These different ideologies of francophone and anglophone inevitably found expression in different patterns of wealth and mobility which, until recently, profoundly marked Québec society. As the Royal Commission on Bilingualism and Biculturalism revealed, the mean income of male wage earners of British ethnic origin in Québec in 1961 was higher than that of all other ethnic groups. It exceeded the mean by 42 percent, while the French ranked twelfth, just above the Italians and the Native peoples, with an income that was 8 percent below the mean. The phenomenon has been given close attention ever since, and while the gap is now diminishing rapidly, if not actually disappearing, its historical significance is not to be questioned.[31]

But the relationship between ethnicity, income, and position in the Canadian space economy explains only part of the Québec paradox. If for Anglo-Québecers cultural identity is related to a particular economic role, expressed in a dual attachment to Canada and to Montréal, the situation is more complex in the case of the francophones. For many francophones, the St. Lawrence Valley and Québec in general constitute a cultural hearth whose sphere of influence has continental dimensions. By virtue of demographic pressure, economic marginality, and the attraction of other regions outside Québec's borders, the people of Québec have often left the hearth in search of work. They, like many of the immigrants to the New

World, assumed the historic role of abundant, cheap, and malleable labour in the development of the continental economy, and particularly in the industrialization of New England.

Geographical mobility — and the creation of a continental diaspora — has become, as a result, an essential feature of the popular collective identity, that is, of Québec's regional consciousness. The francophone élite, while refusing such mobility, has sought periodically to accommodate it in a larger national design. In the past two decades, the idea of Québec as a cultural hearth has been reinforced and is becoming prominent again because of the gradual peripheralization of Montréal and Québec within the continental economic system. Such peripheralization encourages the departure of a significant component of the anglophone community and a partial substitution by francophones, but it also introduces the spectre of the massive departure of francophones in search of employment elsewhere and, once again, the weakening of a nation.

The destiny of Québec remains inextricably linked with that of the continent. At the same time, insofar as Canada is concerned, the character of the cultural hearth and its role in shaping a regional consciousness separates Québec, perhaps more than any other factor, from the rest of the country and draws it closer to the United States.

NOTES

1. The ideas that permeate this chapter owe a considerable debt to the innovative research of Pierre Anctil and Christian Morissonneau. I am also grateful to Dean Louder, with whom I have conducted research on French America over recent years and developed an undergraduate course at Laval on *Le Québec et l'Amérique français.*
2. Raoul Blanchard, *Le Canada français: province de Québec* (Montréal: Librairie Arthème Fayard, 1960).
3. *Ibid.,* p. 65.
4. Paul Claval, "Architecture sociale, culture et géographie au Québec: un essai d'interprétation historique," *Annales de Géographie,* 83 (1974), pp. 394–419.
5. Pierre Biays, "Southern Québec," in *Canada: A Geographical Interpretation,* ed. John Warkentin (Toronto: Methuen, 1968), pp. 281–333.
6. Louis–Edmond Hamelin, "Le Québec: réflexions générales," in *Etudes sur la géographie du Canada: Québec,* ed. F. Grenier (Toronto: University of Toronto Press, 1972), pp. 1–12.
7. Marcel Bélanger, "Le Québec rural," in *ibid.,* p. 35.
8. See, for example, P. Deffontaines, "Le rang, type de peuplement rural au Canada français," *Cahiers de Géographie* (Université Laval) 5 (1953), pp. 3–32; and R. Cole Harris, *The Seigneurial System in Early Canada* (Québec: Les Presses de l'Université Laval, 1966).
9. Paul Claval, "Architecture sociale," p. 418.
10. French Canadians are "... un rameau déraciné du grand arbre français. Elle est née de la France. Pendant plus d'un siècle et demi ses sujets sont tous issus du meilleur sang de la France et depuis deux cents ans leurs descendants se sont, pour la plupart, gardes purs de tout alliage. C'est pour eux un premier titre de noblesse." Anon., *La vocation de la race française en Amérique du nord* Québec: Le comité permanent de la survivance française en Amérique, (1945), p. 25.

11. Groulx's works include *Nos Luttes constitutioneiles* (1916), *La Naissance d'une race* (1918), and *Notre Maître le passé* (1944). For discussions of Groulx, see Jean-Pierre Gaboury, *Le Nationalisme de Lionel Groulx: Aspects idéologiques* (Ottawa: 1970) and Susan Mann Trofimenkoff, *Action Française: French-Canadian Nationalism in the Twenties* (Toronto: 1975).
12. Carl Berger, *The Writing of Canadian History* (Toronto: Oxford University Press, 1976), pp. 181–2.
13. Jean Ethier-Blais in *Le Devoir* (Montréal), 14 February 1981.
14. See, for example O.P. Dickason, "From 'One Nation' in the Northeast to 'New Nation' in the Northwest: A look at the Emergence of the Métis," in *The New Peoples: Being and Becoming Métis in North America,* eds. Jacqueline Peterson and Jennifer S.H. Brown (Winnipeg: The University of Manitoba Press, 1985) pp. 19-36. This article was published previously in slightly altered form, in *American Indian Culture and Research Journal* 6 (1982). The author would like to acknowledge the helpful comments on this article by Dr. Lewis H. Thomas, University of Alberta.
15. C. Morissonneau, "Mobilité et identité québécoise," *Cahiers de Géographie du Québec,* 23 (1979), pp. 29–38.
16. Yolande Lavoie, *L'émigration des Québécois aux Etat-Unis de 1840 à 1930* (Québec: Editeur officiel, 1979).
17. Consider this Great Lakes Métis description of his self identity in the 1850s:

    Où je reste? Je ne peux pas te le dire. Je suis Voyageur — je suis Chicot, Monsieur. Je reste partout. Mon grand-père était Voyageur; il est mort en voyage. Mon père était Voyageur; il mort en voyage. Je mourrai aussi en voyage, et un autre Chicot prendra ma place. Such is our course of life.

    J.G. Kohl, *Kitchi-Gami, Wanderings round Lake Superior* (London: Chapman and Hall, 1860), p. 259.
18. Aidan McQuillan, "French-Canadian Communities in the American Upper Midwest during the Nineteenth Century," *Cahiers de Géographie du Québec,* 23 (1979), pp. 53–72.
19. See, for example, P. Anctil, "La franco-américaine ou le Québec d'en bas," *Cahiers de Géographie du Québec,* 23 (1979), pp. 39–52; and Y. Lavoie, *L'emigration des Québécois.*
20. These observations on the role of the Church are derived from N. Voisine, *Histoire de l'Eglise catholique au Québec, 1608–1970* (Montréal: Fides, 1971).
21. "Votre mission nationale est la conversion des pauvres sauvages et l'extension du royaume de Jésus-Christ; votre destinée nationale, c'est de devenir un grand peuple catholique." Cited in Anon., *La vocation de la race française,* p. 37.
22. For example, Collège Assomption in Worcester, Massachusetts and Collège St-Viateur in Bourbonnais, Michigan.
23. Henri Bourassa, *Réligion, Langue, Nationalité* (Montréal: *Le Devoir,* 1910), p. 16.
24. Major Edmond Mallett, United States Indian Inspector in the late nineteenth century and hence an influential Franco-American as well as a fervent nationalist and, above all, confidant of Louis Riel and Gabriel Dumont, stressed on the occasion of a St-Jean Baptiste rally in Montréal in 1880 that:

    Notre éparpillement nous est très désavantageux, et nous devrions faire un effort pour concentrer sur quelque point donné: comme à partir du Détroit, où il y a déjà une population canadienne considérable, jusqu'à la montagne de la Tortue, dans le Dakota. Cette position offrirait à nos nationaux (les Franco-Américains) de grands avantages naturels et pourrait devenir d'une suprême importance, à nous, ainsi qu'à nos frères de Manitoba, si certains événements venaient à se produire.

    Taken from Pierre Anctil, "L'exil américain de Louis Riel 1874–1884,": *Recherches Amérindiennes au Québec,* 11 (1981), p. 243.
25. The architects of this geopolitical vision were Curé Labelle, Arthur Buies, and Testard de Montigny. C. Morissonneau, *Le terre promise: Le mythe du Nord Québécois* (Montréal: Hurtubise HMH, 1978).
26. Michel Emard in a letter to *Le Devoir,* 9 February 1978.
27. Guy Frégault, *Chronique des années perdues* (Montréal: Léméac 1976), p. 29.

28. This fact is not lost on certain political scientists. Consider the following observation regarding the vocation of the government of Québec that appeared in *Le Devoir,* 10 November 1981:

    Ce n'est pas seulement une province que l'Assemblée nationale et le gouvernement du Québec ont pour mission imprescriptible de défendre et d'illustrer. C'est également et surtout une communauté linguistique originale qui a son assise vitale dans cette province et qui, seulement dans cette province, possède des cadres institutionnels suffisants pour lui permettre d'exister comme société particulière . . . .

29. D. Clift and S. MacLeod Arnopoulos, *The English Fact in Québec* (Montréal: McGill–Queen's University Press, 1979).
30. James and Robert Laxer, *The Liberal Idea of Canada* (Toronto: James Lorimer, 1977).
31. See *Report of the Commissioners, Volume 3. The World of Work, The Royal Commission on Bilingualism and Biculturalism* (Ottawa: 1969); and P. Bernard, *L'évolution de la situation socio-économique des francophones et des non-francophones au Québec, 1971–1978* (Montréal: Office de la langue française, 1979).

PART III
The Hinterland Regions

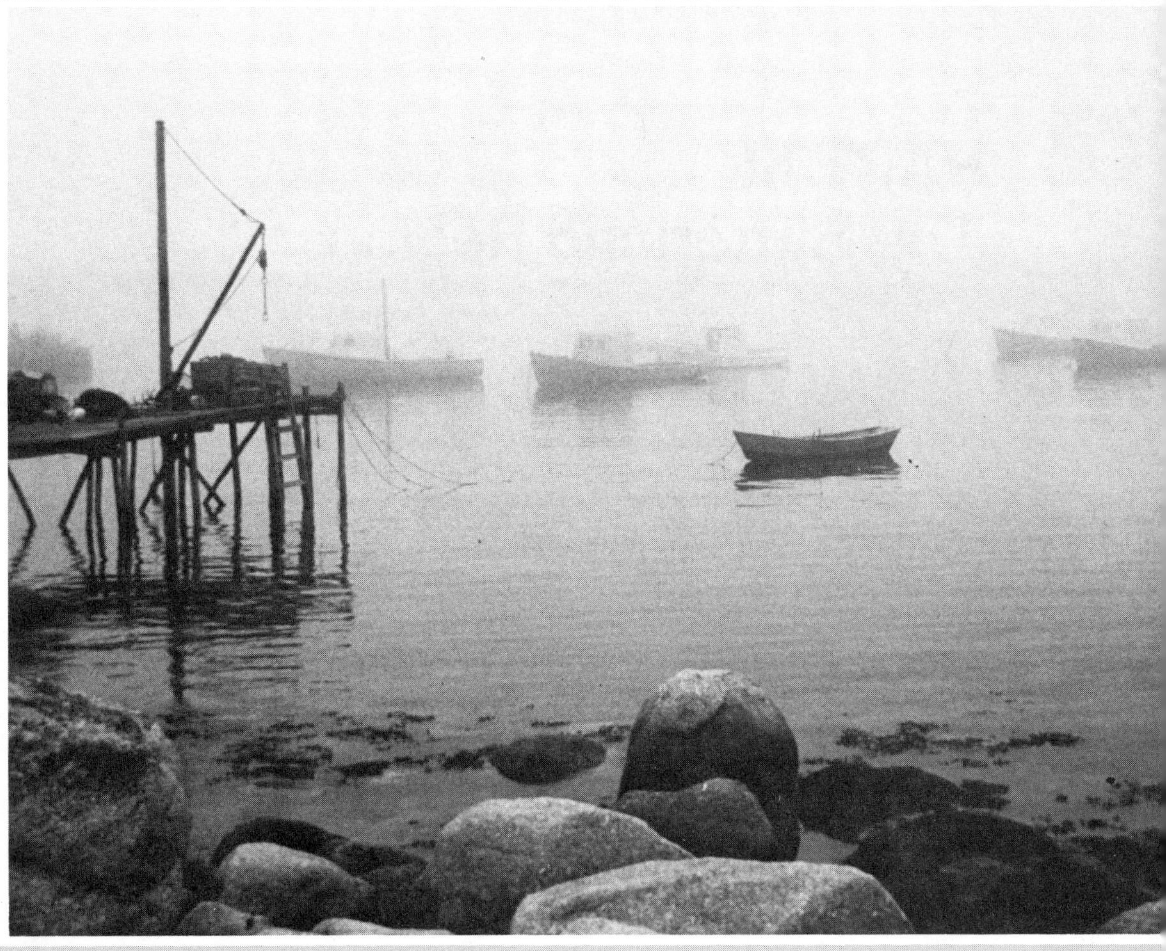

6

The Maritimes: The Geography of Fragmentation and Underdevelopment

Graeme Wynn

Comprising less than two percent of Canada's area, the provinces of New Brunswick, Nova Scotia, and Prince Edward Island form a mosaic of striking physical, economic, and social variety. Even small-scale topographic maps reveal the intricate physical geography of the two larger provinces. Narrow valleys dissect generally forested uplands; steep slopes divide settled lowlands from sparsely occupied plateaus. The area's heavily indented coastline and centrifugal drainage patterns have enhanced isolation and distinctiveness by separating province from province and inlet from estuary: northeastern New Brunswick faces the Gulf of St. Lawrence; southwestern Nova Scotia has had strong ties with New England; insular Cape Breton and Prince Edward Island remain distinct in outlook and identity. Variations in climate, soils, and vegetation — to the extent that upland–lowland transects might identify twenty soil series and half a dozen forest communities in a few score kilometres — reflect differences in location, terrain, surficial material, and precipitation, and further tessellate the natural scene (Fig. 6.1).

The human landscape is equally variegated. Exploitation of a diverse resource base in widely different ways has created a complex economic geography in the Maritimes. Fishing, farming, mining, and forest industries are major resource activities with distinctive distributions. The fishing population is scattered, common on some coasts and sparse on others; agriculture is largely confined to fertile valleys and its distribution is correspondingly linear; pulp and paper mills are dispersed and generally located on the coast; mining is concentrated in a few widely separated locations. Within this matrix, there are regional differences in the species of fish caught, in the most important cash crops, and in the products of

Figure 6.1 The Maritimes region.

the mines. In all but the mining industry there is wide variation in the scale of operations; small family farms, private woodlots, and individual fishing ventures exist alongside large mechanized agricultural operations, corporate forest monopolies, and expensive freezer trawlers. Similar diversity marks the cultural geography of the provinces. Politically divided, ethnically diverse, and differentiated by income, employment, experience, tradition, and religion, people of the Maritimes form a markedly plural society.

Yet there are common elements in the geography of the Maritimes. The sea has integrated the region. Nineteenth century commerce on the sea linked the Miramichi and Charlottetown with Halifax, and both shores of the Fundy Basin with Saint John, creating wide communities of shared economic interest. Moreover, few Maritimers live far from the sea, and those who depend on it for their livelihoods face similar dangers and difficulties, whether in the northeast or the southwest of the region. The United States has shaped the geography of the Maritimes by luring settlers from the area, by competing in commerce and industry, and by providing a ready source of ideas, artifacts, and products for diffusion through the provinces. The region's links to British laws and institutions ordered Maritime lives, and British tariffs and business cycles set the courses of provincial economic development. The significant Acadian minority apart, the present population of the region is overwhelmingly of British descent. Finally, the generally harsh environment has limited both settlement and agriculture in much of New Brunswick and Nova Scotia. Today the legacy of the struggle with this unaccommodating land can be seen in the peripheral distribution of population and in the abandoned farmsteads scattered through the interiors of these provinces. Even where settlement has been successful, it gives, at no great distance, into forest.

GEOGRAPHY OF A HINTERLAND

Compared to the rest of Canada, the Maritime provinces share many basic characteristics.[1] Demographically, they form a region of small numbers, slow growth, and high dependency ratios. Recent estimates show that there are 1.67 million people in the three provinces out of Canada's over 20 million. Between 1976 and 1981, only Newfoundland and Manitoba had a lower rate of population increase than the Maritimes; growth rates of 2 to 4 percent were less than half the Canadian average. Yet fertility rates exceed the national average in all three provinces, and Maritime families are larger than those in all provinces west of Québec.

Migration patterns explain the conundrum. Few immigrants to Canada settle in the Maritime provinces. Until the Canada-wide recession of the early 1980s, there was generally an exodus of Maritimers to southern Ontario, British Columbia, and Alberta. Net losses during the 1960s ranged from 6.1 percent in Nova Scotia to 8.7 percent in New Brunswick. There were some net gains between 1971 and 1976, but losses occurred again in the late 1970s. In 1981–82, the Atlantic Provinces, as a group, lost approximately 10 000 people to the rest of Canada. But with the collapse of the Alberta oil boom and the rising prospects of oil and gas development off Nova Scotia in the mid-1980s, Maritimers began to return home. In 1982–83, the three provinces gained population, and in 1983–84, when Newfoundland lost almost 2500 residents, Nova Scotia added over 4600 and New Brunswick and Prince Edward Island together increased by approximately 1750. Over three-quarters of these migrants came from Alberta. Still, decades of high fertility and net emigration have combined to increase the proportions of young and old in the region. With the working-age group pared by out-migration, youth dependency ratios are among the highest in the country after Newfoundland and the Northwest Territories; old-age dependency ratios far exceed those in the

Territories and Newfoundland, and approximate those in Manitoba, Saskatchewan, and British Columbia.

Measured against the Canadian average of 32 percent, secondary industry — manufacturing, construction, transportation, and utilities — is relatively underdeveloped in the Maritime provinces, where it accounts for 25 to 31 percent of employment. Conversely, tertiary activities — services, finance, trade, and government administration — occupy a greater proportion of the labour force in the Maritimes than in any other region of the country. In 1981, public administration employed more Maritimers (at least 12 000) than logging, sawmilling, and pulp and paper industries combined, more, even, than fishing and fish processing, and almost 50 percent more than the agricultural sector. A similar number of military personnel in the region were on the federal payroll; in the mid-1970s, approximately a quarter of the Canadian forces wage bill was paid in the region. Generally, labour productivity in the Maritimes is low. In manufacturing, provincial productivity is between a fifth and a third less than the national average; overall, the shortfall amounts to 18 percent in New Brunswick and 40 percent in Prince Edward Island.

By Canadian standards, the Maritime provinces are economically poor. Although variations within the region are considerable (with Halifax, Truro, New Glasgow, Moncton, Saint John, and Fredricton generally closer to national levels than the rest of the area), provincial statistics reveal the financially inferior position of Maritime residents. In 1982, average weekly earnings in Nova Scotia were $329; in New Brunswick they were $342; the national average was $391; and the average British Columbian's wage of $445 exceeded that of his Prince Edward Island counterpart by $167.

At the same time, Maritimers had more difficulty finding jobs. The national rate of unemployment in 1984 was 11.9 percent, but seasonally adjusted rates in the Maritimes were between 12.2 and 14.8 percent. Moreover, long-term unemployment is more common in the Maritimes, despite lower workforce participation rates. Seasonal unemployment, which is most severe in Prince Edward Island, is characteristic of all three provinces. According to Statistics Canada's classification of 1980 income data, 13.4 percent of Ontario families were in the $25 000 to $29 999 bracket. In the Maritimes only between 10.5 and 11.3 percent were in this bracket. Even allowing for differences in the consumer price index, housing cost differentials, and the impact of progressive income tax across the country, the disposable purchasing power of New Brunswick families in 1980 was only 84 percent of the Canadian average; by the same measure, Prince Edward Islanders remained 26 percent behind national levels. In 1978, over one-third of Island families spent at least 70 percent of their annual income on food, shelter, and clothing. Low-income families comprised almost 15 percent of all families in Nova Scotia and New Brunswick; nationally they made up 10 percent of all families. In Ontario they accounted for only 9 percent.

Housing, health, and education statistics confirm the lower standard of material life in the Maritimes. Maritimers live in slightly more crowded homes than those of most Canadians; they have fewer telephones than residents of all other provinces but Newfoundland. In 1981, physicians were about half as common, per capita, in New Brunswick as in British Columbia. In addition, fewer 16–year–old boys remained in school in the Maritimes than in the provinces to the west.

Federal–provincial fiscal arrangements, particularly those instituted since 1945 to redistribute a proportion of heartland wealth to "have–not" regions on the periphery, have also helped to shape distinctive patterns of regional life. Through general–purpose transfers (equalization grants) and specific–purpose payments for the provision of health, welfare, and education, the federal government directed almost $875 million per annum into the three provinces during the early 1970s. By 1982 the figure stood at $1980 million. In sum, transfer payments exceeded provincial revenues in Prince Edward Island, and amounted to approximately 80 percent of those in New Brunswick and Nova Scotia. Were federal transfers spread equally among Canadians, they would amount to some $595 per head; on a per capita basis the three provinces received $1540, $1134, and $1157, respectively. In addition, federal government transfers to individuals — old age security and guaranteed income supplements, unemployment insurance, family and youth allowances, veterans' pensions, and employment mobility and training allowances — are above average in the region. Including payments to Newfoundlanders, they averaged almost $540 per capita in Atlantic Canada in the mid–1970s, for example. The national average was $410. In the early 1960s, Nova Scotians derived perhaps 8 percent of their personal incomes from federal transfer payments. Today the proportion almost certainly exceeds 10 percent.

Beyond such direct measures, federal and provincial encouragement of economic growth in the Maritimes has fostered development and created employment in the region. The federal Department of Regional Economic Expansion (DREE) (established in 1969) and its successor the Department of Regional Industrial Expansion (DRIE) (established in 1983) have provided incentives to private industry and have contributed to the development of transport networks, utilities, energy supplies, research agencies, and the infrastructure needed for economic expansion and social adjustment. Between 1969 and 1975, DREE expenditures in the region totalled $520.5 million dollars. Prince Edward Island received approximately $800 per capita, New Brunswick $390, and Nova Scotia $230. By the Department's estimates, these efforts created or maintained 20 000 jobs. Yet critics condemned DREE's "passive" approach to industrial development, dismissing it as a policy of subsidized *laissez faire* lacking the radical impact of more aggressive strategies. Alternatively, they argued, greater risks should have been taken to finance unproven but potentially rewarding industries such as new forms of pulp and paper production or marine technologies. In the mid–1980s, DRIE has renewed an interest in Cape Breton's plight, for example, but the results of its measures are yet to be seen.

Provincial Crown corporations also provide concessions, capital, and services for industrial development. Naive, poorly coordinated strategies and unscrupulous grant–seeking entrepreneurs have vitiated their efforts and they have been equally unsuccessful in transforming the spatial organization of manufacturing. But, together with federal departments (DREE and DRIE), they have stimulated industrial development in the Maritimes. Their combined interest in the creation of growth poles — concentrated development centres — and the encouragement of sophisticated, foot–loose, high–technology manufacturing has initiated a reorientation of regional industry.

Development strategies, modern industrial growth, and the improvement of communications within and beyond the region have thus transformed the economy and society. Today, new and old exist side by side in the region, and are often in conflict. Economic dualism is a marked feature of the region, most clearly reflected in the juxtaposition of capital–intensive, technologically–complex industries tied directly to national or international markets with small–scale, family enterprises linked with provincial or wider markets only through intermediaries. In the regional capitals and growth poles of the Maritimes, the attitudes and practices of modern industrial society have replaced traditional, local ways. National bank executives and corporate lawyers in Halifax are provincial outriders of Bay Street. Government bureaucracies apply heartland regulations to the hinterland circumstances of the eastern provinces. Maritime school curricula reflect pressures to conform to national aims and ideals. Mass–produced goods from distant factories line the shelves and crowd the racks of provincial stores which bear, with increasing frequency, the names of national and international enterprises. Similarly, tourists demand standards of accommodation and service equal to those in the metropolises of Toronto and Boston from which, paradoxically, they seek escape in their visits to the Maritime hinterland. Meanwhile, corporate advertisers increase awareness of heartland standards of living in the hinterland, and young Maritimers migrate to central and western Canada in search of new opportunities and a higher standard of living. Viewed purely in economic terms, their movement is a rational adjustment to circumstances. But their going also has important, and little considered, ramifications in the lives of Maritime communities.

Physical and Cultural Landscapes

The landscapes of the Maritimes are correspondingly intricate and diverse: no brief description can portray their full complexity. But the alert geographical mind will find much of interest in even the most cursory traverse of the region. Halifax, the regional centre of Nova Scotia, backs into scrub forest. High–rise office towers, multi–functional redevelopment complexes, shopping centres, urban freeways, and sprawling suburbs — the characteristic features of modern cities — give way, abruptly, to a rough, rocky, and sparsely settled upland. Along the spine of the province, infertile soils on unconsolidated glacial drift and geologically ancient granites, quartzites, and slates carry a low forest, broken only occasionally by roads, marginal farms, and abandoned clearings. To the west, a bleak interior passes, equally abruptly, into patches of productive farmland. Orchards, pastures, cropland, poultry–sheds, dairy– and tobacco–barns, neat farmsteads, and sedate, tree–shaded villages crowd the narrow Annapolis Valley, flanked by upland brow to the south, and sheltered from Fundy winds and fogs by North Mountain, a 213–metre escarpment of Triassic lava.

South and west, beyond Digby, the coastal settlements fringing St. Mary's Bay form another strand of complexity — Acadia. Here life seems less prosperous than in the Annapolis Valley. There are frequent signs of occupational pluralism: school buses parked alongside farmsteads; lobster traps "out back" on a 20–acre holding; appliance servicemen who also farm. Families are also generally larger. The bald landscape and close, continuous line of settlement is punctuated by large, distinctive churches and is variegated by the bright colours of the dwellings. Acadian and Roman Catholic, the people of this area are different from their English–

The Annapolis Valley: Less than 10 percent of the Maritimes is suitable for agriculture, but the mixed farming of the Annapolis Valley – orchards, dairying, field crops – competes with the best farming areas in Canada. (*Larry McCann*)

speaking neighbours. Distinctive place names define their territory — Belliveau Cove, Comeauville, Surette's Island — and blood ties bind their communities. They can trace their origins to the seventeenth century settlement of Port Royal, to resettlement after the famous deportations of the 1750s, and to on-going migrations within the Acadian realm. The essential elements of their landscape, their sense of community, and their attachment to place, are replicated wherever Acadians predominate in the three provinces, from Caraquet to Chéticamp and from the Memramcook to Madawaska.

Cape Breton's 10 360 square kilometres offer contrasting regional characteristics. Acadian and Scottish settlers occupy markedly different landscapes north and south of Margaree Harbour. On the Island's southern shore, fishermen — hardy, versatile, and intimately aware of their local environment — set their simple, homemade gear from small boats pitching in the wake of supertankers bound for Port Tupper's modern oil refinery, where acres of plant and complex chemical processes are controlled from a single room by a dozen workers. Between the pristine grandeur of the Cabot Trail and Bras d'Or Lake, the dishevelled, polluted townscape of Sydney intrudes. A narrow, slow road winds east from the coke ovens and steel mills eructing smoke over Sydney Harbour.

The Acadian shore of southwestern Nova Scotia: Shoreline lots have been subdivided many times to accommodate the expansion of the Acadian population. (*Graeme Wynn*)

It passes unkempt fields and seemingly endless strings of tiny, narrow-windowed houses lining damp, ill-paved streets. There is little pretension in these old coal mining towns. They are distinctive places. Despite their age,

> no past hangs in the air as in Halifax and there is no romance in the streets as in the seafaring towns such as Lunenburg and Liverpool and Bridgewater. All of those towns, or at least some of their people, made money and built homes with rolling lawns and columned steps. But in [New Waterford, Reserve, Dominion, and] Glace Bay the money went mostly out of town to the men who owned the mines.[2]

In recent years, with Cape Breton mines closing, people retiring, youth outmigrating, and the tax base shrinking, local governments have been hard pressed to sustain even minimal levels of service. The restored eighteenth century fortress of Louisbourg, an industrial park near Sydney, and an ill-fated, enormously expensive, heavy water plant on the outskirts of Glace Bay reflect efforts to provide work for unemployed miners, to attract tourists to Cape Breton, and to modernize the manufacturing economy of Nova Scotia. Yet these projects are incongruous and the Island still lags far behind Nova Scotia and national levels in the provision of many basic amenities. On average, Cape Breton's dentists serve twice as many residents as their counterparts across the country. Even in the early 1970s, diabetes and influenza were 40 percent more common on the Island than in mainland Nova Scotia; the incidence of pneumonia was 175 percent higher. Backhouses are perhaps as common as flush toilets in some fishing villages. The hard lives of those who mine and fish remain exceedingly remote from those of the business-suited, fashionably-clad men and women employed in the banks and offices of Halifax. Yet each day television brings the lifestyles (and expectations) of affluent North Americans into the living rooms of Glace Bay, Ingonish, and Arichat.

In New Brunswick, farmland is rare. More than 80 percent of the province is productive forest. Settled land — a mere 8 percent of the total — skirts the coasts, flanks the St. John River, and only forms a distinctively open landscape between Sussex and Moncton. Yet there is diversity even within the forest. In the Northeast, bogs and barrens are common; "swamps" of black spruce and tamarack alternate with birch and jack pine stands; a red spruce–yellow birch–beech–sugar maple forest occurs on better sites. In the cool north-central uplands, where the frost-free period is but half of Prince Edward Island's 140 days and the mean annual snowfall exceeds 254 centimetres, a spruce–fir forest predominates. Here, as in other mature stands of timber, budworm infestation causes high tree mortality, despite repeated aerial spraying with insecticide. Between the cluttered, moss-strewn spruce–fir forests of the Fundy coast and the left-bank watershed of the St. John River, a well-developed — though now severely culled — mixed forest is characteristic. Sugar maple,

Settlement at the margin: There are many areas of the Maritimes where farms stand abandoned, particularly at the forest's edge. This farmstead near Amherst, Nova Scotia was first settled in the 1780s. (*Larry McCann*)

hemlock, pine, and ash are its dominant species. Basswood, beech, butternut, red oak, and red spruce also occur.

On the fringes of New Brunswick's forest, abandoned farms are common. Each encapsulates a common regional scene. Old fields succumb to the march of aspen, birch, spruce, and fir; barren orchards and exotic ornamental trees straggle unpruned; shabby buildings decay. On average, surviving New Brunswick farms are small and little more than a third of their land has been improved. The practice of mixed crop and livestock production that reduces risk remains common, but the farm consolidation and specialization that marks all Maritime agriculture proceeds, propelled by new technologies and economies of scale. Overall, there is considerable regional variation in the major commercial orientation of New Brunswick's farms. Dairying is the main source of income in the Sussex and Fredricton areas; poultry enterprises cluster near Fredericton and Moncton; most blueberries come to market from northeastern and southwestern corners of the province; potato (and, less markedly, feed grain) production is concentrated in the Upper St. John Valley. Other features compound the fragmentation of this compact 75 520 square kilometre territory and its 700 000 people: the peripheral foci of pulp, paper, and metallic mineral production; the lobster fishing of the Gulf shore; the ethnic differentiation of the province with Acadian hearths in Gloucester, Madawaska, and Westmorland counties; the economic disparities between south and north; and the poor articulation of the urban network; all enhance diversity, yet each reflects broad patterns characteristic of the region.

Measured by the imagery of the tourist industry recently encouraged in all three provinces, Prince Edward Island is a simpler place. With the nostalgic charm of the nineteenth century, it is "a kind of dreamy never-never land that most of us haven't known since childhood — unsophisticated, slow-paced and satisfying. . . ."[3] But this is misleading. Old-settled landscapes; embellished, white-painted, wooden houses; pastoral vistas, and picturesque fishing villages are certainly common. Yet signs of the tension between traditional ways and the pressures of modernity are everywhere. On the Island, as elsewhere in the region, tractors have replaced horses and though harvest efficiency has increased, farmers are less independent and more susceptible to economic and political fluctuations beyond their control. Shopping centres and chain stores proliferate, bringing the goods and advertising practices of North American mass-production and franchise-marketing into competition with the local retailer. Tourism spawns motels. Golf and recreation complexes are created from Island farms and public beaches have been developed for the 600 000 or 700 000 visitors who come to the province,

French Harbour, P.E.I.: Sea and land create the main resource occupations of this insular province. (*Larry McCann*)

whose population is only 120 000, each year. Plans call for the consolidation of fish–processing plants to increase efficiency, but there is often little concern for the fishermen's preferences or requirements. Similar trends have transformed potato farming in the province. Mechanization has increased productivity, but the industry that employed 15 000 in the late 1940s now occupies perhaps a fifth of that number. Many growers are now under contract; a Malpeque Bay processing plant has expanded its payroll and its "stable" of farmers by becoming the supplier of frozen french fries to the northeastern division of North America's largest hamburger chain. Island society is at a divide.

The Maritimes, then, is no simple region. Fragmentation and, by Canadian standards, underdevelopment, may be its defining characteristics. But (to use the terms of the British geographer H.J. Fleure) the Maritimes is also a "region of effort," rather than one of "increment."[4] Strenuous endeavour has generally been necessary for successful settlement in these provinces. Moderately endowed in soil and climate, located on the eastern periphery of an increasingly west–oriented nation, and with coal (its major mineral resource) devalued until recently by preferences for oil fuel and electric power, Maritime Canada is, further, an area poised between lingering past and uncertain future. In this difficult present, modernity challenges tradition; old ways retreat, but often begrudgingly; images of revitalization shimmer, but often as mirages. Saved from the worst consequences of economic decline by national fiscal policy, the provinces have retained but slender control over their destinies. In the view of one historian, they have become "client states of the federal government."[5]

THE EMERGENCE OF A HINTERLAND REGION

Little more than a century ago, the Maritimes was a markedly different region. Its economy was based upon its farms, fisheries, forests, and commercial shipping fleet; its landscape reflected the pre–industrial age of wood, wind, and water; and its society mirrored the isolation and diversity of its fragmented territory. Colonies of a distant British metropolis, New Brunswick, Nova Scotia, and Prince Edward Island had developed relatively prosperous economies finely attuned to the circumstances of the nineteenth century. Together, the provinces had built much of the fleet that made Canada the world's fourth largest shipping nation. Commercial ties linked the region with Britain, the United States, and the West Indies. Lumbering and fishing were basic enterprises. Forest products made up well over half of New Brunswick's exports; wooden sailing vessels accounted for 50 to 75 percent, by value, of all other exports from the province. Nova Scotia possessed a more diverse export base, but fish often exceeded a third of total exports. Farm produce, sawn lumber, and local manufactures such as furniture and shoes diversified the cargoes sold from provincially-built schooners in scattered Caribbean harbours. In the Gulf of St. Lawrence, Prince Edward Island concentrated on farming, sending its surplus to the lumberers of New Brunswick and the schooner masters and merchants of Nova Scotia.

Largely native-born, the people of the region were divided by isolation, ethnicity, and religion. Highland (Gaelic-speaking) Scots, both Catholic and Presbyterian, predominated in Prince Edward Island, Cape Breton, and the Northumberland shore of Nova Scotia. Irish clustered in the major ports, in parts of the St. John Valley, and in the lumbering areas of northern New Brunswick. Settlers of New England descent — including both Anglicans and Baptists — established their influence in Halifax, on both Fundy coasts, and along the St. John River. Acadians settled in discrete blocks throughout the region, the nuclei of more extensive territories occupied today. These ethnic hearths were shaped by the timing of migration flows, the routes of available transport, and variations in economic opportunity across the region. Once established, they were sustained by chain-migration, by the distinctiveness of language and religion, and by the spatial separation attributable to the physical fragmentation of the provinces.

Despite its trans-Atlantic outreach, this was a profoundly local society. Four-fifths of Maritimers were rural dwellers. Although some 40 000 lived in Saint John, there were fewer than 30 000 in Halifax while Fredericton and Charlottetown had populations of only 6000 and 8000 people, respectively. Locally important, these scattered centres were also provincial outposts of British economic and political influence. They served their immediate hinterlands, but none controlled the entire region.

In the countryside, and along the shore, a mixed economy prevailed. Fishermen farmed. Farmers worked a season or two in the woods. In the fishing settlements of the Gulf, 10-acre [4-hectare] farms grew root crops and sustained a few cows and pigs. On the Atlantic shore, sheep were raised on slightly larger farms. Elsewhere, farmers with perhaps 30 to 60 cleared acres [12 to 25 hectares] added grains, hay, and more livestock to their enterprises, the precise combinations varying, to some degree, from community to community. Subsistence was the farmer's prime purpose, even though small surpluses entered local trade. In the fall, a farmer might take a barrel or two of salted meat, a bushel of apples, a firkin of butter, and a load of hay to the nearest storekeeper in payment for sundries purchased on credit during the year. Domestic industry provided many necessities. Tallow candles, home-spun cloth, boots, shoes, and harnesses were made by wives, children, and local artisans. At the census of 1861, there were 13 230 hand looms in Nova Scotia; the value of cloth manufactured in New Brunswick exceeded $700 000. Beyond the farm, village artisans and small town manufacturers met the demands of a nascent market economy. Blacksmiths, skilled makers of tools and implements, thrived. Tanneries and carriage works dotted the provinces. Saw and grist mills at many river-falls provided for local needs.

Recession and Reorientation, 1866–1889

Traditional staple–commodity markets in the United Kingdom and British West Indies survived Britain's shift from mercantilism to free trade in the 1840s, and the economy of the Maritimes benefited from changing international circumstances in the 1850s and early 1860s. Inflated British lumber demands during the Crimean War doubled provincial spruce deal exports between 1850 and 1860. Free trade with the United States, established by the Reciprocity Treaty of 1854, opened new markets for fish, minerals, and forest products. The American Civil War stimulated provincial exports while providing new opportunities for the region's carrying trade after 1861.

But the official end of the Civil War, and the abrogation of Reciprocity, both in 1866, undercut the expansion and prosperity of the preceding years. In 1873, a major international depression constricted remaining American markets for Maritime lumber, and seriously reduced the region's sales of wood and ships to Britain. At the same time, the Maritimes' West Indian trade (which carried fish and lumber to the Caribbean and returned with cargoes of molasses and rum) was jeopardized by the vast surplus of refined sugar dumped on a glutted world market by European and American refineries. The Caribbean economy took a downturn and trade was reduced. This situation in turn threatened the viability of Nova Scotia's fishery as it lost a major market.

Beyond these developments, less clearly perceived changes with telling long–term effects began to undermine the old economic order in the Maritimes. Fast and reliable steamships were forcing sailing vessels from prime trans–Atlantic routes. Iron was winning favour in ship–building and replacing wood in many other types of construction. Territorial expansion carried Dominion interests westward. New technologies of communication and production were harbingers of a more integrated and extensive space economy. Political decisions were reshaping the country's economic environment and the terms of its trade.

Confronted with the effects of world recession in the 1870s, the Canadian government sought to create a strong, relatively self–sufficient economy by promoting inter–regional commerce and fostering domestic manufacturing. To this end, the avowedly protectionist National Policy was implemented between 1879 and 1887. Following American, British, and German models, duties were imposed on imported manufactures, with common consumer goods incurring the heaviest tariffs: in 1879, for example, furniture, woollen clothing, and cotton piece goods were charged approximately 35 percent. Fully manufactured farm implements, such as castings, were levied at about 25 percent. Duties on semi–finished goods –– pig iron, rolled steel — were from 10 to 20 percent. Protection was extended to primary iron and steel in 1883, and its tariffs were raised along with others in 1887. This provided a $3.50 per ton advantage to Canadian–made iron, and further sheltered producers of iron and steel goods. Finally, a 50 cent per ton levy on imported coal (raised to 60 cents in 1880) protected Canadian producers of this prime fuel in the new industrial age.

These altered circumstances reoriented the economies of Nova Scotia and New Brunswick. With the Dominion's only known and viable coal and iron deposits, with maritime access to raw materials, and with the Inter-colonial Railway (completed in 1876) offering year-round connection from Halifax to the expanding markets of central Canada, provincial optimists envisaged a significant place for the region in Canada's emerging industrial order. The general economic upsurge of the early 1880s saw the rapid expansion of secondary industry in the two provinces. Cotton mills, sugar refineries, rope works, steel and rolling mills, and iron and steel manufacturing plants were established or expanded to serve national markets. During the first years of the National Policy, the growth of this continentally-oriented manufacturing sector meshed, remarkably effectively, with the region's traditional Atlantic trading interests. In effect, the Maritimes became the hub of two interlocking and complementary trade systems — one westward to Central Canada and the United States, and one across the Atlantic to Britain and south to the West Indies (Fig. 6.2).

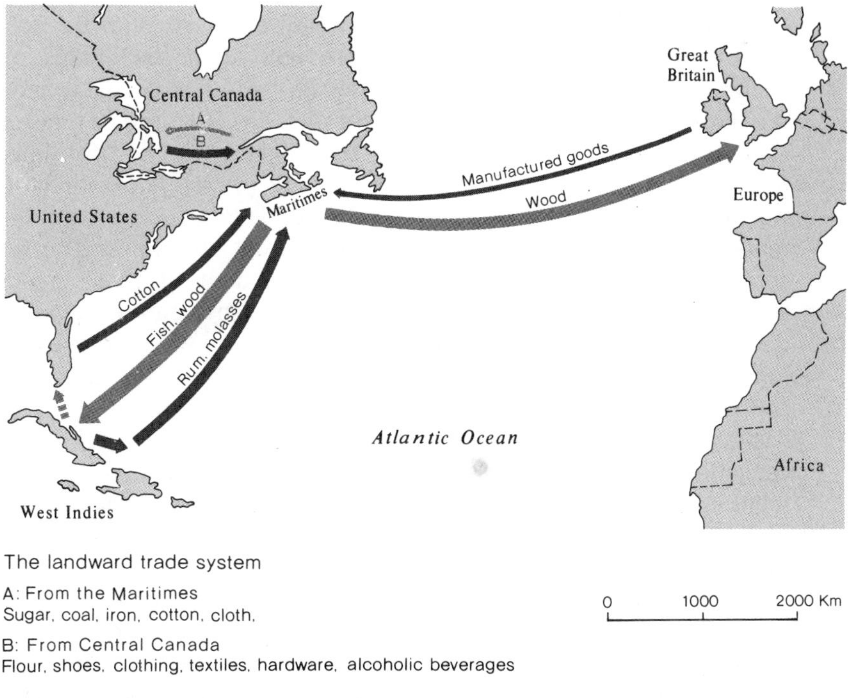

Figure 6.2 The Maritimes: patterns of external trade, c. 1880.

Earnings gained from the Atlantic-oriented import-export trade were essential to pay for central Canadian manufactured goods. If the Atlantic trade failed, as it sometimes did, continental trade was made difficult.

To the west the region's continental trade ran a deficit. Protection and access (enhanced by the Intercolonial's low, developmental rate structure) allowed Maritime manufactures and primary products into the St. Lawrence region. But under the umbrella of the tariffs, rail-borne central Canadian flour and manufactures replaced American and British goods in the Maritime market. Consequently, Maritime imports exceeded exports and the sugar, coal, cotton cloth, iron, and fish sent westward from the Maritime provinces comprised only some 30 percent of all trade in the landward trade system. In the region's Atlantic trade system on the other hand, exports exceeded imports in value and this trading sphere returned a surplus. Seaborne and tied to traditional markets, the system offered an outlet for provincial forest and fishing industries. Moreover, its return cargoes from the sugar islands and southern United States provided raw materials for manufacturing in the Maritimes.

Imbalance, Competition, and Consolidation, 1889–1914

In the early 1880s, the complementarity of the Maritimes' continental and Atlantic trading systems had supported the region's industrial expansion, but the economic balance was precarious. With the decline of the English lumber market in the recession of the late 1880s, and the restoration, in 1886, of American duties on fish lifted twelve years earlier, the balance of regional trade was upset. At the same time, central Canadian markets for cotton cloth and sugar from the Maritimes were threatened by declining demand and falling prices. These circumstances were compounded by American dumping of devalued cloth on a Canadian market barely able to absorb the output of its own mills. The resulting commercial uncertainty led to the development of trade associations which attempted to regulate the cotton industry by controlling production; their failure — precipitated by the refusal of some Maritime producers to limit their output according to association quotas — had far-reaching consequences. Well-financed Ontario and Québec cotton manufacturers decided to stabilize production and secure their interests by industrial consolidation. Their aggressive strategies and locational advantages made them formidable competitors with the generally under-capitalized Maritime enterprises. Central Canadian interests rapidly gained control of most Maritime mills.

Similar developments occurred in other manufacturing industries. Some Maritime companies disappeared, others worked within larger corporate structures. By 1895, only confectionery production and manufacturing tied to the iron and steel and staple industries remained under local control. With this decline of local autonomy, there was a growing tendency for management decisions to be based on profit and loss calculations, rather than on consideration of the fortunes of Maritime communities. From the 1890s on, the Maritimes held a shrinking proportion of a Canadian consumer goods industry that was increasingly concentrated in the Lower Great Lakes–St. Lawrence region, where ready access to both capital and markets enabled producers to realize economies of integration and scale. There was a parallel decline in the Maritimes' tertiary sector as upper echelon service and financial functions concentrated in Montréal and Toronto. Even the region's workshops and artisans producing for local markets gradually succumbed to the competition of mass–produced articles from central Canada, distributed across the region by branches of the Intercolonial and Canadian Pacific trunk–lines. Together, these changes undermined the economic vitality of the province's larger urban centres and left the Maritimes without a regional metropolis.

In the iron and steel industry, large local coal reserves, small quantities of local iron ore, and ready access to the rich Bell Island (Newfoundland) ore deposits opened in the mid–1890s, gave Maritime producers an initial advantage over their central Canadian counterparts. The early twentieth century was a period of industrial ascendency.[6] Primary production was based on the coalfields of Pictou and Cape Breton; iron–using industries — making bridges, railway cars, wire, nails, stoves — clustered in towns along the railroad linking them to the

Evidences of the industrial ascendency of Nova Scotia. (*Ralph Pickard Bell Library, Mount Allison University*)

emerging Canadian heartland. With the expansion of western railways and Prairie settlement after 1896, demand for such products soared. Nova Scotia's pig iron output increased from 32 000 tons in 1896 to 425 000 tons in 1912.

Once again, however, competition among eastern and central Canadian firms resulted in consolidations and the eventual transfer of control out of the Maritimes, thus reaffirming the region's hinterland status. Beginning with the amalgamation of secondary iron manufacturing industries and culminating in the consolidation of Nova Scotia steel producers to form the British Empire Steel Corporation in the early 1920s, ownership of the region's iron and steel industries slipped into international hands. With this loss of control, elimination of the government bounty on iron and steel production in 1912, changing product demands (which required different plant capability), and distance from the growing concentration of industrial output in Ontario, the position of the Maritimes' iron and steel industry declined. Whereas Nova Scotia produced 43 percent of Canadian pig iron in 1913, it accounted for less than 30 percent in 1929, even though output had actually increased.

An extractive industry, coal mining was less footloose than manufacturing, but it, too, was subject to mergers and consolidations engineered for the benefit of expanding corporate capitalism. By 1920, virtually the entire Cape Breton coal field was controlled by the British Empire Steel Corporation. Inevitably, the fortunes of the coal mining industry reflected developments in iron and steel production. But the collieries were never entirely dependent on local markets. Tariff protection made Cape Breton coal competitive in Montréal, and expanding shipments to central Canada through the 1890s employed many Nova Scotian vessels previously displaced by the disruption of Atlantic trade. In 1914, almost 2.4 million tons of Nova Scotian coal, thrice the quantity of 1896, entered the Québec market. And for a brief period during the 1890s, before a smoke abatement law and revisions to the American tariff schedule excluded it from the Boston market, Cape Breton coal was also sold in New England.

External Change and the Traditional Industries, 1889–1914

Evolving technologies and changing product demands altered the traditional fishing, forest, and farming industries of the Maritimes in the quarter century before 1914. Cod fisheries declined. Long-established European markets were lost as improved shipping and advances in the techniques of packing, canning, and refrigeration brought Argentinian and Australian meat into competition with salt fish from Nova Scotia. Caribbean markets for cod also declined as cane sugar producers suffered stiff competition from an expanding sugar beet industry in Europe. Steamships took much of the remaining export trade of the West Indian Islands from provincial schooners.

In home waters, large, expensive Banks trawlers, operating from fewer ports and requiring fewer workers, heightened competition in the cod fishery. Rail links from the Gulf shore brought the fishermen's catches to the holds of steamers in Halifax and bypassed local intermediaries. Yet there were some improvements. Lobster, again in demand for live shipment and for sale to small canneries, offered inshore fishermen another catch. Half-decked, gasoline-powered "Cape Island" boats (named for the area of southwestern Nova Scotia in which they were developed) became more common after 1900, making access to the fishing grounds easier and increasing the range of those fishermen who could afford them. Moreover, special trains and new tariffs led to the development of cold storage warehouses and opened central Canadian markets after 1908. The real value of Nova Scotian fish production nevertheless declined between 1896 and 1913.

Lumbering also reached a plateau during these years. Railroads opened new timber stands in northern New Brunswick. Employment and production increased in provincial sawmills, but with most of the valuable pine gone from the forest, much of the cut was small spruce, and low-valued box shooks and spool wood made up a significant proportion of the industry's output. Heavier capitalization and mechanization set saw-milling in New Brunswick apart from that in Nova Scotia and Prince Edward Island; in the mainland province the impetus was toward pulp production. Here, the heavy investment necessitated by new technologies is apparent. Three small plants producing $108 000 worth of pulp in 1890 were valued at $298 000; in 1911, a dozen plants manufactured pulp worth $1.4 million.

On Maritime farms, grain acreages fell because wheat from the Western Interior produced better and cheaper flour than that grown in the eastern provinces. Subsistence potato growing also declined with the increasing availability of imported foods in the region. Wool and cheese exports to Britain, the latter fostered by the development of cooperative cheese factories after 1870, were challenged before 1900 by large, high quality shipments from Australia and New Zealand. Retrenchment and specialization resulted. Increasingly, in many older settled areas, marginal upland farms once dependent on sheep raising grew back to forest.

But there were some signs of improvement. Apple orchards, concentrated in the Annapolis and St. John Valleys, yielded a profitable crop for the British market and annual exports tended upward. Prince Edward Island farmers formed cooperatives to market butter, eggs, and bacon in the expanding urban centres of New England; a few made fortunes in a fox-ranching industry that reached its most prosperous level on the eve of World War I. More generally, Maritime farmers concentrated on those crops least susceptible to outside competition — fodder and roots for the lumber camps, dairy products for local consumption — or ran their holdings to provide the bulk of their own needs. The combination of farming with other employment remained common. Still, the region lost 20 000 of 134 000 farmers between 1891 and 1911.

Together, the tariffs and the railroads — the building blocks of the National Policy — transformed the Canadian economy between 1879 and 1914. With the industrial development they fostered, and the upswing of the world-economy at the turn of the century, they led to expansion and prosperity in the country. The Maritime provinces were affected by these developments, but the region received a disproportionately small share of their benefits. Despite efforts to realize supposed advantages for the development of manufacturing after 1879, the provinces became increasingly peripheral to the developing St. Lawrence core of the Canadian economy in the quarter century after 1889. External corporate control of primary and secondary manufacturing in the region placed the destinies of local industries beyond the communities in which they were based.

Parallel developments in the financial sector saw the region's mercantile banks amalgamated into national corporations between 1900 and 1920. Improvements in communication technology shook the traditional foundations of provincial economies by subjecting Maritime producers to the competition of outside enterprises whose access to larger local markets allowed them to take advantage of scale economies. Economic shifts and tariff adjustments contributed to the breakdown of the region's connection with traditional markets. By 1914, the provinces were losing ground in the expanding continental economy. Their population grew at barely a fraction of the Canadian rate. Their traditional export industries languished and they slipped far behind the pace of manufacturing expansion.

Artificial Stimulation and Subsequent Decline, 1914–1935

Wartime circumstances reversed many of these trends and restored a degree of prosperity to the regional economy. Coal and steel industries expanded as the demand for munitions and the growth of railroad and steamship transportation generated markets for their products. Lumber prices soared. With the disruption of world trade, Maritime fishermen increased their sales of dried cod fish in the western hemisphere. Fresh fish shipments to central Canada grew as meat prices rose and the government allowed rebates on transportation costs. Local agriculture met less intense competition from distant producers and sheep farming and cotton cloth production increased to meet military needs.

Precipitous economic decline, however, followed the war boom. Again, New Brunswick and Nova Scotia were more directly affected than Prince Edward Island, which was endowed with greater agricultural potential and buffered by its insular position. Yet similar national and international developments shaped the fortunes of all three provinces. The entire region was affected by the shift of industrial dependence and economic development away from coal, iron, and the railroad, to electricity, oil, and the automobile. The coal industry faced a static market in 1918. Cut off from their largest customer, the St. Lawrence market, by the disruption of shipping between 1916 and 1918, Cape Breton's submarine mines now had to compete with the better coal of more efficient American producers. These difficulties increased as inflationary price rises reduced the effective protection of the specific duty (53 cents per ton) on imported coal. Moreover, local coal consumption was down. As railway expansion declined, Nova Scotian steel mills (geared to the production of rails and ingot steel) and their dependent rolling stock manufacturers worked far below capacity.

Meanwhile, Ontario mills, nearer the market, with larger supplies of scrap metal, and favoured by tariff adjustments, adapted to new demands for structural steel and lighter grades of plate. As these mills expanded, the likelihood of takeovers and the eventual phasing out of Maritime production increased. Virtually all established manufacturing plants in the region declined in the 1920s. In 1925, the net value of regional manufacturing output was less than half the 1919 level. Expansion in the newer industrial spheres also passed the region by. Robbed of their energy cost advantage by the turn to new resources, with few good hydroelectric generating sites, and without known reserves of the newly discovered minerals in the Canadian Shield, the Maritimes could not match the growth of Canada's Industrial Heartland.

The business recession that followed spiralling post–war inflation in 1920 also had a profound impact upon the regional economy. Falling prices and protectionist policies affected many Maritime industries. Of the traditional activities, the fishery was perhaps hardest hit. Technologically superior European vessels, selling their catch under the shelter of national tariffs, squeezed Nova Scotia producers out of many markets. World demand for dried cod fell; even West Indian purchases declined as sugar prices dropped again. By 1921 prices for salt cod were half those of two years earlier. In 1919, government subventions for the shipment of fresh fish to Ontario were withdrawn and two years later the United States re–established tariffs on the import of fresh and frozen fish. With the general decline of the economy, and the lack of alternative opportunities within the region, employment in the Nova Scotia fishing industry fell by almost 25 percent between 1920 and 1929.

Lumbering and farming also felt the impact of recession and external competition. After 1918, the Panama Canal allowed Pacific coast lumber into the markets of eastern Canada and the seaboard states. In 1920, the downturn of the British business cycle limited trans–Atlantic sales; and the decline of local construction reduced another outlet. Sawmill employment fell dramatically in 1920–21, and lumber production in Nova Scotia and New Brunswick remained far below pre–war levels during the ensuing decade. Some related industries did prosper, however. Despite economic difficulties in the early 1920s, the pulp and paper industry absorbed labour and logs from the failing sawmilling industry. Improvements in hydro-electricity generation and transmission allowed development of larger pulp and newsprint mills. However, American capital and corporations (such as the International Paper Company) lay behind the expansion, and gradually undermined the leadership of local entrepreneurs in this sector of the economy. Pulp output nevertheless doubled between 1920 and 1929. By 1930 this capital-intensive industry employed 3000 men; many others cut pulpwood for sale to the mills.

Renewed competition from western producers and processed foodstuffs led to a steady decrease in field crop acreage in New Brunswick and Nova Scotia during the 1920s. Dairying remained important for local consumption. Apple exports to Britain continued, although profits fell in the face of competition from British Columbia and the United States, and as a result of disease in Nova Scotia trees. Potato exports rose in the wartime decade, only to encounter higher American tariffs in the 1920s. Further specialization in seed potatoes maintained the viability of New Brunswick and Prince Edward Island growers. But on the whole, Maritime agriculture was in difficulty. The general recession, and the hardship common in the declining industrial towns of the region, reduced local markets for farm produce, pared away many a farmer's slender source of operating cash, and by reducing the diversity of their enterprises, left even those selling export produce more susceptible to external market fluctuations.

Adjustments to the rate structure of the Intercolonial Railroad compounded the consequences of economic and technological change for the region.[7] Initially, in the late nineteenth century, the rate structure was beneficial to the Maritimes. In an effort to overcome chronic financial difficulties, the railroad implemented rates that encouraged long-haul traffic. From a basic rate some 20 percent lower than that on central Canadian lines for hauls of up to 100 miles (160 kilometres), mileage levies decreased proportionately with distance, until shipments of 700 miles or more (1126 kilometres) were charged only half the prevailing central Canadian rate. In addition, traffic bound beyond Montréal was charged an arbitrary rate for the stretch from the Maritimes to Montréal. Westbound rates were approximately 12 percent below those on eastbound goods. Clearly these arrangements extended the westward range of Maritime commodities while providing them with some local protection. They were instrumental in allowing the region's manufacturers access to large central and western Canadian markets before World War I.

Long a focus of contention, the Intercolonial's rate structure came under increasing criticism early in the century. The east–west differential was eliminated in 1912. Management of the railroad was transferred from Moncton to Toronto in 1919, with the creation of the Canadian National

Railway. Soon after, the arbitrary and special commodity rates (applied to sugar and coal) were eliminated. Maritime rates were set at par with those in central Canada. And in 1920 they were included in a general increase necessitated by the rapid rise in prices after World War I. The net effect of these adjustments was to raise rates on the Intercolonial between 140 and 216 percent. With deflation, and the fall in prices that followed, this was a devastating blow. In effect, it crippled the manufacturing sector of a regional economy already lame from the impact of economic change and technological adjustment.

Freight rate adjustments and modifications to trade and tariff policies lessened the Maritimes' difficulties somewhat in the late 1920s. Following the recommendations of a Royal Commission inquiry, railway rates within the Maritimes and on westbound traffic moving beyond them were reduced by 20 percent in 1927. Federal support was offered for the construction of coking plants. Government subventions and bonuses allowed Maritime coal back into Québec and Ontario markets. To encourage Canadian port and railroad traffic, federal harbour commissions were established in Halifax and Saint John; freight-handling facilities were further upgraded; and imports from specified origins were allowed tariff reductions if they entered the continent through selected Canadian ports. Dominion subsidies also fostered a regular steamship service to the Caribbean although a reciprocal trade agreement with the West Indies did not significantly increase Maritime exports. With this government support — a portent of future reliance upon federal investment in the region — and expansion in tourism and primary production, the regional economy turned upward after 1926. Construction boomed. By 1929 manufacturing employment in the region was approximately 45 percent above 1921 levels. Coal sales to central Canada exceeded pre-war totals.

The improvements could not withstand the Great Depression, however. Manufacturing employment fell from 40 000 in 1929 to 24 000 in 1933; in the same period, salaries and wages paid in this sector of the regional economy declined by 40 percent. By 1936 less capital was invested in Maritime manufacturing than in 1917. Coal production dropped by more than 40 percent in the three years after 1929. By 1933 lumber production in the region was 75 percent below the output of 1920. The difficulties of the fishery also continued. In 1933, when Halifax dry cod fish prices were barely one-third those of 1920, the total value of fisheries production was little more than half the 1929 level and only 43 percent of that in 1918.

Farming was just as hard hit. Total farm income in 1932 was barely half that of 1929. Yet farming and fishing sustained a growing proportion of the region's population. Individual small-scale exploitation of land and sea augmented or replaced failing incomes in other sectors. New land was broken in northern New Brunswick; by 1933 there were 10 percent more fishermen than in 1929, and three years later numbers were 20 percent above the pre-depression level. Fishing and farming were combined to provide a meagre subsistence. Farmers — 25 percent of whom reported a principal occupation other than farming at the 1931 Census — eked out livings by cutting pulp wood or taking other work as it was offered.

After 15 years of almost unbroken recession, sectors of the regional population were in distressed circumstances. Overall, the economies of the three provinces were severely afflicted. Largely dependent upon the returns of a few vulnerable export staples; with their manufacturing industries decimated by problems of cost, scale, and competition; and with their best resources depleted or devalued, the Maritime provinces could provide the majority of their people with no more than a meagre, hard-won, and unreliable subsistence.

Revival, Decline, and Federal Amelioration, 1935–70

Economic conditions began to improve in the mid-1930s. Lumbering recovered slowly with the introduction of Imperial preferences and trade agreements with the United States, and more quickly when World War II eliminated competition and spurred domestic construction. Military demand expanded the region's pulp and paper markets. Iron and steel production doubled in value between 1939 and 1942; the gross value of regional manufactures increased 140 percent between 1939 and 1944. Cash incomes from the sale of farm produce more than doubled in the same period. Returns from fish packing and curing virtually tripled. Even in constant dollars, gross values of production rose from 10 to 50 or 60 percent in almost all sectors of the regional economy between 1940 and 1945.

But again, these were temporary benefits of abnormal circumstances. Chronic economic problems reappeared. Although the maturing Canadian economy expanded rapidly after 1945, the Maritimes shared little of the national prosperity. Unemployment rates ran considerably above national levels. Earned incomes in the region, 75 percent of those in the rest of the country in 1945, slipped to 66 percent by 1955. In Prince Edward Island, incomes at the beginning of the decade were a mere 58 percent of the national average, and they fell to 50 percent by 1955. Employment in the region's primary industries declined, and there were no compensating increases in other spheres. As prospects faded, migration from the region increased.

Despite subsidies, mechanization, and changes in control, Nova Scotia's coal and steel industries declined. When the railroads switched from steam to diesel locomotives in the 1950s, coal production fell by a third. Mining ceased on the Cumberland coal field. Mines were closed in Pictou and Cape Breton. Mechanization increased productivity in the industry by almost 50 percent between 1945 and 1955, but extraction costs made it impossible to compete with the selling price of American coal in Ontario. Without market expansion, jobs were forfeit. Employment in Nova Scotia's mines declined from 13 200 in 1946 to 9200 in 1957. Sydney steel production suffered high costs — the burden of outmoded plants — and the loss of established markets. By 1957 industrial Cape Breton was in serious economic difficulty, and the future was dark. Nine thousand people left this area between 1951 and 1956.

Gross output values, calculated in constant dollars, reveal expansion in the region's pulp and paper industry after 1945. Large investments in the New Brunswick forest industry by local–born industrialist K.C. Irving paralleled growing American, European, and British Columbian involvement in pulp and paper production. Within a decade of World War II, output in both Nova Scotia and New Brunswick was up approximately 85 percent. But employment opportunities did not keep pace with this increase, rising by approximately 68 percent and 45 percent, respectively, in the two provinces. In lumber and wood–using industries, employment fell in both provinces, almost completely offsetting the gains in pulp and paper operations. In other manufacturing, there was little expansion in the post–war decade, especially by comparison with manufacturing growth in central Canada. After 1945, Maritime manufacturers competed less and less effectively with their St. Lawrence rivals. Increases in railway freight rates — applied equally across the country but offset by concessions to combat the competition of truckers in Ontario and Québec — enhanced the burden of distance for Maritime shippers through the 1950s. Low traffic intensity and poor road networks (unimproved because provincial revenues were already sorely stretched) restricted the growth of a regional trucking industry whose competition with the railroads might have lowered transport costs. Whereas total manufacturing employment across the country increased by some 310 000 jobs between 1949 and 1957, there was, in contrast, a slight decline in the manufacturing workforce of the Maritime provinces.

Fishing and farming were also affected. Large increases in the output of the fishery stimulated by high prices and a strong domestic market were achieved by increased capitalization and improved productivity. Employment in the fishery remained more or less constant between 1945 and 1955. In farming, too, mechanization maintained output. But limited markets, transport costs — on fertilizers and equipment brought into the region as well as on produce shipped out — and the lure of urban amenities (often beyond the Maritimes) led to widespread abandonment of small holdings. In New Brunswick, agricultural employment fell by 45 percent in the post–war decade. In Nova Scotia, the decline was one–third; in Prince Edward Island it was one–fifth. In all, 36 000 farm jobs were lost in ten years.

Federal transfer payments to individuals — including unemployment insurance, old age pensions, and child allowances — alleviated the worst consequences of this post–war decline. Between 1949 and 1956 these payments accounted for some 10.5 to 13 percent of personal incomes in the Atlantic region. Augmented by new federal–provincial fiscal arrangements to provide more uniform health and education services across the country, they prevented a catastrophic decline in the quality of regional life. Paradoxically, they also permitted the survival of marginal lifestyles as part–time fishermen substituted unemployment insurance payments for subsistence farming or seasonal work in the woods. The federal payments were no more than a papering over of the weaknesses of a hinterland economy. With the downturn of the national economy in 1957, the region's problems were revealed once more. Despite increases of 3 to 4 percent per capita in transfer payments to the region in 1957 and 1958, the personal incomes of Maritimers remained at less than 70 percent of the national average.

Persistent regional disparities within the country prompted new federal initiatives to foster structural changes and economic expansion in the lagging regions. In 1957, equalization payments were introduced. In the 1960s, a series of federal–provincial programmes addressed the problems of unequal development. Among these, the Agricultural Rehabilitation and Development Act (1961) and the Agricultural and Rural Development Act (1965) were intended to alleviate rural farm and non–farm poverty across the country. They offered low–interest loans to farmers and established make–work programmes for community pasture development. A Fund for Rural Economic Development (1966) offered assistance to primary industry, tourism, and manufacturing in Prince Edward Island and parts of New Brunswick, as well as in Québec and Manitoba. Development incentives were offered to firms locating in high unemployment areas. In 1962, the Atlantic Development Board was established to advise on the economic problems of the region and to finance infrastructure development within it. And in 1967 the Cape Breton Development Corporation was charged with rationalizing the coal industry and stimulating economic adjustment in that economically depressed island. Finally, regional development efforts were themselves rationalized in 1969 when the Department of Regional Economic Expansion assumed control of most existing development programmes.

In conjunction with provincial efforts, these initiatives complemented federal transfer payments in gradually improving the economic circumstances of Maritimers through the 1960s. Personal incomes increased slightly in advance of the national rate, and percentage income disparities between Maritime residents and other Canadians were narrowed (although the dollar gap between their incomes increased). Yet migration from the region continued at a high level. Almost 115 000 people left between 1961 and 1969.

The circumstances of the 1960s shaped the face of the region through the 1970s. In the drive to create a more viable economy, high technology industries were encouraged to locate in the region, new industrial parks sought prestigious tenants, primary industries won tax concessions, and tourism was promoted as a potentially lucrative tertiary activity. Meanwhile, the number of bureaucrats administering the new programmes soared, and an increasing proportion of rural dwellers sustained themselves on non-productive farms by supplementing government benefits with seasonal or part-time off-farm work.

A Perspective on Geographical Change

The Maritimes' peripheral location — more than 1600 kilometres from the major demand centres of the national economy — has definitely hindered the competitiveness of its manufacturing and agricultural industries. But the region's problems go deeper than this. The causes of economic retardation in the Maritimes — reflected in lower than average per capita incomes, high unemployment, significant underemployment, and correspondingly low wages — lie in the relatively poor quality of the region's resources, the centralizing tendencies of modern transport and production technologies, and the structure of national tariff policies. All of these factors have tended in the long run to foster economic growth outside the region.

Since the regional economy depends largely on exports, declining world prices for fish and lumber (whether produced by competition or changes in demand) have slowed expansion in the Maritimes. This factor, coupled with the economic marginality and inelasticity of Maritime resources (by comparison with those in other parts of Canada), has reduced the region's attractiveness to capital and labour. Thus migrants and new investment entering the country have tended to bypass the region for the more richly-endowed areas of central and western Canada. Once established, this trend has reinforced itself as the multiplier effects of additional productive capacity have increased the growth rate differential between the Maritimes and other areas of Canada. Indeed, regional perceptions of this differential have impelled the movement of capital and, especially, labour from the Maritimes to more rapidly expanding regions. But this flow — much of it to the United States — failed to raise marginal productivity and per capita incomes in the Maritimes to Canadian levels.

In the long term, the integration of the national economy (attributable to the extension of the railroad), the growth of scale economies in many industries (due to new production technologies), and the advantages of industrial linkages (derived from locational concentration) have undermined the viability of Maritime manufacturing by favouring the development of large plants serving national markets from a more central location.

The broad mechanisms of this process can be illustrated by reference to a simple model. Consider two spatially-separated regions — a small area, A (the Maritimes), and a larger area, B (the Industrial Heartland) — and assume equal density and per capita purchasing power among their populations. Introduce a consumer-goods industry, dependent upon ubiquitous raw materials and therefore free to locate in relation to its market. If under prevailing production and transport technologies, demand in Region A is able to support a plant of optimum size, or if transport costs are sufficiently high to exclude competition from beyond the region, one plant will locate there; two or more will locate in Region B. Now assuming that the number of people in Region A is stable, that the population in Region B is growing, and that production facilities in our hypothetical industry can be upgraded at little cost, any technological advance increasing the size of production units could probably be implemented with profit in Region B albeit, perhaps, with the elimination of one or more established smaller plants; but there would be no return from increased economies of scale in Region A. Theoretically, then, consumers in Region B would pay less for their goods than consumers in Region A.

If this price differential were sufficient to offset the cost of transporting the product from Region B to the nearest part of Region A, consumers there might purchase from Region B more cheaply than from their own plant. The resulting reduction in demand for Region A's output would raise its per-unit costs of production, subjecting its markets to further incursion from Region B. Similar consequences would ensue from reductions in the cost of interregional transportation. Depending upon relative market sizes in Regions A and B, transport rate structures, and optimum plant size, producers might locate away from the centre of Region B towards Region A to minimize their market-access costs. Ultimately, however, the effect of these changes in scale of production and/or transport costs is to subject manufacturers in Region A to growing competition, and to concentrate production in Region B.

The situation depicted here has been realized in Canada by the westward shift of markets that began with the opening of the Prairies to settlement in the late nineteenth century. By enhancing the centrality of the Great Lakes Lowlands, this growth has further favoured Heartland manufacturing over that in the Maritimes. Ultimately, therefore, small Maritime producers of many commodities have found their plant and their limited local market insufficient to sustain their enterprises against the centralizing, consolidating tendencies of modern manufacturing in an integrated national economy. Similar factors have affected Maritime agriculture.

In these circumstances, the long-term effect of the National Policy has been to trap the Maritime provinces in a cost-price squeeze. With much of their gross regional product derived from the sale of primary exports, the provinces have been subject to external competition which produced lower prices in world markets and yielded reduced revenues to their economies. But they have been obligated by national protective tariffs to purchase both producer and consumer goods from sheltered, relatively high-cost Canadian manufacturers. In effect, therefore, the Heartland's failure to absorb the products of Maritime industries except at times when the national economy was operating at capacity — during two World Wars and the boom of 1896–1913 — placed central Canada in an exploitative rather than reciprocal relationship with its Maritime hinterland in the first half of the twentieth century. This relationship only compounded the retardation of a regional economy already disadvantaged by the shift of economic development from dependence upon wood, wind, and water, through reliance upon coal, iron, and steam, to utilization of electricity, oil, and chemicals within little more than a hundred years.

LANDSCAPES AND LIVELIHOODS IN TRANSITION: A HUMAN GEOGRAPHY

Since Confederation, the decline of traditional industries and the growth of new enterprises have transformed working conditions and the nature of individual opportunity in the Maritimes. While economic independence has decreased, economic hardship has become more evident. Improvements in communication have broken down the region's local community character of the mid-nineteenth century. Cities beyond (and more recently those within) the region have lured youth looking for new opportunities. Out-migration has undermined the sense of local community fostered by the settlement of generations in a single locale. The movement of people, the decline of local crafts, and the spread of mass-produced commodities have all reshaped the region's character. These changes have molded the modern human geography of all parts of the Maritimes and added the differential tensions of transition to already complex patterns of land and life in the region.

Population patterns reflect the influence of fluctuating economic fortunes upon the geography of the Maritimes. Overall, the picture is one of stagnation. Rates of population increase have been strikingly low. After per decade increases of 25 percent and 16 percent between 1851 and 1871, the population of 767 000 increased by only 100 000 (13.5 percent) during the 1870s. Between 1881 and 1901 numbers were almost static; not until 1921 did the regional population exceed one million. Despite a 12 percent surge in 1931–41, population increased by less than 50 percent between 1871 and 1941; in the same period, Canada's population rose by 212 percent. Regional increases of 11 and 15 percent per decade thereafter were well short of national levels, and growth rates in the provinces slipped back in the 1960s.

Massive out-migration was the major cause of slow growth.[8] At least 100 000 people left the Maritimes each decade between 1881 and 1931. Between 1871 and 1901, departures of former immigrants exceeded immigrant arrivals, and the exodus of Canadian-born people almost offset the natural increase of the resident population. According to one intriguing case study of the Canning district of Kings County, Nova Scotia, this movement ran slowly in the decade or so after Confederation, but increased dramatically in the mid-1880s. It was dominated by the young and the single and comprised slightly more men (55 percent) than women. It was also structured by family ties, and took the majority of migrants to Massachusetts (Fig. 6.3). Thus, it has been argued, was "established a tradition of leaving school, leaving home, and having to leave the region in search of employment and autonomy which remains today an integral part of the outport Nova Scotian's rites of passage."[9]

Migration continued at a high rate in the early twentieth century. In the difficult decade of 1921–1931, more than 147 000 Maritimers left the region. The massive exodus began in 1920 and most out-migration occurred in the worst economic times, before 1926. That net out-migration fell to almost a third of the 1921–31 level during the 1930s was

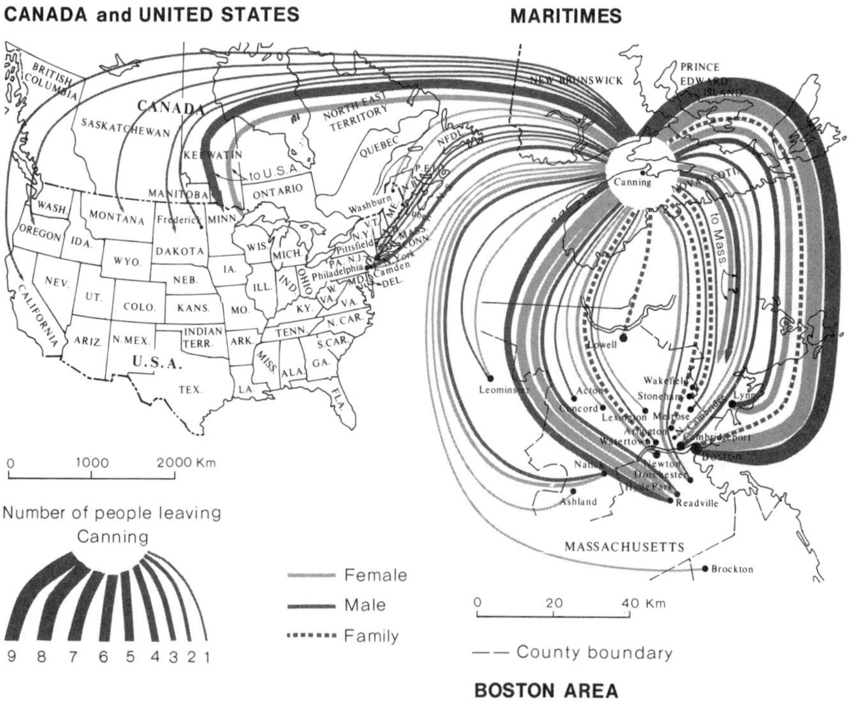

Figure 6.3 Patterns of out-migration from Canning, Nova Scotia in the late nineteenth century.

due more to the general depression of economic conditions elsewhere than to any significant improvement in the Maritimes' economy (at least until the end of the decade). Since World War II the loss of population has continued; although numbers have risen, the increment has been well below the rate of natural increase. During a post-war peak of out-migration between 1961 and 1966, some 80 000 Maritimers left the region.

But population trends were far from uniform across the provinces. Gross figures conceal different patterns at more local scales. At the provincial level, Prince Edward Island was most affected by emigration. Its population declined at every census between 1891 and 1931. Despite subsequent increases, it did not reach the 1881 total until 1966. In contrast, New Brunswick has increased its population each decade since Confederation, and the period from 1921 to 1931 was the only decade of decline in Nova Scotia. Yet out-migration from the mainland provinces began earlier than that from Prince Edward Island, has involved more people, and its dislocating effects have been compounded by considerable internal migration.

Population shifts are most evident at the county level. Almost half of the counties in the region reached their maximum population in 1901 or before. In some of these, out-migration slowed growth rates even in the 1960s. By 1881, population growth in the Annapolis Valley, rural Cape Breton, and neighbouring Antigonish and Guysborough counties was less than the natural increase. People were leaving the lower St. John Valley and Charlotte and Northumberland counties in appreciable numbers, and growth was slowing in Prince Edward Island. Of the region's 36 counties, only 9 returned a larger population at every census between 1871 and 1941, and only 5 of these sustained a numerical increase through each census to 1971. Of the nine, three included urban concentrations (Halifax, Fredericton, and the Cape Breton coalfield). The remainder comprised 6 or 7 counties in an arc through northern and eastern New Brunswick from Victoria and Madawaska through Gloucester to Westmorland. The seventh, Kent County, diverged slightly from its neighbours because its population declined in the 1920s and 1930s.

Including the last agricultural frontiers of the region in Victoria, Madawaska, and Restigouche, these counties also contain the majority of the Acadians whose sustained growth is largely attributable to their high fertility and their tendency to remain and make do in *L'Acadie.* Natural increase, however, has been complemented by migration from Québec to Madawaska and Restigouche since 1871. Today, Acadians comprise almost 40 percent of New Brunswick's population. The province is the country's only officially bilingual jurisdiction. Yet many anglophone New Brunswickers are periodically outspoken in opposition to language policies that they regard as a challenge to their longstanding political and economic pre-eminence.

The pattern of population change is revealed even more clearly by analyzing the region's urban trends. Before 1880 the region was essentially rural; small centres provided services for local settlers, but outside Halifax and Saint John there were few urban Maritimers. Indeed, the absence of a regional metropolis is often cited as both a cause and consequence of Maritime underdevelopment. Yet as overland communication improved, and as mass production and distribution encouraged centralization, the region's urban population did increase. From less than 12 percent in 1871, it reached 38 percent in 1941 and 53 percent in 1971. Urbanization was most evident in Nova Scotia, where urban dwellers increased from 8 to 43 percent of the population between 1871 and 1921. Until 1921, urban expansion reflected the growth of tariff-sheltered industry and focussed on the region's two major ports (with Halifax exceeding Saint John in its rate of growth) and along the line of the Intercolonial Railroad. Moncton, a key node in the region's rail network, grew from 1650 to 19 500 in 50 years after 1871. On the Pictou coalfield, where iron and steel and secondary manufacturing grew rapidly after the National Policy, Pictou and Trenton with approximately 3000 people, Stellarton and Westville with some 5000, and New Glasgow with 9000, formed a dispersed urban cluster of almost 25 000 people by 1921. In Cumberland County the manufactures of "Busy Amherst" supported 10 000 people; nearby Springhill on the coalfield had 5600. And in Cape Breton County, 63 000 urban dwellers lived in Sydney (22 500), Glace Bay (17 000) and the satellite towns of Dominion, New Waterford, North Sydney, and Sydney Mines (Fig. 6.4).

Urban patterns since 1921 may be summarized briefly (Fig. 6.5). Concentration in Halifax, Saint John, and Moncton continued. Slow growth, stagnation, or decline marked the other important centres of 1921. New nodes of growth emerged on the periphery of the region. The populations of Dalhousie, Edmundston, and Fredericton tripled in half a century; that of Campbelltown doubled. Bathurst's population grew slowly until the late 1950s, then tripled in the 1960s. Late in the same decade, Port Hawkesbury more than doubled in size. These developments are attributable to the expansion of pulp and paper production, the expansion of the civil service, the growth of metal mining, and the development of high technology industries. In general, they reflect the resource (and government) dependent character of regional growth since the 1950s.

Thus, the apparent stability of regional population patterns since 1871 conceals a high degree of local flux. Virtually everywhere, the fluctuations of county and parish populations reflect the limitations of Maritime resources. By the end of the nineteenth century, there was insufficient land in the older settled agricultural regions to provide for the third and fourth generations of early nineteenth century immigrant families. As economic conditions made farm subdivision less viable, settlers' sons moved on. Change and hardship in the fishery forced people from that traditional occupation. In southwestern and northwestern New Brunswick, the declining lumber industry further limited the capacity of local economies to employ the offspring of those who had developed the area.

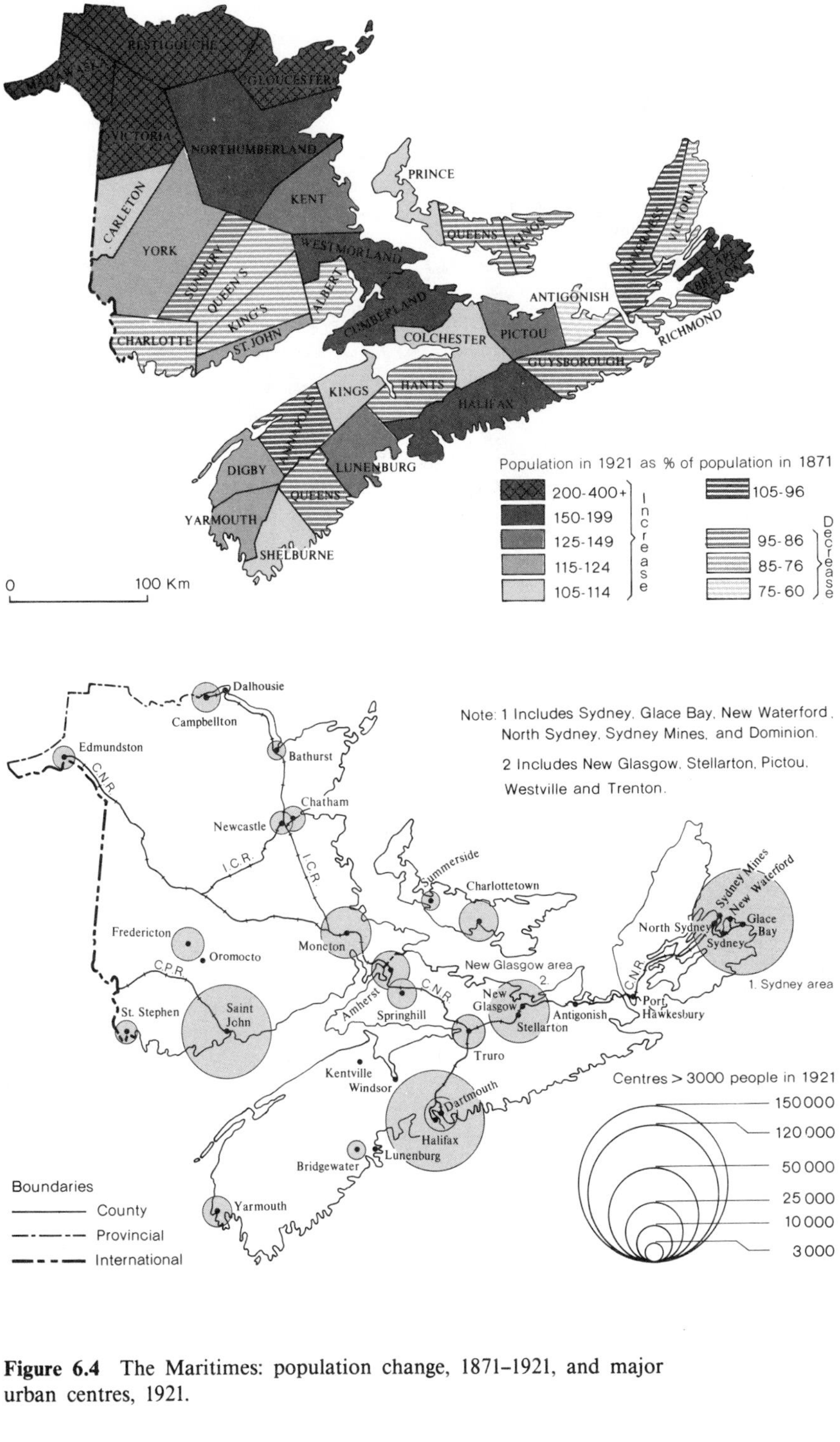

Figure 6.4 The Maritimes: population change, 1871–1921, and major urban centres, 1921.

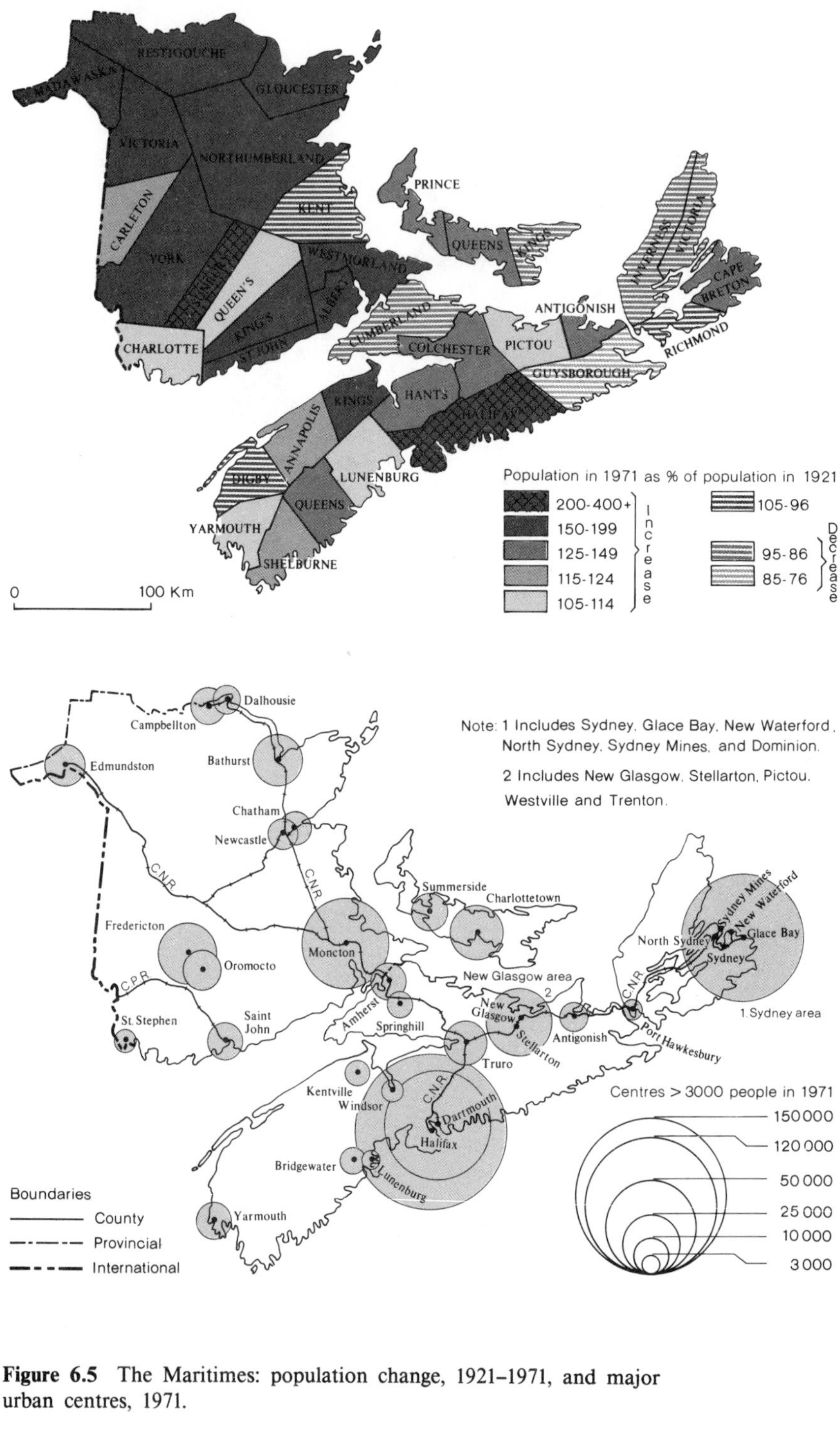

Figure 6.5 The Maritimes: population change, 1921–1971, and major urban centres, 1971.

Again, migration was forced on many of the young. Of those who moved, many gravitated to the region's growing urban areas. There, in time, manufacturing decline or mine closures often necessitated another relocation. Ultimately, the majority of migrants departed for central and western Canada, the United States, and overseas destinations. Propelled by the relative decline of the regional economy, this exodus has robbed the Maritimes of many of its most productive people for a disproportionate share of migrants were young adults, many of them skilled and ambitious. Moreover, migration, whether within or beyond the region, fractured communities and demoralized families. "I'm the worse since you have moved away to stay in the country of coal," lamented bard James Ban Macfarlane on his neighbour's absence from Margaree.[10]

A Landscape Transformed

The Maritimes, in the mid-nineteenth century, was a patchwork quilt of cultural variety. Overland movement was slow and expensive; life was fundamentally local. Religious, economic, ethnic, and physiographic diversity were reflected in varying agricultural practices, in the multitude of churches, and in the proliferation of educational institutions with different denominational affiliations. At a more general level, the basic physical expression of this diversity was in a mosaic of distinctive sub-regions. Recognizably Irish traits — mixed farming, gable chimney houses, and Catholic Church festivals — marked areas in which Irish settlers predominated; elsewhere, Highland place names, widespread use of the Gaelic language, and a concentration upon livestock rather than crop farming revealed Scottish Highland origins. There were even regional variations in the generic names assigned to physical features. Minor rivers, "brooks" in most of Maritime Canada, were (commonly) "creeks" in areas of Loyalist settlement; lowlying, seasonally-flooded riverine tracts were known in different parts of the provinces as "flats," "interval," or "bottom land;" and the "marshes" of some locales might be "lowlands" or "meadows" in others. In sum, separate traditions, distinct patterns of speech, and a considerable degree of group cohesion made the Maritimes in the pre-Confederation era a mosaic of identifiable communities.

Relative isolation and the influence of antecedent circumstances underlay this intricate pattern of Maritime sub-regions. Indeed, the most remote and self-contained communities were generally the most distinctive. During the nineteenth century, and especially after Confederation, improved communication allowed more integration among territories across the region. New characteristics were widely diffused and upheld beside older, essentially local, patterns and practices. Rarely did older traits disappear. But with time, regional contrasts were reduced. Paradoxically, the resulting sub-regions were at once less diverse and yet more difficult to decipher, as reflections of changing technology and fashion were melded with increasingly muted echoes of tradition into the complex landscapes of the late twentieth century.

Types of vernacular housing provide a useful key to these evolving patterns.[11] Although no common house types were exclusive to particular parts of the mid-century Maritimes, discernible regional variations in structural form did exist in the three provinces. Dwellings evoking their builders' previous homelands revealed the distribution of some immigrant groups: Scots in Pictou built stone houses in a form traditional in northern Britain; other Celts erected simple hall and parlour homes reminiscent of Irish and Highland peasant dwellings; Yorkshire immigrants in Chignecto emulated in local brick the substantial late eighteenth century houses typical of the Vale of York from whence they came; New Brunswick Loyalists copied the colonial (or Georgian) forms common in the American colonies they left; and New England immigrants introduced the Cape Cod cottage to Nova Scotia. Here the duplication of forms characteristic of antecedent hearths set a pattern. For the most part these were folk buildings; their design and construction were traditional.

In contrast, self-conscious responses to the dictates of popular taste were evident in the facades of many Maritime dwellings by 1850. Cape Cod cottages, expanded to full storey-and-a-half dimensions, carried a dormer in their roofs. The pitch and decoration of these dormers and their windows reflected the influence of prevailing fashion in the adjacent states. Classical proportions and trim echoed the Greek Revival in American architecture. Gothic treatments stated popular enthusiasm for the romantic revival of that mode fostered by American architects. Similarly, gable-fronted houses with neo-classical trim marked the spread of American inspiration into the Maritime provinces. Yet these influences were most obvious in those areas hard by the American border or flanking the sea routes to the New England states. Elsewhere the fusion of fashion with tradition was less apparent (Fig. 6.6).

In the century after Confederation, the convergence of material culture forms was more marked. With the exception of the hall and parlour house, which continued to be built on the fringes of settlement and in Acadian New Brunswick, folk-housing declined in importance as communication improved and the techniques of mass production superseded craft practices. Set designs, utilizing lumber of common specifications and capable of implementation in almost any setting, replaced the traditional forms of the eighteenth and early nineteenth centuries. Increasingly, the housing stock of the region came to resemble that of New England. By 1900 the townhouses of Saint John's Germain Street were strikingly similar to those built in Boston's inner suburbs during the 1870s. The mansions of the wealthy in Fredericton, Halifax, and Yarmouth, who built their fortunes on the expansion and reorientation of the regional economy in the last quarter of the nineteenth century, were virtually indistinguishable from many houses of similar vintage in

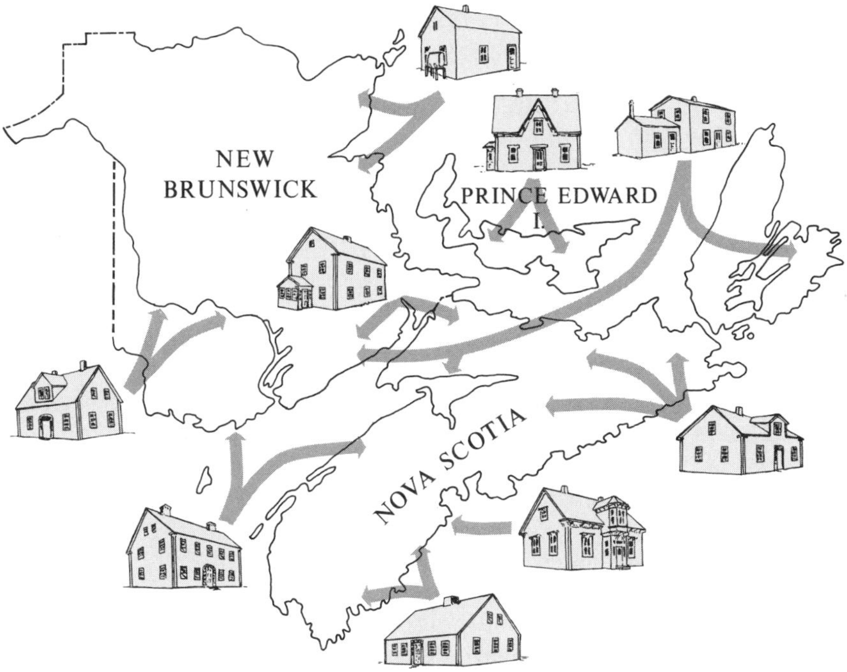

Figure 6.6 Regional distribution of vernacular housing types in the Maritimes.

the northeastern United States. Lower-middle class dwellings and workers' homes in Saint John, Amherst, and industrial Cape Breton differed little from their counterparts in Boston (or indeed from those across the continent in Vancouver a few years later).

In architecture, as in almost all facets of regional life, the impact of industrialism reduced local variety. As the region's landscapes reflected this transformation, an enormous range of folk traditions and regional habits was altered by improved communications, extended market connections, and increased geographical mobility. There is perhaps no more poignant expression of the pervasive impact of these changes than the following description of Neil's Harbour, a Cape Breton fishing village, in the 1950s:

> At four when the mail is sorted there's always a crowd in Alec's. This afternoon there was great excitement as well: [the] ... mail order catalogue ... arrived and every family got a copy of the Wish Book or Winter Bible .... Matt Clipper, his catalogue under his arm, left the store when I did. "I believe it's the catalogues that's causing all the trouble in the world," he said as we walked down the road together .... "People don't read their Boible no more at all, they just sets and

> pages through the catalogue. They sees all the foine things hinto it and wants to have 'em and if they can't get 'em they's full o' misery instead o' bein' happy off with what they has got."
>
> Matt jerked his head towards the houses of the village, "Women round 'ere ain't so much for style but young girls wants to wear thin stockings all through cold weather. They can't put nothing under 'em loike they should do and then they gits sick. . . . Terrible thing, ain't it? Never used to be loike that, it's just since the war. . . . Now seems loike everybody's just for their own self, tryin' to git something more out of the catalogue than the other feller's got." Matt opened his gate and started up his path where his little girls were playing. Seeing the catalogue under his arm, they ran to him and asked for it. He turned back to me, "You see," he said, "even children looks at catalogue and wants dolls when it ain't Christmas."[12]

In all its manifestations, this encroachment of late nineteenth and twentieth century materials, attitudes, and ideas upon older, more local ways of life has been a basic process in the shaping of the modern Maritime character.

Traditional Livelihoods Transformed

Established patterns of rural life broke down as the techniques, goods, and ideas of modern industrial society reached the region from continental and trans-Atlantic hearths. Redefining the nature and purpose of work, modernization undermined the traditional bases of rural settlement in the provinces. And as the scale and cost implications of these changes were felt, so family-centred independence (secured by the possession of one's own land, the provision of the bulk of one's needs, and freedom from onerous financial obligation) became increasingly difficult to realize in the post-Confederation period.

The gradual constriction of individual economic opportunity was apparent even before 1867. In northeastern New Brunswick's lumber industry, the capital costs of steam or large waterpowered sawmills, the financial requirements of remote lumbering ventures, and the demands of overseas markets combined to concentrate control of the industry in the hands of a few important entrepreneurs by mid-century.[13] With the growth of heavily capitalized lumbering operations, it became increasingly difficult for those with only strength and energy to gain an independent foothold in the trade. The cost of exploiting timber, often distant and inaccessible, raised the financial threshold of access to the forest. As early as the 1840s, protests lamented the difficulties this situation presented individuals — recent immigrants, farmers — obliged to work under contract to the leading merchants rather than in independent lumbering ventures. Elsewhere in the province, however, there were more opportunities for independent operations, a situation which continued into the 1860s. Lumbering provided settlers with an off-farm income during the slack months of winter, and allowed recent immigrants greater opportunity to accumulate the capital necessary to purchase farms.

Yet mechanization and specialization, coupled with a relative decline in the importance of lumbering and sawmilling in the regional economy of the twentieth century, reduced the lumber industry's role as a source of part-time employment and additional capital for settlers. The region's workforce became increasingly, if not exclusively, full-time and, working mainly for corporations and with corporate equipment, it became, in effect, an industrial working class or proletariat. To be sure, cordwood production from private woodlots remains an integral element of the region's pulp and paper industry even in the 1980s. In parts of New Brunswick and Nova Scotia it sustains a number of self-designated "farmers." Cordwood sales often constitute the major source of "farm" income, but sales are subject to sudden fluctuations in mill prices and demand. Moreover, there are capital costs — trucks, chainsaws — associated with all but the smallest woodlot operations. Wood prices, held down by the mechanized efficiency of large-scale production, are generally low. Individual returns are often small; today the part-time cordwood operation is a component of economic marginality as often as it provides, or contributes to, an adequate subsistence.

Budworm infestation also threatens these enterprises and the industry in general. The result has been controversy. For sixteen years after 1952 New Brunswick sprayed its forests with DDT in an effort to control the budworm; when this insecticide was banned, chemical larvicides were substituted and remained in use into the 1980s, despite rising concern about their effects on the health of children. Small gains were made by a vigorous lobby of concerned parents in the 1970s: the times and places of aerial spraying are now indicated in advance, and it is agreed that planes should stay away from settlements. Still the infestation remains, and some contend that chemical intervention has only prolonged a problem whose solution lies in less clearcut logging (which encourages the growth of the balsam fir favoured by the budworm) and better silvicultural practice. Spraying is, at best, a short-term palliative; forest management may be a long-term remedy, but the former has been favoured by the industry and the government because it reduces logging costs and saves trees for immediate use. As recently as 1982, however, members of the New Brunswick Federation of Woodlot Owners (who supply approximately a quarter of the province's pulpwood) adopted an anti-spray resolution and recommended the development of a more diverse mixed-species forest. Allied problems surround the use of herbicides to destroy young hardwoods and encourage the softwoods required by the mills. Both 2, 4, 5-T and 2, 4-D (Agent Orange) have been used on the forests of Nova Scotia and New Brunswick in recent years. Individuals and community groups have objected, but control remains with the large, integrated producers and government bureaucrats who are battling with the issue of short-term gain versus ecological balance.

Thus the forest industry has been marked by increasing capitalization on the one hand, and growing marginality on the other. These parallel tendencies have also transformed agriculture in the Maritime Provinces, especially since 1945. Twenty acres [8 to 10 hectares] was enough cleared land for a farmer working with axe, hoe, and ox–drawn implements, when the primary goal was to feed and clothe a family. With perhaps 10 to 15 acres [4 to 6 hectares] of rough pasture, and 15 to 20 acres [6 to 8 hectares] of woodland, a 50–acre [21–hectare] holding offered a comfortable life by mid–nineteenth century standards. But changing values and falling returns gradually undermined the viability of most small family farms in the Maritimes. Those on thin upland soils were first to succumb, while in more fertile lowland areas small mixed farms continued to occupy and sustain many families even until the 1950s. Improved communication — exemplified by the mail order catalogue — brought mass–produced goods into largely self–sufficient communities at prices that made home production unnecessary. Western meat and flour replaced home–barrelled pork and family–harvested grains on farm tables; rising costs of production and competition in local markets kept farm incomes low; long hours of work and lives with few modern amenities appeared less attractive; sons and daughters, if not their parents, left rural life for the cash incomes and apparent attractions of city life.

Specialization and commercialization have drastically altered the nature of agriculture for those who remain on the land. In the nineteenth century, farm ownership was an attainable goal. Modest, landed independence was within reach of the common family when farming was unmechanized and its main purpose was subsistence. But in recent decades specialized commercial agriculture has brought soaring costs. Land costs have increased and specialization has often necessitated heavy investment in buildings and machinery. With steady improvement in farm technology, farmers have had to purchase new equipment and/or enlarge their operations with increasing frequency to remain competitive. Operating costs have escalated with the shift from animal to mechanical power and increased off–farm purchases of feed, fertilizers, fuel, and pesticide.

Together, these changes have multiplied the difficulties of farm financing. Mortgage debt has increased, and short–term credit is a common necessity. An analysis of potato farming — among the most profitable of Maritime agricultural enterprises — undertaken in the 1960s reveals the general pattern. Late in that decade, 160 acres [65 hectares] of cropland was optimal for potato farming in New Brunswick. The capital cost of such a farm — allowing $150 an acre for land, $42 000 for farm buildings and $40 000 for equipment (including two tractors, a harvester, and planters, sprayers and cultivators) — was $106 000. Annual expenditures amounted to some $33 000. Cropping inputs accounted for the largest part of this total. Seed potatoes cost the farmer $5000; fertilizer, applied at a ton per acre to the thin, long-cropped soils in the sloping fields of Carleton and Victoria counties, cost over $6000; spraying to reduce weeds and against blight required a further $1800. The necessary hired hand earned $3000. Seasonal workers, employed to cut seed, to harvest, and to grade and load the crop, raised labour inputs to $7800. Machinery and equipment costs, including depreciation, exceeded $6000. Miscellaneous expenditures such as building depreciation, repairs and insurance, taxes, utility costs, and interest charged on loans to cover cropping inputs amounted to an approximately equivalent sum. At year's end, the net income of an enterprise of this size was $12 000 or $13 000. Allowing a 6 percent return on capital, the farmer's labour income was no more than $8500. Today costs and returns are greater, but the farmer's real income is no larger.

The experience of Brewster and Cathie Keen, of Pictou County, Nova Scotia, summarizes the circumstances confronting many of the region's remaining small farmers in the mid–1980s.

> We're managing a unit that's as large as can be managed as a family unit, and we're not doing the kind of job that we'd like to be doing with it. We're using 12-year-old machinery which has to be kept going because there's simply not enough income to replace it. This means you take care of it — which is good — but you can't use it as you might, and you haven't got the resources to match things up better.[14]

Confronted by rising interest rates and escalating costs in recent years, many farmers have abandoned agriculture. Smaller, less efficient producers moved into nearby towns, leaving the land to deteriorate and buildings to decay. Others remained in the countryside but produced little and faced poverty. In such agriculturally marginal areas as northeastern New Brunswick (Fig. 6.7) — which was said in the 1960s to have only enough good land for 100 viable commercial farms — small, crowded, poorly serviced houses, dilapidated barns, broken fences, and overgrown pastures are graphic testimony to the poverty that was a common result.

In better areas, small farmers were able to sell their properties to large, integrated agri-businesses. Yet others endeavoured to alleviate financial problems by sowing specified crops under contract to corporate buyers (Fig. 6.8). McCain Foods of Florenceville, New Brunswick, for example, is now a multinational corporation, marketing frozen french fries, vegetables, pies, pizzas, and other food products in ten countries, as well as controlling fertilizer, cold storage, transport, and other industries, not to mention thousands of acres of farmland in New Brunswick. The smaller C.M. McLean Company on Prince Edward Island has also increased its land-holdings by purchasing family farms, and has 200 potato growers under annual contract. Reflecting the essentially industrial

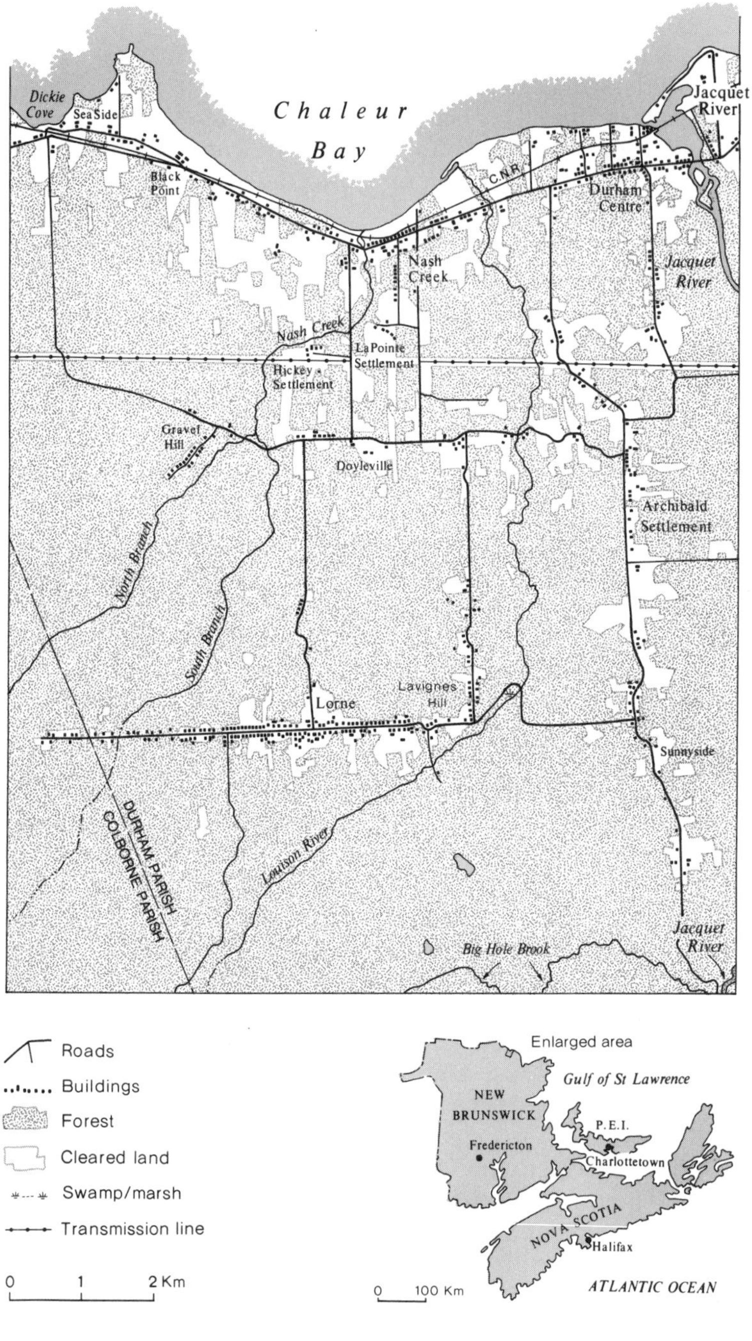

Figure 6.7 Marginal farming and agricultural settlement along Chaleur Bay in northeastern New Brunswick.

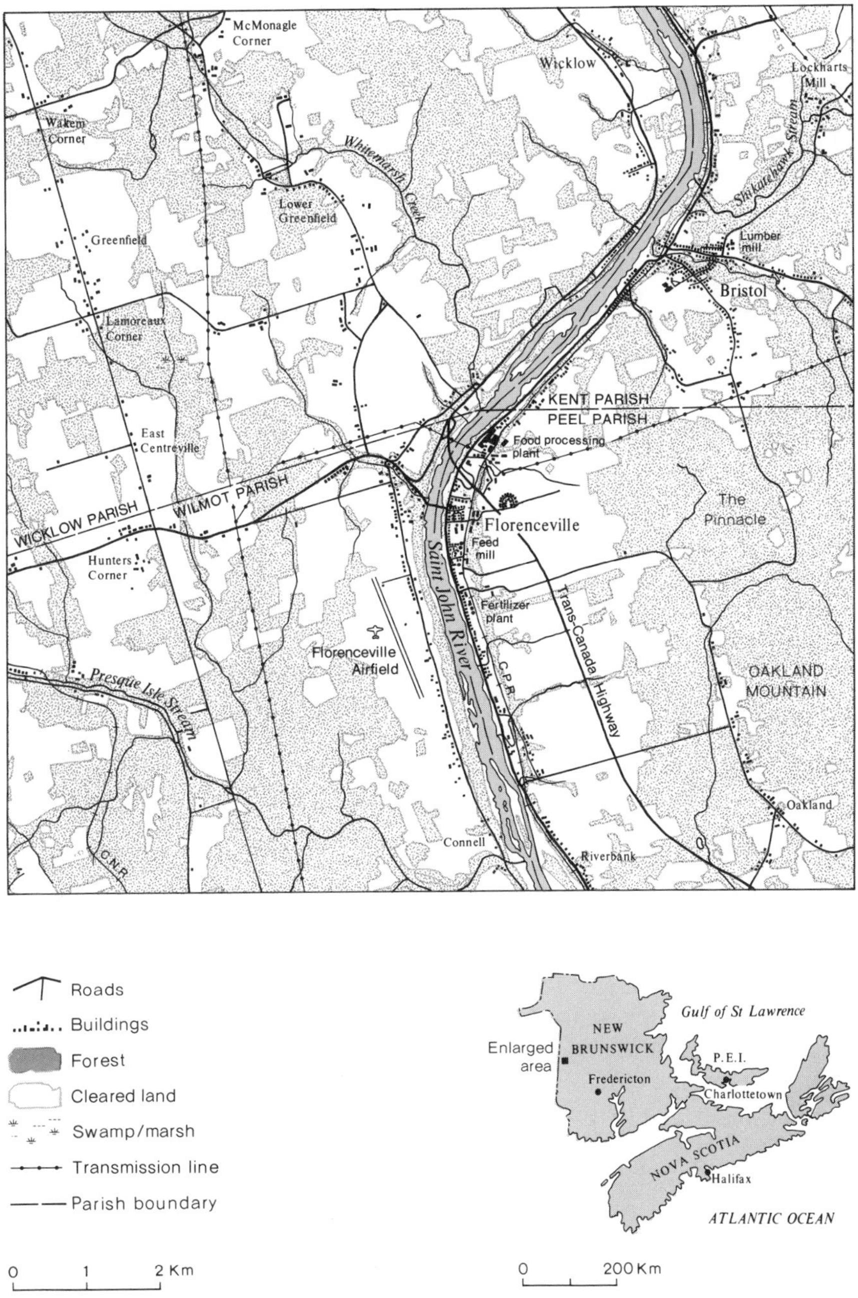

Figure 6.8 Potato farming and agricultural settlement in the Florenceville area, Saint John River Valley, New Brunswick.

A marginal farm in northeastern New Brunswick: The owners of this part-time farming operation also make a living by fishing and cutting pulp wood. (*Larry McCann*)

cast of its operations, the firm holds an annual banquet for its growers and offers premiums for productivity.

The fishery faced changes similar to those that transformed agriculture. In the nineteenth century, fisheries depended upon wood, wind, and human effort; in the twentieth, traditional whalers, dories, and schooners were challenged inshore by motor–driven Cape Island boats and offshore by steam trawlers. Fishermen's protests, and a government ban on further development of the trawler fleet in 1930, allowed diesel–powered schooners to continue hauling long–line trawls on offshore banks into the 1960s; but otter–trawlers, working from side or stern and equipped with electronic navigation and fish–finding gear, have swept them from the seas in the last 20 years. Deckhands in these modern vessels, holding no share in the boat or its gear, are paid according to the catch. In the mid–1970s, a fisherman who spent 200 to 240 days at sea (during which he might work 3500 hours in all weather) on a side–trawler earned $6000 to $8250; for 250 days at sea on a stern–trawler, he might have expected $9400 to $12 000. Data collected for the Kirby Task Force on Atlantic Fisheries (1982) show that the average full–time fisherman earns $11 907 annually. Highliners — the top 10 percent of income earners — made net incomes of $23 350 or more. In a few rich fishing areas such as Cape Sable Island, incomes of over $40 000 are not uncommon. Still, one–third of the households of full–time fishermen (about 8000) have total incomes below Canada's official rural poverty line.

In the offshore fishery, capital has replaced labour; technology has superseded lore. Steel stern–trawlers, operating from a few ports in which processing facilities are concentrated, bring in 180 000 kilograms of iced ground fish after 12 or 14 days at sea. Both vessels and freezing plants are owned by large organizations which control all facets of the trade from catching to marketing. Among them, National Sea Products of Halifax and H.B. Nickerson and Sons Ltd. of North Sydney (now corporately merged) are the regional leaders. The former, with some 50 vessels serving its 14 processing plants in Atlantic Canada (and selling internationally under the brand name "High Liner") was the country's largest–volume fish processing firm in the 1980s. Despite the increasing cost of operating large modern fishing vessels, representatives of the integrated firms insist that sophisticated new freezer trawlers are essential if the opportunities presented by the 200–mile limit are to be realized. Such expansion would further concentrate ownership in, and control of, the fishery. It will also be resisted by inshore fishermen who fear elimination of the remaining small, seasonal processing plants, and depletion of inshore fish stocks by increased offshore catches.

The balance between inshore and offshore fisheries is still debated. Corporate representatives argue that federal quota policies favoured inshoremen through much of the 1970s and 1980s. Certainly some 7500 of Nova Scotia's 10 500 fishermen work inshore. But this proportion has been falling. While early in this century inshoremen outnumbered deep sea fishermen 8 to 1, in 1982 the estimated ratio is 1 to 3. In the 1880s

Lunenburg, Nova Scotia: Lunenburg, a fishing settlement since the mid-eighteenth century, is the site of the National Seafood Products' off-shore trawler fleet and eastern Canada's largest fish processing plant. (*Larry McCann*)

when employment in the provincial fishery peaked at 30 000, the vast majority worked local waters from the hundreds of small, often isolated, settlements scattered along Atlantic, Gulf, and Fundy shores. In the nineteenth century, sales of dried cod fish and of bait to offshore dorymen complemented returns from small farm holdings to provide a simple, if hard-won, subsistence. But the foundations of this existence were gradually eroded. By World War I, newly established freezing plants were centralizing the bait industry. The new fresh fish industry was tied to ports (such as Halifax and Mulgrave) with direct rail access to central Canada. Salt fish markets declined precipitously before World War II. Even in the late 1920s, a Royal Commission investigating the fishery heard of "aging men, discarded gear, abandoned fishing vessels and of fishermen who seemed to have lost the will and the spirit to put to sea."[15]

During the 1930s, the Antigonish Movement spawned a number of fishermen's cooperatives,[16] and local fish buyers and processors sought new markets in an effort to alleviate growing hardship in the small fishing communities. But the most radical impact of changed circumstances upon the inshore fishery came in the 1950s. Larger vessels appeared. Intermediate in size and technology between Banks trawlers and half-decked boats, these 60 foot [18 metre] long-liners, wooden-hulled draggers, and seiners were capable of working longer seasons and in wider areas than those formerly fished by inshoremen. Independently owned by their skippers, these vessels employed crews of three to five. But as long-liners cost between $200 000 and $300 000, very few traditional inshoremen became owners. Spending 60 to 100 days a year at sea on a long-liner in the mid-1970s, a fisherman without a share in the vessel might have earned about $6000.

Today, ownership of a diesel-driven Cape Island or Northumberland Strait boat provides inshoremen more independence but no greater income. Used for lobstering, long-lining, seining, handlining, and gill netting, these versatile 30 to 50 foot [9 to 15 metre] boats are common in the region. Their crews of one or two put out with the dawn and return before nightfall, to sell their catch to buyers at the wharves or to the local fishplants. But returns are low. Two or three months of lobster catching might produce $4000 to $4500. Handlining during the remainder of the nine-month season, in which it is possible to fish from small boats, might yield approximately the same sum. The common practice of combining inshore and offshore work provides additional income. Fishermen's unemployment benefits carry families through the seasonally imposed idleness of winter. But in fishing as in farming communities, the availability of canned and frozen foods and the attractions of modern consumer goods have altered traditional self-reliance.

Coupled with the generally low financial returns from "the hardest life by which men still earn their daily bread,"[17] the impact of modernity has undermined the fisherman's traditional livelihood and fostered frustration and restlessness in the region's small fishing communities. Today, dwellings still cling to the shore in fishing settlements such as those in the Ragged Islands area of southern Nova Scotia (Fig. 6.9). But kitchen gardens and small fields beyond are no longer productive of basic necessities. Houses that sheltered generations of fishermen and their families are now summer places for distant urbanites. And beyond such centres as Lockeport there are generally few obvious signs of the fishery; perhaps a small wharf or two; a few boats, moored or drawn up on the beach; and lobster pots stacked on the strand.

In sum, industrialization has transformed Maritime Canada's traditional industries. In lumbering, farming, and fishing, expensive machinery has replaced manual labour; sophisticated technology has superseded local knowledge. The capital costs of large-scale production have drastically reduced prospects of independent ownership. Wages and contracts have imposed a set structure where before there was at least the illusion of freedom to work when and as intensively as one wished. Fishermen, who once shared their profits with crews of kith and kin, now resemble wage-workers in other industries. Divorcing home and work to the extreme, full-time trawler workers spend twelve of every fourteen days away from their families. Lumberers, who once set out with sons and brothers to fell tall pines in the vicinity of their homes, now denude acres of company-controlled forest during a 40-hour work week spent in the cab of a wheeled skidder or Beloit harvester. Farms on which parents and children followed the oxplough and adapted to the rhythm of the seasons, are now mechanically sown with crops specified by marketing agencies or multinational corporations.

All of these developments have had a profound effect on the regional consciousness of the Maritimes. There is a sense of isolation and intrusion — a feeling that machines have come between the people and their environment and that the decisions of remote and anonymous authorities have impinged upon local life. The changes have reached deep into the texture of rural life.What price the dory fisherman's slowly acquired and intimate knowledge of local seas and skies in all their moods, when radar, sonar, and decca navigators find fish and port in the foulest weather? How common now the farmer's satisfaction that his land "Fits . . . [him] loose and easy, like . . . [his] old clothes"? How rare the comforting reflection: "That rock there is one my father rolled out, and my son's sons will look at these rocks I am rolling out today"?[18]

Urban Patterns

Both portent and instrument of the wider transformation of life within the region, urbanization added further diversity to Maritime society. In the 1860s, small towns dominated the urban pattern. Despite their basic dependence upon external connections for credit, markets,

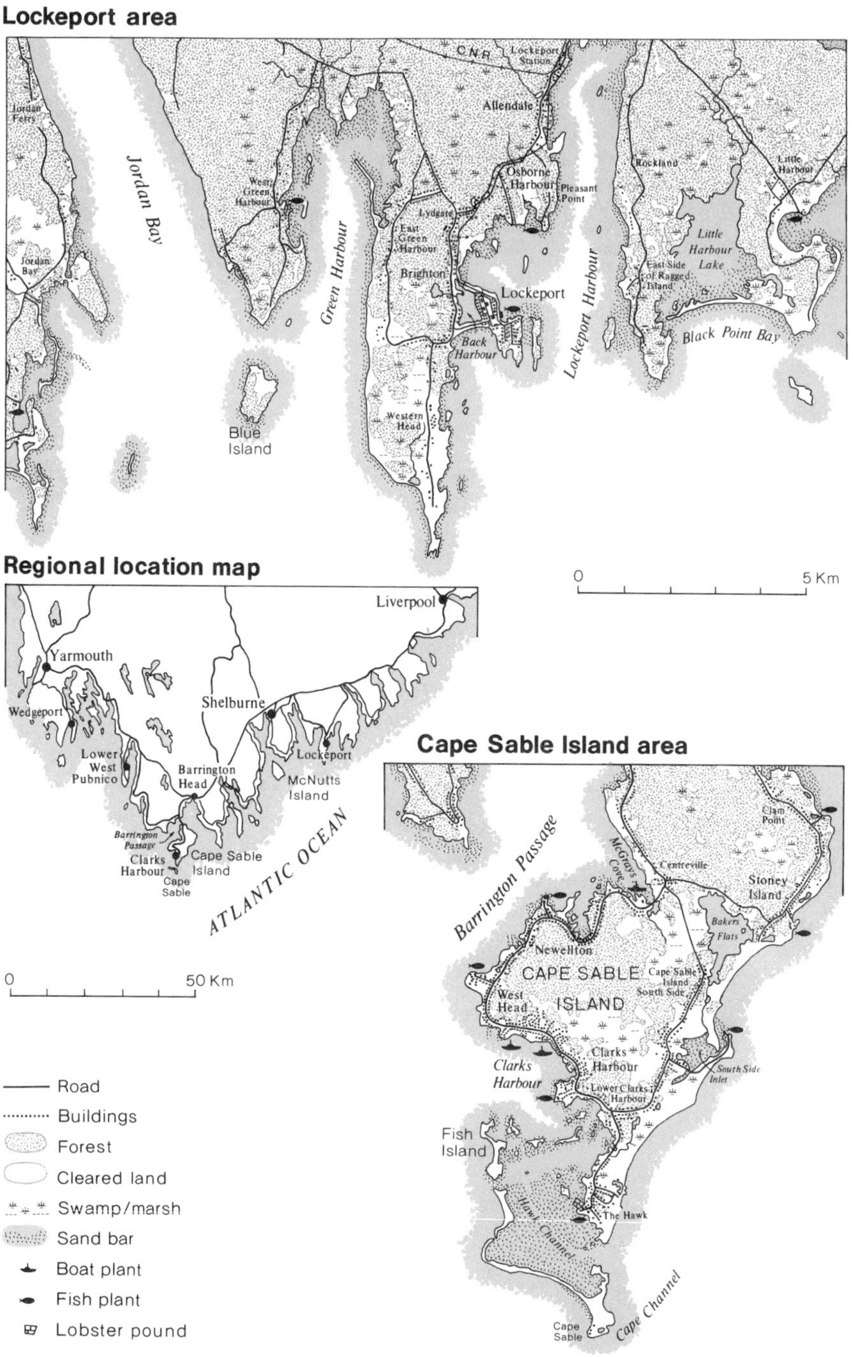

Figure 6.9 Cape Sable Island and Lockeport: fishing communities in southwestern Nova Scotia.

news, and supplies, there was a profoundly local cast to life in these settlements. Town merchants exchanged imported goods for the produce of fields and forests. The smithy, the mill, and the church served the town and its immediate surroundings. However brief, the frequent and repeated contact among town residents reinforced familiarity and a sense of local autonomy. Place and position incorporated families into these communities. Slightly larger centres, such as St. Stephen and Yarmouth, important for lumbering and shipbuilding, had more extensive external links, but differed from their smaller counterparts in degree rather than in kind.

Even in the mid-nineteenth century, Halifax and Saint John were places apart. With populations of some 25 000 and 30 000 they were diverse agglomerations of individuals from many backgrounds, and the lives of most of their inhabitants were correspondingly anonymous. Commercial importance, and in Saint John nascent industrial development, quickened the tempo of life in these cities. And their townscapes revealed wide disparities in the economic and social circumstances of their inhabitants. Prosperous merchants occupied fine, large houses. Behind the wharves, the shipyards, and the sawmills, clustered an urban working class of recent immigrants and native sons with few skills and little capital. Craft workers, artisans, small business operators, and professionals added further dimensions to these socially differentiated and spatially segregated urban societies. Yet shipyards and sawmills apart, large industrial establishments were uncommon in these ports; workshops and manufacturers with annual payrolls of only a few hundred dollars were more typical. If clocks rather than the sun dictated the work discipline of Halifax and Saint John life, these places maintained many ties with their rural hinterlands. Lumberers came to Saint John from the New Brunswick interior to acquire their supplies and to sell their cut; hay and produce markets brought farmers into both cities; garden plots and livestock were part of the urban scene.

Increasing urbanization in the 1880s built on this essentially pre-industrial foundation. New manufacturers, established under the stimulus of the National Policy, located in many of the region's scattered urban centres. Halifax and Saint John led the way; industrial capital investment in both ports more than doubled in ten years; and by 1890 industrial output exceeded $8 000 000 in each city. But the growth rates of smaller places with underdeveloped manufacturing bases in 1880 were even more spectacular. Industrial output in New Glasgow and Yarmouth increased almost five-fold; in Amherst and Milltown-St. Stephen it almost tripled. In all of these centres, the new or expanded sugar refineries, cotton mills, rope works, foundries, and machine shops were local enterprises initiated and financed by entrepreneurs from the community. In Halifax, for example, a committee of merchants trading with the West Indies convinced city business people to invest $500 000 in subscriptions of

$10 000 to $20 000 to establish a sugar refinery. In Yarmouth, three textile firms, two foundries, and a furniture factory were financed by community entrepreneurs. Moncton residents subscribed almost $1 000 000 for the development of manufacturing and utility plants in their town. Citizens of New Glasgow held more than two-thirds of the capital stock in the Nova Scotia Steel Company at its formation in 1882.

By 1900, however, chronic undercapitalization (for most of the new enterprises depended on short-term loans for operating capital), the competitive advantages of central Canadian producers in the expanding national economy, and the rise of the stock market as an instrument of financial organization had led to the transfer of control in most of the region's manufacturing to distant metropolitan interests. With this shift came remote authority. As share certificates held by strangers replaced the investment of neighbours and friends in regional manufacturing, so managers with "neither a communal nor a vocational interest" in the enterprises gained control of their operations.[19] With the ties between economic power and personal reputation in the community broken, the employer's sense of paternalistic responsibility for employees declined. Improvements in communication and increases in the scale of production also encouraged a more impersonal labour market. Jobs were less secure. Wage rates declined and layoffs were not uncommon during downturns in the business cycle. Mechanization gradually eliminated skilled workers (from tailors to sawyers) in many traditional crafts and cyclical unemployment and social distress became more apparent.

The impact of these changes varied by industry and location across the region. Yet the pattern is clear. Traditional and labour-intensive urban trades were less affected by the transfer of control than by mechanization and competition. Employment in the trades fell dramatically as new materials superseded old, and as mass-produced goods from central Canada entered the Maritime market. Between 1880 and 1930, the number of seamstresses, tailors, clothiers, dressmakers, and milliners in the region declined from 6818 to 2394; in Halifax alone, employment in these same trades dropped from 1000 to 212. By 1931, cabinet and furniture makers were barely a fifth as numerous as in 1881; coopers, 1500 strong in 1881, numbered only 580 fifty years later. In short, small manufacturing shops, with masters, apprentices, and journeymen working alongside each other at common tasks, became less typical. Counter to this decline ran the development of new industries. Many of them processed staples and were located in the smaller towns of the region. There were larger enterprises, employing many hands but offering few opportunities for traditional skills. The displaced rural folk and the redundant trades people, who acquired new machine-minding skills or became labourers in the new plants, encountered a work environment governed by contracts and wages. Part of a growing urban working class in the region, they gradually recognized the need for collective action to defend their interests and improve their economic position.

The changing geography of Amherst, Nova Scotia, demonstrates the local implications of this transformation. Hard by the New Brunswick border, pre-Confederation Amherst was a small rural service centre, one of a hundred similar towns in the region. In the 1860s, as in the 1830s,

> [It was] the little focus of attraction for the good people who inhabit[ed] the numerous farm houses . . . spread over the country in every direction around. Here the store (shop) of the petty merchant open[ed] its doors to invite the purchase of a new hat, or a shawl for the "mistress," with the proceeds netted on the last month's drove of cattle . . . Here, too, the everlasting din of blacksmith's anvil, or less noisy operation of the saw and plane, attest[ed] alike the many wants of neighbouring agriculturists, and the encouragement offered to industrious mechanics.[20]

In 1871, the combined value of Amherst manufacturing was less than $750 000. During the 1870s, however, the Intercolonial Railroad was laid through the town. New accessibility stimulated expansion; incorporation followed; industrialization proceeded; and the multiplier effects of new construction sustained an appreciable economic boom. In all of this, developments in Amherst paralleled those in other towns along the Intercolonial — Moncton, Truro, New Glasgow — where production was aimed at national markets under the protection of federal tariffs. By 1910, Amherst was home to 10 000 people, many of them migrants from other parts of Nova Scotia; among the newcomers were some 500 blacks, who had come from Halifax to work in the town's foundries.

Amherst's rapidly evolving townscape reflected these changed circumstances. Large, utilitarian industrial buildings spread out along the periphery of the old town centre. New housing for factory workers — cottages plainly and quickly built, modest in size, and unpretentious in appearance — stood close by. There was little variety in the industrial vernacular styles or the setback of the dwellings to integrate the streetscapes. Across town and across the Intercolonial tracks stood more genteel neighbourhoods with large ornate houses on expansive lots reflecting the social division of the community.

In the first years of the twentieth century, a dozen Amherst industries employed some 4000 people. Manufacturing output, $1 500 000 in 1900, was thrice that by 1905; suddenly Amherst ranked in the top quartile of Canadian manufacturing towns. Shoes, suitcases, pianos, textiles, foundry goods, electric engines, generating equipment, and railway cars were among the products of its plants. Local leaders directed the industrial community. Nathaniel Curry and Nelson Rhodes, for example, returned after working in the United States to establish a small woodworking firm in Amherst in 1877. A rolling mill, an axle factory, and a railroad car plant were added to their inventory in the following decade, and in 1893 they acquired the Harris Car Works and Foundry of Saint John. At its incorporation in 1902, Rhodes, Curry and Company (among the largest secondary iron manufacturers in Canada) employed some 1300 workers and turned out 20 railway cars a day. The Robb Engineering Works was

Workplace and working-class housing in "Busy Amherst." (*Graeme Wynn*)

likewise the product of local initiative. Trained as an engineer in the United States, David Robb turned his father's Amherst foundry to the manufacture of precision machinery and employed 300–400 skilled workers before 1914.

Yet even by 1910, this local leadership was being replaced by outside control. Within 15 years, the expansion and prosperity of the previous decade had passed into decline and depression. In 1909, the Rhodes, Curry enterprise was amalgamated with two Montréal firms to form the Canadian Car and Foundry Company. Orchestrated by stock promoter Max Aitken through his Montréal-based Royal Securities Corporation, this lucrative merger placed control of the Amherst plant in central Canadian hands; within a few years aspects of production were phased out of the Nova Scotia plant. Fearing the development of a monopoly in railroad car production, Halifax interests quickly took over Amherst's second car manufacturer, the Silliker Company. Fears of growing national centralization were borne out. In 1921, the Canadian Car and Foundry Company consolidated its operations in Montréal and Fort William, closing its Amherst plant.

Product obsolescence, created by rapid advances in the technology of electricity generation, and the collapse of wartime demand for marine engines and munitions, forced Robb Engineering to retool after 1918. An arrangement to supply precision parts for kerosene-powered tractors built and assembled by the Dominion Bridge Company failed as tariff protection was removed and as railroad freight rates increased in 1921. A new line of mining machinery did not sell because of economic difficulties in the region's coal industry. Employment in the Robb works was down to

50 by 1926, when David Robb merged his Amherst operations with his Massachusetts based International Engineering Works and became managing director of the American concern. During the economically difficult early 1920s, Stanfields of Truro, which controlled the Amherst textile plant, closed down its looms. With employment dropping, hardship grew. Amherst's residents joined the exodus of the 1920s. By 1931 the town's population was down to 7450 and many of those who remained lived in poverty.

Dissatisfied with inflation, working conditions, and unsympathetic employers, Amherst workers formed the Amherst Federation of Labour in November 1918 to seek improvement. In May of 1919, a general strike brought all but two of the town's industries to a standstill.[21] This unprecedented industrial action stemmed from the Canadian Car and Foundry Company's refusal to pay its Amherst workers at the same rate as its Montréal employees. It also reinforced common demands for recognition of the union, an 8–hour day, and better working conditions in the town's factories. After three weeks of rallies and accusations, acceptable concessions were won in some industries and the labourers returned to work. The material gains of concerted industrial action were small, however. Plant closures, the product of consolidation and regional

A substantial residence of Amherst's elite. (*Larry McCann*)

Industrial Cape Breton: Company housing stands adjacent to the steel works in the Whitney Pier area of Sydney, Nova Scotia. (*Larry McCann*)

economic recession, followed almost immediately. Less tangible consequences — a dawning consciousness of labour as a class, its sense of potential power, recognition of the regional implications of growing economic concentration in central Canada — were ultimately more significant influences on the lives of Maritime workers.

Parallel developments shaped economy and society in industrial Cape Breton. Exploited on a small scale through the nineteenth century, the Cape Breton coalfield became the focus of rapid urban and industrial growth in the 1890s. The population of Cape Breton County doubled, and its urban component increased dramatically as steel plants were established and new mines were opened up. In the 20 years after 1891, the population of Sydney increased more than sevenfold; that of Glace Bay rose almost as sharply. Inevitably, the majority of people in these mushrooming towns were recent immigrants. They were drawn from three sources: the farms and fishing villages of Cape Breton; the British Isles; and other, mainly rural areas of the Maritimes and Newfoundland. Among paternal grandparents of New Waterford residents of the 1960s, only 14 percent were born in industrial Cape Breton; 30 percent came from rural Cape Breton; 15 percent were born elsewhere in Atlantic Canada; and 31 percent claimed British birth. In the coalfield as a whole before 1914, over a third, perhaps 40 percent, of the mineworkers were immigrants to Canada. Native-born Nova Scotians, over 90 percent of the provincial population in 1911, comprised only 65 to 80 percent of those in the mining towns. Yet "Scottishness" — cultural descent from the nineteenth century Highland migration to Cape Breton, vitalized by the influx of miners from Scotland's declining pits — was a distinctive characteristic of these settlements. Over half the people in the towns of Dominion and Reserve claimed Scottish descent in 1921; elsewhere more than 40 percent did so.

For most turn-of-the-century residents of industrial Cape Breton, circumstances were much different from those they had known before their migration. The contrast in its extreme form was echoed in the laments of Gaelic poets, urging their compatriots to return to their farms:

> Oh, isn't it a shame for a healthy Gael living in this place to be a slave from Monday to Saturday under the heels of tyrants, when he could be happy on a handsome spreading farm. . . . [doing] clean work on the surface of the earth, rather than in the black pit of misery.[22]

For the children of crowded and over-cropped hill farms, it was all but impossible to go back to the land. Yet recollections of rural life formed a standard against which existence in Sydney and the mining communities was measured. Certainly, work underground was hard and dangerous. One recent immigrant to Canada told the Royal Commission investigating the mining industry in 1925:

> You work four times harder here in eight hours than you would do in the country I come from. . . . and when you come home from your work you are so darned tired that you cannot hold the children to crawl on your knee you are so sore.[23]

Until 1920, skilled miners had to shove boxes of coal along narrow uneven seams to the mine's larger roadways. It was draining physical labour that reduced their daily output of coal. Before 1914, the fatality rate in the mines was three times as high, per capita, as in Britain. Major disasters in 1917 and 1918 killed 153 workers; between 1871 and 1939, 1600 died in Nova Scotia coal mines. Work discipline in the mines was, however, less rigorous than in many industrial enterprises. Until the introduction of mechanized long-wall mining in the late 1920s, Cape Breton coal mining was labour-intensive and decentralized. Small groups worked at scattered coal face locations; drivers and roadmakers moved through the mines' room-and-pillar geometries; supervisors could not maintain unbroken vigil. Miners had their own conception of a "normal day's work;" labourers broke from their tasks to gather in conversation; they felt their interdependence. Perhaps a third of the miners worked on contract, paid by the ton, rather than by the day, for the coal they mined; occasional "Blue Mondays" punctuated the long weeks of work. The miners had a strong sense of independence, but even contract miners were far from being completely independent. They relied on the mine's steam supply to drive their equipment; they depended on the operator's equitable allowances for variations in geology, drainage, access, and seam thickness in the mines. Collective action was essential to the defence of their individual interests. The mines forged a strong sense of working class solidarity.

Living conditions reinforced the workers' communal consciousness. Shared grievances, the socio-economic homogeneity of the mining towns, and the common dependence upon a single industry fostered local identity. Settlements — despite the incoherence of their townscapes straggling along badly rutted streets between pit heads and town centres — were relatively permanent focal points for the exploitation of submarine seams. Many families had relatives on the coalfield. Migrants from familiar rural communities, fellow Scots, and work mates strengthened connections. Poor housing offered a common cause for protest. Many of the 3500 or so dwellings erected and owned by the coal operators were in need of repair. Cold and damp were common; rain funnelled through ill-fitting doors and cracks in the walls. In 1920, a Royal Commission reported that "the housing, domestic surroundings and sanitary conditions of the miners are, with few exceptions, absolutely wretched."[24]

Five years later, many families still occupied houses too small for their needs, with neither kitchen, cellar, nor sewer. Others lived in temporary shacks, converted to year-round use after being abandoned by workers opening up new mines. Several houses lacked piped water. Low wages limited the miners' abilities to repair their homes, or to seek better accommodation. Early in this century, most miners earned enough to either feed their families or pay general expenses (heat, light, water, clothing, boots) but not to do both. In July 1920, when the *Labour Gazette* estimated food costs for a family of five at $17.09 a week, a surface labourer earned a bare $18.20, while miners paid by the day received $25.00 a week. Only the wages of well-paid contract miners (perhaps $36.00 a week) were sufficient to support a family. In these circumstances, "clothes and shoes went unbought, debts mounted at the company stores [and] bread and molasses or 'potatoes and point' were staple foods."[25] Moreover, infant mortality rates were two or three times the national average.

When recession hit the coal and steel industry in the early 1920s, the miners' union was determined to maintain the economic advantage conferred by a falling cost of living and it resisted company efforts to cut wages by 35 percent. Through the ensuing strikes, Cape Breton's industrial workers united against "the tyranny of capital" in the coal industry. Rejecting private ownership of the mines — as did miners in Britain and America — the cohesive and increasingly radical coalfield communities advocated social control of the industry. Labour poet Dawn Fraser captured the prevailing mood:

> But today it is apparent
> That the Bosses's day is done.
> When I hear the mighty unions
> Proclaim the rights of man,
> and I see the groups endorsing
> The co-operative plan;
> When no more will rank injustice,
> Sustained by greed and lies,
> March boldly down the highway
> Garbed as "free enterprise."[26]

Following the closure of less productive mines, as well as the introduction of shorter shifts in 1924, the cancellation of credit at company stores finally provoked a five-month strike in 1925. Poverty and hardship were widespread; many families left the region. Both the union and the coal industry were severely weakened: through the 1930s, the former was ineffective; the latter's decline continued, despite the replacement of Besco, the British Empire Steel Corporation, with a Canadian corporation and despite government aid to the industry after 1927. This was a struggle without victors. But, a sturdy working-class culture was forged in industrial Cape Breton. This culture, based on opposition to industrial exploitation, shaped the values and sustained the spirit of the region's people through years of depression and war. Weakened since the 1950s by renewed out-migration and a declining oral tradition, but still heard in the affection Cape Bretonners have for their island, this spirit turns on memories of a troubled heritage and resentment of what is viewed as sustained external exploitation.

In the mid-1960s, the problems of external control surfaced once again. Confronting the continued unprofitability of both steel and coal industries, the Dominion Steel and Coal Company (Dosco, which succeeded Besco in 1930 and subsequently became a subsidiary of Hawker Siddeley Canada Ltd.) decided to pull out of both sectors. Redundancy threatened almost 10 000 workers. To ease the consequences of Dosco's decision, its operations were taken over by Crown corporations in the mid-1960s. The federal Cape Breton Development Corporation (Devco) assumed responsibility for the mines; the provincial Sydney Steel Corporation (Sysco) took over the mill. In subsequent years, both the steel and coal industries declined. Sysco's debts mounted. By the mid-1970s, the corporation's losses exceeded $40 million a year; from a 1973 peak of 3500, its workforce fell by a thousand in five years. Employment in the coal industry declined by half in the decade after 1967.

Yet, improvement marked the late 1970s. Despite large annual losses, Sysco fired a new blast furnace and negotiated new long-term sales agreements beyond the region. Upgraded mining operations returned a profit for the first time in decades. Moreover, there were important initiatives in other facets of the Cape Breton economy. Devco's efforts — usually unsuccessful — to provide work for redundant miners by offering grants and subsidies to attract large industries, led to the encouragement of indigenous entrepreneurship and small-scale manufacturing. New plants produced products ranging from ornamental welding to previously imported machinery. Fishery- and marine-related activities were fostered. The rural economy was stimulated by incentives offered to sheep farmers (a once important but long neglected element of local agriculture) and the development of bed-and-breakfast accommodation in Island homes (allowing residents to supplement their incomes without large capital investment and the problems of seasonal use that beset more conventional provisions for the tourist trade). These were significant efforts to turn an economy long dominated by a single industrial complex oriented to external markets into one using diverse local resources to yield considerably more general prosperity and self-reliance. But economic downturn, a conflagration that closed one of the area's pits, and the destruction of a Glace Bay fish plant by fire, pushed unemployment in industrial Cape Breton to excessively high levels in the mid-1980s. This scarred industrial area remains a major centre of economic and social hardship in the Maritime provinces (Fig. 6.10).

Since 1970, Halifax and Saint John have been centres of considerable growth. With rapidly expanding service and construction sectors, they have attracted migrants from the declining urban and rural areas of the region and other Canadian cities. In Saint John, demolition, new construction, and the development of urban freeways have recast the downtown area. Harbour facilities have been upgraded and now include a container port, a general-cargo handling area, and an oil tanker berth

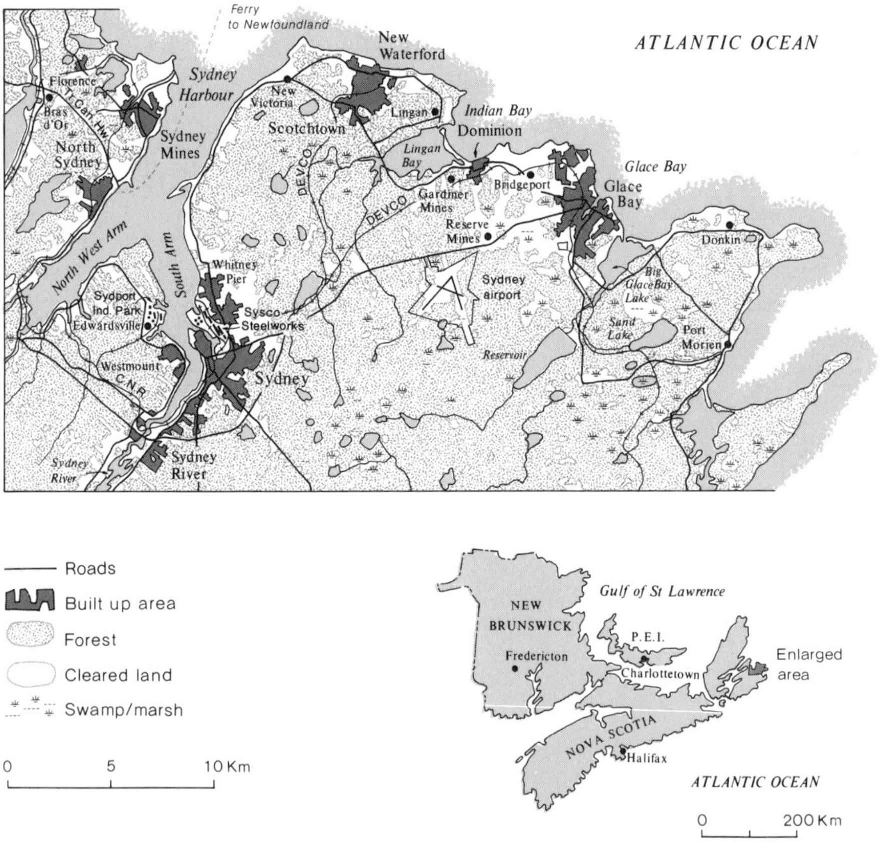

Figure 6.10 Industrial Cape Breton, Nova Scotia.

serving one of the continent's largest refineries. Nearby thermal and nuclear generating plants offer power to a number of newly established heavy and energy-intensive industries located in specially designed industrial parks. Halifax has become the premier city of the Maritimes, a leader in tertiary activities, including research, defence, finance, and transportation. In the 1980s, the servicing of oil and gas drilling ventures on the Scotian Shelf added a further dimension to the Halifax economy. Much has been made of the actual and potential impact of these developments. Claims that almost a quarter of the $630-million exploration budget for 1983 was spent in Nova Scotia likely over-estimate the benefits, however. Government figures suggest that some 1400 Nova Scotians worked on the drilling rigs and in support industries (including rig construction) in 1983. Including jobs created by the expenditure of offshore wages in the province, the impact, in terms of employment, probably accounted for less than 1 percent of the provincial labour force.

New office towers built in Halifax by Canada's leading chartered banks reflect the city's importance as a regional financial centre. Government and commercial facilities created by redevelopment (Scotia Square) and restoration (Historic Properties) have added vitality to, and changed, the character of formerly rundown fringes of the urban core. In both Halifax and Saint John, late nineteenth century business blocks of brick and stone have been replaced by glass and concrete high-rise architecture. Suburbs of single-family detached dwellings have spread, often haphazardly, across peripheral subdivisions. In older residential areas on the fringes of the urban cores, row houses and walk-up apartments are still common. Built mostly of wood in the more compact pedestrian cities of the nineteenth century, many of them have declined in quality, and now house the sizable poor and unemployed populations of these major urban centres.

Elsewhere, urban population growth and the expansion of the tertiary sector have had less dramatic impact. The Bathurst region, stimulated by mining and metal refining, is an exception. The mining sector, in fact, competes with pulp and paper as New Brunswick's leading primary industry and stimulus to urban development. Beyond the pulp and metal mining towns, light industry, warehousing, and distribution have been the most common bases for growth, although research-based firms in agriculture and forestry have been drawn to Fredericton by the university and the federal agricultural research station. Investment incentives, lower wage rates, and a largely unorganized workforce have attracted foreign firms to a few of the region's small towns. The French-owned Michelin Tire Corporation, for example, with plants in Bridgetown and Granton, is the largest private employer in Nova Scotia. It is best known for financial success, strict regulation of its workforce, and a strong anti-union stance. Moncton, at the crossroads of the three provinces and the so-called 'hub' of the Maritimes, has attracted transportation and warehousing activities

Halifax, Nova Scotia in 1985: This regional metropolitan centre is enjoying a renaissance in downtown business development to complement long-standing military and transportation activities. (*Larry McCann*)

to its industrial parks and has benefited from an expansion of federal government employment. Thus the loss of almost 1500 jobs caused by the closure of T. Eaton and Company's catalogue sales operation and the elimination by other employers of almost 400 positions has been offset. The threatened closure of the city's C.N.R. repair shops would be a devastating blow, however.

Slight concentrations of secondary manufacturing in Amherst, Truro, and the New Glasgow area have diversified local economies. Industrial parks, a handful of new commercial buildings, a shopping centre or two, and trailer parks marking the outskirts of most urban places in the region mirror the recent surge of urbanization. But many an effort to attract industrial development has followed a familiar pattern. Offered tax breaks, free water and power, nominal rent, and interest free loans, many companies opened plants with much fanfare but ceased operation only a few years afterwards. Thus Clairtone, Bricklin, Gulf Garden Foods, and the General Instruments electronics assembly plant in Sydney all closed in the 1960s and '70s in the midst of disappointment and, often, controversy. By the end of the 1970s, it was widely agreed that while some gains had been made, the construction boom had peaked, and development would dwindle. Similarly, speculative development associated with offshore oil and natural gas exploration was faring poorly in the mid–1980s. The drop in oil prices in 1986 virtually stopped this development.

Traditional values and modernization at Belledune, New Brunswick: A Roman Catholic Church and modern fertilizer plant stand in contrast. (*Larry McCann*)

LOCALISM AND REGIONALISM IN THE MARITIMES

In the mid-nineteenth century, relative isolation limited the horizons and shaped the regional consciousness of Maritimers. Movement in and between the provinces was slow and expensive. In the 1850s, a 20-hour journey separated Halifax from Pictou. The quickest route to Saint John (via the Bay of Fundy) was equally time-consuming. Overland the stage-coach connection between Halifax and Saint John required 48 hours. In the early 1860s, a railroad across Nova Scotia and a new steamer on the Bay of Fundy linked the two larger cities in 12 hours; a few years later, when railroads replaced the stage for all but the distance between Truro and Moncton, the isthmus journey still consumed a full day; its cost was perhaps four times the average daily wage of a blacksmith, or about the sum a common labourer might earn in a week. Beyond the main routes, and the immediate vicinities of towns and villages, rough roads through stumps and tangled roots, trails, and bridge paths were the arteries of overland traffic. Even on the road from Moncton to Saint John, the stage coach journey undertaken by the English visitor Isabella Lucy Bird in 1854 was uncomfortable enough:

> Seven gentlemen and two ladies went inside, in a space where six would have been disagreeably crowded. . . . The road was very hilly, and several times our progress

> was turned into retrogression, for the horses invariably refused to go up hill.... The passengers were therefore frequently called upon to get out and walk ... the ice was the thickness of a penny; the thermometer stood at 35°; there was a piercing north–east wind; and though the sun shone from a cloudless sky, his rays had scarcely any power. We breakfasted at eight, at a little way–side inn, and then travelled till midnight with scarcely any cessation.[27]

Of course, people and information moved through the region. The sea connected the provinces. Individuals travelled to markets to purchase goods or to conduct business with the government. Peddlers traversed the provinces bringing goods and news to isolated locations. Information diffused through the settlement network. But for the most part, long–distance movements were special and sporadic and information spread neither far nor fast. Regular access to a weekly newspaper was the privilege of a minority. In any case, most provincial papers focussed on practical and parochial concerns. Reports from provincial legislatures and, in the 1860s, discussions of impending Confederation, appeared regularly, but moral homilies, agricultural instruction, commercial intelligence, and community information were the stock–in–trade of the provincial press. Such material might be complemented by reports of the American Civil War, British politics, Crimean battles, and Imperial ventures in India, but local boosterism was an integral element of mid–nineteenth century journalism.

Lives were lived within local horizons. With the exception of the region's literate, political, and economic leaders, most Maritimers probably felt little connection with events elsewhere in British North America. Indeed, Thomas Haliburton, the Nova Scotia satirist, argued that mid–nineteenth century Nova Scotian society was profoundly individualistic. It was a society with "no hamlets, no little rural villages, no collection of houses, but for the purpose of trade ... [with] no mutual dependence for assistance or defence," a society in which "Every one live[d] by himself and for himself" to the extent that "interest predominate[d] over affection and the ties of friendship ... [were] weak."[28] Haliburton exaggerated. Elsewhere he noted the cooperative spirit of "bees" and "raisings." Towns and villages, with their churches, societies, and administrative officers were more than purely commercial centres. Provincial identities were recognized. But for most maritimers, in the years before Confederation, the immediate and the familiar, the intensely local world of everyday experience, were pre–eminent.

After Confederation, improvements in communication facilitated personal movement and increased the range of information available to Maritimers. Yet well into this century the lives of most Maritimers continued to turn about the villages and small towns so common in the provinces. Conceptions of the world beyond were often shaped by local experience. "Where does that road go to ...?" asked an American visitor of a Cape Breton girl in 1885. "It goes to the Strait of Canso, sir, and on to Montana — that's where my brother John is workin' on a ranch — and I don't know where else it goes," she replied.[29] Families from the fishing community of LaHave Island, located off the southwestern coast of Nova Scotia, travelled the 15 miles to Bridgewater but once a year to buy provisions. Such expeditions aside, daily life proceeded within familiar limits: members of the community gathered at church; dances and tea meetings broke workaday routines; chance encounters in the store or on the wharf reinforced familiarity; in many a hamlet and village "all the people bunched toget'er somehow, somewhere or anot'er, an' had a little party or surprise party or somethin'. Got toget'er, y'know, for a visit. Card party, mat hookin' party an' a wood party . . . whatever, it was a party."[30] Even in the 1950s, similar islands of everyday existence, bound by kinship and shared experience, as well as by relative isolation from the society beyond, were a significant facet of life in the three provinces.

Today, most Maritimers still owe their first allegiance to local communities steeped in shared experience, places in which memories are entrenched and names are kept alive by their connection to everyday features. These places are the fishing villages in which official insistence on common access to marine resources is discounted because "the lobster bottoms were distributed . . . before any of us can remember and the grounds my father fished were those his father fished before him and there were others before and before and before."[31] They are the farming communities in which

> the 'Bart Ramsey place' . . . [will] always be the 'Bart Ramsey place', however often it change[s] hands. . . . The fire that plundered the forests for miles around when it escaped from George Rawding's pipebowl the day the falling hemlock knocked the pipe from his mouth in the tinder August . . . [will] always be known as 'the George Rawding fire.' The brook through Peter Herald's meadow . . . [will] be 'Pete's Brook' as long as water [runs].[32]

They are the settlements to which migrants are drawn to return by the firm bond between people and place. They are the villages and towns at the core of the Maritime experience. "We come from Petit de Grat," said an Acadian girl to author Silver Donald Cameron at a Halifax party; but she and her parents before her had been born in Halifax. "No matter," concluded Cameron, "her ancestors probably fled the siege of Louisbourg in 1758 . . . and after two centuries they are from Petit de Grat however long they may live in . . . [Halifax]."[33]

A sense of common identity nonetheless overlies the local scale of life in the Maritime Provinces. Facilitated by advances in the technologies of transportation, printing, and broadcasting, and focussed by the apparent deterioration of the provinces' positions within Confederation, heightened regional awareness has strengthened shared values and common interests among Maritimers. Early in this century, no resident ever claimed to be from the *Maritimes*; the very notion was a figment of imaginations unfamiliar with the area. But Canada's territorial expansion and the economic recession of the 1920s provided Maritime residents with a common cause. Facing the relative decline of their political influence and economic importance in the westward-growing nation, Maritime business people and professionals sought to defend regional interests. Under the banner of Maritime Rights, their campaign for better terms brought the region's difficulties to national attention and won wide support in the three provinces. Those who saw the problems of the Maritimes in other than financial terms challenged Ottawa's rhetorical embrace of "the wheat economy" and the opportunity of Prairie land as defining features of the country on the eve of "Canada's century." They urged Maritime Canadians to secure their place in the nation by sharpening their sense of distinctiveness.

Revealingly, such clarification was contingent upon loosening "the old pride of ancestry;" those who clung to their Scottish, English, or French roots would have to recognize that they were "a special kind of Canadian — Maritimers."[34] Articulated at public meetings and in the regional press at a time when Maritime localism was in retreat before modern technology, these ideas precipitated a strong, and unprecedented, sense of regional consciousness among some Maritimers during the inter-war years. Yet even this sense of the region faded rapidly when anticipated concessions failed to materialize.

Since 1945, the growing centralization of the national economy, increases in the scale of production, and the spreading influence of gigantic corporations have worked against the development of a distinct sense of Maritime regionalism. After World War II, modern technology's rationalizing tendencies abruptly brought the area's remaining enclaves of local existence — farming communities in the Annapolis Valley, fishing settlements on Gulf and Atlantic shores, Island villages — into a framework of national existence. There was less to hold individual allegiance at a regional level. As national directions were added onto local concerns, so identification focussed on both local and national levels. In recent decades, as earlier, provincial identities have been important, though distinct internal identities still hold. In Cape Breton, Halifax is regarded with more suspicion than Ottawa, and the distinction between Gulf and Fundy shores of New Brunswick remains sharp. Nor has there been any broadly based sympathy for the recurrent notion of Maritime Union, which for all its advantages threatens traditional emotions. A handful of cooperative initiatives on specific issues among their premiers aside, the provinces remain separate and apart, their policies and their politics tied mainly to their particular interests and traditions.

Today, Maritime regionalism has a negative emphasis. It echoes the sense of regional injustice embodied in the Maritime Rights campaign, and it builds upon current problems of regional economic disparity in

Canada. Beyond the provinces' dependence upon federal payments, and the persistent gap in incomes between central and eastern Canada, Maritimers have denounced the lack of a national energy policy as spiralling costs of imported fuel pushed upward the costs of electricity from oil–fired generators. The drop in world oil prices in 1986 eased this concern somewhat, but the region still pays the highest oil and gas prices in Canada. Maritimers have also protested proposals to remove federal rail subsidies for the export of grain through Maritime ports. And they have decried the tendency of central Canadians to regard the Maritimes as an appendage of a transcontinental nation extending from Vancouver to Montréal. Urgency was added to these concerns in the 1970s by the election of the Parti Québécois in Québec and by the increasingly strident tones of western Canadians, flexing their new resource strength.

Opinions still divide upon the consequences of Québec independence for Maritime Canada. The collapse of Confederation is regarded with foreboding by those who see the region reduced to destitution by the elimination of transfer payments and subsidies. Others place hope in accommodation with Québec. Optimists suggest a bright future for a sovereign Atlantic nation, economically comparable to Norway or Sweden. As significant for Maritimers are the implications of growing opposition in the "have" provinces to federal policies of fiscal redistribution. Calls for decentralization and the devolution of more power to the provinces are gaining currency. On the surface, such changes would seem to satisfy the demands of Québec and the West; in certain spheres decentralization would be commendable. But the economic independence sought by certain provinces is almost the converse of sovereignty association, and its corollary, emasculation of federal fiscal authority, would grievously affect economic conditions in the Maritime provinces. For all the dissipation of separatist momentum in Québec and the pinning of local hopes on offshore energy development, in the mid–1980s, the Maritime Provinces remain vulnerable and uncertain. These circumstances are hardly conducive to the development of a more positive allegiance to the region. And paradoxically, in the short term at least, Maritime interest may lie in support of a strong federal government so long reviled for its role, or acquiescence, in the manipulation of national policies to the disadvantage of the Maritimes.

THE PAST AND THE FUTURE

For all its past–shaped complexity, the Maritimes confronts a singular future. The region, and its people, are apparently at a crossroads. Should economic growth be pursued in an effort to overcome the region's underdeveloped, hinterland status? Or should the benefits of underdevelopment be recognized? Should the region break away from its historical roots? Or should the distinctive legacy of the region's past be nurtured and protected? On the one hand there is the promise of more employment, higher wages, a more broadly based economy, a better standard of material life; on the other, there is environmental pollution, urban concentration, and a general decline in the quality of Maritime living. On the evidence of recent decades, there is no easy resolution of the alternatives. To pose the question as one of Nova Scotia's industrial development agencies did, "How do you equate the crash of industry with the cry of the loon?"[35]

The choice has divided Maritimers. Regional development strategies, the designation of growth poles, and the quest for "propulsive industries" all reveal that politicians, business people, developers, and planners have generally embraced the cause of economic expansion. "In Province House and on the hustings," writes Malcolm Ross ("an old reconstructed Maritimer," who taught English at Dalhousie University), "the cry is 'Forward' — on to that brave new world of super-port and oil spill, with offshore the nuclear island, and on-shore the twelve-lane highway obliterating the village and valley it takes the tourist to."[36] Yet Ross's ironic tone adumbrates a rising local critique of destructive progress — a critique echoed by opposition to the ready assumption that life in the region should be patterned on developments in the rest of North America, and reflected in the conclusion that "Chicago, Detroit, Jersey City, Hoboken and even Hamilton, Ont. look nothing at all like the New Jerusalem."[37]

Growth — the underlying assumption of North American life for generations — was the ambition of the Maritimes in the 1960s and 1970s. Did not the Industrial Heartland owe its prosperity to its strong, broadly-based, and expanding manufacturing economy? Might not the hinterland secure similar benefits by promoting similar development? Prevailing conviction hailed forced growth as the regional panacea. "Catch up" was the game plan. The Maritimes was to be brought more squarely into the mainstream of the modern industrial world. Yet this direction was charted just as a growing number of North Americans began to question the wisdom of continued economic growth. Rachel Carson, Paul Ehrlich, E.F. Schumacher, the scientists of the Club of Rome, and others raised public consciousness about desecration of the environment, the exhaustability of resources, the fragility of our planetary ecology, and the need for conservation.[38] At the same time, many turned away from the technological materialism and pressure-filled existence of mid-twentieth century North American society to live lives at a less punishing pace in surroundings less austere than those of the large, modern metropolis. Some among them (writers, professionals, and members of the counter-culture) settled in the Maritimes, where they added weight to local unease at the passing of traditional livelihoods and the decline of community life. Thus, the central dilemma of the region was clearly defined by the close of the 1970s.

Now, in the 1980s, the terms of regional underdevelopment are commonplace. The signs are everywhere: in the broad regionalization and external control of economic activity; in the disappearance of local breweries; in the declining small towns suffering from competition with growing regional centres; and in the consolidated schools that "rationalize" the delivery of education, but only by dependence on school bus systems and at the expense of community facilities. The underdevelopment of the Maritimes is a product of these circumstances. It was fashioned out of the improvements in transport and technology that favoured large producers over small, that fostered centralization, and that based the organization of land–use and productive capacity on economic principles of a national scale. Within this matrix, as we have seen, the Maritimes contributed resources and felt the growing impress of heartland dominance.

Since the mid–1970s, however, transport costs have risen dramatically; they will almost certainly continue to do so. The implications will be profound. Inter–regional exchange will become more costly. The competitive reach of heartland manufacturers will decline. Producers will gain a measure of protection in local markets. There will be a tendency towards the decentralization of industry enhanced by the advantages many engineers and planners see in modern technology's capacity to allow the economic production of many goods in small units. Agriculture will also be affected by rising costs of movement. Regional specialization based on the optimum use of soil and climate, and predicated on the assumption that needs and preferences for locally "marginal" crops can be met by imports, is likely to decline. Diversified production for local requirements will become characteristic.

The prospects of such change for the Maritimes are intriguing and warrant brief review. Farming in the region might be reoriented and revitalized. As rising local demand reduces the Maritime farmer's need to compete in specialized national or continental markets, so today's reliance upon expensive technology could give way to less capital–intensive production. With their financial requirements reduced, family farms would no longer be threatened by corporate consolidation; abandoned land might be reclaimed; and the decline of rural population might be reversed. The prospects for the fishery are less clear. Smaller processing plants, more responsive to local needs, might emerge. More fishermen's cooperatives might be established. Perhaps the saltfish industry — abandoned in the Maritimes since 1945 despite the relative buoyancy of the international saltfish trade after World War II — could be revived. With care for the quality of the product and an effective marketing organization, it might again provide a "cottage–style industry" in the region's small fishing settlements. No longer need industrial development strategies necessarily incline toward attracting large, highly specialized activities, or feel compelled to hold out massive incentives to more commonplace industries, in order that they be competitive in the national market. Instead, a variety of smaller plants, dispersed even within the region, might provide for local demands.[39]

The environmental consequences of such developments would be far less severe than those of the large-scale operations currently encouraged. The smaller scale and dispersion of industry would reduce the tendency toward urban concentration. With more intensive cultivation of smaller farms, the heavy application of chemical fertilizers so common in modern agriculture could be reduced. Almost by definition, smaller industrial plants are less damaging to the environment than massive operations whose impact often transcends the recuperative capacity of nature. Moreover, the return to smaller production units, and the probable corollary of local control, are likely to encourage more careful management of the environment than is characteristic of the operations of anonymous mega-corporations; exploitation might be tempered by a sense of stewardship.

Decentralization and "down-sizing" would also influence the social dimensions of regional life. Small places, once considered redundant, could again become the foci of daily lives. Opportunities to participate in government and decision-making at the local level would increase the attachment of people to place. Integration of residents into their communities would occur in many ways. Consider a single example of the prospects. Today, residents of the Belfast district of Prince Edward Island are represented on the Island School Board by a single individual. Several generations ago there were 17 school districts and some 50 trustees in the same area. Decentralization need (indeed should) not revert to the latter extreme. But without denying the advantages of modern educational facilities, there would seem to be scope for, and purpose in, actively involving more area residents in the planning and administration of their children's education. Similarly, familiarity (and interaction as individuals rather than as functionaries) would reinforce the sense of place that lingers in much of the Maritimes.

Thus, it may be the region's peculiar advantage to confront these changing circumstances from its present underdeveloped position. Misfortune may be turning into benefit. Arguably, backwardness by the standards of today offers a headstart for growth attuned to late twentieth century circumstances. Relatively untrammelled by the technological infrastructure of big industry, Maritimers may well set to improve their economic position without destroying their countrysides and their beaches, without undermining the distinctive qualities of regional life, without, in short, welcoming "the Trojan Horse of troubles that has already wrecked much of the pleasure of being alive in so many cities of the world."[40]

Of course, this vision of the future — community-oriented, environmentally sensitive, and offering a more humanely satisfying life for Maritimers than many of them now know — may be unattainable. But it is surely worth contemplating. First, it demonstrates the importance of context and connection in shaping the changing geography of area. Second, it suggests that the centralizing tendencies of modern industrial society may be fading, and that rising costs of movement may ultimately lead toward the more decentralized, locally self-sufficient, communal, and personally fulfilling societies envisaged by many of those disaffected by the consequences of modern industrialism. Third, the perspective offered here reminds us that human happiness and achievement are not defined in material terms alone. And, finally, this view emphasizes the need for both wisdom and vision in shaping the future of the Maritimes. For despite the years of out-migration, and the underdevelopment and economic disadvantage of recent decades, there is much of value in the region. The challenge ahead is to shape a viable future for both the people and the land, with intelligence and judgement.

NOTES

1. The basic reference for comparison of economic, demographic, and social conditions in the Maritimes with those in the rest of the country is The Economic Council of Canada, *Living Together: A Study of Regional Disparities* (Ottawa: Ministry of Supply and Services, 1977). Data have been updated by using the 1981 *Census of Canada* and the *Canada Year Book 1985* (Ottawa: Statistics Canada, 1985).
2. Kenneth Bagnell, "The Evening Town I Knew as Morning," *The Globe Magazine* (Toronto), October 10, 1970.
3. *The Financial Post* (Toronto), May 2, 1970, p. 16.
4. H.J. Fleure, "Human Regions," *Scottish Geographical Magazine,* 35 (1919), 94–105.
5. T.W. Acheson, "The Maritimes and 'Empire Canada'," in *Canada and the Burden of Unity,* ed. David Jay Bercuson (Toronto: Macmillan, 1977), p. 103.
6. The urban-industrial development of the Maritimes in the late nineteenth and early twentieth centuries is discussed in T.W. Acheson, "The National Policy and Industrialization of the Maritimes, 1880–1910," *Acadiensis,* 1 (1972), 2–34; David Frank, "The Cape Breton Coal Industry and the Rise and Fall of the British Empire Steel Corporation," *Acadiensis,* 7 (1977), 3–34; L.D. McCann, "The Mercantile-Industrial Transition in the Metals Towns of Pictou County, 1857-1931," *Acadiensis,* 10 (1981), 29–64; and *idem,* "Staples and the New Industrialism in the Growth of Post-Confederation Halifax," *Acadiensis,* 8 (1979), 47–49. See also David Alexander, "Economic Growth in the Atlantic Region, 1880–1940," *Acadiensis,* 8 (1978), 47–76, for a more general treatment of patterns of economic development.
7. Ernest Forbes, "Misguided Symmetry: The Destruction of Regional Transportation Policy for the Maritimes," in *Canada and the Burden of Unity,* ed. D.J. Bercuson (Toronto: Macmillan, 1977), pp. 60–86.
8. On this and related points see Alan A. Brookes, "Out-Migration from the Maritime Provinces, 1860–1900: Some Preliminary Considerations," *Acadiensis,* 5 (1976), 26–55.
9. A.A. Brookes, "The Golden Age and the Exodus: the Case of Canning, Kings County," *Acadiensis,* 11 (1981), 82.
10. Charles W. Dunn, *Highland Settler: A Portrait of the Scottish Gael in Nova Scotia* (Toronto: University of Toronto Press, 1953), p. 131.
11. Peter Ennals and Deryck Holdsworth, "Vernacular Housing and the Cultural Landscape of the Maritime Provinces — A Reconnaissance," *Acadiensis,* 10 (1981), 86–106.

12. Edna Staebler, *Cape Breton Harbour* (Toronto: McClelland and Stewart, 1972), p. 94.
13. Graeme Wynn, *Timber Colony: A Historical Geography of Early Nineteenth Century New Brunswick* (Toronto: University of Toronto Press, 1981).
14. *New Maritimes* (Enfield, Nova Scotia) Vol. 3, No. 4 (December 1984–January 1985), p. 10.
15. MacLean Royal Commission, 1927–8, cited by Jim and Pat Lotz, *Cape Breton Island* (Vancouver: Douglas and McIntyre, 1974), p. 100.
16. The Antigonish Movement was started in the era of World War I by M.M. Coady and J. Tompkins, both priests associated with St. Francis Xavier University. Directed from the university's Extension Department, the Movement involved large numbers of farmers, fishermen, and coal miners in cooperative ventures to alleviate local conditions of distress and malaise in eastern Nova Scotia. See R. James Sacouman, "Underdevelopment and the Structural Origins of the Antigonish Movement Cooperatives in Eastern Nova Scotia," *Acadiensis,* 7 (1977), 66–85.
17. Father Thomas Morley of Bras d'Or, cited by Silver Donald Cameron, *The Education of Everett Richardson: The Nova Scotia Fishermen's Strike, 1970–71* (Toronto: McClelland and Stewart, 1977), p. 29.
18. Ernest Buckler, *The Mountain and the Valley* (Toronto: McClelland and Stewart, 1961), p. 157.
19. Acheson, "The National Policy and Industrialization of the Maritimes," p. 24.
20. Captain W. Moorsom, *Letters from Nova Scotia: Comprising Sketches of a Young Country* (London: 1830), pp. 327–8.
21. Nolan Reilly, "The General Strike in Amherst, Nova Scotia, 1919," *Acadiensis,* 9 (1980), 56–77.
22. Dunn, *Highland Settler,* p. 132.
23. Cited by David A. Frank, "Coal Masters and Coal Miners: the 1922 Strike and the Roots of Class Conflict in the Cape Breton Coal Industry," (unpublished M.A. thesis, Dalhousie University, 1974), p. 45.
24. Cited by Eugene Forsey, *National Problems of Canada: Economic and Social Aspects of the Nova Scotia Coal Industry,* McGill University Economic Studies, No. 5 (Toronto: Macmillan, 1926), p. 49.
25. Frank, "Coal Masters and Coal Miners," p. 43. "Potatoes and point": a Scottish expression offering wry comment on a meal of potatoes in which the only variety was provided by pointing at illustrations or empty containers of other foods.
26. Dawn Fraser, "Mon Père," in *Echoes From Labour's War: Industrial Cape Breton in the 1920s,* eds. David Frank and Donald Macgillivary, (Toronto: New Hogtown Press, 1976), p. 89.
27. Isabella Lucy Bird, *The Englishwoman in America,* foreword and notes by Andrew Hill Clark (Toronto: University of Toronto Press, 1966), pp. 71–2.
28. Thomas Chandler Haliburton, *The Old Judge or Life in a Colony* (Toronto: Clarke, Irwin and Company, 1968), pp. 200–1.
29. Charles H. Farnham, "Cape Breton Folk," (1886), reprinted with an introduction by Stephen F. Spencer, *Acadiensis,* 8 (1979), pp. 97–8.
30. Peter Barss, *Images of Lunenburg County* (Toronto: McClelland and Stewart, 1978), p. 78.
31. Alastair MacLeod, "The Boat," in *Stories from Atlantic Canada,* ed. Kent Thompson (Toronto: MacMillan, 1973), p. 102.
32. Ernest Buckler, *Ox Bells and Fireflies* (Toronto: McClelland and Stewart, 1968), p. 88.
33. Cameron, *The Education of Everett Richardson,* p. 22.
34. Cited by Ernest R. Forbes, *The Maritime Rights Movement, 1919–1927: A Study in Canadian Regionalism* (Montréal: McGill-Queen's University Press, 1979), p. 36.
35. Cited in Atlantic Provinces Economic Council, *The Atlantic Economy: Sixth Annual Review* (Halifax: 1972), p. 58.
36. Malcolm Ross, "Fort, Fog and Fiddlehead: Some New Atlantic Writing," *Acadiensis,* 3 (1974), p. 120.

37. *Ibid.*, p. 121.
38. Rachel Carson, *Silent Spring* (Boston: Houghton Mifflin, 1962); Paul Ehrlich, *Eco-catastrophe* (San Francisco: City Light Books, 1969); and E.F. Schumacher, *Small is Beautiful: Economics as if People Mattered* (New York: Harper and Row, 1973).
39. *The Essential Kropotkin,* eds., E. Capouya and K. Tompkins (New York: Liveright, 1975) provides a fascinating critique of modern industrial society and offers an intriguing basis for comparison with and reflection upon the circumstances of the modern Maritimes.
40. Atlantic Provinces Economic Council, *The Atlantic Economy,* p. 58.

7

Newfoundland: Economy and Society at the Margin

Michael Staveley

Most Canadians have at least a vague feeling for the distinctiveness of Newfoundland, that strangely shaped island jutting aggressively into the Atlantic. They would likely agree that the accession of Newfoundland to Canada in 1949 completed with some propriety the notion of a country professing "Dominion From Sea unto Sea." Many of the more thoughtful, however, must have been uneasily aware that they were adding to their vast country of widely separated regions — already imperfectly integrated with the core — yet another and more intractable periphery which differed not only in degree but also in kind from the other provinces of eastern Canada. Indeed, it is important not to underestimate the differences between Newfoundland and its neighbouring provinces. These distinctions have a long history. Looking at nineteenth century economic life, for example, we see that in 1884 the harvest of the sea accounted for 67 percent of goods production in Newfoundland, but for only 13 percent in the Maritime Provinces (and 2 percent in Canada). This dependence on the sea is described lyrically by the historical geographer J.D. Rogers:

> Newfoundland from within reveals only a fraction of its nature. Its heart is on the outside; there its pulse beats, and whatever is alive inside its exoskeleton is alive by accident. The sea clothes the island as with a garment, and that garment contains the vital principle and soul of the national life of Newfoundland.[1]

This dependence on the sea, both economic and spiritual, had diminished by 1949, but it was still sufficiently strong to clearly distinguish the new province from its neighbours. Even today, economic diversity is characteristic of the Maritime provinces but not of Newfoundland. Newfoundland has little agriculture and secondary manufacturing. It lives by the sea. Other forces have also left their mark: "policies, geography and economy have kept Newfoundland eccentric and peripheral in the British North American scene."[2] With the qualification that eccentricity now relates to a wider world, this generalization captures much of Newfoundland's lot *vis-à-vis* the evolving political and economic systems of the North American heartland. Life at the margin has been difficult for Newfoundland; it is characterized by traits of underdevelopment and dependency.

DEVELOPMENT IN A DIFFICULT PHYSICAL ENVIRONMENT

In large measure, economic development has been hindered by a difficult and restrictive physical environment. An island situated in the North Atlantic, Newfoundland is far from mainland markets and its northern location adjacent to the cold Labrador Current contributes to a climatic regime that restricts agriculture, stunts tree growth, and through fog makes the inshore fishery hazardous. Moreover, the heavy flow of icebergs along the eastern coast of the island threatens offshore oil development in the Hibernia field.

Climate varies considerably throughout the province, ranging from the cool and dry subarctic conditions of Labrador, where winter temperatures average −20°C and summers about 10°C, to the marine influenced climate of St. John's (−3.8°C in January; 15.3°C in July). Inland temperatures on the island are more extreme, but they are still insufficient to support a viable agricultural base. Nor do soils, which are generally coarse and immature, enhance this sector. The soils show the effects of continental glaciation that covered the island during the Pleistocene era, the last stages of which are now dated to 7000 years ago. It is only in certain areas such as the watersheds of the Humber, Gander, and Churchill rivers where surface deposits are fairly deep that good forest stands appear. The forest is made up of species common to the boreal forest that stretches across Canada. Black spruce is the most common type. Many areas of the province, however, are poorly forested. These include extensive boglands across south-central Newfoundland and, of course, the tundra regions of Labrador.

But it is the marine environment and the coastal physiography that sustain the popular image of Newfoundland as a region of small fishing outports, isolated in coves set against a rocky shore. Economic livelihood in the outports is singularly dependent upon the cod fishery (Fig. 7.1). The physiography of Newfoundland is dominated by uplands, especially in the western half of the province, where plateau surfaces over 600 metres high

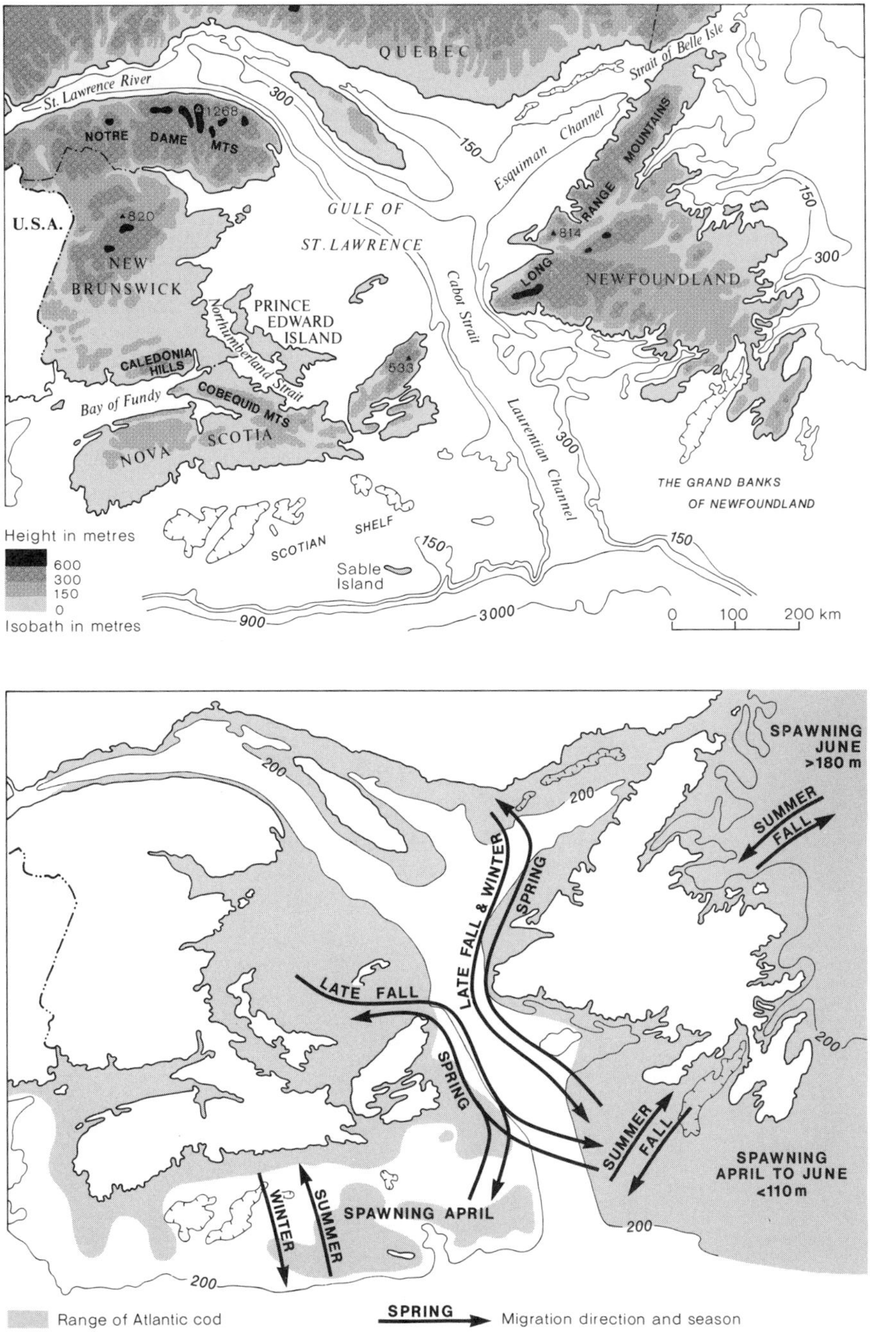

Figure 7.1 The physiography of Newfoundland and the migration of Atlantic cod. (Reprinted from "The Physical Geography of the Atlantic Provinces" by Ian Brookes in *The Atlantic Provinces* ed. Alan G. Macpherson with permission of the author and University of Toronto Press. © University of Toronto Press 1972.)

are broken by steep-sided valleys. Even in eastern Newfoundland, where elevations are lower, topography is broken and frequently rugged. Small valleys break this surface and at their seaward ends provide shelter and some agricultural land for fishing settlements. These settlements are equally fixed in space by the nature of the adjacent marine environment, particularly the ocean shelves such as the Grand Banks off southern and eastern Newfoundland. The density of settlement is highest here around Placentia, Saint Mary's, Conception, Trinity, and Bonavista Bays, all areas that have supported an abundant fishery.

However, just as the prairie areas of the Western Interior of Canada suffer from variability of precipitation — leading to drought and poor crops — these coastal areas are susceptible to variability of water temperatures, with equally devastating results. Should the bottom waters fail to warm above 5°C, migrating cod may fail to strike home and spawn. This situation happens all too often, particularly when the Labrador Current prevails over the warmer waters of the Gulf Stream. As a consequence, the inshore fishery is poorly stocked with cod, catches are low, and even land-based operations such as fish processing plants work well below capacity. Such problems have plagued Newfoundland throughout its historical development.

Little Port is an example of a summer fishing village on the French Shore of eastern Newfoundland. Fishermen work the inshore for cod. They live in these tilts for only a few months of each year and return to such places as Corner Brook to work at other jobs. (*Larry McCann*)

TERRITORY AND IDENTITY IN NEWFOUNDLAND'S DEVELOPMENT

In the spring of 1921, William Smith, an Ottawa civil servant, was sent to Newfoundland to investigate the Labrador territorial dispute on behalf of the Canadian government. In a private report to his Minister of Finance, he described the social and economic disarray current in Newfoundland. In his view, "conditions in the Island may compel the [Newfoundland] Government to approach this [Canadian] Government with a view to relieving that situation." This was the Canadian view, but there were other prescriptions of salvation. Smith reported that the Leader of the Opposition would have resort to the "Old Mother" — Britain. The Premier, however, was said to be "pro-American," and was quoted as saying that if the British Colonial Secretary "attempts any of his games with us, we would go right over to the States." The prospect of appealing for sustenance to Canada was admitted, but at best with a diffidence which was well expressed in Smith's somewhat contradictory appraisal:

> The feeling as regards Confederation is not more favourable than it ever was. When it is desired to stigmatize a man as unworthy of any confidence, he is called a confederationist. But, at the same time, the admission is freely made that they may be compelled to seek terms with Canada, and while they are still jealous of their independence, I do not think the old bitterness against Canada exists, and they look at the prospect with more equanimity than they did.[3]

Smith's analysis neatly describes Newfoundland's position throughout most of the century preceding union with Canada. That Newfoundland aspired to a "jealous independency" but never functioned truly independently of Britain, the United States, and Canada, influenced the region's character both directly and indirectly. Although dependent on these three larger nations in a number of political and economic spheres, Newfoundland was *marginal* to their major concerns. Its structural and institutional marginality was compounded by a peripheral location. This view is not to claim that Newfoundland was isolated. In many respects, especially in the mid-nineteenth century, it was much less isolated than many parts of the North American mainland; in some institutional forms (for example, dollar currency, Canadian banking, ecclesiastical and educational affiliations) it gradually aligned itself with its continental neighbours. Inevitably, however, as the continent became more integrated and economically developed, Newfoundland's marginality increased relative to the mainland.

Thus, increasing dependence and marginality are interconnected themes in Newfoundland's development. They are the product of prolonged international conflict. Newfoundland's dependency may be measured roughly by the growing dominance over the region's trade by the three metropolitan powers. In 1866-70, the majority of Newfoundland's exports (56 percent) went to countries lying outside the metropolitan bloc, but by 1945-49, this proportion had fallen to 36 percent. Since imports were always dominated by the metropolitan economies (over the same period their share rose from 86 to 97 percent), it is not surprising that their control of total trade shifted from 66 percent in 1866-70 to 82 percent in 1945-49.

These composite values mask a further and telling pattern of concentration. In the early period, Newfoundland's largest single trading partner was Britain (35 percent); on the eve of Confederation, almost 70 percent of total trade was with the United States and Canada (but only 12 percent with Britain). And this was before any formal political alliance had been cemented. The degree and advance of Newfoundland's economic enmeshment in North America was masked, at least in the popular imagination, by separate political status. Until 1949, a series of protracted territorial conflicts had helped to strengthen feelings of national identity. Newfoundland ranged herself in particular against France, the United States, and Canada, and in general against Britain which, as the reluctant vehicle of Newfoundland's foreign policy, was often perceived as thwarting Newfoundland's just aspirations. But conflict distracted attention from the long-run move towards continental dependence.

The first constitutional conflict forcing Newfoundland to adopt an adversary position against the metropolitan world is commonly referred to as the French Shore Question, which arose from the terms of the Treaty of Utrecht of 1713. By this treaty, the French were permitted to fish and dry their catch on a remote but extensive part of the shores of Newfoundland. As population in Newfoundland grew throughout the nineteenth century, the moving frontier of settlement came into conflict with the rights of the French who defended their position by asserting that these rights were exclusive. Newfoundland countered by claiming that the rights could only be concurrent. The final resolution of this disagreement was reached in 1904 when an Anglo-French convention extinguished French rights in Newfoundland in exchange for concessions in other parts of the British Empire.[4] But the lesson is clear: the resolution of Newfoundland's problems was subordinate, or marginal, to larger Imperial or European affairs. The impact of the 1904 decision on territorial claims and on patriotism and nationalism should not be underestimated, however, Newfoundland was confirmed as sole possessor of a large and potentially rich territory, an acquisition not wildly dissimilar in scope to the transfer of Rupert's Land to Canada in 1870. As to the meaning of this victory for the national psyche, the words of the Premier, Sir Robert Bond, express eloquently how this accession captured the national imagination:

> This island, which some of us love so dearly . . . may henceforth be hailed not only as our native land, but our own land, freed from every foreign claim, and the blasting influence of foreign oppression — ours in entirety — solely ours.[5]

Conflict with the United States centred on the issue of sovereignty over resources. Although not of the same magnitude as the French Shore

Question, this conflict was nevertheless substantial enough to heighten Newfoundland's self-consciousness. As this issue was contested concurrently with the struggle against French rights, it contributed to the image of a beleaguered Newfoundland. The conflict stemmed from an Anglo-American Fishery Convention signed in 1818 which granted the Americans the right to "dry and cure fish in any of the unsettled bays, harbours and creeks of the southern part of the Coast of Newfoundland." Clearly, in a Newfoundland of expanding settlement, this clause was rife with potential problems that time and again caused clashes between Newfoundland and the United States and *pari passu,* the "Old Mother," Britain. A settlement was finally reached on this issue in 1912, when the United States agreed to forfeit its claims.[6]

Newfoundland's contests with Canada were no less important for formulating a sense of separate identity. In 1890, Newfoundland engineered a Treaty of Reciprocity with the United States, perceived as likely to confer substantial economic benefits upon the colony. The treaty, however, was disallowed by Britain at the behest of Canada. A contemporary observer minced no words in describing the strength of local feeling:

> Sir John A. McDonald's (sic) opposition to the arrangement and his imperious order to the Home Government to put an end to it, was given on the eve of election; it was done to secure his Government's return ... our rights as an independent colony have been made entirely subservient to the political exigencies of the Dominion ... Nothing did more to stir up a hostile feeling against the great Dominion than this interference in our affairs.[7]

This hostility was further exacerbated by another controversy a decade later. In 1902, Québec contested the right of Newfoundland to issue licences for the cutting of timber at the head of Hamilton Inlet in Labrador. This initiated a diplomatic and legal contest between Canada and Newfoundland over the ownership of Labrador. For nearly 25 years, the issue remained in limbo as the two sides researched their cases, until, in 1927, judgement was given in favour of Newfoundland, and the colony's territories were at last rounded out. Ironically, Newfoundland — the island core — was now endowed with its own disadvantaged periphery, though at the time, the differences between the two areas were, perhaps, less obvious.

The fact that such a small colony, with a turn-of-the-century population of well under a quarter of a million, could take on the Goliaths of the international trading and diplomatic world and gain substantial concessions from them was an item of no little pride to Newfoundlanders. It helped mold and foster their national identity. In a practical sense, too, these early territorial accessions helped to give Newfoundland a concrete identity which has lasted into the latter half of the twentieth century. But, at the time they were fought out, these struggles may have distracted

Newfoundlanders from other serious problems. Peter Neary observes, for example, that "to the extent that their obsession with the French Shore problem led the merchants to imagine that their difficulties had a simple solution, it was an irrational and retarding influence on Newfoundland's development."[8] The same may be said of Newfoundland's other political victories. Politico-geographic triumphs have disguised — even compensated for — economic weakness, and may have hastened the slide towards a precarious dependence.

THE TRADITIONAL NEWFOUNDLAND ECONOMY

The fervour of nationalism at the turn of the century did not wholly blind the more reflective of Newfoundland's leaders to the plight of the economy. Even in the moment of triumph over the French Shore question, the Premier, Sir Robert Bond, voiced the reservations felt by many. In his celebrated speech, quoted previously, he added a qualification to his euphoria: "This island, which some of us love so dearly *despite its backwardness,* its isolation, its ruggedness, physical and climatic. . . ." [emphasis added]. Newfoundland *was* backward, and the reasons for this condition have been much debated.

It is clear to many scholars, however, that some level of explanation is to be found in the core-periphery thesis. Interestingly enough, in precisely the same year — 1904 — that Newfoundland secured the French Shore, the famous geographer Halford Mackinder made one of the first prophetic analyses of centre-periphery relations, an analysis with portentous implications for small countries like Newfoundland. Indeed, A.L. Mabogunje has noted that by the beginning of the twentieth century, Mackinder had recognized that the concentrating effects of transportation and communications technology had telescoped the world into "a single political system where . . . 'every explosion of spatial forces . . . will be sharply re-echoed from the far side of the globe, and *weak elements in the political and economic organism of the world will be shattered in consequence.*' He [Mackinder] contended that it was probably some half-consciousness of this fact that was at last diverting much of the attention of statesmen in all parts of the world *from territorial expansion to the struggle for relative efficiency*" [emphases added].[9] Newfoundland stands as a classic example of this crude, early model of the centre-periphery thesis. The country was torn between the imperatives of "territorial expansion" and the urgent need to improve her "relative efficiency." Newfoundland advanced in the former, but failed substantially in the latter, remaining, in political and economic terms, a 'weak element;' and, to pursue the Mackinder metaphor further, was "shattered in consequence."

What was it in the social, economic, and physical geography of Newfoundland that contributed to this backwardness and weakness? Were the problems inherent in Newfoundland, or were they forced on the colony from outside? The answers to these questions, if answers there be, may be approached through a closer analysis of Newfoundland's human geography as it evolved through the nineteenth and early twentieth centuries, particularly of the development of the traditional economy — the fishery. Newfoundland is distinctive because of its dependence on the sea. Marine resources, as noted previously, accounted for 67 percent of the value of the national product in 1884. In terms of exports, however, the country was even more heavily marine dependent. In 1911-12, when a modest diversification of the economy away from the fishery had begun, the fishery still accounted for 77 percent of exports by value. Earlier, in 1900-01, the amount was 86 percent, and throughout most of the nineteenth century, the proportion would certainly have been higher than 90 percent. Even today, with the added promise of offshore oil development, the sea remains the livelihood of the province.

The Settlement Pattern

The patterns of spatial and social organization developed to exploit the resources of the sea are equally distinctive. The cod fishery in Newfoundland began in the sixteenth and seventeenth centuries as a migrant fishery. Merchant houses in southwestern England (and later southeastern Ireland) sent fishing ships to exploit the cod stocks of the Grand Banks from summer shore bases on the coasts of Newfoundland. In essence, these firms were vertically integrated. They controlled the catching, processing, and marketing of the salt cod fishery, and regarded Newfoundland territory as a *de facto* extension of the metropolis.[10] Towards the end of the eighteenth century, the cost benefits of this ship (or migrant) fishery diminished, and it was gradually replaced by an indigenous small-boat fishery prosecuted by a sedentary population. This transition was basically completed by the end of the first quarter of the nineteenth century. Then, in 1832, Newfoundland attained representative government. Regardless of political control, well-being was still derived mainly from a flourishing, one-product, and domestically-controlled economy — the fishery.

The exploitation of the fishery by the sedentary population was facilitated by two developments which had profound, long-term effects on Newfoundland's society and economy. The transition from a migrant to an indigenous fishery encouraged a wide scatter of settlements from which small boats, of limited range, worked mainly inshore. The resource was widely distributed in space, but less so in time. Settlements were small and numerous, located to command the widest possible area of coastline when the feeding cod 'struck-in' for the brief early summer season. These settlements were known as "outports," the name itself suggesting some kind of hierarchy in which the outport occupied a subsidiary role.

The second development was essentially a corollary of the first. The withdrawal of the vertically integrated British firms left a vacuum in the catching and processing operations which was filled by household and family units working in the outports. The marketing aspects were gradually concentrated in the hands of major merchant houses in St. John's and a few of the larger outports. Acting as intermediaries between catching and processing on the one hand, and marketing on the other, were several hundred outport merchants who outfitted the local fishermen on credit at the beginning of the season, and who were themselves bound in credit relationships to the larger merchants. The settlement pattern and population distribution attributable to these developments is of profound importance for any understanding of Newfoundland's human geography. Conventional views and the popular imagination, however, have exaggerated certain aspects of these patterns, particularly the primacy of St. John's and the fragmented nature of the settlement distribution.

An understanding of the reasons for Newfoundland's backwardness cannot rest solely on these general notions. Table 7.1 offers some new evidence on population distribution and settlement frequency. During the period 1857 to 1945, population grew by a factor of 2.6. The fastest growth, calculated as a rate, came in the first three decades (column 1), but a depression in the fishery in the late 1880s caused a steep decline in the growth rate. From the 1890s, growth continued at a steady but unspectacular rate of slightly under one percent per annum.

More interesting than simple growth is an examination of elements of persistence and change in the distribution of population. Column 2 demonstrates that the concentration of population in the area of initial settlement — the Avalon Peninsula — diminished over the entire period, at first sharply but later gradually. This diminution naturally accompanied the spread of population into the previously unsettled frontiers, especially along the northern and western coasts. Even so, when Newfoundland faced the beginning of its most enduring economic crisis during the 1880s, more than half the population was concentrated on the relatively restricted Avalon Peninsula. It is hard to argue convincingly that the fragmentary pattern of settlement was a prime cause of Newfoundland's economic malaise.

Column 3 provides more material for reflection on the distribution of population. Conventional views suggest that over time the capital city, St. John's, held increasing proportions of unproductive economic factors (those not concerned directly with the production of fish), and thus became a parasite on the healthy and industrious body politic of rural Newfoundland. If this were so, it is not apparent from an examination of population data. What is remarkable is the retention by St. John's of a

TABLE 7.1 POPULATION DISTRIBUTION AND SETTLEMENT SIZE FREQUENCY IN NEWFOUNDLAND, 1857–1945

			Percentage of Population Living in			*Percentage of Settlements with Population of*			
Date	*Total Population*	*Average Annual % Increase over Intercensal Period (1)*	*Avalon Peninsula (2)*	*St. John's (3)*	*Number of Settlements (4)*	*0–199 (5)*	*200–499 (6)*	*500–999 (7)*	*≥1000 (8)*
1857	122 638[a]	—	64.4	20.3	615	79.8	12.7	5.9	1.6
1869	146 536	1.6	55.2	15.4	662	74.7	16.2	7.1	2.0
1874	161 374	1.8	56.6	14.8	801	77.8	14.7	5.1	2.3
1884	197 335	2.3	53.7	15.8	1 052	81.0	12.7	3.9	2.4
1891	202 040	0.3	51.8	14.4	1 183	82.2	12.3	3.9	1.7
1901	220 984	0.9	49.2	13.9	1 372	81.5	13.2	3.9	1.4
1911	242 619	1.0	47.5	14.1	1 447	81.1	13.7	3.6	1.6
1921	263 033	0.8	46.4	14.5	1 440	78.5	15.8	4.4	1.6
1935	289 588	0.7	43.5	13.9	1 387	75.2	17.3	5.3	2.2
1945	321 819	1.1	42.8	14.0	1 379	72.6	19.5	5.8	2.1

[a]No data for Labrador.

Source: Calculated from data in *Census of Newfoundland*.

consistent share of the colony's population at about 15 percent. If the data reveal any trend at all, they demonstrate a slight decline in the proportion of population held by the capital. Clearly, this is no picture of rapid urbanization, or of developing primacy. For nearly 80 years, only one in seven of the country's population was resident in the largest urban centre.

Detail on the size frequency of settlements is illustrated by data in columns 4 to 8. The framework is admittedly coarse, but sufficient detail is presented to show how traditional interpretations of Newfoundland's settlement distribution have some credence. Most settlements were indeed small; at any date, about three-quarters of all settlements had fewer than 200 inhabitants. Moreover, the number of settlements increased markedly over the period at roughly the same rate of increase as the colony's population. Even allowing for difficulties in census interpretation of what actually constitutes a settlement, this is a remarkably consistent pattern. The overall figures disguise important regional variations, however. By far the greatest proportion of these tiny places existed in areas of recent settlement on the northern, western, and southern coasts. In 1911, for example, at the time of the maximum expansion of the settlement frontier, 44 percent of these tiny settlements hugged isolated bays and coves on the French and American Shores, and in Labrador. Other concentrations characterized Twillingate and Placentia Bay. In general, settlements became smaller with increased distance from the initially settled core of the Avalon Peninsula and the North-East Coast.

Another perspective on the settlement pattern, the degree of urbanization, is portrayed in Table 7.2. Assuming that, in Newfoundland, "large" settlements are those with more than 500 persons, the population is aggregated into "large" settlements and "urban" settlements, that is, those which conform to the contemporary Canadian definition of more than 1000 persons (columns 1-3). It is clear that a sizable proportion of the population lived in these two classes of settlement. In the mid-nineteenth century, 57 percent of the total population resided in settlements of over 500 people, and 37 percent lived in urban centres. The urban component later declined during the period of frontier expansion at the turn of the century, but regained its strength in the 1920s to the 1940s.

Even if the non-metropolitan population is considered alone, eliminating St. John's (as in columns 4-6), on average, four out of every ten people lived in large places, and two out of ten in urban centres. These data make an interesting comparison with the urbanization of the Canadian heartland in Québec and Ontario. If columns 7 and 8 are assessed against column 2 (with which they are a fair comparison), the population of Newfoundland in the 1850s and '60s was more urbanized. Even when the level of urbanization in the Industrial Heartland is compared with that of non-metropolitan Newfoundland (column 5), the urban base of this, the Newfoundland hinterland, was larger than that of central Canada. All of this is not to argue that Newfoundland possessed an

TABLE 7.2 NEWFOUNDLAND POPULATION LIVING IN LARGER SETTLEMENTS AND URBAN PLACES, 1857–1945

		Percentage of Total Population Living in Settlements of			*Percentage of Non-metropolitan Population Living in Settlements of*			*Percentage of Central Canadian Population Living in Settlements of ≥1000*	
Date	*Total Population*	*500–999 (1)*	*≥1000 (2)*	*Total (3)*	*500–999 (4)*	*≥1000 (5)*	*Total (6)*	*Ontario (7)*	*Québec (8)*
1850	—	—	—	—	—	—	—	14.6	14.7
1857[a]	122 638	19.9	36.8	56.7	25.0	20.7	45.7	—	—
1860	—	—	—	—	—	—	—	16.9	16.8
1869	146 536	22.1	34.5	56.6	26.1	22.6	48.9		
1870	—	—	—	—	—	—	—	20.2	19.2
1874	161 374	18.1	37.4	55.5	21.3	26.5	47.8	—	—
1884	197 335	15.1	37.8	52.9	17.9	26.1	44.0	—	—
1891	202 040	15.6	32.8	48.4	18.2	21.5	39.7	—	—
1901	220 984	14.9	29.8	44.7	17.3	18.5	35.8	—	—
1911	242 619	15.3	28.5	43.8	17.6	18.4	36.0	—	—
1921	263 033	17.2	30.1	47.3	20.1	18.3	38.4	—	—
1935	289 588	17.6	33.4	51.0	20.4	22.7	43.1	—	—
1945	321 819	17.2	34.3	51.5	20.0	23.6	43.6	—	—

[a]No data for Labrador.

Source: See Table 7.1; and J. McCallum, *Unequal Beginnings: Agriculture and Economic Development in Quebec and Ontario until 1870* (Toronto: University of Toronto Press, 1980), p. 55.

A Newfoundland outport, c. 1890: Epworth on the Burin Peninsula (population c. 190) was characteristic of many of the smaller outports on the south and west coasts. The photograph shows cod fish drying on fishing flakes, as well as subsistence agriculture. (*Memorial University of Newfoundland, Department of Geography Collection*)

Fogo, Newfoundland, c. 1900: With a population of over 600, Fogo was a substantial settlement on the northern fringe of the Newfoundland 'core.' Clearly shown are flakes for drying fish, 'rooms' for gear, the small gardens of subsistence agriculture, a good number of small inshore fishing boats and schooners, and in the outer harbour, several larger, square-rigged vessels. (*Memorial University of Newfoundland, Department of Geography Collection*)

urban base more powerful or inherently superior to that of the Industrial Heartland. Quite clearly, there was a different scale and a different dynamic to the developing urban and economic systems of the Canadian heartland, such that any extended comparison of the systems would be profitless. But the comparison is useful because it reminds us that the picture of Newfoundland as a scatter of tiny, isolated settlements is not entirely accurate. There was a substantial base of small towns in Newfoundland which, during the third quarter of the nineteenth century at least, was as important as its Canadian counterpart.

Dependence on the Fishery

Just as the economy of Newfoundland was focussed to an unusual degree on a single enterprise — the fishery, so too, was the fishery dependent on a single species — the cod. Given the species' widespread distribution, almost every settlement centred on the cod fishery. For this reason, many scholars have viewed the province as a monolithic unit and have discussed its economy and society as an undifferentiated whole. But economic specialization does not necessarily create regional uniformity. In 1900-01, when fishery products made up 86 percent of the value of all exports, cod alone totalled 78 percent of the value of fish exports. The other species exported were seal products (10 percent), lobster (6 percent), herring (3 percent), salmon (2 percent), and whale products (1 percent). There were subtle gradations in the product mix and technologies of the fishery which, together with variations in the developed pattern of settlement, have created a differentiated system of regions in Newfoundland. In St. George's Bay on the French Shore, herring was an important element in the fishery. On the South Coast, the lack of winter ice allowed a longer fishing season, but the deeper waters discouraged the use of fixed traps and encouraged a more mobile fishery. Lobster was significant for the economy of Placentia Bay, and the offshore bank fishery was important on the Burin Peninsula. On the North-East Coast, migratory fishing trips to Labrador had become an essential element of lifestyle. Many areas of the Northern Peninsula prosecuted the land-based seal fishery. In all regions, despite the general importance of cod, the seasonality of the cod fishery forced people into a pattern of occupational pluralism, in which different resources were harvested in a seasonal round. This pluralism had the advantage of not only maximizing the total yield of resources, but also protecting society against the not infrequent failure of any one element in the resource complex. It was a natural and sensible adaptation to the environment.[11]

If there is one region which may be viewed as typical of traditional Newfoundland, it is the North-East Coast. The North-East Coast includes Conception Bay, Trinity Bay, Bonavista Bay, and possibly the Fogo and Twillingate districts, but excludes St. John's. It is the region that

Brigus, Conception Bay, c. 1890: With a population of about 1500, Brigus was one of a large number of prosperous small towns which dominated the economy of the North-East Coast, but which went into decline in the twentieth century. (*Memorial University of Newfoundland, Department of Geography Collection*)

St. John's, c. 1900: The dominant economic and political centre of Newfoundland. The mercantile houses on the waterfront controlled much of the Newfoundland fishery, providing credit, and marketing fish. (*Memorial University of Newfoundland, Department of Geography Collection*)

developed and institutionalized, to the greatest extent, the adaptations necessary for wresting a pluralistic livelihood. Naturally, the inshore cod fishery was basic to the economy. Onto this base were grafted the migratory Labrador fishery and the spring seal fishery. Later, in the early twentieth century, pulp wood cutting became an additional part of the seasonal round. By the mid-nineteenth century, this combination of indigenous economic activities supported a large and flourishing population, as well as the majority of the colony's small urban centres. It was, in a sense, the true economic core and cultural hearth of Newfoundland (Fig. 7.2).

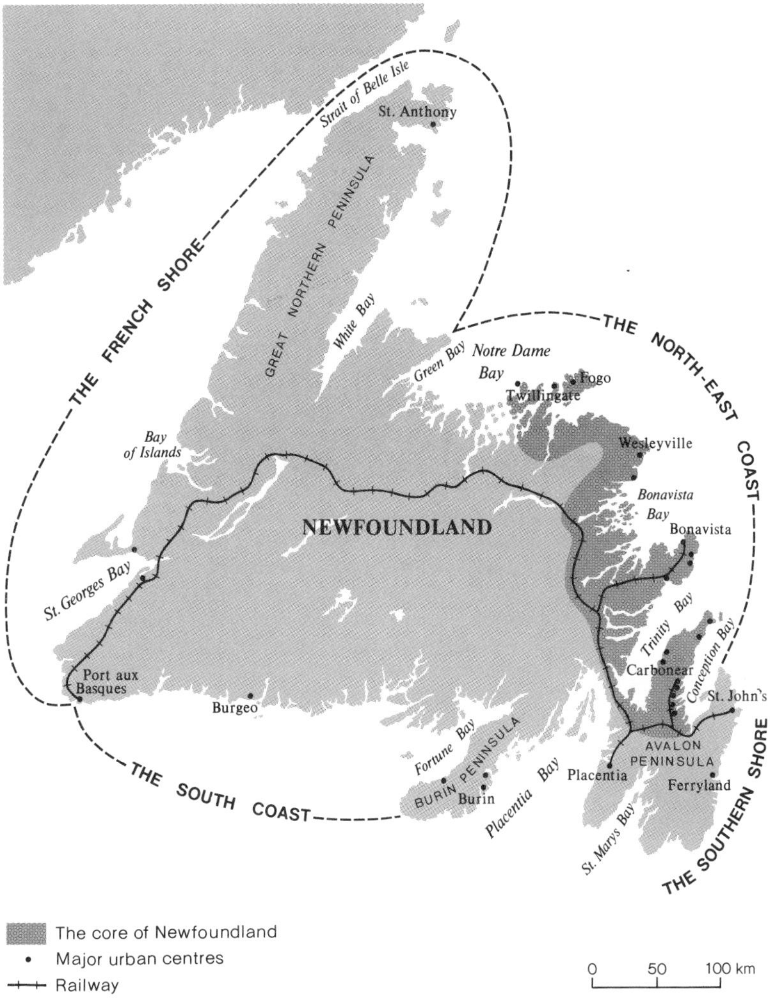

Figure 7.2 Newfoundland at the end of the nineteenth century.

The basis for identifying the North-East Coast as the pivotal Newfoundland region, therefore, lies in the complex of traditional adaptations made by the local population. Other regions of Newfoundland had their distinctive adaptations, but in most cases these were shared with non-Newfoundlanders. The bank fishery, for example, was dominated by American and Nova Scotian fishermen, as was the herring fishery; the lobster resource was locally important, but nowhere as important as in Maritime Canada. The North-East Coast combined the three elements in which Newfoundlanders excelled and dominated: the inshore cod fishery, the Labrador fishery, and the seal fishery. On this basis, the region was the engine which drove the traditional Newfoundland economy. Beyond this, it was a cultural and emotional symbol of all that Newfoundland had become.

THE ROOTS OF UNDERDEVELOPMENT

What are the roots of underdevelopment in Newfoundland? Too frequently, explanations of the region's problems have been presented in simplistic, singular — and hence misleading — terms. The Newfoundland

The Newfoundland seal hunt, c. 1910: The seal hunt was an important element in the economy of Newfoundland, particularly on the North-East Coast, which provided most of the ships and men. Three groups of sealers pick their way across the treacherous sea-ice surface at the 'Front,' the whelping ground of the seals about 160–320 kilometres offshore. The men carry gaffs, used for both killing seals and safety on the ice. (*Memorial University of Newfoundland, Department of Geography Collection*)

Royal Commission of 1933, for example, was one of the most thorough and well-intentioned of the many inquiries made into Newfoundland's condition. The Commission found that the immediate cause of difficulty lay in human failings, and expressed its findings in language graced with a strong moral overtone of disapproval:

> the Island's difficulties are largely due to the reckless waste and extravagance, and to the absence of constructive and efficient administration, engendered by a political system which for a generation has been abused and exploited for personal or party ends.[12]

This analysis isolated only immediate causes and misconstrued them as root causes.

Another explanation for the sustained low level of development is based on environmental limitations. A subtle variation on this theme has been presented by Ellsworth Huntington, who compared and contrasted developments in Newfoundland and Iceland. He concluded that Newfoundland suffered greatly from "negative selection" — the tendency of the more able to emigrate — and that this factor had lowered the intellectual capacity of the populace. The net effect, surmised Huntington, was that "Newfoundlanders live in a physical environment which is too difficult for their innate capacity."[13] A more recent and closely argued example of the single factor explanation has been advanced by the economist S.D. Antler. Eschewing the notion of limitations in physical geography as the explanation of regional disparity, Antler adopts a Marxist mode of analysis by assigning dominant roles in Newfoundland's underdevelopment to the opposing interests of the various classes: "it appears that Newfoundland's class structure, rather than her geography, accounted for her poverty."[14]

Antler's argument shows insight into Newfoundland's conditions and is persuasive in analytic detail, but slender evidence suggests critical deficiencies. It is Antler's thesis that the surplus value accumulated by the Newfoundland economy was, because of the lopsided relationship between merchant and fisherman, captured by the merchant class and exported rather than reinvested in local development. This thesis of colonial exploitation is, of course, a particular form of the centre-periphery relationship. The case advanced rests on the assertion that Newfoundland's capital stock in 1884 was worth only $1.2 million. If all of the surplus accumulated in the colony over the previous four decades had been retained in Newfoundland, however, the capital stock should have totalled between $3.2 and $4.7 million. The critical deficiency in this array of fact lies in the unwarranted, narrow assessment of the 1884 capital stock. The figure of $1.2 million is based on census data for the value of the manufacturing plant. This is a poor base for a meaningful assessment of Newfoundland's capital stock. Investment in shipping and mining, for example, not counted in the 1884 Census, would increase the $1.2 million figure enormously.[15]

A most thoughtful and constructive analysis of Newfoundland's economic development has been made by David Alexander. In a series of incisive and perceptive essays, he offers a balanced critique of Newfoundland's underdevelopment and dependency.[16] Alexander focusses on the deterioration of a one-product economy after the mid-nineteenth century when population growth outstripped advances in productivity and prices. He also reviews the attempts to diversify a faltering, export-led economy, first through import-substitution and later, in the twentieth century, by opening resource opportunities to multinational corporations. To Alexander, the thesis of exploitation is less convincing than the incapacity of the elite to "mobilize the country more effectively." Later, Alexander refined this analysis and suggested that a general unwillingness or inability to devote sufficient resources to education resulted in extremely low levels of literacy, and that this condition limited the supply of imaginative and innovative leadership necessary for sustained advance in a world in which Newfoundland was becoming increasingly disadvantaged. This particular analysis suggests that Newfoundland's problems were home-grown, but Alexander's complete findings emphasize how external forces exacerbated underdevelopment and dependence.

How can geographic analysis amplify or qualify the findings of the economic historian? Let us examine the economic geography of the traditional economy, to determine whether Newfoundland's regional patterns shed light on problems of development and dependency. The most promising approach lies in the investigation of productivity. Productivity is a measure of the way in which a society creates goods and services from scarce resources to produce wealth or value. It is significant, therefore, that both Antler and Alexander explain declining productivity and increasing poverty as a function of the failure of human agencies. Antler is unwilling to perceive any direct relationship between population pressure and resources because "the rate at which Newfoundland's fisheries resources were exploited depended directly on the merchant's willingness to extend credit to fishermen."[17] Alexander, in turn, suggests that "there is no evidence that, at the time, the resource was overexploited."[18] Yet, given the fact that productivity apparently lies at the root of Newfoundland's economic weakness, it is surprising that no thorough attempt has been made to calculate variations in productivity in time or space. Indeed, it is unlikely that weaknesses in the traditional economy were experienced uniformly throughout Newfoundland. Thus, an examination of variations in productivity both by regions and by sector should offer insights into the problems of underdevelopment and dependency.

Table 7.3 offers the first of a series of such analyses. Assigning the per capital value of fisheries production for the whole of Newfoundland an index value of 100, the per capita value for each district is expressed as a percentage of this index for each of the five census years from 1884-1920.

The districts of the North-East Coast were generally low in productivity;[19] the districts of the South Coast and the French Shore almost always had above average labour productivity.[20] The regional problem created by this uneven distribution in productivity is summarized in Table 7.4, which portrays the demographic and economic decline of the North-East Coast. The region's share of the colony's population decreased only slightly over the forty years, but its share of the labour force engaged in fishing declined at a faster rate. Even more sobering is the fact that the value of production declined more severely. Clearly, returns to at least the labour factor of production were relatively diminished, probably because of an increasing disparity between population and resources. Over the 1884 to 1920 period, then, the North-East Coast declined in productivity and became impoverished. It was the economic weakening of this region that contributed massively to Newfoundland's overall demise. Equally important, the decline of this region dealt a severe blow to the self-image of Newfoundlanders. Insofar as it was the archetypal Newfoundland region -- the "core" of Newfoundland — its decline had a subtle emotional as well as a broader economic significance.

Antler's analysis of the merchants' role in the economy prompts an examination of the relationship between merchants and productivity. Selected districts portraying high, medium, and low productivity (as revealed in Table 7.3) were analyzed for each of the five census years. In each district, all settlements with merchants or traders were aggregated and classed as "merchant communities;" those without any trading establishment were labelled "non-merchant communities." The average productivity of each class of settlement was then calculated and the results set out in Table 7.5. The results show a strikingly consistent pattern. In all cases, the group of merchant communities was more productive than the non-merchant group. Moreover, disparities in productivity between the two groups tended to widen over time, if only slightly.

What is the significance of this finding for our understanding of Newfoundland's traditional economy? It is not unreasonable to surmise that a settlement pattern is one of the tools society (i.e. population) uses to mediate its relationship with the environment (i.e. resources). In a system of agricultural settlement, for example, it is possible for population to place too heavy a burden on the resource base. Imagine the difficult economic situation resulting from a Prairie settlement system granting just a quarter of a quarter-section to a homesteader. It is equally possible for a settlement system exploiting an open-access resource such as a fishery to become overextended. With this in mind, we can expand our analysis of merchant and non-merchant communities. There are two possible explanations for why merchant communities were the most productive settlements: either the presence of merchants stimulated greater economic activity; or the settlements were inherently more productive by virtue of their resource endowment, and thus attracted a group of merchants.

TABLE 7.3 PER CAPITA VALUE OF FISHERY PRODUCTION, 1884–1920 (by district and percentage of annual Newfoundland average)

District	*1884*	*1890*	*1900*	*1910*	*1920*
St. John's	66	453	427	455	161
Harbour Main	61	59	52	34	23
Port de Grave	114	91	105	38	82
Harbour Grace	89	119	80	81	80
Carbonear	201	75	110	54	96
Bay de Verde	74	49	61	86	111
Trinity Bay	86	59	62	82	61
Bonavista Bay	70	55	66	52	64
Fogo	83	71	77	60	92
Twillingate	52	72	92	74	69
St. Barbe	52	106	74	92	109
St. George's	264	265	160	79	227
Burgeo-La Poile	138	147	97	119	102
Fortune Bay	163	142	99	125	107
Burin	143	109	150	125	141
Placentia-St. Mary's	115	113	108	131	112
Ferryland	127	95	103	114	98
Newfoundland	100	100	100	100	100
Value of per capita production	£18.68 (c. $90)	$150	$155	$213	$294
Calculated by	Persons catching and curing fish	Males catching and curing fish			

Source: Calculated from data in *Census of Newfoundland*.

TABLE 7.4 PRODUCTIVITY IN THE NEWFOUNDLAND FISHERY: THE REGIONAL PROBLEM OF THE NORTH-EAST COAST, 1884–1920

Date	*Percentage of Newfoundland Population*	*Percentage of Newfoundland Fishery Labour Force*	*Percentage of Total Production Value*
1884	48	61	50
1890	48	62	39
1900	48	56	42
1910	45	53	35
1920	45	52	39

Source: See Table 7.3.

TABLE 7.5 FISHERY PRODUCTIVITY IN MERCHANT AND NON-MERCHANT COMMUNITIES, 1884–1920

Date	Class of Community	*High Productivity* (1)[a]	(2)[b]	*Medium Productivity* (1)	(2)	*Low Productivity* (1)	(2)
1884	Merchant	£32.63	107	£23.72	110	£13.50	103
	Non-merchant	29.16	95	19.48	90	12.69	97
	All	30.54	100	21.56	100	13.14	100
	District	Fortune Bay		Placentia-St. Mary's		Bonavista Bay	
1890	Merchant	$256.83	124	$223.74	138	$104.57	118
	Non-merchant	119.82	58	89.99	55	69.35	78
	All	207.11	100	162.62	100	88.64	100
	District	Burgeo-La Poile		Burin		Trinity Bay	
1900	Merchant	$285.87	123	$181.22	113	$112.64	111
	Non-merchant	131.00	56	136.61	86	82.75	81
	All	233.22	100	159.76	100	101.73	100
	District	Burin		Ferryland		Bonavista Bay	
1910	Merchant	$330.53	118	$260.14	107	$162.20	103
	Non-merchant	172.77	62	224.72	93	152.52	97
	All	279.40	100	242.61	100	156.92	100
	District	Burin		Placentia-St. Mary's		Twillingate	
1920	Merchant	$533.67	128	$445.27	141	$222.79	125
	Non-merchant	290.82	70	211.54	67	150.81	85
	All	416.42	100	315.15	100	177.54	100
	District	Burin		Fortune Bay		Trinity Bay	

[a]Column 1: value of fishery per capita of labour force in the fishery. Data are in current pounds or dollars.
[b]Column 2: percentage of all districts.

Source: See Table 7.3

This second possibility is the more likely explanation. Merchant location mattered little. What Table 7.5 shows is that there was an economic hierarchy in which some communities were clearly more productive than others, and that there was a substantial and growing fringe of settlements characterized by sustained low productivity. This latter condition was widespread, but was particularly evident on the North-East Coast where there was a concentration of larger settlements. Even with resort to expedients such as the seal fishery and the Labrador fishery, these settlements were characterized by low returns to both labour *and* capital. Without either revolutionary innovations in technology or a large shift in the terms of trade, these settlements had clearly surpassed the capacity of the local resource base to sustain them at a constant, or increasing, level of return.[21]

With this argument, we do not intend to substitute a geographical causation for political, economic, and social factors. Indeed, it seems more sensible to think of problems as resulting from a complex of causes. In the case of Newfoundland, however, the one aspect which has received frequent casual mention, but little analysis, is the inability of the settlement system, on both regional and district scales, to remain in equilibrium with the resource potential. Although there was no clear indication of a reduction in the resource base in the period 1884-1920, the overall growth of population and its increasing disposition in both tiny scattered fishing camps and in large settlements suggests that as disequilibrium grew and productivity stagnated or fell, the margin between rural prosperity and hardship became slender indeed.

MODERNIZATION THROUGH INDUSTRIALIZATION

We have to this point emphasized the social, spatial, and economic underpinnings of the fishery, as an aid to understanding traditional Newfoundland. The fishery affected, either directly or indirectly, the well-being of everyone in the colony down to the eve of Confederation in 1949, and beyond. The fishery *was* the engine of economic growth. Nevertheless, attempts were made, beginning in the 1880s and 1890s, to diversify and modernize the economy through industrialization.

An infrastructure of railroads was an essential prerequisite for any industrial strategy. In 1881, construction of a narrow gauge railway began, but by 1884 only the 135-kilometre section from St. John's to Harbour Grace had been built. By fits and starts, and amid sustained political turbulence, the line was eventually completed to Port aux Basques in 1897 (Fig. 7.2). The cost of the railway to the public purse was considerable, forcing the colony for the first time into foreign debt. Even the economic benefits were dubious. Roughly twenty years after its completion, the cost of moving freight on the Newfoundland Railway was approximately ten times more than that of the Canadian Pacific Railway. Accumulating annual deficits were later instrumental in pushing the colony towards bankruptcy.[22] Nevertheless, by the turn of the century, a modest transportation infrastructure, of which the railway was the major component, was in place to encourage economic development. It is doubtful whether the ensuing development was engendered or particularly facilitated by such an expensive infrastructure, but the new century did usher in a phase of industrial development based on mining and forest industries financed by international corporate capital, a novel experience for Newfoundland.

The first major assault on land-based resources began in the 1890s when a Canadian corporation, The Nova Scotia Steel and Coal Company, started to mine iron ore on Bell Island in Conception Bay for use in its Pictou County, Nova Scotia, metal-making operations.[23] The nature of this mining operation, and its corporate structure, are of particular interest because the pattern of development exhibits several characteristics common in Newfoundland's modernization strategy. First, the developing agency was an "outside" company seeking sources of raw material supply for its larger, extra-Newfoundland operations. Local control and initiative were therefore virtually non-existent. Second, the Scotia Steel enterprise depended on both the availability of a rich, easily-won natural resource and the use of a relatively unskilled supply of cheap labour. Third, the company's mining operation was clearly adapted to the system of occupational pluralism common in Newfoundland. Two six-month shifts were employed. One group of men worked in the mines in winter and fished during the summer. The other shift worked in the mines during the summer and cut wood in winter. In this way, Scotia Steel reinforced, rather than competed with, the prevailing mode of occupational pluralism, and also hindered the build-up of a large and specialized industrial labour force. Finally, like most other trans-national companies that entered Newfoundland, Scotia Steel was able to deal with the Newfoundland government from a position of strength. These companies paid virtually no direct taxes and royalties into the national revenue, and were largely unresponsive to development incentives.

Hopeful of overturning the underdevelopment of its iron resources, the Newfoundland government pressed for change, but failed. In 1903, the government passed an act authorizing the payment of bounties for iron and steel actually fabricated in the colony. The proposed amount of bounties was directly related to the amount of Newfoundland ore, fuel, and flux utilized in the manufacturing process. The bounties were designed to depreciate over a 7-year period, the hope being that an iron and steel complex would be built early in the period to take advantage of the higher rates. The offer was not taken up; the bounty system proved ineffectual.

The Newfoundland government then attempted another tack. In 1910, a modest royalty of 7½ cents was imposed on each ton of iron ore exported abroad. This was, at the time, the only direct tax imposed on Newfoundland's natural resources, and it remained in force for 10 years, providing only an exiguous contribution to colonial revenues. Then, in 1921, a similar though bolder act was passed combining the "carrot and stick" methods of tax-free incentives and discriminatory taxation. Realizing that Newfoundland resources were being exploited by the British Empire Steel Corporation to supply a secondary manufacturing process on neighbouring Cape Breton Island, the government increased the royalty on ores exported to Nova Scotia to 25 cents per ton. At the same time, it permitted duty free exports of ore to any other part of the world, provided that the exporting company would build a plant in Newfoundland capable of smelting 100 000 tons of pig iron a year and operate it at full capacity. Failure to do so within an agreed time span would result in export taxes of 10 cents per ton on ore exported anywhere other than Nova Scotia. As before, the Canadian company found it more profitable to ignore these incentives and to continue exporting unprocessed iron ore both to its Cape Breton plant and to world markets.

The experience of mining development on Bell Island was repeated, though in a modified form, in the forest products industries. In 1905, the colonial government entered into an agreement with the Anglo-Newfoundland Development Company which wanted to build a pulp and paper operation in central Newfoundland at Grand Falls. Generous incentives were offered to the company: complete water and timber rights over an area of 2000 square miles at a rental of $2.00 per square mile "not to be payable on swamp or barren lands;" a renewable 99-year lease; full mining rights for a scant 5 percent of net profits from mineral operations; no municipal taxation; and no duty for 20 years on materials imported for use in construction and development. The company's obligations were minimal, including a royalty of 50 cents on every 1000 feet of sawn lumber cut, and modest capital expenditures. Similar, if slightly less generous assistance, was later provided to encourage the development of pulp and paper operations at Deer Lake and Corner Brook, and a mining operation at Buchans on the Anglo-Newfoundland Company's leased territory.

The precise impact of government assisted development is difficult to assess. Diversification did occur; the Gross Domestic Product was increased; and per capita gains in productivity were significant. In the period 1884 to 1939, real output in Newfoundland's forest industries grew by 8 percent per annum, which was much better than the performance of either the Maritime provinces or Canada. Similarly, gains in mining productivity, which averaged 4.5 percent per annum, compared well with those of the Maritimes. Furthermore, at both a personal and aggregate level, the impact of wages supplied by the new industries was significant. Despite gains in productivity, and despite the generally good relations engendered by the companies (especially the paper companies) in a colony with high unemployment and underemployment, there is much evidence to criticize the foreign companies for their poor conservation practices and their tendency to export unprocessed wood products. In 1925, for example, the Newfoundland Board of Trade complained: "This process of denuding our forests provides a minimum amount of employment for our people, and leaves but a fraction of what should be distributed among the producers."[24]

The real deficiency in the programme of industrial and resource development was the government's inability or unwillingness to make

Corner Brook, Newfoundland: This regional centre was originally developed by the Bowater Mersey pulp and paper company in the 1920s. Difficult world markets in the early 1980s almost forced closure of this mill, and government assistance was necessary for plant operation to continue under new management. (*Larry McCann*)

these new agents of development contribute more to national revenue. Newfoundland's financial crisis of the early 1930s was a function of declining revenues and increasing debt loads, but there was virtually no direct taxation of the most prosperous and productive sectors of the economy (mining and forest industries, for example). An assessment of the revenues produced by the resource towns demonstrates just how small their contribution to the public purse was (Table 7.6). Mining and forestry contributed little to relieve the mounting pressures of financial crisis. In fact, it is reasonable to infer that profit and secondary advantage accrued outside the colony.

The policies of enticement and appeasement developed early in the century were, either of necessity or habit, continued in the 1960s and '70s. The ill-fated oil refinery at Come-by-Chance, the failed linerboard mill at Stephenville, and the sellout of hydroelectric power in Labrador resulted from these policies. A comprehensive economic analysis of Newfoundland, conducted between 1978 and 1980 by the Economic Council of

TABLE 7.6 SOURCES OF REVENUE AND VALUE OF EXPORTS IN NEWFOUNDLAND, 1910–1930

Source		*Percentage*
Gross government revenues	$150 738 000	100.0
Gross revenue from royalties[a]	891 000	0.6
Gross revenue from customs in resource towns[b]	8 494 000	5.6
Gross value of exports	500 031 000	100.0
Gross value of iron ore exports	30 089 000	6.0
Gross value of forest products exports	117 970 000	23.6

[a]Almost all from Bell Island iron ore.

[b]Customs revenues paid by new resource industry towns — Bell Island, Grand Falls, Corner Brook, Botwood, Bishops Falls, Curling, Deer Lake.

Source: Calculated from Newfoundland records on revenues and customs.

Canada, concluded that "huge sums of money in the form of forgone revenue from natural resources are leaving the province." The report went on to suggest that this may be explained, in part, by the poor bargaining position of successive Newfoundland administrations *vis-à-vis* the more footloose and flexible multinational corporations: "experience has demonstrated that . . . the politicians and their advisers were no match for the shrewd and highly knowledgeable promoters and industrialists with whom they were negotiating." This pattern replicates that situation of core-periphery relations in which the poor hinterland region, desperate for economic development and diversification, is forced into agreements for minimal, short-term gains. Ultimately, of course, "the costs [are] far greater than the sum of all the direct and indirect economic benefits."[25]

A turbulent three-quarters of a century of efforts to diversify the economy could have left a legacy of changes in Newfoundland's economic geography. By the end of the 1970s, as Table 7.7 shows, the value of goods produced in both mining and construction exceeded the value produced in the fishery, and the value of forest production was not far behind. At the same time, however, the fishery was still the largest single employer of labour, and for a number of reasons (wide spatial distribution, high degree of domestic ownership, and as an underpinning of Newfoundland's traditional culture), it remained the most pervasive element in Newfoundland's social and economic geography.

THE FISHERY IN DECLINE

Compared with the strong gains in land-based resource development by foreign corporations, the performance of the indigenous marine

TABLE 7.7 GROSS DOMESTIC PRODUCT AND EMPLOYMENT IN THE GOODS-PRODUCING SECTORS IN NEWFOUNDLAND, 1979

Sector	Value ($ millions)	Percentage of Total	Employment	
			Years of Labour	% of Total
Agriculture	18.6	1.5	1 100	2.3
Forest	185.5	15.2	5 200	10.7
Fishing	232.2	19.0	16 100	33.1
Mining	342.2	28.0	5 900	12.1
Manufacturing[a]	134.9	11.0	6 400	13.1
Construction	309.3	25.3	14 000	28.7
Total	1 223.7	100.0	48 700	100.0

[a]Excluding fish and forest products.

Source: Government of Newfoundland and Labrador, *Managing All Our Resources* (St. John's, 1980), p. 12.

economy in the period 1884-1939 was disastrous. Until 1911, the fishery grew sporadically: over the period 1884 to 1911, the average annual growth rate was 1.2 percent. Thereafter, from 1911 to 1939, the growth rate declined at an average rate of — 2.3 percent per annum. Because the fishery was the main source of regional employment, this collapse had marked effects on the social and economic well-being of the colony, and contributed largely to the political and economic crisis of the 1930s.

A nexus of factors, both external and internal in origin, precipitated the collapse.[26] The root of external causes lay in the declining comparative advantage of Newfoundland fish on the international market. As protection in the world-economy replaced free trade in the depression years, as the convertibility of currency became more difficult, and as the North American dollar (in which Newfoundland purchased most of her imports) became more expensive, the returns on fishing, at both individual and aggregate levels, became more marginal. These problems were exacerbated by the domestic organization of the industry which, in terms of production, processing, and marketing, clung to traditional nineteenth century ways. As a result, Newfoundland lost ground to more sophisticated competition, particularly in Norway and Iceland. Only during the two World Wars was the return on fishing sufficient to offset the general picture of poor returns, though with the advent of peace, prices once again fell to marginal levels.

It is now apparent that small colonies like Newfoundland could not control the force of external factors. Newfoundland is a good example of a peripheral region which is squeezed out, or more likely ignored, in difficult times by the larger core preoccupied with the defence of its own interests. Yet, some small countries managed to survive and even profit. Iceland is cited as the example Newfoundland might have followed. The analogy, however, is not entirely valid. While accepting that Newfoundland may have profited by pursuing Iceland's course of development, the point must be made that because Newfoundland was tied to the North American market economy, it was not free to manoeuvre at will. Iceland, on the periphery of the non-dollar trading world, had more flexibility in its trading relationships. Newfoundland, poised uncomfortably on the edge of two trading blocs, fell between the two.

Could Newfoundland have overcome this peripheral disadvantage by improving the domestic organization of its indigenous economy? The general consensus is that whatever should have been done, was not done, largely because of inertia and "obscurantist conservatism." After the loss of self-government in 1934 and the switch to government by Commission, however, some substantial internal improvements were made. In 1935, a Newfoundland Fisheries Board was established. This organization regulated the catching and processing aspects of the industry, and despite depressed conditions, helped solidify Newfoundland's position in world markets. During World War II, market conditions changed radically in Newfoundland's favour. Even the anticipated post-war slump was countered with the formation, in 1947, of a marketing organization known as the Newfoundland Associated Fish Exporters Limited (NAFEL).

By these means, Newfoundland rectified some of the worst problems of her indigenous industry. Serious internal problems still persisted, and control of external conditions remained virtually impossible, but Newfoundland did emerge from the post-war period with a restructured industry capable of re-establishing former market dominance. However, by the end of the 1940s, much of the potential of this restructuring was vitiated by two factors, one political, the other technological. In 1948, the people of Newfoundland voted by a narrow margin to enter Confederation with Canada. Of no less significance was the move towards fresh frozen fish production, away from salt fish production. The combined effect of these two factors severely compromised success in the fishery.

It was neither fashionable nor popular in the immediate post-Confederation period to decry the advantages accruing from union with Canada. Most Newfoundlanders were impressed by the largesse which became immediately available. Family allowances were a welcome novelty in a traditionally cash-poor region. Newfoundland families were large, and the average monthly benefits ($16.38) were the highest in Canada. The reservations about political union held by the older, more traditionally minded Newfoundlanders were muted by the receipt of old-age pensions. Before Confederation, a largely grace-and-favour system had provided some 3000 senior citizens with $18 a quarter; after Confederation, 10 000 or so people received $30 a month, a figure which quickly was raised to $40 a month. At the institutional level, the new provincial government gained munificent transfer payments and inherited approximately $40 million which had been garnered during the prosperous war years by a parsimonious Commission of Government.

Union with Canada also brought difficulties, however. The long-term prospects for growth in the fishery, still Newfoundland's basic industry, were clouded by Confederation. One fundamental reason for this lies in the nature of jurisdiction exercised over the fishery resource. In any Canadian province in which manufacturing is not a major sector of the economy, prosperity is largely a function of natural resource endowment over which the provinces have, by constitution, sole ownership and control. Fisheries, however, because they are mobile and a common property resource, are an exception to this rule. By entering Confederation, it was Newfoundland's misfortune to lose control of its most important resource industry. This loss need not have mattered had the federal government pursued a fisheries policy that sustained the positive developments initiated by the Commission of Government, but Canada had neither experience nor sympathy in dealing with the idiosyncratic and traditional nature of the Newfoundland fishery. In the 1950s, benign neglect by Ottawa and internal structural problems arising from divided jurisdiction ensured that the fishery would slip further into decay. The fate of the NAFEL is but one example. Ruled unconstitutional under the British North America Act, its role was at first restricted, and eventually it was entirely phased out. As a result, marketing initiative and expertise slipped from Newfoundland's control, never to be replaced. The prospects of the fishery were further dimmed by growing dependence on the American market and its particular demands for fresh frozen fish. Deficient in capital and technical expertise, Newfoundland held no comparative advantage in this trade, and was unable to adjust adequately to compensate for losses in the salt fish trade to European countries.

Canadian foreign policy affecting the fishery perpetrated even more serious problems. After World War II, there was a marked increase in the number of foreign trawlers fishing the Grand Banks, arguably the spawning and breeding grounds of the world's richest fish stocks. The traditional Newfoundland method of exploiting this resource had been to wait for the feeding fish to migrate shoreward during the spring and early summer, and to harvest the resource as an "inshore," small-boat fishery. In principle, this is a labour-intensive operation, well-suited to a labour-rich, capital-poor economy. The expanding and aggressive assault on the offshore fishery through the 1950s, therefore, soon affected the size of stocks coming inshore. Clearly, offshore fishing by huge foreign fleets restricted the domestic inshore catch. The North-East Coast, the core Newfoundland region, was hardest hit, renewing seemingly endemic depression.

The Canadian response to this development was both slow and deleterious to the inshore fishery. At first, Canada failed to establish meaningful controls over the foreign offshore fleets, and the stocks quickly diminished. It was not until 1977 that Canada established a 200 mile economic zone for purposes of control and fisheries management (see Fig. 7.4). Equally important, federal policy favoured the development of a corporate, deep-water trawler fleet to compete against the foreign fleets in the offshore grounds. This was a capital-intensive solution which did little to answer the problems of Newfoundland's numerous inshore fishermen. In addition, federal funds were made available to assist in the resettlement of large numbers of rural Newfoundlanders, eroding further the basis and necessity of a labour-intensive inshore fishery. The irony is that at the time, the returns to capital and labour were greatest to the small, inshore boats and to the midwater fleet, and not to the offshore trawler fleet.[27]

The catch statistics for the critical decade from 1969 to 1978 illustrate some of these processes (Fig. 7.3). Until 1977, foreign fleets dominated Canadian waters and the combined Canadian catch averaged only about 42 percent of the total. At the same time, the total catch fell steeply from 2.43 million metric tons in 1969 to 1.41 million in 1978. The decline was universal throughout Canada's Atlantic waters, but was proportionately more marked in the areas subject to heavy foreign fishing: in the Labrador Sea (Area 2), the 1978 catch was only 18 percent of the 1969 total; in the Newfoundland zone (Area 3), the catch was down to 58 percent; but in Nova Scotia and Gulf of St. Lawrence waters (Area 4), the decline to 76 percent was more modest. In brief, the statistics illustrate that federal policy was diffident and that the Canadian fishery suffered as a result. When an effective policy was implemented, it was beneficial mainly to the corporate fleets of Nova Scotia, and gave relatively little assistance to the large inshore fishery of Newfoundland. To counter this trend, the Newfoundland government attempted to establish increased provincial jurisdiction and control, but by the end of the decade had met with little success. The closing of the seal fishery in the early 1980s as a result of foreign protests emphasized the impotence of the periphery in the development of its own resources.

The long-run decline of the fishery was masked by the establishment of the 200-mile economic zone in 1977. For three or four years in the late 1970s and early 1980s, with immediate foreign competition removed, fish prices were strong, and capital poured into the fishery from both large corporations and small business investors. But the boom was short-lived, and high interest rates together with weakening markets in the early 1980s decimated the industry. Decisive federal intervention on two levels — massive fiscal support for corporate restructuring and much firmer police action in the economic zone to protect the resource from foreign depredation — partially rectified the situation. By the mid-1980s, a cautious optimism had returned to many sectors of the industry, but the future of the traditional inshore fishery remained in doubt.

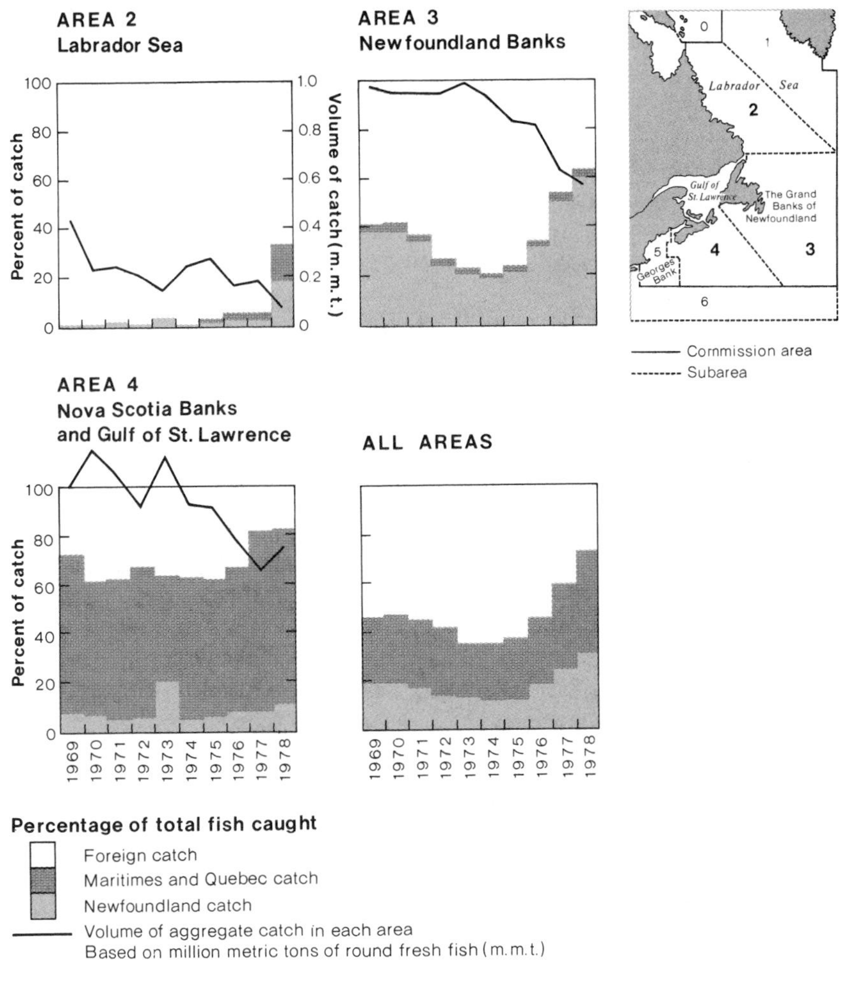

Figure 7.3 Regional trends of fish caught off Canada's eastern coast, 1969-1978.

CURRENT RESOURCE ISSUES

Newfoundland's confrontation with the federal government over the fishery was exacerbated by other differences of opinion, the most important focussing on the development and disposal of Labrador hydroelectric power and the ownership and control of offshore mineral resources (Fig. 7.4). The development of the Upper Churchill River in Labrador in the early 1970s created one of Canada's largest and cheapest sources of hydroelectric power. Unfortunately, Québec refused Newfoundland the right to transmit power to market across its territory, and insisted that any power generated be sold primarily to Hydro Québec at the border. The contract, signed in 1967 for a 65-year period, gave power to Québec for less than three mills per kilowatt hour, a price that will actually be reduced towards the end of the contract. By the end of the 1970s, the market price of the electricity sold for three mills was 30 to 40 mills per kilowatt hour, and the economic rent thus captured by Québec was worth between 50 and 60 percent of Newfoundland's annual revenues.

The "unconscionable inequities" contained in the Upper Churchill power contract were, by the early 1980s, the subject of embarrassing legal manoeuverings in St. John's and Ottawa. Further development of large Labrador hydroelectric power resources has been stymied by the intransigence of Québec over the transmission of power. Newfoundland requested that the federal government invoke its powers to require the unrestricted transmission of electricity as a commodity across Québec. The province argued that if oil and gas could be transmitted by inter-provincial pipeline, then any commodity of inter-provincial trade could not, unreasonably, be denied transmission rights. By denying these rights, Newfoundland felt that Québec was acting unconstitutionally. The federal government's response has been ambiguous; it has urged Newfoundland and Québec to settle the matter on their own. Successive federal governments have been unwilling to offend Québec, a base of their political power.

Newfoundland's requests for assistance from the federal government have not been helped by growing disagreement over the question of ownership and control of the offshore zone. This controversy first erupted over the question of fisheries jurisdiction when Newfoundland pressed Canada to limit the depredations of foreign fishing fleets. Had Newfoundland been an independent state, it is reasonable to assume that it would, like Iceland, have enacted 200 mile legislation at an earlier date to control the plundering (Fig. 7.4). As a part of a federal state, however, Newfoundland quite properly had to wait for Canada, which was constitutionally responsible for foreign affairs, to effect change. While conceding Ottawa this responsibility, Newfoundland adamantly claimed ownership of the seabed resources on the Continental Shelf, just as other provinces controlled land resources. Newfoundland argued that because it entered Confederation as a Dominion equal in status to Canada, it possessed territories both on land and under the sea. Canada countered by stating that the submarine lands in question accrued to Canada after Confederation. The outer boundary of the shelf is still in dispute.[28] While the claims are simple in principle, the legalities are more complex, and Newfoundland's moral case may be just as important as its legal case. Whatever the legal outcome of the resource ownership question, Newfoundland's movement into Confederation unquestionably endowed

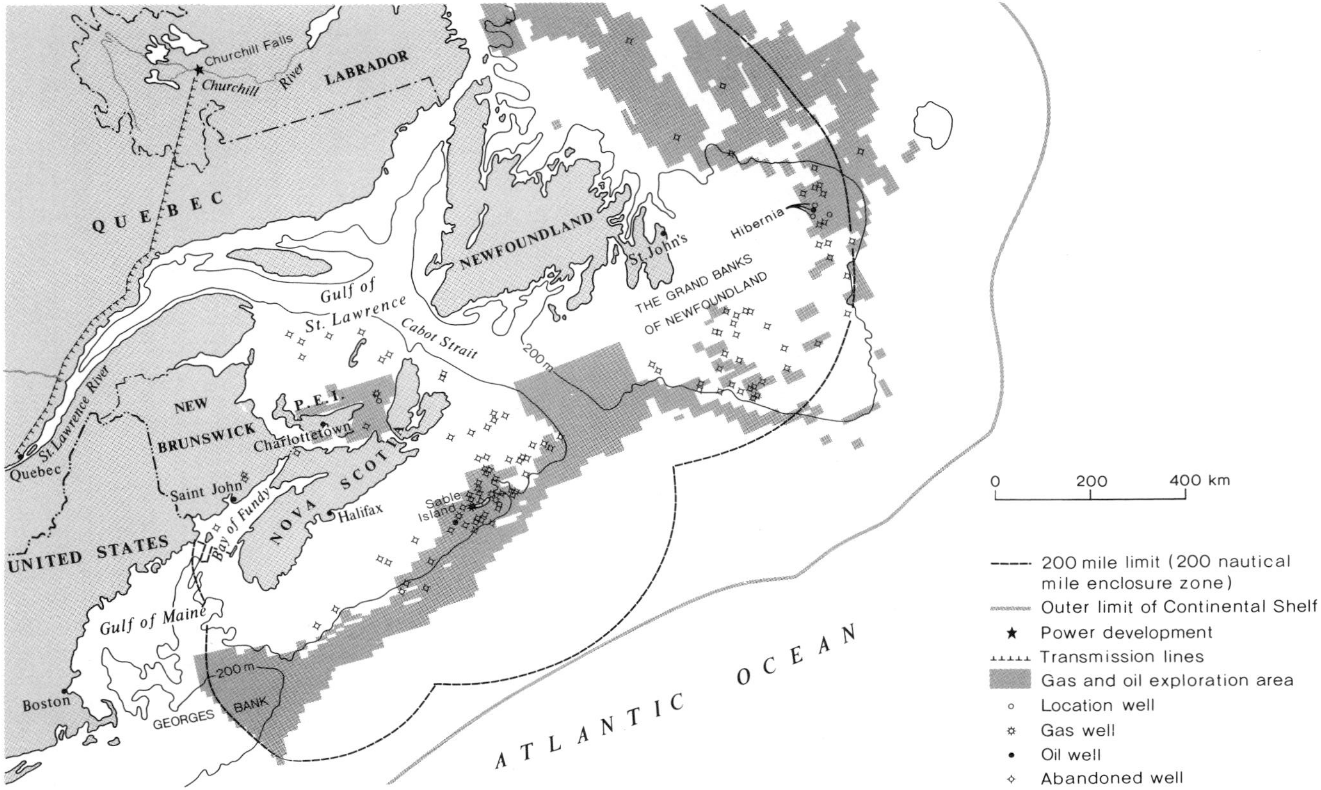

Figure 7.4 Location of major resource developments in Atlantic Canada, c. 1980.

Oil and the future of Newfoundland: Will offshore oil discoveries change Newfoundland from a "have not" to a "have" province? Regardless, when oil production finally replaces the current phase of exploratory drilling, Newfoundland's economy and society will undergo marked change. (*Mobil Oil Canada, Ltd.*)

Canada with the region's resources. As a "disadvantaged" part of Canada, many argue that Newfoundland maintains a moral right to primacy in the utilization of these resources to foster economic development.

The disagreement over offshore ownership lay dormant for most of the post-Confederation period. It was only in 1966, when the first exploratory well was drilled in the search for offshore oil, that the question began to resurface. In 1974, significant discoveries of gas were made on the Labrador Margin. In 1979, a large oil strike was made in the Hibernia field, just 164 nautical miles east of the Avalon Peninsula (Fig. 7.4). In the early 1980s, other substantial, commercially viable finds were made. These promising finds made the dispute between the two governments all the more significant, for the unresolved conflict inhibited exploration and virtually prohibited commercial development of the offshore oilfields until the issue was resolved. The eventual outcome was a compromise: Canada secured legal title by Supreme Court decision, but in the Atlantic Accord signed in 1985, ceded a substantial share of resource control and revenue to Newfoundland.

CONCLUSION

It would be incorrect to infer from the above arguments that Newfoundland has not benefited from Confederation. Short-run benefits have been numerous, and at least to older Newfoundlanders, they have been obvious. After nearly 40 years of Confederation, there are signs that the power of the centre, as manifested in policies and practices engendering sustained development, may be moving in Newfoundland's favour. Nevertheless, Confederation has placed constitutional and political constraints on the development of Newfoundland. These constraints did not result from malign intent or benign indifference; rather, larger considerations of national and international significance — foreign policy, international trade obligations, federal-provincial relations — have prevailed over Newfoundland's problems and priorities. There is nothing new in this pattern. For nearly 150 years, Newfoundland has functioned at the margin under various forms of self-government, and as a small and peripheral entity it has always been subjected to domination by metropolitan countries. Newfoundland has been the disadvantaged partner in a series of core-periphery relationships. But if the Newfoundland example suggests one element more than any other, it is that the relationship is primarily political in nature. Core-periphery structures are frequently described as a set of immutable economic laws; the Newfoundland case suggests that political relationships can be the more potent causes of underdevelopment and dependency.

NOTES

1. J.D. Rogers, *A Historical Geography of the British Colonies: Newfoundland* (Oxford: The University Press, 1911), p. 170.
2. G.E. Gunn, *The Political History of Newfoundland, 1832-64* (Toronto: University of Toronto Press, 1961), p. 188.
3. Quoted in E.R. Forbes, "Newfoundland Politics in 1921: A Canadian View," *Acadiensis*, 9 (1979), pp. 95, 99, 101, and 102.
4. The definitive work on this affair is F.F. Thompson, *The French Shore Question in Newfoundland: An Imperial Study* (Toronto: Macmillan, 1961), p. 222.
5. Sir Robert Bond, speech in House of Assembly, April 20, 1904.
6. For a concise and balanced account of these two struggles, see Peter Neary, "The French and American Shore Questions as Factors in Newfoundland History," in *Newfoundland in the Nineteenth and Twentieth Centuries*, eds. J.K. Hiller and Peter Neary (Toronto: University of Toronto Press, 1980), pp. 95-122.
7. D.W. Prowse, *A History of Newfoundland from the English, Colonial and Foreign Records* (London: 1895), p. 532.

8. Neary, "The French and American Shore Questions," p. 118.
9. A.L. Mabogunje, "The Dynamics of Centre-Periphery Relations: The Need for a New Geography of Resource Development," *Transactions, Institute of British Geographers,* 5 (1980), p. 277.
10. For a good account of the operations of such a merchant house, see M. Chang, "Newfoundland in Transition: The Newfoundland Trade and Robert Newman and Company, 1780-1805" (unpublished M.A. thesis, Memorial University of Newfoundland, 1975).
11. For a discussion of the cod fishery and occupational pluralism, see W.A. Black, "The Labrador Floater Cod Fishery," *Annals of the Association of American Geographers,* 50 (1960), 267-93; and C.W. Sanger, "The Evolution of Sealing and the Spread of Permanent Settlement in Northeastern Newfoundland," in *The Peopling of Newfoundland,* ed. John Mannion (St. John's: Institute of Social and Economic Research, Memorial University, 1977), p. 137.
12. United Kingdom, *Newfoundland Royal Commission, 1933* (London: 1937), p. 223.
13. Ellsworth Huntington, *Mainsprings of Civilization* (New York: Mentor, 1945), p. 155.
14. S.D. Antler, "The Capitalist Underdevelopment of Nineteenth Century Newfoundland," in *Underdevelopment and Social Movements in Atlantic Canada,* eds. R.J. Brym and R.J. Sacouman (Toronto: New Hogtown Press, 1979), p. 197.
15. In 1891, for example, the value of mines (buildings, plant etc.) was recorded as $582 000, but capital invested to secure this amount was $5 115 000. There had been significant mining exploration and development before the 1880s, however, and were mining investment figures available for 1884, they would doubtless considerably increase Antler's figure of $1.2 million. Similarly, the capital flow into shipping must have been a major element of re-investment in the local economy. An approximate value attributed to Newfoundland shipping in 1891 might be $2.5 or $3 million. This latter point has been addressed by Eric Sager in "The Merchants of Water Street and Capital Investment in Newfoundland's Traditional Economy," in *The Enterprising Canadians: Entrepreneurs and Economic Development in Eastern Canada,* eds. Lewis Fischer and Eric Sager (St. John's: Memorial University Press, 1979), pp. 75-96. The ultimate objection to the capital export thesis of colonial exploitation is qualitative, not quantitative. As David Alexander suggests, the proponents of such a thesis must demonstrate that "retention of capital would have had positive, dynamic effects on national income through a higher investment ratio," and that Newfoundland was accordingly more disadvantaged than other colonies. David Alexander, "Literacy and Economic Development in Nineteenth Century Newfoundland," *Acadiensis,* 10 (1980), pp. 3-34. Quotation is from p. 5.
16. David Alexander, "Development and Dependence in Newfoundland," *Acadiensis,* 4 (1974), pp. 3-31; *idem,* "Newfoundland's Traditional Economy and Development to 1934," *Acadiensis,* 5 (1976), pp. 56-78; *idem,* "The Political Economy of Fishing in Newfoundland," *Journal of Canadian Studies,* 11 (1976), pp. 32-40; *idem,* "The Collapse of the Saltfish Trade and Newfoundland's Integration into the North American Economy," *Canadian Historical Association Historical Papers,* (1976), pp. 229-48; idem, *The Decay of Trade: An Economic History of the Newfoundland Saltfish Trade, 1935-65* (St. John's: Memorial University Press, 1977); *idem,* "Economic Growth in the Atlantic Region, 1880-1940," *Acadiensis,* 8 (1978), pp. 47-76; *idem;* "Literacy and Economic Development."
17. Antler, "Capitalist Underdevelopment," p. 193.
18. Alexander, "Development and Dependence," p. 12.
19. The major exception to this is St. John's District, which recorded leading values in three of the five years. This occurred because the harvest of the seal fishery was landed and registered in St. John's, a function of growing capital and entrepreneurial concentration. Many of the sealing crews came from the districts of the North-East Coast and their earnings should properly contribute to the "productivity" of their home districts. See Sanger, "Evolution of Sealing," p. 150.

20. There are two possible explanations for this situation. First, in simple environmental terms, the South Coast has a longer fishing season. Second, there may have been a greater capital investment in larger offshore boats on the South Coast. The relevant statistics, however, do not support this latter suggestion.

	North-East Coast	South Coast
Avg. size of boats >20 tons, 1900	37	35
Avg. size of boats >20 tons, 1910	39	42
Tons per man c/c fish, 1900	2.04	1.48
Tons per man c/c fish, 1910	1.95	1.90

Although over this period the South Coast Fleet (Burin, Fortune, Placentia, and St. Mary's) was increasing in size faster than that of the North-East Coast (Trinity, Bonavista, and Twillingate), there is no case for saying that there was a substantial difference in capital investment between the two areas. As our intention is to show variations in wealth accruing to particular regions, it seems important to relate the returns to persons rather than to capital. This, of course, does not prove that individual fishermen on the South Coast, for example, received greater individual returns for their efforts, but it is difficult to believe that they did not profit from the generally higher levels of income.

21. This argument, of course, has no direct bearing on Antler's thesis which deals with the mechanisms for the appropriation of surplus, rather than with simple productivity. It is still possible that higher productivity in merchant communities meant no added benefit to fishermen but merely allowed for higher appropriation to merchants. But the argument cannot be true both ways: if the presence of merchants tended to increase productivity, then the chances are that this would benefit fishermen at some stage; if, on the other hand, merchants were irrelevant to productivity, then the spatial variations in productivity must be related to variations in resource potential. The latter seems more likely.

22. J.K. Hiller, "The Railway and Local Politics in Newfoundland, 1870-1901," in *Newfoundland in the Nineteenth and Twentieth Centuries* (Toronto: University of Toronto Press, 1980), pp. 123-47.

23. Scotia Steel's corporate evolution is traced in L.D. McCann, "The Mercantile-Industrial Transition in the Metals Towns of Pictou County, 1858-1929," *Acadiensis*, 10 (1981), pp. 29-64. See also D.W. Mercer, "Bell Island: An Economic Analysis" (unpublished B.A. honours thesis, Memorial University, 1963); and Peter Neary, *Bell Island*, Canada's Visual History, Vol. 12 (Ottawa: National Museum of Man, 1974).

24. Council of the Newfoundland Board of Trade, "Sixteenth Annual Report," *Journals of the House of Assembly* (1925), p. 458.

25. Quotations are from the Economic Council of Canada, *Newfoundland: From Dependency to Self-reliance* (Ottawa: 1980), pp. xii and 12.

26. The best exposition of this deterioration and of the counter measures taken is Alexander, "The Political Economy of Fishing," and *idem, The Decay of Trade.*

27. Alexander, "The Political Economy of Fishing," p. 37.

28. The outer limit of the Continental Shelf, as shown in Fig. 7.3, has been interpreted by Dr. Hal Mills, an Ottawa - based consultant, from an examination of Article 76 of the *Draft Convention on the Law of the Sea Conference* (New York: United Nations, 1979). I am grateful to Dr. Mills for providing this interpretation.

8

The Western Interior: The Transformation of a Hinterland Region

Brenton M. Barr and John C. Lehr

The Western Interior has traditionally been viewed as a region dominated by the economic force and political power of central Canada which, in turn, has been guided by similar and equally strong forces in Britain and the United States. The chief commodities of the region, including primary agricultural and mineral products, have been subject to burdensome transportation costs, inequitable tariffs, and alienating market prices determined far beyond its boundaries. Moreover, the regional economy has advanced by using labour and capital imported from developed regions. Even though the influx of immigrant farm labour diminished during the Depression of the 1930s, the development of energy and mineral resources after World War II continued the tradition of relying on metropolitan sources of capital and entrepreneurship. Many of the advanced skills and the technology necessary to develop highly productive petroleum reserves still come, for instance, from the Texas Gulf region. Borrowed capital, technical expertise, and entrepreneurial skills have also brought organizational dependence on, and subordination to, multilocational and multinational firms, whose chief interests focus on the spatial integration of a hinterland's resources with its own industrial and management systems in other regions and nations. From a heartland-hinterland perspective, therefore, the Western Interior has shown many characteristics of hinterland dependency. In this world order, change and innovation are diffused from developed regions into areas struggling with remoteness, environmental obstacles, and limited social and economic opportunities.

Historically, the most direct lines of dependency have been to central Canada. The West, most of which was settled during the period of intensive immigration between 1896 and 1914, was initially agricultural in character and supplied primary products to distant industry in central Canada and overseas markets. For decades after Confederation, efforts to develop an even limited industrial base were unsuccessful mainly because of inequitable freight rates, isolation, and remoteness from markets. Federal government policies tended to reflect the realities of Canadian demography — the power of the electorate lay in Ontario and Québec — and concentrated on nurturing the growing financial and industrial interests of the Heartland, often to the disadvantage of the West. In the debate before World War I over reciprocity between Canada and the United States, for example, Ontario and Québec favoured a protectionist stance, defending what they viewed as their fragile industrial structure. By contrast, the West favoured reciprocity and access to cheaper American goods, especially farm machinery. Reciprocity was defeated: the Heartland's gain was the West's loss.

A similar polarization of objectives between western and central Canada is evident in the 1980s. In the debate over free trade with the United States, Ontario and Québec again generally oppose the move. American competition and ownership is perceived as a threat to central Canada's economic base. The western provinces, including British Columbia, on the other hand, favour access to even wider world markets. They see economic advantages in exporting raw materials and primary manufactures to American and world markets and in importing capital equipment (such as electrical turbines, computers, and urban public transportation equipment) and consumer goods (such as automobiles, personal and domestic electronic commodities, and clothing) from non-Canadian heartlands such as Japan, the European Economic Community and the U.S.S.R., and from the People's Republic of China and the "Newly Industrializing Countries" (NICs) of southeast Asia. Under such a system, not only would exports likely increase bringing greater profits to the region, but production costs would likely decrease.

The prospects for prosperity in the West, however, have wavered considerably over the past decades. In the decade preceding the early 1980s, rapid changes in the social, economic, and political fabric of the Western Interior seemed to be presaging a new relationship between the region and its traditional core areas of subordination.[1] The abrupt change — some would say return — to more customary levels of economic activity after 1982 suggests, however, that the heartland-hinterland paradigm still describes many of the forces binding the region to its markets and suppliers. The Western Interior by the 1980s was on the verge of a new-found maturity in the self-control of its internal development because its resource-exploration, development, extraction, and marketing activities were generating attendant activities such as processing, management, finance, research, and investment control within the region. And many of these activities were controlled by firms based in the Western Interior.[2]

Provincial control over numerous aspects of the regional economy and its resources has also generated a noticeable degree of vertical integration associated with primary commodity production. Head office functions involving administration, research, control, and finance have grown in the region through the establishment of provincially-owned Crown corporations or through governmental policies aimed at patriation of the tertiary and quaternary sectors of the economy from non-regional private corporations. Accepting that all levels of government in Canada generally spent approximately 40 percent of the Gross National Product in the early 1980s, the degree of control by the region over its own activities was much greater in mind and in practice — as evidenced by the rapid rise to power by entrepreneurs based in the Western Interior, "the prairie super rich" — in 1980 than in 1940.[3] A study by G. Friesen also suggests that large government-owned enterprises such as "the three prairie telephone corporations, the two power corporations, the Alberta airline (Pacific Western), the Alberta Energy Company and Treasury Branches, the Saskatchewan Crown Investments Corporation, the Alberta Heritage Fund, and ... NOVA — an Alberta Corporation, were subject to government directives"[4] that protected regional interests. Sixty Western Interior corporations were included in the 1981 *Financial Post* list of the 500 most important industrial organizations in Canada, 17 Western Interior firms were among the *Financial Post* 1981 50 Big Subsidiaries, and 5 of Canada's 10 largest Crown corporations had bases in the Western Interior. Cooperatives and credit unions have also played a large part in the regional economy: "5 of Canada's 10 largest cooperatives were based in the prairie West and the prairie credit unions possessed assets of nearly $7 billion" in the early 1980s.[5]

Thus, by the early 1980s, the population had become aware of local and regional forms of development and had become more conscious and articulate of the need to take control of its external cultural, political, and economic affairs. Such relatively unfettered optimism, however, was shaken when the realities of Canadian and world geographical distribution of political and economic power were reasserted in the 1980s in the form of the federal government's National Energy Policy enunciated in 1979 (aimed at reducing American control of the oil industry), the collapse of world energy prices after 1981, and the severity of economic recession and protectionist attitudes in one of the region's most important energy and resource or primary-manufacture markets, the United States.

All of these major events have had repercussions on the viability of the spatial economy in the Western Interior in the 1980s. Much of the previous buoyancy was predicated on continuing strong export sales and the service-sector spin-offs from investment in capital and domestic construction. Although any significant upturn in the spatial economy must stem from the major oil and gas sectors, other energy sources such as coal, uranium, and hydroelectricity; the primary agricultural sectors of grain and livestock; lumber and wood products; and non-ferrous metals; all complement the extent to which the spatial economy, including the region's metropolitan areas and smaller communities, can sustain growth and continue the process of achieving maturity in internal development.

Diversification since World War II within the resource sector and the specialized related service industries has helped the region weather the economic crises of the 1980s. Farming is no longer the major source of employment and regional income. Friesen, for example, observes that although half of the Western Interior's residents lived on farms in 1941, only 10 percent did so in 1981. During the same period, the five metropolitan centres grew to house over half the region's population. Agriculture contributed one half of census value added in 1941 but less than 15 percent in 1978.

This change is attributable to the growth of mining. Mining (including oil and gas production) contributed only 8 percent of census value added in 1941 but two-fifths in 1978. The proportion of the labour force engaged in agriculture declined from about one-half of the total in 1941 to about one-tenth in 1981. The slack was taken-up by the tertiary sector, with its special links to the oil and gas industry, as managerial, professional, clerical, sales, and service workers grew from 30 to 59 percent of the paid labour force between 1941 and 1981.[6] Urbanization and tertiary-led growth have therefore combined to reduce the region's dependency on wealth generated by world demand for primary and semi-finished commodities.

Although dependency on the primary sector has been reduced, it has not been eliminated. Diversification is not broadly based, despite some significant individual examples of specialized and internationally competitive activities such as Manitoba's aerospace industries, Saskatchewan's agricultural and biological research prowess, and Alberta's transportation and communication firms. The Western Interior remains dependent on the Industrial Heartland and on other world centres. Diversification is made difficult by the region's remoteness and vulnerability to swings in the national and world-economy. The reasons are clear enough: many manufacturing industries cannot function competitively because of their high wage levels; access to external markets is hampered by long distances and expensive transportation systems; and foreign ownership of economic activity means that the welfare of the Western Interior is often of secondary importance. Nevertheless, as Alberta in particular illustrates, the emergence of an indigenous entrepreneurial class can improve and widen the base of a regional economy.

It is clear, therefore, that the Western Interior is still a hinterland region within the Canadian space economy and the world-economy. The heartland-hinterland paradigm is a valid framework for assessing the development of the Western Interior. In this chapter, we emphasize the historical perspective and analyze in particular those factors shaping the geographic character of the region. The Western Interior is treated as a conceptual unity, recognizing fully that the three provinces have distinct characteristics. Their unifying features of a common past and general world status are emphasized in the context of the heartland and hinterland pattern. We begin by describing those essential features of the region's physical geography that have influenced its economic and cultural development.

THE PHYSICAL MOLD OF THE WESTERN INTERIOR

The Western Interior of Canada is the northern extension of the central lowlands of the United States (Fig. 8.1). It is a part of a massive physiographic unit bounded by the Rocky Mountains on the west and by the Appalachian and Shield systems on the east. The plains between sweep northwards from the Texas Gulf Coast to the arctic margins of the Mackenzie Delta. The international boundary, which bisects the region along the line of the 49th parallel, divides the land politically, but physically it remains a cohesive unit. Differences of nomenclature — Great Plains and Prairies — cannot obscure the natural linkages wrought by geology and topography.

Geologically, the Western Interior of Canada is a massive, crescentic sedimentary basin located between the crystalline rocks of the Shield and the sedimentary folds of the Rocky Mountains.[7] This basin is composed of gently warped limestones, shales, sandstones, and evaporites, ranging in age from the Cambrian to the Tertiary. The deposits deepen westwards. In Alberta, where deposits of over 3000 metres are found, oil is present in vast amounts in Devonian reef systems. In the Fort McMurray-Athabasca area, thousands of hectares of oil-bearing sands are found at shallow depths, sometimes outcropping on river banks and seldom overlain by a glacial overburden of more than 100 metres. Natural gas is found in conjunction with conventional oil reservoirs and independently at shallow depths in sand beds in the southern part of Alberta. These oil and gas reserves are the heart of Alberta's rich resource base. The wealth generated from their development has sparked the economic growth of the region, particularly through the world energy crisis of the 1970s and into the 1980s.

Topographically, the settled area of the Western Interior is not one landscape but three, for the region consists of three great plains each separated by gentle escarpments (Fig. 8.1). The first level runs from the Shield to the rise of the Manitoba escarpment. Here the cuesta of resistant Cretateous sediments has been dissected by eastward flowing rivers into a series of picturesque hills: the Tiger, Riding Mountain, Duck, Porcupine,

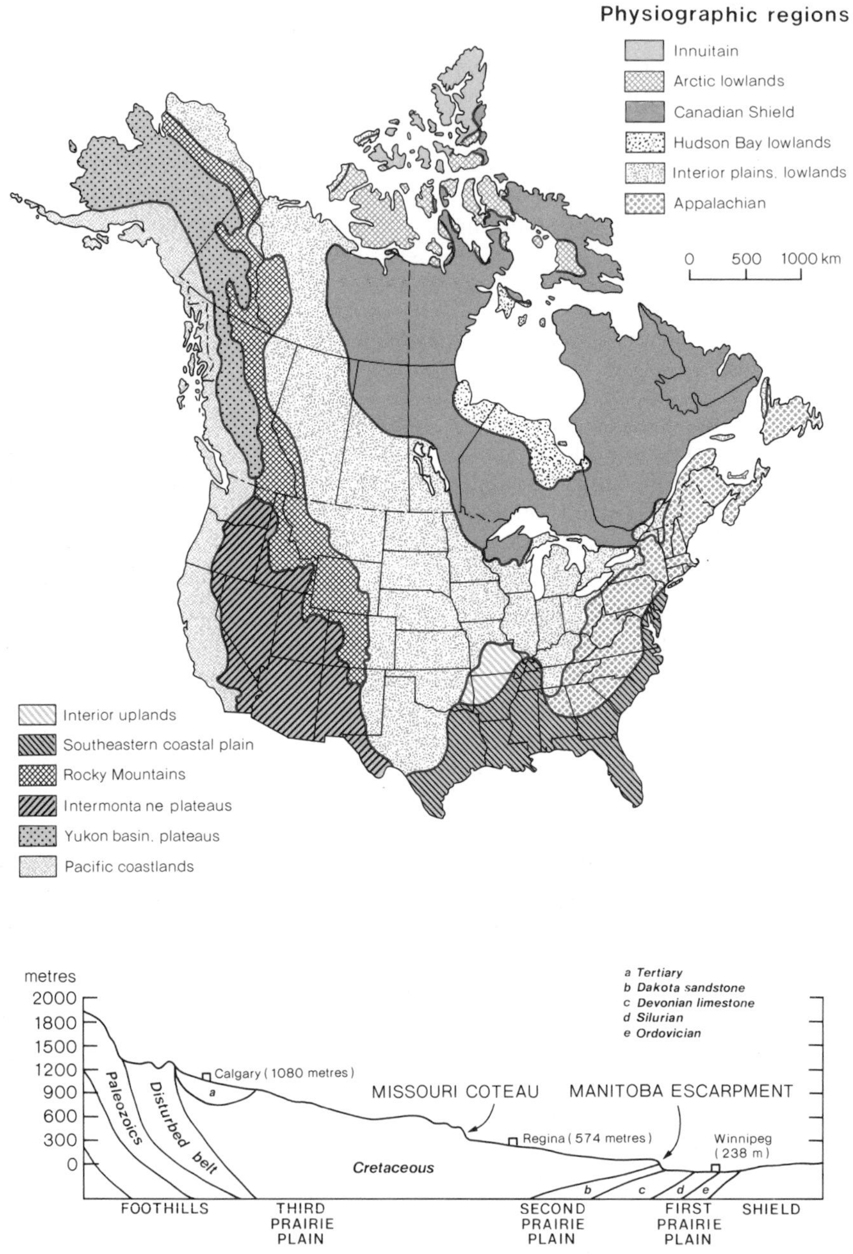

Physiographic regions
Innuitain
Arctic lowlands
Canadian Shield
Hudson Bay lowlands
Interior plains, lowlands
Appalachian
0 500 1000 km
Interior uplands
Southeastern coastal plain
Rocky Mountains
Intermontane plateaus
Yukon basin, plateaus
Pacific coastlands
metres
2000
1800
1500
1200
900
600
300
0
a Tertiary
b Dakota sandstone
c Devonian limestone
d Silurian
e Ordovician
Calgary (1080 metres)
MISSOURI COTEAU
MANITOBA ESCARPMENT
Regina (574 metres)
Winnipeg (238 m)
Paleozoics
Disturbed belt
Cretaceous
FOOTHILLS
THIRD PRAIRIE PLAIN
SECOND PRAIRIE PLAIN
FIRST PRAIRIE PLAIN
SHIELD

Figure 8.1 The physical setting of the Western Interior.

and Pasquia Hills. The terrain rises by 250 metres to the second level, a rolling plateau of over 500 metres above sea level cut by deeply incised rivers and levelled by many post-glacial lake sediments. The western limit of this level is marked by the less defined rise of the Missouri Coteau, a low line of dirt hills running from Weyburn to Moose Jaw, then following the line of the Saskatchewan-Alberta boundary. Westwards the third prairie level rises from 670 metres above sea level in the northeast to 1200 metres above sea level at the base of the Rocky Mountain foothills.

The topography of each of these "prairie steps" owes much to glacial and fluvio-glacial process. In the Quaternary period continental ice-sheets invaded from the northeast, covered virtually all the interior, and at their maximum size joined with the Alpine glaciers probing eastwards from the Rocky Mountain heights. This ice left a discontinuous cover of stony and stratified till to depths of 320 metres and deposited thick accumulations of end moraine. Stagnant ice moraines dotted with "myriad kettle lakes" and rolling till plains are common in the southern part of all three prairie provinces, as are the wide, steep-sided, flat-bottomed glacial spillways now occupied by misfit streams, sinuous lakes, and swamps.[8] These offer some of the most magnificent scenery in the Canadian West.

The most characteristic prairie scenery — the level plain — was formed by the damming or glacial melt waters (glacial lakes) in pre-glacial troughs. The largest of these lakes is Lake Agassiz, which, at its maximum extent, covered parts of the Lake of the Woods region in Ontario, most of southern Manitoba, and extended into east central Saskatchewan. It left a series of gravelly beach ridges — strandlines — at the foot of the Manitoba escarpment and left deep deposits of lacustrine clays across southern Manitoba. The old lakebed constitutes one of the most fertile, and to some unsympathetic eyes, most monotonous regions of the prairie.

In post-glacial times the Western Interior has been drained by two major river systems. The Nelson-Saskatchewan basin extends from the international boundary to 54° north, while the basin of the Mackenzie-Athabasca-Peace system drains the northwestern plains. Though the escarpment and hills were important to the course of native and European occupation, the river systems were the single most important geographical feature of the region. They dictated the flow of communication, the path of trade, and the tide of exploration and early settlement.

Since the rivers flow north and east, delayed ice breakup in the north makes many river valleys prone to spring flooding when melt waters hit icebound territory or ice-jammed rivers. In sparsely settled areas this flooding merely disrupts agricultural activity, but in the densely settled Red River Valley spring flooding causes considerable social and economic disruption. Ironically, the phenomenon which has awarded the Valley its great fertility constitutes its most serious natural hazard, one which has led Winnipeg to construct a massive flood diversion channel to deflect the waters around the city.

The vegetation and soils of the Western Interior reflect both the climate and topography of the region (Fig. 8.2). Short grasses form most of the cover on the less fertile brown chernozems of Palliser's Triangle. In the extreme south of the region sage and common cactus are also found. Bordering this short grass zone is an arc of mixed grass prairie developed on more fertile dark brown chernozems. Here precipitation levels are higher and more reliable. At the eastern extent of this arc of vegetation, on the Agassiz plain, lies the true prairie — a lush cover of tall grasses some 1.5 metres in height developed on black chernozems and gleysols. Between the mixed grass prairie and the boreal forest, sits the parkland belt where aspen bluffs and prairie clearings developed on dark brown and black chernozems, and gleysols. These gradually merge northwards into continuous deciduous woodlands and coniferous boreal forest developed mostly on dark grey chernozems and grey luvisols.

The climate of the Western Interior is cool continental, marked by hot summers and extremely cold winters. Climate has been a major obstacle to the successful agricultural settlement of the region. Late and early frosts restrict the growing season from 120 days in the south to 100 or less in the north, a period which was insufficient to ripen wheat in the early years of settlement, even in the best regions.[9] Today, despite the development of early maturing varieties, the growing season on northern margins of the region is barely adequate for successful cereal cultivation. Other climatic hazards include hail from severe convectional summer storms, the occasional tornado which wreaks havoc in the southern margins and, of course, drought, which is usually most serious in the water deficient areas of the prairies north and south of the Cyprus Hills.

The severity of the climate is tempered in the extreme west by chinooks that sweep down from the Rocky Mountains and raise temperatures dramatically over short periods, clearing the snow cover from the range lands which lie east of the mountains. Microclimatic variations assume importance in local agricultural endeavours, as, for example, at Morden, Manitoba, where apple orchards survive in the shelter of the escarpment.

The Western Interior is, as many prairie authors have observed, a stark land of haunting beauty, a land of contrasts and extremes in climate, vegetation, and topography; one which places a vertical man on a horizontal land and pits the puny skills of mankind against the immensity of the plain and the unpredictable vagaries of an unforgiving continental climate.[10] Many perceptive writers of the prairie provinces have attributed the attitudes and opinions held by the region's inhabitants to the environment in which they live. This may be facile determinism, but it is clear that the historical evolution of the Western Interior as a hinterland region has done little to dissipate the westerners' perception of themselves as a people beset by a harsh environment.

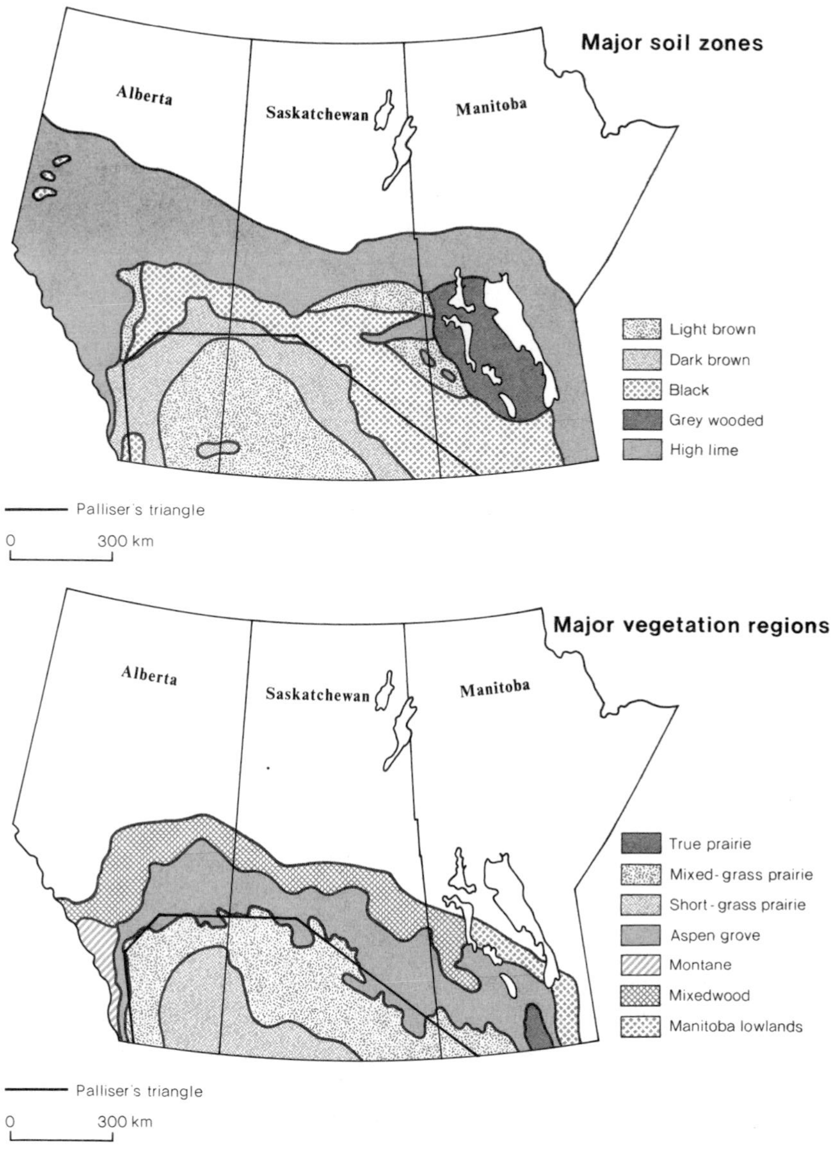

Figure 8.2 Vegetation and soils of the Western Interior.

CASTING THE PATTERN

Two corporations, the Hudson's Bay Company and the Canadian Pacific Railway, cast the initial geographical patterns of the Canadian West. Indeed, as Harold Innis has pointed out in *The Fur Trade in Canada,* the present political boundaries of the region are, in large measure, a reflection of the efficiency of the Canadian fur trade.[11] In 1670, the Hudson's Bay Company was awarded a royal charter to trade through Hudson Bay. It received proprietary title to Rupert's Land, a vaguely defined territory that came to be equated with the drainage basin of Hudson Bay. Within this area, the Company enjoyed the privilege of monopoly trading and, apart from the small area of colonial Canada, it was for two hundred years the sole agent of British Imperial authority. From the beginning, the Company focussed its activities upon the prosecution of the fur trade. To the extent that it did colonize, it did so only with the view of increasing the efficiency of its staple trade. Agricultural settlement was incompatible with the efficient harvesting of furs, but the company did establish a small colony on the Red River near its confluence with the Assiniboine River at the present site of Winnipeg. The Selkirk settlement, as it became known, may have attained the philanthropic objectives of its founder, but the Company accepted it with reluctance, viewing it only as an agricultural and labour supply base for its wilderness trade.

The Company's greatest impact was in its permanent reorganization of aboriginal occupance patterns over much of the northern half of the continent. This European geography imposed by the Company was characterized by three distinct patterns of occupance and trade. Initially, from 1670 until 1774, settlement was confined to fortified entrepôts located on the estuaries of the major rivers flowing into Hudson Bay. The Company remained on the coast, depending upon Native intermediaries for the extension of company trade to the outer limits of the fur trade hinterland. The placement of these forts eventually drew the Native population north and west in search of access to the central routeways to the Bayside. This movement in turn provoked intertribal conflict. The Cree and Assiniboine tried to retain their supremacy in the north by maintaining their role as agents of the fur trade, but in doing so, they denied the Gros Ventre, Blackfoot, and Chipewyan access to the Bayside forts. The diffusion of trade goods and manufactures from a European core wrought havoc among the aboriginal population, transforming the native economy and altering the human geography of the region.[12]

The second phase of Hudson's Bay Company occupance was marked by the movement of trading posts inland, away from Bayside, in an attempt to counter rival fur trade companies seeking to divert the flow of furs eastward to the St. Lawrence. Compelled to move into the interior, the Company did so selectively, establishing forts and posts at strategic locations to control the rivers — the arteries of the fur trade. Finally, the amalgamation of the North West Company and the Hudson's Bay Company in 1821 terminated rivalry and ushered in an era of fur trade consolidation. Many of the strategic post locations identified in the heat of competition consolidated their positions. Some, such as Fort Garry and Fort Edmonton, served as springboards for urban growth when Rupert's Land was acquired by the Dominion of Canada in 1870.

During the two centuries of company jurisdiction, Native society and economy were transformed. Often within a generation, the Native peoples' independent way of life was changed by the fur trade to a life of dependency upon European mercantile interests. Thus, to the uncertainties of the fisheries and the hunt were added those of supply and demand in Europe. The vagaries of the European market were felt keenly in the emerging West.

Early Settlement, 1870-1895

Three years after Confederation, the government of Canada acquired Rupert's Land. It received a territory where the fur trade reigned supreme, where agriculture was either for subsistence or designed to provision the fur trade, and where, along the banks of the Red River, the few Selkirk settlers and the Métis maintained a tenuous hold on the easternmost fringes of the prairie. The most pressing demand on the Dominion government was to settle this vast virgin territory, because settlement would check the aspirations of the United States for territorial aggrandizement in the Northwest. In addition, settlement of the West promised to stimulate the sluggish economy of central Canada.

Any settlement of the Western Interior depended on three prerequisites: establishment of a land survey, creation of reservations for Native people, and construction of a rail link to eastern Canada. Before 1869, agricultural settlement followed a river lot survey system not unlike that used in Québec. This system was expeditious, for the river was an essential part of a settler's life. But, although the river lot system offered social and economic advantages for the early settler, it was deemed unsuitable for the territory as a whole. Instead, the township system, modelled upon the American Survey system, was chosen to facilitate "the rapid and accurate division of the prairie region into farm holdings."[13] The township survey usually preceded settlement and superimposed a rigid, stereotyped pattern across the landscape without regard for topography (Fig. 8.3). In only rare instances did the system deviate, as it did to accommodate Métis demands for local river lot surveys.

With the completion of the survey, one major obstacle to settlement was removed. The conclusion of a series of treaties, which placed Native people on reservations as wards of the Crown, removed another. The third, most difficult obstacle still remained: Manitoba and the Northwest

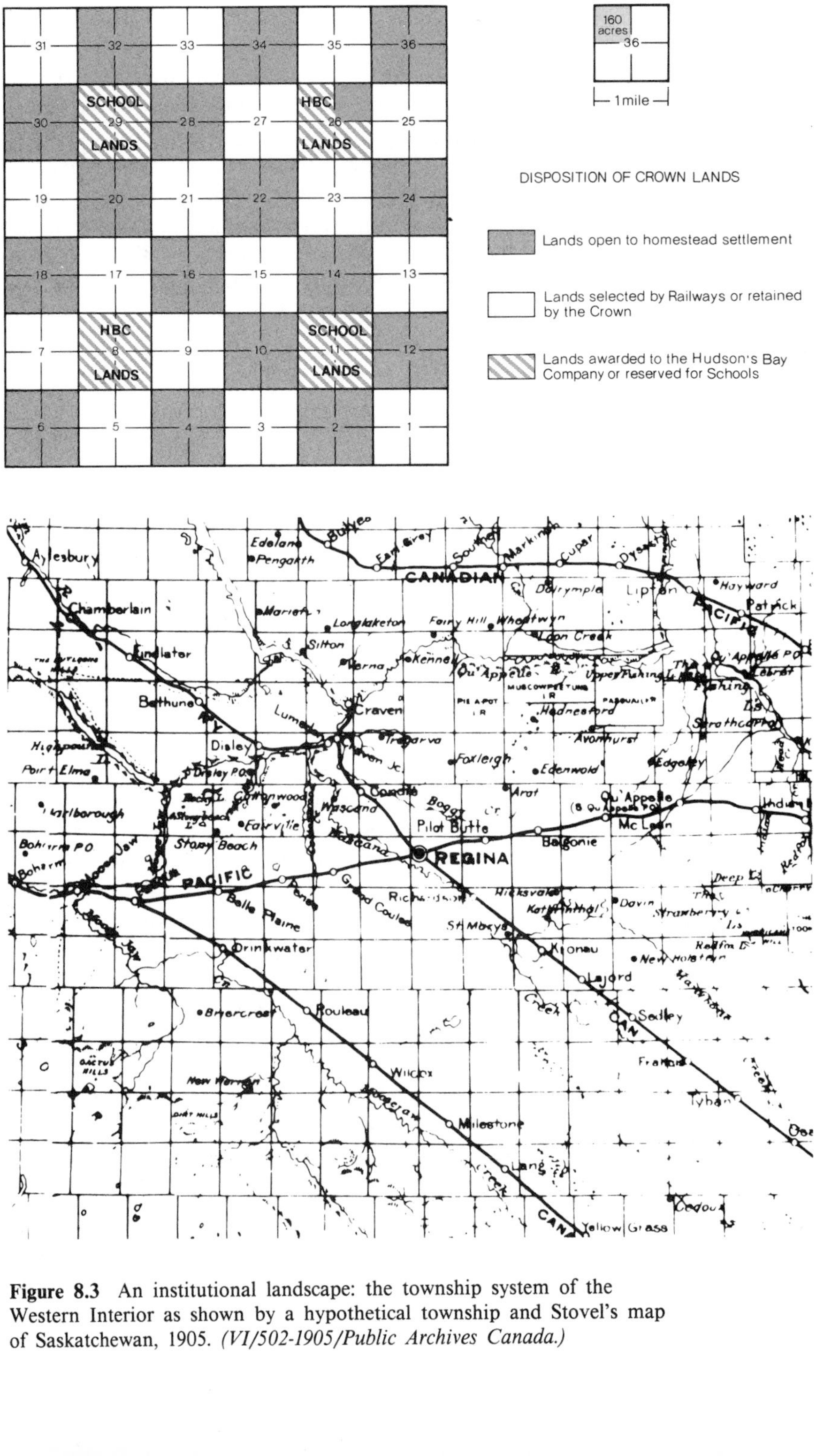

Figure 8.3 An institutional landscape: the township system of the Western Interior as shown by a hypothetical township and Stovel's map of Saskatchewan, 1905. *(VI/502-1905/Public Archives Canada.)*

Territories were isolated from central Canada by tracts of forest, swamp, and rock. None of the existing routes into the West was easily traversed. The two all-Canadian routes — the Hudson Bay-Lake Winnipeg route and the Dawson route via Lake of the Woods and the Great Lakes — were both arduous. The alternative route, by rail to Moorehead, Minnesota, and then by boat north along the Red River to Emerson or Winnipeg, was easier; but it was not until Winnipeg obtained a rail link with the United States railhead at Emerson in 1878 that the communications barrier was truly broken.

Settlers did enter Manitoba and the Northwest before the completion of this rail link, but they were few in number and settled mainly in the Red River Valley and on the prairie margins. The government had stimulated settlement by encouraging the immigration of ethnic and religious groups, for whom special reserves of land were set aside, creating a mix of individual and colony settlement in the first phases of regional occupation. In one instance, beginning in 1874, Mennonite settlers from the Czarist Ukraine were attracted to western Canada by the Dominion government's guarantee of freedom of conscience, exemption from military service, and the exclusive use of an eight-township block of land in the Red River Valley. In the same year, French Canadians from New England were given land reservations to facilitate their settlement in blocks; and in subsequent years similar reservations were granted to other ethnic and religious groups which the Dominion government was anxious to attract into the West, including peoples from England, Scotland, Iceland, Belgium, and Russia.

Although the government experienced some success with its group colonization policy (for example, over 6000 Mennonites alone entered Manitoba between 1874 and 1878), for several reasons the general rate of settlement remained disappointingly slow. In the 1870s, the limitations of Red River farming had yet to be overcome. With little exception, new settlers were either reluctant or unable to leave the security of the rivers or woodland fringe to challenge the open prairies. The fact that the government granted the Mennonites eight townships of land east of the Red River illustrates the conventional attitudes to land evaluation. The area chosen was only 50 kilometres southeast of Winnipeg and well endowed with wood and water, but it possessed large areas of swamp and gravelly soils. It was a good location for a typical settler of the time — a settler who lacked experience in farming the open prairie, who depended on wood for fuel, building, and fencing, and who relied on surface streams and ponds for watering stock. But for the Mennonites experienced in farming the Ukrainian steppe, it was an inferior environment giving limited potential and opportunity for sustained economic progress.

More suited to the Mennonite experience and needs were the 22 townships of the West Reserve, opened for their exclusive settlement in 1875. There, on rich chernozem soils, they used adaptive strategies

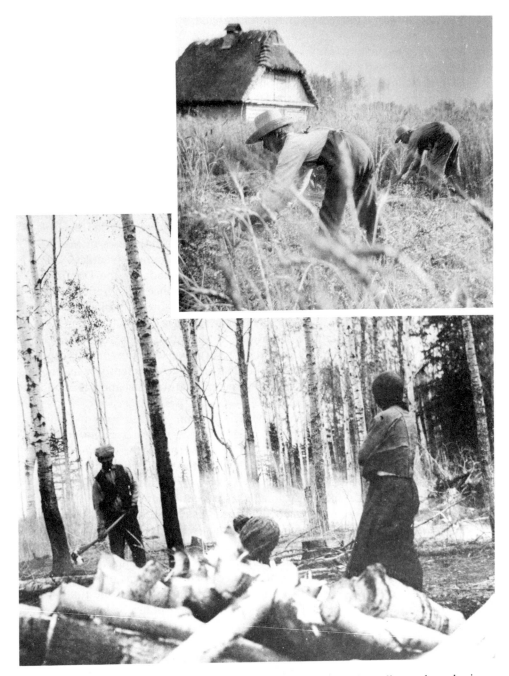

The initial phase of settlement: For many of the earliest settlers, clearing the land and reaping the first harvest were difficult experiences. Farming was often done without the aid of sophisticated tools, as shown by these pioneering families in Manitoba. (*W. J. Sisler Collection, Manitoba Archives*)

evolved on the Ukrainian steppe. The use of dung for fuel, the employment of temporary sod buildings, and the communal herding of stock reduced their dependence on timber for fuel, building, and fencing. But to other potential settlers, lacking not only the necessary agricultural technology and adaptive strategies, but also access to eastern Canadian markets, the West held little attraction. The situation became worse in 1875 when plagues of grasshoppers destroyed the standing crops of southern Manitoba and further discouraged immigration. Additional uncertainty was added by the malaise of economic depression then afflicting the industrial world.

The completion of the rail link between St. Paul, Minnesota, and Winnipeg in 1878, together with the easing of the world economic situation, soon renewed the flow of immigration into the Western Interior. By 1881, most of highland Manitoba south of the Riding Mountains had been occupied. So, too, had the Canadian base of the parkland crescent lying in the western section of the province. Lands to the west remained generally void of activity. Settlement was still confined to areas where wood, water, and hay were readily available; to districts easily accessible by rail; or to those areas with good prospects for the imminent development of rail communications. Although some 1 092 000 hectares of land had been occupied by 1881, only a fraction of that, a mere 113 000 hectares, was actually improved for agriculture.

The linking of Winnipeg with eastern Canada by the Canadian Pacific Railway (C.P.R.) in 1883, and the completion of the transcontinental route in 1885, initially failed to meet settlement expectations. Many of the homestead entries in Manitoba and in adjoining parts of the Northwest Territories between 1883 and 1890 were speculative ventures. From 1874 to 1896, homestead entries averaged under 3000 a year. In some years there were as many cancellations as there were new entries, partly because the Dominion Lands Act allowed relocation if the initial homestead proved disappointing. Of more serious concern was the contrast in settlement rates with the Dakotas to the south, which were being settled rapidly, in large part by emigrant Canadians. The *Winnipeg Times* complained that the trails from Manitoba to the States were "... worn bare and barren by the footprints of departing settlers."[14]

The paucity of settlers in the 1880s was understandable. The memory of the grasshopper plagues was still fresh and the uncertainty of cereal production in the region began to diminish only in 1885 with the introduction of early-maturing Red Fife wheat. The price of manufactured goods from central Canada was high, and cheap American imports were denied access by tariff walls erected to protect Canadian manufacturing. Transportation costs were excessive and wheat prices depressed. Credit costs were steep, as were farm mortgages: both inhibited settlement, especially settlement of the prairie drylands which required large investments of capital. Thus, settlement clung to the Red River Valley, the park belt within Manitoba, and the Qu'Apelle region of the Assiniboia district. It advanced only slowly towards the prairie lands, clinging to the lifeline of the C.P.R. as far as Moose Jaw, where the move into the arid conditions and rougher lands west of the Missouri plateau was halting and tentative. The prevailing official view was that most of the Palliser Triangle was fit for settlement, but few were willing to risk farming in this semi-arid environment.

Other factors besides natural and economic conditions were responsible for the slow rate of settlement. Contemporary critics, admittedly partisan, pointed to the lacklustre promotion of the West by the Department of the Interior, which they claimed did little to promote Western settlement. Clifford Sifton, Liberal member of parliament who later became Minister of the Interior, offered a stinging critique: "[It is] a department of delay, a department of circumlocution, a department in which people could not get business done, a department which tired men to death who undertook to get any business transacted with it."[15] The C.P.R. also promoted Western settlement, but despite an apparently energetic and imaginative campaign, it, too, experienced little success before 1896. It seems, therefore, that the failure of the government to promote settlement was due more to economic conditions beyond its immediate control, than to departmental inaction.

In order to finance the building of the transcontinental link between central Canada and the Pacific, in 1881 the federal government gave the C.P.R. a subsidy of $25 000 000 and 25 000 000 acres of land, in addition to a grant for roadway and station sites. This land was assigned in alternative, odd-numbered sections of 640 acres from territory extending 24 miles from each side of the railway. The railway company was free to select its lands from those "fairly fit for settlement" at a rate of 12 500 acres per mile for the first 900 miles of track, 16 666 acres for the next 450 miles, and 9615 acres for a final 640 miles. Although the C.P.R. built 652 miles of its total track through Ontario and 268 miles in British Columbia, it selected its lands primarily in Manitoba, Saskatchewan, and Alberta: 2 183 084, 6 216 784, and 9 805 446 acres respectively. It was a heavy burden for these provinces to bear. The system of securing alternate sections retarded the introduction of irrigation, dispersed settlement, and removed a substantial portion of potential taxation revenue from government sources. Alberta and Saskatchewan were hit particularly hard, because the railway companies selected land which promised the greatest appreciation in value. Six railroad companies, running no track in Saskatchewan, chose their grant from that province. Alberta relinquished over 9 800 000 acres to the C.P.R. alone, yet only 336 miles of track actually crossed its territory.[16]

To westerners, the C.P.R. enjoyed the unenviable reputation as a rapacious agent of eastern Canadian capitalism. Not only had the company alienated millions of acres of potential homestead land, but its real estate offices often manipulated station locations to ensure maximum profits.[17] Even more galling to westerners was the fact that much of the C.P.R.'s land holdings in the burgeoning urban centres was tax exempt. The C.P.R.'s land-disposal policy, based on delaying the sale of the land in the more northerly areas until the improvements of homesteaders had caused a sharp appreciation in the value of railway sections, was, of course, in the best interests of the corporation, but not of western progress. Indeed, the C.P.R. delayed selecting lands "fairly fit for settlement" to avoid paying taxes on entitled but unpatented lands. By doing this, settlement was effectively prevented in some of the most promising farming areas, because the Department of the Interior could not open for homesteading those lands which the railway might eventually select as part of its grant. Exacerbating this situation, the C.P.R.'s promotional schemes centred on lands located adjacent to its transcontinental line, where accessibility had obviously increased land values. These sites could only be developed by settlers with considerable capital and experience, the most elusive type of immigrant in the 1880s and 1890s.

The C.P.R.'s freight rates were also a controversial issue. Westerners called them discriminatory, because they forced settlers to bear the brunt of transportation costs on both exports and imports. The C.P.R. was viewed as an expensive alternative to American railways. The burdensome rates, however, were also a result of the hinterland status of the West. Relying on exports of raw materials and facing strong competition from other established suppliers, the western farmer had to bear the cost of transporting goods to distant markets. The absence of manufacturing industry in the Western Interior created a relatively inelastic demand curve for imported manufactures, so freight costs were borne by the consumer — the western farmer.[18]

The laggardly pace of early western settlement and economic growth is attributable in large measure to such economic circumstances. To what extent governments of the day can be blamed is more difficult to assess. Nevertheless, by the mid-1890s progress had been made: over three million hectares had been occupied, of which a little over one-fifth had been improved by agriculture. In Manitoba, the base of the parkland crescent land had been settled, and in the shadow of the Rocky Mountains, a small group of Mormon settlers had established a tenuous bridgehead on the plains in the Cardston area. Still, it was a disappointingly low level of achievement for 15 years of effort. One disillusioned Westerner described the region in the early 1890s as having "... a small population, a scanty immigration, and a north west empty still."[19]

The Sifton Years, 1896-1905

The mid-1890s were watershed years in the settlement of the Western Interior. At a time when the international economic climate was improving, political change in Canada made Clifford Sifton Minister of the Interior in the newly elected Liberal government of Sir Wilfrid Laurier. More than ever before, one man's personality and policies dramatically shaped the geography of a region. To Laurier, the twentieth century belonged to Canada, but to Sifton it belonged to the Canadian West. Soon after joining the new government in November, 1896, Sifton reappraised his department's objectives and policies in the area of immigration. He was determined to create a settled and prosperous West as a foundation for Canadian economic prosperity.

Previous administrations had attempted to secure immigrants from Great Britain and northwestern Europe, emphasizing qualities such as loyalty to the Crown, cultural affinity, and assimilative potential, while generally overlooking both the financial and occupational factors which ultimately determined the success of an immigrant. Indeed, attempts to secure immigrants with agricultural experience and capital were largely misdirected when focussed on the highly urbanized British Isles. Many Britons came to Canada as artisans with no farming experience; they subsequently failed in agriculture and drifted to urban centres. When Sifton took office, Canada's immigration policy was, therefore, general in scope and very lenient. Entry was prohibited only to the diseased, the criminal or vicious, and those likely to become public charges. Sifton did not directly change this policy, but he recast the net for immigrants and pursued the agricultural immigrant with single-minded determination. To Sifton, the ideal settlers were Canadian or American farmers. They were usually blessed with capital, were familiar with North American agricultural practices, were independently minded, and posed no problems of assimilation. Even though the Americans may have been "tainted by republicanism," Sifton thought them to be ". . . of the finest quality and the most desirable settlers."[20] But because they could not be acquired in sufficient numbers, Sifton looked towards the peasant heartland of central Europe.

The most notable, and controversial immigrants to settle in the West during Sifton's tenure were the Slavs, mostly Ukrainians and Doukhobors, but Hungarians, Germans, Poles, and Romanians came as well. Convinced that a ". . . stalwart peasant in a sheepskin's coat, born on the soil, whose forefathers have been farmers for ten generations, with a stout wife and half a dozen children is good quality,"[21] Sifton encouraged Slavic immigration and gave his blessing to the formation of a clandestine organization of steamship agents, known as the North Atlantic Trading Company, to promote Canadian immigration in areas where, for political reasons, the Canadian government could not openly conduct business. Thus, the peasant heartland of Europe was scoured by agents of the North Atlantic Trading Company, all propagandizing Western Canada as the place of free land, equality, and opportunity. Sifton even paid a bonus on the head of each agricultural immigrant booked to Canada. The amount reflected his perception of their potential as pioneers: $5.00 for a Ukrainian male adult but only $1.75 for a British agriculturalist!

The social geography and ethnic character of the Prairie West were forged during the nine crucial years of Sifton's tenure as Minister of the Interior. His policies gave unity and presence to the region. Although the foreign immigrants entering Canada in this period never threatened to overwhelm those of British extraction, in some years Slav immigrants comprised almost half of those who passed through the Winnipeg gateway. But their foreign ways and peasant dress, combined with their arrival by train in large groups, often on successive days, exaggerated their impact to English-speaking westerners. The question of Slavic immigration, indeed the future direction of western settlement, became a national issue. The Conservative press, and even some elements of the Liberal press, furiously attacked Sifton's importation of Slavic "peasants." Even the pro-Liberal elements, while stoutly defending the Slav immigrants against racist invective, voiced the opinion that the newcomers should be assimilated, and demanded that they reject their cultural heritage as proof of loyalty to their adopted country.[22]

The great majority of Slav immigrants were Ukrainian peasants from the then Austrian provinces of Galicia and Bukovina.[23] The social background and poor economic status of the typical Ukrainian peasant immigrant led to a remarkably uniform pattern of settlement. Coming almost entirely from the hills and forests of the Western Ukraine, they lacked experience in steppeland farming and craved the security of parkland habitats. There, the penurious settler could find the essential resource base of wood, water, and meadowland which was vital for successful subsistence farming in the early years of settlement. These immigrants also sought the social advantages of settling together to preserve a milieu of familiar religious, cultural, and linguistic characteristics. The spectre of "little Ukraines and Polands" arising in the West caused alarm in the anglophone society, both in the West and Ontario. The British character of the new lands seemed to be in danger. The early years of Sifton's tenure were accordingly marked by frantic efforts to prevent the growth of large blocks of ethnically homogenous settlement immune to assimilative pressures.

From 1896 until 1900, therefore, the government worked diligently, and generally with success, to accommodate the wishes of the immigrants and to appease the demands of an anglophile Canada. Slavic, Scandinavian, German, and Anglo-Celtic blocks were intermixed across the northern fringes of the parkland belt. Unfortunately, the singular determination to settle adjacent to friends and kin led later Ukrainian arrivals to disregard the environmental quality of the land they were settling, and to move on to progressively poorer land close to their compatriots. Sifton's detractors subsequently charged that the Slavs were deliberately placed on sub-marginal territory as a matter of policy, but this

The transfer of material culture from the Old World to the New: Galician settlers, Theodosy Wachna and family, near Stuartburn, Manitoba. The first generation of Ukrainian immigrants frequently built traditional houses and barns, such as the thatched roofed buildings shown in the photo, but by the second or third generation, these forms were replaced by pattern book and even prefabricated styles. (*PA-6005/Public Archives Canada*)

action does not seem characteristic of a Minister dedicated to the development of western resources and western markets for Ontario manufacturers. In fact, Sifton's immigration and settlement policies played a key role in establishing the macro patterns of the Western Interior's social geography.

Sifton's foreign campaigns to attract immigrants were matched in Canada by his manoeuvers to free as much land as possible for settlement. By the mid-1890s, millions of acres of potential homestead land remained in the grip of railway companies and land speculators. The railways were granted 28 500 000 acres of land, but in 1896 had selected and patented only some two million. Huge reserves of land "fairly fit for settlement" remained unsettled (Fig. 8.4). Realizing that this untaken land was detrimental to the progress of settlement, Sifton attacked the legal foundation that allowed the situation to exist. He forced the railways to complete their selection and patenting of lands in 1900, thereby opening up vast areas for homesteading. He also cancelled time sales, and thus both freed further areas for settlement and discouraged speculation in

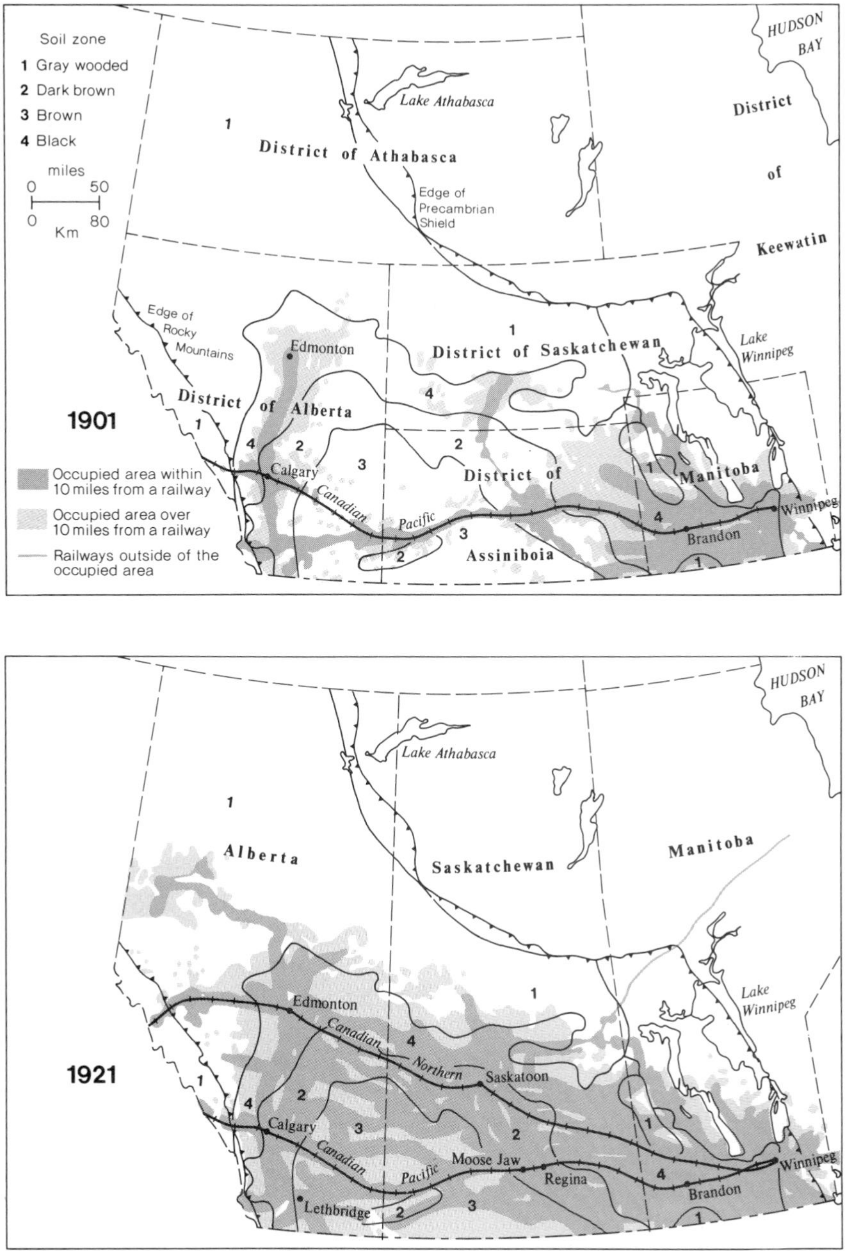

Figure 8.4 The changing pattern of settlement in the Western Interior, 1901 and 1921.

unsettled land. There was little to be done about underdeveloped patented lands — the results of unchecked speculation in the 1880s — and this situation continued to prevent the settlement of some of the better soils in Manitoba.

Sifton's policies, however, did not alter the general direction of economic development in the Western Interior. Although population grew rapidly, and the area of land brought into agricultural production expanded dramatically, the West remained a producer of primary products and an importer of manufactured goods. Urban development was based on service to the primary sector, and what little industrial growth took place was similarly oriented. Winnipeg, for example, experienced rapid growth in warehousing and transportation functions, but there was little processing of the materials shipped to eastern Canada. Sifton's conception of a prosperous West did not encompass vigorous industrial growth; the West's destiny lay in the achievement of prosperity through fulfilling the needs of the Industrial Heartland. Nevertheless, by 1905 when Sifton resigned as Minister of the Interior, the position of the West had been consolidated and the social fabric established. Within a few years, settlement would reach the last frontiers and people would strive to exploit the semi-arid plains in the heart of the Palliser's triangle, enter the boreal forest, and penetrate the grasslands of the Peace River District (Fig. 8.4).

The Last Frontier

As more attractive lands became increasingly scarce, homesteaders moved boldly toward the open prairies of southern Alberta and Saskatchewan. Two important innovations contributed to this movement: the adoption of Red Fife wheat and the employment of black summer fallow. American technology, including the chilled steel plow, steel windmill, barbed wire, and self-binding reaper, facilitated the costly move into these drier and drought-prone regions. Capital costs of settlement were high. The peasant immigrants from Europe were excluded by financial constraints, although some second generation Slavs did move into these areas — around Prelate in Saskatchewan, for example. As with most movements onto new lands, this westward thrust was undertaken in a spirit of enthusiasm and optimism. Technological adaptations were made, but the old institutional framework based on the quarter-section farm unit (160 acres), more suitable for humid regions, was maintained. In the drier areas, even the half-section (320 acres) was not economically viable as a farm unit, and from the start it was clear that many of the homesteaded areas of the shortgrass prairie were marginal. Droughts, frosts, and grasshopper infestation triggered farm abandonment even in the early years of settlement, but it was not until the 1930s that many finally realized, or admitted, that the arable frontier had extended beyond wise environmental limits.

But not all settlement was forced to retreat. Irrigation in southwestern Alberta was introduced by Mormon settlers in the 1890s. Based at first on the small-scale flooding of river flats, a series of large-scale irrigation ventures was established in 1897 by the Mormon Church in cooperation with both the Alberta Coal and Railway Company and several Utah-based sugar producers. In the shadow of the Rockies, irrigation was undertaken largely to ensure fodder crops in the event of drought, but east of Cardston and south of Lethbridge it was used to cultivate sugar beets. The significance of Mormon irrigation lies not in its areal component, but in its precedent, for it paved the way for the later and larger schemes of the C.P.R. and the Prairie Farm Rehabilitation Act.

The Peace River Block — 8000 square miles (20 500 square kilometres) in extent — was the last sizable part of the Western Interior to be colonized. Settlers began moving into the area in earnest about 1910, just ahead of the railway, which did not reach High Prairie until 1914 and Peace River townsite until 1915. The Peace River district's remoteness, climate, and soils encouraged dependence on wheat as a staple crop, but mixed and subsistence farming prevailed in the northern fringe areas where the risks of early frosts curtailed crop yields. A short growing season forced Peace district farmers to face problems already overcome in more southerly areas by the introduction of Red Fife wheat. Indeed, it is by no means clear whether settlement was *drawn* into the Peace district by the perceived attractiveness of the land, or was *forced* into the area by the shortage of favourable land elsewhere in the prairies. Certainly some second generation Ukrainian farmers, who left the marginal bush country of southeastern Manitoba just before World War I, chose the challenge of the Peace, bypassing the intervening opportunities of dryland farming in southwestern Saskatchewan.

As in the prairie region to the south, settlement in the Peace River district has been characterized by four well-defined stages. Until World War I, the region was locked in the outpost stage. Agriculture was insignificant, though not totally absent. In the next phase of agricultural expansion, immediately before the outbreak of war, settlement was beset with problems such as distance to markets and lack of winter feed for livestock. With the arrival of the railway, the region entered a stage of expansion and integration. Security of tenure increased for most farmers, and many expanded their operations until the malaise of the depression years necessitated retrenchment. The final stage, which in some measure is still in process, has been marked by regional centralization, focussing on the growth of regional service centres. However, it is a measure of the region that even in the 1980s, there is not one clearly dominant service centre. The broken topography and variety of soil types in the Peace River district have created widely separated settlements. Low rainfall and

The last frontier: The Peace River district of Alberta continues to attract agricultural settlement even today. Movement to the Peace Country began at the turn of the century, and attracted considerable numbers during the 1930s, such as this family en route to the Rolling Hills Settlement Project. (*Western Canada Pictorial Index, University of Manitoba*)

climatic uncertainty continue to prevail against the viability of the small farmstead. Off-farm jobs — insurance against the vagaries of nature — are commonplace. These elements have all added to the region's sense of being an agricultural, as well as a resource, frontier.

Agricultural Progress in the Inter-War Period

The economic boom which accompanied the settlement of the Western Interior ended in 1912, but two years later the outbreak of war boosted demand for wheat. Prices rose and remained relatively high through most of the 1920s. The resumption of immigration after the hiatus of the war stimulated a last burst of land settlement and railway building, and by the end of the decade there was little settled territory that was not within ten miles of a railway (see Fig. 8.4).

But this flowering also carried the seeds of disaster. Encouraged by high wheat prices, marginal land in the dry belt was broken, and wheat production continued to increase. At the same time, overseas markets, which previously had absorbed a large proportion of the wheat crop, began to close down as Europe recovered its agricultural productivity and established protectionist policies. The stock market crash of 1929 further reduced foreign and domestic markets for Canadian grain: prices fell dramatically (wheat dropped from $1.02 to $.35 a bushel between 1929

Dust storm near Lethbridge, Alberta, c. 1940: Farmers in the Western Interior face a difficult environment: hail and dust storms, crop-killing, frosts and soil drifting, variability of precipitation and insect infestations to name several difficulties, can spell ruin to the farmer. (*Glenbow Archives*)

and 1931), and farmers suffered. A series of dry years heightened the tension. The dry belt was hardest hit; here wheat farmers were faced with the erosion of both land and income. Ironically, certain prosperous areas such as Moose Jaw, Saskatchewan were hit worst by the drought and ensuing depression. Cash flow dependence affected the commercial farming population more than the marginal farmer who, located on the northern fringes of settlement, could easily fall back on a subsistence way of life. This fact prompted some farmers to migrate northwards from the dried-out areas to the fringe of settlement.

By 1935, the agricultural calamity had assumed such dramatic proportions that the provincial governments were unable to cope effectively with the host of escalating problems. The federal response was the creation of the Prairie Farm Rehabilitation Administration (P.F.R.A.), which was designed to reconstruct the social and economic fabric of the drought-stricken and eroding areas of the prairies. The Administration was an example of Heartland support for the West. The P.F.R.A. encouraged dryland farmers to adopt conservationist techniques such as strip farming and plowless fallow (trash farming); to switch from grain to grass; and in the worst hit areas, to resettle on P.F.R.A. irrigation projects. Within eight years, over 60 700 hectares (ultimately some 1 112 910 hectares) of sub-marginal land were recovered from grain farming and turned into community pastures managed by the P.F.R.A. Initial P.F.R.A. action was mostly consultative, based on the diffusion of information from experimental farms to various Agricultural Improvement Associations which initiated and coordinated community action. In keeping with this stance, early P.F.R.A. efforts were typically small in scale and directed at the individual farmer or community; but subsequent projects became more complex when, for example, the P.F.R.A. cooperated with the Alberta Eastern Irrigation District to provide resettlement opportunities for displaced farmers. Eventually, P.F.R.A. projects increased in size to the scale of the St. Mary's River Project in southern Alberta, where over 89 000 hectares of land were irrigated to diversify crops and add value to local production.[24]

The years of drought and depression were also years of rural population loss. From 1931 to 1951, Saskatchewan experienced an absolute decline in population, and natural increases in Manitoba and Alberta barely balanced losses from out-migration. Before the 1930s, some rural-urban drift had been evident (the percentage of the prairie population classed as rural fell from 75 in 1901 to 63 in 1931) as a consequence of farm consolidation and the gradual elimination of the inefficient quarter-section. But the Depression left a deeper, more lasting scar on the psyche of the regional farmer. The abandoned farmhouse on the dry prairie bore witness to the vagaries of nature; to the suffering farmers it stood as a symbol of the indifference shown by the banks and mortgage houses of central Canada. From this discontent in Saskatchewan and Alberta sprang the Western populist protest movements of the Cooperative Commonwealth Federation (C.C.F.) and Social Credit, two radically different responses to a common western perception of regional ills.

The Urbanizing West

For the most part, widespread urban development in Western Canada was a product of the railway age. Although the Hudson's Bay Company had established a delicate tracery of routes and a scatter of posts across the West, this structure had little impact upon initial urban development. The railway companies, in fact, virtually dictated the geography of urban growth. Station halts or shipping points for grain exports — the life-blood of a railway — were placed at 16 kilometre intervals and became the nuclei of rural service centres. Major centres emerged at divisional points where railway maintenance facilities were located.

For obvious financial reasons, the railway companies preferred to establish townsites on their own lands. The C.P.R., for example, steered clear of Hudson's Bay Company sites. Even the choice of the southerly Kicking Horse route placed the C.P.R. well away from established H.B.C. posts in the parkland belt. As a result, the C.P.R. established new towns in many different areas: Brandon, Moose Jaw, and Regina were all creations of the C.P.R. When a self-interested railway company located a station upon its own land a few kilometres outside an existing settlement, as was the case both at Calgary and Vegreville in Alberta, then the existing settlement moved to the railway site. Winnipeg narrowly escaped eclipse only by offering the C.P.R. lucrative concessions, including a cash bonus of $200 000, free land for a station site, and exemptions from municipal taxes in perpetuity, as an inducement to route the line through its borders. Originally the line was to pass 32 kilometres north, through Selkirk.[25] Not until the building of the Canadian Northern and the Grand Trunk did the northern tier of settlements based upon fur trade posts rise in importance, and only then was the Hudson's Bay Company able to capitalize on its entitlement to a land reserve surrounding each post.

Only four prairie settlements had more than 1000 inhabitants in 1891: Winnipeg (30 000), Calgary (4000), Brandon (3800), and Portage La Prairie (3400). Winnipeg and Calgary benefited from their strategic locations at the extremities of the prairies and assumed rudimentary metropolitan functions shortly after the turn of the century. Winnipeg, especially, capitalized on its location at the eastern edge of the prairies and on its initial advantage as an established urban centre. The gateway function of the city was bolstered by a discriminatory freight rate structure that made it cheaper to ship goods west from eastern Canada through Winnipeg, rather than directly to other prairie centres. The city's entrepôt function would undoubtedly have arisen without this rate structure, but it certainly encouraged the rapid growth of Winnipeg's wholesaling and warehousing function.

At the same time, the city exploited its natural advantages in the financial and commercial sphere. Following the major rush of immigration by 1912, Winnipeg boasted the Winnipeg Grain Exchange (1887) and the Winnipeg Stock Exchange (1903), as well as an array of other financial and insurance companies. Although most railway privileges had been removed by 1914, weakening a monopoly on trans-shipment functions, Winnipeg's position as the leading city of the West was firmly established. But, even as the major city of the Western Interior, with a population of 128 000 in 1911, it was still firmly linked to the economy of central Canada. West of Winnipeg, the emerging urban centres of Saskatchewan and Alberta were equally in the shadow of the Industrial Heartland's economic strength. Their growth stemmed from servicing the local hinterland. The benefits of Western agricultural expansion were reaped largely by the manufacturers, suppliers, and financial institutions of Ontario and Québec.

The outbreak of war in Europe in 1914 failed to stimulate urban growth in the Western Interior as it did in the manufacturing cities of eastern Canada. Not only did war terminate the injection of immigrant capital into the supply centres of the West, but the region also failed to benefit from military expenditures. In the early stages of World War I, military contracts were let to civilian contractors without tender, the

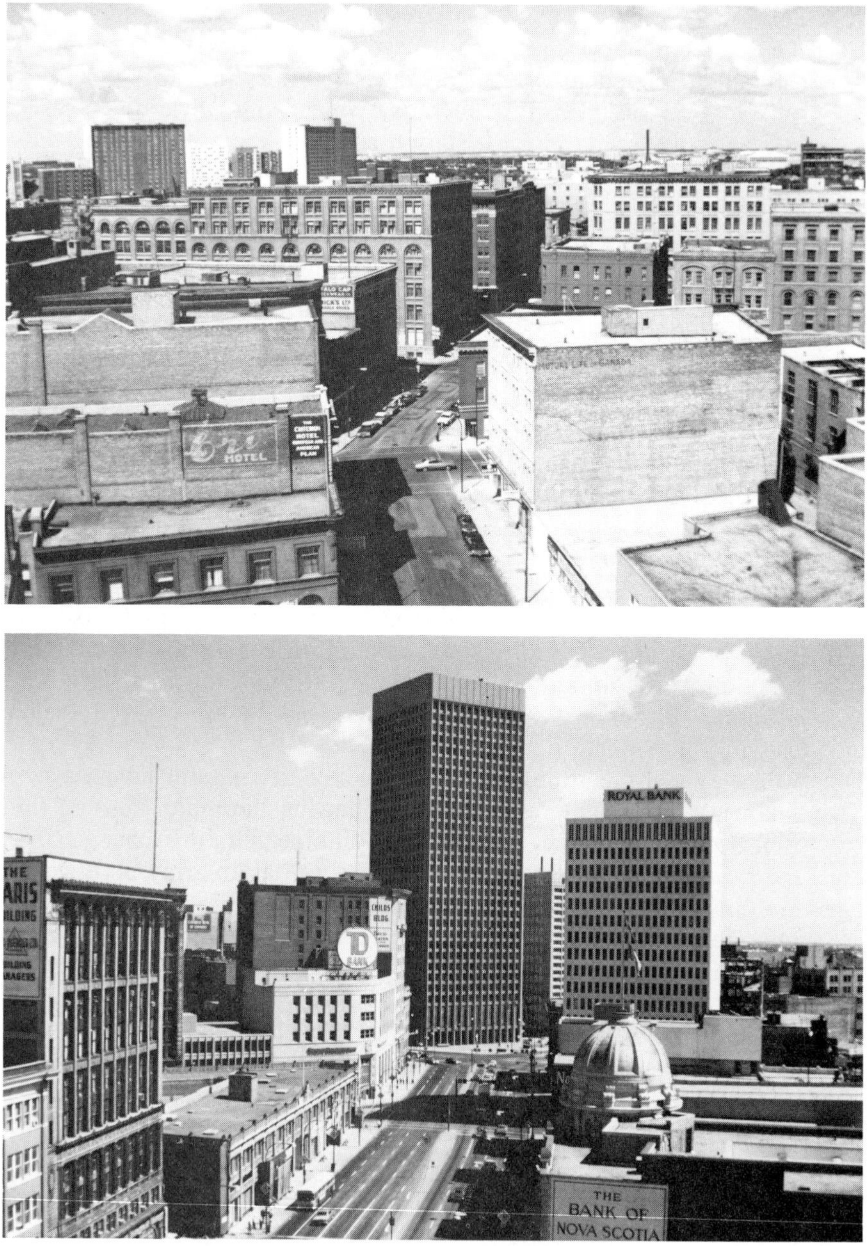

Winnipeg, Manitoba, the ''Gateway City'': Although Winnipeg's leading position in the Western Interior has been challenged by Calgary and Edmonton, the city remains an important distribution, financial, and government centre. These photographs show the pre-World War I wholesaling district and the headquarters of the Richardson family's financial enterprise at the corner of Portage and Main. (*Larry McCann*)

emphasis being placed on rapid delivery. Western cities suffered under the double disadvantage of having a poorly developed industrial capacity and a paucity of political friends in the high councils of the Militia Department. The federal government explained its wartime economic policies as the rational allocation of resources; in its view, the Western Interior should concentrate on production of wheat, eastern Canada on munitions manufactures. It did "not consider it to be in the interest of the Empire to encourage the erection of plants for forging shells in Calgary when there [were] sufficient plants already in the Dominion."[26] This continuation of the subservient hinterland status of the Western Interior was rational economic planning to the Ottawa bureaucrat, but to the westerner it was simply protection of established economic interests, and a clear reaffirmation of Sir John A. Macdonald's discriminatory National Policy

During the inter-war period, urban growth advanced little; the advance would come after World War II (Fig. 8.5). Winnipeg remained the dominant centre despite slow growth, increasing by only 2 percent between 1931 and 1941. The city used its strategic position to diversify a manufacturing industry which strongly reflected the hinterland status of the region it served: processing of agricultural products (meat packing and flour milling), the manufacture and repair of railway equipment, the production of a variety of consumer goods (especially clothing), and the manufacture of farm equipment. Edmonton and Calgary achieved moderate size at this time. Edmonton had been selected as provincial capital and used this position to secure the University of Alberta. Calgary, which coveted both, did not fare badly, however. It was a C.P.R. divisional point and in 1911 the company located its major western repair shops in the city. Soon after, oil was discovered 40 kilometres to the southwest in the Turner Valley, and in 1921 western Canada's first oil refinery was set up in the city. Still, little diversification followed, and Calgary remained, like other western cities, a transportation and distribution centre and a limited processor of primary products.

In marked contrast stood Saskatchewan, the most rural of the three interior provinces. The province had the largest total population but the smallest urban population. Regina and Saskatoon were overshadowed by Winnipeg, so their growth was determined by the demands of the limited agricultural hinterlands which they served. Until the 1950s, they remained only small centres in a "have-not province."

ECONOMY AND SOCIETY IN TRANSITION

From the beginning of the pioneer era, the settled landscape of the Western Interior was a landscape of institutional efficiency. The system of survey, the selection of the quarter-section as the optimum size for the

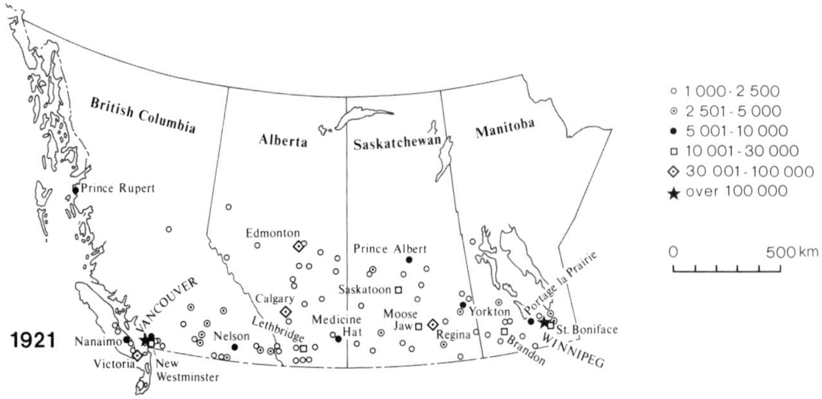

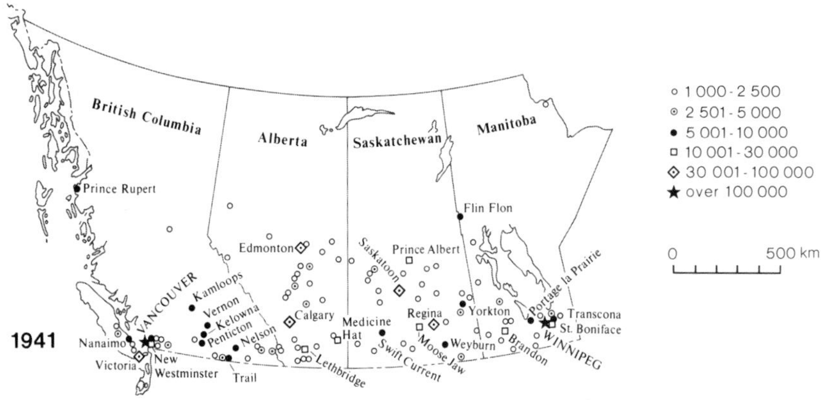

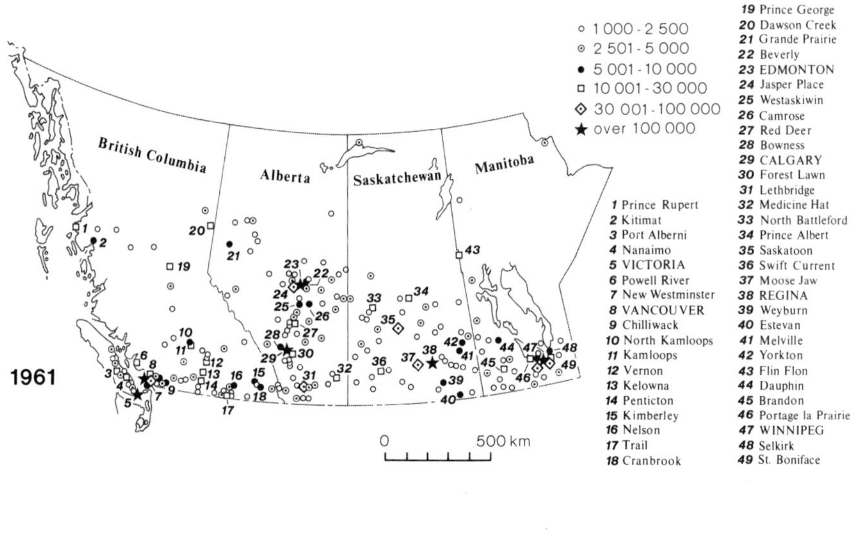

Figure 8.5 Urban population growth in the Western Interior, 1921, 1941, and 1961.

homestead unit, the rigid geometry of communications, and the regular spacing of villages and towns along railway lines, all reflected corporate and governmental concern for the efficient management of a new colonial territory. The framework of the landscape was clearly of metropolitan origin.

The material culture of the region, in contrast, was derived from the placement of a polyglot population on this institutionalized landscape.[27] Since most immigrants preferred to settle with others of their own nationality, early settlement was marked by the transference of material culture from the Old World to the New. For the most part, ephemeral or transient elements distinguished the pioneer landscape: domestic vernacular architecture, formal religious architecture, farm building arrangements, and fence types. With few exceptions, traditional village forms disintegrated under the rigid system of land survey. Only those who secured the privilege of officially sanctioned group settlement, such as the Doukhobors and Mennonites, or those who arrived independently but were united by strong religious bonds, as were the Mormons, were able to overcome the constraints of the sectional survey and retain their old-world village systems. But even the ephemeral signs of ethnic occupance began to disappear within a decade or two of initial settlement, as pattern book and even prefabricated houses became commonplace, replacing traditional vernacular forms.

The social fabric, however, has been more enduring (Table 8.1). The stability of rural society has resulted from a slow rate of economic change in the countryside. Out-migration has only helped to maintain the social status quo, enabling rural-urban migrants in the burgeoning cities to idealize rural life as a repository of basic moral and social values. A measure of continuity in the rural Western Interior, therefore, is the extent to which the social geography of ethnic occupance has remained intact. After World War II, the boundaries between ethnic groups in rural areas blurred a little and social environments became homogenized by the assimilation of the second and third generations into the mainstream of Canadian culture. But southern Alberta is still "Mormon country;" southwestern Manitoba is Ontario-British; Manitoba's Interlake district is Icelandic and Ukrainian; and Mennonites remain on the reserves set aside for their settlement in the 1870s. Even in the cities, patterns of ethnic segregation have shown surprising longevity. In the pioneer era, a proportion of immigrants from all groups preferred to stay in the cities, to seek work rather than land. For example, Winnipeg's "North End," the Slavic and Jewish immigrant section of the city, was well defined by 1914. There was some mobility out of these ghettos in the inter-war period, but social patterns remained little changed, as Jews and Central Europeans again formed areas of concentration in the suburbs. Their old neighbourhoods have been taken over by rural in-migrants, particularly the Métis and Native people fleeing the poverty of the reserves to seek opportunity in the city.

TABLE 8.1 BIRTHPLACE AND ETHNIC ORIGIN CHARACTERISTICS OF THE WESTERN INTERIOR, 1911–1971 (by percentage of total population)

Birthplace	*1911*	*1951*	*1971*
Canadian-born	*51.6*	*77.1*	*84.6*
Maritimes	1.7	.8	1.1
Québec	2.5	1.4	.9
Ontario	17.1	5.1	3.6
Manitoba	14.9	22.2	22.3
Saskatchewan	7.9	25.3	25.6
Alberta	5.7	21.4	29.3
British Columbia	.2	.9	1.6
Yukon and N. W. T.	.1	.1	.1
Foreign-born	*48.4*	*22.9*	*15.4*
Great Britain	17.5	7.4	3.9
United States	12.6	4.2	2.4
Scandinavia	3.2	1.2	.6
Germany	1.4	.7	1.3
Russia	9.6	3.5	1.5
Poland	n.a.	2.4	1.3
Italy	.2	.2	.5
Asia	.4	.4	.6
Other	*5.0*	*2.8*	*3.4*
	100.0	100.0	100.0

Ethnic Origin	*1911*	*1951*	*1971*
Asian	.3	.5	.8
British	53.5	45.8	44.2
French	5.6	6.8	6.7
German	10.5	11.7	15.1
Italian	.2	.3	1.1
Jewish	1.1	1.0	1.1
Netherlands	.6	4.0	3.2
Polish	1.4	3.7	3.2
Russian	11.1	1.7	.7
Scandinavian	5.9	6.5	5.6
Ukrainian	n.a.	10.4	9.5
Indian and Eskimo	2.3	2.8	3.6
Others	6.2	4.8	5.5
	100.0	100.0	100.0
Total population	1 328 121	2 547 770	3 543 370

Source: Calculated from data in the *Census of Canada*.

Despite the resilience of neighbourhood communities, the Western Interior has shed many of its former characteristics. It is now a highly urbanized society. The majority of its population is made up of newcomers who know little of the pioneering phase. With the advance of transportation and communication, isolation has diminished in importance as an integrating force of regional consciousness. The region is undergoing a new phase of economic development and social and cultural change have followed economic changes. Agriculture shaped the initial social and economic character of the Western Interior, and was still of fundamental importance through the Depression and war years. But in the post-war period, energy resources — particularly oil — have transformed the region. An urban way of life has superseded the rural past, as energy resources took on new dimensions of national and international significance.

Before the 1960s, economic growth in the Western Interior proceeded largely in response to external factors originating in Europe, the United States, and central Canada. But this once ineluctable position has changed in the past two decades. In the 1970s, the resource-generated boom gave the region a degree of maturity and independence and strengthened its role in the national and world-economy. In the 1980s, subordination to national and international heartlands is still evident, but the range of alternative heartland markets, suppliers, sources of capital, technology, and corporate linkages has been broadened and diversified to include those of east and southeast Asia. The region has also gained greater control over the ownership, sale, transportation, and export of its primary commodities through intraregional provincial policies, intervention, and regulatory supervision. Federal agencies continue to participate in the national and international marketing of the region's commodities, however, and many of the federal programmes are guided by the objectives of Canada's two most populous provinces whose economic sectors and policies are based on different premises from those of the Western Interior.

Traditional supply and demand relationships for the region's primary commodities have also changed. The dynamism and optimism associated with the 1970s resource boom appeared to refute an earlier observation that "the self-sustaining development of many prairie industries, based on independent private capital, is being superseded by government financial support for so-called 'hothouse industries' in which total benefits appear to be less than actual costs, . . . and that the demand for many prairie products is not growing quickly enough to ensure sufficient provision of new industrial employment."[28] While some companies (for example, the Winnipeg bus manufacturer, Flyer Industries) continue to receive financial support in the anticipation of eventual fiscal viability, the dramatic increase in the demand for the region's primary commodities in the 1970s so altered the region's role in world markets that it placed high priority on satisfying that external demand. Many assumed that the buoyancy of world markets, the strength of export sales, and the attendant demand for many related manufactured goods would continue to ensure fiscal viability for many of the region's industries, particularly those producing agricultural equipment, pipe and pipeline equipment, and building products.

Events subsequent to 1982, however, demonstrate that the region's market for resource-related industrial commodities has not changed substantially. Markets continue to be variable and fragile from one time period to the next. Distance and peripherality penalize the region by increasing the delivered price of some bulk primary export commodities such as coal, grain, and livestock and by hurting the competitive strength of regional manufactures through high freight rates (such as in flour processing) and weak external economies of scale (important to aerospace industries, for example). Provincial governments of the Western Interior and programmes supported by federal departments such as the Department of Regional Industrial Expansion (DRIE) and the Ministry of State for Science and Technology, although active in earlier periods, have not by the mid-1980s effected new policies or measures for sustaining *and* encouraging manufacturing within the Western Interior. They have not offset the malaise affecting levels of growth and employment in the primary and secondary industrial sectors of the Western Interior economy.

The assertion of provincial jurisdiction in external economic and political affairs, however, has affected the relationships of different parts of the Western Interior to each other. Some attempts at coordinating economic development among the three provincial governments, including seminal events such as the Western Economic Opportunity Conference in 1973 and the regular meetings of the provincial premiers, do occur. For the most part, however, given their competition for scarce investment capital and limited external market opportunities, the provinces strike individual courses. They insist on controlling resource ownership and associated revenues and taxes though the federal government became involved in petroleum and natural gas sales through the National Energy Program instituted in 1979. Multinational corporations must therefore deal with both federal and provincial authorities though the gains accrue to the provinces on an individual basis.

Thus, provincial governments now intervene regularly in their own internal economic development and investigate the environmental, economic, and social impact of resource development. They allocate "windfall profits" to Heritage Funds for reinvestment in "social development" and some basic and infrastructural economic schemes; they create special agencies with concerns for indigenous populations and peripheral areas; and they promote or supervise economic opportunities in selected municipal and sub-regional districts of their jurisdiction. With few exceptions, the initiative and responsibility for developing natural resources and employment opportunities lie with individual provincial

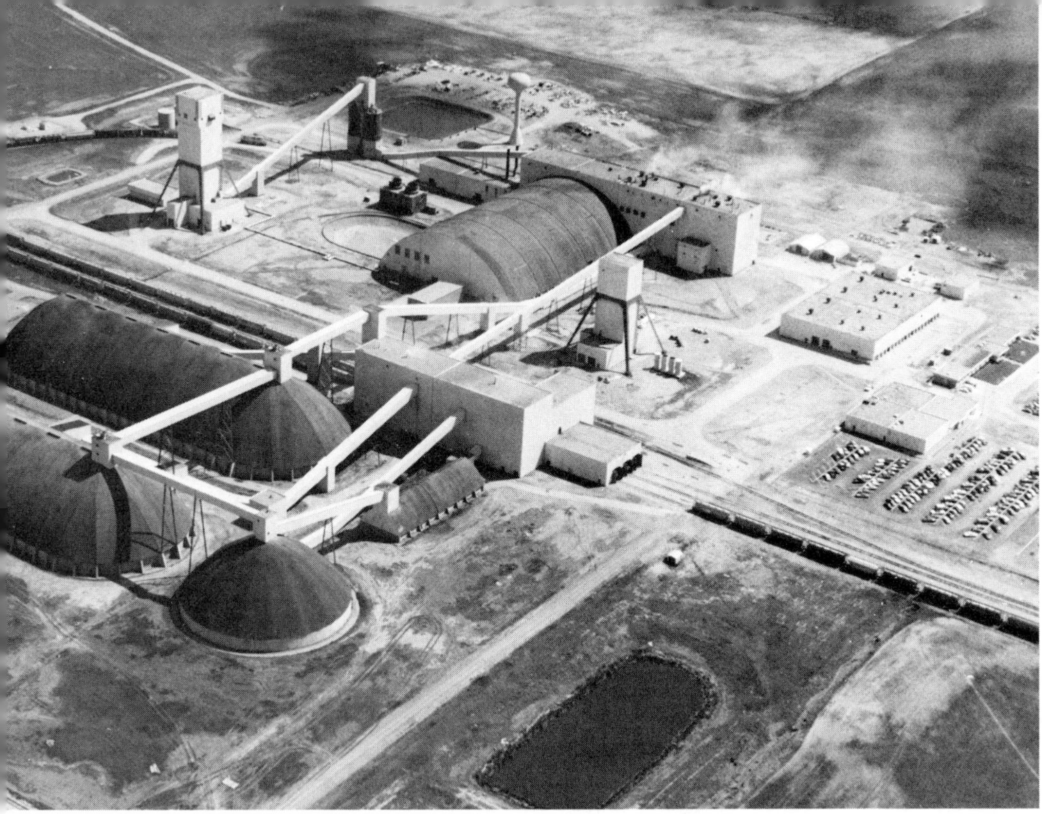

A new generation of staples: The economy of Saskatchewan has been buoyed and diversified by the recent development of the potash industry, which is heavily financed and managed by the provincial government. (*Government of Saskatchewan*)

governments, rather than with a unified regional agency or the federal government. Many of Ottawa's regional development personnel were decentralized to separate provincial offices in the mid-1970s in a move partly reflecting the growing proprietary role of the provincial governments in regional economic development.

A significant shift in strength between the national political heartland and the provincial governments has thus taken place. Sub-areas in the Western Interior, however, remain subordinate to provincial political jurisdictions. Provincial agencies have been reluctant to delegate power or jurisdiction to their constituent regions and have, thereby, enhanced core-periphery relationships at an intra-provincial level. Although the physical distance which separates internal sub-regions from the centres of decision-making has been reduced, and the number of competing demands diminished, conflict still separates centre and periphery in individual provinces. Alberta is attempting to decentralize some public institutions, but the other provinces have not taken concrete steps in this direction. The region's metropolitan centres nevertheless show positive signs of completing the transition from limited administrative or branch-office locations to dynamic and mature centres of power, administration, innovation, and economic growth. In short, they have assumed roles of national significance. They have an immediate but also comprehensive spatial and functional relationship with their hinterlands, and have become important centres both for retaining many of the creative energies of the region's population and for directing further growth and investment within the region and beyond. Calgary, for example, has taken an active role in the oil development of the North, the United States, eastern Canada, the North Sea, southeast Asia, the Middle East, and North Africa.

The Western Interior's frenetic economic development during the 1970s, which carried the promise of considerable political independence and economic maturity, now appears to have been an exciting but nevertheless short-lived aberration in the region's traditional role as a resource-producing hinterland. Although increased control over its raw materials has led to some economic expansion and diversification, the region has not experienced a permanent change in its manufacturing and service economy. The expectation that a reliance on staples would give way to a regional economy based on industries spun-off from the original resource activities has not been realized. Expansion and stability in the region's economic base depends, of course, on the prowess of the region's entrepreneurial and political acumen, on alternative investment opportunities in Canada, the United States, and abroad, and on the long-term outcome of significant but still not clearly perceived global changes in relationships among the world's heartland and hinterland regions. Thus, while the 1970s witnessed an important shift in focus of Canadian political power, economic activity, and population migration toward the Western Interior, the ambiguity and confusion long prevalent in the region are again evident in the 1980s.

THE ADJUSTING SETTLEMENT PATTERN

Population and Migration

The population of the Western Interior grew throughout the 1970s approximately three times faster than the national average and comprised just over 17 percent of the Canadian population at the 1981 Canadian Census. This growth in the 1970s appeared first to halt, and then later to reverse the region's previous relative decline in the share of national population. Growth rates, however, differed among the provinces. As the result of a prolonged period of growth associated with petroleum exploration and development, and the attendant growth in construction and services, Alberta grew most rapidly at a rate approximately four times the national rate (1976-1980). Manitoba grew at less than one-tenth the national average, while the increase in Saskatchewan almost coincided with that of Canada as a whole. Saskatchewan's previous population decrease was turned around by the strong demand in the 1970s for grain, potash, petroleum, and uranium — all elements which offer the possibility of slow but perhaps steady population growth in the future.

In addition, as a result of the attraction to Alberta, the Western Interior registered a strong positive balance of net migration between 1971 and 1981. Except for a brief period in the early 1960s, Alberta has shown positive net migration for all intercensal periods since 1951; Manitoba and Saskatchewan, however, both registered negative net migration for every intercensal period since 1951 (Table 8.2). Initial estimates, however, of annual net migration since 1981 reveal that all three provinces have had positive balances. Furthermore, the net migration rate for Manitoba and Saskatchewan from 1982 to 1983 exceeded that of Alberta and appears to reflect the stability of non-petroleum sectors in cushioning the regional economy from the otherwise disastrous downturn in world demand and prices for petroleum in this decade. More recent analyses suggest, however, that Alberta's net migration had become negative by 1982-83 and may indeed have surpassed -40 000 for 1983-84, reflecting a dramatic end to the hectic period of immigration associated with the oil boom.[29]

With the exception of Alberta's negative net migration rates in the mid-1980s, the region's population growth has been testimony to its economic strength. In the early 1970s, the Western Interior received approximately one-seventh of Canada's immigrants. This same proportion was registered in 1981-82 and 1982-83. These rates of international migration to the Western Interior bracketing the boom years of the 1970s thus seem to indicate a reasonable average for the region. Central Canada, particularly Ontario, continues to attract between three-fifths and two-thirds of all international migrants.

TABLE 8.2 MIGRATION CHARACTERISTICS IN WESTERN CANADA, 1971-76 and 1976-81

Migration	*1971-76*			*1976-81*		
Characteristic	*Manitoba*	*Saskatchewan*	*Alberta*	*Manitoba*	*Saskatchewan*	*Alberta*
In-migration	57 165	52 555	175 045	54 030	63 395	336 830
Out-migration	83 765	82 700	113 185	97 620	69 220	139 180
Total net internal migration	-26 600	-30 145	61 860	-43 590	- 5 825	197 650
Immigration	28 265	9 885	61 895	24 410	11 275	75 485
Net migration	1 665	-20 260	123 755	-19 180	5 450	273 135

Source: Canada Year Book, 1978-79 and 1985 (Ottawa: Statistics Canada, 1978 and 1985.)

In the mid-1970s, despite their considerable differences in economic and population size, Ontario and Alberta each attracted approximately one-fifth of all migrants within Canada, a proportion far above that of any other single province. Migration within the Western Interior and between the region and other areas of Canada in the 1970s was an indicator of the region's increasing importance within the country. Central Canadians responded to job opportunities in the West at higher rates than ever before in the post-World War II era.

Within the Canadian urban system, a study by Simmons and Bourne notes that "the marked regional variation is evident and there is no systematic relationship between rate of growth and city size within regions. The variability of urban growth . . . declines with population size, but increases from east to west." Furthermore, between 1976 and 1981, the Canadian urban system displayed "increased regional differentiation of urban growth, due largely to the boom in Alberta," indicating that the national urban system reveals a "dominant impression" of "ebb-and-flow of growth . . . over relatively short periods of time."[30]

The urban system of the Western Interior recognized by Simmons comprises five levels based on size, situation, and economic role (Fig. 8.6).[31] There are three major fourth-order metropolitan centres: Calgary, Edmonton, and Winnipeg. Saskatoon and Regina, census metropolitan areas, serve as third-order urban places subordinate to Winnipeg. In addition to these five metropolitan areas, the system has three second-order and 13 first-order urban centres. Altogether there are 21 centres in the Western Interior urban system (including one in the Northwest Territories and one in far-northwestern Ontario). The Western Interior thus appears to have three urban subsystems, each transcending the familiar provincial political units. But these subsystems are ultimately linked not to each other, but to Toronto, one of Canada's two highest order centres (the other is Montréal).

Linkages within the urban system thus represent not only inter-urban connections, but also diffusion of growth, talent, information, and general levels of opportunity, patterns of migration, and expressions of similar interest and political affiliation. Simmons notes, however, that "the institutions of government in Canada . . . make no explicit recognition of either the urban centre's region, or its organization within the urban system. Although the public policy outputs can be clearly linked to the characteristics and dynamics of the urban system, on the input side the focus is on the parliamentary constituency or the province." He adds that "provinces make unwieldy geographical regions by any criterion."[32]

In population movement, for example, domestic and foreign migrants are attracted to the diverse opportunities of the largest centres and to the specialized resource towns. The economic activity of such places seems to enhance the region's dependence on, or subordination to, the heartland

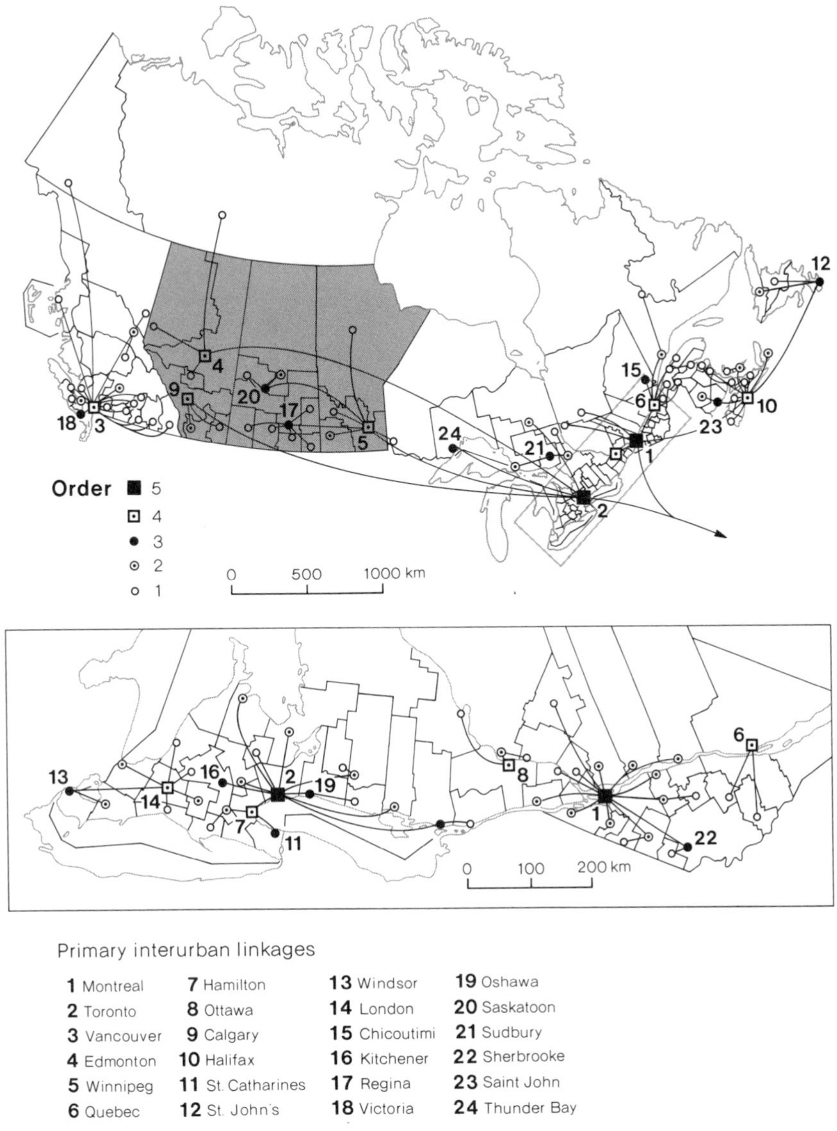

Figure 8.6 The Canadian urban system. (Adapted from J.W. Simmons, *The Canadian Urban System as a Political System, Part I: The Conceptual Framework,* Research Paper No. 141 (Toronto: University of Toronto, Centre for Urban and Community Studies, 1983.)

economies. Continued in-migration, of course, can help the region's urban system adjust relatively quickly to new spatial opportunities and to achieve the transition from simplicity, through deepening specialization, to mature or complex technological prominence. According to Simmons and Bourne, the in-migration rates of metropolitan areas have a much greater range (5 to 34 percent) than those for out-migration (9 to 21 percent), reflecting the greater diversity of age and geographical origin of in-migrants. They also note, however, that out-migration is very high in the most rapidly growing centres due to the relatively large share of single, young in-migrants who contribute to unusually high turnover. In the 1976-1981 period, for example, "approximately one-fifth of the initial population moved away from Saskatoon and Calgary. . . . The flow of in-migrants was equivalent to *one-third* of the 1976 population in Calgary and to *one-quarter* of Saskatoon's 1976 population."[33]

Although recent population gains may be offset by the economic downturn after 1982, the gains registered in the 1970s and very early 1980s indicate that the Western Interior has the potential to increase its status as an upward transitional hinterland with specialized heartland functions. Indeed, Calgary has already become a major financial centre and its entrepreneurs have made significant innovations in petroleum technology and the management of energy resources. Calgary has achieved many features of a metropolis. The Western Interior passed through the middle stage of the growth process in the 1970s. With additional population and economic growth, and with the continued concentration of heartland functions in the region's centres, it could become a major focal point of Canadian economic power, playing the role of national and even international innovator and creator of employment.

The Role of Cities

The transformation of society and economy in the Western Interior is most apparent in the urban and quasi-urban landscape. Despite the phenomena of "counter-urbanization" noted in previous studies of the region,[34] the growth of urban areas continues to far exceed that of the rural population in all provinces. The urban population of just more than three million now comprises over seven-tenths of the region's population. The rural farm population of all three provinces declined both in absolute numbers and relative share of the regional population between 1971 and 1981, though the rural non-farm population increased. The former comprised 11 percent of the regional total in 1981, the latter nearly 18 percent, or over one-sixth of the total regional population. The rural non-farm share ranges from 9 percent in Manitoba and 14 percent in Alberta, to 23 percent in Saskatchewan. Approximately 9 percent of Alberta's population is rural, but the share in Saskatchewan is nearly 19 percent. Good highway and secondary road linkages enable a significant share of urban and rural workers — including farmers — to live close to large and medium-size urban places and commute to places of employment.

As Table 8.3 shows, two distinct influences are noticeable in the growth between 1976 and 1981 of the Western Interior's five major Census Metropolitan Areas (CMAs): natural increase and net migration. The modest growth of Winnipeg and Regina was due mainly to natural increase, indicating that negative net migration adversely affected Winnipeg while a small positive net migration contributed to Regina's growth. The other three CMAs grew significantly from both natural increase and net migration. Furthermore, the average growth of the five Western Interior CMAs was significantly higher than that of the 23 Canadian CMAs for the same period. The Western Interior underwent a period of burgeoning urban growth in the 1970s.

What might these figures indicate for the future? If the growth of the region's cities in the 1980s should resemble that of the other Canadian CMAs, and if the general forces propelling the expansion of Canadian CMAs remain about the same as in the recent past, then we might expect to observe between 1981 and 1986, for example, an average growth for the five Western Interior CMAs of two-fifths to one-half that of the late 1970s, and a relative share of natural increase about twice that of net migration. According to such a scenario, the growth prospects for the five CMAs would resemble that of Regina between 1976 and 1981.

The urban system of the Western Interior has long been dominated by its five largest metropolitan areas that now comprise nearly three-quarters

TABLE 8.3 GROWTH OF CENSUS METROPOLITAN AREAS (CMAs) IN THE WESTERN INTERIOR, 1976-1981

Census Metropolitan Area	*Growth* %	*Natural Increase* %	*Net Migration* %
Winnipeg	1.1	3.3	- 2.2
Regina	8.7	6.0	2.7
Saskatoon	17.0	6.9	10.1
Edmonton	18.1	6.4	11.7
Calgary	25.7	6.1	19.6
Average growth for 23 Canadian CMAs to 1981	5.8	3.8	2.1
Average growth for 5 Western Interior CMAs 1976 to 1981	12.2	4.6	7.6

Source: Compiled from D. Hopper, J.W. Simmons, and L.S. Bourne, *The Changing Economic Basis of Canadian Urban Growth, 1971-81,* Research Paper No. 139 (Toronto: Centre for Urban and Community Studies, 1983), p. 28.

of the region's urban population and just over half of the total population. In Alberta and Manitoba, metropolitan centres alone make up nearly three-fifths of the total population; in Saskatchewan, they account for one-third. In Manitoba, Winnipeg comprises 80 percent of all urban population. In Saskatchewan, the share of the two CMAs is 57 percent; Alberta's two CMAs make up nearly three-quarters of the urban population. In all provinces of the Western Interior, metropolitan places increased their relative share of provincial population in the 1970s. As shown by data in Tables 8.4 and 8.5, the five metropolitan centres play a major role in shaping the regional character of the Western Interior. They dominate the region's urban system, population, and economic prowess; they are located in commanding regional and provincial positions on the transcontinental railways and highways; and they serve as the most important places for directing and administering the space economy of their provinces or of the entire region.

The number of urban places in the region has also increased dramatically since the early 1950s, largely through the development of the region's non-agricultural resources.[35] Prior to this growth, most urban places were small, their size determined mainly by their basic role of providing services to a surrounding farm population. Other small urban places performed additional functions such as mining (Flin Flon), military services (Prince Albert), food processing (Lethbridge and Red Deer), oil and natural gas (Lloydminster and Medicine Hat-Redcliffe), and manufacturing (Brandon). Still, these activities were not enough to stimulate widespread urbanization. During the last quarter-century, however, the urban system has changed substantially: many existing places have become larger and other new centres have been established, while many very small non-urban places have ceased to exist (Table 8.6). Overall, the variety of functions performed by most urban places is much greater than in the past. Urban places now offer more residential and specialized support service functions including health, recreational, and educational functions. This growth has resulted largely from improved transportation and communication systems and a trend toward centralization.

The other geographically widespread resource-based industries such as oil, natural gas, coal, potash, and timber have also generated important road systems, allowing many associated urban places to offer increasingly numerous and specialized services. In some areas, resource industries have developed in conjunction with agriculture and residential services. Small urban places such as Morris, Fort Macleod, Claresholm, and Brooks have thus developed an important manufacturing profile, which has taken advantage of local entrepreneurial talents and regional market opportunities. In other areas, resource development has drawn the urban system away from its previous spatial association with farmland. Grande Cache, Fort McMurray, and Redwater in Alberta, for example, have developed on the rough terrain and in the forested areas of the region's sedimentary

TABLE 8.4 EMPLOYMENT STRUCTURE OF MAJOR CENSUS METROPOLITAN AREAS, 1984

Type of Industry	Winnipeg No.[a]	Winnipeg %	Regina No.	Regina %	Saskatoon No.	Saskatoon %	Calgary No.	Calgary %	Edmonton No.	Edmonton %
Forestry	–	–	–	–	–	–	–	–	–	–
Mines, quarries, and oil wells	–	–	–	–	–	–	27.1	11.0	1.2	0.5
Manufacturing	39.6	17.4	5.9	9.7	6.8	11.3	22.9	9.3	23.2	9.6
Construction	8.6	3.8					13.3	5.4	12.9	5.4
Total Goods Producing	*48.2*	*21.3*	*5.9*	*9.7*	*6.8*	*11.3*	*63.3*	*25.8*	*37.3*	*15.5*
Transportation, communication, and utilities	25.5	11.3	8.8	14.4	4.5	7.5	25.2	10.3	20.1	11.7
Trade	47.2	20.7	13.6	22.3	13.8	22.9	41.3	16.8	51.2	21.3
Finance, insurance, and real estate	17.4	7.6	5.6	9.2	2.8	4.6	17.4	7.1	14.5	6.0
Community, business, and personal services	85.8	37.7	22.6	37.0	20.3	46.9	93.6	38.1	102.4	42.5
Public administration										
Total Services	*170.9*	*78.6*	*50.6*	*82.0*	*49.4*	*81.9*	*182.4*	*74.2*	*201.5*	*83.7*
Total above industries	224.1	98.5	56.5	92.5	56.2	93.2	240.8	98.0	233.5	97.0
Total all industries	227.5	100.0	61.1	100.0	60.3	100.0	245.7	100.0	240.8	100.0

[a]Thousands of employees

Source: Statistics Canada, *Employment, Earnings, and Hours* (Ottawa: May, 1984).

TABLE 8.5 EMPLOYMENT STRUCTURE OF PROVINCES IN THE WESTERN INTERIOR, 1984

Type of Industry	*Manitoba* *No.*[a]	*%*	*Saskatchewan* *No.*	*%*	*Alberta* *No.*	*%*	*Western Interior* *No.*	*%*
Forestry	1.0	0.3	0.6	0.2	1.7	0.2	3.3	0.2
Mines, quarries, and oil wells	4.9	1.4	8.4	3.1	58.3	7.2	71.6	5.0
Manufacturing	50.1	14.3	19.7	7.2	69.0	8.5	130.8	5.0
Construction	12.7	3.6	13.3	4.9	46.0	5.7	72.0	5.0
Total Goods Producing	*60.7*	*19.6*	*42.0*	*15.4*	*175.0*	*21.6*	*205.7*	*19.9*
Transportation, communication, and utilities	45.0	12.9	20.0	10.3	84.6	10.4	157.6	11.0
Trade	64.4	10.4	56.8	20.9	140.3	17.3	261.5	18.3
Finance, insurance, and real estate	20.7	5.9	17.2	6.3	47.2	5.8	85.1	5.9
Community, business, and personal services	124.0	35.5	104.2	38.2	294.5	36.4	522.7	36.5
Public administration	26.8	7.7	24.3	8.9	68.5	8.5	119.6	8.4
Total Services	*200.9*	*80.4*	*230.5*	*84.6*	*635.1*	*70.4*	*1136.5*	*80.1*
Total all industries	349.6	100.0	272.5	100.0	810.1	100.0	1432.2	100.0

[a]Thousands of employees

Source: Statistics Canada, *Employment, Earnings, and Hours* (Ottawa: May, 1984).

TABLE 8.6 NUMBERS OF URBAN PLACES BY SIZE CLASS, WESTERN INTERIOR, 1956-1981

Minimum Population	*1956*	*1966*	*1976*	*1981*
100 000	3	5	5	5
25 000	4	6	7	9
10 000	8	6	10	13
5 000	10	11	17	24
2 500	26	47	49	56
1 000	83	90	100	111
Total	134	165	188	218

Source: Compiled from P.J. Smith, "Urban Development Trends in the Prairie Provinces," in A.W. Rasporich, ed., *The Making of the Modern West: Western Canada Since 1945* (Calgary: The University of Calgary Press, 1984), p. 136.

basin. Other urban places, such as Lynn Lake in Manitoba, have grown in the boreal forest and around the mineral deposits of the Canadian Shield. In still other places, such as Hinton, Grande Prairie, Fort Saskatchewan, and The Pas, growth has been associated with large, capital-intensive projects — pulp mills and metal refineries, for example — that use regional raw materials but employ modest numbers of industrial, extractive, and service personnel. In all cases, the urban system is dependent upon an extensive rail and pipe transportation system for the movement of commodities and equipment, and upon comprehensive air links for personnel support, access to extra-regional amenities, and maintenance of effective supplies of food and replacement equipment. All these specialized economic activities and related smaller urban places, however, are subordinate to, and ultimately dependent upon, the core areas of the Western Interior — the major metropolitan centres.

Continuing trends indicate that the metropolitan centres will maintain their dominance in the decades ahead by directing provincial political and economic affairs, by developing additional agglomeration economies, by retaining a high regional manufacturing profile, by functioning as the destination of intraregional migration, and by extending their supervision, administration, control, and distribution of technology into other regions of Canada and beyond. As R. Thompson notes:

> ... the change in accessibility patterns, primarily due to an improved highway network, has hastened the trend to centralization in the higher-order urban places ... to the detriment of smaller centres as regards functions. ... As a result the higher-order centres of Winnipeg, Edmonton, and Calgary and to a lesser degree Regina and Saskatoon are increasing their functional dominance through centralization and polarization tendencies within the Prairie urban system. Rather than the persistence of a single primate centre for the Prairies, there is a triumvirate of centres, each dominating a specific area.[36]

In many spheres, however, competition within the provinces produces regional asymmetries, suggesting that dominance corresponds not to a triumvirate, but rather to a troika. The major urban centres — Winnipeg, Regina, Saskatoon, Calgary, and Edmonton — do not function interdependently. They are organized on a provincial basis and even within the three provinces, internal competition can be fierce. In a national context, an analysis by Simmons and Bourne indicates that growth in the 1976-1981 period has contributed to additional reordering of the entire Canadian urban hierarchy:

> Toronto has strengthened its position at the top of the hierarchy; Calgary and Edmonton have pushed past Winnipeg to dominate the Prairies. ... These relationships are particularly important when they indicate a change in the role of competing service centres, such as between Toronto and Montréal or among western cities, and when they mirror a restructuring of networks of interaction and dependence.[37]

It is a sign of the maturing character of the Western Interior that the metropolitan centres of Calgary, Edmonton, and Winnipeg are widely recognized as places of considerable innovative strength. Not only do they anchor the core-periphery patterns of the region, but they also dominate critical activities of the Canadian space economy. Despite its recent limited growth, Winnipeg is still of international importance in the world grain trade. In a similar way, the oil and gas industry has propelled Calgary and Edmonton onto the world stage. Growth has also had significant effects at the regional level. Edmonton's government and university activities have stimulated a variety of localized functions (eg. manufacturing and business services). Winnipeg is an important cultural centre. Calgary's administrative importance has created numerous linkages (eg. computer services) that mark it as a post-industrial city. Clearly, the cities of the Western Interior have assumed a leadership role in the ongoing development and transformation of the region's economy and society.

Sectors of Economic Growth

By the early 1980s, the Western Interior had increased its share of Canadian primary and secondary production from about one-sixth in 1971 to one-quarter of total value added (Table 8.7). The region is now Canada's chief primary producer, dominating in agricultural and fuel commodities. The construction sector accounts for nearly one-third of the Canadian total. Still, the production of natural resource commodities (other than those of agriculture and fuels) and manufactured goods remains well below expected levels, based on the region's share of the Canadian population. Indeed, manufacturing in the 1980s continues to rely heavily on food processing, general manufacture, and custom fabrication related to construction and resource extraction.

TABLE 8.7 VALUE ADDED IN SELECTED ECONOMIC SECTORS, 1971, 1976, and 1981

	Western Interior Percentage			*Canada Percentage*			*Western Interior's Percentage Share*		
Sector	*1971*	*1976*	*1981*	*1971*	*1976*	*1981*	*1971*	*1976*	*1981*
Agriculture	21.9	18.3	18.1	6.7	7.3	8.5	54.8	58.7	54.0
Mining	29.5	38.3	40.0	9.6	13.8	14.4	51.8	64.9	66.6
Other natural resource industries and production of electricity	4.3	3.0	5.5	6.5	5.9	10.0	11.0	11.6	13.7
Total primary industries	*55.7*	*59.6*	*61.6*	*22.8*	*27.1*	*32.9*	*41.1*	*51.4*	*47.2*
Manufacturing	23.3	18.0	19.2	58.1	51.9	52.0	6.7	8.1	9.3
Construction	21.0	22.4	19.2	19.0	21.1	15.1	18.6	24.8	31.9
Total secondary industries	*44.3*	*40.4*	*38.4*	*77.2*	*72.9*	*67.1*	*9.7*	*12.9*	*14.4*
Total	100.0	100.0	100.0	100.0	100.0	100.0	16.8	23.3	25.2

Source: Statistics Canada, *Survey of Production, 1976* (Ottawa: 1978); and *Provincial Gross Domestic Product by Industry, 1981* (Ottawa: 1983) (formerly entitled *Survey of Production*).

The region's manufacturing profile, therefore, reveals two basic characteristics: a continuing reliance on production of primary commodities for shipment out of the region, and the expansion of a population with a rising share of national per capita income and increasing requirements for consumer goods. The region plays its key role in Canadian primary production. It could expand its national share of manufacturing if levels of intraregional producer and consumer demand were to reach critical thresholds, and if the constraint of distance on the movement of finished commodities to extra-regional markets were reduced.

Levels of activity within the Western Interior vary considerably among the provinces. Each province is dominated by a specific goods-producing sector: petroleum production in Alberta, agriculture in Saskatchewan, and manufacturing in Manitoba. Each of these activities reflects the general dilemma faced by the region in overcoming its peripheral position and its own small market. Alberta relies heavily on distant markets in the United States and in central Canada to sell its natural gas and crude oil (Fig. 8.7). These markets, including those for Saskatchewan and British Columbia producers, traditionally have been expensive to reach by overland pipeline systems and have been protected in the United States by quotas and institutional barriers. The pipeline systems have, however, been extended in the four decades following the major discovery at Leduc in 1947 to service central Canada, British Columbia, the United States northwest, upper midwest, and Great Lakes States. The networks collect gas and oil from throughout Alberta and British Columbia, and reach into the Yukon and Northwest Territories.

Concentration on extra-regional markets for Alberta's oil and natural gas, however, tends to discourage manufacturing of related products within the Western Interior, and companies based outside the region generally resist moving their processing facilities into the West. Alberta is thus forced to export large quantities of raw materials to sustain its current level of prosperity, despite recent programmes designed to promote industrial diversification.

The Western Interior's and in particular Saskatchewan's reliance on the export of agricultural commodities has been a traditional source of income, as well as of discontent, for nearly 100 years. The region is particularly subject to the vagaries of world markets, and must also cope with a frequently unreliable rail transportation system for the movement of its products to tidewater. Of particular concern to producers in all provinces are the frequent proposals to shut down prairie rail branch lines and the continuing turmoil over the cost of moving grain. The lack of agreement among farmers, producer organizations, grain companies, and the railways over the appropriate recipient, use, and level of government subsidies does little to aid the situation.

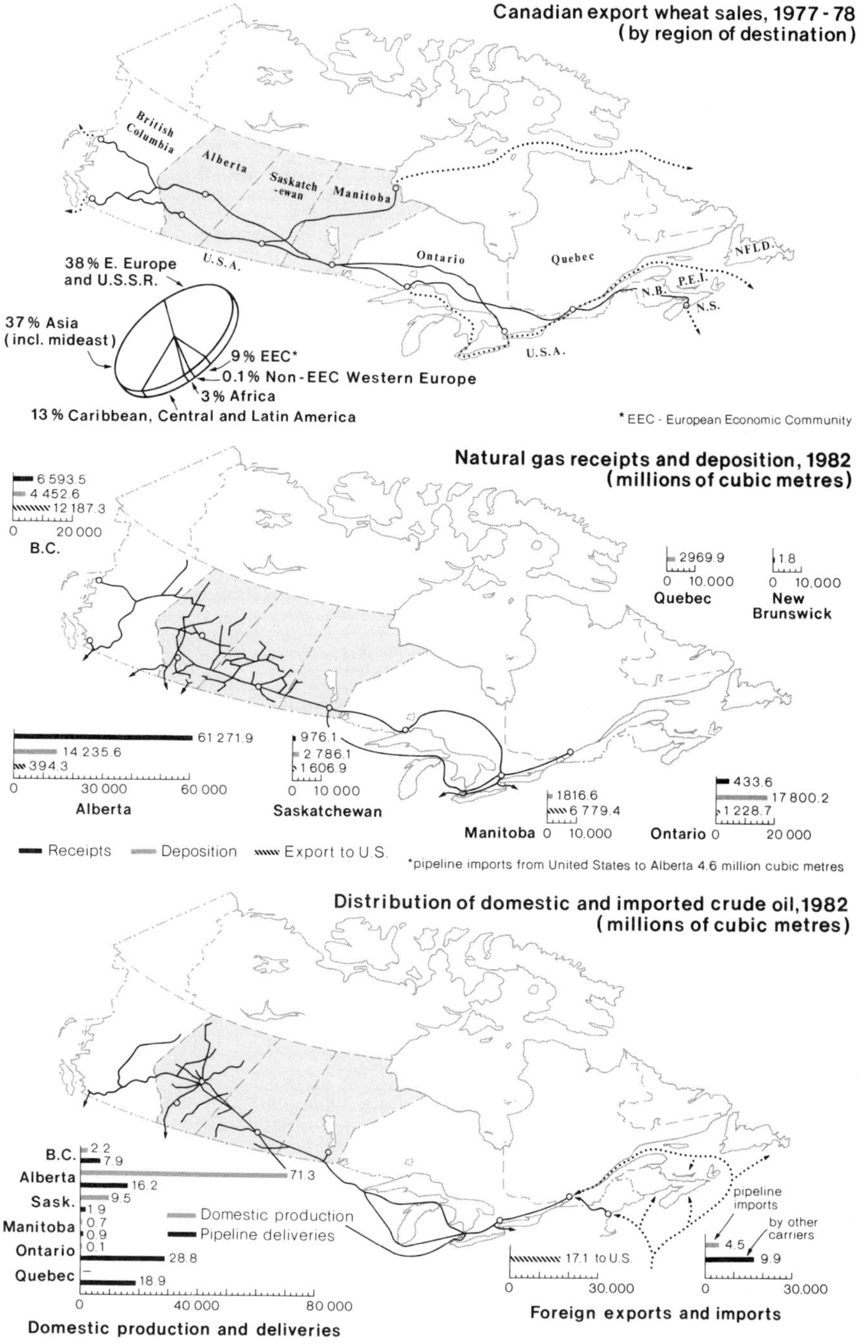
Canadian export wheat sales, 1977 - 78
(by region of destination)
British Columbia
Alberta
Saskatch -ewan
Manitoba
Ontario
Quebec
NFLD.
P.E.I.
N.B.
N.S.
U.S.A.
U.S.A.
38 % E. Europe and U.S.S.R.
37 % Asia (incl. mideast)
9 % EEC*
0.1 % Non-EEC Western Europe
3 % Africa
13 % Caribbean, Central and Latin America
*EEC - European Economic Community
Natural gas receipts and deposition, 1982
(millions of cubic metres)
6 593.5
4 452.6
12 187.3
0
20 000
B.C.
2969.9
0
10,000
Quebec
1.8
0
10,000
New Brunswick
61 271.9
14 235.6
394.3
0
30 000
60 000
Alberta
976.1
2 786.1
1 606.9
0
10 000
Saskatchewan
1816.6
6 779.4
Manitoba 0
10,000
433.6
17 800.2
1 228.7
Ontario 0
20 000
Receipts
Deposition
Export to U.S.
*pipeline imports from United States to Alberta 4.6 million cubic metres
Distribution of domestic and imported crude oil, 1982
(millions of cubic metres)
B.C.
2.2
7.9
Alberta
71.3
16.2
Sask.
9.5
1.9
Manitoba
0.7
0.9
Ontario
0.1
28.8
Quebec
–
18.9
0
40 000
80 000
Domestic production and deliveries
Domestic production
Pipeline deliveries
17.1 to U.S.
0
30,000
pipeline imports
by other carriers
4.5
9.9
0
30,000
Foreign exports and imports

Figure 8.7 Staple commodities of the Western Interior in the world-economy.

Nor has the passage of the Western Grain Transportation Act in 1983 stopped the dissension among these groups. The federal government is still trying to keep rail transportation costs for all producers roughly equal by artificially denying the differences in location accessibility. In the rate system, low freight costs on trunk lines in the densely settled agricultural areas are added to higher transportation costs from peripheral districts and averaged to avoid penalties being incurred by distant producers. Distances and rates are also "managed" by government and transportation companies to avoid penalizing particular ports and coastal destinations, or to promote movement through some ports and alleviate congestion at others. Opponents of such geographical manipulation in the subregional space economy charge that, in a highly competitive international market for Western Interior grain, costs are nonetheless kept high for all producers.

Stability in a region of change: Despite the transformation of the economy and society, the dominant visual landscape of the Western Interior remains one of farms, fields of grain, and the geometry of the township survey system. (*Government of Saskatchewan*)

Just as Alberta supports its petroleum-related manufacturing, the Saskatchewan and other regional governments have become involved in the upgrading of terminal and port facilities, particularly on the Pacific Coast, and in the purchase and maintenance of rail cars which were once the strict prerogative of the railway companies. Rationalization of the rail transportation system, however, cannot proceed in isolation. The viability of numerous small communities within the Western Interior's urban system would suffer from hasty construction of large inland terminals at such places as Edmonton, North Battleford, and Saskatoon. They would do away with the need for many country elevators and attendant rail lines and hence small urban places.

The area of arable land within the Western Interior also requires careful management. The major agricultural region extends in a crescent-shaped pattern from southeast Manitoba through central Saskatchewan. It bends around Edmonton and continues southward in a band through central Alberta, terminating between Calgary and Lethbridge (Fig. 8.8).

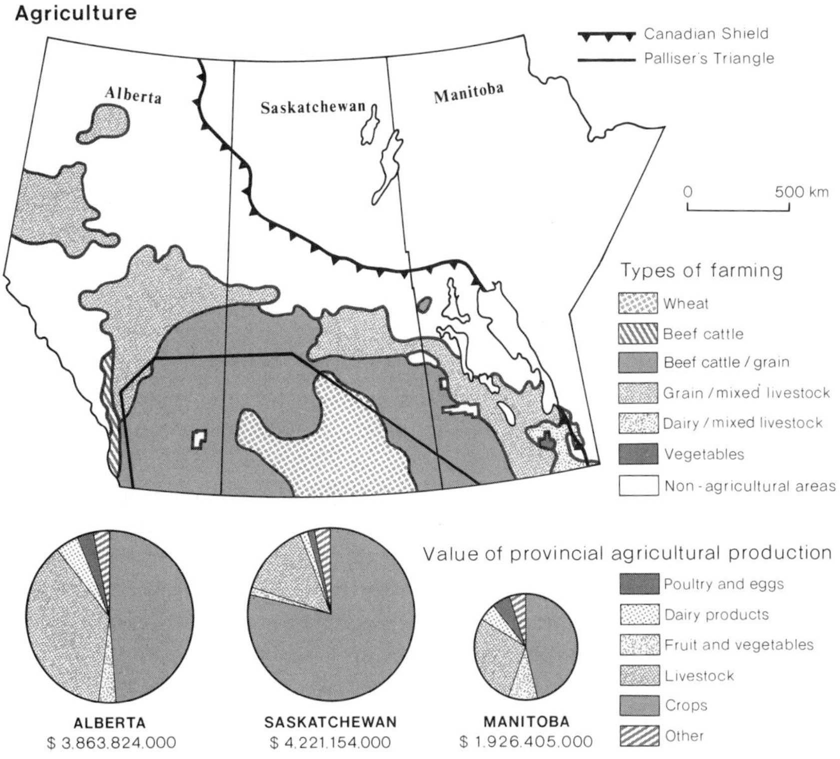

Figure 8.8 Agricultural production in the Western Interior.

This area corresponds to the most favourable natural combination of heat, moisture, and soils in the region. To the south of this arc the environment is too dry, the climate is too variable, and much of the terrain is characterized by irregular glacial deposits. Cost-effective farming cannot persist without supplementary moisture and careful soil and crop management. To the north and west, the fertile soils give way to the Canadian Shield, to the swampy land of the interior sedimentary basin, or to the eastern slopes of the Rockies. Land clearing (mainly in capital-intensive operations) is still proceeding in some northern margins of the Western Interior's agricultural ecumene, particularly in Alberta, and in some important outliers of activity in the Peace River territory of Alberta and adjacent British Columbia, but northern agriculture faces lower heat budgets, greater surplus moisture, heavier need for fertilizer, and shorter growing seasons.

The upgrading of the agricultural ecumene north and south of the major mixed livestock and grain farming belt of the region, and even on some of the hitherto under-utilized lands within it, is encouraged when sales of Canadian farm products are strong. But it is subject to severe retrenchment and financial hardship during times of unfavourable world markets and high interest rates on loans. Approximately 2.5 million improved hectares were added north of the main prairie agricultural area between 1961 and 1981 however; over half of this addition accrued to Alberta, one-quarter to Saskatchewan, and approximately one-fifth to Manitoba.

While still heavily dependent on wheat production, the Western Interior has developed important markets for other grains and a significant portion of the agricultural activity is associated with mixed farming.[38] Intensive horticulture shows some spatial relation to the major metropolitan markets, but is found mainly in the southern Western Interior. Here can be found the fertile glacial lake soils of the main agricultural belt and the irrigated land in the otherwise dry farming region where the heat budgets and length of growing season are most favourable for sensitive crops.

Despite the region's potential for much greater horticultural activity, however, the area devoted to vegetables fluctuates from one decade to another, and has declined significantly from 8505 hectares in 1961 to 6425 hectares in 1981 (although the area in 1971 was much lower yet at 5483 hectares). Small general regional markets and competition from seasonally earlier and usually cheaper American and Mexican imports restrict further production. As of 1981, Alberta held a 63 percent share of vegetable production; Manitoba followed with 28 percent. Although impossible to predict, the significance of this form of intensive land use could increase in the future to satisfy regional markets if levels of demand in the United States and Mexico started to match or even exceed available supplies, and if international Canadian alternatives were uneconomic. The advent of such a scenario could be hastened if fruit and vegetable exporting countries were faced with increases in their own population, shortages of water, and alienation of agricultural land for industrial and urban growth.

Two other factors affect the continued productivity of agricultural land in the Western Interior: the expansion of irrigation projects, and the problems of water and soil conservation and salinity damage. The area of irrigated land in the Western Interior more than doubled between 1971 and 1981 (to nearly 610 000 hectares), and studies predict that by 1990 approximately 2.5 percent (or 890 000 hectares) of the region's improved cropland will be irrigated.[39] Irrigation and conservation measures such as stock watering dams and runoff retention ponds have battled the problems of drought and poor soil drainage, but water supplies are limited and saline seepages have already seriously damaged large areas. Some 200 000 hectares of Alberta dry farmland — approximately 2 percent of the province's total cultivated area — has been affected by salinity, and seepages are increasing at an annual rate of 10 percent, presently about 20 000 hectares. Consequently, more intensive use of the soil resource, as with other renewable regional resources such as water and forests, will require increasingly careful management if basic productivity is to be maintained or enhanced.[40]

Economic activity in Manitoba — particularly in the fertile southern region and in the city of Winnipeg — centres on wholesaling, manufacturing, and finance. The province is the gateway to the Western Interior; people and investment from central Canada and Europe have traditionally flowed across its borders, stimulating economic development. Today, Winnipeg is still a major wholesaling, manufacturing, and financial centre despite recent incursions by the Interior's other four metropolitan centres. In terms of manufacturing, Winnipeg still enjoys advantages of size, agglomeration, and access to the region, to central Canada, and to the American Midwest, but suffers by being neither adjacent to the dominant regions of manufacturing in North America nor near the expanding markets of the Western Interior. Because the need for break-in-bulk or intermodal transshipment of commodities is no longer a critical factor, Winnipeg is now primarily a provincial manufacturing centre. However, several activities, including those related to the aerospace industry, transportation equipment production, and food processing, do participate in national and international markets. But Winnipeg will continue to suffer because of its relatively unproductive northern hinterland, because of vicissitude in the demand for provincial mineral products (nickel, copper, and zinc), and because of the penetration into its regional and national markets by foreign manufacturers who remain unimpeded by an ineffective national economic and manufacturing strategy.

Finally, while the Western Interior's occupational structure confirms a heavy reliance on primary industry and a relative lack of manufacturing, it also demonstrates that the region has a comparatively high employment rate in tertiary industries, matching the Canadian average. Nearly two-thirds of the labour force in each province is engaged in the tertiary sector. The Western Interior thus seems to possess the necessary social and economic infrastructure to achieve specialized metropolitan status. Studies have shown that the region's CMAs have become increasingly able to support complex regional growth. With the exception of Winnipeg, the employment growth rates of Edmonton, Calgary, Saskatoon, and Regina between 1971 and 1981 in their secondary, tertiary, and quaternary spheres were generally above the Canadian CMA average. In addition, Calgary grew by 228 percent in the mining sector, about 200 points above the Canadian average. In fact, Calgary and Edmonton together accounted for over half of the increase in employment change from 1971 to 1981 of all the Canadian CMAs.[41]

Commodity Flows and Regional Integration

Inter- and intra-regional commodity flows are a measure of the way in which the region is integrated, both internally and with the world-economy at large. Shipments of exports are dominated by grain, oil, natural gas, and other staple commodities (Table 8.8 and Fig. 8.9). In aggregate, such exports indicate that the Western Interior is tied more to foreign economies than to the Industrial Heartland. Indeed, exports to the West Coast (and hence to international markets) are greater than those moving eastward (67 versus 30 percent). The principal imports are processed food and wood products, most of which (52 percent) come from eastern Canadian sources, rather than through Pacific Coast centres (43 percent). These data suggest that the Industrial Heartland is dependent on the Western Interior for support of its industrial and commercial economy. If the international trade of the Western Interior falters, the economy of Ontario and Québec will suffer accordingly. Within the region, the majority of commodities moved are classed as general freight, perishable and processed food, and petroleum. There is little movement of manufactured goods.[42]

The degree to which the Western Interior functions as a system and is tied to other regions can be illustrated further by inter-urban rail and truck transportation shipments.[43] Externally, the region's urban centres have direct rail links with the Pacific Coast and central and eastern Canada. Flows of commodities over these routes are non-hierarchical and all centres demonstrate a similar pattern of external connections (Fig. 8.8). Connection with the West Coast became stronger in the 1970s and early 1980s due to the Western Interior's regional economic growth, reducing the region's historical subordination to Ontario and Québec.

Thus, the dual pattern of commodity movements characterizes a region which is neither functionally integrated nor unified as an urban system. Saskatchewan is the watershed between the two principal shipping

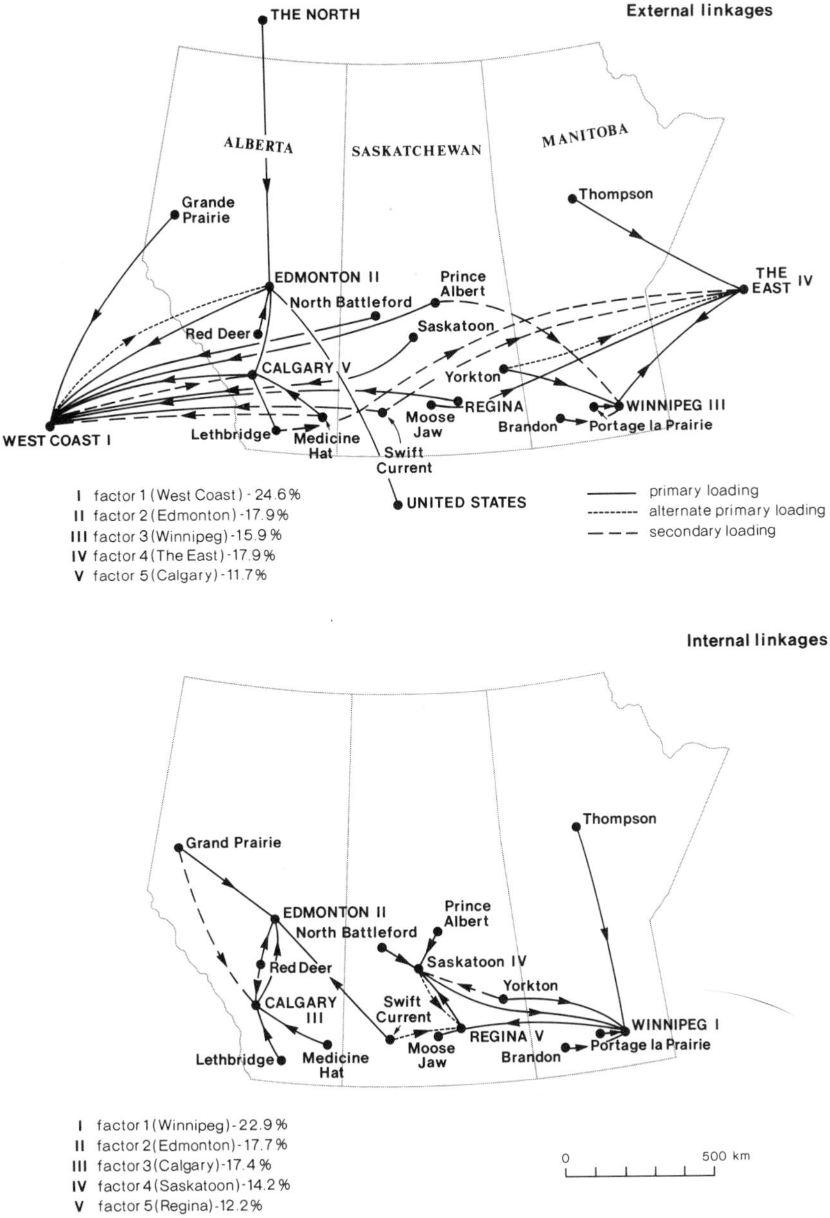

Figure 8.9 Commodity flows and regional integration in the Western Interior (Adapted from R. Thompson, "Commodity Flows and Urban Structure: A Case Study in the Prairie Provinces," unpublished doctoral dissertation, University of Calgary, 1977, by permission of the author.)

TABLE 8.8 MAJOR EXPORTS OF THE WESTERN INTERIOR

Stage of Fabrication	*Value in 1977*
Raw or crude stage	
Wheat[a]	$1 759 000 000
Crude petroleum	1 743 000 000
Natural gas	1 614 000 000
Other unmilled cereals	445 000 000
Coal	252 000 000
Fabricated and semi-processed	
Fertilizers and materials	512 000 000
Petroleum and coal products	335 000 000
Softwood lumber	77 000 000
Wood pulp	76 000 000
Newsprint	25 000 000
Manufactured	
Tractors[b]	42 000 000
Motor vehicle parts (excl. engines)	40 000 000
Drilling, excavating, and mining machinery	15 000 000
Trucks and chassis	3 000 000
Materials handling machinery and equipment	1 000 000

[a]Based on exports to the region's largest trading partners.
[b]Estimated.

Source: Department of Regional Economic Expansion, *Economic Expansion in Western Canada* (Edmonton, 1979), p. A4.

areas, each of which is attached to focal points on the West Coast or in the East. The internal pattern also suggests that the region is not functionally unified. Instead, three separate systems, circumscribed by provincial boundaries, are apparent. The Western Interior sustains internal core-periphery relationships based upon communication linkages, transportation routes, and the movement of goods and services within each of its three provinces. Such relationships suggest the need to reconsider the regionalization of the Western Interior. Particularly over the last decade, Alberta, Saskatchewan, and Manitoba have developed distinct identities, despite their general physical and economic similarities.

CHALLENGES AND DILEMMAS IN A CHANGING HINTERLAND

The heartland-hinterland paradigm, as applied to the Western Interior, offers a classic example of peripheral dependence on developed core areas. Throughout much of its history, the Western Interior has been subordinate to central Canada, Great Britain, and the United States. Two centuries of colonial rule through the Hudson's Bay Company set the basic pattern for the region's development, a pattern which was entrenched by the C.P.R. in the pioneer settlement era. The region came to depend on the importation of labour and capital from developed regions and to rely on the export of a limited range of raw commodities, or staples, to metropolitan markets.

In the 1970s, however, the region gained more control over its development than ever before. Although some retrenchment followed in the early 1980s, the precedent set by change in the 1970s and the experience gained by business, government, and political leaders suggests that development in the Western Interior will proceed on the basis of autonomy, not subordination. The large reserves of capital and investment expertise now resident in the region, particularly in Calgary and in public institutions in the three provincial capitals, indicate that the infrastructure is already in place for ensuring active regional control over future growth.

Many of the processes which shaped the growth of the Western Interior still characterize the region, or operate within it in somewhat different forms. Large organizations such as the Hudson's Bay Company and the C.P.R. have been joined by numerous other corporations which seek to integrate the region into their multiregional and multinational concerns. Natural resources remain the basis of the regional economy and the stimuli for urban growth. Immigration remains vital to the region, but the immigrant's search for land has been replaced by the need for a plethora of technical skills and scientific expertise, making the urban centres and their immediate surroundings the focus of population growth. Migration, abrupt waxing and waning of economic growth within short periods, natural resources, and large corporations (both private and public) direct and shape the space economy and settlement pattern of the region; the dimensions of these forces, however, have been much more diverse and comprehensive during the past decade and a half than in previous periods of the Western Interior's development.

Prior to the 1970s, for example, the resources exported from the Western Interior did not yield premium revenues to the region, even though they were its *raison d'être.* With the advent of worldwide energy shortages in the 1970s, particularly those related to oil, natural gas, and coal, the income gained by exporting such raw materials to industrial markets enhanced the region's status in Canada and in the international economic order. In 1982, for example, the Western Interior produced 93 percent of Canada's mineral fuels, of which nine-tenths originated in Alberta. Nearly 60 percent of Alberta's coal exports in that year went to Japan; 12 percent to countries such as Argentina, Brazil, Chile, Germany, Holland, Sweden, India, Korea, Mexico and Taiwan; just over 20 percent to other Canadian provinces; and the remainder to intra-provincial consumers.

These energy exports, plus the potential of others, have supported strong urban economies in Saskatchewan and Alberta. These two provinces dominate Canada's hydrocarbon reserves. At the end of 1982, the region had 78.5 percent of Canada's established crude oil reserves, 90 percent of its natural gas liquid reserves, and two-thirds of its marketable natural gas reserves. The region maintains nearly one-fifth of Canada's stocked, productive forest land, and one-fifth of the forested land area. Thus, in the 1970s, these two provinces became the focus of migration from the Canadian heartland, particularly from Ontario, and they attracted an increasing number of Canada's international migrants. The Western Interior's rich resource base permitted its inhabitants to share in levels of prosperity usually associated with the world's successful industrial metropolitan economies. In contrast, the capital equipment and settlement structure of Canada's traditional Industrial Heartland, like its spatially adjacent American regional counterparts, became increasingly vulnerable to the technological superiority of industrial Europe, America, and Japan, and to the low-wage manufacturing industries of the Third World, especially those of newly industrializing countries (NICs) in southeast and east Asia.

In repudiating the yoke of perceived subordination to central Canada, the Western Interior established a sense of self-confidence and prowess which remains in place even though international economic factors have posed temporary setbacks to the region's development in the 1980s. This expression of regionalism is marked at the provincial level — irrespective of the political persuasion of governments in power — by on-going governmental intervention in the region's society and economy. The relocation of many corporation headquarters and investment centres to the Western Interior from central Canada suggests that the region is firmly engaged in the process of upward transition toward a state of maturity and equality with other areas of Canada, and is achieving closer integration with the advanced economies of Europe and Asia.

However, while many of the traditional relationships of adversity between the region and external core areas have diminished, they have not completely disappeared. The constraining fetters of the past in the West are loosening rapidly, but they will only be removed when the distribution of decision-making in Canada becomes entrenched in a viable constitution or related legislative schema, and when both international corporations and world trade are firmly managed to ensure effective regional participation, not subordination. In terms of the national and international political economy, the Western Interior is at a crossroads — vulnerable to external forces that demand wisdom and political expertise from those who represent the region's interests. Control and ownership of the region's natural resources must be wisely managed to ensure that the monetary benefits accruing from national and international markets are effectively repatriated and are equitably redistributed throughout the region.

Dilemma in a changing hinterland: Mining of uranium, as shown in this photo of the AMOK mine at Cluff Lake, has diversified Saskatchewan's economy. But Eldorado Nuclear, a Crown Corporation, closed its mine at Uranium City. The closure is a forceful reminder of the vulnerability of any hinterland economy. (*Government of Saskatchewan*)

The process of ensuring that the Western Interior benefits from the sale of its resources abroad will not be complete, however, until key elements within the region also effectively participate in its social structure and economy. Many crucial issues evident at the time of initial settlement were not resolved, but were swept aside by the momentum of development; today, they have emerged as problems to test the region's political fabric and weigh on its social conscience. The exclusion of Native people from the mainstream of economic development and their relegation to special areas and inferior socio-economic status now poses grave problems. Native people face problems of identity within the structure of the urban industrial society surrounding them. Continuing rural poverty, difficulties with education and health care, and futile migration to the region's urban areas, all suggest that the general prosperity of the West has eluded this important group. The lack of participation by indigenous peoples in the socio-economic structure continues to tarnish the region's otherwise notable achievements, and is one of the important issues which will have to be addressed in the political arena.

The general direction of future economic development will be determined by the region's ability to effect change in several areas of discontent. Despite numerous attempts, for example, the region has not been able to revise the institutionalized freight rate structures that affect its competitive relations with other Canadian regions — especially those rates favouring the regional export of raw materials over processed or finished commodities. This structure continues to discourage the development of a diversified economic base. Grain and young (feeder) livestock, for example, are still shipped as primary commodities to related industries in central Canada where value is added through market-oriented manufacturing or finishing and processing (livestock).

An example — the flour milling industry — of this discrimination is provided in evidence produced by the Hall Royal Commission, set up in the mid-1970s to examine Canada's grain industry and grain transportation problems. The Commission found that

> the application of certain government programmes, of Canadian Wheat Board selling practices, and of ancillary rail charges offset the natural geographic advantage Western mills should enjoy.[44]

Western mills were required to pay unequal interest, storage, and railway stopoff charges.

The Western Grain Transportation Act passed in 1983 has alleviated some of these inequalities by abolishing the Crows Nest Freight Rates. The new rates and subsidies should guarantee railway companies adequate returns so that they can expand to meet the growing needs of the region and the new opportunities in international markets. The Act also helps to protect farmers from low world grain prices and high domestic interest rates by guaranteeing that their share of the rail transport cost should not exceed 10 percent of the 1988 price of grain.

Problems still remain, however. Subsidies paid for statutory grain transportation increase the price of grain and hence stimulate its production over other farm products. The subsidies also raise the price of feed grain in the Western Interior, thereby negating some of the natural advantage of the region's livestock producers. Further, rail transportation of grain is subsidized over movement by road. Critics argue that production efficiency could be enhanced if payments were made not to the railways, but directly to farmers, who could then determine what crops to produce and what modes of transportation to use.

How then does the heartland-hinterland paradigm apply to the Western Interior in the late 1980s and 1990s? Undoubtedly tensions still exist between the West and the Industrial Heartland. The federal government's management of subsidies and freight rates continues to hinder the movement of both agricultural and energy resources in the West's view. The policies are barriers to the development of a diversified economic base. They are continuing sources of discontent and of regional alienation and seem to lock the West into its hinterland status.

The traditional relationship between central Canada and the Western Interior is changing dramatically, however. The western provinces' growing representation abroad is a telling symbol of the ability of many regions to bypass Ottawa in their dealings with the world's heartlands. The growth in trade between Western Canada and the Orient demonstrates that many goods do not have to pass through central Canada on their inward or outward movements to world markets. The increasing penetration of foreign airlines and banks directly into the Western Interior further demonstrates that the region is gradually, but persistently, loosening its physical connections with central Canada. These political and economic changes signify the emergence of a new set of relationships between the Western Interior and the Industrial Heartland. Growing attention to uranium, heavy oil, deep tar sands, and northern electricity, in addition to the continuing significance of conventional oil, natural gas, and coal deposits, suggest that international interest in the region's resources will eventually expand across the energy spectrum, bringing increased regional income and associated political confidence. These in turn will put greater pressure on Ottawa for the effective redistribution of political and economic power within Canada.

Events in the 1980s such as the patriation of the Canadian constitution, abolition of the Crows Nest Freight Rates, election of a national government consistent with western electoral preferences, and apparent repudiation of the inimical 1979 National Energy Policy may have temporarily defused some regional alienation, but they have not eliminated the discontent and the inequities. Western attitudes toward regional economic development, including full provincial autonomy in ownership and control of natural resources, are likely to find increasingly sophisticated political expression. Canadians must recognize that western frustration and the pursuit of regional goals are not simply parochial intransigence. They represent the need for a fundamental change in the region's economic status *within* Canada to ensure future harmonious relationships within the federal system. Many of the issues and problems underlying the grievances of the Western Interior, including those of its own minorities such as native and non-native ethnic groups toward the region's provincial centres of power and authority, require resolution before attitudes become intractable.

In the late 1980s, therefore, the human and economic geography of the Western Interior as viewed through the heartland-hinterland paradigm suggests the following: (1) the region's relationships with foreign heartlands are in a state of flux, but they are likely to become more comprehensive and sectorally diverse throughout the rest of this century; (2) the region's traditional dependence on the central Canadian Heartland has lessened, but the relationship is still restrained by unresolved and deep-rooted obstacles; and (3) within the Western Interior serious spatial imbalances exist in the urban hierarchy, between urban and rural regions, and in levels of economic and social participation among important ethnic groups.

NOTES

1. Perspectives on this and related problems are provided by J. Richards and L. Pratt, *Prairie Capitalism: Power and Influence in the New West* (Toronto: McClelland and Stewart, 1979); and C. Caldarola, ed., *Society and Politics in Alberta* (Toronto: Methuen, 1979).
2. R.K. Semple, "A Geographical Perspective of the Prairies: The 1980s," in *The Prairie and Plains Prospects for the '80s,* ed. J.R. Rogge (Winnipeg: The University of Manitoba, Department of Geography, Manitoba Geographical Series No. 7, 1981), pp. 106-23.
3. Marsha Gordon, *Government in Business* (Montréal: 1981), p. 1. Quoted in G. Friesen, "The Prairie West Since 1945: An Historical Survey," in *The Making of the Modern West: Western Canada Since 1945,* ed. A.W. Rasporich (Calgary: The University of Calgary Press, 1984).
4. G. Friesen, "The Prairie West Since 1945," pp. 3-4.
5. *Ibid,* pp. 4 and 26-32.
6. These data are from Friesen, "The Prairie West Since 1945," p. 1. For a current historical interpretation of the Canadian Prairies, the reader is referred to Gerald Friesen, *The Canadian Prairies: A History* (Toronto: University of Toronto Press, 1984).
7. One of the most readable descriptions of the physical geography of the Western Interior is still that of W.A. Mackintosh, *Prairie Settlement, The Geographical Setting,* Vol. 1 in *Canadian Frontiers of Settlement,* eds. W.A. Mackintosh and W.L.G. Joerg (Toronto: Macmillan, 1934).
8. Peter B. Clibbon and Louis Edmond Hamelin, "Landforms," in *Canada: A Geographical Interpretation,* John Warkentin, ed. (Toronto: Methuen, 1968), p. 72.
9. C.F. Shaykewich and T.R. Weir, "Geography of Manitoba," in Government of Manitoba, *Manitoba Soils and their Management* (Winnipeg: Manitoba Department of Agriculture, n.d.).
10. Laurence Ricou, *Vertical Man/Horizontal World* (Vancouver: University of British Columbia Press, 1973).
11. Harold Innis, *The Fur Trade in Canada: An Introduction to Canadian Economic History* (New Haven: Yale University Press, 1946), pp. 386-92.
12. See Arthur J. Ray, *Indians in the Fur Trade: Their Role as Hunters, Trappers and Middlemen in the Lands Southwest of Hudson Bay, 1660-1870* (Toronto: University of Toronto Press, 1974); and Arthur J. Ray and Donald Freeman, *Give us Good Measure: An Economic Analysis of Relations Between the Indians and the Hudson's Bay Company before 1763* (Toronto: University of Toronto Press, 1978).
13. Canada, *Report of the Department of the Interior 1892,* Sessional Papers XXV, No. 13 (Ottawa: 1893).
14. *Winnipeg Times,* quoted in John W. Dafoe, *Clifford Sifton in Relation to His Times* (Freeport, N.Y.: Books for Libraries Press, 1971), pp. 103-4.
15. Clifford Sifton, quoted in Joseph Schull, *Laurier* (Toronto: Macmillan, 1967), p. 336.
16. Chester Martin, *Dominion Lands Policy* (Toronto: Macmillan, 1934; reprinted, Toronto: McClelland and Stewart, Carlton Library Series, 1973), pp. 46-7.
17. Douglas Hill, *The Opening of the Canadian West* (Toronto: Longman, 1973), pp. 233-48.
18. Kenneth H. Norrie, "The National Policy and Prairie Economic Discrimination, 1890-1930," in *Canadian Papers in Rural History,* Vol. I, ed. D.H. Akenson (Gananoque, Ont.: Langdale Press, 1978), p. 16.
19. Edward Blake, letter to the electors of West Durham, 1891. Quoted in Dafoe, *Clifford Sifton in Relation to His Times,* p. 316.
20. Clifford Sifton, "The Immigrants Canada Wants," *Maclean's,* 1 April 1922, p. 16.
21. *Ibid.*
22. John C. Lehr and D. Wayne Moodie, "The Polemics of Pioneer Settlement: Immigration and the Winnipeg Press," *Canadian Ethnic Studies,* 12 (1980), 87-101.
23. John C. Lehr, "The Rural Settlement Behaviour of Ukrainian Pioneers in Western

Canada, 1891-1914," in *Western Canadian Research in Geography: The Lethbridge Papers,* ed. B.M. Barr (Vancouver: Tantalus Press, 1975), pp. 51-60.
24. Canada, Department of Agriculture, *PFRA* (Ottawa: Queen's Printer, 1961).
25. Alan F.J. Artibise, *Winnipeg: A Social History of Urban Growth, 1874-1914* (Montréal: McGill-Queen's University Press, 1975).
26. Quoted in John Herd Thompson, *The Harvests of War* (Toronto: McClelland and Stewart, 1978), pp. 52-3.
27. For an excellent review of the literature on ethnic diversity in the Western Interior, see Hansgeorg Schlictmann, "Ethnic Themes in Geographical Research in Western Canada," *Canadian Ethnic Studies,* 9 (1977), 9-41.
28. B.M. Barr, "Reorganization of the Economy," in *The Prairie Provinces,* ed. P.J. Smith (Toronto: University of Toronto Press, 1972), p. 67.
29. Statistics Canada, Postcensal Annual Estimates of Population, Vol. 1, Catalogue 91-210 (Ottawa: Supply and Services Canada, 1984).
30. J.W. Simmons and L.S. Bourne, *Recent Trends and Patterns in Canadian Settlement, 1976-1981,* Major Report No. 23 (Toronto: University of Toronto, Centre for Urban and Community Studies, 1984), p. 28.
31. J.W. Simmons, *The Canadian Urban System as a Political System, Part I: The Conceptual Framework,* Research Paper No. 141 (Toronto: University of Toronto, Centre for Urban and Community Studies, 1983), pp. 9-13.
32. *Ibid.,* p. 13.
33. Simmons and Bourne, *Recent Trends and Patterns in Canadian Settlement,* p. 31.
34. P.J. Smith, "Urban Development Trends in the Prairie Provinces," in *The Making of the Modern West.*
35. *Ibid,* p. 135.
36. R. Thompson, "Commodity Flows and Urban Structure: A Case Study in the Prairie Provinces" (unpublished doctoral dissertation, University of Calgary, 1977), p. 86.
37. Simmons and Bourne, *Recent Trends and Patterns in Canadian Settlement,* p. 33.
38. Observations and data reported in this and the previous paragraph are based upon J. Lewis Robinson, *Concepts and Themes in the Regional Geography of Canada* (Vancouver: Talonbooks, 1983), pp. 237-39.
39. W.J. Carlyle, "Prairie Agriculture in the '80s," in *The Prairie and the Plains,* pp. 32-5.
40. J. Lilley, *Dryland Salinity in Alberta* (Edmonton: Environment Council of Alberta, 1982), pp. 14-6.
41. D. Hopper, J.W. Simmons, and L.S. Bourne, *The Changing Economic Basis of Canadian Urban Growth, 1971-1981,* Research Paper No. 139 (Toronto: Centre for Urban and Community Studies, 1983), pp. 16 and 22.
42. B.M. Barr, "The Importance of Regional Inter-industry Linkages to Calgary's Manufacturing Firms," in *Calgary: Metropolitan Structure and Influence,* ed. B.M. Barr (Victoria: University of Victoria, Department of Geography, Western Geographical Series, Vol. 11, 1975), pp. 1-51; B.M. Barr and K.J. Fairbairn, "Calgary and Edmonton Manufacturers' Perception of Economic Opportunity in Alberta," *Edmonton: The Emerging Metropolitan Pattern,* ed. P.J. Smith (Victoria: University of Victoria, Department of Geography, Western Geographical Series, Vol. 15, 1978), pp. 29-57.
43. R. Thompson, "Commodity Flows," pp. 41-2 and 68. The basic evidence is drawn from Thompson who analyzed rail and truck transportation patterns for the region's seventeen largest urban centres accounting for 56 percent of its 1971 population and the majority (seven-tenths) of its road and rail (excluding grain) traffic. Nearly two-fifths of road and rail traffic is shipped within the region; the remainder flows to the Pacific Coast, eastern Canada, and the United States. The total movement of traffic is dominated by the railways (some 55 percent). Nearly four-fifths of the intra-regional traffic is carried by road, and three-quarters of the extra-regional traffic by rail.
44. Hall Commission, *Grain and Rail in Western Canada,* Vol. 1 (Ottawa: 1977), pp. 284-311.

9

Alberta Since 1945: The Maturing Settlement System

P.J. Smith

In the years since World War II, Alberta has experienced the characteristic late stages of economic modernization that W.W. Rostow has called the "drive to maturity" and the "age of high mass-consumption."[1] In fact, the two stages may have collapsed into one, so sudden was the transition from the rural and agricultural economy of the 1920s and 1930s to the more diversified, urban-centred economy of the 1960s and after. But while the provincial economy has clearly matured, in the sense of being able to meet the ever more sophisticated demands of a rapidly increasing population, it is not yet mature in the sense of balanced or broadly-based development. For all the prosperity it has generated, and the expanded opportunities it affords, Alberta's economy continues to be dominated by trade in a limited range of primary and partially-processed products. It is still a typical hinterland economy.

This chapter sets the economic modernization of a hinterland region in geographical context, by describing the major adaptations that have been made to Alberta's settlement system.[2] The approach is based on the close correspondence that exists between the economic bases of a region and its geographical organization or structure. This relationship is expressed in the idea of the *space-economy,* which can be defined as the arrangement of economic activities in geographical space. To understand the principles on which a regional space-economy is organized, it is helpful to think of it as a system made up of thousands of individual places (the "settlements") where economic activities are located. In a modern economy, every settlement, no matter how large or small, specializes in certain kinds of activities which determine its *function.* All settlements also depend, in varying degrees, on functions performed by other settlements, and it is this condition of interdependence that integrates them into a *settlement system.* It follows that the basic structure of a settlement system is formed by the pattern of functional relations among the different kinds of settlements of which the system is composed. The pattern will also change over time, as settlements assume different functions in response to the pressures of modernization and growth.

These theoretical ideas set the general framework for an interpretation of Alberta's changing geography. The main emphasis in this chapter is on the period since 1945, but it is first necessary to fix the modern developments in an evolutionary context if the structure of the contemporary settlement system is to be understood. It is also important to establish that Alberta's modern geography cannot be expressed solely in terms of economic functions. Alberta is foremost a political region and its distinctive identity, in the minds and hearts of Albertans, is grounded in its jurisdictional autonomy. The chapter therefore begins with a discussion of the factors that make Alberta distinctive to Albertans, and the implications for the province's relations with the rest of Canada.

OTHER MINDS — ANOTHER REGION

Canada's Western Interior, it has been said, is a "region of the mind." The idea of a single, unified region implies a sense of cohesion and common identity, derived from a shared experience. The Interior, it is believed, poses special challenges to the human will and psyche, and offers special rewards to those who dare its space and dangers. But this belief stems primarily from a particular historical experience, the opening-up, to staple trade and pioneer agriculture, of a vast settlement frontier on the North American continent. While the notion of a distinctive western mentality, rooted in some common perception of this historical experience, is by no means without foundation, it is increasingly remote from the realities of contemporary life. Modern Albertans, as urban, industrial mass consumers, are likely to see their world from a different perspective.

In one important sense, Alberta has always been a distinctive region within the Western Interior. From the time provincial status was attained in 1905, the governments of Alberta have consistently pursued an independent course. They have generally paid little heed to the doctrines of their neighbours, to either east or west. Alone among the four western provinces, for example, Alberta has never had a socialist government. Although it contributed to the radical farmers' movements of the 1910s and 1920s, it did not follow Saskatchewan into the cooperative commonwealth, but turned, instead, to the monetarism of C.H. Douglas.

Alberta's distinctive identity also has its roots in another movement. The support the Social Credit movement drew from the evangelical churches during the 1930s was a vital part of the Albertan experience, leaving its moral stamp on all the Social Credit governments.[3] Above all, in keeping with one of the most basic tenets of evangelical faith, an ethic of individualism prevailed. No matter what the popular pressure for social controls, Alberta governments, including those before and after Social Credit, have tended to bow slowly and unwillingly. Freedom of enterprise and individual responsibility have persisted as cardinal virtues. To some, they appear as marks of a frontier mentality that should long since have been outgrown, but the religious undertones suggest that these values are both more fundamental and more enduring.[4]

Whatever the link between political and religious thought, there can be no doubt that independence has long been a central element of Alberta's political culture.[5] In part, this independence stems from the sentiments of alienation and exploitation upon which the whole of the Western Interior has brooded for so long. But a shared sense of grievance alone is not enough to override provincial loyalties. Indeed, from the Albertan perspective, the injury of regional misunderstanding is compounded when outsiders speak of the three prairie provinces as one, imposing on them a common identity, a common purpose, and a common set of behaviours.[6] These assumptions touch local sensitivities to the quick, especially if British Columbia is seen to be so fundamentally different that it must stand apart. To Albertans, this view of the West is profoundly offensive; to geographers, it represents a retreat to environmental determinism. It is based on the assumption that the "geographical reality" of Canada is its physical geography — not its political geography -- and that the great barriers to explorers, voyageurs, and railway builders are still barriers to regional intercourse, and thus shape regional consciousness. In this perspective, the "prairie region" is still cut off from the heartland by the "wastes" of northern Ontario; and British Columbia still huddles, in maritime isolation, behind its mountain ramparts.

But the mountains also range into Alberta and are a vital part of its self-image, particularly as it is projected to the outside world. Jasper National Park, mountain scenery, and internationally famed resorts are all features of Alberta's Rocky Mountains and are promoted as Alberta attractions. When Albertans idealize their physical environment, they may think first of its spaciousness. But the space is not boundless, unhorizoned, featureless, as it tends to be in external images of Saskatchewan, the prairie archetype. It is bounded, structured, and westward oriented. This sense of bounded space has long been expressed as a visual metaphor for Alberta. Fields of grain dominate the foreview, but at no great distance they give way to green hills with open pasture on the lower slopes, forest above. Then, beyond the summits of the hills, defining the edge of Alberta's territory with absolute authority, loom the massive blocks of the mountain ranges.

There is a corollary, as well. This Albertan self-image has little connection with the conventional "prairie" image. There seems even to be a deliberate rejection of that image, as having little relevance to the

Albertan experience, particularly as it has been shaped in the decades since World War II. Development policies have emphasized urban-industrial growth, transportation links with British Columbia, even medical research. Alberta is a province rich in a diversity of resources — oil in particular has superseded the agricultural base of a prairie region.

Insofar as there is a regional consciousness or sentiment extending across the Western Interior, it too is rooted in the physical environment — or at least that part to which the vast open plains of popular imagining belong. But it is an environment occupying a comparatively small share of the prairie provinces, so-called, and even less of Alberta. Its expression is chiefly artistic and is epitomized in the prairie tradition of landscape painting, with its aesthetic of light and space, now becoming increasingly abstract. There is also a distinctive prairie literary tradition, in both creative and biographical writing, although its significance is essentially historical. It draws its strength from the primordial struggle against nature, and springs from the common experience of ill-prepared settlers in a demanding and unpredictable land.

Albertans have contributed as much as other westerners to this literature, but not so as to forge a regional sensibility to which all

Alberta's bounded landscape: The physical milieu of Alberta, including plains, foothills, and towering mountains, sets the region apart from Saskatchewan and Manitoba. (*Government of the Province of Alberta*)

Albertans feel committed. The hardships of the pioneers are already remote, even to their descendants. To more recent Albertans, whose cultural heritage lies elsewhere, the pioneer experience has no personal meaning. In 1981, about 380 000 of the province's 2.3 million people were immigrants who had arrived in the 1970s. A further 310 000 had arrived in the 1950s and '60s. If these people have planted their own roots in Alberta, it is not because they have found nourishment in the rich soils that were heaven on earth to the first generation of settlers. Their promised land is in the cities, or on the new resource frontier, with its juxtaposition of mass amenities and wilderness. When urban Albertans turn to the land for recreation, it is not the prairie they seek. When they idealize the past, in their folk festivals, the Calgary Stampede, and Edmonton's Klondike Days, it is not the world of the pioneer farmer they are trying to recapture, even in myth. Today the land of the settlers is domesticated, increasingly trim and suburban. The physical environment with the greatest appeal is that *not* converted by the settlers — the wilderness of forest and mountains, lakes and rivers, still remote and difficult to encounter, still challenging, even in its most subdued corners.

The notion of a prairie region is an abstraction for most Albertans in their everyday lives. Neither environment nor history has created an overriding bond, or burned some experience into the collective consciousness in an enduring way. The converse is more evident. Insofar as Alberta shares a common environment with Saskatchewan and Manitoba, it is a force of division rather than union. Albertans compete with their eastern neighbours for grain and cattle markets, investment capital, and tourists. There may be common problems associated with the difficulty of breaking out of a resource-extractive economy in a sparsely settled, comparatively isolated, continental interior location; and there are obvious advantages in adopting joint positions on specific issues, such as grain transport. But these are not sufficient in themselves to foster a common regional will. In their outward orientations, Albertans look west, south, and north, but only rarely east, to their immediate neighbours.

Modern Albertans find more reason to identify themselves with British Columbia. Like British Columbians, they are closely linked to their American counterparts in the Pacific Northwest, California, and the sunbelt states. The best highway connections in the province are north-south (in the Edmonton-Calgary-Lethbridge axis) and westward to the mountain passes from Edmonton and Calgary. The air service network of Western Canada is dominated by movement between Alberta and British Columbia, and by the new southern connections to Houston, Denver, Las Vegas, Phoenix, Los Angeles, and San Francisco.

For relaxation and retirement, and increasingly for business therefore, Alberta's outlook is west and south. Albertan expertise gained from the oil industry is used in the United States, and modular homes from Calgary are sold in British Columbia's resource camps. Even in their patterns of competition, Alberta and British Columbia display a converging interest, particularly in the north. Traditionally, there have been three northern service areas — Winnipeg-Keewatin, Edmonton-Mackenzie and Vancouver-Yukon — but the two western areas are becoming less distinct. Services in Edmonton and Vancouver are now equally accessible and the two cities are competing to service the north.

Converging interest is also manifest in Alberta's promotion of itself, not just as a western province, but as a Pacific province. In both trade and tourism, Albertans are actively developing connections with Japan, China, and Korea, and Albertan markets are being courted in return. Yet, as Alberta has become more aggressive as an independent trading agent, its landlocked situation has become more confining and frustrating. Alberta's offshore exports — chiefly grain, oilseeds, coal, and sulphur — are routed mainly through British Columbia, along railway lines notorious for their slips and blockages, and through a port notorious for its delays. Dreams of an Alberta port have therefore become more urgent, and have led to the resurrection of an older dream, the development of Prince Rupert as a deep-water facility to rival Vancouver. The expansion of Prince Rupert and the improvement of its railway access could benefit the whole of the Western Interior, including northern British Columbia. But the major initiative is coming from Alberta, another sign of the vigour with which the province is pursuing its independent interests.

No issue has done more to underline this point for Canadians in recent years, or to crystallize the feelings of Albertans, than the pricing and sale of petroleum and natural gas. To those Albertans who are aware of earlier battles over natural resource ownership, this issue stirs up past frustrations and resentment. When Alberta and Saskatchewan were carved from the Northwest Territories in 1905, they did not receive the same control over their own resources as the other provinces did — the government of Canada retained its ownership of Crown land and subsurface rights. To the two provinces, this was a base inequity. It was eventually redressed in 1930, but the memory of that old constitutional battle has not faded. Reaction to recent challenges against provincial government control over natural resources has therefore been intense, particularly in Alberta. Since only one resource has been involved to date, and since one province has been chiefly affected, any attempt by the central government to insist on the ultimate right to determine how much oil and natural gas will be sold, where, and at what price, is easily taken as an affront to Alberta's provincial autonomy. This threat to autonomy has underlain Alberta's position throughout the constitutional and economic debates of the 1970s and 1980s.[7]

The traditional view of Alberta as a hinterland region has also added to the controversy. The economic strength of Canada has historically been vested in a few major export staples — the furs, grain, pulp, lumber, and minerals of a vast, richly-endowed hinterland. The exploitation of these staples required a high order of entrepreneurial skill, which has been concentrated in central Canada. As a result, resource-producing regions have traditionally been viewed as economically subordinate to the centre. On the contrary, however, the wealth generated by hinterland resources has facilitated the industrialization of southern Ontario and the St. Lawrence Lowlands. The heartland is directly dependent upon hinterland resources (the petrochemical industry of Sarnia, for example, depends on Albertan oil) and the trade in hinterland resource staples has created an economic climate in which domestic manufacturing could be protected. J. Tait Davis has argued, for example, that the Canadian heartland depends more for its prosperity on the hinterland than does the hinterland upon the heartland, although this is not the view that is commonly presented.[8] Rather, there is a tendency to assume that the development of the hinterland is a consequence of the economic demands of the heartland. Interdependence is more the case. A strong heartland economy naturally increases the market for hinterland resources, just as a strong hinterland market is vital to the manufacturers of Ontario and Québec. In the larger perspective, however, it is the external demand for the hinterland's resource-based products that stimulates the Canadian economy.

Many popular and political attitudes have thus been shaped by erroneous perceptions of the role of heartland and hinterland in the Canadian economic system. The broadly-based, diversified economy of central Canada, with its general prosperity and stability, its concentration of political and economic institutions, and its large population base, stands in such striking contrast to the vast peripheral regions — sparsely settled, often impoverished, and economically fragile in their dependence on the vagaries of weather and international markets. The Canadian hinterland, in short, has long displayed the marks of economic under-development, and Alberta has been no exception. In the view from the West, it seems that the benefits from hinterland staples have remained chiefly in central Canada, and the resource-producing regions have been held in check by subjection to the directives of banks and investment houses, transport companies (particularly the railways), and manufacturers of central Canada. Some see the relationship as a form of colonial exploitation, in which the centre is blind to the true source of its strength. Nor has the perception been helped by a long series of national governments with little support in the West, and no apparent sensitivity to western concerns and aspirations.

The energy crisis of the 1970s heightened the tension between Alberta and central Canada. Almost overnight, Alberta oil was transformed from a neutral trade commodity, which had made a modest penetration into American and Ontario markets, into a cornerstone of national economic strength and security. In extreme political hyperbole, oil suddenly became part of "the birthright of all Canadians," to be managed in the "national interest." To Albertans, however, it was difficult to separate the national interest from the central interest, especially when Albertans heard their own arguments for increased prices, as an essential condition for energy self-sufficiency and the development of alternative energy sources, attributed to parochialism and greed.

For the first time in its history, however, Alberta was in command of a resource needed by central Canadians, with the prospect of large capital accumulation — capital that might be invested to broaden and strengthen the province's economic base.[9] The petroleum resource became a symbol of Alberta's constitutional rights and the key to its long-term security. With this double value at stake, to suggest that natural resource control could be pre-empted by central government fiat was regarded as the ultimate humiliation for Albertans, as serious a threat to their distinctive place within Confederation as the erosion of the French language is to Québec. No issue is better guaranteed to give Albertans the will to assert their right of self-determination, and none can more effectively unite them. Despite the mid-1980s decline in world oil prices, Albertans continue to assert this right — a sign of regional maturity.

The oil issue, however, has also brought the negative side of regionalism to the fore. It has caused regional sentiment to be focussed on a siege mentality rather than on the sense of organized community responsibility that a region should possess if it is to assume a political identity. The individualism of political regions, however, is not unique to Alberta; it is a national issue rooted in the history and geography of the individual provinces and the country as a whole.

FOUNDATIONS OF THE ALBERTA SETTLEMENT SYSTEM

Although a sense of independence and political relationships serve to define Alberta as a distinctive entity within the federal state, they do not, of themselves, require the province to follow any particular pattern of spatial organization. However, if Alberta is to be a functional region as well as a political one, its settlement system must have a coherent form determined by the structure of its *internal* relationships. These relationships are important; without them, there would be no means of knitting the region together into a functioning unit, and there would be no settlement system.

Functional relationships can take many forms, but communication is always a basic element. People, goods, and messages flow between pairs of places, and thus communications facilities are as much part of the settlement system as are the places they connect. The simplest way to display the basic form of any settlement system is to map these communications flows; they serve as indicators of the amount of interaction between places within the system. Highway traffic volumes provide a particularly useful illustration in Alberta (Fig. 9.1). Not only are

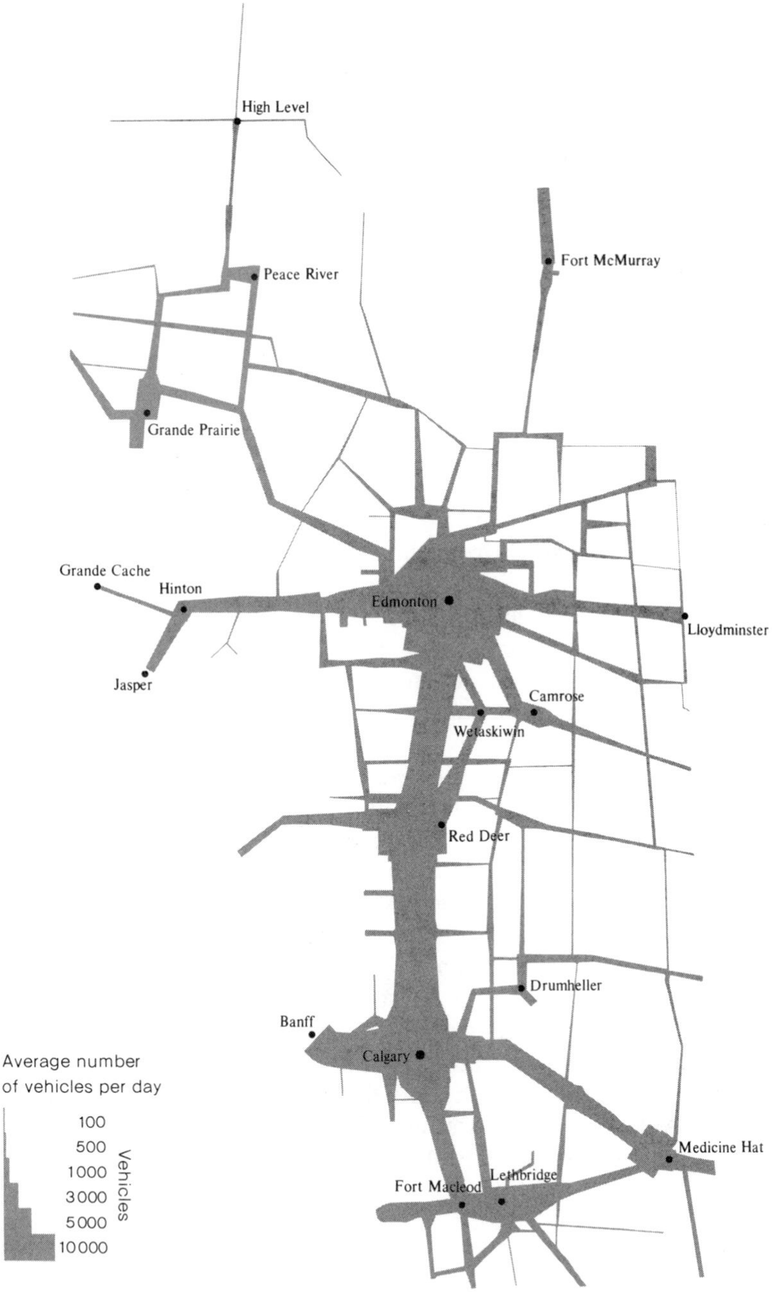

Figure 9.1 Diagrammatic representation of highway traffic volumes in Alberta, c. 1980.

they derived from a mode of communication that is universally accessible, but they indicate internal interactions between Albertans.

As a matter of general principle, any functional region will have an identifiable core or cores around which the settlement system is organized in some consistent way. Figure 9.1 demonstrates this organization in two respects:

(i) The dominance of Edmonton and Calgary is vividly portrayed. As a functional region, there can be no question that Alberta is organized around the two large cities on which all routes eventually converge. The map also gives some suggestion of a hierarchical ordering of urban places, as a basic characteristic of Alberta's space-economy. Lethbridge stands out as the major secondary node, and lesser nodes can be identified at such cities as Medicine Hat, Camrose, and Grande Prairie. In large part, this structure is based on the central place activities — banking, retailing, personal and business services — which, historically, have been the dominant functions of Alberta's urban settlements. A central place provides services to a surrounding trade area, and the need for hierarchical sorting arises from the differing levels of demand for different kinds of services. The less a service is required, the fewer the places in which it will be available. The most specialized services are provided only in Calgary and Edmonton, and their trade areas for those services cover the whole of Alberta and beyond.

(ii) The greatest traffic volumes are recorded on the highways in the Edmonton-Calgary corridor. These volumes reflect a high level of interaction between the two cities, but they are also a function of what, in total, is a considerable amount of movement among the corridor's other urban centres. The corridor has become a complex interaction system in its own right, and the core element of the larger Alberta system. As pointed out in Chapter 1, the heartland-hinterland model can be applied at all geographical scales. Here, at the regional scale, Fig. 9.1 appears to have identified an Alberta heartland.

If this observation is to be substantiated, it should be possible to invoke another principle from settlement theory — the principle of historical advantage — to show that the pattern of central dominance was forged at the beginning of the settlement period, and that the functional region of Alberta evolved around its original cores. Again, the evidence can best be presented graphically, employing a model developed by Peter Haggett to describe the spatial transformations that accompany economic modernization.[10] In Alberta, the initial penetration by European commercial interests (Stage I in Fig. 9.2) took the form of a disconnected series of fur-trading posts along the major waterways. These fortified posts were widely distributed throughout the northern two-thirds of the province, in the parkland and forest zones (Fig. 9.2). They all communicated directly with the major collection points, such as York Factory and Fort Garry. Eventually, however, it was Fort Edmonton, at the head of steam

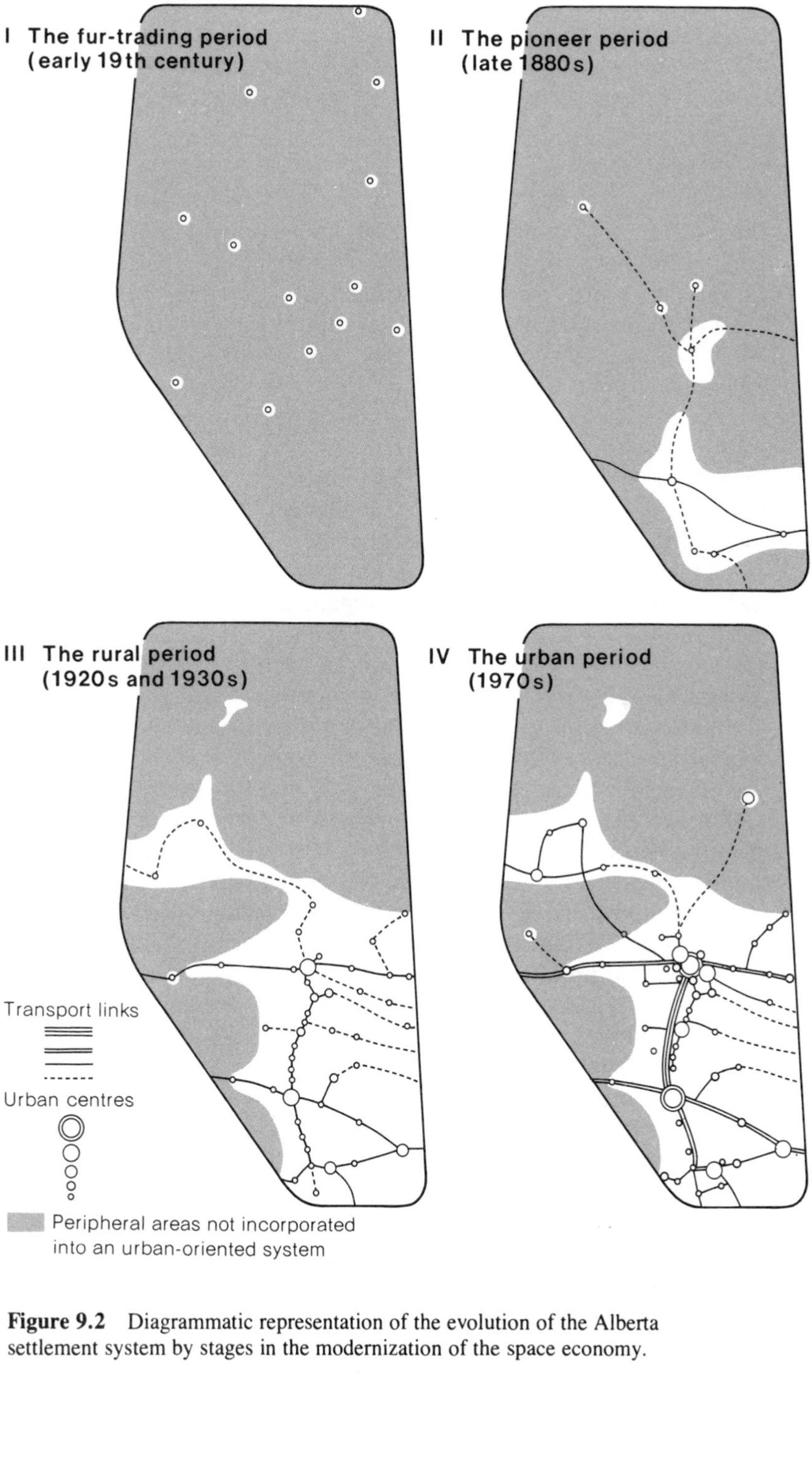

Figure 9.2 Diagrammatic representation of the evolution of the Alberta settlement system by stages in the modernization of the space economy.

navigation on the North Saskatchewan River, that secured the position of regional entrepôt for the western plains.

With the first trickle of agricultural settlers, in the third quarter of the nineteenth century (Stage II), transportation began to shift to the overland trail system. Two main routes met at Fort Edmonton, one paralleling the river from Winnipeg and the other linking Edmonton to Fort Benton, Montana, at the head of navigation on the Missouri River. By the 1870s, the southern end of the Benton Trail had given rise to a string of trading and police posts — Fort Whoop-up (Lethbridge), Fort MacLeod, Fort Calgary — which marked the spread of American influences and the countervailing spread of Canadian authority, represented by the North West Mounted Police. Then came the construction of the Canadian Pacific Railway's trans-continental line across southern Alberta in 1883. Predictably, the point at which the old and new transport facilities crossed became the hub of development for the huge territory opened for settlement. The dependence on Fort Benton was broken but so, too, was Edmonton's historical dominance in the western plains. Calgary was now the easiest point-of-entry to the region.

At first, agricultural colonization was concentrated in the area south and east of Calgary and was accompanied by a rapid expansion of the local rail network. Even at this early stage, however, the established attraction of Edmonton could not be denied, particularly as central Alberta had an environmental advantage that was eventually to give rise to a closer mesh of rural and small town settlement than was feasible in the Calgary area. Both cities are located in the famous black soil zone that sweeps through the southern half of Alberta from Lloydminster to Lethbridge (Fig. 9.3). But Edmonton, by virtue of its more northerly location, is also in the best watered part of the parkland ecosystem, where the natural vegetation is a mixture of grassland and poplar groves, grading into the boreal forest. In its moisture characteristics, this region is classified as subhumid rather than semi-arid, with obvious consequences for agricultural productivity and population density. A railway north from Calgary was logically an early need. It was opened in 1891, and was followed immediately by a new surge of settlement in a wide radius around Edmonton.

In the census of 1901, Calgary and the twin cities of Edmonton-Strathcona (the railhead on the south bank of the North Saskatchewan River) each recorded populations of 4000, but their small size was not a fair guide to their relative importance. These cities were already the dominant places in the immature settlement system. Lethbridge, their nearest rival, had only 2000 people and its secondary status was dramatically demonstrated during the great immigration boom at the beginning of the new century. Between 1901 and 1921 the population of Alberta experienced an eight-fold increase, from 73 000 to 588 000, but for Edmonton and Calgary the increase was fifteen-fold. From twice the size

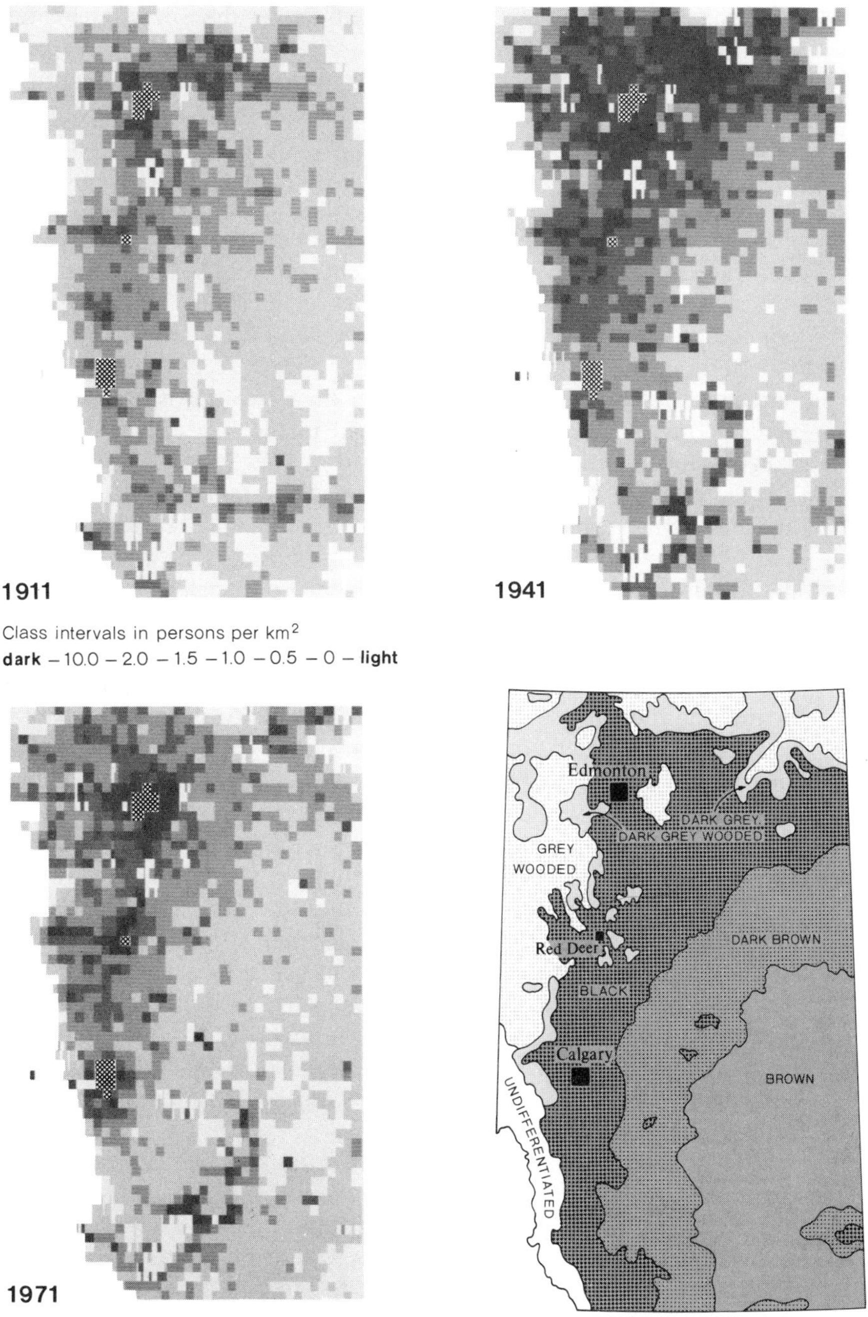

Figure 9.3 Major soil zones and rural population density by townships in the southern half of Alberta, 1911–1971.

of Lethbridge at the start of the growth surge, they jumped to well over five times its size by 1921.

Growth was not confined to the nineteenth century communities, either. Many small urban centres appeared for the first time in the censuses of 1911 and 1921, as a network of central places appeared over the great arc of the cultivated plains. The rural settlement pattern filled out as well, and supported a farm population that was at its climax, demographically and spatially, in the decades between the two world wars. The influence of the physical environment on the spatial distribution of Alberta's population was also at its greatest in this period. Rural population was concentrated in the black and dark brown soil zones, and especially in the more humid parkland (Fig. 9.3). Of the total provincial population of 800 000 in 1941, more than two-thirds was rural and 58 percent (rural and urban) was clustered in the five census divisions that roughly covered the parkland zone, from Calgary to Lloydminster.

Despite the strength of the settlement system's rural base, however, and the spatial expansion and intensification that occurred between 1901 and 1941, the central importance of Edmonton and Calgary was undiminished. As the twin apexes of the provincial hierarchy, they were also the foci of all those service demands contained within the settlement system. Every step in the modernization of the Alberta economy (Stages II and III in Fig. 9.2) served to reinforce their dominance, a point underlined by the way the pattern of transport facilities evolved. First, railway service was prominent. After Edmonton was provided with its own transcontinental line (the Canadian Northern Railway in 1905), the network expanded quickly in a radial pattern, with Calgary and Edmonton as the twin hubs. Then, in the 1920s, as the railway system reached its development climax, the modern highway system began to take shape, demonstrating even more vividly the focal roles of Edmonton and Calgary. Unlike the railways, which were initiated by external interests and served first as links to the outside world, the highway system was a local response to internal needs and, thus, to the interrelationships already built into the settlement system. Again, the double radial pattern prevailed from the outset, but in the highway improvement programmes of the 1920s and 1930s it was the connection between Edmonton and Calgary that received the highest priority.

That there was a particular attraction to the Edmonton-Calgary corridor was plain. From the 1890s on, there was a high concentration of relatively large urban places between Edmonton and Calgary, and the early highway developments served to string these places together, like beads. Their favoured situation was also manifest in another spatial characteristic that is imprinted on the economic landscape to this day. Because of the unusually close spacing of the corridor towns, the normal arrangement of trade areas never developed there. Instead of being roughly circular, the trade areas took the form of elongated ellipses at right angles to the transport axis. Similar distortions did not develop elsewhere, where the towns were further apart, so it must be concluded that the corridor zone has always exerted a special influence on the form of Alberta's settlement system.

There is theoretical support for this conclusion, in the idea that settlement systems evolving around core areas will display development gradients from core to periphery. A variety of measures might be used to identify these gradients, but Figs. 9.1 to 9.3 provide enough information to illustrate the validity of the principle for Alberta. There is, to begin, a cultural gradient that can be inferred from Fig. 9.2. In its hypothetical extremes, the cultural gradient ranges from unmodified tradition, or the culturally closed system, to total openness at those points of penetration that are exposed to an unchecked flow of innovations and external influences. In this construction, the core areas act as filters through which new cultural elements have to pass before they can be diffused into the larger settlement system. At an early stage of a system's evolution (Stage II in Fig. 9.2), when communication is still difficult, neither the range nor the force of cultural penetration is likely to be great. Traditional societies can persist with comparatively little change, particularly if they are protected by isolation in the remote extremities of the territory, as the Woodland Cree were in the northern half of Alberta. The Alberta experience also shows how the original settlers imposed their distinctive cultural traditions on their new land, while those remnants of the aboriginal population which remained within the areas of European settlement experienced a profoundly disruptive acculturation. Although afforded some security by the reserve system of land grants, their traditional way of life was lost forever.

Yet the colonists were no more successful in protecting their traditional practices than the plains Indians, particularly as their cultures became increasingly embedded in the North American market economy. Even the Hutterian Brethren, whose colonies constitute the closest approximation to a closed culture to be found in Alberta, have made themselves masters of the technology of twentieth century agriculture. In other words, as the Alberta economy evolved through the decades before World War II, the force of tradition (whether indigenous or introduced) was steadily weakened. Even in modified form, traditional ways of life could survive only by being insulated from the points at which cultural change originated. There were two ways of achieving this effect: physical isolation in remote and inaccessible communities, chiefly in the forests of northern Alberta (the physical periphery); or social isolation in artificially maintained communities, such as the Indian reserves of southern Alberta or the Hutterite colonies (the cultural periphery).

Concomitant with the cultural gradient (and part of it), an economic gradient is also to be expected, if only because of the effects of economies of scale and agglomeration. The number, size, and variety of economic activities all decline with distance from the regional cores, with obvious consequences for such intimately related phenomena as population density (Fig. 9.3) and traffic flows (Fig. 9.1). In general, the economies of the peripheral regions are characterized by their comparative simplicity and narrow bases, specializing in a limited product range that is relatively insensitive to the distance factor in transport costs. A strong emphasis on primary industry, or, at most, the initial processing of primary products, is the most probable outcome.

In Alberta, during the evolution from Stage I to Stage III of the Haggett model, two main economic activities were prominent: extensive agriculture and mining. Agriculture was based on two main forms: grain monoculture on the subhumid and semi-arid plains, supplemented by irrigation on the dry margins from an early date; and cattle ranching in the foothills of southwestern Alberta and in the driest plains areas. Mining also took two main forms. The first commercial exploitation of oil and natural gas occurred in the Turner Valley district, south of Calgary, shortly after World War I, but it was coal that provided the main interest from the beginning of the railway period. Brown coals were tapped at many points on the plains, including Edmonton and Lethbridge, but the most distinctive mining communities were along the valley of the Red Deer River in the vicinity of Drumheller, and in the foothills and front ranges of the Rocky Mountains, where high-grade coking and thermal coals were found.

STRUCTURAL CHANGES IN THE MATURING SYSTEM

In the preceding section, the basic structure of the Alberta settlement system was placed in its evolutionary context, up to about 1940. Next, we turn to a more detailed consideration of the latest phase in the modernization process, which carried Alberta from Stage III to Stage IV (the contemporary pattern) in Fig. 9.2. Over this period there were radical changes in social and economic activities, in the size and distribution of population, and in the functions of settlements. The geographical consequence has been a massive restructuring of Alberta's space-economy and, simultaneously, a further evolution of the settlement system into a more complex form.

A specific framework for reviewing these changes is provided by Michel Boisvert's scheme of development regions for Canada.[11] Like Fig. 9.2, this scheme is based on the theory that there is a close correspondence between a region's stage of economic development and the form of its settlement system. Boisvert divided Canada into 20 city-centred regions, which he classed, in evolutionary sequence, as resource, transformation, and fabrication regions. The last corresponds to the Industrial Heartland and is limited to two regions, centred respectively on Toronto and

Montréal. Eleven regions have reached the intermediate or transformation stage, and the remaining seven, including Alberta, are still classified as resource regions. Alberta is also unusual, however. It is a binodal region, organized around two cities rather than one; and it is now close to completing the transition from a resource region to a transformation region (Fig. 9.4).

In economic terms, the basic point of difference between resource and transformation regions is that resource regions are driven by the export of staples in raw or unprocessed form, whereas transformation regions have been able to retain a large amount of processing activity. These characteristics have important implications for urban growth and the structure of the settlement system. Resource regions are characterized by comparatively low levels of urbanization; by a comparatively small concentration of population in the primate centre (Edmonton and Calgary combined, in Alberta); by an urban hierarchy in the shape of an upside-down T; and, excluding central place relationships, by comparatively low volumes of interaction among the region's urban places. The evolution to a transformation region is marked by changes in all these features: the level of urbanization increases substantially; the regional metropolis grows rapidly and increases its dominance over the regional system; the number of intermediate-sized cities increases, giving the urban hierarchy a more pyramidal shape (△); and the growth of the industrial base gives rise to an increased degree of interdependence, and hence interaction, within the urban system. Alberta has shown all these tendencies in the recent past.

Figure 9.4 Canadian regions in development. (Adapted from Michel Boisvert, *The Correspondence Between the Urban System and Economic Base of Canada's Regions* (Ottawa: Economic Council of Canada, 1978.)

Urbanization, Urban Growth, and Rural Development

The outstanding feature of Alberta's modern development is the sheer scale of its economic and population growth. The first signs of this growth appeared in the late 1930s, with a renewed interest in oil exploration and a fresh spurt of migration to Edmonton and Calgary. Both trends accelerated during World War II, but the major stimulus for long-term growth was the discovery of a group of oilfields in the vicinity of Edmonton. The first discovery was the Leduc field in 1947.[12] The scale of the Leduc discovery stimulated further exploration for oil in the Edmonton region. Within a few years hundreds of wells were being drilled and fields were discovered at Redwater and Pembina. The immediate outcome was a powerful development impulse, which was translated directly into a high rate of population increase (Fig. 9.5c). In general, that trend has persisted, although there have been periodic interruptions at times of economic recession.

The growing population, however, has been unevenly distributed. As Fig. 9.5 shows, between 1941 and 1981 Alberta's total population increased from 800 000 to 2 200 000, and its urban population grew from 300 000 to 1 700 000. Alberta's entire population increase since 1941, therefore, has been urban increase (Fig. 9.6). In 1941, at the end of the rural development period, only 38 percent of the population was classified as urban by the Census of Canada; 40 years later, the urban proportion had risen to 77 percent. Moreover, this figure excludes the whole of the rural non-farm population, much of which lives in villages or country subdivisions within commuting range of Edmonton, Calgary, and the secondary cities.

Urbanization began suddenly in the late 1940s and was closely associated with the expansion of the petroleum industry. More basically, urban-industrial growth marked the beginning of a major adjustment in

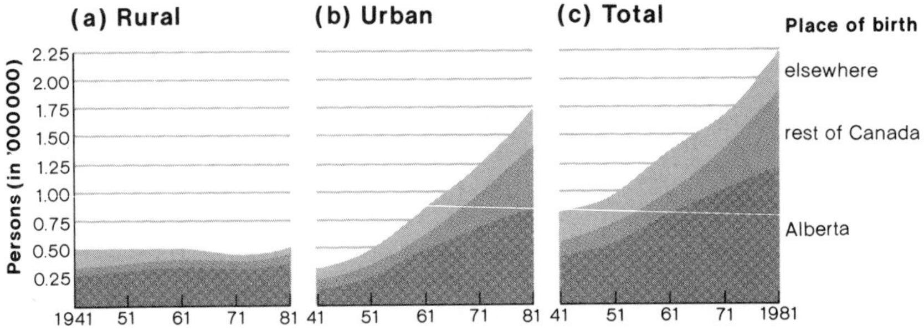

Figure 9.5 Rural, urban, and total population of Alberta, classified by place of birth, 1941-1981.

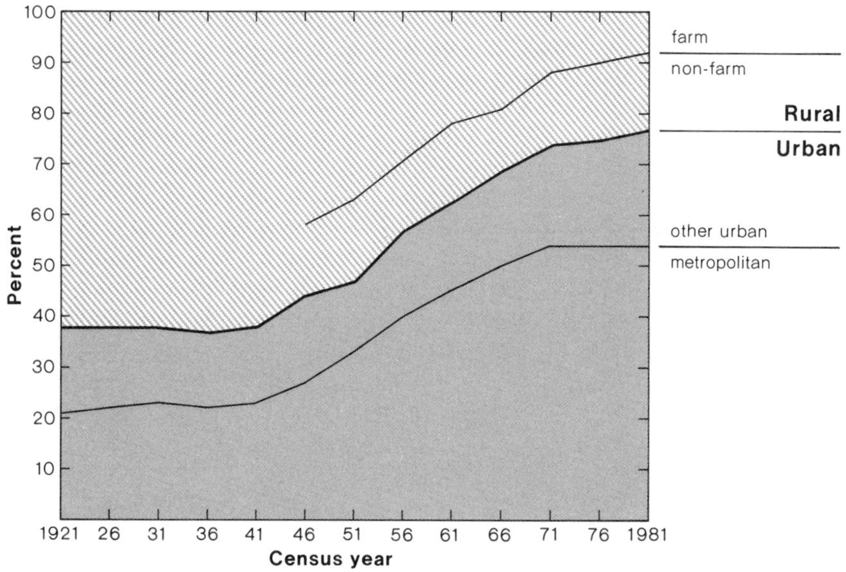

Figure 9.6 The rural-urban distribution of Alberta's population, 1921-1981.

what has been referred to as Canada's "demo-economic space" — the geographic relationship between population and economic patterns. A generally strong demand for the primary products of the westernmost provinces, and environmental attractions that invite comparison with American sunbelt states (meaning access to the Rocky Mountains in Alberta's case), encouraged migration to Alberta. The regional growth in employment has thus been above the national average for most years since the 1940s. Population in Canada has shifted westward and inter-provincial migration, related to structural changes at the national scale, has been a major contributor to Alberta's urban population increase. This increase was especially evident in the period 1961-81 (Fig. 9.5b).

Within Alberta, another structural change, directly related to the concept of modernization, also had a significant impact on the urbanization process. This change was the development of residentiary industry, or the production of goods and services for the local Alberta market. Under the joint impact of increasing affluence, improving living standards, and rising expectations, all indicators of the "age of high mass-consumption," an explosive new source of economic demand was generated. This demand has taken in everything from the manufacture of cardboard cartons to the most sophisticated surgery. It has also had a localizing effect which is of geographical significance. Residentiary industry is an urban phenomenon. The more specialized the goods and services that are made available, the more they will be concentrated in the largest cities. The

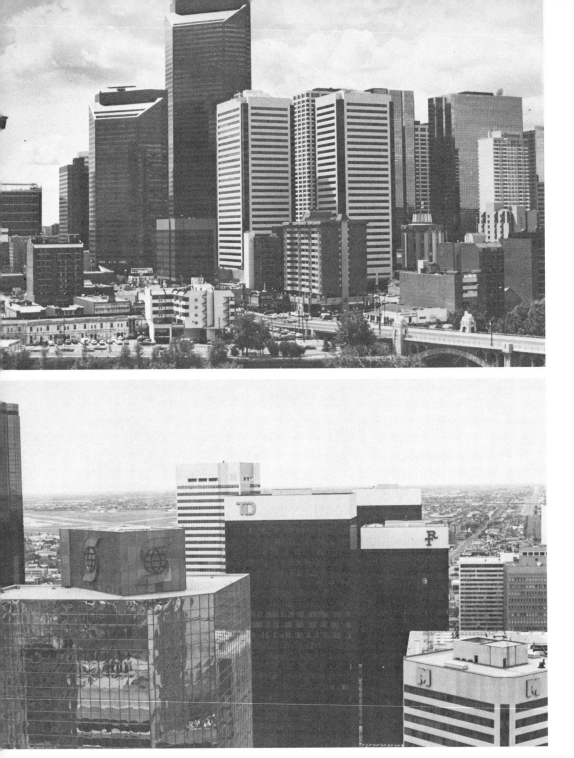

The Central Business Districts of Calgary and Edmonton: A booming resource economy has restructured the downtown cores of these two metropolitan centres. Oil offices in Calgary (top) and space for government agencies in Edmonton (bottom) have led this revitalization. (*Larry McCann*)

result is clearly visible in the various business districts of Edmonton and Calgary, now many times larger and more diversified than they were in the 1940s.

In the agricultural areas of the province, by contrast, economic modernization has caused populations to fall. Steep rises in productivity, in relation to the inputs of land and labour, have resulted in sharply reduced labour needs. The total rural population has hovered close to half a million ever since 1941 (Fig. 9.5a), but the farm sector fell from 340 000 in 1946 (the first year it was recorded in the census) to 190 000 in 1981. By then, only 8 percent of Alberta's people lived on farms.

The spatial outcome of this trend is illustrated by changes to the density distribution pattern of rural population between 1941 and 1971 (Fig. 9.3). As expected, depopulation has been most pronounced in those peripheral parts of Alberta where agriculture is the economic mainstay. While comparatively high rural densities are still found around Edmonton and along the Edmonton-Calgary corridor, chiefly because of increases in the non-farm population (particularly urban commuters), the huge agricultural zone to the east and south has become more uniformly and sparsely occupied. In the census decade 1966-76 alone, the farm population in the area dropped by 30 percent.

These trends in urban and rural population change also indicate that rural-urban migration has been a factor in the urbanization process. Since 1941, the net out-migration from rural areas has equalled the entire natural increase of the rural population. It is impossible to know how many of these migrants settled in the towns and cities of Alberta, or if they stayed there, but recent census statistics suggest that the flow to the cities was significant. As late as 1981, when the rural population was only three-tenths as large as the urban population, and could no longer account for a substantial share of urban population increase, some 40 000 urban residents reported that they had been living in a rural community in Alberta five years before. The same number had been living in rural areas in other Canadian provinces (Fig. 9.7). The flow of rural-urban migrants may be relatively small in the 1980s, but its effect on the urban population base is still significant.

Centralization and Time-Space Convergence

Alberta's generally high rates of economic and urban growth, and the evidence of large-scale migration into its urban places, point to a highly mobile population. In the censuses of 1961, 1971, and 1981, 30 percent or more of the urban population reported that they had moved to their present community within the previous five years. Many had come from other places in Alberta, even in 1981 when the census recorded the climax of an intense period of interprovincial migration. Indeed, Fig. 9.7 establishes that there is a considerable amount of migration *within*

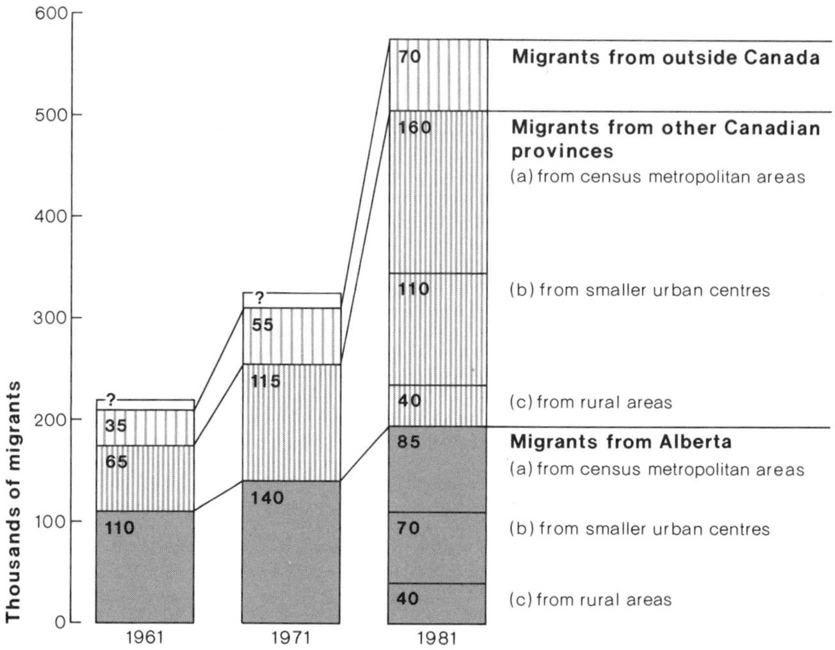

Figure 9.7 Previous place of residence of census migrants in Alberta's urban population, 1961, 1971, and 1981. According to the Census of Canada, a "migrant" is anyone five years of age or older who lived in a different community five years before the date of the census.

Alberta's urban system. There are various reasons for this trend, but the most significant in terms of structural change is the process of centralization. While centralization has been operating for several decades, its major effects were felt in the 25 years between 1946 and 1971.

Centralization refers to the tendency for a few central places to become increasingly dominant in the provision of services throughout a settlement system. This process is a predictable accompaniment of urbanization and the development of residentiary industry, since population size is a critical determinant of the thresholds and ranges of central place activities. Very simply, the larger the city, the more specialized its services and the larger the trade area it is able to command. Conversely, anything that permits a city to enlarge its trade area will also allow it to increase its service specialization and, thus, contribute to its growth. This factor introduces a second structural phenomenon that has influenced Alberta's urban system since the 1940s — time-space convergence, or the shrinking effect of reduced travel times on distance. The most accessible places in the transport network are given a special growth advantage because as transport facilities are improved, these places can be reached by more people with no increase in travel time.

From the perspective of the rural resident, time-space convergence means that it is possible to travel further in a fixed time and so have more convenient access to larger centres with their varied amenities. It also follows that centralization is a manifestation of deepseated changes in rural society as it, too, absorbs the values of mass-consumption. Television has played a major role, and not just in the sense that it has been dominated by images of an urban-centred culture. Almost overnight, rural households were introduced to mass advertising of brand name products. Increasing affluence and mobility also played vital roles, bringing the promise of the advertisers within easier reach, financially and spatially. More and better cars, cheap and plentiful gasoline — these increased the potential for growth, especially when blended with the rising expectations of the 1950s and 1960s. They led provincial and municipal governments of the day to place high priority on improvements to the rural highway network, with two objectives: to maintain the attractiveness of rural life by ensuring that the rural population had access to the same amenities that urban residents had; and to strengthen the economic bases of the small towns of Alberta, particularly in areas of rural depopulation, by maintaining their accessibility from viable trade areas. Thus, a healthy regional centre was to be the mark of a strong rural community.

Unfortunately, there was a dark side to the rural roads policy: the demise of the smallest central places seemed inevitable. As distance from the larger centres became less of a disadvantage, the smallest centres became less competitive. A 1965 study of the prosperous mixed-farming area between Camrose and Red Deer surveyed all the business people in a number of hamlets, along with a selection of farmers from the surrounding trade areas. The verdict, from both sides, was unanimous. The farmers were visiting their small, nearby centres less frequently, and were doing less of their business there. As a result, many business establishments had closed and most of the survivors had lost trade.[13]

Table 9.1 indicates some of the consequences for the Alberta urban system, although centralization was not the only factor contributing to the pattern of decline. In the decade 1961-71, when the urban population of Alberta increased by 30 percent, half the incorporated urban places either decreased or did not grow. This experience was concentrated on the smallest urban places, a trend that would have appeared even more pronounced if the table had included all the unincorporated hamlets at the bottom of the central place hierarchy. In the Red Deer trade area alone, 30 of these small communities are known to have disappeared between 1941 and 1971. Thus, it is clear that under the dual impact of a decreasing farm population and time-space convergence, fewer central places were needed.

Concomitantly, centres such as Camrose and Red Deer, whose accessibility was enhanced, experienced a selective growth effect. By

TABLE 9.1 POPULATION CHANGE BY URBAN SIZE CLASS IN ALBERTA, 1961-1971

			Type of Population Change 1961-1971			
Level in Hierarchy	*Size Class*	*Number of Places in 1961*	*Number of Places That Increased in Population*	*Number of Stable Places*[a]	*Number of Places That Decreased in Population*	*Number of Places in 1971*
1	More than 100 000	2	2	–	–	2
2	20 000-100 000	2	2	–	–	3
3	5 000-20 000	4	4	–	–	8
4	2 500-5 000	20	17	3	–	28
5	1 250-2 500	29	20	4	5	24
6	625-1 250	41	31	8	2	38
7	Less than 625	142	46	22	74	137
	Totals[b]	240	122 (51%)	37 (15%)	81 (34%)	240

[a]"Stable" means that the place's population in 1971 was within 5 percent (plus or minus) of the 1961 population.
[b]N=240 incorporated places that appeared in both censuses.

Source: 1971 Census of Canada, Bulletin 1.1-2, "Population: Census Subdivisions," Table 2.

becoming "more central" they obtained an advantage over their smallest neighbours. As Table 9.1 shows, all the largest places increased their populations, and there was an upward shift in size classes as the number of small and medium-sized cities (classes 2, 3 and 4) increased by 50 percent (from 26 to 39). The hierarchy of urban places was still more like an upside-down T than a pyramid, but the middle levels were filling out. The growing centres were able to increase their competitive attractiveness further by offering enriched arrays of services. In Red Deer, for example, the number of service establishments increased from about 150 in 1941 to almost 500 in 1971, while the number of *different* service functions increased from 56 to 80.[14]

The larger implication of all these effects is that centralization is a process of structural rationalization by which central place systems adapt to cultural and technological changes. In Alberta, through the 1950s and 1960s, there was a steady evolution to a condition in which fewer, larger, and more widely-spaced centres were able to offer increasingly specialized services to the whole population. Even some very small centres were able to grow, as they captured the trade areas of their less effective neighbours.

Metropolitanization

Ultimately, any tendency to centralization in a central place system is reflected in the growth of the cities at the top of the hierarchy. In Alberta, for example, the combined population of Edmonton and Calgary, including their suburbs, was only 190 000 in 1941; 40 years later, the respective totals for the official census metropolitan areas (CMAs) were 657 000 and 593 000. In fact, both counts were low. If all the detached, satellite communities had been included, and all the rural non-farm commuters, Calgary's population would have been increased by about 20 000 in 1981 and Edmonton's by about 50 000. On this basis, the two cities accounted for 80 percent of Alberta's population increase over the period 1941-81, and their share of the total population increased from 23 percent to 60 percent (Fig. 9.6).

These trends have two main implications. First, Edmonton and Calgary have clearly increased their dominance over the rest of Alberta, thus satisfying another of Boisvert's conditions for a transformation region. Second, even at the national scale the growth of Edmonton and Calgary has been extraordinary, indicating that they have been increasing the scope of their influence in relation to other Canadian cities. When the Alberta settlement system was in its rural climax condition (Stage III in Fig. 9.2), Edmonton and Calgary were no more than large central places. They were service and distribution centres for huge tributary regions, and were chiefly distinguished by functions such as transportation and wholesale trade that reflected Alberta's distance from the heartland production centres. They seemed firmly embedded in the third rank of

Canadian cities, along with places like London, Halifax, and Victoria. In the west, only Vancouver and Winnipeg were in the second rank, singled out, in J.W. Maxwell's benchmark study, as "major metropolitan centres."[15] But if Winnipeg deserved such honour in the 1940s, so, surely, did Edmonton and Calgary in 1981. They were then the fifth and sixth largest CMAs in Canada, whereas Winnipeg had fallen to seventh place.

The notion of metropolitanism introduced by this change of national status is attractive but vague, at least in North American usage. In Victorian Britain, *the* metropolis was London, but in Canada and the United States "metropolitan" has become synonymous with relatively large size. For statistical purposes, metropolitanism has been reduced to a technique for aggregating the populations of urban areas that are fragmented into several jurisdictions. But while it is useful to think of a *metropolitan area* in this administrative sense, it is also useful to think of the *metropolis* as having some of the historical qualities of pre-eminence in political and economic affairs. Both ideas contribute to an understanding of what has happened to Edmonton and Calgary since the 1940s.[16]

There are two main ways in which the cities' change of status has become manifest. The first is most obviously a function of size, or what is known as the critical mass effect. The larger a city becomes, the more growth it attracts. Both Edmonton and Calgary are now large enough to sustain a significant volume of creative and innovative activity. This activity embraces artistic and intellectual achievement, such as the production of feature films, and book and magazine publishing, but the greatest impact has come from entrepreneurs who first developed their skills in Alberta and then applied them on a larger stage. For example, Alberta firms have had leading roles in North Sea oil exploration and development, in the construction of prefabricated buildings for Middle East town sites, and in downtown redevelopment in a number of American cities. In technology, too, Alberta innovators have made major contributions — to the processing of heavy oils and oil sands, to offshore oil exploration (particularly in northern oceans), and to the development of new products in plastics and pharmaceuticals. These activities illustrate the widespread significance of a highly specialized labour force such as Edmonton and Calgary now possess.

The second mark of changed status is the national prominence into which Edmonton and Calgary were catapulted by OPEC and the energy crises of the 1970s. In some degree, as the leading centres in the Canadian petroleum industry, they have had a distinctive national role since the 1940s, but that role went largely unnoticed as long as energy, from all sources, was relatively cheap and abundant. The situation changed abruptly after 1973. Before a decade had passed, some of the most powerful institutions and relationships of Confederation were beginning to shift in Alberta's favour. The national banks committed themselves to major relocations of staff and decision-making authority, to take advantage of the investment opportunities afforded by new perceptions of energy needs. Other corporations, large and small, made similar moves, either by relocating their head offices or by establishing major regional offices with considerable independence.

Calgary was the principal destination, reflecting its long established role as the administrative centre of the Canadian petroleum industry. In 1979, for instance, 526 of the 612 Canadian-based exploration and production companies had their head offices in Calgary. That pattern was extended through a long and complex chain of business activities, all dependent in some way upon the needs of the petroleum industry. Edmonton, meanwhile, experienced comparable growth in its traditional roles as a processing and service and supply centre, particularly as exploration and development shifted northward. In the national context, though, it is Edmonton's political role that has done most to enhance its prominence. Since energy resource development and public policy are interrelated, the decisions made by governments, provincially and federally, are as crucial to regional development as the decisions of financiers and industry executives.

The influx of numerous new corporations as a result of this economic and political activity has had massive physical consequences, particularly in the central areas of the cities where redevelopment has taken on a radically new scope. Calgary was affected first, but before the 1970s were over, the building trend was well established in Edmonton as well. Projects far larger and more elaborate than those of earlier decades were undertaken, in a construction orgy unprecedented among middle-sized Canadian cities.

This general similarity aside, however, there has been a significant difference in the redevelopment experiences of the two cities, reflecting their different relations with the petroleum industry. In Calgary, since the early 1950s, the industry's direct impact has been concentrated in the city centre, in the dense ranks of office towers built by and for the petroleum corporations and the firms that serve them. That pattern intensified in the 1970s, and Calgary's new status was accompanied by the symbolic importance of "prestige" buildings. Edmonton has neither this corporate power, nor its accompanying architecture. Since Edmonton's central area expansion has resulted chiefly from the multiplier effects of the petroleum industry, with a particularly heavy demand for office space by agencies of the provincial government, speculative building by developers has been more characteristic. Nondescript office buildings house the "byproducts" of the oil boom — exploration companies, computer consultants, and civil servants. There are few major head offices. Calgary's central core is more confined with narrower streets. When the resulting pattern of compact, intensive development is combined with the greater number of office buildings, the smaller city actually projects more of a "big city" atmosphere in its central area.

In Edmonton, the direct effects of the petroleum industry have always been most evident in the outer reaches of the metropolitan area. Since the first post-war oil strikes were close to Edmonton, it was the logical location for the associated transport and processing systems. Pipeline terminals, refineries, petrochemical plants, and manufacturers with massive fuel needs (e.g. a nickel smelter), were soon drawn there, mostly downstream from the city, on the North Saskatchewan River. This area has now become the site of the largest industrial complex in Alberta.

This location of early industrial development outside Edmonton's boundaries has also contributed to the varying development of the two cities. Edmonton has acquired the classic symptoms of a fragmented metropolitan area, whereas Calgary has deliberately contained its development within the city boundaries. The boundaries have been extended regularly, to ensure that the city's territory would always be large enough to prevent overspill development in the rural-urban fringe. In the Edmonton area, on the other hand, regional planning policy has encouraged some dispersal of development on the British new-towns model. Industries have located in satellite communities to relieve congestion in the metropolitan centre and to meet the growth aspirations of the many small towns surrounding the city. This trend might be described as an after-effect of the initially denser pattern of rural settlement in the Edmonton area, reinforced by the tax advantages bestowed on some municipalities by industrial overspill.

As a result, the Edmonton metropolitan area is now an elaborate constellation of autonomous communities. Calgary, on the other hand, is a statistical anomaly — the only CMA in Canada that contains nothing but a central city (Fig. 9.8). Yet even in the Calgary area, there are signs that dispersal may be inevitable. The population of Airdrie, for example, increased six-fold (from 1400 to 8400) between 1976 and 1981, indicating a movement outward from the city core.

Spatial Concentration and Corridor Development

As the foci of the centralizing tendencies in the Alberta central place system, and the only cities in the province to have taken on metropolitan characteristics, Calgary and Edmonton have been the focus of population redistribution for several decades. As suggested by the diagram for Stage IV in Fig. 9.2, the growth of Edmonton and Calgary has drawn population to many nearby towns, creating a highly-urbanized subregion. By 1981, 16 of Alberta's 35 next-largest urban places were found either in the two metropolitan zones or in the corridor between them (Fig. 9.8). Some 70 percent of all Albertans live in this subregion, on only 5 percent of the province's territory.[17]

Such a concentration of population has major implications for the structure of the Alberta settlement system, and particularly on the pattern

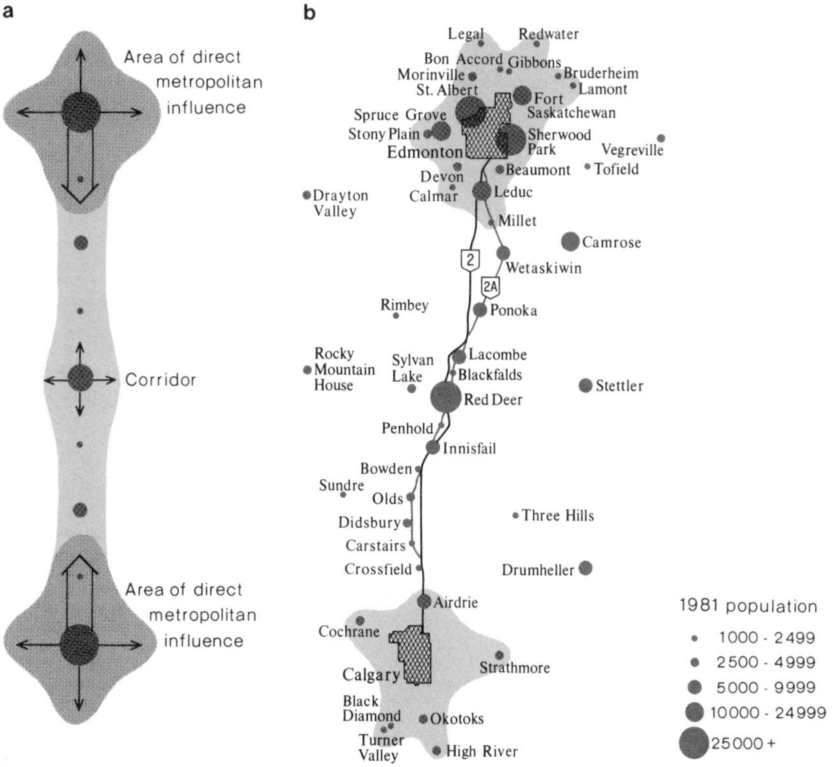

Figure 9.8 Organization of the Edmonton-Calgary corridor.

a. Hypothetical structure of a binodal corridor system with a four-level hierarchy of urban places. The arrows indicate the directions of major and minor spread effects.

b. Actual development pattern in the Edmonton- Calgary subregion based on the 1981 census.

of linkages and interactions described in Figs. 9.1 and 9.2. As regional service centres of roughly equal size, Edmonton and Calgary have always played independent, competitive roles, matching each other in the array of services they have provided to their discrete hinterlands. Interaction, however, presumes *inter*dependence; and interdependence, in its turn, presumes complementary specialization. A simple proposition can therefore be constructed, employing the theoretical principle that the interaction potential between any two places is a function of their population sizes and the distance between them. As the largest cities in the Alberta system, there will always have been some gravitational attraction between Edmonton and Calgary, and that attraction will have increased with their populations. If the attraction (interaction potential) is to be capitalized upon, however, transport facilities have to be upgraded, thus reducing the travel time between the two cities in another illustration of time-space convergence. As the effective distance is reduced, there is a further increase in the interaction potential and, simultaneously, in the potential for complementary specialization and further growth.

That there has been an upgrading of transport connections between Edmonton and Calgary is easily demonstrated. Beginning in the mid-1950s, a completely new, high-speed highway was constructed, bypassing all the intervening towns and almost halving the safe travel time for inter-city traffic. As well, air service between the two cities has been increased repeatedly, with dramatic consequences for the volume of interaction. As early as 1965, the Edmonton-Calgary air route was the third busiest in Canada, with about 100 000 trips per year. By 1979 that total had jumped to 750 000, and Edmonton-Calgary had become the second busiest route in the country. Even on the national scale, then, the level of interaction between the two Alberta cities is particularly high.

More specific evidence of the complementary specialization that underlies the high volumes of road and air traffic can be found in census employment statistics. In their general industrial structures, which continue to be dominated by the characteristic service activities of central places, Edmonton and Calgary are similar. Their differences, as recently as 1981, occurred chiefly in three employment categories: mining (which includes the firms in the petroleum industry) employed three times as many people in Calgary as in Edmonton; financial services showed a small imbalance in Calgary's favour; and the provincial and federal governments had 2.5 times as many employees in Edmonton as in Calgary. There was also some finer specialization within these categories. Thus, government and financial services associated with the petroleum industry have increasingly been concentrated in Calgary. Corporations with either their head offices or their main Alberta offices in Calgary have tended to centralize their administrative operations in that city. Conversely, Edmonton has become the largest oil refining centre in western Canada. The city's three major refineries expanded in the 1970s, while smaller units in Calgary and elsewhere were closed. No great additions accrued to the labour force, but by other criteria, such as value added or value of shipments, Edmonton makes a substantially stronger contribution than Calgary to the manufacturing economy of Alberta. Edmonton's manufacturing base focusses on the processing of petroleum and petrochemical products.

These observations have considerable significance for a heartland-hinterland interpretation of the structure of Alberta's settlement system. In its earlier stages (II and III in Fig. 9.2), the system was organized around two cores, the cities of Edmonton and Calgary. In fact, in terms of central place activities there were two more or less separate systems, and it was only Edmonton's specialized functions of provincial capital and university

Oil refineries and associated industry on the eastern outskirts of Edmonton: Calgary is the administrative and financial centre of Alberta's petroleum industry, but Edmonton is the focus for servicing the oil and natural gas fields and for manufacturing petrochemical products. (*Government of the Province of Alberta*)

seat that imposed an overriding unity. Then, as the regional economy expanded after 1940, the two cities became the loci of new activities through which they have filled increasingly specialized or complementary roles. At that point in their relationship, the friction of distance, which historically separated them, was largely overcome and they functioned like a single city. They began to form a binodal heartland within the Alberta settlement system.

More recently still, there have been signs that an even more complex unit is evolving, as some of Edmonton and Calgary's growth impulse has been channelled into the towns along the Edmonton-Calgary corridor. In part, this is a direct metropolitan effect, although one that reaches well beyond the CMAs as defined by Statistics Canada. Leduc and Airdrie, for example, are thoroughly suburbanized, and even more distant communities, such as Camrose and Wetaskiwin, now fall within Edmonton's commuting zone and have businesses pitched at the Edmonton market.

The evidence that Edmonton and Calgary's growth effects are spreading further along the corridor is still sketchy, but there have been indications of growth throughout the late 1970s and early 1980s. Even the smallest and most neglected towns have shown signs of coming back to life; main streets have been rehabilitated, new businesses have been opened, derelict railway properties in the town centres have been redeveloped, and mobile home parks became attached to communities. In most towns, large new residential subdivisions were opened to builders. A regional water supply system was installed, to remove the major constraint on the expansion of the string of towns between Red Deer and Calgary, and a variety of other public expenditures helped to increase the development potential of the corridor. New industries also appeared: a lamb packing plant in Innisfail, a brewery in Red Deer and, most significant, a world-scale petrochemical complex at Joffre, near Red Deer. In fact, as these examples suggest, Red Deer's experience is especially revealing. It lies at the mid-point of the corridor, where there is maximum opportunity to benefit from interaction with both the major cities and, at the same time, to capitalize on their competitive weaknesses. Not only has Red Deer experienced exceptional growth — from a population of 3000 in 1941 to 46 000 in 1981 — but the growth effect has spilled over into its nearby towns. Highway traffic flow data reveal that Red Deer has become the hub of its own interaction system within the larger corridor system.

Recent population trends also indicate that some of Edmonton and Calgary's growth impulse may be shifting into the corridor. Between 1971 and 1981, for example, the rate of population increase in the two CMAs was still high by national standards but, as with other metropolitan areas across the continent, they were lower than they had been. For the first time in four decades, the Albertan cities increased at about the same rate as the provincial population, showing that the trend to metropolitan concentration had at last been checked (Fig. 9.6). Meanwhile, the corridor towns, as a group, raised their rate of increase from 34 percent in 1961-71 to 87 percent in 1971-81. They then formed the most rapidly growing group of urban places in Alberta. In the province's settlement system, they stand out as a concentrated, closely-spaced series that has defied the differential growth effects imposed elsewhere by centralization. The effect of falling oil prices in the mid-1980s on growth in the corridor, however, has yet to be measured.

The Revaluation of the Periphery and the Resource Base

In contrast to the changes in the Edmonton-Calgary region, peripheral Alberta in the 1960s seemed well on the way to becoming the rump of the province, valued less for its productive capability than for the leisure-time amenities it could offer to an urban world. The settlement frontier was no longer advancing; the agricultural economy was threatening to collapse under a burden of overproduction; rural population was decreasing; small town life was generally in decay; the coal mining industry was struggling to survive; and there was little market incentive for petroleum exploration. Growth and investment of all kinds were concentrated in Edmonton and Calgary — the two cities seemed to have taken on a dynamic energy of their own as the engines of the Alberta economy.

In the 1970s, however, and coinciding with the world energy crisis, Alberta's natural resources underwent a radical revaluation, accompanied by a renewed appreciation of the periphery's role in the Alberta settlement system. Just as no one could doubt, in the 1930s, that the prosperity of the agricultural areas was vital to the prosperity of Edmonton and Calgary, so no one could doubt, in the 1970s and 1980s, that their fortunes were directly dependent on the resource-based industries.

The contemporary importance of primary production to the Alberta economy is illustrated in Fig. 9.9. The figure also indicates the substantial growth in the petroleum industry, both directly — in the increased contribution of mining to the Gross Domestic Product (GDP) — and indirectly. The size of the finance sector, for example, and the increase in its share of GDP between 1973 and 1983, owes much to petroleum royalty payments. In dollar terms, oil and natural gas account for 95 percent of Alberta's mineral production, but these products have also taken on an increasing national significance. In 1973, Alberta petroleum products

Mining oil sands: After the forest cover and overburden have been stripped away, giant machines cut into the oil sands, feeding conveyor belts which in turn move the sands to processing plants. Each tar sands project represents an investment of many hundreds of millions of dollars. (*Government of the Province of Alberta*)

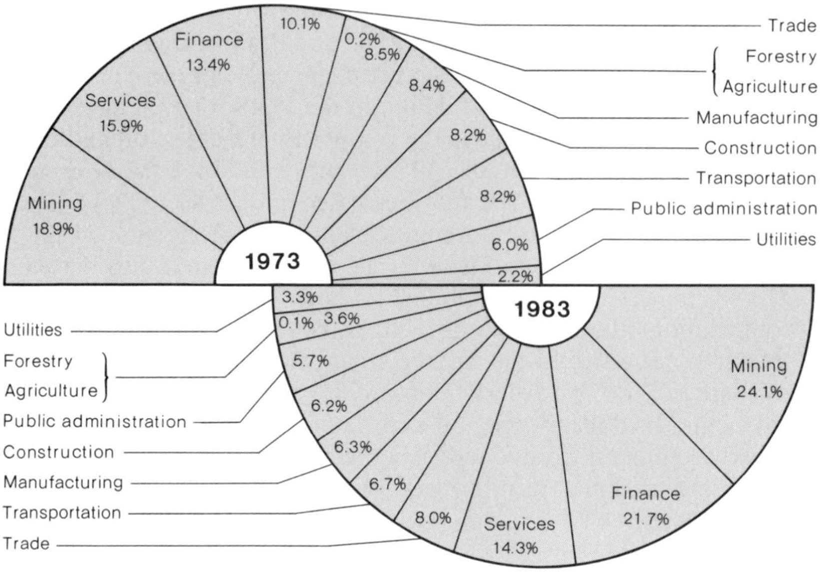

Figure 9.9 Gross domestic product of Alberta, by industry, 1973 and 1983.

accounted for just over 30 percent of the value of all mineral production in Canada; in 1983, their contribution was almost 60 percent (Table 9.2).

The increased "value" of Alberta's petroleum products, to both Alberta and Canada, is essentially a function of higher prices rather than greater production (Table 9.3). Crude oil production was actually at its height in 1973, the year of crisis in the international marketplace, while natural gas production has fluctuated within narrow limits since the early 1970s. In the meantime, concern over the long-term security of Canada's petroleum supplies has been heightened by the realization that Alberta's conventional oil is a rapidly depleting resource (Table 9.3). Despite an intense exploration effort through the 1970s and into the 1980s, reserves are declining steadily and major new strikes are not likely. Indeed, one argument holds that the best means of improving Alberta's reserves is to continually increase the price of gasoline, since this increase would expand production in the existing fields and facilitate the use of enhanced recovery methods. No matter how the financial climate changes, however, future development must turn to more costly alternatives, particularly the oil sands and heavy oils of northern Alberta (Fig. 9.10a), which could not be viewed as feasible resources until gasoline came to be accepted as an expensive commodity. Even so, the economic, political, and technical problems of development are enormous. The first processing plant came into production in 1967, and the second in 1978, but there have been no

TABLE 9.2 VALUE OF ALBERTA MINERAL PRODUCTION IN 1973, 1978, and 1983 (in millions of dollars)

	1973	*1978*	*1983*
Fuels			
Coal	60	257	462
Natural gas	389	3 591	6 228
Natural gas byproducts	340	1 033	2 523
Crude oil	1 895	4 913	12 283
Totals	2 684	9 794	21 496
All other minerals	76	293	722
Totals	2 760	10 087	22 218
Share of Canadian production	33%	50%	62%

Source: Alberta Statistical Review, Fourth Quarter, 1984.

others and none are likely until the late 1980s at the earliest. By then, Alberta's conventional oil production may have fallen to half its peak level of 1973.

On the positive side, the accelerated pace of exploration has brought a substantial increase in the known reserves of natural gas (Table 9.3). Yet, despite the major contribution that natural gas and its byproducts make to Alberta's GDP (Table 9.2), the new discoveries have not resulted in more production. Natural gas has the potential to replace crude oil in Alberta's staple trade, but it is proving difficult, for a variety of political and economic reasons, to expand the markets for Alberta gas in eastern Canada and the United States (Fig. 8.7). Albertans, therefore, tend to place more value on natural gas as a raw material. It could form the basis of a sophisticated chain of petrochemical industries, but the first links have not yet been built. In the long run, this development should be the most significant element in Alberta's evolution as a transformation region.

Coal is undergoing a similar revaluation, both as a fuel and as an industrial raw material. Annual production increased steadily from 8.5 million tonnes in 1973 to 21 million tonnes in 1983, and the reserves can only be described as enormous — 14.8 billion tonnes in 1984. Coal production aims at three main markets. First, the huge shallow beds of sub-bituminous coal (Fig. 9.10b) supply a rapidly expanding market within Alberta for electricity. The sub-bituminous beds account for two-thirds of annual production. Second, there has been a renewed, if erratic, demand for the coking coals found along the mountain front. These are exported chiefly to Japan, Korea, and Brazil. Finally, the high-quality thermal coals of the foothills are used mainly in the electricity industry of Ontario and the northeastern United States.

TABLE 9.3 ESTIMATED RESERVES AND ANNUAL PRODUCTION OF LIQUID HYDROCARBONS AND NATURAL GAS IN ALBERTA, SELECTED YEARS, 1965-1983

	Estimated Reserves[a]			*Annual Production*			
	Liquid Hydrocarbons (million m³)		*Natural Gas (billion m³)*	*Crude Oil (million m³)*			*Natural Gas (billion m³)*
	Conventional Crude Oil	*Natural Gas Liquids*[b]		*Conventional*	*Oil Sands*	*Total*[c]	
1965	965	200	776	37	–	45	35
1969	**1 223**	**348**	1 273	44	2	56	47
1971	1 174	326	1 223	56	2	72	60
1973	1 051	327	1 377	**83**	3	**104**	74
1975	951	287	1 451	68	2	87	74
1977	830	293	1 478	61	3	79	79
1979	760	302	1 646	69	5	90	**82**
1981	696	321	1 723	57	6	77	76
1983	658	325	**1 900**	56	**9**	78	75

*Peak years are picked out in bold type.

[a]Oil sands are not included in the reserves because it is not yet possible to calculate the likely limits of commercial production. The four major deposits (Fig. 9.9a) hold an estimated 200 billion m³ of bitumen, but only 5.2 billion m³ are currently recognized as recoverable reserves.

[b]Natural gas liquids comprise propane, butanes, and pentanes plus, which are obtained from processing raw gas or condensate.

[c]The total production of crude oil includes natural gas liquids.

Source: Alberta Industry and Resources, periodical publication of The Department of Economic Development; *Alberta Statistical Review,* Fourth Quarter, 1984; and Energy Resources Conservation Board, *Alberta's Reserves of Crude Oil, Oil Sands, Gas, Natural Gas Liquids, and Sulphur,* Reserve Report Series, ERCB-18, 1984.

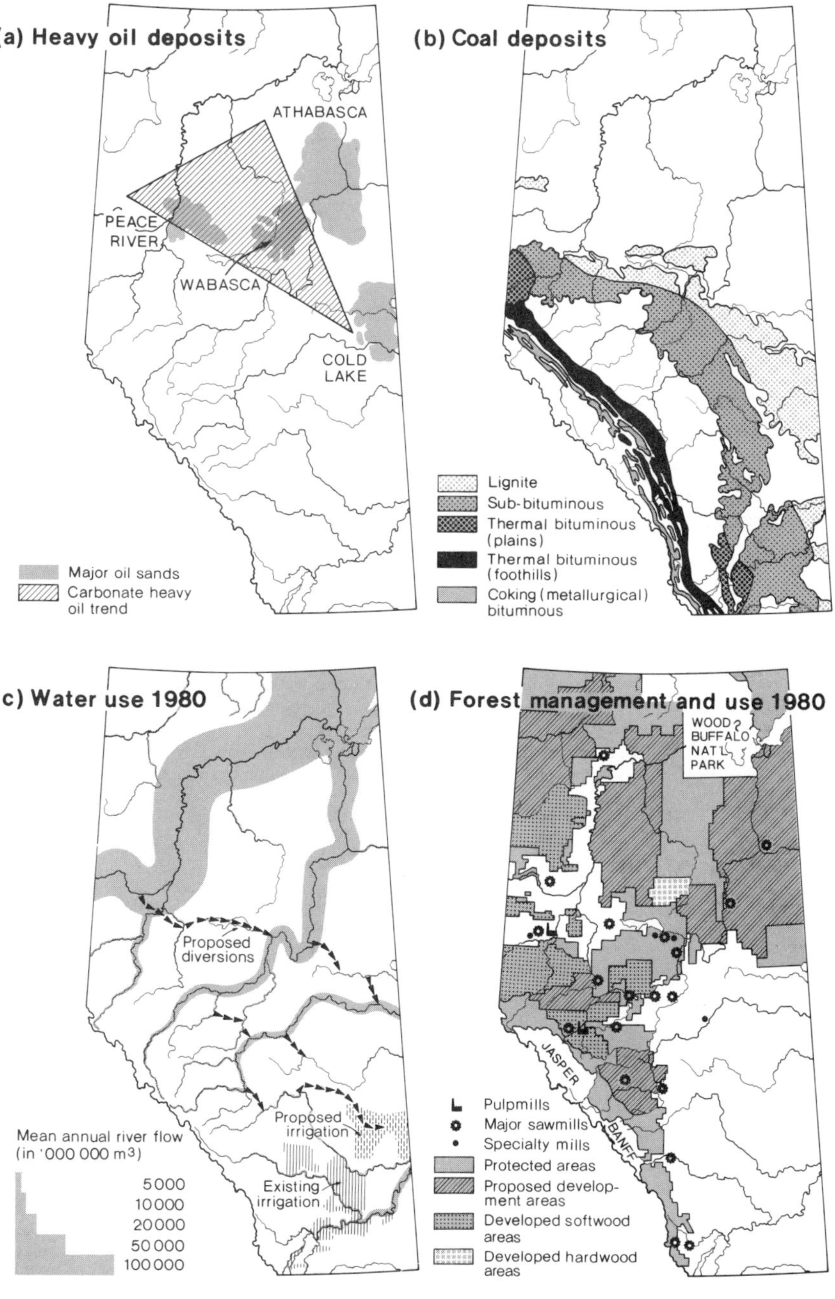

Figure 9.10 The distribution and use of some of Alberta's major natural resources: heavy oils, coal, water, and forests.

Two other natural resources — water and forests — are becoming increasingly important to Alberta's resource economy. Both are renewable resources. Neither is heavily exploited yet, but their potential value has been heightened by the well-publicized decline in oil reserves and the awareness that Albertans cannot rely for the long term on non-renewable resources. It is argued, for instance, that the development of hydroelectric generating sites on the great northward-flowing rivers (the Peace and Athabasca) could provide Alberta with a new export commodity. In addition, hydroelectricity could be substituted for thermal power, thus freeing some of the coal reserves for use in the distillation of gasoline and related petroleum products. Water diversion schemes have also been discussed for many years (Fig. 9.10c). The immediate objectives would be to increase industrial water supplies in central Alberta and to extend the area of irrigation agriculture on the semi-arid plains. Furthermore, there is the possibility that the diversion projects could be used to export water to the United States. All these suggestions are controversial on environmental, economic, and political grounds, but they persist and the fierceness with which they are debated indicates the prime importance of the province's water resources.

In a similar way, Alberta's forests are now seen as multi-use resources, thus enhancing their value from a variety of perspectives. Permanent forest on Crown land makes up 60 percent of Alberta's area (Fig. 9.10d), but commercial exploitation has proceeded slowly. Development in the softwood forests has been limited by environmental conditions such as difficult terrain (principally muskeg), slow growth, and small tree size, while the poplars of the northern hardwood forests were long regarded as useless for timber. The delay, however, has worked to Alberta's advantage, since the government was able to enforce scientific management practices when large-scale development began. The first pulp mill was opened in 1954; the second, 20 years later. The third is expected late in the 1980s, as part of the planned development of a huge timber reserve between the Peace River region and the Athabasca River. Two large sawmills are also to be included in this project, and milling is now a characteristic activity in the towns along the forest margin. Technological changes in lumber processing and the construction industry have played an important role in this trend, particularly since the increasing use of plywood and flakeboard has converted the poplars of northern Alberta into a valued resource.

In combination, these recent developments in the resource-based industries have brought major changes to the Alberta settlement system. As a group, the province's secondary cities experienced a substantially higher growth rate than Edmonton and Calgary in the period 1971-81. Even the old agricultural zone was affected, as larger central places like Medicine Hat and Lloydminster took on substantial functions as service, supply, and processing centres for the petroleum industry. Insofar as there was a tendency toward stagnation and decline, it was concentrated in the smallest communities of the agricultural districts. Generally, the pattern was one of growth (Table 9.4). The urban hierarchy also continued its evolution toward the pyramidal form of a transformation region. Sixty-seven places moved up the hierarchy between 1971 and 1981; 28 of them were in the Edmonton-Calgary region and 23 were on the resource frontier to the west and north. In some individual cases, the population increases were nothing less than spectacular: Fort McMurray's population increased from 6850 to 31 000; Grande Prairie's from 13 000 to 24 250; and Hinton's from 5000 to 8350.

Rapid growth, however, has had some negative effects. Economic and social dislocations were accompanied by shortages of skilled labour, housing, community services, effective public management, "front-end" money, and even land for building purposes. As a consequence, Alberta governments have taken an active part in the planning and development of resource-based communities. A New Towns Act was adopted in 1955, when the growth problems of the first energy boom became clear. The Act governs the location, physical planning, local government organization, and financing of new resource towns. It has also been used many times to provide technical and financial assistance during the initial growth years of new or expanding towns.

Large public investments have been made in transport facilities as well. Two long railways were built in the 1960s. The first, the Great Slave Lake Railway, runs north for some 600 kilometres from Grimshaw to Hay River, in the Northwest Territories; the other, the Alberta Resources Railway, traverses 350 kilometres of wilderness between Hinton and Grande Prairie. Both were justified by the desire to exploit specific mineral deposits — the lead-zinc ore body at Pine Point and coal at Grande Cache — but their larger purpose was to open frontier areas to development. Funding has also boosted airport construction. Airports, however, have tended to follow development, demonstrating the dependence of modern resource exploitation on easy communication with distant urban bases, almost regardless of cost. A dense network of air routes now radiates northwards from Edmonton, enhancing the city's historic role as a transport centre. Frontier road construction has also advanced rapidly. Every resource town, no matter how remote, must be accessible by all-weather highway, more perhaps for social reasons than for economic ones. While resource products can be shipped by pipeline or railway, for people, a highway represents a lifeline to the outside world.

This dependence reveals much about life on the modern resource frontier. It underlines the basic settlement problem: how to induce stability and permanence in an unstable environment. Today's resource towns, even those based on a single non-renewable resource, are not designed to be tomorrow's ghost towns. They are meant to be permanent communities, where people invest their lives and raise their families with hope and security. Close contact with the larger world is critically

TABLE 9.4 POPULATION CHANGE BY URBAN SIZE CLASS IN ALBERTA, 1971-1981

Level in Hierarchy	*Size Class*	*Number of Places in 1971*	*Type of Population Change 1971-1981*			*Number of Places in 1981*
			Number of Places That Increased in Population	*Number of Stable Places*[a]	*Number of Places That Decreased in Population*	
1	More than 100 000	2	2	–	–	2
2	20 000-100 000	3	3	–	–	6
3	5 000-20 000	9	9	–	–	21
4	2 500-5 000	28	28	–	–	30
5	1 250-2 500	27	26	1	–	31
6	625-1 250	41	34	7	–	40
7	Less than 625	142	109	18	15	122
	Totals[b]	252	211 (84%)	26 (10%)	15 (6%)	252

[a]"Stable" means that the place's population in 1981 was within 5 per cent (plus or minus) of its population in 1971.
[b]N=252 incorporated places that appeared in both censuses.
Source: 1981 Census of Canada, Catalogue 93-909 (Vol. 2–provincial series), "Alberta," Table 4.

Opening the wilderness: The Alberta Resources Railway has opened, in the past decade, a vast area of western Alberta to resource development, particularly coal mining and the forest industry. (*Government of the Province of Alberta*)

important, since the isolation of frontier life is generally regarded as inimical to family and community alike. If the new frontier is to attract the permanent commitment desired by physical and social planners, it must meet demands for most of the amenities of urban life. As yet, no formula for long-term stability has been discovered, although efforts are focussing on a broadening of the economic base. Two of the earliest oilfield towns, Devon and Drayton Valley, have shown that a future can be secured, though their circumstances are special; Devon is close enough to Edmonton to have been converted into a dormitory suburb, and Drayton Valley was accidentally placed in a vacant niche in the central place system. In most frontier situations, it is difficult to see beyond the exploitation of other, preferably renewable resources. Most expansion will likely concentrate on the forest industry, supplemented, in favoured locations, by tourism and recreation.

Increased pressure on a limited array of environmental resources is thus replete with problems. Programmes for development are constantly in conflict with the growing desire to conserve and preserve. Debate has centred on a number of issues in recent years: Do hydro development and river flow regulation pose a threat to the Peace-Athabasca delta, which is so large a part of Wood Buffalo National Park? Do the needs of the power industry for coal warrant the destruction of productive farmland? How seriously do oil and gas exploration and development damage the forest resource? Issues of this kind became commonplace as Alberta became more affluent, and they concentrated in particular on the area known as the Eastern Slopes, the last remaining belt of near-wilderness between the Rocky Mountains and the agricultural margin. Commercial exploitation there is already intense; natural gas, sulphur, coal, limestone, cement, pulp, lumber, and hydroelectricity are major products, and their associated processing plants are prominent features of the landscape. Cattle grazing is also widely permitted, on Crown leases, although biologists worry about conflict with wild animal populations and irreplaceable wildlife habitats. Furthermore, much of the area lies at high elevations, providing an environment that is at once extremely fragile and vitally important to the flow regimes of the plains rivers. The proximity of the Eastern Slopes to a large urban population has also sparked conflict. To many people, the region is a huge playground, and not just for urban Albertans; international tourism is being promoted on an increasing scale, as congestion becomes acute in Banff and Jasper National Parks. The result is a paradox: a "wilderness" that has to be planned and managed in the interest of a largely urban public.

Beyond the settlement frontier, in the vast forests of northern Alberta, the wilderness is less exposed to urban contact (Fig. 9.2). Here, the last remaining approximation of a traditional way of life — the Native mode of production — is found among the indigenous population. Trapping for furs is still a cash staple, though an uncertain one, commonly supplemented by subsistence hunting. Poverty is rife; health and housing standards are far below the level that would be tolerated in the rest of the province; and physical and social services of all kinds are difficult to provide. In part, this is a consequence of physical isolation, but only in part. Physical isolation can be overcome by communications technology, but the barriers imposed by cultural isolation are proving far more difficult to break through, on the reserves of agricultural Alberta as well as in the north. Thus, there is another paradox. On the one hand, the preservation of a distinctive culture, protected by territorial separation, is seen as the best hope for the Native people. On the other hand, on all but a few reserves, cultural isolation has led to severe cases of social and personal breakdown.

The dilemma is profound, no less for the white population than for the Native community. In the special context of natural resource development, for instance, social issues are just as troubling as the more popular environmental ones. Should special attempts be made to assimilate Native labour into the resource-based industries, or would such a move simply destroy any chance the Native people have of building anew on their cultural base? Can the material benefits of resource exploitation be shared by the Native people through anything other than the wage-labour nexus, since the alternative ways of transferring wealth would have too much in common with the welfare syndrome that already prevails? Can the hunting and trapping rights of a few people stand in the way of a multi-billion dollar oil sands plant; and, if not, how can those people ever be compensated for the way of life they have lost? Unfortunately, there are no clear-cut answers to questions of this kind.

On a more positive note, recent resource developments have brought prosperity to once-marginal agricultural areas. The most striking example is in the Edson district, west of Edmonton, where the Yellowhead transportation corridor encouraged an unusually deep penetration by homesteaders into the podzol soil zone. Generally, however, the farms were too small to be viable, and breaking in new land was slow and expensive. The opportunities for off-farm employment were also limited, and although a high proportion of farmers supplemented their incomes by part-time or seasonal jobs, poverty seemed to be endemic.[18] In 1963, the area was selected for a pilot project under the Agricultural Rehabilitation and Development Act (ARDA), with modest success. Then, with accelerating development of oil, gas, coal, and forest resources, poverty began to fade and agriculture was strengthened. Marginal farmers no longer had to cling to their land, farm consolidation increased, and the clearance of new land accelerated.

A considerable amount of Alberta's forest land could be cleared for agriculture, but the market incentive is weak and the land with the greatest agricultural potential is also best for sustained-yield forest production. The agricultural frontier is therefore basically frozen, and changes to the agricultural system are limited to the area originally occupied between the 1880s and 1920s. At the same time, the size and productivity of this area bears emphasis. Excluding the Peace River region, the agricultural block extends almost unbroken for 600 kilometres north from the American border and for 350 kilometres from the Eastern Slopes to Saskatchewan. In all, only 30 percent of Alberta's land area is in crop and livestock production, and little more than half of that is actually cultivated (Fig. 9.11a). Still, the total agricultural land use area is about 200 000 square kilometres, which accounts for about 20 percent by value of Canada's agricultural production.

Agriculture's enduring importance to the Alberta economy has been easily overlooked in recent years, because of the publicity attached to energy resources. So, too, has it been easy to overlook the dynamic nature of the agricultural industry. The grain elevator is still the most obvious symbol of the cash crop economy, but today the grain is as likely to be barley as wheat, and a great deal of the total output is channelled into livestock production (Fig. 9.11b). As the Canadian market became more affluent and more selective, the demand for high quality animal products, particularly beef, increased significantly. Alberta's cattle population, and the numbers of cattle slaughtered in local packing plants, tripled between

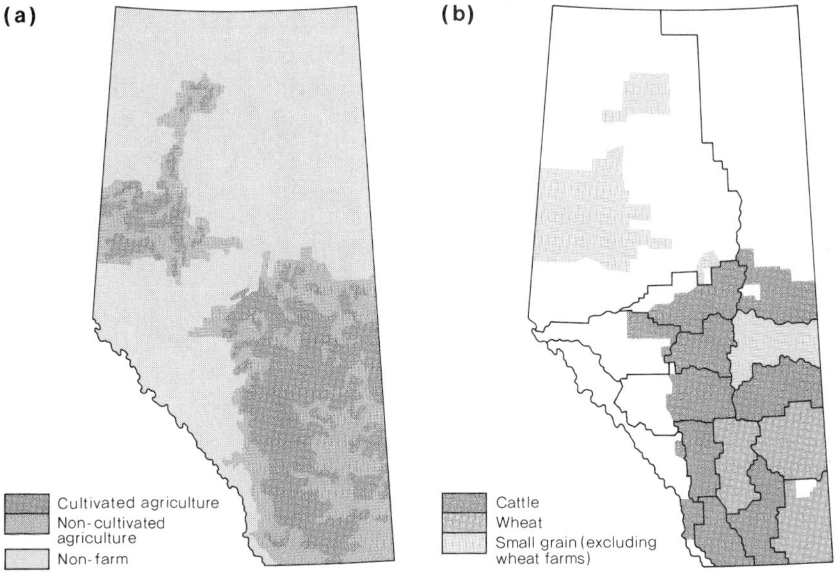

Figure 9.11 Generalized pattern of land use in Alberta and predominant farm type by census division, 1981. (Based on data from the Environment Council of Alberta, *Maintaining and Expanding the Agricultural Land Base of Alberta,* summary report, 1984; and *1981 Census of Canada,* Catalogue 96-920, "A Profile of Canadian Agriculture," Map 17.)

1951 and 1981. In step with this trend, the feed lot, where cattle receive their final fattening, came to rival the grain elevator as the visual symbol of Alberta agriculture.

Other notable changes in agricultural patterns owe less to the changing demands of Canadian consumers than to the application of scientific and technological improvements. Although the industry continues to be subject to climatic and economic uncertainties, which can cause considerable fluctuations in production patterns from year to year, its overall proficiency has increased significantly since the 1940s. The total amount of improved land, for example, increased by 50 percent, from 8 to 12½ million hectares, between 1951 and 1981. Increases in cropland accounted for most of this rise, though the area in improved pasture also increased by one-third. New crops have been developed, adding welcome diversity and stability to the agricultural system. The most successful has been rape or canola, an oilseed whose bold yellow flowers seem to be everywhere in the cultivated plains in mid-summer. The range of specialty crops in the Lethbridge area, where the combination of well-textured soils

Agriculture in transition: This cattle feed-lot operation in the parkland zone of central Alberta is symbolic of recent changes in the agricultural economy of Alberta. Livestock production and slaughtering in local packing plants are now commonplace, new cash crops such as canola have taken on prominence, and a trend to corporate farming is discernible. (*Government of the Province of Alberta*)

and a relatively long growing season has favoured the development of the most intensive irrigation agriculture in Alberta, has also been extended substantially. Tomatoes, green peppers, and a variety of vegetable crops have been added to the established sugar beet and potato crops.

Agriculture everywhere in Alberta has become more scientifically managed, more mechanized, and more capital-intensive. In addition, productivity per capita has climbed even more steeply than productivity per hectare, contributing to the rural depopulation trend. Fewer farm workers and larger farm units have been inevitable consequences. The average farm size in Alberta increased from 220 hectares in the early 1950s to 320 hectares 20 years later, although the trend has levelled off since, reflecting the importance of the family farm in Alberta. About 90 percent of all farms are still operated as family ventures, and they account for almost 80 percent of the total farm area. The adjustments in farm size that accompanied the modernization of Alberta agriculture can therefore be interpreted as an attempt, by individual farmers, to achieve a balance between an area large enough to be economically viable and small enough to be physically manageable.

THE FUTURE IN PERSPECTIVE

Since 1946, and most notably since 1973, Alberta's resource wealth has stimulated growth and prosperity. Alberta is now firmly established as the fourth largest province by population, and in GDP it ranks third, having surpassed British Columbia in 1978. It has also gained steadily on Québec and Ontario, as the following ratios indicate:

GDP 1972	Québec: Alberta = 2.9:1	Ontario: Alberta = 5.0:1
1977	2.1:1	3.4:1
1982	1.6:1	2.6:1

This trend has given Alberta a much stronger national position than is usual for a resource region in a hinterland location. Yet, Alberta's economic position continues to be fragile, in both the short and long terms. Conventional oil production is already in decline and the eventual exhaustion of the other hydrocarbon energy resources is merely a matter of time. The economic and political significance of this insight is now well understood in Alberta; indeed, it is by far the most threatening cloud over Alberta's long-term prosperity. What will Alberta be without its oil and natural gas reserves? The fear is that it will be no more than it was in the 1920s and 1930s: a food-producing appendage of central Canada, held in check by disadvantageous freight rates and the tariff walls protecting central Canadian manufacturers. Agriculture may be Alberta's greatest renewable resource industry, but it could not, on its own, sustain the province at its present level of development through an indefinite future.

Out of this and related concerns there has emerged a new sympathy in Alberta for long-range economic planning. Repeatedly, since it was first elected in 1971, the Conservative provincial government has declared its support for two basic development goals: the diversification of the economy and the decentralization of Alberta's settlement system beyond the major metropolitan centres. The first reflects the traditional fear of hinterland regions, that an export economy dominated by a limited range of raw or semi-processed staples is at the mercy of a fickle and callous marketplace. A broadly-based economy is thus seen as a mark of maturity, and a path to long-term security. At the same time, the peripheral areas of Alberta are considered to be in greatest need of diversification, partly because people there live directly on the knife-edge of dependence on a single resource, and partly because the concentration of growth in Edmonton and Calgary was thought to be at the expense of the province's smaller centres.

These goals point the Alberta settlement system in a particular direction. The implication is that any development suited to the aim of diversification should be directed away from the "overdeveloped" core to the "underdeveloped" periphery. It is still too early to judge whether this conception is either useful or realizable. The government's attempts at intervention have been tentative, in keeping with its belief in individual enterprise. Even in their present vague form, however, these goals emphasize the value of the periphery to Alberta's way of life and the need to ensure its long-lasting vitality. There is also a parallel here, in the relationship between Alberta and the Canadian heartland. Alberta is still a peripheral region in the national scheme, but it is also essential to the national well-being and it is an integral part of the political, economic, and cultural character of the country. So, too, in the Albertan scheme of things, core and periphery are equally important, equally necessary, and equally deserving of regard; they are inseparable complements in the functional region that is Alberta.

Alberta's undervalued periphery: Small settlements in Alberta, such as Marshall, must diversify beyond a single resource or activity to ensure long-term security and well-being. (*Larry McCann*)

At one and the same time, then, the revaluation of Alberta's resource base has given rise to a sharpened appreciation of the province's geographical unity and of its distinctiveness within the Canadian federation. Above all, in the context of this essay with its theme of economic modernization, it is important that the structural transformation of the Alberta settlement system and the changing perceptions of the province's regional identity have focussed on a politically-defined territory. The spatial organization of that territory is a reflection of its functional unity. It is also reasonable to infer a connection between the strengthened integrity of the Alberta settlement system and the confidence with which regionalism and provincial interests are equated in the national councils. To Albertans, there is no question that Alberta is a region of concern, as distinct as British Columbia, Ontario, or Québec. But that distinction depends on more than the arbitrary boundaries that divided the vast area of Western Canada in the late nineteenth and early twentieth centuries. As the economic and settlement systems evolved, and particularly as they took on their modern form in the years after World War II, the distinctiveness of the political territory was enhanced. It came to embrace a uniquely-ordered space, a functional system tightly organized around its own core area which, in turn, is an important symbol of Alberta's growing authority.

NOTES

1. W.W. Rostow, *The Stages of Economic Growth* (Cambridge: The University Press, 1960).
2. A fuller development of the information contained in this chapter is available in B.M. Barr and P.J. Smith, eds., *Environment and Economy: Essays on the Human Geography of Alberta* (Edmonton: Pica Pica Press, 1984).
3. W.E. Mann, *Sect, Cult, and Church in Alberta* (Toronto: University of Toronto Press, 1955).
4. The following books deal with the ethic of conservatism in Alberta's political culture, and the implications for economic and urban development: John A. Irving, *The Social Credit Movement in Alberta* (Toronto: University of Toronto Press, 1959); C.B. Macpherson, *Democracy in Alberta: Social Credit and the Party System,* 2nd ed. (Toronto: University of Toronto Press, 1962); John J. Barr, *The Dynasty: The Rise and Fall of Social Credit in Alberta* (Toronto: McClelland and Stewart, 1974); David G. Bettison, John J. Kenward and Larrie Taylor, *Urban Affairs in Alberta* (Edmonton: University of Alberta Press, 1975); Carlo Caldarola, ed., *Society and Politics in Alberta: Research Papers* (Toronto: Methuen, 1979); and Allan Hustak, *Peter Lougheed: A Biography* (Toronto: McClelland and Stewart, 1979).
5. J.R. Mallory, *Social Credit and the Federal Power in Canada* (Toronto: University of Toronto Press, 1954).
6. The argument that prairie regionalism was at its peak between 1905 and 1939, and has since been replaced by strong provincial sentiments, is developed by Roger Gibbins, *Prairie Politics and Society: Regionalism in Decline* (Toronto: Butterworths, 1980).
7. G. Bruce Doern and Glen Toner, *The Politics of Energy: The Development and Implementation of the NEP* (Toronto: Methuen, 1984).

8. J. Tait Davis, "Some Implications of Recent Trends in the Provincial Distribution of Income and Industrial Product in Canada," *The Canadian Geographer,* 24 (1980), 22-36.
9. The implications of capital accumulation in Alberta were the subject of a special issue of *Canadian Public Policy,* 6 (1980), 141-280.
10. Peter Haggett, *Geography: A Modern Synthesis,* 3rd ed. (New York: Harper and Row, 1975), pp. 508-10.
11. Michel Boisvert, *The Correspondence Between the Urban System and the Economic Base of Canada's Regions* (Ottawa: Economic Council of Canada, 1978).
12. Eric Hanson, *Dynamic Decade: Evolution and Effects of the Oil Industry in Alberta* (Toronto: McClelland and Stewart, 1958).
13. James Anderson, "Change in a Central Place System: Trade Centres and Rural Service in Central Alberta" (unpublished M.A. thesis, University of Alberta, 1967).
14. Charles L. Keys, "Spatial Reorganization in a Central Place System: An Albertan Case" (unpublished Ph.D. thesis, University of Alberta, 1975).
15. J.W. Maxwell, "The Functional Structure of Canadian Cities: A Classification of Cities," *Geographical Bulletin,* 7 (1965), 79-104.
16. For discussions of Calgary and Edmonton as metropolitan centres, see Brenton M. Barr, ed., *Calgary: Metropolitan Structure and Influence,* Western Geographical Series, Vol. 12 (Victoria: Department of Geography, University of Victoria, 1975); and P.J. Smith, ed., *Edmonton: The Emerging Metropolitan Pattern,* Western Geographical Series, Vol. 15 (Victoria: Department of Geography, University of Victoria, 1978).
17. The development of the Edmonton-Calgary subregion is analyzed in P.J. Smith and Denis B. Johnson, *The Edmonton-Calgary Corridor,* Studies in Geography (Edmonton: The University of Alberta, 1978).
18. Patricia Sheehan, *Social Change in the Alberta Foothills,* The New Canadian Geography Project (Toronto: McClelland and Stewart, 1975).

10

British Columbia: Metropolis and Hinterland in Microcosm

John Bradbury

Resource enterprise and a unique physical environment have shaped the geographic character of Canada's west coast province. British Columbia is a staple-producing hinterland for industrial markets throughout the world, yet it has also developed a prosperous internal economy. A diversity of mineral, forest, and marine resources have supported continuous economic growth, which in turn has been fueled by large infusions of people, capital, and technical expertise from metropolitan economies. The physical environment is of further importance because topographic elements have dictated a settlement and communication pattern that concentrates human activity in the southwestern corner of the province around Vancouver. The role of Vancouver as the metropolis of the region — the natural intermediary between world markets and a vast resource hinterland — mirrors much that is characteristic of core and periphery in the world-economy.

THE PHYSICAL ENVIRONMENT

The physical geography of British Columbia is dominated by mountains, ocean, and forest — all of which have set the context for patterns of human activity. The Rocky Mountains, stretching northward from Montana, running along the Alberta-British Columbia border and terminating in the plains surrounding the Liard River, act as a powerful physical and, some say, cultural (even psychological) barrier between British Columbia and the rest of Canada (Fig. 10.1). The Rockies rise abruptly above the foothills of Alberta, and some mountains tower more than 3000 metres above sea level. To the west of the Rockies lies the

Rocky Mountain Trench, one of the longest continuous valleys in the world. Two other mountain systems, the Columbia and the Cassiar-Omineca, run parallel to the Trench. The geological history of these systems is generally similar. Sedimentary rocks of the Paleozoic and Proterozoic ages, subsequently folded, warped, and glaciated, are most characteristic. In some areas, such as the Kootenays of southeastern British Columbia, well-mineralized sedimentary and intrusive rocks of Cretaceous, Triassic, and Jurassic ages have yielded considerable mineral wealth.

Dividing the interior of the province into other physiographic units are more mountain ranges, plateaus, and river valleys. The Interior Plateau is British Columbia's largest physiographic region, covering about 191 800 square kilometres. Four of the province's six major river basins — the Fraser, Columbia, Skeena, and Peace (but excluding the northern Stikine and Liard river basins) — drain its highly variegated surface. The plateau surfaces are by no means flat, but the overall appearance is that of a basin. The Coast Mountains, running the western length of the Plateau and rising quickly from the Pacific Ocean, enhance this appearance. Vancouver Island, too, is dominated by a mountain spine, but the Island shares other common landscapes of the province — plains, valleys, fiord-like inlets, and drylands. Here as elsewhere, the effects of glaciation are

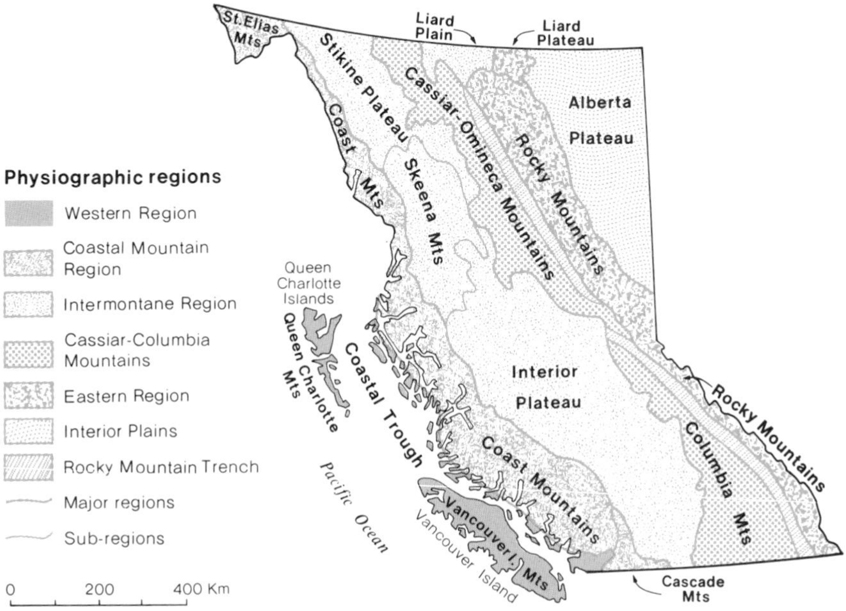

Figure 10.1 The physiographic regions of British Columbia.

The Kootenay region of British Columbia: Mountains and valley define the boundaries of regions within British Columbia. (*Larry McCann)*

everywhere apparent. All of British Columbia was once under a thick sheet of ice; cirques and fiords, terraces and benches, and ground moraines are common features created by retreating ice some 12 000-15 000 years ago.

The physiographic structure of British Columbia is largely responsible for the patterns of soils, vegetation, and climate that distinguish the province. The two most basic regions are "the Coast" and "the Interior," but variations mark valleys and uplands as well as northern and southern areas. Less than 5 percent of British Columbia has soils suitable for agriculture. As in most mountainous areas, these are concentrated in the flood plains, terraces, and deltas of river valleys, most notably in the fertile Lower Mainland of the Fraser River Valley. This region also enjoys a climate favourable for agriculture. Like other southern coastal areas, it enjoys mild winters and warm summers — both moderated by the relatively warm air masses of the Pacific Ocean. The Interior, by contrast, experiences cold winters and hot summers similar to those of Alberta and Saskatchewan. In fact, the Coastal Mountains shield the dry Interior from the heavy precipitation that distinguishes the Coast. Whereas the Vancouver area receives 170-250 centimetres of precipitation annually, the interior Okanagan region receives only 25 centimetres.

Such differences in climate and precipitation influence types of vegetation. The forests of coniferous trees in coastal British Columbia — Douglas fir, western cedar, Sitka spruce, balsam fir, and hemlock — are the most substantial in Canada. Species of the Interior such as lodgepole and ponderosa pine, white spruce, and balsam fir are much smaller in dimension and volume, but nevertheless support a highly productive forest industry.

The diverse physical environment supports distinct regions of economic enterprise. Logging and lumbering on coastal mountain slopes give way to irrigated agriculture in the Okanagan (apple and soft fruit orchards), Similkameen (vegetables), and Thompson (alfalfa for hay) Valleys. To the east, the valleys of the Columbia River system are dammed for energy production. The provincial government has invested heavily in the production of hydroelectricity for export to coastal cities, as well as to cities and industries in the northwestern United States. The East and West Kootenays have a mining base (coal, lead, and zinc) and some forest industry, but little agriculture.

The presence of enterprise pales in northern British Columbia. Multinational oil companies exploit natural gas and the provincial government generates hydroelectric power in the Peace River District, but beyond, in the vast areas of tundra and low forest cover, there is little evidence of human activity. Further south is Prince George, the "hub of the north," the centre of the forest industry in the Interior and of an extensive road and rail network built by the provincial government. The Central Interior and the Thompson-Kamloops region support some small farms and extensive cattle ranches, but the forest industry and mining form the backbone of the economy.

On the Pacific Coast, at Prince Rupert, the salmon fishery is the most important industry. Along the Northwest Coast, the Lower Coast, and on Vancouver Island, lumbering and pulp and paper production predominate. Giant corporations — some of the largest in the world — run integrated logging, sawmilling, and pulp and paper operations, shipping products to worldwide markets. Fishing here is of secondary importance, although it produces more in value than its Atlantic counterpart. Enterprise in British Columbia is indeed resource-oriented, for one-half of provincial income is generated by the forest industry alone.

These patterns of resource enterprise, in a rich and diverse physical environment, support the structure of metropolis and hinterland within the province. Virtually any criterion illustrates the commanding position

The Okanagan Valley near Vernon in British Columbia: Ranching and the orchard industry mark the limits of settlement in this dry interior valley and topographic control is preeminent. (*Larry McCann*)

of Vancouver in the region's geography: population distribution, concentration of manufacturing activity, location of corporate headquarters, the confluence of transport facilities, share of provincial wealth, and control of political power. These characteristics are suggested by the distribution of urban population (Fig. 10.2), and above all else, outline the metropolis and hinterland pattern in which Vancouver is the mainspring of the provincial space economy. It is the centre for resource extraction, processing, and servicing, and also the focus of trade, corporate management, and, along with Victoria, of government operations. On a world scale, the province is a vast resource hinterland for a number of world metropolises, with business interactions centred in Vancouver. The pervasiveness of this pattern of metropolis and hinterland, set against the context of resource enterprise and the natural landscape, forms the challenge basic to an interpretation of British Columbia's regional geography.

METROPOLIS AND HINTERLAND IN EVOLUTION

British Columbia has always been oriented to staple production. A succession of natural resources — fur, gold, coal, lumber, base metals, pulp and paper, hydroelectricity, and natural gas — have propelled the region through successive phases of growth and diversification, both internally and in the world-economy.

Integration Within the World-Economy

The exploitation of these resources, and the shaping of society and economy in British Columbia, took place essentially in the late nineteenth century. Earlier calls on the resource base were not insignificant. Mid-nineteenth century markets for fur, gold, and coal, for example, reinforced lines of communication and political association with Great Britain and fostered commercial connections with California. The flow of financial capital, labour, and merchants from both places was substantial, but these early ties were limited by difficulties of isolation and the high costs of exporting products, for British Columbia functioned at the margin of the industrial world's search for raw materials. It is, therefore, not difficult to explain the initial emphasis on commodities such as furs and gold, or the interest in canned salmon immediately after Confederation. The high value and limited bulk of these commodities could sustain the considerable costs of transportation.

The concentration of settlement in the southwestern corner of the province, still important today, also took shape in this early period. The primacy of Victoria, however, was eclipsed after 1886 by the meteoric rise of Vancouver, and other early patterns were also soon modified. Lumbering and mineral production acquired prominence; the ecumene took on new dimensions by expanding into most areas of the province, casting the now familiar pattern of core and periphery; and new trading connections and sources of development capital appeared. Despite these changes, British Columbia would remain a peripheral — albeit wealthy — region of the world-system.

This hinterland dependency on external markets and institutions thus assumed many of its present characteristics in the period between 1886 and 1914. The arrival of the Canadian Pacific Railway (C.P.R.) in Vancouver in 1886 opened lines of communication and trade with the

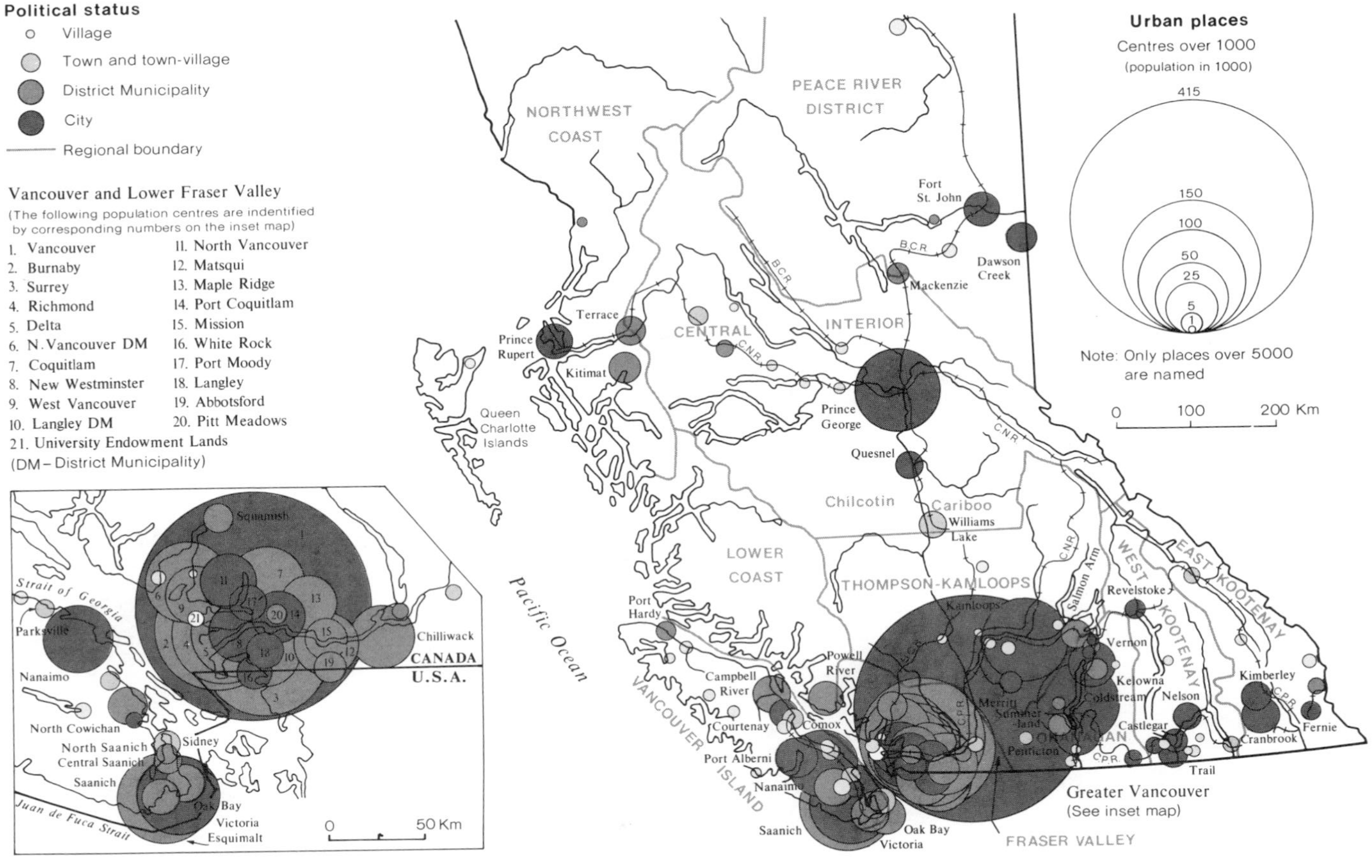

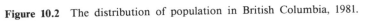

Figure 10.2 The distribution of population in British Columbia, 1981.

First train in Vancouver: When the Canadian Pacific Railway reached Vancouver in 1886, it not only ensured that the "Terminal City" soon controlled the provincial hinterland, but also that British Columbia entered the continental economy. Soon thereafter, the Western Interior became the leading market for the province's forest products. (*No. 1091, Vancouver Public Library*)

North American economic community. Even after joining Confederation in 1871, British Columbians had to travel through the United States to reach eastern Canada. The railway, therefore, was the critical integrating force. At first it did little to tie British Columbia commercially to eastern Canada, but it did link the coastal area of the province to parts of the Interior, and created the means for supplying lumber to the expanding market of the newly settled Western Interior.

By the eve of the World War I, the "Canadian prairies had become the most important, almost the only, outside market for British Columbia lumber."[1] Economies of scale and lower transfer costs for producing lumber ensured that Vancouver would remain the province's leading sawmilling centre, but the prairie market nevertheless stimulated the growth of interior mills along major transportation routes. Much of the capital and entrepreneurship employed in the forest industry — to the extent of two-thirds in the interior and one-third on the coast — came from the United States. American capital and mining technology were initially prominent in the Kootenay mining boom of the 1890s as well, but after 1897 British and eastern Canadian financial capital played the leading role. Canadian funds were similarly important in the reorganization of the coast salmon canning industry in 1902, by which time the banks and manufactured products of the Industrial Heartland had made significant inroads, replacing once important British institutions. Eastern Canada also supplied considerable entrepreneurial talent and labour, complementing the traditional British element on the coast and the American presence in the southeastern interior.[2]

Patterns of integration within the world-economy changed again following World War I. The volume and diversity of staple exports increased, but trade patterns often shifted dramatically (Fig. 10.3). The lumber market of the Western Interior had declined appreciably during and following the war as settlement there subsided, but the slack in this trade was more than compensated by expanding overseas markets and increased demand in the United States. In addition, pulp and paper — representing a new generation of staples — became an important export commodity and the basis for resource town development along the coast. For the first time, too, grain from the Western Interior flowed through British Columbia's ports in significant quantities as a direct result of the opening of the Panama Canal in 1914. The salmon canning industry also benefited from this development, although it never regained its late nineteenth century role as the leading provincial export. Mining consolidated its position in the provincial economy as well. The Kootenay boom subsided early in the twentieth century, and although coal from the Fernie district and lead and zinc from Kimberley were still important export commodities, further advances in this sector occurred only after World War II.

All of these export trades suffered a brief decline at the beginning of the Depression, then quickly recovered, only to decline again during World War II. These swings illustrate both the resiliency and the weakness of British Columbia's position in the world-economy. Throughout the inter-war period, while traditional sources of financial capital remained constant, new and significant sources were developed within the region, notably in the forest industry. Still, there were no regional banks and other local financial institutions were few in number and small in scale. Technology followed a similar course: most mining innovations were borrowed from elsewhere, though local advances in logging and sawmilling were significant. Throughout the inter-war period, the various provincial governments trumpeted and supported resource development in the "company province" by granting generous leases for resource exploitation and by supporting railway construction.[3]

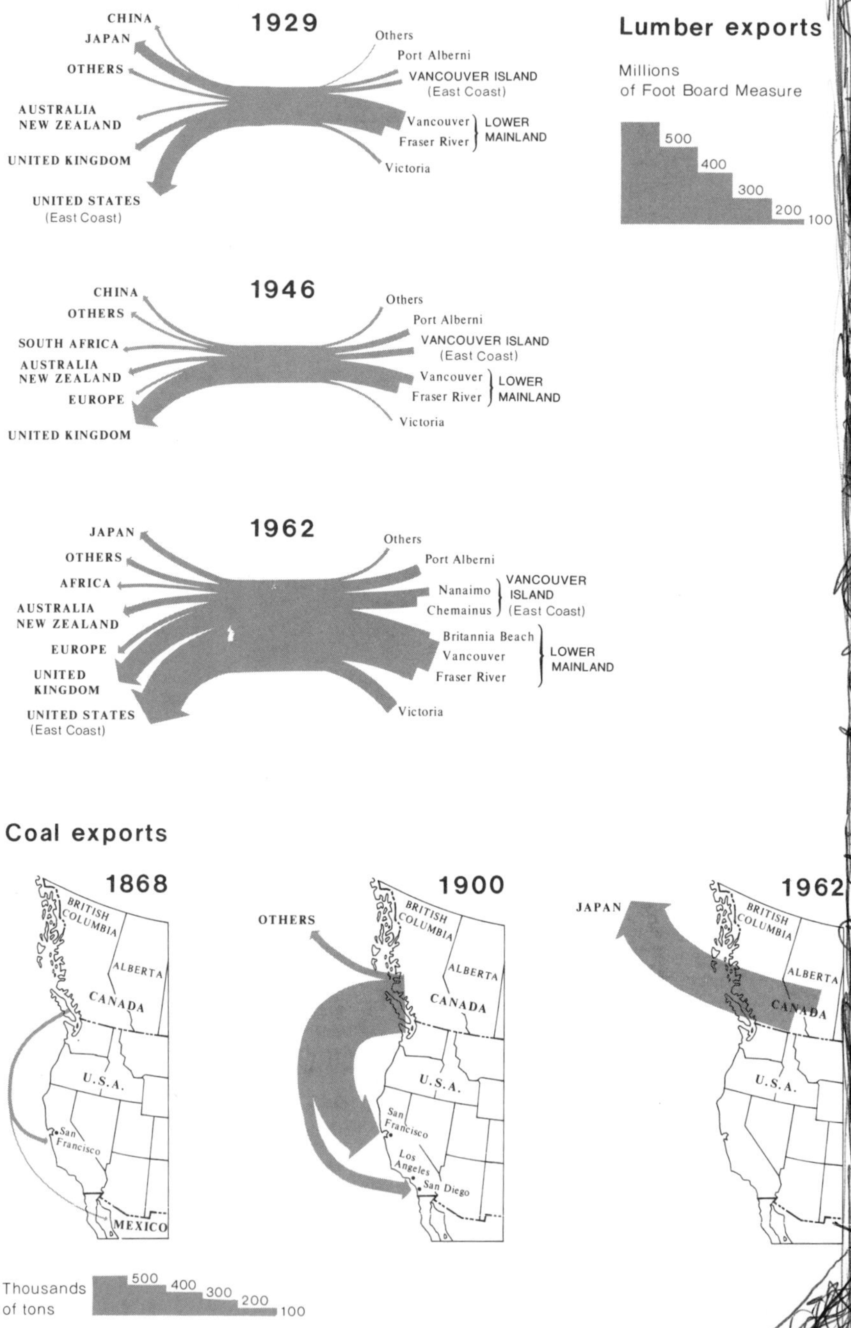

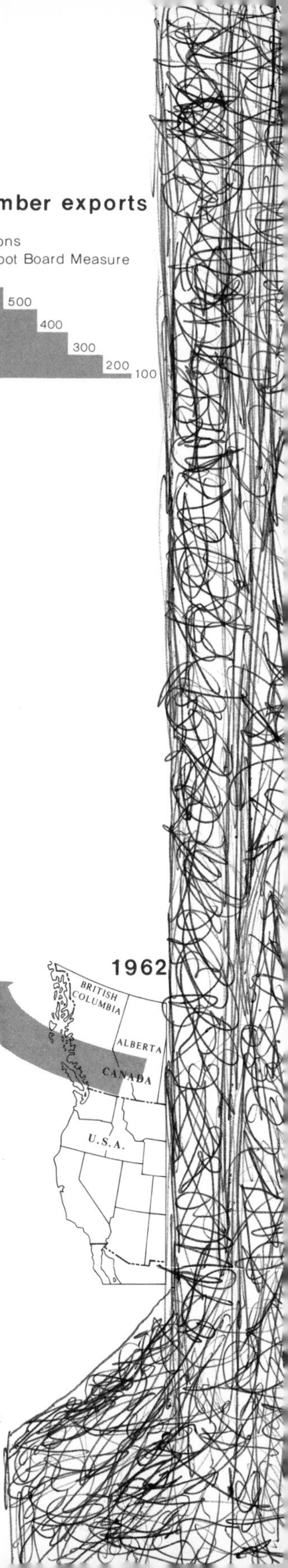

Figure 10.3 Lumber and coal shipments from the ports of British Columbia.

Regional Integration

Writing of British Columbia in 1895, a discerning visitor noted not only the potential, but also the obstacles to be overcome in developing the staple economy:

> No province of Canada so little admits of indiscriminate immigration . . . the good farming land is limited in quantity and, compared with that in other provinces, [is] expensive. The vast deep-sea fisheries of the coast, on account of their distance from markets, can only be developed by degrees. . . . Mines can only be worked with capital, and capital which does not demand a quick return. The same is true of the timber industry with the further problem of access to foreign markets.[4]

But these obstacles *were* overcome. British Columbia suffered no shortage of capital and technical expertise in its drive to economic prosperity. All sectors of the provincial economy advanced markedly before World War II. Growth was propelled by the staple industries, including resource-based manufacturing, but commercial, financial, and transportation activities — essential for servicing the staple economy — also made appreciable gains. Secondary manufacturing remained weakly diversified, however, a victim of the limited size of the local market.[5]

These economic changes altered the social make-up of the province. Nearly 700 000 people were counted in the 1931 Census, a seven-fold increase over 1891. Most lived in cities — the province has always been strongly urban-oriented — and the majority were British, chiefly English. But in 1931 the ethnic mix was more diverse than ever before, including Scandinavian, Russian Doukhobor, and German immigrants. The size of the Japanese community had also grown, but the Native people and Chinese populations had generally stabilized. The impact of this immigration and ethnic make-up was felt in three main ways: in the rise of a new business acumen based on national corporate enterprise; in the confrontation between labour and management; and in outbreaks of racism. British Columbia developed in an era of expanding industrial and financial capitalism, and there was little in community-oriented values to halt the advance of large-scale corporate enterprise. Of the many immigrants coming to the province, most were English and many were from urban and industrial settings and had strong ties with organized labour. Thus, coinciding with industrial growth, clashes between labour and management shaped the province's regional consciousness. In a similar but sadder way, nativist hostility towards Chinese, Japanese, and East Indians in particular has scarred ethnic relations.

The essential geographic development in the period before World War I was the emergence of a core-periphery design as the governing principle of the regional space economy.[6] Urban places in the Georgia Strait region — notably Vancouver — constituted the core, while resource centres in the

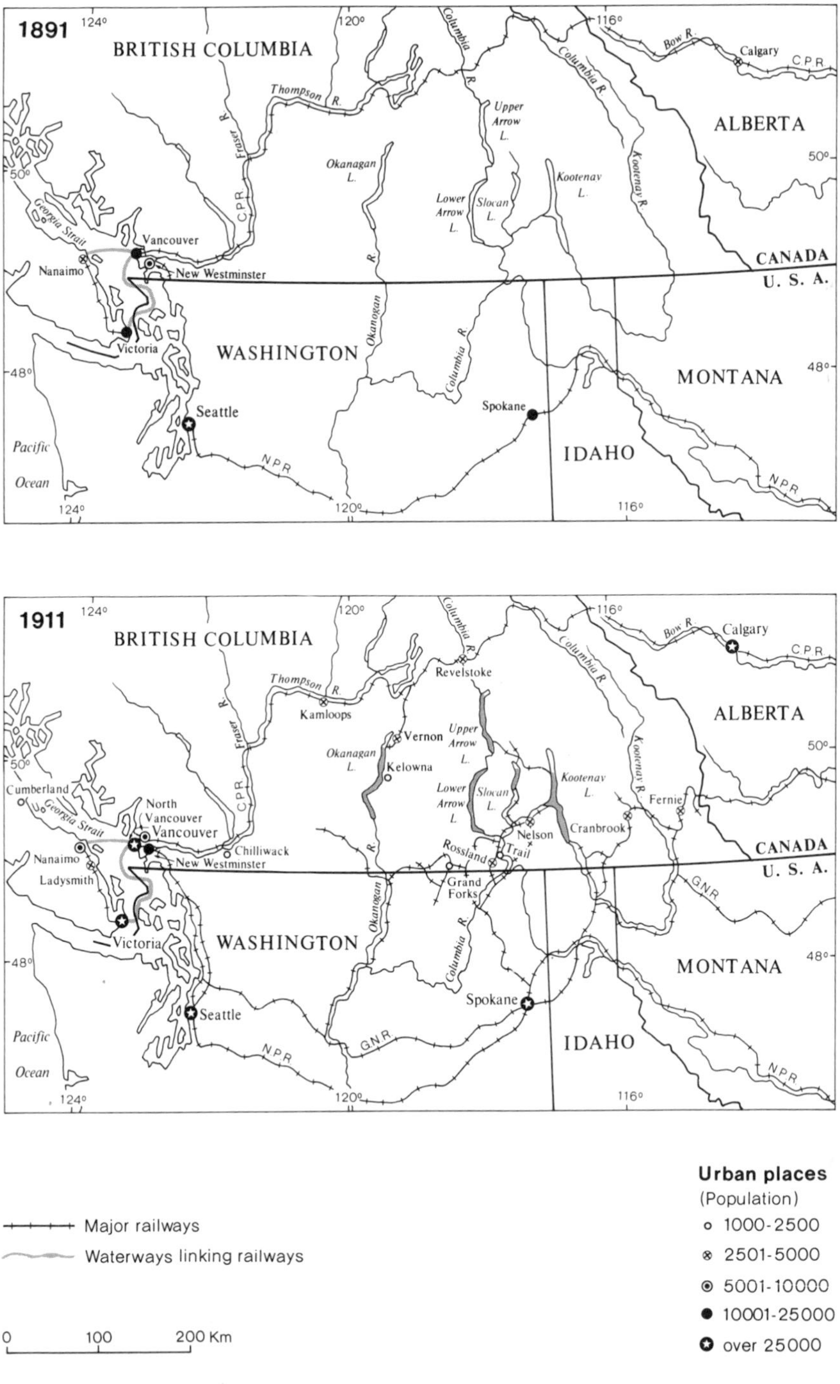

Figure 10.4 The changing pattern of urban settlement in British Columbia, 1891 and 1911.

Technology and industrial enterprise at the Hall Mine, above Nelson, 1896: British Columbia's regional character has been shaped strongly by the forces of industrial and financial capitalism. Beginning particularly in the late nineteenth century, economic development has depended on large infusions of foreign capital, labour, and technology. Nowhere is this more apparent than in the mining sector. (*Saskatchewan Archives Board photograph*)

interior comprised a weakly articulated peripheral system (Fig. 10.4). Regional patterns of resource extraction in existence today were clearly in evidence by the close of this period. Settlements rimming the coastal waters between Vancouver Island and the mainland supported the province's largest sawmills and pulp and paper operations, with the Vancouver area as the focal point. Not only did it have excellent transportation facilities, but new technological advances in logging and transporting and processing raw materials ensured that Vancouver would hold this position. In a similar way, the consolidation of the salmon canning industry at the mouth of the Fraser River, near Vancouver, and at

Prince Rupert, was the product of technological advances in boat design and factory operations (for example, refrigeration) which favoured larger plants and concentration in urban areas with good accessibility to markets. The consolidation and concentration of resource-based industries thus fueled the growth of Vancouver.

The city rose to prominence in other sectors as well. It gained control over the import-export trade largely through preferential freight tariffs arranged by the C.P.R. Vancouver was thus clearly favoured as a location for those manufacturing, transportation, and trading services linked to the export base. It also won prominence as a financial and management centre. The depression of the mid-1890s forced many British banks headquartered in Victoria to withdraw, thus weakening that city's financial base and giving Vancouver the advantage. Expanding eastern Canadian corporations, including the banks and other financial institutions, usually sought locations in Vancouver rather than Victoria. This shift in the spatial direction of capital flows consolidated Vancouver's pre-eminence in financial affairs. It thus controlled the region's transportation, commercial, manufacturing, and financial activities. The foundations of its metropolitan status had been laid. The city's population reached some 100 000 in 1911, three times that of Victoria, and by 1931, it had expanded to nearly 250 000 people.[7]

Despite this growth, Vancouver's control over the resource hinterland remained incomplete. The interior forest industry, characterized by small mills and limited capacity, developed wherever settlement and good timber stands existed along major transportation routes, but its markets were mainly local, not primarily export-oriented, and its products were not shipped through coastal ports. Agriculture followed a similar pattern. Like lumber milling, it was confined to the southern and interior valleys of the province, with an outlier in the Peace River District. Cattle ranching was extensive throughout the Interior Plateau, running from the Nicola Valley north into the Cariboo and Chilcotin country, but Kamloops was the industry's main service and transportation centre.

The major thrust of economic activity in the Interior had been in the southeastern corner of the province where the search for silver and other metallic ores had drawn the mining towns of the West and East Kootenays into the orbit of Spokane's influence. Indeed, direct rail links between the Kootenays and Vancouver did not exist until World War I, and even then, the region often looked elsewhere, to Calgary and Winnipeg, for servicing and provisions. In many ways, therefore, the interior regions were only weakly integrated into the regional space economy. There was recognition of Vancouver's prominence, but communication ties were weak. The period of greatest economic and population growth would come after World War II, when the provincial government embarked on an intensified programme of road and railway building and resource promotion, designed to further integrate and consolidate the provincial economy. Only then would Vancouver assume more complete control over the provincial hinterland.

Government and Post-War Resource Development

After World War II, the character of enterprise in British Columbia took on new forms. Some provincial companies, such as the forestry giant MacMillan Bloedel, became multinational in scope. Others, chiefly externally-controlled resource corporations, eliminated older, regional companies to achieve prominence. But most important, the provincial government was instrumental in facilitating vast resource developments.

Under the Social Credit government of W.A.C. Bennett, in power from 1952 to 1972, and during subsequent New Democratic Party and Social Credit terms in office, resource extraction was encouraged by favourable government policies. Early governments had also promoted economic growth, but the Social Credit Party was at the centre of development at the very time British Columbia's resources achieved a marked comparative advantage in world markets. The Bennett government therefore set out to develop the province's resources by establishing liaisons with large corporations and financial houses willing to invest in a resource extraction economy; by building an infrastructure of railways, roads, and electricity through government spending; and by providing a fiscal policy, a tax structure, and a legal framework which encouraged multinational corporations to invest chiefly in the forest and mining sectors. Direct government investment was not envisaged, at least not initially. The object instead was to provide the necessary physical and economic infrastructure for profitable enterprise. During the 1950s and '60s, therefore, the provincial government often promoted British Columbia as a resource hinterland by sending the Premier and his Ministers throughout the United States and Europe to attract new investment. This policy meshed with that of John Diefenbaker and other federal leaders who saw unlimited resource potential in the Canadian northlands.

If resources in British Columbia were to be exploited, then access to them had to be assured. Extensive government surveys first pinpointed resource areas, and then development plans were put in place by both business and government. Penetration into resource areas through government-managed highway and railroad building followed. Finally, while the government made plans for specific industrial developments such as pulp mills and aluminum smelters, private enterprise became engaged in the actual extraction process. Government involvement was instigated not only on the northern frontier of the province, but also in the southeast Kootenay region and in the Central Interior, around Prince

George. The strategy was generally successful, for the 1960s and early 1970s were boom years, although some would argue that government policies served only to entrench the province in its position as a staples-extracting hinterland.

A major part of this development was the construction of the government-owned and financed British Columbia Railway, then called the Pacific Great Eastern Railway (P.G.E.). Facilitated by a special Loan Act of 1954, work began in 1955 to push the railway 232 kilometres north of Prince George, and also to connect Fort St. John and Dawson Creek in the Peace River region. From Prince George the line proceeded north through Pine Pass to a junction at Little River where it then divided, one branch extending to Fort St. John, the other to Dawson Creek where it connected with the Northern Alberta Railway. The P.G.E. thus became both a critical agent for integrating metropolis and hinterland and the basis of a resource corridor for tapping the gas, oil, mineral, and forest potential of northern British Columbia.

Another major development project instigated by the provincial government was the $500-million Alcan project, begun in 1953, to smelt aluminum at Kitimat from hydroelectricity generated nearby at Kemano. The provincial government also acted to ensure the existence of a workforce in hinterland resource areas such as Kitimat. Where a workforce was not present, for example, the government promoted permanent settlements to accommodate the workers who would migrate there from the cities, or from other resource frontiers. A number of resource towns like Kitimat were constructed during the 1960s, facilitated by the government's passage of the Instant Towns Act in 1965 which established local governments in all single-enterprise communities.

Electricity, like railways, highways, and towns, was an important element in the government's development strategy. Electricity was used both as a source of energy for new industry and as a commodity for export to the United States. Several major hydroelectricity schemes were initiated in the 1960s. In 1961, the provincial government took over the British Columbia Electric Company and acquired the rights to produce power on the Peace River. In conjunction with several private companies, this government project was completed in 1968 and had the capacity to produce some 2.4 million kilowatts, making it one of the world's largest power schemes.

Further south, on the Columbia River, a series of dams was constructed to provide for local industrial and residential consumption, as well as for sales to the American market. The biggest undertaking was the Mica dam project, completed in 1976. The initiative for developing the Columbia had come from the United States Army Corps of Engineers who argued that the full potential of downstream dams in the United States could not be realized without Canadian participation. The scheme remained under debate for a considerable period until the Columbia River

Treaty provided a resolution in 1964. Under the Treaty, Canada agreed to build three storage dams at an estimated cost of $410 million. The dams have since proven more expensive than anticipated, and the financial and energy benefits somewhat less. Nevertheless, selling energy as a staple, rather than using it to produce finished goods for export, marks British Columbia as a hinterland region.[8]

Most of the forest in the province (about 95 percent) is owned by the Crown and allocated to companies on long-term, tenure arrangements: 12.8 percent to the largest company, MacMillan Bloedel; 58.7 percent to the ten largest firms; and 95.5 percent to the 75 largest companies.[9] Government policy in the forest industry is based on a sustained yield programme of forest management. Companies are permitted to cut only certain areas and amounts of timber to keep the forest in perpetual growth. Reforestation must also be practiced. Timber areas have therefore been set up on a regional basis, to sustain a permanent population of logging and milling companies.

Tree Farm License Areas are one specific administrative device by which private industry incorporated state policies. By this method, public timberlands are allocated to private companies in perpetuity, but the company must use sustained yield practices, provide fire protection, disease and pest control, and maintain access. Public Sustained Yield Units (P.S.Y.U.) cover areas of publicly owned land and lands under direct government control on which the rights to harvest timber are sold, by auction, to individual operators. The first P.S.Y.U. was formed in 1950; there were 30 in 1953, 58 in 1957, 78 in 1968, and by the early 1980s, the number totalled over 100. Timber is sold to competitive bidders, both small logging firms and large conglomerates, with awards generally accruing to the latter. A third category, the Pulpwood Harvesting Area, is designed to encourage the establishment of the pulp and paper industry in the interior of the province.

By the early 1970s, the provincial forest industry, including pulp mills and lumber operations, was dispersed throughout the province, but was basically controlled by vertically-integrated, multinational firms based in Vancouver. The move to this structure became apparent by the early 1950s, with the post-war construction of coastal mills at Port Alberni, Prince Rupert, Harmac, Elk Falls, and Crofton. In 1961, a mill built at Castlegar, situated on the Columbia River in the southeast interior, marked the first major move away from a coastal location. This move was soon followed by the construction of several mills in the Central Interior, principally at Prince George, and later by the massive enlargement of the Kamloops mill. By the mid-1970s, the interior forest industry was producing more in value than the coastal industry. Vancouver still remains the focal point of the provincial forest industry because of historical inertia, concentrated investment in physical plant and regional head offices, and ample transportation and auxiliary services.[10]

Pollution control in the interior forest industry: Shown in the photo is a 50-acre aeration pond for waste waters from two of the three pulp mills located near Prince George. As the fluid flows toward the Fraser River, jets of air stir the liquid to promote bacteria action which is so complete the effluent is almost pure by the time it reaches the river. (*Prince George* Citizen)

In a similar way, Vancouver has attracted the operation, exploration, and executive functions of the mining industry. Mining development was stimulated by favourable government policies (except between 1972 and 1975 when high royalty charges temporarily held back exploration and development) and by the penetration of national and foreign firms. In the early post-war period, new mining activities were generally confined to tidewater sites. If companies did venture inland, they usually stayed within 80 kilometres of the international border in areas across southern British Columbia. High transportation costs and difficulty of access dictated this pattern, but by the mid-1960s, high prices on the world market encouraged development of quality deposits located outside these limits. Copper in the Highland Valley, located just south of Kamloops; molybdenum from Fraser Lake near Prince George; and natural gas and oil from the Peace River District, are representative of recent advances.

The government imperative in resource development was not limited solely to solicitation and promotion, nor to the provision of an infrastructure of roads, railways, towns, and sustained yield timber areas. The government also sold bonds and obtained loans on the national and international money market. The Social Credit Party argued that to maintain a boom and expand the natural resource and extractive industries, large volumes of foreign capital were essential. The bulk of this investment came from the United States, Europe, and Japan, thereby increasing the diversity of international capital, while entrenching the

Mining in the Highland Valley of British Columbia: Copper for world markets, especially for Japan, is exported from this open-pit mining area located south of Kamloops. (*Larry McCann*)

staples orientation of the regional economy. At the same time, this investment strengthened corporate and executive linkages between the metropolitan forces of government and business in British Columbia, and the functional dependence between Vancouver and the hinterland regions of the province.

The penetration of British Columbia by foreign investment after World War II, especially in the early 1960s, was part of the worldwide search by industrial economies for raw materials. The mining and forest industries of the province competed with these same export sectors in other parts of the world. Such competition is influenced by factors of comparative advantage, including technological change, shifts in supply and demand relations, variations in labour conditions and costs, state and business coordination, problems of pollution control, and fluctuations in energy costs. The cyclical patterns of these factors in the world-economy have repercussions in British Columbia. The export record is therefore an indicator of a region's growth within the world-economy. By the early 1960s, the United States was still the major destination of the province's staple exports; the United Kingdom remained second; Japan came next; and Australia, which took less than 5 percent of the province's exports, was a distant fourth. To the United States went chiefly forest products, some minerals, and natural gas. The United Kingdom bought lumber and plywood. Japan was a new purchaser of copper, coal, and forest products. Australia was interested in small quantities of lumber, aluminum, wood pulp, newsprint, and asbestos fibres. By the early 1980s, however, several new trends in staple exporting were evident: the United Kingdom market was declining relatively; Japan was importing more forest products, coal, and other mineral products than ever before; and Western Europe, India, and Australia were increasing their imports of minerals, particularly asbestos fibres (Table 10.1).

The case of Japan illustrates that countries desperately in need of raw materials will seek out stable political environments. As political tensions in the world-system mounted in the post-war period, Japan increasingly looked eastward to the resources of British Columbia to fuel its industrial expansion. Exports of coal to Japan rose rapidly from 640 000 to 8 300 000 tons between 1962 and 1976, but Japan also imports considerable quantities of copper from the province, despite the fact that it holds copper interests elsewhere — for example, in the Philippines, Uganda, and Indonesia. These countries, however, have been wrought by political instability, and Japan thus favours British Columbia instead as a stable supply area.

Recent developments have reinforced commercial ties. In 1980, an agreement was signed to open the Sukunka coal fields north of Prince George, proposed jointly by the provincial government and several Japanese multinationals. These rich deposits will supplement coal already drawn from the East Kootenays where Japanese demand promoted the first direct foreign investment by Japanese steel makers in an overseas source of coking coal. A consortium of ten Japanese corporations, under the umbrella of the Mitsubishi Trading Corporation and including seven steel makers, agreed in 1966 to an initial investment of some $27.5 million, an amount that has increased considerably in recent years. Thus, Japan was largely responsible for reviving British Columbia's long-dormant coal industry. But as the province, like the rest of Canada, entered a recession in the late 1970s and early 1980s, the Japanese consortium rewrote contracts and substituted prices in the coal to be exported from the northeastern coal fields. Both the provincial and federal governments had spent large sums of public money to set up the infrastructure of towns, railways, and ports for this mega-project. Such was the extent of the recession that major losses were incurred by all levels of government and the Canadian mining partners in the coal fields. Much of the province's mining industry suffered in the same manner with closures, unemployment, and production losses.

Nevertheless, during the 1970s and early 1980s, the government has supported a number of mega-projects. These have included more coal mining operations, metals processing, and natural gas processing (Table 10.2). The government's plans were in keeping with past measures to

TABLE 10.1 TRADE THROUGH BRITISH COLUMBIA PORTS, 1983
(in thousands of dollars)

Destination	*Fish and Marine Animals*	*Forest Products*[a]	*Metals in ores and ingots (iron, copper, lead, zinc, etc.)*	*Crude Non-metallic minerals (excluding fuels)*	*Coal, Crude Petroleum and Natural Gas*	*Chemicals and Related Products*	*Grain and Cereal Products*	*Other Products*	*Total*
United Kingdom[b]	21 987	293 930	49 300	10 091	–	636	396	21 655	397 995
Other Common Market[b]	62 910	640 112	72 102	73 211	44 013	45 126	30 576	35 918	1 004 268
Other Western Europe	9 369	27 568	10 573	23 521	7 357	1 648	75	7 897	88 008
Eastern Europe	25	6 741	6 045	23 405	–	–	490 378	2 567	529 161
Middle East	308	29 325	12	20 913	–	211	7 617	9 443	67 829
Other Africa	1 324	107 178	1 215	124 517	3 480	6 159	–	2 517	246 390
Japan	138 162	792 407	603 843	1 676	871 731	239 267	556 207	699 423	3 902 716
China, People's Republic of	92	159 216	85 530	24 182	1 302	59 718	931 815	4 148	1 266 003
South Korea	63	34 874	58 529	33 359	154 740	51 231	23 554	67 492	423 842
India	–	12 295	250	27 661	–	49 071	25 506	32 533	147 316
Other Asia	2 481	111 328	148 075	44 751	62 327	121 704	110 154	120 930	721 750
Australia	12 792	94 162	2 020	43 848	–	30 350	1 768	38 565	223 505
New Zealand	4 541	7 816	2 743	16 270	–	6 703	21	13 169	51 263
Other Oceania	46	1 078	–	–	–	24	–	3 610	4 758
South America	8	31 808	7 922	88 493	41 563	48 035	2 265	12 227	232 421
Central America and Antilles	1 072	32 598	2 903	11 106	–	11 932	54 433	21 380	135 424
Greenland	–	–	–	–	–	–	–	14	14
St. Pierre	–	–	–	–	–	–	–	–	–
United States	46 974	1 787 680	265 222	25 202	2 385 047	215 950	10 972	1 511 523	6 248 570
Total	302 154	4 170 416	1 316 284	592 208	3 571 558	887 768	2 245 739	2 605 011	15 691 233
Estimated British Columbia Content (percentage)	100.0	100.0	81.0	26.0	95.0	15.0	0.4	61.0	71.0

[a]Includes crude wood, fabricated wood, wood pulp, paper and paperboard.
[b]Common Market = United Kingdom, Ireland, Denmark, Belgium-Luxembourg, France, West Germany, Italy, the Netherlands, and Greece.
Sources: British Columbia, Ministry of Industry and Small Business Development, *British Columbia Exports* (Victoria, 1985), p. 5-8.

encourage resource extraction and to extend the processing base. However, many of the projects were not completed or became too expensive.[11]

CORPORATE ENTERPRISE AND THE CONSOLIDATION OF METROPOLIS AND HINTERLAND

The structure and strategies of Canadian and foreign corporations operating in British Columbia's forest, mining, and fishing sectors illustrate many of the mechanisms at the basis of the metropolis-hinterland process. These mechanisms have shaped and consolidated both British Columbia's role in the world-economy and its internal patterns of core and periphery.

The Forest Sector

The Tahsis Company, which operates a pulp mill at Gold River on Vancouver Island, exemplifies one form of external control. A long-established and family-run firm, Tahsis was jointly purchased in the late 1960s by the East Asiatic Company of Denmark and the International Paper Company of Montréal which, in turn, was wholly owned by the International Paper Company of New York. The structure of indigenous management was quickly dismantled and replaced by a regional management team, based in Vancouver, which was responsible to a board of directors headquartered outside the province. In 1981, Canadian Pacific Enterprises of Montréal gained control of Tahsis. These shifts away from regional control over industries reinforce British Columbia's hinterland function in the world-economy.

However, concentration, amalgamation, and takeover in the forest sector have also been practiced by some regional companies, creating ambivalence in Vancouver's role as regional metropolis and world intermediary. MacMillan Bloedel, the leading Canadian producer of lumber and newsprint, the second largest manufacturer of plywood, and an important processor of kraft pulp and other wood products, is the most important example of this process.[12] Now a multinational corporation operating in the United States, Europe, and East Asia, MacMillan Bloedel originated in three long-established and family-run businesses: the MacMillan Export Company, incorporated in 1919 as a lumber trading concern; Bloedel, Stewart and Welch, founded in 1911 as a logging company; and the Powell River Company, incorporated in 1910 to manufacture newsprint. The first two companies merged in 1951 to form MacMillan Bloedel, which then merged with the Powell River Company in 1959, creating the MacMillan, Bloedel and Powell River Company, subsequently changed to MacMillan Bloedel in 1965. Although each company had achieved limited vertical integration before the mergers,

TABLE 10.2 NEW AND PROPOSED BRITISH COLUMBIA MEGA-PROJECTS DEVELOPED TO SUPPLY THE PACIFIC RIM

Project	*Phase*[a]	*Participants*	*Description*
Northeast Coal	5	Quintette Coal (owned 50% by Denison, 12.5% by Mitsui 10.5% by Tokyo Boeki, 5% by Sumitomo Shoji, 10% by Japanese steel mills, 12% by Charbonnages de France)	Metallurgical coal mine near Chetwynd producing about 6.3 mill. tonnes/year when in full production for sale to Japan
		Teck Bullmoose (owned 51% by Teck, 39% by Lornex, 10% by Nissho Iwai)	Thermal and metallurgical coal mine near Chetwynd producing about 1.7 mill. tonnes/year when in full production for sale to Japan
Methanol Plant	5	Ocelot Industries	Near Kitimat; selling about one-third of product to Japan
L.N.G. Plant	2	Dome, TransCanada PipeLines, Nova, Nissho Iwai	Planned for 1987 near Prince Rupert; will sell natural gas to 5 Japanese utility companies
Petrochemical Complex	1	Dome, Westcoast Transmission, Canadian Occidental Petroleum, Mitsubishi	Planned plants at Prince George and Prince Rupert
Ferrosilicon Plant	1	Cominco, Mitsui	Planned plant at Kimberly; decision depends on economy
Monkman Coal Project	2	PetroCanada, Canadian Superior Oil, McIntyre Mines, Sumitomo	Metallurgical and thermal coal mine planned near Chetwynd, aiming for Japanese market
Willow Creek Coal Project	3	David Minerals, Ssangyong of South Korea	Planned thermal coal mine near Chetwynd, aiming for South Korean market
Cinnabar	1	Cinnabar Peak Mines	Planned metallurgical coal mine near Chetwynd, aiming for Pacific Rim and European markets

Sage Creek	2	Sage Creek Coal (owned by Rio Algom and Pan Ocean Oil)	Planned thermal coal mine year Fernie, aiming for Pacific Rim market
Elk River	1	Elco Mining (owned by Stelco, Home Oil, and consortium of European steel mills)	Planned metallurgical coal mine near Elkford, aiming for Pacific Rim markets but postponed at present

[a]Phase 1 = Preliminary project proposal.
Phase 2 = Preliminary project design.
Phase 3 = Project design.
Phase 4 = Final engineering and construction.
Phase 5 = Operational.
Source: Compiled from J. Maund, *The Implication of the Japanese Procurement Strategy for Staple Resource Regions: An Examination of Coal Mining in Southeastern British Columbia,* M.A. thesis, University of British Columbia, 1984, p. 13.

their joining together created a strong pattern of functional integration and substantial economies of scale which, in turn, provided the necessary capital to achieve multinational status.

The spatial pattern of MacMillan Bloedel's merger scheme reveals much that is characteristic of the coastal forest industry (Fig. 10.5). Processing operations — sawmills, pulp and paper mills, plywood and veneer plants, and other manufacturing units — are concentrated in the Georgia Strait region, and often at one integrated site such as Powell River or Port Alberni. Logging operations take place well away from this industrial core, on northern Vancouver Island, and as distant as the Queen Charlotte Islands. Integrated processing facilities, utilizing virtually all of the raw material inputs, guarantee substantial production economies which, together with improved transportation technologies such as the self-dumping barge, more than compensate for the cost of transporting logs from distant supply areas. Industrial concentration has, in turn, influenced the location of head offices, research facilities, and other service activities, most of which have tended to centre, over time, in Vancouver.

The Mining Sector

The Lornex Mining Company of Vancouver, which operates an open pit copper and molybdenum project in the Highland Valley, located just south of Kamloops, represents another form of corporate structure and strategy — that of interlocking directorships and intermeshed financial arrangements. Production capital was provided to Lornex by Rio Algom Mines and Yukon Consolidated Gold Corporation of Toronto, three Canadian banks, and nine Japanese smelting and trading companies. By 1978, Rio Algom held 66.5 percent of the common shares of Lornex, and

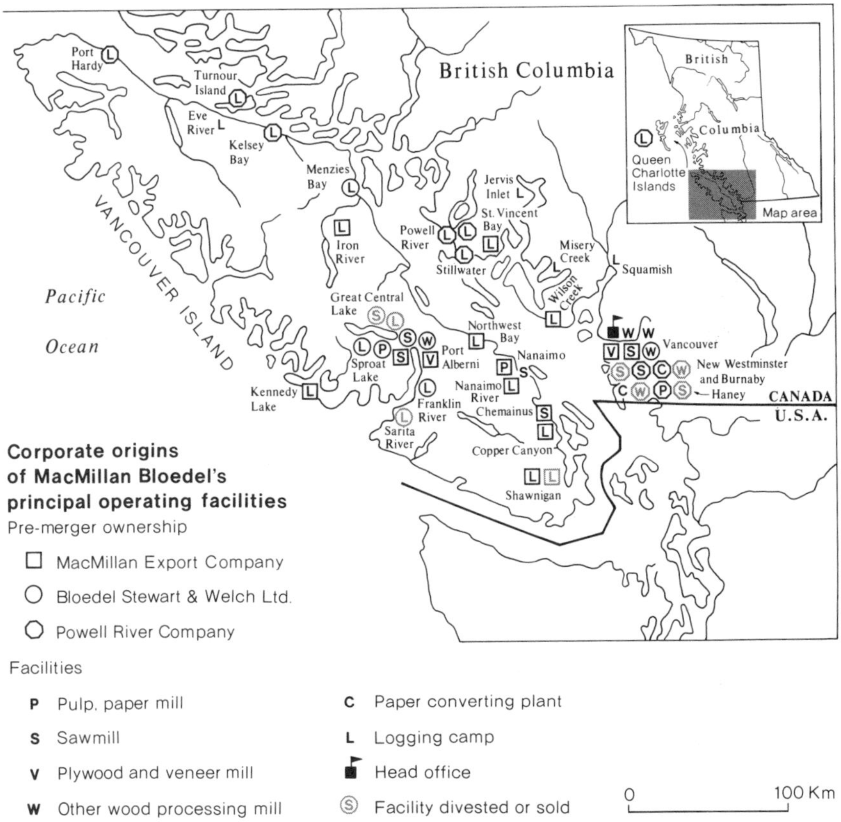

Figure 10.5 Corporate change and spatial integration in the British Columbia forest industry: the case of MacMillan Bloedel. (Adapted from Roger Hayter, "Corporate Strategies and Industrial Change in the Canadian Forest Products Industries," *Geographical Review,* 66 (1976), by permission of the American Geographical Society.)

Yukon Consolidated nearly 21 percent. Under a long-term agreement with the Japanese companies, Rio Algom was required to hold no less than 50 percent of Lornex's common shares, giving it clear control of Lornex. Both Lornex and Rio Algom share similar officers and directors in Toronto and Vancouver, including the company president, secretary, treasurer, and vice-presidents of exploration and marketing, as well as several directors. But the extent of control reaches further afield. Control of Rio Algom, totalling 51 percent, is held by the Rio Tinto-Zinc Corporation of London, England, through its wholly-owned subsidiary, Tinto Holdings of Toronto.[13]

Another example of metropolitan control, whereby raw materials are shipped out of the hinterland for processing elsewhere, is provided by Noranda Mines, a Toronto-based multinational formed in 1922. Through subsidiaries and associated companies, it conducts a fully integrated mining, smelting, refining, marketing, and exploration enterprise. Like so many other mining companies, Noranda expanded the geographic scope of its operations in the euphoria of the 1960s. In 1972, it opened one of its first British Columbia projects, the Bell Mine located just west of Prince George at Fraser Lake, at an estimated cost of $44 million. Copper concentrates from this mine are shipped to Noranda's smelter in Québec for further processing, restricting the diversification of British Columbia's industrial base. However, at the insistence of the NDP government, a smelter was built in 1979 near Kamloops to service Highland Valley copper mines, countering the policies of companies such as Noranda.

The Fishing Sector

The fishery achieved prominence in the late nineteenth century when numerous canneries were established along the coast, focussing on Victoria for supplies, management, and working capital. The number of canneries fluctuated considerably from year to year, but most were located close to the fishing grounds. After 1900, changes in transportation, processing techniques, and ownership patterns revolutionized the industry, and as a consequence, the Vancouver area became the centre of the industry. In particular, reduced transportation costs and the use of refrigeration meant that fish could be moved greater distances without spoilage. Catch areas could therefore be separated from processing facilities, and canneries became more mechanized and capital intensive. Competition among smaller plants and against a few larger units soon forced many firms out of business, reducing the number of companies from about 65 to just 15 by the close of the 1970s. Virtually all were concentrated at the mouths of the major spawning grounds, the Skeena and Fraser Rivers.

B.C. Packers, now controlled by George Weston Limited (83 percent of common shares), a central Canadian industrial and holding company with worldwide linkages to food processing, wholesaling, and retail chains, emerged during this period of change and concentration. The company started in a small way as the B.C. Packers Association, and in 1902 it absorbed a number of competitors to become a leading integrated production unit. In the late 1920s, it took over several other fishing and packing companies, and subsequently, in 1937, it built more processing facilities and acquired the important reduction plants and fishing fleets of Butterfield, Mackie and Company and the Quathiaski Canning Company. During the 1940s, in a move towards further diversification, the company built fish meal and oil plants at Steveston on the Fraser River and at Port Edward on the Skeena River. By the mid-1950s, B.C. Packers had taken on a multinational dimension, operating in the United States and Peru. Later, in the early 1970s, the company became involved in tuna fishing off the Philippines. B.C. Packers is therefore engaged in the catching, processing, and marketing of a wide range of fish and seafood products for both domestic and foreign markets. Its major processing operations are located in British Columbia, but it maintains distribution outlets across North America and engages in fishing in other world areas.

B.C. Packers, however, is not alone in this pattern of development. Canada Packers, another giant of the industry, has followed a similar course of expansion and diversification both in British Columbia and abroad. The inter-industry linkages of the fishery are not widespread. For the most part they are concentrated within the province, chiefly in the Vancouver area, which has important tin can manufacturers, boat repair yards, marketing agencies, and other service facilities. The fact remains, however, that majority control and ownership of the industry lie outside the region.[14]

MANUFACTURING AND TERTIARY SERVICES IN A RESOURCE ECONOMY: DIVERSIFICATION OR SPECIALIZATION?

Vancouver, the Lower Fraser Valley, and the southern tip and eastern coastal fringes of Vancouver Island are major geographical locations for both resource- and consumer-oriented manufacturing. The Lower Mainland region alone accounts for about 50 percent of the total value of provincial manufacturing. Manufacturing industries in the interior are also resource-based, but they are scattered, rather than concentrated. Overall, wood products account for almost one-half of British Columbia's total added value in manufacturing (Fig. 10.6).

The manufacturing sector is therefore characteristic of a hinterland region, for not only is there an emphasis on resource processing and narrow specialization, but dependence on export markets is high. British Columbia ships over 40 percent of its output to foreign purchasers and just 15 percent to domestic markets. Ontario, by comparison, exports about 20 percent of its products abroad, but over one-quarter to other provinces. Wood industries, paper and allied products, and primary metal goods are the most critical elements of British Columbia's international trade in manufactured products. Fully 54 percent of all wood products go to foreign markets. At the national scale, customers in Ontario and Québec purchase some of the province's wood products, textiles, rubber and plastic goods, and transportation equipment and machinery (especially items related to resource extraction, such as lumber transporters

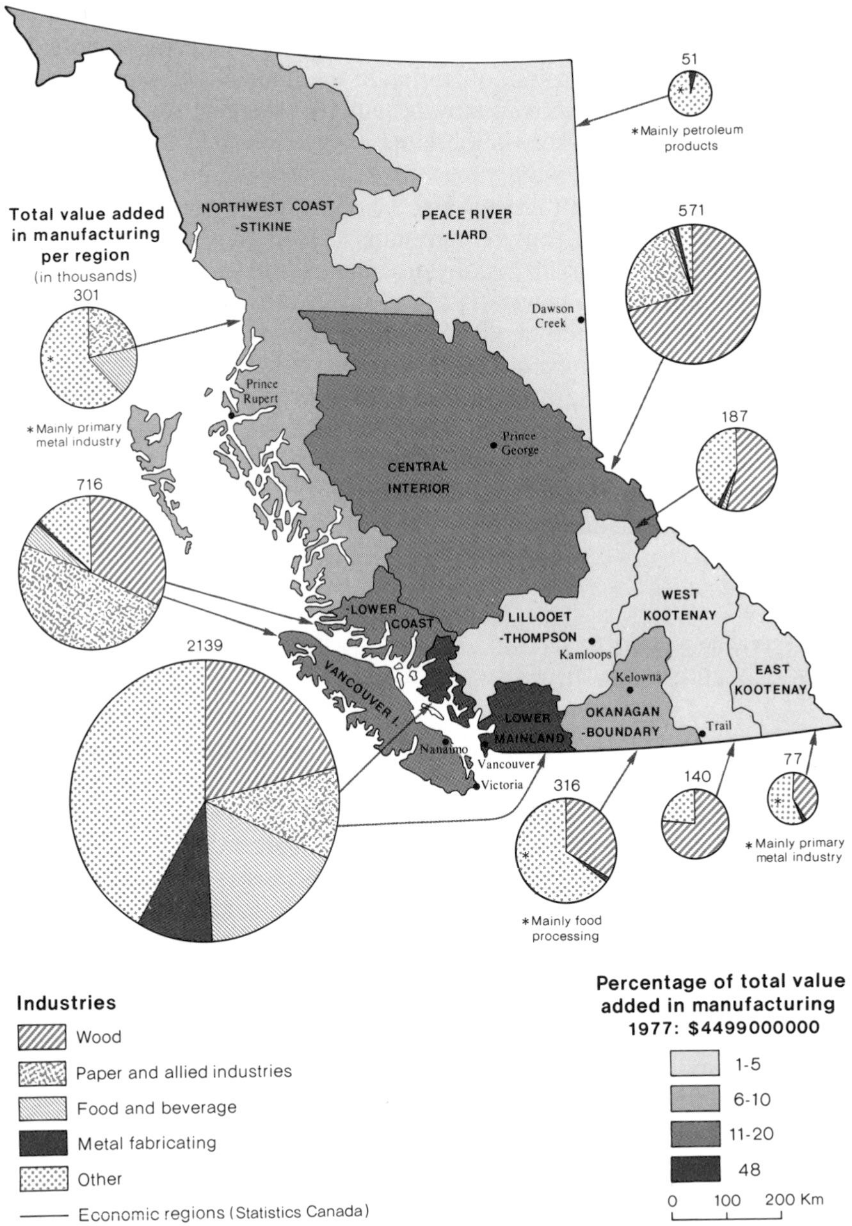

Figure 10.6 The distribution of manufacturing in British Columbia by region and type of industry.

and processing machinery). Alberta and Saskatchewan buy small amounts of electrical products, transport equipment, textiles, plastics, and food and beverages. Atlantic Canada imports little from British Columbia.

What is the explanation for this manufacturing condition which emphasizes resource processing for export abroad? Clearly, economic development in Canada has led to the emergence of certain territories of secondary manufacturing such as Ontario, and other regions of raw material processing. Primary and secondary manufacturing generally only coincide spatially when the profitability of firms can be raised to a level that merits investment in the same region. This coincidence has not occurred in British Columbia. Even in the Vancouver area, the range of manufacturing activities is underdeveloped and deceptively narrow. When compared to cities of similar size throughout North America, Vancouver has not advanced far beyond the primary level of food, wood, and mineral processing, and of component assembly (Fig. 10.6). Indeed, dependence on a supply of materials from throughout the province is pronounced, linking metropolis and hinterland. Manufacturing in Vancouver is therefore closely related to resource extraction, particularly to the forest industry, but also to agriculture and fishing. Vancouver's secondary manufacturing, to the extent it exists, is attracted by the advantages of a sizable local market and transfer economies. When central Canadian or foreign manufacturers of consumer goods contemplate a branch plant in British Columbia, they rarely consider any location other than Vancouver.

Primary and secondary manufacturing, although somewhat arbitrary divisions, are valuable nonetheless for distinguishing the manufacturing types of the provincial hinterland. In the Kootenays, primary forest and metal processing are key sectors of the manufacturing base. There are some local manufacturers who supply a limited trade area and employ a small labour force, but most consumer and producer goods are imported. A similar pattern prevails in the regions focussing on the urban centres of Prince George and Kamloops. Fully two-thirds of central British Columbia's manufacturing labour force, some 15 000 workers, is engaged in sawmilling and pulp and paper production. Elsewhere across the province, the bulk of manufacturing (nearly 90 percent) consists of sawmilling in many small and widely scattered settlements. Secondary manufacturing is limited to dairy products, bakery goods, and repair industries, all of which tend to fluctuate with the boom and bust cycles of the resource extraction sector. The fortunes of these small interior firms are further influenced by stiff competition from some Vancouver companies and by national marketing and supply agencies. In short, the limited markets of hinterland areas make it difficult for industrial diversification and the development of secondary manufacturing catering to regional consumers, even in Vancouver.

Vancouver's continued economic dominance is now supported by the growing importance of tertiary activities, for it is the centre of trade, transportation, banking, and corporate administration, even of some provincial and federal government activities. But in these spheres as well, specialized orientation to resource development, rather than diversification, is the characteristic pattern.[15] Banking has been of particular importance. Strong linkages exist between financial institutions, including the regional Bank of British Columbia, and hinterland companies. These institutions lend capital to manufacturing firms, logging companies, and mining concerns, as well as to suppliers of goods and services in the resource sector. For larger transactions, especially those related to multinational companies in mining and forest exploitation, linkages with central Canadian banks and foreign institutions are more pronounced. In these cases, Vancouver serves an intermediary or comprador function between the external core areas and the British Columbia hinterland. Not only does Vancouver lend or distribute capital, but it also generates working capital through the actions of the Vancouver Stock Exchange, particularly in mining promotions. Vancouver has also grown as a management centre. Corporations in the metropolis advance Vancouver's sphere of influence in the tertiary and quaternary sectors by increasingly making decisions of national and international importance.

PEOPLE AND PLACES IN A RESOURCE HINTERLAND

The population of British Columbia is largely urban — 80 percent of the people live in cities and nearly 50 percent of the province's 2.5 million people live in metropolitan Vancouver. As a counterpoint, both functionally and demographically, nearly one-third of British Columbia's non-metropolitan population reside in single-enterprise communities. The post-industrial era of tertiary growth is little felt in the hinterland of the province where staple industries are still the basic enterprise. In fact, British Columbia, with at least 100 single-enterprise communities representing about 50 percent of its non-metropolitan places, has the highest ratio of single industry towns to total settlements of any Canadian province. Most are based on lumbering, pulp and paper, or mining activities, and although many have come and gone, a considerable number have survived. The case of Trail, incorporated in 1907 and dependent on the Cominco smelter operation, is but one example. Others are associated with pulp and paper production — Port Alice on Vancouver Island and Powell River located northwest of Vancouver, both built before World War I.

Between 1962 and 1972, six "instant towns" including Logan Lake, Granisle, and Gold River were planned and developed by resource companies during a global commodities boom.[16] Each community was carefully laid out to provide modern housing, retail facilities, recreation

The "Company Province": The top photograph illustrates company housing at Cumberland, a coal mining community on Vancouver Island, c. 1889; the bottom photograph shows Kitimat, a comprehensively planned resource town, built by Alcan in the mid-1950s. British Columbia has the highest ratio of single enterprise towns to total settlements of any Canadian province. (*Top: Provincial Archives of British Columbia; Bottom: Aluminum Company of Canada*)

areas, and other "metropolitan" amenities. Families were attracted by promises of well-paying jobs, which also enticed many single people, mostly young men. These instant towns were given municipal status, along with a local government and elections. In this way, resource companies achieved a long-term goal by transferring the costs of running and organizing these townsites to the communities themselves and to the provincial government. Although it is true that planning has improved the physical appearance and livability of these resource towns, little can be done to alleviate their physical isolation and social and economic dependence on a single enterprise.

In the resource towns of the province, life is oriented to mine and mill. As well as the seasonal turnover in employment, there is a peculiar vitality in the daily pattern of shift work. Despite the attempts in the 1960s to create independent settlements rather than company towns, the resource town as company town is still in evidence. Not only is there a singular dependence on the resource company operating in the community, but there is a shared consciousness that economic and social affairs are manipulated by managers and decision-makers in distant metropolitan centres.[17] Fluctuations in world prices for major resource commodities such as forest products, copper, coal, molybdenum, or asbestos are felt directly in these hinterland communities. Today's boom in production and corresponding high wages can readily become tomorrow's economic downswing, with low profitability, layoffs, and unemployment. Resource town dwellers are conscious of these industrial swings and have organized to achieve security. Continuing a long-standing tradition in British Columbia, union membership is generally high and an intense working-class consciousness is extant. But even in some union organizations, the metropolis-hinterland structure is evident because decisions affecting local people are frequently made elsewhere, perhaps by a foreign representative of an international union.

Along the mainland coast, between Vancouver and Prince Rupert, the economy is also based on staples. Where loggers once lived in temporary floating camps and felled trees directly into the water to be floated to sawmills, today personnel are often flown in daily to work the high steel booms, now located further inland, which gather the fallen trees to be placed on giant trucks for the journey to tidewater dumping grounds.

Coastal forests also shelter the secrets of earlier Native occupation. Brush and forest cover much of the material evidence of a rich culture of Haida, Tsimshian, and other Native groups. Once dependent on the salmon, the cedar tree, and the sea, these people now live on reserves or in small coastal communities; or if they have fled the region, they often live in the slums of cities where they ply the trades (or draw on the unemployment payments) of a competitive society. The coastal region also hosts specialized fishing communities, most small and isolated, many abandoned or clinging to reduced activity — the result of industrial concentration at the mouths of the Skeena and Fraser Rivers. But there are also larger communities. Prince Rupert is the port city for northwestern British Columbia with rail linkages to the Western Interior. Fishermen work out of Prince Rupert, along with vessels carrying wheat, lumber, and mineral products. Nearby is Kitimat, the "instant town" constructed for Alcan, a Canadian-based aluminum smelting company. Originally conceived to support a population of about 50 000, it houses only some 12 000. It is a suburban presence in the north, created by southern town planners for a modern industrial workforce.

Interior settlements also owe much of their vitality to a resource-based economy. Towns in the Okanagan Valley, including Vernon, Kelowna, and Penticton, service fruit farming, ranching, forest, and tourist operations. In the long and narrow valleys which fragment southeastern British Columbia, many places are, or were, associated with mining that dates back to the late nineteenth century. These centres collectively support many thousands of people, but they tend to be relatively isolated, situated in areas usually devoid of agricultural settlement. Further north, in the corridor connecting Prince George to coastal Prince Rupert, towns are associated with agriculture, lumber, mining, or tourism. In the Peace River country to the northeast, the four largest places (Fort St. John, Dawson Creek, Hudson's Hope, Chetwynd) are based on agricultural, hydroelectric, or petroleum development. Even on Vancouver Island, town life is supported by the forest industry, fishing, mining, or tourism. The strength of the staple economy is all-pervasive.

In these hinterland areas and resource-tied communities, there are visible signs of the inequities of the metropolis-hinterland process, for there is a common lack of cultural facilities, and social and economic opportunities are limited. The economy of the hinterland is truncated, displaying an unbalanced occupational structure when compared with more diversified metropolitan economies. But there are also distinctive differences between farming communities and single-enterprise towns. Daily life on farm and ranch is focussed on tending crops and feeding animals; seasonal life is bound by routines of planting, maintenance, and harvesting. The year is punctuated by rodeos, fairs, and forays to the city. Settlement is dispersed, as in the ranching country of the Cariboo, Chilcotin, and Kamloops districts, and where towns do exist, they house a different social fabric and culture than that of either metropolis or resource town. In these places, jobs require a lower skill level, and unionism and working-class culture are replaced by the particularism of place and conservatism of rural life. High population turnover is commonplace, particularly when jobs become available in resource areas situated a short distance away. Farmers sometimes work part-time in local businesses and industries. These service centres therefore reflect an unease

Ranching near Kamloops in the Interior Plateau region of British Columbia: The American influence is strongly present in the layout of this cattle ranch. (*Larry McCann*)

of occupational pluralism, as people move from one area to the next, or from one occupation to another.

As part of their metropolitan function, Victoria and Vancouver provide jobs for people in public administration, commerce, transportation, manufacturing, finance, culture, and tourism. The class structure of the two places is therefore different from that of the service centre or resource town. The people have a wider range of incomes and there are more obvious signs of affluence, cultural activity, and class differentiation; the material aspects of life are more pronounced than elsewhere. The inner city houses people who are far below the poverty line, as well as those who are far above. The pace of life is quicker and opportunities are more varied. Vancouver, in particular, hosts numerous foreign and interprovincial migrants, and is cosmopolitan in character. Cultural aspects are therefore varied, including both indigenous and imported entertainment. From the major centres of the world come visiting orchestras, entertainers,

The emergence of Canada's West Coast metropolis: Towering high-rise apartments and office buildings have replaced houses and businesses in downtown Vancouver. Combining functions of transportation, distribution, manufacturing, and finance, Vancouver is the core of the provincial space economy, and a metropolitan centre of international importance. (*Top: No. 2999, Vancouver Public Library; Bottom: Greater Vancouver Convention and Visitors Bureau*)

and sporting events. However, there is also a strong current of local talent and initiative in sports, crafts, art, and music. The region that was host to the painter and writer Emily Carr is now home to a modern group of artists. Vancouver has developed a major symphony orchestra.

Throughout its history, British Columbia has attracted migrants, especially people looking for work in Vancouver or in the primary resource industries. For many years the province received more migrants from eastern Canada than any other western province, but in the late 1970s Alberta became the major focus of migration. In fact, out-migration data indicate that in 1980-81, 3813 people moved from British Columbia to Alberta, and 2023 to central Canada. Nevertheless, migration into the province exceeds the outward flow. Foreign immigrants gather chiefly in Vancouver, where they contributed as much as 45 percent of the annual population increase in the late 1960s and in the 1970s. Despite recent surges of people from western and southern Europe, the ethnic composition of the province still reflects a long-standing British emphasis, and this emphasis has influenced the cultural values and landscape of the region.[18] The proportion of French people in the province is small. Historically, there has been little migration of people from Québec, though the community of Maillardville, established prior to World War I in suburban Vancouver, is an exception.

The ethnic profile of the rest of the province reflects a variety of immigrant backgrounds. Many people came from Europe in this century to establish model farms and communities. German immigrants went to the Peace River country to homestead. Italians settled in the mining towns of the Kootenays. Doukhobors grouped communally near Grand Forks after leaving Saskatchewan in 1910 to maintain their religious beliefs. In the 1950s, Dutch farmers took up marginal land in the lower Fraser Valley where they revitalized the dairy industry and built essential dikes. Thirty years before, Mennonites had also moved to the rich agricultural lands of the Yarrow area, east of Vancouver, but later moved to Clearbrook, further afield. Earlier still, in the 1880s, the Japanese had migrated to coastal lumber mills and later stayed to help establish Steveston, a fishing and canning community at the mouth of the Fraser River. Chinese and Sikhs were also early members of the labour force supporting the province's staple economy. The Chinese generally worked on the railroads; the Sikhs found employment in sawmills.

Many of these ethnic groups have retained some of their original identity through such means as voluntary associations, language, and religious practices. But because these groups are relatively small, the general tendency has been toward assimilation. The province and its people have been drawn into the industrial process of resource extraction and associated activities. There has been little time, opportunity, and perhaps, willingness either to embrace or to encourage ethnic and cultural diversity. The melting pot of the frontier — of the mine, the mill, and the sea — is more characteristic than the cultural mosaic.

CONCLUSION

British Columbia is a hinterland region within North America and the broader world-economy, though it has become prosperous through the diversity and value of resource extraction. It would be misleading, however, to claim that the entire province is wealthy — resources are spread unevenly across the landscape and returns from the staple economy are not distributed equally among all social classes. Thus the core-periphery system has a varied effect on the region. Within the province, it tends to undermine local economies and to sustain or create uneven economic and space development, despite the overall appearance of well-being. The general level of affluence is almost as high as Ontario, but although British Columbia is a high-wage region, with above average personal income and high net in-migration, it is also plagued by above average unemployment. Moreover, resource industries are constantly subject to the vagaries of business cycles. The interior regions of the province, those most specialized in resource extraction, are affected most by cyclical growth and decline. In the late 1970s, for example, unemployment throughout the interior was 30 percent higher than in the rest of the province, and over 40 percent higher than in Vancouver. The provincial average was frequently above the Canadian average.

What is the future of staples production in the development of British Columbia? As we have seen, the provincial economy is based largely on resources — some renewable, some not. Little diversification has taken place. How these resources are used and owned is vitally important for the well-being and employment of British Columbians. Staples such as coal and gold have been exhausted and in some cases, markets have turned to alternative sources. These situations could occur again despite the commitment of both government and industry to promote sustained and well-managed resource development. Moreover, capital can readily shift to alternative, more profitable sites, even though current investment in British Columbia appears secure. Brazil, for instance, has cheap and plentiful supplies of lumber that could infringe on British Columbia's share of the market. Similarly, there are alternative sources of coal, copper, and other minerals. And as the record of the late 1970s and early 1980s shows, British Columbia's staples economy is still susceptible to downswings and to recessions with little opportunity for diversification. Primary, secondary, and tertiary industries suffered during this period, experiencing high levels of unemployment, production declines, and losses of income. Indeed, the period demonstrated the problems of a resource dependent economy, particularly as external linkages weaken, deficits increase, and unemployment unrest rises (Table 10.3).

Since Confederation, British Columbia has grown as a metropolis and hinterland in microcosm. It has developed the character of a "company province," pioneered not by farmers, but by mine and mill workers and, most especially, by industrial capital and large corporations. The isolation

TABLE 10.3 SELECTED INDICATORS OF ECONOMIC GROWTH IN BRITISH COLUMBIA, 1970-83

Year	*Population (000s)*	*Forest Products*	*Employment in Selected Sectors (000s)*			*Value of Exports Produced in British Columbia[c] ($ millions)*	*Average Personal Income*	*Unemployment Rate (%)*
			Mining	*Secondary[a]*	*Tertiary[b]*			
1970	2 128	20.6	11.7	159.8	351.3	2 032	$3 045	7.7
1971	2 185	22.3	12.0	171.5	359.6	2 192	3 745	7.2
1972	2 241	18.6	12.8	180.8	383.6	2 759	4 201	7.8
1973	2 302	22.9	14.1	197.5	411.6	3 821	4 921	6.7
1974	2 376	22.1	13.9	200.6	439.7	4 177	5 761	6.2
1975	2 433	18.7	13.9	195.4	466.1	3 872	6 489	8.5
1976	2 467	21.7	13.2	199.0	469.2	5 270	7 372	8.6
1977	2 494	23.0	14.1	205.5	492.4	6 307	8 128	8.5
1978	2 530	23.2	14.3	203.9	514.3	7 558	8 861	8.3
1979	2 570	24.7	15.0	219.8	534.5	9 413	9 821	7.7
1980	2 666	25.2	16.9	224.7	569.0	9 653	11 133	6.9
1981	2 744	19.9	18.3	226.7	598.1	9 152	12 835	6.7
1982	2 790	17.4	16.2	195.6	579.0	8 755	13 811	12.1
1983	2 823	20.2	13.1	180.0	564.6	n.a.	n.a.	13.8

[a]Manufacturing and construction.

[b]Trade, services, and public administration and defence.

[c]Estimated value of exports of British Columbia products shipped through all Canadian customs ports.

Source: British Columbia, Ministry of Industry and Small Business Development, *British Columbia Economic Activity: 1980 Review and Outlook,* Vol. 32-34 (Victoria: February 1981; 1982), Tables 1, 4, 5, 6, and 31; British Columbia, Ministry of Small Business Development: *British Columbia Industry Review: 1983,* Vol. 1 (Victoria: 1983), Tables 2, 3, 8, 30, 32.

of the province from the rest of Canada has decreased dramatically over the past one hundred years, just as the isolation of the interior of the province from Vancouver has decreased, though integration is not complete. Vancouver dominates the regional economy, but, to a degree, is subject to the calls of external decision-making centres. The structure of metropolis and hinterland is well established both within the province and in the region's relationship to the world-economy.

NOTES

1. W.A. Carrothers, "Forest Industries of British Columbia," in *The North American Assault on the Canadian Forest,* ed. A.R.M. Lower (Toronto: Macmillan, 1938), p. 271.
2. For a useful overview of regional economic development, see Robert A.J. McDonald, "Victoria, Vancouver and the Evolution of British Columbia's Economic System, 1886-1914," in *Town and City: Aspects of Western Canadian Urban Development,* ed. Alan F.J. Artibise (Regina: Canadian Plains Resource Centre, 1981), pp. 31-55.
3. Martin Robin, *Pillars of Profit: The Company Province, 1934-1972* (Toronto: McClelland and Stewart, 1973).
4. G.R. Parkin, *The Great Dominion: Studies of Canada* (Oxford: 1895), p. 162.
5. Ronald A. Shearer, "The Economy of British Columbia," in *Trade Liberalization and a Regional Economy,* eds. Ronald A. Shearer *et al.* (Toronto: University of Toronto Press, 1968), pp. 3-42.
6. J. Lewis Robinson and Walter G. Hardwick, *British Columbia: One Hundred Years of Geographical Change* (Vancouver: Talonbooks, 1973).
7. L.D. McCann, "Urban Growth in a Staple Economy: The Emergence of Vancouver as a Regional Metropolis, 1886-1914," in *Vancouver: Western Metropolis,* ed. L.J. Evenden, Western Geographical Series, Vol. 16 (Victoria: Department of Geography, University of Victoria, 1978), pp. 17-41.
8. Neil A. Swainson, *Conflict Over The Columbia* (Montréal: McGill-Queen's University Press, 1979).
9. L.W. Copithorne, *Natural Resources and Regional Disparities* (Ottawa: Economic Council of Canada, 1979), p. 57.
10. Roger Hayter, "Forestry in British Columbia: A Resource Basis of Vancouver's Dominance," in *Vancouver: Western Metropolis,* pp. 95-115. See also A.L. Farley, "The Forest Resource," in *British Columbia,* ed. J. Lewis Robinson, Studies in Canadian Geography (Toronto: University of Toronto Press, 1972), pp. 87-118; and Walter G. Hardwick, *Geography of the Forest Industry of Coastal British Columbia,* Occasional Papers in Geography No. 5 (Vancouver: Tantalus, 1963).
11. For comments on recent resource and other developments see: T.I. Gunton, *Resources, Regional Development and Provincial Policy: A Case Study of British Columbia,* (Ottawa: Canadian Centre for Policy Alternatives, 1982); J.K. Maund, "The Implications of the Japanese Resource Procurement Strategy for Staple Resource Regions: An examination of Coal Mining in Southeastern B.C.", M.A. Thesis, The University of British Columbia, 1984.
12. The following analysis is drawn from Roger Hayter, "Corporate Strategies and Industrial Change in the Canadian Forest Products Industries," *The Geographical Review,* 66 (1976), pp. 209-28.
13. Information on Lornex Mines has been drawn from the service files of *The Financial Post.*
14. Information on B.C. Packers has also been drawn from the service files of *The Financial Post.*

15. E.M. Gibson, *The Urbanization of the Georgia Strait Region,* Geographical Paper No. 57 (Ottawa: Environment Canada, 1976).
16. John Bradbury, "Instant Resource Towns Policy in British Columbia, 1965-1972," *Plan Canada,* 20 (1980), pp. 19-38.
17. *Idem,* "Class Structures and Class Conflicts in 'Instant' Resource Towns in British Columbia, 1965-1972," *B.C. Studies,* No. 37 (Spring, 1978), pp. 3-18.
18. Alfred H. Siemens, "Settlement", in *British Columbia,* ed. J. Lewis Robinson (Toronto: University of Toronto Press, 1978), pp. 9-31.

11

The Canadian Shield: The Development of a Resource Frontier

Iain Wallace

The Canadian Shield, unlike other hinterland regions identified in this book, is delineated by boundaries which are physical rather than political. The significance of this fact in an era which has seen substantial growth in the power and influence of the state (primarily, in the domestic Canadian context, of provincial governments) is that the Shield lacks the institutional structures through which its inhabitants' common regional interests can be focussed and pursued. The region is fragmented among five provinces (six, if a small area in northeastern Alberta is included) and this definition excludes the extension of the Shield into the Northwest Territories. These politically separate "provincial norths" constitute relatively sparsely populated frontier hinterlands with limited influence in their respective legislatures.

The same lack of influence characterizes the Shield at the national level. Despite occupying over 40 percent of Canada's territory, it is the home of only 8 percent of the population and of only 1 percent of the country's 500 largest corporations.[1] To a considerable extent, the region is spatially and functionally peripheral to the urban, industrial economy of heartland Canada, which in turn has the capacity to utilize only a limited proportion of the Shield's resources. At the international level, the vulnerability of the region to fluctuations in external markets is the most apparent characteristic of its hinterland status. Despite the Shield's relatively rich and varied endowment of natural resources, its attractiveness as a source of these products has been eroded in recent years. New sources of supply, many in Third World nations, have been developed and offer strong competition in world markets. The changing structure of the global economy (its declining resource-orientation) and the weakened competitive position of the United States (notably in steel production) have reduced the stimulus to resource exploitation in the Shield. On all three levels — regional, national, and international — heartland-hinterland relationships result in economic activity that is invariably initiated and controlled by groups external to the region.

The Canadian Shield effectively covers the bulk of Ontario and Québec, Labrador, and the northern portions of Manitoba and Saskatchewan. Its rugged terrain has always been viewed as a barrier, rather than as a link, in a country uniting people "from sea to sea." Nevertheless, the Shield has contributed significantly to the evolution of a distinctive Canadian consciousness and historiography. Its landscape is central to much of the painting of the Group of Seven.[2] Historically, the myth of Canada as "the true North, strong and free" was given an objective basis in the environmental conditions of the post-Confederation northern frontier. Initially, emphasis was placed on the severity of winters in the Shield and the qualities of rugged self-reliance engendered in those who made the region their home.

With the development of an industrial economy, the principal theme became the apparent inexhaustibility of the Shield's resources, which would assure Canadians of a prosperous future. As recently as 1958, John Diefenbaker's vision that Canada's destiny lay in embracing the challenges and reaping the rewards of harnessing its northlands found popular acceptance. Academic interpretations of the history and economic growth of Canada have given comparable weight to the influence of the Shield. Donald Creighton and other historians of the "Laurentian School" have explained the evolution of the nation in terms of the strategic importance of the St. Lawrence waterway and the resources, notably the furs and forests of the Shield, to which it gave access. Harold Innis recognized that one of the crucial characteristics of Canada's staple export economy was that it depended upon and entrenched a relationship of metropolitan dominance over hinterlands such as the Shield.

THE PHYSICAL ENVIRONMENT

The Shield therefore has played a major role in shaping our national consciousness and in dictating patterns of resource development. Canadians, of necessity, have been forced to deal imaginatively with both the potential and limitations imposed by this unique physical environment, not least in building liveable resource communities for a highly transient population.

As Canada's largest physiographic region, the Shield covers an area of some 4.6 million square kilometres. Its geological structure and glaciation record are major distinguishing traits (Fig. 11.1). It is a mosaic of geological provinces in which Precambrian rocks (many over 2.5 billion years old) are most common. Over three-quarters of the surface is made of granite gneiss: "the sameness of Shield scenery over vast areas must be explained by this constancy of rock type."[3] The presence of greenstone belts (metamorphic basic volcanics) within the southern Shield, containing the region's principal gold and base-metal deposits, determines the location of mining settlements.

The landscape of the Shield may be described as a generally rolling, lake-dotted upland with elevations averaging about 650 metres above sea level. The bare rock, thin soils, and muskeg are telling signs of the widespread imprint of glaciation (Fig. 11.1). The southern portions of the Shield felt this imprint less than 10 000 years ago; the remainder about 13 000 years ago. Soils are predominantly of low fertility. Shallow, permeable soils, developed on coarse material exposed by the Pleistocene ice sheets, are widespread and are better suited to forestry than crop cultivation. Where post-glacial lakes resulted in the deposition of sedimentary material, most notably in the so-called Clay Belts of Ontario and Québec and in the Lac St. Jean Lowland, acidity and poor soil drainage have impeded the expansion and productivity of farming. In these farming areas, a short frost-free season and the modest accumulation of heat units restrict agricultural land use to pasture and fodder crops. These inhospitable environmental conditions, which do much to discourage permanent agricultural settlement, at the same time account for the importance Native people attach to their land-extensive subsistence economy. Having survived by living off the limited resources of the natural environment, they logically oppose developments that would imperil its fragile ecological balance.

Although the homogeneity of the major forest belts (especially the boreal forest as illustrated in Fig. 11.2), the frequency of lakes, and the widespread occurrence of rocky outcrops suggest environmental uniformity, there are regional variations. The faulted escarpment of the Shield which overlooks the valleys of the lower Ottawa and St. Lawrence Rivers, for example, provides a distinct visual contrast to the gently-sloping sedimentary lowlands and thinning tree cover extending towards Hudson Bay in northern Ontario and Manitoba. The barren upland plateau of Québec-Labrador is also different from the agricultural landscape of the Lac St. Jean Lowlands.

Such features of the physical environment have shaped a discontinuous pattern of settlement. Native people occupy small villages or reserves but often roam over huge territories to fish and hunt. Most residents of the Shield live in larger but isolated settlements based upon resource extraction — mining, pulp and paper, and hydro. These single-enterprise communities are usually found along rail lines where small whistle-stops house the railroad workers who maintain the cross-Canada lines of the C.P.R. and C.N.R.

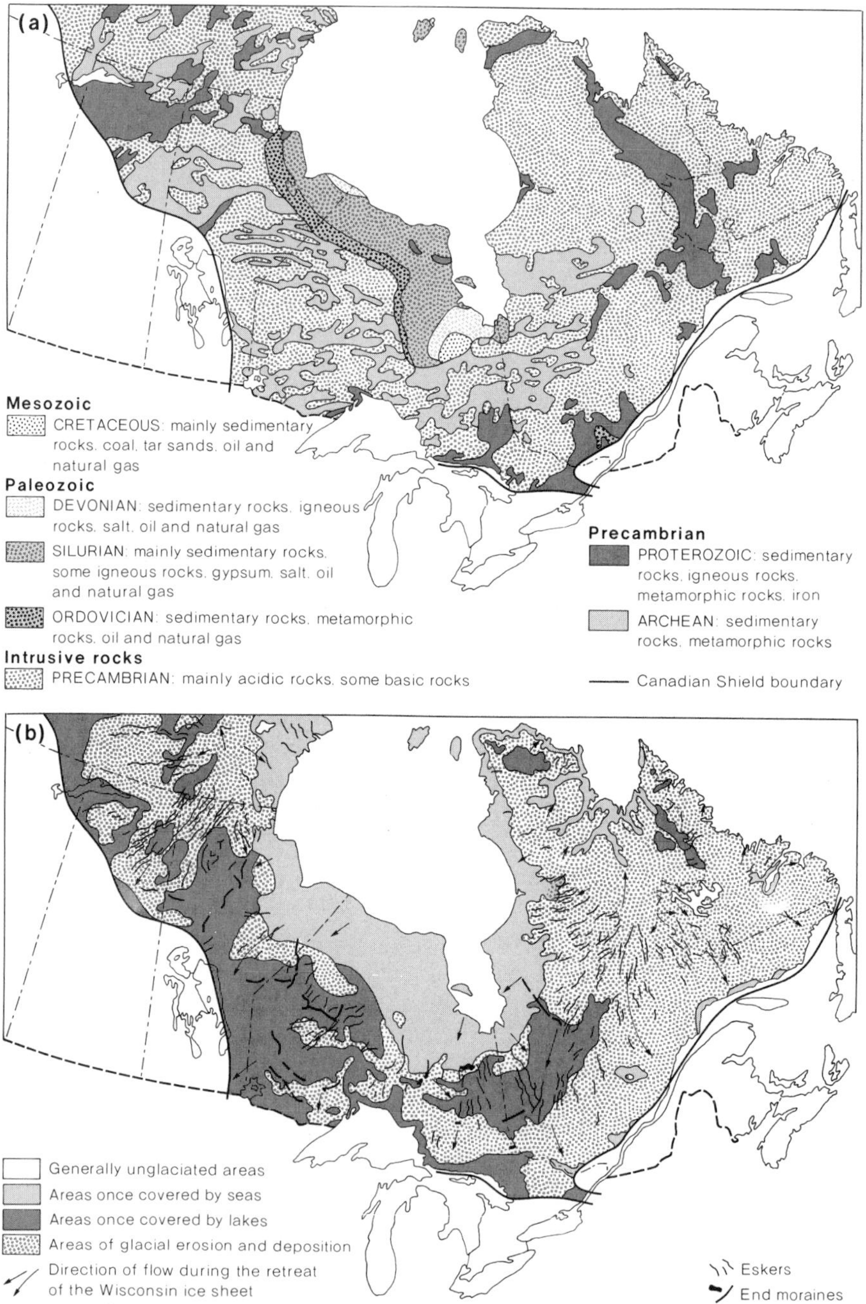

Figure 11.1 The physical geography of the Canadian Shield.

More specifically, the distribution of population within the Shield can be characterized by three components. The first is the widespread encroachment of settlement at points along the Shield's southern boundary from more productive agricultural areas in the St. Lawrence Lowlands. Here, farming communities occupied the land in the wake of the advancing commercial lumbering frontier as it progressed westward during the nineteenth century. The Ottawa Valley was the principal axis of this movement. Similarly, the Lac St. Jean Lowlands were opened up by colonists from the St. Lawrence Valley, although here, in a more subsistence-oriented economy, the chronological distinction between the movement of the lumbering frontier and the subsequent advance of agriculture was less clear cut.

The second component of the Shield's population distribution consists of the ribbon-like settlements which followed the construction of transcontinental railways during the years 1880-1915. The crowded sequence of station names that appears on the railway map across northern Ontario and along the Québec section of the former National Transcontinental Railway belies the sparsity of residents along these corridors. On the other hand, Sudbury, Thunder Bay, and a number of smaller, resource-industry towns came into being or acquired their modern significance as a result of this phase of development.

The third component includes the most recent additions to the ecumene and is distinguished from the other two by conception rather than spatial pattern. In the second phase of development, the transcontinental railways stimulated settlement and resource developments within the Shield quite incidentally to their primary purpose of linking east and west. In the third phase, however, the building of the Temiskaming and Northern Ontario Railway (now the Ontario Northland), the subsequent settling of an agricultural population in the Clay Belts, and the construction of numerous rail lines and mineral-based resource towns in the 1950s and 1960s, from Lynn Lake in the west to Schefferville in the east, were all enterprises undertaken specifically to tap the Shield's resource potential. Regardless of its conception, however, settlement is discontinuous and thinly scattered across the Shield.

The result of this sequence of settlement is a vast region, inhabited by some two million people, but lacking either a political or a geographical focus. The population is predominantly urbanized, but many of the smaller single-industry towns offer a limited range of social and occupational opportunities. The three sub-regional capitals — Thunder Bay, Sudbury, and Chicoutimi-Jonquière — have stronger links to larger metropolitan centres external to the Shield than they have to each other. The mining and forest-based industries which dominate the region's economy are almost entirely in the hands of firms controlled from Toronto, Montréal, or the United States. Provincial governments, whose policies have had, and still do have, a major influence on the region's inhabitants, are situated in a physical and cultural environment far removed from that experienced by many residents of the Shield.

The 1970s and 1980s have witnessed limited steps towards granting more influence over the future course of development in the Shield to those who live there, but the region still remains a hinterland of five provinces, Canada, and the capitalist world-economy. External demands and external perceptions shape its human geography. The frustrations and alienation which arise in this dependent and fragmented hinterland region are not, in themselves, sufficient to establish a common regional identity or a coherent voice in the broader political arena. Hence, this chapter focusses primarily on the resource development undertaken in the Shield by external heartland interests, and considers the impact of this activity on the character of the region's settlements and the life of its inhabitants.

THE FOREST INDUSTRIES

Forest dominates the landscape of the Canadian Shield, and the industries it supports have long been the foremost component of the regional economy. The first period of commercial exploitation extended from the early nineteenth century until World War I and was based on lumber production. The second period began in the early twentieth century and was devoted almost entirely to pulp and paper manufacturing. Insofar as recent developments justify the recognition of a third period, which is essentially a continuation of the second, it is distinguished by an emphasis on the full utilization of available wood supplies through the integration of pulp and paper manufacture with a revival of commercial lumber production. The initial period was characterized spatially by the movement westward of exploitation, as the forest was selectively and wastefully mined, rather than harvested. The second period, in contrast, was based on the establishment of pulp and paper mills at fixed locations, each one fed with timber from within defined catchment areas. Had forest regeneration been pursued more rigorously in these catchments over the past 70 years, there would be less pressure in this most recent period to extend commercial operations northward.

British demand for Canadian lumber grew rapidly at the beginning of the nineteenth century when access to Scandinavian forests was severed by Napoleon's blockade of the Baltic. The cutting of squared timber from virgin stands of pine, which, together with hemlock and birch, make up the mixed forest of the Great Lakes-St. Lawrence region (Fig. 11.2), was encouraged by preferential tariffs and financed by British merchants based in Québec City. Operations in the woods, however, were brought progressively under the control of Canadian entrepreneurs based in Ottawa-Hull, where, as the frontier advanced up the Ottawa Valley, log rafts were assembled for dispatch downstream. Impoverished French-

Canadian and Irish workers constituted the bulk of the labour force and bequeathed to the Ottawa Valley its distinctive ethnic mix.

By the early 1840s, changing external conditions began to reorient the Shield's forest industries to a new market. Britain, no longer cut off from Baltic lumber and interested in free trade, removed its tariff protection for Canadian shipments. As a result, squared timber exports began a prolonged decline. Simultaneously, the rapidly growing industrial economy of the northeastern United States was emerging as a new heartland,

Major forest regions

- Tundra and alpine tundra
- Tundra and boreal forest transition
- Boreal forest
- Great Lakes - St.Lawrence forest
- Acadian forest
- Deciduous forest
- Parkland (boreal and grassland transition)
- Grassland (tallgrass and shortgrass prairie)

Pulp and paper mills

Size

△ □ ○ Small
▲ ▣ ◉ Medium
▲ ■ ● Large

Product

△ ▲ ▲ Newsprint
□ ▣ ■ Pulp
○ ◉ ● Other paper/paperboard

– – – – Canadian Shield boundary

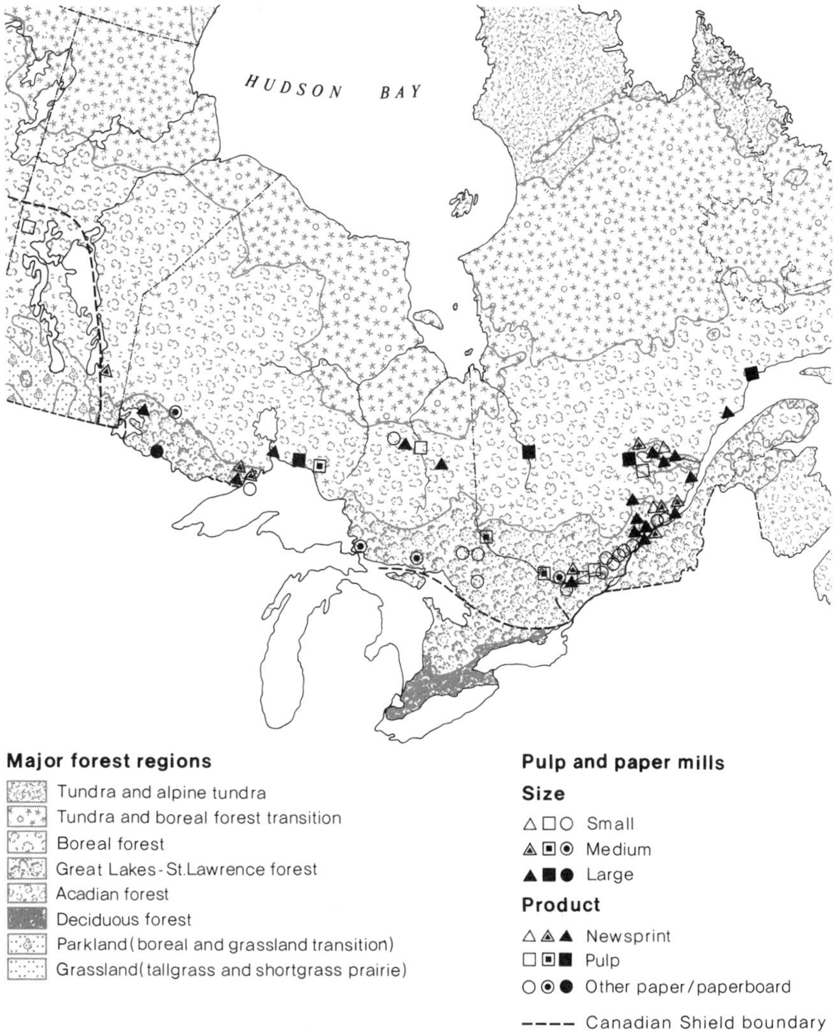

Figure 11.2 The distribution of pulp and paper mills in the Canadian Shield.

whose demand for constructional sawn timber was outstripping its domestic supply. The composition and destination of shipments from the Shield's forests thus gradually switched at the same time as the frontier of exploitation maintained its westerly momentum. From the 1850s, sawmills increased in size and in levels of mechanization, and the largest concentrations emerged at strategic locations such as Ottawa and Parry Sound. By the close of the nineteenth century, the focus of timber production had moved beyond the Ottawa River catchment, through the Georgian Bay region, and on to the North Channel shore of Lake Huron.

This geographical shift was matched by significant changes in the industry's structure. The long-established firms of the Ottawa Valley made little attempt to extend their control over production further west, where newer and smaller firms predominated and competition from United States interests was more direct. Eventually these western firms, particularly vulnerable to adverse developments in trade relations between Canada and the United States, felt constrained to seek government help.

A period of relatively free trade in forest products, beginning in 1890, saw a sudden rise in the export of unprocessed logs from the Ontario shore, towed in rafts across to sawmills in Michigan. This threat to the prosperity of the Ontario mills intensified in 1897, when the United States reimposed duties on Canadian timber, but not on sawlogs. In appealing to the provincial government for support, the mill owners were able to capitalize both on the significance of forest revenues to the Ontario treasury and on growing popular sentiment in favour of strengthening the province's expanding industrial economy. The time was ripe for "Empire Ontario" to curtail the export of unprocessed primary products typical of a resource hinterland, and to increase the amount of domestic manufacturing. An amendment to the Crown Timber Act, "the manufacturing condition," specified that all pine cut on Crown land in Ontario was to be sawn into lumber in Canada. This move, ensuring that the revenues and employment generated by the upgrading of a provincial resource remained within the province, immediately stimulated sawmill construction all along the North Channel and Georgian Bay shores, as well as in the Lake of the Woods area.[4]

The second major phase of forest exploitation was already underway by the turn of the century. Technological advances had established the viability of wood-based paper production and a growing demand for pulpwood soon developed to offset the declining availability of quality sawlogs. Spruce replaced pine as the species attracting most attention in the forest industries, aided by the growing railway network, expanded northwards towards the boreal forest belt. Early pulp and paper mills were concentrated in the Ottawa and St. Lawrence Valleys, close to the metropolitan newspaper markets of the northeastern United States. By 1910 the distribution of mills extended from Sault Ste. Marie to Chicoutimi.

As was the case in the sawn timber trade, the earliest newsprint markets were focussed in New York, to be joined later by those centred in Chicago. Ontario's attempt to enforce "the manufacturing condition" against the export of pulpwood logs was unsuccessful in the absence of parallel legislation in Québec, then the chief source of shipments to American markets. But by 1911, foreseeing an inadequate domestic wood supply, leading newspaper publishers in the United States successfully persuaded their government to permit the duty-free entry of Canadian newsprint. This move immediately resulted in investment by both American and Canadian interests in pulp and paper mills north of the border and laid the foundations for the industry's dramatic growth in the 1920s. By that time, too, the eclipse of the Shield's lumber industry was being accelerated by the growth of West Coast lumber producers.

The geographical distribution of pulp and paper mills has been remarkably stable since the early 1920s, when a brief period of extremely high newsprint prices stimulated massive over-investment in production capacity. Between 1925 and 1930, for example, newsprint consumption increased by one-fifth, but production capacity doubled in response to the momentum of earlier capital commitments. Naturally, this excess capacity brought about a disastrous fall in prices which merged into the broader economic dislocation of the Depression. From a high of $137 in 1921, the price of a ton of newsprint fell to $57 in 1931, and to a low of $40 in 1934. These developments created severe problems for the financially overextended pulp and paper manufacturers; for the Canadian banks whose loans were at risk; for the many single-industry communities whose livelihoods were totally dependent on employment generated by the local mill; and for the provincial governments who faced demands from each of these other interests. Attempts were made, first by Montréal-based banks and subsequently by the premiers of Ontario and Québec, to enforce a cartel on the industry in an effort to prorate production and eliminate price competition.

These measures by Canadian heartland institutions to bring stability to the hinterland resource economy met with limited success. One obstacle was the divergent interests of those American firms, notably the International Paper Company, whose corporate linkages gave their Canadian mills guaranteed newsprint markets and hence relative immunity from the dislocations suffered by Canadian-owned producers. Stronger markets eventually reappeared in the late 1930s, but not before towns such as Espanola and Pine Falls had endured heavy unemployment and attendant communal stress. In general, institutional responses to the industry's plight did more to protect heartland stock and bond holders than hinterland woods and mill workers from financial insecurity.[5]

Those pulp and paper mills which use the forest resources of the Shield (for many mills in the valleys of the St. Lawrence and the lower Ottawa are physically beyond the Shield's edge) are concentrated in the

Lac St. Jean area, along the St. Lawrence Valley between Trois-Rivières and Québec, in the lower Ottawa Valley, and at Thunder Bay. Elsewhere, the location of isolated mills reflects the alignment of transcontinental railway lines; in the case of northeastern Ontario, at the points where they cross northward flowing rivers. Three mills were constructed during the 1940s along the northern shore of Lake Superior, representing a new production sub-region made viable by changes in pulping technology that permitted extensive use of jack pine. Precisely these technological advances, however, helped to reduce the overall appeal of the Shield as a locus of post-war investment by pulp and paper companies serving the American market. The pine forests of the southeastern United States have emerged as a competitive source of raw material, giving producers there several advantages (including lower wood, labour, and transportation costs) over competing Canadian suppliers.

New pulp and paper mills were built in the Shield in the late 1960s and early 1970s, but their locations were more peripheral than those of earlier mills, and their financing involved considerable amounts of public money in the form of federal or provincial regional development incentives. Taken together, these two factors go a long way towards explaining the relatively unsuccessful, if not disastrous, early careers of the

Pulp Mill, Thurso, Québec: This air photo illustrates the integrated operations that now characterize many wood products operations. The waste products from the sawmilling division are used in the pulping process. (*La Compagnie James MacLaren Limitée*)

projects involved. Large mills at The Pas, Manitoba; Port Cartier, Québec (closed since 1979 and likely to be dismantled); and Stephenville, Newfoundland ran into debt at least partly because of the uncompetitively high costs of wood supply in regions of slow and low-density tree growth. The environmentally-based economic difficulties were generally discounted by an excessive political commitment to encourage investment and create jobs.[6] The small pulp mill at Prince Albert, Saskatchewan has fared better than the grandiose schemes just mentioned and the paper mill opened at Amos, Québec in 1982 has broken the sequence of unpromising investments at new locations in the Shield.

To maintain the competitiveness of existing mills, especially in view of the recent expansion of the pulp and paper industry in the southern United States, it has been necessary to invest heavily in new paper machines (wider and faster than those they replace, so reducing unit labour costs) and in pulping technologies that are less polluting and make better use of the available wood fibre. With the assistance of a federal-provincial programme of grants in the early 1980s, some form of upgrading has been carried out at nearly every production location, securing the long-term future of an albeit reduced workforce; but in a few cases there has been no viable alternative to closing a mill (at Hawkesbury and one of the two at Kapuskasing, for example). At Temiskaming, an obsolescent American-controlled mill which was to have been closed in 1972 has subsequently, in the hands of locally-based owners (Tembec), regained profitability by steady investment in innovation.[7] In 1986, the firm opened a second mill in the town which was the first in North America to produce bleached chemi-thermomechanical pulp (CTMP). CTMP is ideally suited to the Shield, for it recovers twice as much fibre from the wood supply as existing kraft pulps and is capable of utilizing a wider range of raw materials (including poplar and aspen). It is a relatively heavy user of electricity, but the Shield enjoys a continental comparative advantage in electricity production.

The greatest threat to the Shield's forest-based industries in the immediate future is a shortage of economically accessible wood fibre. Both the industries and their landlords, the provincial governments, have been negligent in their past approach to forest regeneration. Inadequacies in collecting basic resource information and in implementing effective renewal policies have created a situation in which the current annual cut cannot be sustained in some areas. The problem is most acute in northwestern Ontario, where three-quarters of manufacturing employment is dependent on the forest sector and where there could be a shortfall of more than 20 percent in meeting the industries' wood requirements by the year 2000. Fewer difficulties are anticipated in northeastern Ontario and the Abitibi region of Québec, although the transportation costs of obtaining pulpwood from more northerly regions will rise.[8] Concerted efforts by industry and government to establish an effective programme of forest regeneration are now underway, but the legacy of past shortsightedness will not disappear overnight. The governments of Ontario and Québec, in reviewing their forest legislation, are attempting to promote both a fuller utilization of the wood supply and (especially in Québec) a more rational spatial pattern of raw material flows from timber limits to processing plants.

By the early 1980s, approximately 60 pulp and paper mills, representing 40 percent of the national total, drew upon the forest resources of the Shield (Fig. 11.2). These mills account for almost 70 percent of Canadian newsprint capacity and over half of national woodpulp capacity. Following the pattern established in the interior of British Columbia, pulp production in the Shield is relying increasingly on wood chips to supplement logs. Backward integration by large paper companies into the more fragmented sawmilling industry has prompted government moves, particularly in Québec, to ensure that the small-scale operators are protected under new forest management arrangements.

There are, however, significant economies of scale in lumber production. The large sawmills in the Shield are modern plants, incorporating technologies which greatly improve the economics of processing small trees. As a result, despite remaining a higher-cost source of timber than western forests in Canada and the United States, the Shield has improved its competitive position in the major metropolitan markets of central Canada and the American Midwest. The United States continues to consume almost 90 percent of the Shield's pulp and paper production, although Canada's share of the American newsprint market has gradually declined (to just over 60 percent) as a result of growing output in southeastern states. Further substantial erosion of the Shield's market share south of the border is unlikely, but the profitability of Canadian pulp and paper sales is sensitive to variations in the exchange rate on the American dollar, over which the hinterland manufacturers have no control.

MINING

Mining, no less than the forest industry, has been developed in the Shield primarily in response to the demands of non-Canadian markets. As a permanent element of the regional economy, the industry dates only from the last decade of the nineteenth century. The first major investments in mineral resources accompanied the initial construction of railways across the Shield. These routes often hit upon rich deposits more by accident than design, as the Canadian Pacific Railway did at Sudbury (1883), and the Temiskaming and Northern Ontario Railway did at Cobalt (1903). However, with the exception of precious metals and of nickel (in which Sudbury quickly acquired a near-monopoly of world supply), the minerals of the Shield faced weak markets: at that time, the United States, in particular, had no shortage of accessible domestic supplies. After World War II, however, this situation changed and the mining industry of the Shield underwent a prolonged period of sustained expansion. The production capacity of established mining regions was enlarged, and new metals from new regions, notably iron ore from Ungava, were added to the spectrum of mineral output (Fig. 11.3). Foreign competition, the high cost of borrowing capital, and the drop in the price of gold brought this growth phase to a halt in the 1970s. Similarly, the severe recession of the early 1980s left the mining industry of the Shield smaller in size and facing an uncertain future.

Limited demand was thus one factor that delayed the emergence of a mining industry in the Shield; a second was the complex composition of many of its mineral deposits. Whereas the nineteenth century gold rushes in British Columbia and the Yukon were based on placer (alluvial) material, accessible to the lone miner, the gold of Porcupine and Kirkland Lake could only be separated by a capital-intensive chemical process such as cyanidation. Even more challenging were the nickel-copper ores of the Sudbury basin. The technological breakthrough which finally made possible the separation of the two metals was achieved by an American company (a forerunner of INCO) which had the expertise, the financial backing, and a secure market in its domestic armaments industry, all factors absent in the hinterland Canadian economy. Armed with this technological monopoly, the company was able, quite easily, to frustrate Ontario's attempt in 1900 to apply "the manufacturing condition" to the export of ores. Refining facilities remained firmly situated in the United States until changes in refining technology (from a coal-based to an electrolytic process), and the prospect of having its properties expropriated during World War I, prompted the company to establish a Canadian refinery at Port Colborne in southern Ontario, using Niagara power.[9]

The third factor which has influenced the pace of mineral development in the Shield is accessibility. With few exceptions, mineral products are of low value in relation to their bulk. In inland areas they are therefore dependent upon cheap rail transportation for commercially viable shipment. The spread of mining in the Shield has thus been directly linked to that of an expanding railway network. Prior to the 1920s, railways were built through the Shield to serve a variety of national and provincial purposes unrelated to mining, although significant mineral discoveries were made in the process. Thereafter, as the development of bush flying gave prospectors a new-found mobility, mineral deposits could be evaluated well in advance of railway construction. Subsequent decisions to develop a mine then identified the specific transportation infrastructure required. Mining activity in the Shield is therefore most intense where an expanding core region meant that only small investments had to be made for the necessary transportation network. The history of development in

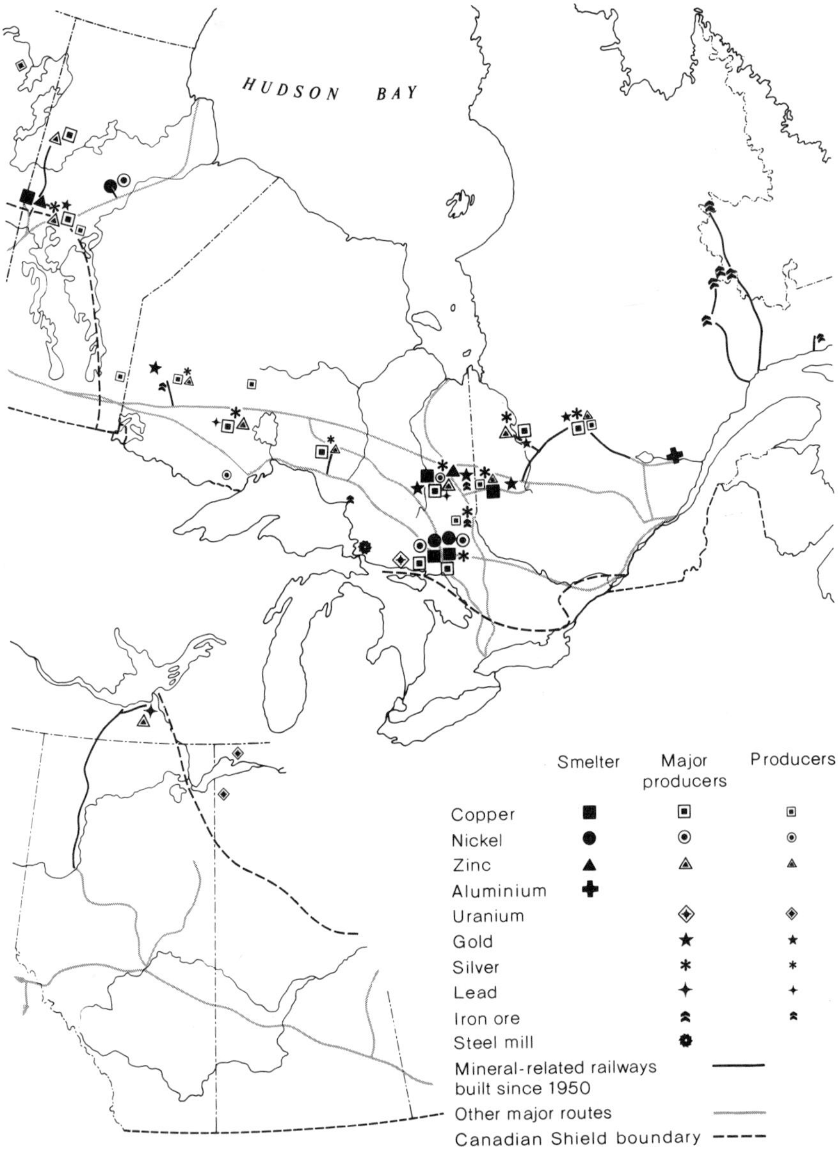

Figure 11.3 The distribution of mining activity in the Canadian Shield.

the Cobalt-Timmins-Noranda area prior to 1930, and in northwestern Québec and northern Manitoba in the decade prior to 1965, demonstrates this pattern.[10]

In contrast, the most distinctive feature of the dramatic expansion in the Shield's mineral economy which began in the early 1950s was the massive investment in railway construction undertaken to bring distant and isolated deposits into production. Development of the Québec-Labrador iron fields required laying 1155 kilometres of railway, as well as building related port facilities at Sept Îles, Port Cartier, and Havre St. Pierre. Altogether, over five thousand kilometres of railway carrying significant mineral traffic were built in Canada between 1950 and 1975, nearly half serving mines in the Shield.[11] Only a number of gold mines in northwestern Ontario and northwestern Québec and uranium mines in northern Saskatchewan have been able to sustain production solely on the basis of road (including winter road) and air transport.

The Shield is one of the largest and most diversified mining regions in the world. After a century of production, it still contains extensive reserves of a variety of minerals and continues to attract investment in new mines. Yet the prosperity, and hence the expansion, of the region's mining industry has become increasingly sensitive to changes in its external

Iron ore carrier at Sept Iles, Québec: Raw materials such as iron ore from the Québec-Labrador mining area are carried by large lake carriers via the St. Lawrence Seaway to industrial markets in the Industrial Heartland. (*Iron Ore Company of Canada*)

environment, both in Canada and the world. Canada's share of world mineral markets has declined for the past 30 years as a result of the tremendous growth of output in the Third World and Australia. From the global perspective of heartland mining companies, including Canadian-owned multinationals, the Shield is now only one resource hinterland among many. The comparative attraction of investment in the Shield, as opposed to elsewhere, is influenced by such factors as the relative richness of particular deposits; comparative operating and infrastructure costs; Canadian mining taxation (a severe deterrent for most of the 1970s, in contrast to the previous decades); the marketing behaviour of state-owned mining companies in the Third World, where the hard currency earnings from mineral exports are critical; and the geographically differential impacts of changes in technology and markets.

Nickel provides a singular illustration of the significance of these factors for the Shield's mining industry. In the 1950s, the Sudbury basin produced over 80 percent of world supply and INCO monopolized the world market. Yet despite expanded output at Sudbury and the development of a large deposit at Thompson, Canada's share of global output shrank to less than one-third in the late 1970s and dipped to only 14 percent in 1982. What accounts for this dramatic shift, especially considering that in 1980 the Shield's nickel industry remained the world's lowest-cost producer by a comfortable margin?[12] First, continuous growth in world demand had come to a sudden end and as a result there was a global surplus of production capacity. Many of the new sources of supply, planned before the slowdown, maintained or even increased their output (even though this has helped to lower world nickel prices) either to provide their governments with hard currency or to maintain a cash flow to service their high debt load. Canada's private-sector producers have found it increasingly difficult to compete with these predominantly state-controlled or state-subsidized enterprises.

The second reason for the slowdown is that Canadian firms (INCO and Falconbridge) have invested in nickel production overseas to protect specific markets, to some extent at the expense of their Shield operations. Certainly, the simultaneous start-up of an Inco property in Indonesia and major redundancies at its Sudbury and Thompson mines in 1977 led to accusations that the company was exporting jobs, and there were calls for its nationalization by Ottawa. Assuming that world nickel markets revive from the depths that they reached in the early 1980s, it is still not expected that employment in the Shield will show any significant increase. By 1984, INCO had reduced its Sudbury labour force to 7150, from 20 700 in 1971. The increasingly widespread adoption of bulk mining methods has brought major improvements in labour productivity and research is proceeding into the application of robot technology to some of the more hazardous tasks underground.[13]

The Shield's iron ore deposits have never been as commercially attractive internationally as its nickel and the reduction in output brought about by the recession of the early 1980s may prove to be permanent. This conclusion is reinforced by the decline of the United States steel industry, whose demand for raw materials in the 1950s was the principal thrust behind the large-scale investment which opened up the iron fields of the Labrador Trough. The original mine and settlement at Schefferville, at the northern end of the Québec North Shore and Labrador Railway, was closed down in 1982-83. Mines were also closed at Fire Lake and Gagnon on the Québec-Cartier Railway in 1984-85.[14] Overall, ore production in the Québec-Labrador region dropped by almost half between 1979 and 1983, to approximately 28 million tonnes. Smaller mines in Ontario (at Atikokan, Capreol, and Red Lake) have also closed in recent years.

The Shield's copper mines, which are distributed in a continuous arc from Lynn Lake to Chibougaman, have also been subject to severe financial pressures in recent years. Copper prices in the early 1980s were higher in real terms than in the Depression of the 1930's. Again, the problems are less the result of changes in mining conditions in the Shield than of a world market transformed by the expansion of Third World production which is frequently subsidized by producer governments. Only

Kidd Creek mine site, Timmins, Ontario: This newly developed copper mine sends materials to a nearby smelter and refinery. However, the refined copper is sent out of the region to be processed into producer and finished consumer goods elsewhere in Canada, the United States, and even Europe and Asia. (*Kidd Creek Mines*)

the fact that the Shield's copper is invariably found in mixed deposits — with zinc, nickel, or precious metals — has saved the region from widespread mine closures, although prices for many of these co-products were low in the mid-1980s. The Sudbury basin accounts for over one-fifth of Canadian copper production and supports two local smelters. Smelters at Noranda and Flin Flon also process ore from a number of mines in their respective regions, whereas a third, at Timmins, draws primarily on the output of the nearby Kidd Creek mine. This zinc-copper deposit was discovered only in 1964, but was quickly developed into one of the largest and most lucrative base-metal properties in Canada. The Shield's zinc smelters are located near Timmins and at Flin Flon, although there is also a substantial flow of concentrates to the smelter at Valleyfield, near Montréal.

Gold and uranium were the metals primarily responsible for new mine developments in the Shield in the difficult economic conditions of the early 1980s. Despite the uncertain future of the nuclear power industry in many parts of the world, interest in securing long-term access to uranium supplies remains strong. Intensive exploration in northern Saskatchewan in the 1970s, involving much European capital, revealed high-grade deposits whose exploitation has begun. Despite the closure in 1982 of the mine at Uranium City, after over 30 years of operation, uranium output in Saskatchewan could overtake that in Ontario in the coming decade, although the mines at Elliot Lake, currently the centre of production, are far from exhausted. A new uranium refinery, complementing the facilities at Port Hope in southern Ontario, was opened at Blind River, near Elliot Lake, in 1983. Northern Ontario has also witnessed the most recent example of a Canadian gold rush, occasioned by the discovery of rich and easily accessible deposits at Hemlo, east of Marathon. This area promises to develop into one of the largest gold-mining centres in the Shield. Other substantial ventures, notably at Detour Lake, have also begun production in the established mining areas of northeastern Ontario and northwestern Québec.

HYDROELECTRICITY

Had it not been for the widespread distribution of substantial hydro power potential, the pulp and paper and mining and smelting industries of the Shield would have developed later and less extensively than they did. With the exception of the currently unworked lignite deposits of Onakawana, in the James Bay Lowlands, the Shield is devoid of fossil fuels. The delivered cost of coal (significant prior to 1950) and of petroleum products to industries in the Shield rises rapidly with increasing distance from the distribution network of shipping on the St. Lawrence and Great Lakes. Natural gas became available to most of the industrial communities in northern Ontario (and Noranda) on completion of the Trans-Canada Pipeline in 1958, but cheap hydroelectricity has been basic to any comparative advantage enjoyed by resource processing industries in the Shield. Increasingly, however, the stimulus to harnessing the region's power potential has passed from these internal markets to the steady growth of electricity demand in the urban-industrial heartland to the south. Technological advances in long-distance, high-voltage transmission have helped to make increasingly remote hydro generating sites economically preferable to market-oriented thermal power stations.

Despite the uniform context of hydroelectricity development throughout the Shield, the evolution of the industry within each province has been different. Québec, Manitoba, and Newfoundland have this point in common, that 80 percent or more of their total provincial electricity generating capacity consists of hydro stations located in the Shield. In contrast, the equivalent figure in Ontario is 15 percent. The relatively limited hydro potential of the Ontario Shield, as compared to that of the other provinces, stems primarily from regional variations in physical geography (Fig. 11.4). The Hudson Bay-Atlantic drainage watershed is so located as to produce only minor southward-flowing rivers in northern Ontario but a large number of high-potential rivers draining south off the Shield in Québec (and the Churchill River in Labrador). In addition, of the rivers draining into Hudson Bay, those in Ontario have their major breaks of slope further upstream than those in Manitoba and Québec, thus reducing their hydro development potential. As a result, Ontario, which has the highest provincial demand for electricity, has the most restricted opportunity for generating hydro power in the Shield. Under prevailing cost conditions, the commercially attractive potential has been fully developed; and with its southern hydro resources, notably at Niagara, already exploited, the province has been forced since 1960 to look increasingly to thermal generation. Ontario Hydro's substantial commitment to nuclear power must be seen in this light.

Interprovincial variations in the institutional framework of hydro development have also been important. Electricity generation in all four provinces is in the hands of public utilities, though in Québec and Newfoundland this development has come about only in recent decades. Throughout the Shield, because of their need for electricity in locations remote from existing distribution grids, many resource industries build and retain private hydro plants. Ownership of this captive capacity, even if it is now supplemented by power purchases from the provincial utility, can provide important cost savings. Links between pulp and paper and power production are most numerous (e.g. the Maclaren group, International Paper-Gatineau Power), but by far the largest industrial producer of electricity is Alcan, whose aluminum smelting and refining operations in the Lac St. Jean region depend on the output of 2350 megawatts of captive capacity (about 10 percent of the Québec total).

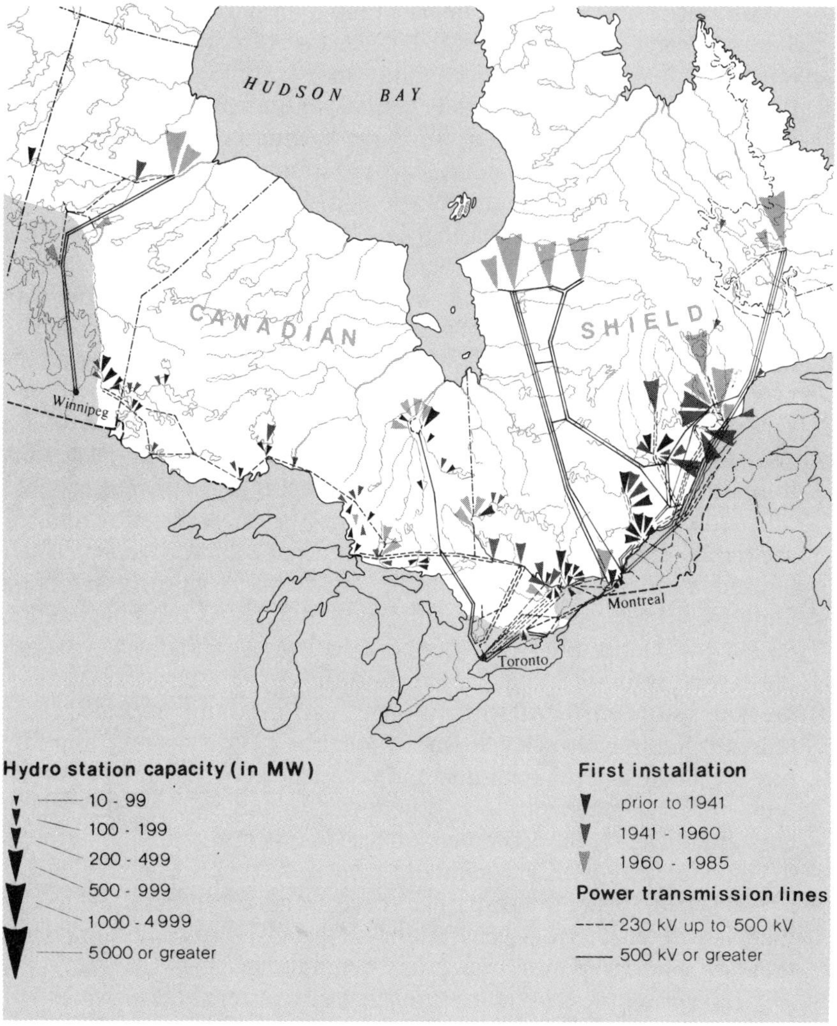

Figure 11.4. Distribution of hydroelectric developments in the Canadian Shield.

The Shield became a source of hydroelectricity for metropolitan markets in the central Canadian heartland much earlier in Québec than in Ontario. Early power development in Ontario was concentrated at Niagara, and it was the inherent monopoly position enjoyed by the owners of generating capacity there which led to the pioneering creation of a provincial public electrical utility in 1907. In contrast, the first major hydro developments in Québec took place at Shawinigan, where there were no immediately obvious captive consumers. Rather, the private utility had to create its markets, which it did by attracting power-intensive industries and by pioneering long-distance transmission of electricity to distant urban markets (145 kilometres to Montréal by 1903). In fact, the first move by Ontario Hydro to tap the hydro potential of the Shield for the Toronto region was through a power purchase contract from a Québec utility, the Gatineau Power Company. But thereafter, Ontario Hydro began to develop power sites in the north of the province, primarily to meet the growing industrial demand in the Sudbury region. Construction of power plants on the Ottawa River was delayed until the post-World War II period by intergovernmental disputes concerning jurisdiction over the river.[15]

Rapid growth in electricity demand from urban-industrial heartland markets has, since 1950, been the prime stimulus to further exploitation of the Shield's hydro potential. Ontario soon found itself without significant undeveloped sites, despite some water diversion in catchments north of Lake Superior, and was forced to concentrate on market-oriented thermal generation. Québec and Manitoba, however, were in a position to embark on ambitious schemes to harness remote sites. In Manitoba these schemes have involved sequential development of the Nelson River on a scale well beyond that necessitated by domestic provincial demands. High-voltage transmission corridors bring power not only to southern Manitoba (with links to Saskatchewan and northwestern Ontario), but also to American utilities in the upper Midwest. In Québec, the systematic exploitation of river basins which are increasingly distant from the major markets of the Montréal region has been both a major influence on the province's economy and a symbolic statement of the technological expertise of contemporary French-Canadian society. Successive dam construction on the Betsiamites, Outardes, and Manicouagan Rivers culminated in the massive $15 billion James Bay development, which will have a total capacity of 10 269 megawatts when it is completed in the late 1980s.

Controversy has surrounded the James Bay project since its inception in 1971. The provincial government established a separate organization (the James Bay Development Corporation) to undertake construction, but also gave it such comprehensive powers over such an extensive territory (350 000 square kilometres) that it was likened to an autonomous republic. The technical and economic aspects of the hydroelectric scheme underwent numerous changes in the course of its development. The final version involves doubling the flow of the La Grande River by diversions from four other rivers, and increasing the peak power generating capability at the expense of some of the firm (base-load) power capability initially planned for. This latter change indicates that growth in electricity demand has been less than anticipated in Hydro Québec's projections, despite the enhanced attractiveness of hydro power over alternative energy sources, both in price and reliability.

From the beginning, the size of the project raised questions about where the markets for such a large block of power might be found. The fact that exports to New York State were clearly involved strengthened the opposition of groups who saw the scheme as another example of the degradation of the Canadian environment to meet the demands of consumers in the United States. In addition, having had their interests initially ignored, the Native peoples directly affected by the project won a court battle to establish their rights in the region, and after protracted negotiations with the provincial government, they reached a land claim settlement.

Although located in Labrador, the Churchill Falls power plant (the largest single-site hydroelectric scheme in the Western hemisphere) is functionally integrated with the Hydro Québec network. This integration has long been a contentious issue between the governments of Newfoundland and Québec. Rights to harness the potential of the Churchill

Power for the Industrial Heartland: The Daniel Johnson Dam (Manic V) was built by the state-owned Hydro-Québec power agency on the Manicouagan River in northeastern Québec. One of the world's largest multiple vault dams, it generates hydroelectricity for customers in southern Québec and American utility companies. (*Hydro-Québec*)

(formerly Hamilton) River were part of a substantial bundle of concessions granted in 1953 by the Smallwood government of Newfoundland to Brinco, a consortium of European financial interests headed by the Rothschilds. Construction of the 5225 megawatt generating station waited, however, upon the identification of distant markets for its power. Advances in long-distance transmission technology made New York State a potential customer, but necessarily one that could be reached overland only via the province of Québec, and thus only on terms acceptable to that province. Québec was dissatisfied with the 1927 ruling on its border with Newfoundland and this issue compounded the problems associated with complex financial considerations. To purchase power from Brinco "at the border" would appear to sanction Newfoundland's claim, yet by 1966 Hydro Québec saw the need to purchase large amounts of Churchill Falls power to meet projected provincial demand. In the ensuing negotiations Hydro Québec obtained, in a 65-year contract, 90 percent of the power generated, at a rate which throughout the 1980s has been about one-tenth that of the true market value.

The government of Newfoundland, which nationalized Brinco's water power rights in 1974, made determined efforts to obtain a more equitable share of these revenues. However, the Supreme Court of Canada ruled in 1984 that it had no legal basis for breaking the existing agreement. Some political accommodation may still be reached, but meanwhile this cheap power provides a substantial proportion of Hydro Québec's total system needs, giving the Québec government freedom to attract electricity-intensive industry and to pursue lucrative sales of power to adjacent parts of the United States.[16]

RESOURCES OF LAND AND LAKE

No less than the industrially-defined resources reviewed in the preceding sections, the land of the Shield has been subject to appraisal and exploitation from the perspective of the metropolitan society to the south. What most concerned the Ontario government around the turn of the century was that the transcontinental railways, which were opening up the southern Shield to economic activity, were also inviting "the sons of Ontario . . . [to] seek a home in another Province." Surveyors' reports of "excellent agricultural land" in the so-called Clay Belts indicated that these potential emigrants could, with some assistance, be retained to create a prosperous "New Ontario" in the north.[17] The government's decision, in 1902, to undertake construction of the Temiskaming and Northern Ontario Railway as a colonization line was a direct result of this concern. Settlers quickly discovered the constraints of northern agriculture, but official publications nevertheless conveyed a promising image throughout the 1920s. In Québec, Church and State collaborated closely, and acted more directly than did the Ontario government to promote rural colonization as a culturally idealized way of life. Demographic pressure in the farming communities of southern Québec had already prompted substantial out-migration to the industrial, commercialized, and secularized society of Montréal and to the mill towns of northern New England.

Inter-provincial differences in the degree of support for, and perceived role of, agricultural colonization in the Shield are reflected in contrasting spatial patterns of settlement. These are particularly evident in the northern Clay Belt, which is bisected by the provincial boundary. The systematic creation of contiguous parishes linked by a regular and dense pattern of rural roads in the Abitibi region of Québec contrasts with the more sporadic and lower density settlement on the Ontario side, where colonization proceeded under an essentially *laissez-faire* regime.

The final thrust to promote farming in the Shield took the form of a desperate but ill-conceived response to the massive urban unemployment of the 1930s. Various federal and provincial measures aimed to assist northern settlement so that the unemployed might at least feed themselves; but the measures did little more than transfer the burden from municipal welfare rolls in the heartland to ill-equipped individuals in an unpromising hinterland. "[A] class of pseudo-farmers was introduced on to the land without capital and real knowledge of farming, usually in units too small to allow capital formation and subsequent farm enlargement and specialization."[18] These essentially subsistence holdings were rapidly abandoned after World War II, initiating a more general shrinkage of the farming population which has continued at a decreasing rate.

The agricultural ecumene of the Shield comprises, in addition to the continuous belt of farmland on its southern margins, three principal regional concentrations. In 1981, the largest of these was the Clay Belts, containing 373 000 hectares north of Lake Temiskaming and along the axis of the transcontinental railway from Cochrane to Senneterre. The Lac St. Jean area contained 213 000 hectares, and in northern Ontario three distinct subregions, focussed on Thunder Bay, Rainy River, and Dryden, made up a further 136 000 hectares. Agricultural activity is similar in all three regions, with differences primarily reflecting variations in accessibility to metropolitan markets. Thus, the percentage of farmland improved is about 45 in northwestern Ontario, 55 in the Clay Belts, and 65 around Lac St. Jean.

Of the crops, hay is dominant throughout, followed far behind by oats. Dairying is important around the urban centres of the Lac St. Jean region, the Clay Belts, and Thunder Bay, but it has declined in volume in recent years, whereas beef cattle have better maintained their numbers. Beef production has long been dominant in northwestern Ontario, but it has achieved growing significance in the Clay Belts, partly as a result of the increasing agricultural intensity of southern Ontario and Québec. A number of established livestock farmers have moved north, where the land they need for forage is considerably cheaper than in the heartland. Farms in the 100-160 hectare size range are the modal class in almost every census division. Despite the continuing trend to improve the viability of farming in the Shield by increasing the size of remaining holdings, the majority of farmers in Ontario census divisions are part-timers, deriving other income from a wide variety of occupations. Levels of off-farm work are somewhat lower in Québec, especially in the Lac St. Jean region.

Proximity to heartland cities underlies the spatial pattern of tourist and recreational activities in the Shield. From the Laurentian Hills to Muskoka, its southern boundary is within day-trip distance of the major metropolitan centres between Québec City and Toronto and, except in provincial parks, its lakeshores have been incorporated into vacation properties. The metropolitan populations of Winnipeg, Minneapolis-St. Paul, and other American cities in the upper Midwest have created a similar concentration of seasonal homes in northwestern Ontario and southeastern Manitoba. Camping, canoeing, sport fishing, and, in the fall, hunting are the major attractions for those who come to the Shield to enjoy more than the scenery of lake and woods. Accessibility by road is a major factor in determining the detailed pattern of these activities, but hunting and sport fishing also attract a substantial clientele willing to pay for fly-in tourist facilities at remote sites. Especially in northwestern Ontario, these lodges and camps provide a significant source of employment for Native people, as guides.

Seasonal employment of Native people in the tourist, forest, and other industries of the Shield does not destroy the distinction, made by Mr. Justice Hartt, that "Indian people live in the land, while non-natives live on it."[19] Especially in the north, traditional activities such as trapping, hunting, and fishing yield an important part of Native food consumption, and provide the means of earning supplementary income. In the Kenora area, wild rice harvesting represents a similar combination of cultural ritual and source of economic independence, one which the Ontario government acted to protect in 1978 against demands by non-natives that the crop be more fully exploited commercially, with mechanized harvesting.

The use and enjoyment of land and lake by Native people and non-Natives alike has not escaped the negative environmental impacts of the Shield's industrial economy. For many decades, the pollution of water-courses by pulp mill effluent or mine tailings, or of the atmosphere by smelting operations, was simply allowed to go on. The resolve of governments to enforce even minimal control measures eroded at the threat that such action would destroy the economic basis of single-industry communities. Today, as a result of increased public awareness and more stringent environmental legislation, adverse industrial impacts have been reduced. There remain, however, significant loopholes which weaken effective control over industry practice, and the threat to the Shield's natural environment is not confined to forms of pollution originating within it.

Contemporary concern focusses primarily on acid rain, which, by reducing or destroying the biological productivity of lakes and forest, directly threatens the viability of the Shield's tourist and forest product industries. The nickel smelters at Sudbury are (when operating at full capacity) the largest single source of sulphur dioxide emissions on the continent, but to continue the programme of emissions reduction which proceeded during the 1970s requires heavy investment at a time when the industry has been severely squeezed financially. Meanwhile, international consultations to reduce the cross-border movement of pollutants from the United States into the Shield have produced few tangible results. Construction of INCO's "superstack" in 1972 did improve the air quality around Sudbury (at the expense of more distant areas downwind) and contributed to a noticeable improvement in vegetation growth locally. It has become apparent, however, that the particulate content of atmospheric emissions, leading to metal contamination of the soil, has as negative an impact on plant life as acid rain.[20]

A summer Inuit hunting camp near Nain, Labrador: Many Inuit still migrate seasonally between a permanent home and a hunting camp such as this on the shores of Davis Strait. (*Jean Cameron*)

URBANIZATION

The resource economy of the Shield has influenced the nature and pattern of its human settlement. A limited agricultural land base and the predominance of basic employment in mines and paper mills combine to make industrial towns the most characteristic centres of population. These industrial towns are markedly different from the urban centres of the heartland. Most hinterland communities exhibit limited economic diversification, owing to their dependence on a single major employer. This relationship similarly constrains occupational diversity, which is in most cases further reduced by the truncated managerial hierarchy of the local (branch) plant, and by the limited variety of service sector employment in a small town. Except in northeastern Ontario and the Lac St. Jean area, individual urban centres are widely separated. Such isolation contributes to the strength of community organizations, which many residents regard as an attractive feature of these settlements; but it nevertheless limits the scope of social and employment opportunities, often forcing young people to migrate. The Shield's resource towns often display dramatic growth in their early years, but thereafter they are prone to stagnate, both in size and socio-economic composition. This decline in turn reduces their subsequent chances of achieving industrial diversification and self-sustaining growth.[21]

Single-industry communities, varying in size from less than 1000 to more than 10 000 inhabitants, are found throughout the region. Larger urban centres, where employment is more diversified but still mainly dependent on the resource industries, are concentrated close to the Shield's southern margin. (Along the lower Ottawa and St. Lawrence River valleys the definition of a town as a Shield community is unavoidably arbitrary. In Fig. 11.5, for instance, the pulp and paper town of Gatineau is excluded, as part of the Ottawa-Hull metropolitan area, but Trois Rivières is included.) The main rail routes by which heartland interests traversed and penetrated the Shield determined the precise location of most towns, and the external metropolitan centres of Montréal, Toronto, and Winnipeg continue to exert a pervasive influence. Sudbury, Chicoutimi-Jonquière, and Thunder Bay, with 1981 populations of 150 000, 135 000, and 121 000 respectively, are the foci of the three most populated sub-regions.

Construction of the Canadian Pacific Railway consolidated Montréal's position as the dominant metropolis of the Shield in the nineteenth century. Sudbury, Sault Ste. Marie, Thunder Bay, and Winnipeg were connected to Montréal by rail for almost 20 years before railway links from Toronto offered any substantial competition. That city's emergence as a rival metropolis to Montréal for control of the Shield economy was directly associated with the rise of the mining industry and thus (albeit fortuitously) with the construction of the Temiskaming and Northern Ontario Railway. From the 1880s, financiers in Toronto had shown an interest, not shared by their Montréal counterparts, in promoting mining properties, and in 1898 two small mining exchanges amalgamated to form the Standard Stock and Mining Exchange. Its stature as the centre for mining industry financing in Canada was solidly entrenched in the aftermath of the Cobalt silver discoveries (1903) and the Porcupine and Kirkland Lake gold discoveries (1911-12) in northeastern

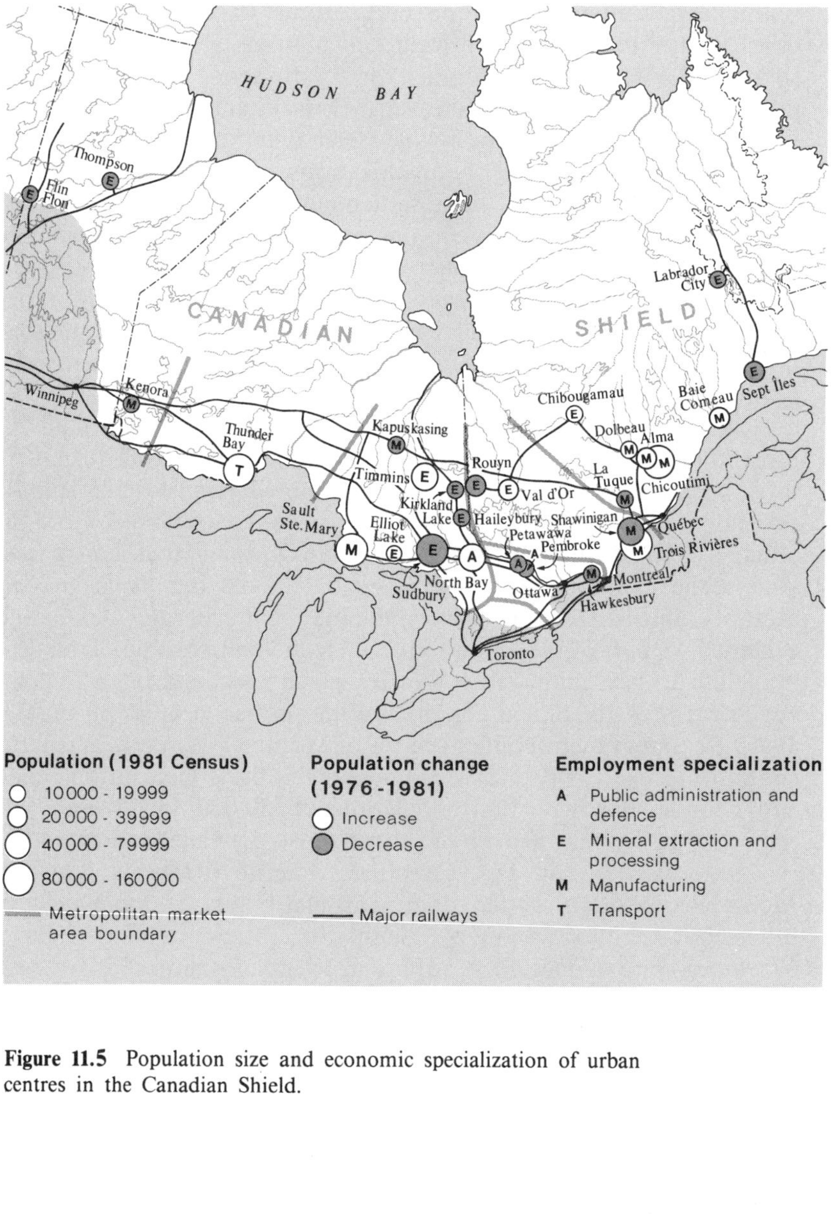

Figure 11.5 Population size and economic specialization of urban centres in the Canadian Shield.

Ontario. Nearly all subsequent expansion of the non-ferrous mining industry in the Shield has been organized from or through (in the case of foreign-controlled firms) Toronto.[22] The weak presence of Québec-based interests in the mining industry of their own province was symbolically confirmed in 1928 when the Ontario-owned, Toronto-controlled, Temiskaming and Northern Ontario Railway linked the Rouyn mines to its system, despite legal opposition from the Québec government. Had it not been for the creation of Soquem (the provincial mineral exploration company) in 1965, Toronto's control over the non-ferrous mining industry in Québec would still be virtually complete.

It would be misleading, however, to view the Shield as a region locked into an unchangeable pattern of heartland-hinterland relationships. These relationships are subject to changes in the national economy. As a result of corporate mergers in the 1970s, for example, Toronto has reduced Montréal's dominant control over the Shield's forest industry. The same westward shift of power has seen the Vancouver Stock Exchange assume some of Toronto's role in the promotion of junior Canadian mining companies. The increased willingness of provincial governments to enforce their constitutional rights in the resource sectors and to participate actively in production has resulted in further challenges to Toronto's hold over the Shield's economy. For example, the significance of Saskatoon has been enhanced by the Saskatchewan government's substantial involvement in the province's growing uranium industry. (In contrast, with the exception of the forest industry complex at The Pas, Winnipeg controls none of the forest or mining industry in its Shield hinterland.)

Nevertheless, the fact that the critical decisions of Alcan, INCO, Abitibi-Price, or Hydro Québec are made in Toronto or Montréal clearly limits the power of hinterland cities to direct the course of the Shield's economy. Sudbury, Thunder Bay, and Chicoutimi act primarily as major, sub-regional service centres, a role which gives their urban economies some resilience to the ups and downs of resource industry cycles. At Sudbury, for example, the downturn in the nickel market in 1977-78, followed in turn by a prolonged strike at INCO, proved two points. The municipality's fortunes are not totally dependent upon the mining industry payroll; but at the same time, its population remains vulnerable to shrinkage (by 6500 or 4.5 percent in those two years) as a result of fluctuations in the mineral economy. Smaller centres are less cushioned, especially if they are remote and dependent on an inevitably finite mineral deposit.

The cessation of mining at Uranium City (1982) and Schefferville (1983) illustrates the problems. The workers and their families directly affected by the closure of a mine face major upheavals, but in many respects they are the least disadvantaged group in the community. At Uranium City for instance, the United Steelworkers of America, representing the miners at the Eldorado uranium mine, was able to secure full relocation expenses, severance pay, and the cancellation of various household debts owed to the company. Within a few months of the closure announcement, over 60 percent of the mine employees had been recruited for other jobs. In contrast, the owners of private businesses such as drug stores or restaurants were faced with the sudden loss of their livelihood and of the capital (often their life savings) tied up in it. Neither the mining company nor the provincial government had specific obligations to protect their interests, although some assistance was provided. Within a year, the population of Uranium City shrank from 3000 to 700 and about 90 percent of its buildings fell vacant. The closure of the Iron Ore Company of Canada mine at Schefferville, where over one-third of the permanent workforce had accumulated 25 years of seniority, had similar consequences.[23] The community survives only because the Native people, most of whom did not work in the mine but in hunting and fishing, stayed on.

That these problems will inevitably arise at some stage in the life of many hinterland resource communities has forced both governments and corporations to reconsider their role in planning resource towns. Generally, it was the pulp and paper manufacturers who first found themselves in the position of having to establish new communities. Unlike many of the early, small-scale mining enterprises, whose activities sponsored unplanned and ephemeral collections of makeshift structures, pulp mills represented large-scale capital investments which employed substantial numbers of people on a continuing basis to process a renewable resource. As a result, a firm had to undertake at least a minimum of community development. Unimaginative urban layouts and housing which entrenched the social hierarchy of the workplace were at first the norm, but after World War I, experimentation with British Garden City planning concepts took place at Temiskaming, Kapuskasing, and Dolbeau. In the inter-war period, the large-scale mining and smelting operations of the Sudbury basin, together with smaller concentrations at Flin Flon and Noranda, gave rise to planned company towns. Later, during the major post-war expansion of the Shield's mining industry, many new communities such as Labrador City and Thompson were developed in remote areas on the basis of comprehensive planning principles devised and used in southern metropolitan centres.[24]

Resource towns in the Shield share many features which distinguish them from similar-sized settlements in southern Ontario and Québec. Whether comprehensively planned or not, most of them came into being over a period of a few years, as the industry on which they depend established its operations. Their initial population structure was dominated by male workers, and even where a mature community has developed, providing the facilities for family life and employment opportunities for women, adult males remain over-represented in comparison with the population composition of urban Canada as a whole. After the initial attraction of migrants, which typically brought together workers from a variety of geographical origins and ethnic backgrounds (population is less diverse in the Québec Shield, where French-Canadians clearly dominate the urban population), the settlement's population tends to stabilize. Not all who are attracted to well-paying jobs in the resource industries from less isolated centres in the south find themselves at home in the Shield, however. The restricted range of social and employment opportunities for women, together with limited educational and occupational facilities for older children, prompts many families to return to heartland centres after only a few years. Both the community and the major employer suffer if the rate of population and employee turnover becomes excessive, and cooperative attempts to improve the quality of life in resource towns are widespread.

Resource production in the hinterland: An aerial view of Inco's New South Mines, with the Copper Cliff smelter in the background. The Sudbury Basin is one of the world's largest nickel-producing areas. (*NFB Phototheque*)

Some mining towns have acquired functional importance as regional service centres (Thompson for northern Manitoba and Matagami for the James Bay developments). Others, such as Val d'Or, can look to a relatively secure future of continuing mineral production. But given the uncertainties of contemporary markets, the mining industry no longer chooses to create new communities around mines which may have an active life of 30 years or less. Increasingly, therefore, it has become the practice, wherever possible, to designate an existing community as the home base for miners employed at a new, remote mine site. This may involve considerable daily commuting, as between Mattabi Mine and Ignace (160 kilometres round trip), or else "fly-in" commuting, on a 7 days in, 7 days out basis, as at the Rabbit Lake uranium mine in northern Saskatchewan. There, an air shuttle service moves personnel from as far away as Saskatoon (690 kilometres) to live in motel-type units at the mine site. Although this arrangement is estimated to cost more than construction of a townsite, it is more appealing to the majority of miners and their families, and thus reduces the costs and social disruption associated with the high rates of labour turnover typical of remote resource communities.[25]

Despite their common dependence on resource-based employment, the larger urban centres of the Shield exhibit relative diversity (Fig. 11.5). Those places which lost population between 1961 and 1981 included mainly single-industry communities based on mining (Flin Flon, Kirkland Lake, Rouyn) and paper-making (Kenora, La Tuque), although some diversified centres, such as Shawinigan and Pembroke, also declined. Until the late 1970s, consistently growing centres included relatively new resource communities (Labrador City grew from 537 to 15 871 between 1961 and 1976), as well as all the cities of over 50 000 population except Shawinigan and Sudbury. Since then, cutbacks in mineral production have reversed the fortunes of such centres as Sept Îles and Labrador City. The population of Sudbury and Thompson has risen and fallen with the market for nickel. Population growth at Sault Ste. Marie levelled off progressively after 1966, even though production capacity at the Algoma steelworks expanded significantly in the early 1970s. (This hinterland producer, unlike the heartland Hamilton mills, has not attracted local metal-using industries). North Bay has grown steadily since 1961 and has diversified its economy in recent years by attracting new manufacturing investment. Shawinigan, in contrast, has experienced pronounced industrial decline. Plant obsolecence, loss of localized production economies (increased electricity costs as a result of Hydro Québec's zonal pricing system), a period of poor labour relations, and low priority for highway improvements to the Montréal region have all been contributing factors.[26] Some potential growth has been lost to the nearby larger city of Trois Rivières.

These diverse experiences indicate that although industrial incentives have been offered throughout the southern Shield by the federal government and the various provinces, secondary manufacturing employment in the region has not grown substantially. The more accessible and diversified communities, such as North Bay, have benefited more from government incentives than the isolated single-industry towns.

The three Census Metropolitan Areas (CMAs) which act as the Shield's sub-regional capitals — Sudbury, Chicoutimi-Jonquière, and Thunder Bay — are equally distinctive. One of their few common characteristics is that since 1961, they have grown more slowly than the Canadian CMA average, a rate which only Sudbury's more erratic expansion has at times exceeded. In 1971, the three cities also ranked lowest among CMAs in the aggregate educational experience of their population, although the benefits of local universities established since 1957 are now being felt.

Otherwise, however, each city reflects its prominent position in broad cultural and economic patterns which reach beyond the boundary of the Shield. Despite its setting and its paper mills, Thunder Bay could lay claim to be a city of the Prairies. Ethnically, only half its population is of English or French origin and it boasts the largest concentration of Finns in North America. Functionally, its storage and transshipment role in the grain economy of western Canada is the most highly specialized element in an otherwise diversified employment base. Chicoutimi-Jonquière is the most exclusively French by ethnic origin of all Canadian CMAs, and shares with Québec City the distinction of experiencing the highest linguistic assimilation of born anglophones. Its spatial structure is that of a multi-centred linear conurbation, in which Chicoutimi serves as the regional service centre, and various former company towns (Kenogami and Port Alfred with their paper mills, Arvida with its aluminum smelter) retain their manufacturing orientation. An equal mix of English and French ethnic groups makes up three-quarters of Sudbury's population, reflecting both its location and its period of initial settlement. Although the city's growth has been directly tied to that of the nickel industry, from the beginning Sudbury developed as a service centre for a region of scattered mining communities (subsequently consolidated in company towns such as Copper Cliff, Coniston, and Levack) rather than as a mining town itself.[27]

Communications flows and migration movements link these CMAs to heartland metropolitan centres more directly than to each other. Chicoutimi-Jonquière has had the least favourable net migration ratio (within Canada) and the lowest external immigration ratio of all Canadian CMAs. Like Thunder Bay, it has gained migrants only from non-metropolitan areas of its own province, which suggests that these CMAs act as intermediary points for those moving outwards and (socio-economically) upwards from the hinterland to more dynamic heartland cities. Migration and communications flows link Chicoutimi most strongly to Québec City and Montréal, just as they do Thunder Bay to Toronto and, to a lesser degree, Winnipeg. Sudbury's interaction with the central Canadian city system is more complex, but links with Toronto are most prominent. The main scheduled air services mirror these patterns, fostering north-south contacts between Shield and heartland, rather than east-west links between hinterland centres. The principal attempt to redress this imbalance has been the creation, by the Ontario government, of Norontair, which has built up networks of local air services in northeastern and northwestern Ontario, linked together by a route connecting Sudbury, Sault Ste. Marie, Thunder Bay, and Fort Frances.

THE HINTERLAND EXPERIENCE

Having examined heartland interest in the resources of the Shield and the nature of the urbanization to which it has given rise, we now consider the consequences for the hinterland population. An analysis of northwestern Ontario by G.R. Weller provides a useful analytical framework for our discussion.[28]

According to Weller, the resource-based economy is organized by, and principally serves, metropolitan interests. The myriad effects of this *economics of extraction* (sub-regional fragmentation, selective out-migration, the alienation of local control, etc.) cumulatively weaken the capability of the hinterland to define and pursue its own goals. This process results in the *politics of extraction,* an unequal struggle between heartland and hinterland. Hinterland interests attempt to bring about fundamental change in their relationship with the heartland (*the politics of futility*), whereas heartland interests seek to maintain hinterland acquiescence in the status quo through the *politics of handouts.* Repeated failure of the hinterland to change its status within wider economic and politically systems affects the character of intra-regional public life. Hence the *politics of frustration* expresses itself in the appeal of politically radical groups and of fringe movements, such as the regional separatists of the New Province Committee of Northern Ontario. Alternatively, this frustration is sublimated into the degenerate *politics of parochialism,* best exemplified by the rivalry which kept Port Arthur and Fort William independent (and uncooperative) municipalities for almost a century.

The Shield's future will undoubtedly be marked by continued dependence on an economy of forest products, mining, and tourism. Employment will remain cyclical, in varying degrees of severity, in all these industries. Increasing capital intensity in the mining and forest sectors means that greater output is achieved by a smaller workforce. The occupational structure and limited backward linkages of the tourist industry will do little to weaken the pressures on young people to migrate to regions where more buoyant and diversified economies exist. Incentive programmes have been in place long enough to demonstrate that heartland manufacturers (outside of the resource-based sectors) do not rate the Shield highly as a location for branch plant production. A more diversified employment base will come into being only through concerted efforts encouraging local entrepreneurs to exploit their opportunities. This path is being pursued in the Sudbury area, along lines both predictable (manufacture of equipment for the mining and forest industries) and unconventional (growing tomatoes in greenhouses warmed by exhaust air from mineshafts). La Sarre, 600 kilometres from both Montréal and Toronto, and with only 5000 inhabitants, may be exceptional, but it proves that the hinterland need not be a backwater. Here, two local firms have grown to become, respectively, the largest lumber producer east of the Rockies and one of Canada's largest trucking firms.

Local initiative can combat hinterland conditions, but it cannot fundamentally change the region's dependent status. Hinterland problems are still often seen from a heartland perspective. Around 1970, for example, much publicity was given to the Mid-Canada Corridor, a concept perpetuating the myth of the north's "inexhaustible resources". As a band across a map it was suggestive, but the inferred processes of massive population growth and industrialization ran directly counter to the actual dynamics of demographic and economic change within the region.[29] Growth centre strategies, such as those outlined in the Ontario government's *Design for Development* studies, represent a more modest approach to stimulating the economy of the Shield, but rather than growth they merely promote the orderly provision of services in a region of static or declining population.

Evidence of heartland control over the hinterland economy is pervasive. Corporate marketing strategies are such that no metals refined in the Shield are sold on an f.o.b. refinery basis (a price at the plant, to which any transportation costs would need to be added), so consuming industries have no particular incentive to locate in the region. Similarly, gasoline sold in Red Lake, Ontario, retails at the Sarnia price plus freight to Red Lake (2050 kilometres), although the town is only 500 kilometres by road from the Winnipeg refineries. Hinterland frustrations are also manifest in other ways. For example, the residents of Matagami told Ontario's Royal Commission on Electric Power Planning in 1976 that whereas they appreciated the benefits of electricity, they were "still puzzled that although their community had to be relocated in 1921 in order that a dam for hydroelectric power generation could be built, it was only five years ago [in 1971] that electricity was installed in their community."[30]

Hinterland alienation has in some instances fostered a radical reaction. The effectiveness of such a response within the broader political and economic system has been limited, however, by the numerical weakness of the hinterland population and the fragmentation of its protest. Early unionization of resource industry employees was hindered by ethnic diversity, with each group conscious of its separate identity and often at odds ideologically. Active management opposition meant that unionism took root more slowly in paternalistic company towns, such as those of the Nickel Belt, than amongst Cobalt and Timmins miners, who generally lived away from the company's premises. Having finally established itself in Sudbury in the 1940s, union activity was hampered for the next 20 years by internal rivalry. Only in recent years, by directing attention to such vital issues as the occupational health and safety record of the mining industry, have significant improvements in working conditions been secured.

Parliamentary protest has been no better coordinated. In the 1984 federal election, for instance, Shield ridings in Québec, Saskatchewan, and northeastern Ontario returned Conservatives, ridings in Manitoba and northwestern Ontario New Democrats, and ridings in north central Ontario and Labrador Liberals. Provincially also, there has been as much tendency for Shield residents to support governing parties as those in opposition. The most successful channels for voicing hinterland concerns in recent years have been those initiated by Native peoples in response to proposed large-scale development projects with potentially far-reaching disruptive social and environmental effects.

The James Bay agreement, whereby the Native people affected by the massive hydroelectric scheme accepted $225 million (to be paid over a 20-year period) in exchange for relinquishing land claims to over half the area of Québec, illustrates both the possibilities and frustrations of greater hinterland autonomy. The financial settlement is generally viewed as satisfactory and funds derived from it have been used to begin or to assess the feasibility of a wide variety of Native business ventures. Lake Mistassini Enterprises, for instance, is a Cree cooperative with activities in forestry, tourism, and mining exploration.[31]

The administrative aspects of the settlement, on the other hand, have been characterized as a "nightmare of legal wrangles and bureaucratic red tape."[32] The process of persuading heartland governments to grant Native northerners greater self-government was more conflict-ridden than it might otherwise have been because of intense federal-provincial struggles. Only in the 1960s did the government of Québec begin to take an active interest in the administration of its "provincial north," where the Native population was serviced by a strong federal (and anglophone) presence.[33] Much of the tension and acrimony surrounding the James Bay agreement in its early years was caused by the failure of the federal and provincial governments to live up to their undertakings, frequently placing responsibility for problems on one another. Native perception of the growing provincial presence in the region has focussed on the fact that they have

Nain, Labrador: Poorly constructed housing and streets characterize an area of Native settlement in this coastal community. (*Jean Cameron*)

only one government department to deal with in Ottawa, whereas in Québec City, for example, their concerns have been shifted from ministry to ministry.

That sense of frustration soured the attitudes of the Native people of northern Ontario to the provincial Royal Commission on the Northern Environment, established in 1977. Initially charged to study a proposal by the Ontario government to release the last large tract of uncommitted Crown forest to the paper company whose Dryden mill had been responsible for mercury pollution of the English-Wabigoon river system, the enquiry's mandate was broadened to cover the whole range of social and economic problems of the "provincial north." An interim report, issued in 1978, documented the concerns of a region where two-thirds of the residents are Indians.[34] Having neither traditional nor industrial skills, and therefore poorly integrated into the heartland-oriented economy, much of the predominantly youthful population experiences an alienating culture of discrimination and welfare-dependence, showing all the symptoms of social disorientation such as alcoholism, delinquency, and early mortality.[35] Nobody pretends that the region's problems have simple solutions, but the Royal Commission dragged on into the mid-1980s without presenting a final report. Natives, who initially welcomed the enquiry, came increasingly to see its protracted existence as a sign that the government was avoiding direct, effective action.

Since 1970, the voice of hinterland residents, especially of its Native peoples, has received increased attention through the media and through official enquiries. If there is now greater sensitivity to the vulnerability of the Shield's economy and of important segments of its society, this awareness comes at a time when reduced economic growth and fiscal constraint make it difficult to compensate for intrinsic regional handicaps and past neglect. Undoubtedly, the resource-based economy which has been created across the rugged expanse of the Shield is a major achievement of heartland society. But it is also, to some degree, an indictment of that society.

NOTES

1. Seven companies listed in *The Financial Post 500* (1984), some of them subsidiaries of larger groups, have their corporate headquarters located in the Shield: two each in Sault Ste. Marie and La Sarre, Qué.; one each in Thunder Bay, Kapuscasing, and Temiscaming.
2. Douglas Cole, "Artistics, Patrons and Public: An Enquiry into the Success of the Group of Seven," *Journal of Canadian Studies,* 13 (1978), 69-78.
3. J.B. Bird, *The Natural Landscapes of Canada,* 2nd ed. (Toronto: John Wiley and Sons Canada, 1980), p. 184.
4. H.V. Nelles, *The Politics of Development: Forests, Mines and Hydro-electric Power in Ontario, 1849-1941* (Toronto: Macmillan, 1974), chap. 2.
5. Nelles, *Politics of Development,* pp. 443-64; Gilles Piédalue, "Les groupes financiers et la guerre du papier au Canada, 1920-1930," *Revue d'histoire de l'Amérique française,* 30 (1976), 223-58.
6. Philip Mathias, *Forced Growth: Five Studies of Government Involvement in the Development of Canada* (Toronto: James Lewis and Samuel, 1971), chap. 6.
7. *The Financial Post,* October 1, 1983.
8. F.J. Anderson and N.C. Bonsor, *The Economic Future of the Forest Products Industry in Northern Ontario* (Thunder Bay: Lakehead University, for the Royal Commission on the Northern Environment, 1981).
9. Nelles, *Politics of Development,* pp. 326-35, 349-61; Jamie Swift, *The Big Nickel: Inco at Home and Abroad* (Kitchener, Ont.: Between the Lines, 1977), pp. 21-8.
10. J. Lewis Robinson, *Resources of the Canadian Shield* (Toronto: Methuen, 1969), pp. 23-7 and Fig. 3.1.
11. Iain Wallace, *The Transportation Impact of the Canadian Mining Industry* (Kingston, Ont.: Centre for Resource Studies, 1977), pp. 22-8. Calculations are based on a revised form of Table 3.
12. *Mineral Policy: A Discussion Paper* (Ottawa: Energy, Mines, and Resources Canada, 1981), p. 43.
13. *The Globe and Mail,* October 9, 1984; March 8, 1985.

14. John H. Bradbury and Isabelle St.-Martin, "Winding Down in a Québec Mining Town: A Case Study of Schefferville," *Canadian Geographer,* 27 (1983), 128-144.
15. John H. Dales, *Hydroelectricity and Industrial Development: Québec 1898-1940* (Cambridge, Mass.: Harvard University Press, 1957), chaps. 3, 4, 7; Nelles, *Politics of Development,* pp. 464-87.
16. R.C. Zuker and G.P. Jenkins, *Blue Gold: Hydro-Electric Rent in Canada* (Ottawa: Economic Council of Canada, 1984). The authors estimate that the economic rent enjoyed by Québec on power purchased from Churchill Falls exceeded half a billion dollars in 1979. J.B. Bird, *The Natural Landscapes of Canada,* 2nd ed. (Toronto: John Wiley & Sons Canada, 1980), p. 184.
17. Albert Tucker, *Steam into Wilderness: Ontario Northland Railway, 1902-1962* (Toronto: Fitzhenry and Whiteside, 1978), p. 7, quoting Ontario Premier George Ross.
18. Ivor G. Davies, "Agriculture in the Northern Forest: The Case of Northwestern Ontario," *Lakehead University Review,* 1 (1968), 129-53. Quotation on p. 133.
19. Justice E.P. Hartt, *Royal Commission on the Northern Environment: Issues Report* (Toronto: Queen's Printer, 1978), p. 54.
20. K. Winterhalder, "Environmental Degradation and Rehabilitation in the Sudbury Area," *Laurentian University Review,* 16, No. 2 (1984), 15-47.
21. L.D. McCann, "Canadian Resource Towns: A Heartland-Hinterland Perspective," in *Essays on Canadian Urban Process and Form II,* eds. R.E. Preston and L. Russwurm, Department of Geography Publication Series, No. 15 (Waterloo: University of Waterloo, 1980), pp. 209-67.
22. Because the Québec-Labrador iron mines are mainly vertically-integrated elements of United States steel corporations, they are largely independent of the Toronto mining and financial communities. The Iron Ore Company of Canada, for instance, maintains an office in Montréal, but its executive office is in Cleveland, Ohio and its head office is in Wilmington, Delaware.
23. Bradbury and St.-Martin, "Winding Down."
24. L.D. McCann, "The Changing Internal Structure of Canadian Resource Towns," *Plan Canada,* 18 (1978), 46-59.
25. Wallace, *Transportation Impact,* pp. 47-9.
26. Normand Brouillette, "Les facteurs de declin industriel de Shawinigan, province de Québec," *Cahiers de géographie de Québec,* 17 (1973), pp. 123-33.
27. D. Michael Ray, ed., *Canadian Urban Trends, Metropolitan Perspective,* Vol. 2 (Toronto: Copp Clark Publishing in association with the Ministry of State for Urban Affairs, Ottawa, 1976) contains the data from which the social statistics are derived.
28. G.R. Weller, "Hinterland Politics: The Case of Northwestern Ontario," *Canadian Journal of Political Science,* 10 (1977), 727-54.
29. Mid-Canada Development Foundation, *Essays on Mid-Canada* (Toronto: MacLean-Hunter, 1970); Ivor G. Davies, "The Emergence of Mid-Canada," *Lakehead University Review,* 3 (1970), 75-97.
30. Ontario Royal Commission on Electric Power Planning, *The Meetings in the North* (Toronto: Queen's Printer, 1976), p. 14.
31. *The Financial Post,* March 5, 1983.
32. *The Globe and Mail,* March 8, 1983.
33. G.R. Weller, "Local Government in the Canadian Provincial North," *Canadian Public Administration,* 24 (1981), 44-72.
34. Hartt, *Issues Report.*
35. Anastasia M. Shkilnyk, *A Position Stronger Than Love: The Destruction of an Objibwa Community* (New Haven, Conn., Yale University Press, 1985).

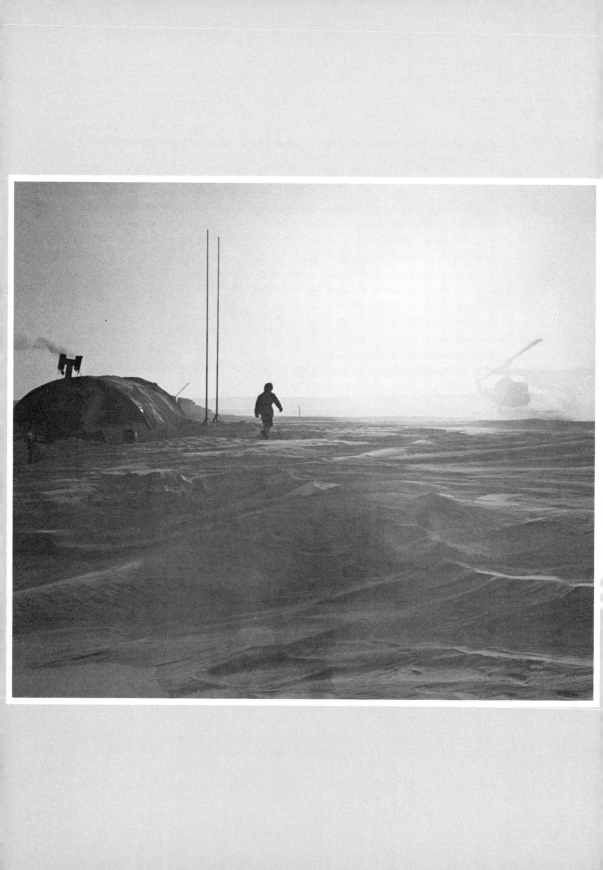

12

The North: One Land, Two Ways of Life

Peter J. Usher

The North is a region that has been of enduring fascination to many Canadians, but few have any experience of it and even fewer live there. The North comprises a large part of our country in area and differentiates Canada from most other nations. Not only do the North's physical, biological, and human attributes differ from those of other parts of the country, but they have also inspired a special view of the future. Our national mythology suggests that our identity and purpose lie in the North, that a truly distinctive Canadian nationality will only be achieved through the development and settlement of our northern lands. Some say that the North is our last frontier, that developments there will be new, different, and better. To the North lie not only our economic destiny, but also our moral and spiritual renewal. This chapter examines the origin and validity of these notions.

THE NORTH AS A REGION

Our focus in this chapter is on the territorial North: the Yukon and the Northwest Territories (N.W.T.). This is at once a political and an economic definition, and one which emphasizes the North's special status within Canada. It is a hinterland unlike any other region south of the sixtieth parallel. Politically, these territories have not had the full range of self-governing institutions that the provinces enjoy, and the central government in Ottawa guides their destiny to a degree unparalleled elsewhere in Canada. Economically, the territorial North is an internal Canadian colony. Unlike the provinces, the territories do not have jurisdiction over their mineral and energy resources. Instead, these resources are owned, and policies for their development devised, by the federal government in trust for all Canadians. Control over economic resources and political institutions is thus a major issue in the North.

The territorial North is indeed distinct from the rest of Canada. The Yukon Territory, with an area of 536 000 square kilometres, and the Northwest Territories, with an area of 3 367 000 square kilometres, contain 40 percent of Canada's land surface. The Arctic coastline is longer than the Atlantic and Pacific coastlines combined. The same applies to the area of Canada's Arctic territorial waters. Although estimates vary, some geologists believe that the territorial North holds as much as 50 percent of Canada's potentially recoverable oil and gas and perhaps 40 percent of its potential mineral wealth (not including sand, gravel, and fossil fuels). Despite this potential resource wealth, the territorial North cannot support significant agricultural, forest, or fishery production. The region receives relatively little solar radiation. It is characterized by low temperatures, by low precipitation in most areas, by poorly developed soils which are also permanently frozen (permafrost), by low species diversity, and with few exceptions, by cold and relatively stable marine waters which are frozen over for much of the year.

Accordingly, the North is a region of low biological productivity. At the same time, with populations of 23 075 and 45 535 respectively, the Yukon and N.W.T. accounted for only 0.3 percent of Canada's population in 1981. Of the total population in both territories, 21 and 23 percent were, respectively, Native peoples of Dene and Inuit descent.[1] The Northwest territories are unique in Canada in that the Native population outnumbers non-Native inhabitants. There is a high turnover of the non-Native population, for many are transient rather than permanent residents.

Yet the territorial North has similarities with the northern parts of the provinces. The northern areas of all but the Maritime provinces also constitute regional resource hinterlands and, many residents feel, political colonies of the more populous southern regions. The same sense of remoteness and powerlessness that is felt in the territorial North is also felt by residents of the northern areas of British Columbia, Manitoba, Ontario, and Labrador. To many southern Canadians, both the territorial and provincial parts of the North seem isolated, cold, dark, and uncomfortable.

The ways in which contrasting perceptions of the North have developed is the subject of much of this chapter. The view of the North as a distant and distinctive hinterland — but one which somehow illuminates the future of the nation — is the metropolitan view of the North. It is characteristic of the North's hinterland status that we know more about how southerners view the North than of the regional consciousness of those who live there. There are, however, essentially two other views of the North held by its inhabitants. One is the frontier view, commonly held by non-Native residents. This view tends to unite these people, often of diverse origins and backgrounds, in terms of their reasons for being there and the nature of their lives there. The other is the homeland view,[2] a perspective held chiefly by Native northerners — Indians and Inuit — who view the North neither as a hinterland nor as a frontier, but as their ancestral home which has undergone a continuing transformation due to the progressive encroachment of non-Native peoples and their social and economic institutions.

Physical Definition

How then are we to define the North? What are its boundaries? The territorial boundary at the sixtieth parallel is a political one which does not differentiate the character of the physical environment or the nature of human settlement north of that line. Similarly, the Arctic Circle is merely the latitude north of which the sun does not rise on the shortest day of the year and does not set on the longest. Lines of latitude tell us relatively little. Places such as Great Whale River on the eastern shore of Hudson Bay and Hopedale in Labrador, both just north of 55°, seem more barren and harsh than Dawson City or Fort Good Hope in the Western Interior, which are at 64° and 66° respectively.

Geographers and other natural scientists have therefore used certain bio-climatic criteria to define the North. They have identified two major natural environments: the Arctic and the Subarctic. The boundary between the two is usually defined as either the 10°C isotherm for July on land (surface waters consistently at or near their freezing point for the marine environment), or the tree line (in fact not a line at all, but a zone in which trees become fewer and smaller, until they are finally found only in the most favourable sites). The 10°C isotherm for July is nearly coincident with the treeline (Fig. 12.1).

The Arctic is treeless, whereas the Subarctic is commonly considered to consist of the northern forest zone, ranging from closed Crown forest, in the south, to open woodland in which tundra vegetation predominates, in the north. Coniferous species, especially spruce, dominate the Subarctic forest. Subarctic summers can be occasionally hot, but are always brief (not more than four months with a mean temperature exceeding 10°C). The winters are long and cold, although not as extreme as in the Arctic. The Arctic therefore includes very little of the Yukon, only the northern and eastern parts of the N.W.T., but also parts of northern Manitoba, Ontario, Québec, and Labrador. The Subarctic includes all of the remainder of the territorial North, plus the northern parts of all of the provinces except the Maritimes. A major physical attribute of the northern environment is permafrost, soils or rock frozen at all times of the year. In the Arctic, permafrost tends to be universal, whereas in the Subarctic, it is more likely to be discontinuous in its extent.

One of the distinctive features of the northern environment, and of the physical processes in it, therefore, is ice. On land, ice is not simply the result of a cold and long winter. Ground ice is a significant geomorphic agent. The occurrence of permafrost results in a specific hydrologic and

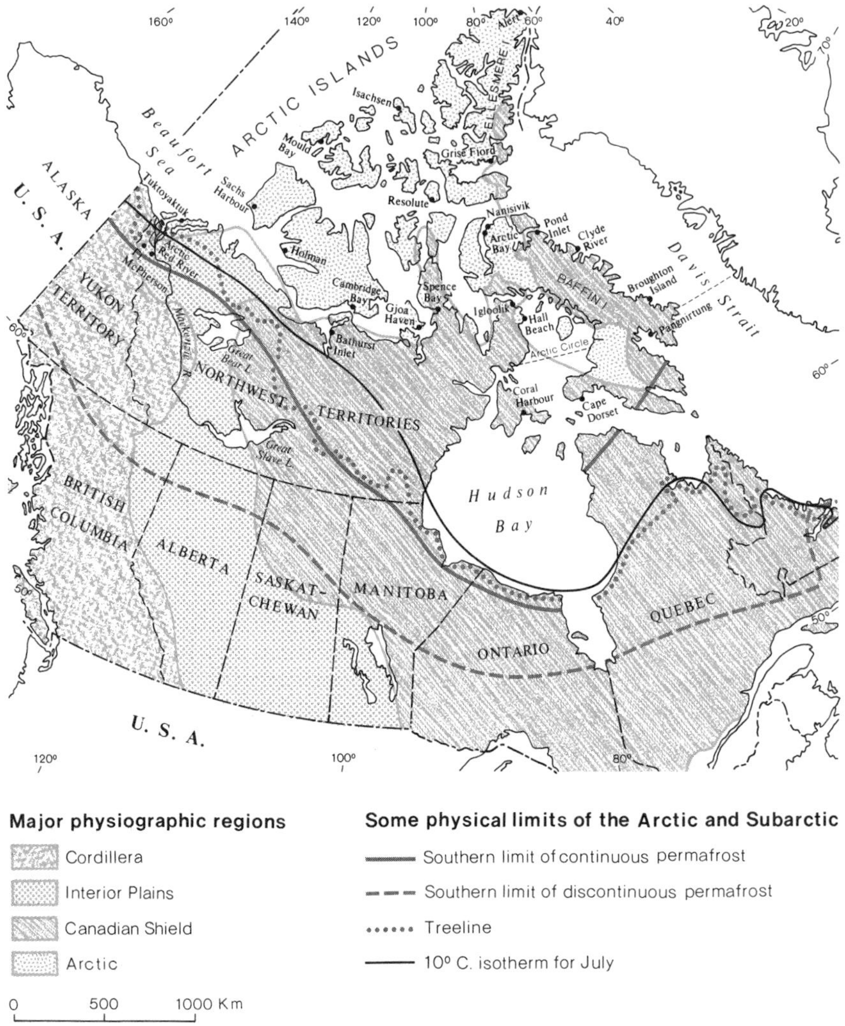

Figure 12.1 Selected physical characteristics of the North.

groundwater regime: water cannot flow at depth at any time of year, and consequently surface water must either run off entirely or saturate the active layer above the permafrost. Neither wells nor buried sewage lines are possible in such conditions. Permafrost with high moisture content, if melted, subsides unevenly, with the result that the construction of buildings, airfields, roads, and pipelines must be done so as to maintain the thermal regime at depth. Clearly, permafrost poses special problems for construction.[3]

At sea, the presence of heavy ice for much or all of the year is a distinctive feature of the Arctic environment. The southern Beaufort Sea in the Western Arctic, and Hudson Bay and Strait and Davis Strait in the Eastern Arctic, are ice-free for approximately 100 days. From October, however, they are generally covered by ice which reaches a maximum depth of two metres by late winter. This cover is punctuated by pressure ridges of jumbled, tilted, and rafted ice which pose formidable obstacles to travel, whether by dog team, snowmobile, or icebreaker. In less favourable waters, for example in the Central and High Arctic, the ice pack often fails to dissipate completely during the summer, with the result that heavier, multi-year ice is frequently encountered. Northwest of the Arctic Islands, there is a permanent cover of ice, in constant counter-clockwise motion in the western part of the Arctic Ocean. Icebergs, which consist of freshwater ice breaking off the glaciers of Greenland and Ellesmere Island, are encountered off the Eastern Arctic coast, and drift as far south as Newfoundland before melting completely. The existence of these various forms of ice in the ocean pose unique problems and possibilities for the human use of the Arctic seas.

The biological regime in the North, and especially the Arctic, is characterized by low species diversity, relatively simple food and energy chains, instability of populations, and slow growth rates. Many species are characterized by population cycles of dramatic amplitude. Arctic fox catches, for example, are known to vary by as much as ten-fold in large areas over a four-year cycle. The larger mammals, whether marine or terrestrial, tend to travel great distances; they either migrate seasonally in herds, or they wander as individuals over a large territory. In the Subarctic, by contrast, and especially in the more densely wooded areas, the larger terrestrial mammals do not range as widely. Fire, however, is a continuing ecological determinant there, and there is, over time, a shifting distribution of ecotypes from recent burns to mature forest. Consequently, the distribution of animals varies greatly within a region. The differences between Arctic and Subarctic fish and bird populations are less dramatic. It is a distinguishing feature of both environments, however, that population instability and slow growth rates place special limits on the human use of wildlife. These features, along with the instability of permafrost soils and slow vegetative recovery, account for the North's reputation as a "fragile" environment.

Aboriginal Occupation

The environmental differences between Arctic and Subarctic are reflected in the history of aboriginal occupation in the North. The Arctic is inhabited by the Inuit, a people oriented chiefly to the harvesting of marine resources and large migratory herds of terrestrial mammals. They developed a specialized technology, capable of converting such locally available materials as stone, bone, hides, animal oils, and snow into shelter, clothing, heat, light, tools, and transport. United by a common language (but with widely varying regional dialects), Eskimo peoples extend from the eastern tip of Siberia to eastern Greenland, and only about 20 percent live in Canada where they are known as Inuit. The Subarctic is occupied by various Indian peoples who belong to two major linguistic groups, the Athapaskan in the west and the Algonkian in the east. Within these groups there are a number of distinct peoples and languages. Nevertheless, they are united by a technology based on the snowshoe, the birch bark canoe, and the toboggan. All are peoples of the forest, relying chiefly on the harvesting of a combination of large and small game, and fish.[4]

From a non-Native point of view, however, the distinctions between Arctic and Subarctic are matters of degree rather than substance. Neither environment has offered the possibility of significant settlement based on agriculture. Moreover, as one progresses northward in the Subarctic, forest potential becomes extremely limited. Both Arctic and Subarctic have been perceived as sources first of animal wealth, in the form of furs, oil, baleen, and ivory, and more recently of mineral and energy wealth. Despite significant differences between the Arctic and Subarctic in terms of bio-climatic characteristics, animal populations, and aboriginal occupancy, the problems of colonizing and settling each are similar in terms of the difficulty of the environment, the distance from settled and familiar parts of the world, and the inhabitation by a Native population.[5]

COMMON HERITAGE, SHARED CONSCIOUSNESS?

The Arctic and Subarctic, in particular the northern forest and tundra beyond the fringe of agricultural settlement in Canada, have had a common history in several important respects. First, the Native inhabitants of the region originally derived virtually all of their food and clothing from fur, fish, and game. They were primarily hunters, relying on meat and fish for sustenance. Yet their remarkable hunting skills were not enough to free them from risks of periodic hunger or even starvation. Northern Native people ranged widely over the landscape in pursuit of game rarely found in sufficient concentration to allow permanent settlements of any size. Residential groups consisted of a few families, all engaged in primary production. There was no concept of private land or resource ownership in the European sense, although there were systems by which access to land and resources was recognized between, allocated within, and managed by, human groups.

Second, northern Native peoples share a common history of contact with white society, based chiefly on the fur trade. In most cases this contact has been with the Hudson's Bay Company because much of northern Canada was under charter to it until 1870. (However, early contact and trade with many Inuit groups occurred primarily through the search for the Northwest Passage by the British Navy, and the expansion of British and American whaling into Canadian Arctic waters during the nineteenth century. The fur trade was mainly a twentieth century phenomenon.) Throughout this period, many Native people abandoned their own technology and became increasingly dependent on trade for material goods which they were incapable of producing. As well, Christianity and English law were brought to bear on the consciousness of Native people.

The third element of common history is that northern Native people occupied territory never used for agriculture. Their lands were never widely or densely settled by whites and were never sub-divided or fenced off in private hands. Until recently, the landscape was not significantly altered by human exploitation. Given these circumstances, Native northerners have been able to hunt, trap, fish, and travel widely and without obstruction over "unoccupied Crown lands" practically to the present day. These circumstances also imply both a geographic and a social isolation from the settled parts of Canada, again until very recently.

Other factors stand out in the common history of the Arctic and Subarctic. Throughout the area during the 1940s and 1950s, the fur trade was in crisis. There was a sharp and persistent drop in the value of furs related to the cost of imported goods, and in some areas, a decline of fur and game stocks. During this crisis, Native people became both urbanized and more numerous. The predominant residence of most Native families is no longer the small, seasonal encampment; virtually all now live in centralized settlements of two types. One is the small, largely Native community, on or off the reserve. The other is the larger but predominantly white community, which by southern Canadian standards would be classed as a small town. As well, there has been a rapid growth in Native population in recent decades, to the point where in many northern communities, over half of the Native inhabitants are under the age of 16. The North, in sum, is an area in which Native people are a significant presence, one never far from the consciousness of neighbouring white residents.

For northern Native people, the post-World War II period has witnessed significant changes: a declining dependence on trapping as the central focus of life; increasing participation in some form of wage labour; and, in daily life, increased and more varied contact with non-Native people and institutions. At the same time, there has been a rapid growth of government intervention in the lives of Native people, as administrations at all levels have developed major programmes for, and spent rapidly growing amounts of money on, health, housing, municipal services, education, training, welfare, and job creation. These programmes are often directed specifically towards Native people and their communities.

These historical developments have also changed the circumstances of white migration to the North. The early explorers were almost all sponsored by national governments. During the commercial era, whites came as company traders, as missionaries for the major churches, and later, as members of the national police force. On the southern fringes of the Subarctic, small farmers, loggers, and prospectors were able to settle, and for a time, white trappers as well, although for many years now northern fur resources have been allocated chiefly to Native people. Independent traders and small businessmen are relative latecomers to the North, especially to the Arctic. Whites have come to the North in significant numbers only since World War II, chiefly in the employ of governments (especially in the Arctic), or to work in single-purpose resource towns (chiefly in the Subarctic). Most whites, however, migrate to the North as temporary residents, either to fill a particular job or to achieve a certain financial objective. Most eventually move south again. Few see their descendants establish themselves in the North; fewer still die there of old age.

Out of this northern experience there have emerged two viewpoints of what it is to be a northerner. Native people see the North as their ancestral homeland; a heritage they will never lose, wherever they might be. Their sense of community and identity is rooted in common descent and a shared history. They have a growing political consciousness, particularly concerning the question of control over land, resources, and political institutions, and the impact of development initiatives by government and large corporations. Theirs is the consciousness of the North as a homeland. For non-Natives in the North, community and identity are generally matters of choice and intent. People can and do define themselves as northerners on the basis of even a few months' residency. There is a growing regional consciousness among non-Natives in the North, fed in part by their small numbers, by their mobility, and by their restricted occupational structure. All of these factors create a remarkable continuity of personal acquaintanceship. Newly arrived residents in both administrative centres and resource towns, if they have been to other northern centres before, commonly discover other residents whom they knew previously on some other job in some other place in the North. The common experience of a harsh climate, high prices, limited amenities, and isolation from family and friends in the south unites non-Native residents. They are also united by a sense of common purpose, a feeling that they are indeed modern day pioneers, the advance guards of civilization and development in a hostile land. Theirs is the experience and the consciousness of the North as a frontier.

Yet the regional consciousness of both Natives and non-Natives is fragmented because the North is not an autonomous region with strong internal linkages. Its various parts are tributary to southern centres. The Yukon is part of Vancouver's hinterland, the Mackenzie Valley part of Edmonton's, the Keewatin part of Winnipeg's, and Baffin Island part of Montréal's. Contemporary air transport routes reflect this situation, building on patterns established earlier by surface transport. Even satellite communication links emphasize this regional dependence. Regional administrative centres, established at the northern termini of these metropolitan linkages, have tended to reinforce north-south orientation at the expense of east-west ties. To overcome this fragmentation, both Natives and non-Natives have attempted to develop pan-northern institutions and linkages. Native political and cultural organizations such as *Inuit Tapirisat* have arisen over the last decade, and have attempted to unite the interests of their members over broad areas of the North. The N.W.T. government has attempted to focus the consciousness of all northern residents, from Aklavik to Frobisher Bay (2900 kilometres west to east) and from Grise Fiord to Sanikiluak (2250 kilometres north to south) on a common administration based in Yellowknife. Despite these efforts, links remain tenuous, and the quest for a greater degree of shared consciousness remains largely unfulfilled.

TWO MODES OF PRODUCTION IN THE NORTH

The contrasts in consciousness of Natives and whites arise not only from their varying historical experiences, but also from their different circumstances in the present. The two ways of life in northern Canada are manifestations of two distinct *modes of production.* A mode of production encompasses not only the resources and technology by which a people make their living, but also the social organization and ideological system which combine the factors of production — land (including resources), labour (including skills, knowledge and technique), and capital (fixed investment in tools, buildings, transport, i.e. the means of production) — into a functioning productive system. It is the means by which a people provide not only for their material needs — food, clothing, and shelter — but also for their social and spiritual needs. To understand the dynamics of a mode of production, we must examine not only the factors of production, but also the ways in which human groups manage labour tasks, organize the ownership and use of production factors, and handle the distribution of product and surplus.[6]

The two modes of production in the North today are the domestic and the capitalist. The capitalist mode has been superimposed on the pre-existing domestic mode, but the latter survives in modified form. The two coexist not as isolated, unconnected enclaves, but rather as interrelated parts of a larger social formation, that of industrial capitalism on the frontier. Wherever two modes of production coexist, however, one is dominant. The Canadian North is no exception. As in all cases of capitalist expansion, the relationship between the two modes is mediated by capitalist relations of exchange, regardless of the internal dynamics of the non-capitalist mode. The industrial capital mode is the dominant and expanding one in the North today, and the domestic mode has been

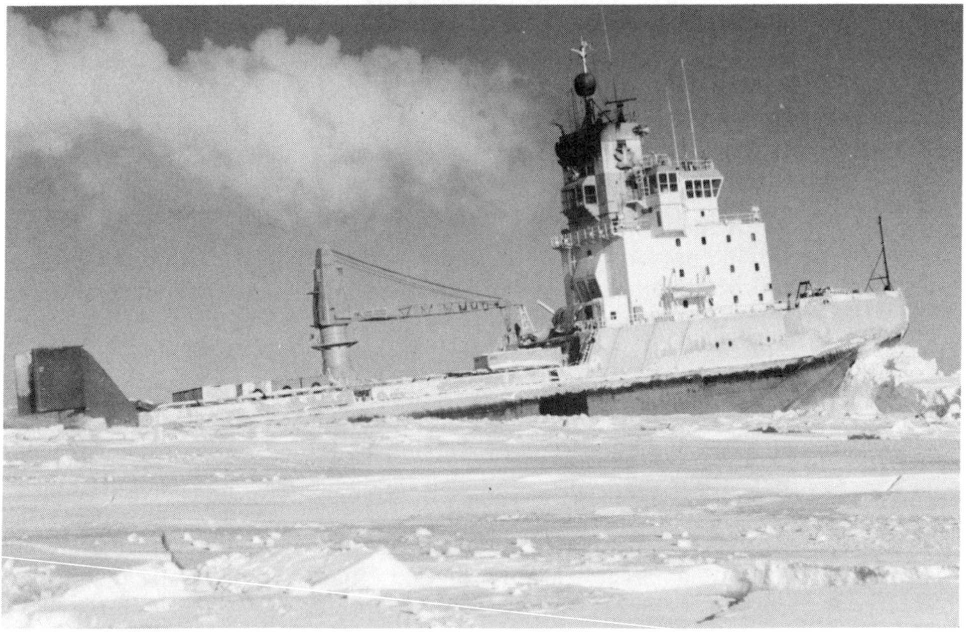

Two modes of production in the North: (Top) An Indian woman standing beside a fish wheel illustrates well the Native or domestic mode of production. (*Yukon Archives*). (Bottom) The industrial economy is characterized by complex technologies, capital intensive industries, corporate enterprise, and support from the state. (*Dome Petroleum Limited*)

rendered, to a large degree, dependent on it. This situation is the result of metropolitan penetration and domination of the frontier, a process best understood from an historical perspective. Before engaging in this discussion, however, we need to identify these modes (or economies) more precisely. One is variously called the Native, traditional, bush, subsistence, domestic, or household economy. It exists in contrast to the so-called industrial, modern, market, money, or capitalist economy. For convenience, we refer to these throughout as the Native and industrial economies.

The Industrial Economy

The industrial economy consists essentially of three sectors: government, corporate, and resident small business. The government sector is the largest, but relatively little of it is under direct local control. Central governments tend to aim for the orderly development of the frontier by and for metropolitan interests. The government agencies best represented on the frontier are those concerned with Native administration and services and with resource development; these are largely the responsibility of central governments — provincial south of the sixtieth parallel, federal north of that line.[7] The responsibilities of local governments, whether regional, territorial, or municipal, tend to focus primarily on the more immediate concerns of the white settler population and the resident business sector.[8] There tends, as a result, to be a conflict between local and senior levels of government, the former constantly seeking more power and autonomy. In any event, senior governments play an important role in the northern industrial economy by any measure — labour force, expenditure, or authority.

The corporate sector consists of large, externally-controlled organizations which extract, process, and export goods. Multinational oil companies exemplify this type. The more isolated the locale and the more difficult the environment, the more sophisticated and capital-intensive the corporate sector is likely to be; and the larger and more influential its individual members become.

The third sector — the resident small business group — rarely produces goods. If tourism and recreation are well developed, this sector may be significantly independent of its government and corporate counterparts. Otherwise, it will function in a dependent relationship with these sectors by providing them with retail, professional, transport, and other services. In general, the resident small business sector is both more developed and more independent in the southerly and accessible parts of the Canadian North.

The industrial economy in general is motivated by the search for staple resource exports by metropolitan interests. It is organized by corporate enterprise and is supported by the apparatus of the modern state. The mode of production, being capitalist, is reliant on external support systems and productive factors, which include enormous capital investments, specialized managerial and labour skills, and a complex infrastructure of transport, communications, and administration. In its goods-producing sector, the industrial economy is capital and energy-intensive and technologically sophisticated; in its service and administrative sectors, it requires less capital and technology but more labour. Money is the exclusive medium of exchange and prices are determined by market forces, except where power is sufficiently concentrated to allow any party to overcome these forces. Income is distributed unequally in the form of wages, salaries, profits, interest, and rents. The manner in which this income is spent, saved, or reinvested in productive factors is strongly influenced by the largest economic units in the system.

The tendency of any mode of production is to strengthen, both practically and ideologically, the ties and obligations involved in the social relations of production. In the industrial mode, this means strengthening attachments and obligations between owner and employer, between corporation and community, and between the job and the individual. The industrial economy, especially in the North, requires a labour force that is mobile and individualistic. Northern development needs people who are prepared to move from job to job and from place to place, sometimes frequently and on short notice. A premium is placed on personal mobility. Ties of family and friends and the desire for a stable community life are at odds with the needs of industrial development. While it is not impossible for industry in the North to reduce some of these problems, for example by improving living conditions outside the work place, reducing labour turnover, and providing transport to and communications with home, these measures are inevitably viewed as costs of production and must be justified as such.

The Native Economy

The Native economy, under modern conditions, consists generally of two sectors: a commodity or exchange sector and a subsistence or domestic sector.

The commodity sector was developed significantly by trade relations first with Europe and later with metropolitan North America (however, almost all northern Indian and Inuit groups had developed long distance trading relations among themselves for specialized products in aboriginal times). Some have argued that the establishment of these trade relations represents the adoption of capitalist productive relations by northern Native peoples. There is no question that the exchange sector has provided the underpinnings for the Native economy for decades, if not for centuries. It provided the means by which Native people related their own economy to the growing capitalist economy of North America. The key link in that relationship throughout the North was, until very recently, however, not the sale of labour but the sale of commodities. Although the relations of exchange were determined by European capitalism, the ownership of the means of production thus remained in the hands of Native people.

The subsistence sector produces goods for direct domestic consumption, while the exchange sector produces goods for trade, either for other goods (rarely services) or for cash. The organization of production is generally similar for each. The division of labour is based on sex and age, and occurs within rather than between productive units, which are typically households. Thus, it is possible to discuss the dynamics of both sectors under the rubric of the Native economy as a whole.

The Native economy exploits a combination of readily available resources and opportunities primarily for local consumption and benefit. It is organized predominantly by household units of production, although for certain purposes several households may cooperate in production. Essentially, labour is recruited and organized, and produce is distributed, according to the system of kinship. Suprahousehold political organization, for example at the band level, is relatively informal in most cases. The economy is neither capital nor energy-intensive, but relies instead on relatively small and simple productive factors that may be reproduced or purchased and maintained by the individual household. Money is one of several media of exchange, along with domestically produced goods. Value is determined only partially by market forces, as these are understood by most economists, with cultural and political considerations also playing an important role. Internally, value is derived from the utility of an object, rather than by its exchange value. Income, in the form of domestic produce, is distributed in more or less egalitarian fashion amongst an extended group. Cash income, derived from commodity exchange, tends to accrue to the producer, but there are means, such as sharing and gambling, which promote a rapid circulation and distribution of cash throughout the community. Savings are virtually nonexistent, reinvestment decisions are made at the household level, and there is a high propensity to spend cash income soon after its realization.

The Native northerner finds it difficult, in this economic mode, to accumulate capital on anything more than the modest scale required to obtain essential productive equipment (for example, boats, motors, snowmobiles, rifles, and fishing gear), most of which depreciate rapidly. Consequently, the Native economy suffers from a chronic shortage of capital and is much more labour-intensive in its goods-producing sector. It has virtually no service or administrative sector, except insofar as household labour might be classified as such.

The terms "Native" and "industrial," it should be noted, by no means imply a strict ethnic separation of economic activity. At present, virtually all non-Native residents of the North participate exclusively in the industrial economy, but very few Native people are totally dependent on the Native economy. Instead, they rely on some combination of the two. The above descriptions are intended to provide interpretive models. The nature and consequences of their interaction are best illustrated by reviewing the historical development of the North since European discovery.

THE PROCESS OF NORTHERN DEVELOPMENT

The North, since the time of European exploration, has undergone three major phases of development, whose timing and duration have varied considerably from one region to another. The transition from one phase to the next has often been gradual because, while new modes of production and the exploitation of new staple commodities soon displaced earlier ones, they did not always eliminate them. The initial phase consisted of discovery and commercial penetration first by Europeans and later by southern Canadians. The second was marked by the establishment of administrative colonialism by the Canadian government. The third and current phase is characterized by the development of an industrial mode of production, dominated and controlled by the Canadian heartland, and by extension, other centres of commerce and power in the western world.

Phase 1: Discovery and Commercial Penetration

The first phase, beginning with the voyages of discovery, led to an awareness of the North in Europe, to the establishment of direct trade relations with the indigenous peoples, and to the exploitation of the North's marine resources (chiefly the whale fishery). Aside from probable sporadic visits by Norsemen in the eleventh century, these voyages (mostly British) began as early as the sixteenth century in the Davis Strait area. Explorations continued into the early twentieth century in the more inaccessible parts of the Central Arctic and the interior of Keewatin, although by that time it was less a matter of discovery and more the extension of commercial relations to the last untouched groups of Inuit, and the extension of the concomitant influence of church and state.

Throughout most of this phase, the North was a European hinterland, but it differed from southerly parts of the Americas chiefly because its access and habitation were more difficult. It therefore became a frontier of exploitation rather than of settlement, requiring little or none of the apparatus of colonial administration. It was also, with certain exceptions – such as the early French fur trade in the eastern Subarctic and the nineteenth century American whale fishery in the Beaufort Sea and Hudson Bay — a British hinterland. The fur trade, the first great staple to be exploited, was organized by large European-based companies, the chief of which was the Hudson's Bay Company of London. This enterprise required only isolated trading forts that, except for local meat provisioning, were supplied entirely from overseas. Native labour produced the furs. Indeed, the company traders could afford, by and large, to wait for the Indians to bring their furs to the forts. Not until the Montréal-based Northwest Company was established in the 1770s was the fur trade aggressively brought to the Indians, and the northern interior explored by whites. The early fur trade was based on the beaver. The Subarctic was therefore drawn into this trade much earlier than the Arctic, where beaver are absent. The fur trade reached Great Slave Lake in the late 1700s and was then extended down the Mackenzie River and into the Yukon in the nineteenth century. The Inuit did not become involved in fur trapping until the early twentieth century. For them, the Arctic fox became the staple commodity.

Until 1870, the North was not a part of Canada. Rupert's Land, comprising the entire area draining into Hudson Bay, as well as the Northwestern Territory, was administered by the Hudson's Bay Company under monopoly charter from the Crown. The Arctic Islands, in turn, had been claimed by Great Britain. With the sale of Rupert's Land to Canada in 1870 and the transfer of the Arctic Islands to Canadian jurisdiction in 1882, control of the entire North passed to the new Canadian nation. A new era of commercial development soon began.

Direct overseas control of the North ended, but some features of the era remained. The major coastlines and rivers of the North had been charted, due as much to the quest for the Northwest Passage as to the pursuit of the fur trade. The fur trade, though a minor aspect of British imperial activity around the globe, had resulted, even by 1870, in the extraction of considerable wealth from the Canadian North. Initial metropolitan penetration had encouraged Native people to produce goods for exchange in addition to subsistence, which previously had been the almost exclusive objective of production. European trade goods were in most instances sufficient to induce this change, since metal knives, traps, firearms, pots, and similar items were obviously of great advantage to Native people in harvesting and processing fur, fish, and game. Aside from this reorientation, however, European economic interests sought neither to displace the North's Native inhabitants nor to disrupt their way of life, although both sometimes happened (chiefly through the spread of epidemic diseases and the establishment of intermediary trade relations among tribes, both of which caused major demographic shifts). The colonial powers did not need an elaborate administrative structure either to enforce a new system of law or to protect a large settler or resident population. Religious interests did seek to convert the Native inhabitants to Christianity, but as long as the fur trade and whaling interests prevailed, they were given little opportunity or encouragement to do so. (Northern Labrador, where the Moravian Mission controlled both religious and commercial activities, was an exception.)

The Canadian government's immediate objective in purchasing the territory of the Hudson's Bay Company was to gain access to the Prairies for agricultural settlement and development. Obtaining the Subarctic in the bargain was almost incidental. The subsequent acquisition of the Arctic Islands was spurred largely by the purchase of Alaska by the United States from Russia in 1867, and hence Canada's fear of further American encirclement. As Edward Blake, a former premier of Ontario and a leading nationalist and expansionist of the day, observed in a report to the Colonial Office in London: "... the object in annexing these unexplored territories to Canada is, I apprehend, to prevent the United States from claiming them, and not from the likelihood of their proving of any value to Canada..."[9] Thus, the new Dominion had, in a short time, acquired half a continent. Most of this acquisition consisted of land that, in the popular view, must have ranked among the most fearsome and inhospitable environments on the face of the globe. For the new country, focussed on the extreme southern parts of Ontario and Québec, the first task was the construction of the transcontinental railway and the settling of the Prairies. It could afford to do little else. With no external threat, it did not have to. The North could remain as a vast reserve for the future, its land and inhabitants left undisturbed until national policy deemed otherwise.

The transfer of Rupert's Land terminated the fur monopoly, thereby opening the region to settlement and other forms of economic exploitation. In succeeding years, numerous but small mining, logging, and commercial fishing enterprises were established north of the agricultural fringe, chiefly in areas accessible to the transcontinental railways or to major waterways. In the less accessible areas, however, commercial resource exploitation remained impractical unless the commodity had an extraordinary value relative to its mass. This, of course, was the basis of the fur trade. Not surprisingly, then, the first mineral development north of the sixtieth parallel was the Klondike Gold Rush of 1898. In anticipation of further settlement and development, the provincial boundaries were gradually extended northwards, to the sea in the east, and to the sixtieth parallel in the west. The present political division of the North dates from 1912 (except for the Québec-Labrador boundary that was defined in 1927). The Yukon was created as a separate territory in 1898. Railways pushed north in the new provincial extensions: to the Athabasca River in the early 1920s, to Churchill in 1929, and to Moosonee in 1932. The short but difficult railway from Whitehorse to tidewater at Skagway, Alaska, was completed in 1900.

The first permanent federal presence in the North, the Royal Northwest Mounted Police (R.N.W.M.P.), came as a response to the gold rush in the Klondike. During the early twentieth century, several more R.N.W.M.P. detachments were established across the North and in the High Arctic, and the federal government also dispatched expeditions to

Old mission at Fort Resolution, N.W.T., 1920: Anglican and Roman Catholic missionaries have always been present in the North, and appeared in the earliest phases of settlement, catering to the spiritual, educational, and medical needs of Native communities. (*PA-101517/Public Archives Canada*)

conduct geological surveys, scientific research, and exploration. The chief purpose was to show the flag. The Americans and the Danes had also sent expeditions to the far North, creating the fear that Canadian sovereignty there could be challenged. Otherwise, however, the federal government maintained no presence in the North. Even 50 years after Confederation, there were no publicly employed doctors, teachers, or administrators in the Northwest Territories.

This complacency was shaken in 1920, however, by the discovery of oil below Fort Norman on the Mackenzie River. Mindful of the experience of the Yukon gold rush, when good luck and the dedication and competence of a tiny police force and civil service had maintained Canadian law and sovereignty in that district, the government moved hastily to establish its presence in the Mackenzie District. First, it created, in 1920, the Northwest Territories and Yukon Branch of the Department of the Interior to deal exclusively with the territorial North. Administrative offices were located at Fort Smith, the head of navigation on the Mackenzie River. Second, it arranged a treaty with the Dene. These events heralded further commercial development. The fur trade became well established even among the most remote Inuit, due in part to greatly improved river and coastal shipping. The airplane made it possible to travel easily and quickly about the North. Gold, silver, and radium mines were discovered and developed in the Yukon and in the Mackenzie District. A rudimentary administrative and commercial infrastructure was established, along with regular shipping and mail services. Business and commerce could be conducted more easily.

Yet there remained a conspicuous lack of official concern for the Native inhabitants. The government had sought to remove any encumbrance to land title and settlement and the police maintained law and order. Beyond these measures, however, the government showed little responsibility for those people over whose territories it had assumed control. Responsibility for the Inuit, with whom no treaties were ever signed, was shifted from one agency to another in government. In the case of northern Québec, the provincial and the federal governments fought each other all the way to the Supreme Court in 1939 to shift responsibility for the Inuit to the other party. The federal government lost, and was forced to assume fiscal responsibility for Inuit health and education.[10] As in other parts of the North, however, these services were actually provided by the Catholic and Anglican missions which, during the preceding decades, had become well established in the North, gaining influence among Native people. In the twentieth century, the colonial administration of the North came to be personified by the trader, the police officer, and the missionary.

This period of more intensive commercial penetration, from within Canada, brought many changes to the Native inhabitants of the North. Disease and trade-induced demographic changes continued and in some areas intensified. By the early twentieth century, many believed that northern Indians and Inuit were, along with the other aboriginal inhabitants of North America, vanishing peoples. The economic life of Native peoples was increasingly disrupted by both intended and unintended overkilling of fur and game populations. Some overkilling was caused by white trappers and whalers, some by Native people in response to commercial incentives. Overharvesting was made easier by the introduction of new technology such as the rifle. There were also changes in the material culture and observable behaviour of Native people. They had come to adopt many items of Euro-American technology, dress, and food, while certain traditional skills and practices atrophied. More spoke English and observed Christian rites.

Yet despite these changes, the Indians and Inuit of the North continued to engage in the traditional mode of production: hunting and fishing for subsistence, trapping (and sometimes fishing) for exchange. In some areas, unskilled seasonal wage labour became common, but this was for the most part easily integrated with the traditional mode. Work in sawmills or at trading posts and in guiding and survey parties became another way of obtaining trade goods at the store, during a season when trapping was not possible or profitable. The new economy allowed people to stay on the land and to live by their traditional skills and values. Indeed, it often rendered that life easier and more secure. In many respects, the period was one of social and economic stability. It was an era today's middle-aged and older Native people still remember in much of the North, and which they regard as traditional. It was the time when their consciousness as a people, and their relations with the non-Native world,

The traditional economy: This photo of a Native family near Hudson's Bay, was taken in 1910, illustrates both change and stability in the Native mode of production. The caribou and the dress of the woman and children are traditional food and cultural elements of this hunting society, but the man's clothes and cleaning knife symbolize interaction with an exchange, or capitalisic, economy. (*Yukon Archives*)

were formed. Nonetheless, it was an era in which the traditional mode of production became dependent on external mercantile, and later capitalist, economies. These metropolitan societies set the terms of trade (and consequently could extract an economic surplus for use elsewhere), and brought their civil and religious order to the hinterland. It became evident to Native people that "outsiders," though few in number, wielded authority. The creation of economic dependence was a deliberate policy on the part of the trading companies, for when the quality of trade goods was not a sufficient inducement for Native people to produce a surplus for exchange, the destruction of traditional food resources was encouraged.[11]

Phase II: Administrative Colonialism and the Welfare State

The second phase of metropolitan incorporation came with the central government's full assumption of sovereignty. As before, change occurred largely in response to external pressures. World War II brought a new appreciation of the strategic significance of the North, an appreciation that continued to grow with the Cold War of the 1950s. Airfields and bases were established in the northwest to link the United States with Alaska, and in the northeast to provide staging points for Europe. The northwestern link was strengthened by the construction of the Alaska Highway in 1942. In the post-war years, joint Canadian-American weather stations were established in the High Arctic. In the mid-1950s, two major radar lines were built across the North. The Mid-Canada line followed roughly the fifty-fifth parallel, and the DEW line the seventieth. The threat to Canadian sovereignty came most alarmingly from Germany, Japan, and later the Soviet Union, but most immediately from the United States, which built and controlled most of the airbases and radar stations, and which was eager to extend its sphere of influence.

The construction of these facilities brought a level of technology, investment, and productive organization previously unknown in the North. At about the same time the military arrived, there developed a crisis in the fur trade, due chiefly to a long, steady decline in fur prices accompanied by a sharp increase in the cost of imported goods. Metropolitan fur interests cut their investment in the northern trade by reducing credit both to trappers and to local independent traders, and by closing smaller or less profitable posts. No longer able to outfit themselves by trapping, many Native people gravitated to the new military installations in search of employment, or in more desperate situations, in search of food and other goods.

The collapse of the fur trade in the post-war years was accompanied by an increasing awareness (promoted by writers, journalists, and government reports) on the part of southern Canadians that there were fellow citizens in the North who suffered from economic want, and who also lacked the modern conveniences and opportunities enjoyed by most

Canadians. The post-war feeling against traditional colonialism, along with a growing ethic of "equality of opportunity," created a climate ripe for change in the far North. The publicity surrounding a few dramatic incidents of suffering and starvation, particularly among the Keewatin Inuit in the 1950s, demanded action. The federal government could no longer maintain a laissez-faire approach to the North and its inhabitants. Capitalism had suddenly failed Native people, and in the context of the dawning welfare state, the government was widely seen as having no alternative but to intervene.

Thus began a period of significant government intervention in northern life. It was initiated by the extension of family allowances and old age pensions to Native northerners in the late 1940s. The construction of federal schools and nursing stations followed during the 1950s and 1960s, and the provision of public housing and municipal services (water, power, fuel delivery, and waste disposal) in the 1960s and 1970s. Similar services and benefits were extended to Native communities in the provincial North, often with the cooperation of the federal government. Some argue that these measures have led to a peculiar form of government totalitarianism, in which virtually no facet of Native life remains uninfluenced by the state.

Yet there can be little doubt either of the need for at least some of these government initiatives, or of the humanitarian motives behind them. Native health and housing conditions had become appalling in many parts of the North by the 1950s. Government involvement sparked an influx of teachers, nurses, and administrators, all of whom had to be fed and sheltered. In the smaller settlements, the civil servants received modern housing and services long before these were extended to Native residents. But since these large investments were most economically and conveniently administered in larger centres, government had to select and develop the necessary growth points. The construction of new towns, such as Inuvik and Frobisher Bay, and the transformation of established mining centres, such as Yellowknife, into administrative capitals stemmed directly from this second phase of northern development. In retrospect, it is evident that government programmes were implemented according to metropolitan perceptions. Northern needs in health, education, shelter, and welfare were identified by the government and responded to by the government. Though intentions were humanitarian, programmes often proceeded in ignorance of how the Native people lived and therefore often did not solve fundamental problems.

The consequences of these changes for Native people have been profound. The two most important were a shift in population from the temporary camps to permanent settlements and a major upheaval in Native culture and institutions. Both changes made living on the land more difficult. Whereas previously it had been in the interests of the fur trade for Native people to live on the land and away from the settlements, it was now in the interest of the government for Natives to move off the land and into the settlements. When explaining this movement, many observers have emphasized the attractions of these central places: greater security of income and health; the opportunity to obtain cash, either through casual labour or welfare payments, more easily than through trapping; and the range of goods, services, and amenities available there. For many, however, the move to the towns was not voluntary. Compulsory schooling (which meant that to stay on the land was to be separated from one's children), and the lack of alternatives to casual employment and welfare as a means of supplementing hunting and fishing, compelled many to make the move. So depressed was the traditional economy that the most unskilled and lowest paid Native employee in town could live in more security and comfort than a highly skilled and esteemed hunter and trapper.

Federal, provincial, and territorial administrations of all political persuasions had come to a common understanding of the problem of Native people in the North, and determined what to do about it. They concluded that the traditional way of life was fast dying, and that the only avenue for Nateve people was to forsake their traditional ways and take up those of the modern world. The immediate solution to the crisis was in health and welfare programmes. The long-run solution was to educate Native people and give them wage employment. These policies led, particularly in the larger centres, to the growth and entrenchment of a largely ethnic-based class structure. Good jobs, benefits, housing and services, and high cash incomes went mainly to non-Native government employees and business people. There were few Native people in the new resource- or transport-based towns.

The dependency of Native people increased as a consequence of this second phase of metropolitan incorporation. The maintenance of the traditional economy, formerly dependent on the production of furs for exchange, became more difficult. Subsistence production remained important (although it was temporarily interrupted in some areas), but it was virtually unnoticed and unacknowledged by non-Natives. The exchange sector was weakened. The production of furs declined sharply, but in some areas commercial fishing, handicraft production, and similar activities still provided some economic support. The continuing need for trade goods was met by a combination of seasonal (summer) wage employment, family allowances, pensions, and welfare payments. The problem with transfer payments, however, was that they were obtained not by traditional skills and organization, but from bureaucrats of whom Native people had little understanding and even less control. Although Native people remained primarily oriented to their traditional mode of production, they became dependent on the government for shelter, heat, and power, and for the education of their children.

Phase III: The Transition to an Industrial Mode of Production

The third phase began in the 1950s and 1960s and has since gathered momentum. It is characterized by the ascendancy of the corporate sector's large-scale resource exploration and development. At least as important is the expectation, support, and encouragement given this sector by both the government and resident small business sectors. Once again, therefore, external pressures have played a leading role in metropolitan advance. Earlier mineral developments, in contrast, were often the result of personal initiatives. Typically, they received only marginal attention from the industry as a whole and little support (and indeed, little response) from governments. These earlier developments were rarely seen as strategic to the national economic or military interest. When they were seen as such, as in the case of the radium mine at Great Bear Lake during World War II, the central government did not hesitate to take command.

Since World War II, the dwindling resources of the United States have forced it, as well as the European Economic Community and Japan, to rely increasingly on hinterland sources. In this search for new materials, northern Canada has received growing attention. For example, the needs of the American steel industry led to the opening in the early 1950s of the Labrador-Ungava iron mines. World demand for lead and zinc resulted in the development in the mid-1960s of the Pine Point mine south of Great Slave Lake. These developments heralded even more massive projects designed to extract the mineral and energy resources of the North, almost entirely for foreign rather than Canadian consumption.

Most of the important development projects recently completed or in progress in northern Canada are related to energy, chiefly hydroelectric power development in the east and fossil fuel extraction in the west. The former includes two of the largest power stations in the world — at Churchill Falls, Labrador and on La Grande Rivière in Québec — and the development of the Churchill and Nelson Rivers in Manitoba. The latter includes the steady exploration for and, in some cases, development of oil and gas fields in northern Alberta (including tar sands developments), British Columbia, the Mackenzie Valley, the Beaufort Sea, and the High Arctic. Only the more southerly of these have been brought into production, but the exploration and planning phases of hydrocarbon development in the territorial North have already brought unprecedented investment and change to that region.

Significant reserves of oil and gas have been found in the North and there is every expectation that commercial quantities will also be found in various parts of the western and northern Northwest Territories. Exploration is also occurring in the eastern offshore regions from Lancaster Sound to Labrador. In general, the investment capital for resource development has come from abroad or has been amassed from

Canadian sources by foreign-based multinationals. The development of a Crown-owned integrated oil company (Petro-Canada), along with policies designed to encourage Canadian investment and ownership, however, has been an important exception to this trend.

Since the late 1960s, there have been numerous proposals for means to transport oil and gas from the North. The voyage of the Manhattan, an American tanker, through the Northwest Passage in 1969 heralded the possibility of a commercial shipping route to bring Alaskan oil, and potentially oil from the Canadian Arctic, to the eastern United States. More recently, there have been proposals to transport liquified natural gas by ship from the High Arctic to southern markets. However, pipelines are generally considered the safest and most cost-efficient mode of transport and there have been numerous proposals for pipeline developments. The most important follow three major routes: the Mackenzie River Valley route to bring gas from Prudhoe Bay in Alaska and the Mackenzie Delta in Canada to the American Midwest; the Alaska Highway route through the Yukon, designed for the same purpose; and a route from the High Arctic west of Hudson Bay, running south through Ontario to the Great Lakes region.

These gas and oil transport proposals are subject to extensive government review processes, chiefly by the National Energy Board, but also by environmental agencies and sometimes by public inquiries established to determine the regional social and economic impacts. The best known of the latter was the Mackenzie Valley Pipeline Inquiry which, in 1977, recommended that no pipeline be built along that route for at least ten years to provide time for the settlement of Native claims and the development of programmes and institutions that could minimize the risks and maxamize the benefits of development.

Later that year, the Canadian and American governments approved the Alaska Highway route in principle, but construction never proceeded due to financial difficulties. Although several proposals have since been put forward for the transport of both gas from the High Arctic and oil from Alaska and the Western Arctic, the only one implemented to date has been the small-diameter oil pipeline south from Norman Wells along the Mackenzie Valley. That line, based on the expansion of the existing Norman Wells oilfield in production for over 40 years, began operation in 1985.

The development of the mining frontier was less dramatic during this period. Declining prices for many minerals, and the development of lower cost mines in Third World countries, have been important factors. Major developments in the Canadian North have included two lead-zinc mines in the Arctic (Nanisivik on northern Baffin Island in 1976 and Polaris on Little Cornwallis in 1981), and uranium mines in northwestern Saskatchewan. However, other proposals such as uranium mines in Labrador, iron mines on northern Baffin Island and in the northern Yukon, and coal

The resource frontier: Increasingly since the late 1950s, metropolitan-based multinationals have forced the industrial mode of production on the North. The search for oil and natural gas and the eventual exploitation of these resources will have a tremendous impact on the social and economic structure of the region. (*Dome Petroleum Limited*)

mines in northern Ontario, have come no closer to fruition even though developers have known about some of these deposits for many years.

These developments, actual and proposed, require an enormous deployment of labour and capital and often involve innovative technology. They have attracted much public attention and have led many to believe that a "breakthrough" in the exploitation of northern resources is close at hand. Often, one major project such as a gas pipeline or oil tanker route is seen as the wedge that will quickly open the door to many other developments, by providing essential transport and other infrastructure requirements. A review of the last decade, however, suggests that this may not be the case. Of the numerous major proposals for either mineral and energy developments or related transport systems, few have actually been brought into production or operation. Even those which at one time had the full backing of the federal government, as a national priority, have been abandoned or delayed. No new oil and gas fields have yet been brought into production in the territorial North.

The distribution of mineral production is also little changed. Most mines are still to be found in the south central part of the Yukon and around Great Slave and Great Bear Lakes. Although the value of mineral production in the N.W.T. and Yukon approximately doubled between the early 1970s and the early 1980s, this increase was due mainly to inflation. The actual volume of production declined for almost all minerals except gold. Yet the last decade has seen steady progress in establishing an inventory of the North's mineral and energy resources. Seismic exploration and exploratory drilling increased during the 1970s, peaking first on land and later on the continental shelf. Mineral exploration also increased significantly. There is now a much greater corporate commitment to the development of these resources, in terms of capital investment, exploration, ownership or lease rights, and research.

The rate at which this development will occur, however, may be slower than was anticipated a decade ago. Instead of a series of spectacular "megaprojects," there may be a more gradual and incremental infilling along already established lines. The fact remains that the North is a high-cost and comparatively disadvantaged environment in which to work. Physically, its harsh climate, permafrost, and marine ice conditions are major barriers to development. In human terms, it remains an unfamiliar environment situated far from the core of settlement. Distance from manufacturing and consuming centres, and the difficulties of overcoming that distance, whether on land or on sea, remain powerful deterrents to northern resource development. Major developments, which would add significantly to national resource production, are still more likely to occur in the Subarctic than in the Arctic.

A survey of major developments in the North does not, however, reveal much of the process of metropolitan incorporation in the frontier. Nor does it convey the changes which proceed regardless of whether any particular development proposal is implemented. For these concerns, we must return to our model of the industrial economy and examine the penetration of its various features in the North. Each of the three major sectors — corporate, government, and resident small business — have become more firmly entrenched in recent years.

This penetration has taken several forms. First, exploration activity alone, during the last decade, has offered industrial employment opportunities to Native northerners on an unprecedented scale. Particularly in the territorial North, federal government policy has stressed that the private sector provide industrial training and employment.

Second, although industrial development in the territorial North did not reach anywhere near the proportions that it reached in neighbouring Alaska — or even in the northern parts of Alberta, Québec, or Labrador — both the expansion in exploration activity and the anticipation of future developments promoted rapid growth in the government and resident small business sectors. In the N.W.T., the transfer of responsibilities —

such as financial management, education of Native people, and social services — from the federal government in Ottawa to the territorial government, newly established in Yellowknife, has proceeded rapidly in the past decade. (The transfer of these functions occurred earlier in the Yukon, and their growth has been rapid there as well.) In the early 1960s, Yellowknife was basically a mining town where small government offices were housed in modest, two-storey wooden buildings. Since the official seat of government was moved there from Ottawa in 1967, it has become a regional administrative centre and has tripled in population. Now, numerous federal and territorial government agencies operate out of modern high-rise office buildings.

Third, the non-Native population of the North has increased in recent years and has concentrated either in administrative centres such as Whitehorse, Yellowknife, Inuvik, and Frobisher Bay, or in resource centres such as Fort McMurray, Labrador City, and Churchill Falls. While there is both a growing non-Native population in the small communities and reserves and a continuing drift of Native people into the larger centres (chiefly the administrative ones), there is also a growing distinction between large centres whose population is chiefly non-Native and smaller centres inhabited primarily by Native peoples. The turnover of population is much higher in the larger centres. Indeed, the bulk of the non-Native population in the territorial North must still be classed as transient.

Those who do remain in the North tend to be involved in the small but growing resident small business sector.[12] This sector's growth is a direct result of the increase in the non-Native population and in spending by both the government and corporate sectors. Consequently, although this sector frequently espouses an ideology of frontier individualism, free enterprise, and autonomy from central governments, it is dependent on the extension of metropolitan institutions and control into the frontier. The emergence of this business sector typifies a pattern already well established in the history of Canadian frontier settlement: the central government, rather than a class of independent frontiersmen, usually opens the way for development and settlement. Later, once there is a well established group of settlers, and particularly a local business and professional elite, it is typically the territorial rather than the federal government which most actively advances their interests. By the same token, the Native population might see its interests more directly threatened by both the local settler population and the local government, rather than by the central government. This is particularly true when lands and resources are alienated directly to settlers, and apparently less so when these are alienated to large metropolitan corporations.

The growth of government employment and spending in the North now proceeds on the assumption of steady and imminent progress toward the industrialization of the region's economy. Industrialization in this context means not just the establishment of industry or the growth of blue-collar employment, but rather the widespread establishment of capitalist relations of production. In this system, the bulk of personal income will be derived from wage employment rather than the production of goods for subsistence or exchange. Industrialization of this kind involves the establishment of a full range of welfare state machinery, including pensions, unemployment insurance, and government programmes for job training, employment creation, labour allocation, and regional economic development. As well, it requires an appropriate banking and financial infrastructure. The introduction of these structures, rather than the development of industry as such, has characterized the last decade in the territorial North, and has integrated the region more fully into the national economy. No longer are government functions concentrated in one department of northern administration, a characteristic feature of the era of administrative colonialism. Instead, the apparatus of the welfare state and the industrial economy is increasingly handled by the full array of government and corporate agencies in southern Canada.

COMPETITION BETWEEN THE TWO MODES OF PRODUCTION

When large-scale resource development and modern government centres first appeared in the North, many regarded the native and capitalist economies as independent because, although they existed in close geographic proximity, there were few linkages between them in terms of cash or commodity flow, transport, labour, or technology. The chief point of contact appeared to lie with the capitalist economy's employment of Native peoples, and even this was restricted largely to the resident business sector (chiefly tourism and recreation) and to the government sector (chiefly unskilled labour). Such employment was mostly available in the larger settlements, where Native people were incorporated into the lowest and least secure levels of the occupational structure.

The apparent independence of the two modes of production gave rise to the notion of a dual economy. Since economic growth (or measures to promote it) in the industrial or modern sector failed to stimulate growth in the Native or traditional sector, it was assumed that the two sectors were functionally separate. The concomitant solution to the problems of the "moribund" Native economy, therefore, was to move people out of it and into the modern economy. Not surprisingly, then, one prevailing view among governments has been that mineral and energy development is not only the way in which the North will make the greatest possible contribution to the national (or provincial) economy, but also that such development offers the only viable economic option to an apparently "impoverished and unproductive" Native population.

Despite the few direct linkages between the two modes of production however, both have always been dependent on, and functionally related to, the metropolitan economies of the south. The modern economy in the North has direct economic and transport links to the metropolitan economy. The Native economy is by no means an aboriginal enclave; it is directly connected to the metropolis by virtue of its exchange component. The two economies have always been so connected. Recently, the advance of industrial development in the North has resulted in widespread conflict over land use, resource management, and the allocation of public and private funds, as well as in the concerted encouragement of Native people to join the industrial labour force. In short, direct competition has arisen between the two economies for the essential factors of production — land, labour, and capital. The Native economy is thus directly affected by the capitalist economy, precisely because of the structural linkages between them.

Competition for land, labour, and capital has arisen in several ways and has generated many of the contemporary concerns and conflicts in the North. During the first phase of northern development, in which furs were the staple export commodity, Native people were an integral part of the production process. They were encouraged to retain their ties to the land and their way of life. During the second phase of development, the locus of contact between whites and Natives was restricted to the administrative and trade centres. The intrusion of non-Native society and authority, massive as it was, was limited in geographical extent to a few tiny dots on the enormous map of the Northland. Life on the land remained basically unchanged, and Native people continued to enjoy relatively free access to the land and its resources. The third and most recent phase of development, however, has introduced a new dimension — the practical implementation of non-Native ownership and control of the land.

Certain land-oriented activities, such as the exploration for oil and gas and the development of hydroelectric power, are not restricted to a particular site. They are widely dispersed and have broad environmental implications. Seismic exploration crews in the Western Arctic and Mackenzie Delta, their use of explosives and heavy equipment, poor trail construction and garbage disposal practices, and their occasional interference with traplines and bush camps, raised fears among Native people that the land — their chief source of livelihood — was being threatened. Similar problems, as well as the prospect of extensive flooding, have accompanied hydroelectric development in northern Québec, and raised parallel concerns among the James Bay Cree. Since the early 1970s, stricter environmental regulations have been enacted, and the performance of many companies engaged in exploration and development in the North has improved. Yet, it seems inevitable that large-scale development in the North will eventually lead to reduced species diversity and to smaller populations and reduced ranges for many surviving species, especially the larger mammals. Industrial pollution may also threaten certain country food sources (game, fowl, and fish).

Concurrently, as the non-Native population of the North grows, competition will increase for the fur, fish, and game that remain. Although Native people have always had exclusive or prior harvesting rights to these resources, this special status is now questioned both by resident non-Natives, who seek the commercial, recreational, or subsistence benefits of these resources, and by non-residents, who increasingly see the North as a last wilderness, whose wildlife and wildlands should be preserved, not exploited. As well, anti-trapping and anti-hunting lobbies in southern Canada and other industrial nations pose a threat to traditional economic activities in the North.

Competition for labour stems chiefly from government and industry employment policies. The decline of trapping as a central focus of life in many areas, the intensified schooling of young Native people, and the more general effects of change in the North, all have clearly led Native people to increase their demand for wage employment. At the same time, however, there is a concern that these employment opportunities be consistent with continued participation in hunting and fishing, and with continued residence on the reserves or in the small communities. Employment in the resource industries is frequently incompatible with these objectives: long periods away from home and community may be required, and the employee may be in no position to provide country food for his family. In some situations, employers have been willing to negotiate special arrangements, but these are not always possible. This same flexibility is not evident in government employment programmes, in which jobs are conceived within the framework of an industrial rather than a domestic or exchange mode of production. Employment opportunities made available by government initiative in the North thus tend to ignore the question of compatibility with the traditional mode, and thereby increase the pressure on Native people to abandon traditional livelihoods.

There is also competition for capital resources, in the sense that as programmes and policies become more oriented to an industrialized economy, less public capital is available to finance or modernize the Native mode of production. Both public and private sector spending, the control of which frequently lies outside of the territories or at best in the large, regional administrative centres, are becoming more oriented to the concepts of investment, business, and employment that prevail in the more industrialized parts of Canada. As a consequence, relatively less capital is available for Native enterprise, and the inequalities between the two modes become institutionalized.

As the Native mode of production is increasingly hobbled, despite its continued support by many Native people, metropolitan dominance and hinterland dependency are increased. The two are inevitably linked; and the pattern, well-established on the Canadian frontier since European discovery, has been replicated in the North. Native dependency has deepened progressively with each phase of northern development. The demand for Native peoples' produce was replaced first by the demand for their souls and allegiance and more recently for their land and resources. Where there were formerly only a few outsiders in the North, many dependent for their personal survival on Native people, there are now many outsiders, only some dependent on Native people for their jobs, and none dependent on Native people for their survival.

As the non-Native communities in the North have become able to meet their own material and social needs, they can now achieve, in collaboration with metropolitan interests, their objectives on the frontier independently of the Native population. There is definite concern that Native people will be transformed from an essential element in the productive life of the North to a "problem" of northern development. Some believe that this has already happened. Native people can rely less on their traditional resources, organization, and skills. They depend more on jobs, shelter, and social services that they cannot control. Many Native people fear that the process of industrial development, whatever benefits it may bring in the form of jobs, commodities, and services, will in the long run leave them poorer and more dependent. Earlier experiences in construction, in operational or maintenance jobs at military bases, on road, dam, or town site construction, or in mines or forestry operations, suggested that industrial employment was often unreliable and unstable. Frequently, the best jobs went to outsiders who eventually left, taking their money and experience with them, while Native people filled the marginal, low-paid positions. Many also fear that non-renewable resources will be taken out of the region, creating wealth in distant places, but leaving their own lands and waters polluted, degraded, and unable to sustain fur, fish, and game resources in traditional abundance.

Some of these past experiences may have been unavoidable. Some of these fears for the future may prove unfounded. They have, nonetheless, influenced Native peoples' perceptions of contemporary industrial development in the North. There is a considerable difference between the perceptions of Natives and whites about the costs and benefits of industrializing the North.

THE CONTEMPORARY NORTH

The North is changing rapidly and any account of its current situation quickly becomes dated. The material and technological changes are the most evident and the most startling. In the 1960s, there were few telephones and no televisions in the North. Now these are found in virtually every home, made possible by satellite transmission. No one had refrigerators or freezers or electric lights in the smaller settlements. Now these are commonplace due to a near universal supply of electricity. Many communities boast modern water and sewage facilities (often installed at enormous expense due to the engineering problems created by cold temperatures and frozen soil), where 15 years ago the most primitive systems were used. For most people, daily life in the North has become, by southern standards, more comfortable and convenient. But technological advance is only one aspect of change. Changes in the social organization of production — in the persistence, expansion, and disappearance of modes of production — are more fundamental. Shifts in these modes mark the epochal changes in human societies.

Persistence of the Native Mode of Production

There has been a widespread view among non-Native observers that Native people no longer live on the land nor spend much time hunting and trapping, and that they appear to have developed increasingly conventional customs and tastes. Past economic statistics seemed to indicate that trapping was for many years in decline, while wage income accruing to Native people was at the same time increasing. Recent research suggests, however, that these data are misleading.[13] First, Native people still live extensively on the land. Although there have been many specific changes in land use patterns, and some areas are used both less frequently and less intensively than before, vast areas of land are still in use. Second, the rate of Native participation in traditional hunting and fishing activities is still comparatively high. The figures are masked by conventional economic measures of employment and income, because the majority of these Native people are at the same time participating in wage employment. Modern hunting and fishing techniques allow many people to assume casual or even full-time employment and still produce much of their own food. Income-generating functions within the family are also becoming increasingly specialized. Third, conventional methods of data gathering by government wildlife agencies on the harvesting of fish and game, particularly by Native peoples, tend to underestimate actual harvests by a significant degree. Finally, commodities produced for domestic consumption, and which therefore do not enter the marketplace, are either not evaluated at all or are under-valued by conventional economic systems of measurement.

Thus, we can draw several conclusions. One is that vast tracts of unaltered lands and waters continue to be essential for the traditional mode of production. Second, Native northerners' per capita consumption of meat and fish is substantially higher than the national per capital consumption of these foods (Table 12.1). Third, while Native northerners now spend more time at, and derive more income from, non-traditional pursuits than was the case a generation ago, they are still producing much of their own food. Lastly, in some areas at least, the total volume of food produced for domestic consumption has risen over the past 15 years.

Adaptation in the Native mode of production: The use of modern equipment, such as ski-doos, allows many Inuit and Dene people to assume casual or even full-time employment and still produce much of their own food requirements. (*NFB Phototheque*)

These findings are clearly inconsistent with the notion of declining subsistence activity. It now appears that although the exchange component (trapping and commercial fishing) of the Native economy did in fact decline during the 1950s and '60s, the domestic sector (hunting and fishing for local human consumption) did not suffer any long-term decline except for temporary disruptions due to rapid urbanization or localized game shortages. With effective replacement values for country food now running from $5.00 to $20.00 per kilogram in the North, country food production contributes hundreds and perhaps thousands of dollars to real per capita income. This estimate also does not include the imputed value of domestically consumed furs, hides, fuelwood, building materials, and the like.

These figures are particularly significant when compared with Native peoples' cash incomes. Without such a calculation for domestic production, hunting and trapping communities often appear poverty stricken,

TABLE 12.1 ANNUAL PER CAPITA COUNTRY FOOD PRODUCTION BY NORTHERN NATIVE PEOPLES (VARIOUS YEARS, 1970-1983)

Region or Place	*Edible Weight (kg)*
Arctic Québec (Inuit)	439
James Bay, Québec (Cree)	139
Northern Labrador	131
Northeast Saskatchewan	532
Pond Inlet, N.W.T.	204
Baffin Region, N.W.T.	216
Baker Lake, N.W.T.	320
Keewatin Region, N.W.T.	214
Mackenzie Valley and Western Arctic, N.W.T.	109
Ross River, Yukon	284
Canada (per capita-) consumption of meat and fish, 1980-81)	117

Note: These figures are from a variety of sources and were not gathered according to uniform criteria and methods. They are, therefore, of varying reliability, but nonetheless indicate that native per capita production of country food for subsistence use is higher than the national per capita consumption.

Sources: James Bay and Northern Québec Native Harvesting Research Committee, *Research to Establish Present Levels of Harvesting by Native Peoples of Northern Québec,* various unpublished reports (Montréal); P.J. Usher, *Renewable Resources in the Future of Northern Labrador* (Nain: Labrador Inuit Association, 1982); P. Ballantyne *et al., Aski-Puko (The Land Alone)* (n.p., 1976); E. Treude, trans. by W. Barr, "Pond Inlet, Northern Baffin Island: The Structure of an Eskimo Resource Area," *Polar Geography,* 6(1977), 95-122; Government of the Northwest Territories, Interdisciplinary Systems Ltd., *Effects of Exploration and Development in the Baker Lake Area* (Winnipeg: 1978); R.L. Gamble, *A Preliminary Study of the Native Harvest of Wildlife in the Keewatin Region, Northwest Territories,* Canadian Technical Report of Fisheries and Aquatic Sciences No. 1282, Dept. Fisheries and Oceans (Winnipeg: 1984); T. Berger, *Northern Frontier, Northern Homeland,* Voi. 2 (Ottawa: Supply and Services Canada, 1977); P. Dimitrov and M. Weinstein, *So That The Future Will Be Ours* (unpublished report prepared for the Ross River Indian Band, 1984); and Statistics Canada, *Apparent Per Capita Food Consumption in Canada* (Ottawa: 1982).

with income derived mostly from fur sales and welfare, in inadequate amounts. Hence, the conclusion that even small amounts of wage labour will generate great increases in total income. A clear evaluation of domestic production, on the other hand, radically alters this view of Native income and accordingly of the need for wage employment. Recent calculations for many parts of the North show that income from fur, fish, and game provided as much as 50 percent of Native income, with game generally being the most important source.[14] Also significant is the fact that wage income is not always a net addition to total income, so that the net benefits from wage employment are not necessarily as great as

TABLE 12.2 ETHNIC COMPOSITION OF THE POPULATION OF THE TERRITORIAL NORTH, 1981

Ethnic Group	*N.W.T.*	*Yukon*	*Total*
Dene[a]	10 520	4 045	14 565
Inuit	15 890	-	15 890
Other	19 125	19 030	38 155
Total	45 535	23 075	68 610

[a]Dene includes Métis.
Source: Census of Canada, 1981.

standard economic indicators might suggest. Beyond these measurable economic facts are the important social and cultural values Native people attach to both the production and consumption of country food, and to the way of life those activities represent.

These differences in economic activity are reflected in the distribution of human settlement and in the patterns of land use of Natives and whites in the North (Figs. 12.2 and 12.3). The approximately 30 000 Native people in the territorial North reside in about 85 different locations, not including seasonal camps (Table 12.2). About 60 of these locations are predominantly Native and have populations of less than 1000, although there are several thousand Native people living in major regional centres that are predominantly non-Native in character. Of the approximately 38 000 non-Native residents in the territorial North, over 27 000 live in the 6 major regional administrative and transport centres — Frobisher Bay, Fort Smith, Hay River, Yellowknife, Inuvik, and Whitehorse. Nearly 8 000 more live in such mining towns as Pine Point, Tungsten, and Faro, or in such smaller regional centres as Dawson, Watson Lake, or Fort Simpson.

Table 12.3 illustrates the variation in ethnic composition of settlements by size and function in more detail for the N.W.T. There, nearly 88 percent of non-Natives live in regional centres or resource towns, while over 75 percent of Native people live in predominantly Native communities. If one assumes that the majority of Native people living in the latter communities is heavily involved in the Native economy, we have a rough approximation of the minimum Native involvement in the traditional mode of production. The fact that less than 2 percent of the population of the resource towns in the N.W.T. is Native indicates the low Native involvement in the mining industry on a full-time basis. Figs. 12.2 and 12.3 show that there is a considerable overlap between traditionally used areas and the areas presently undergoing non-renewable resource exploration and development.

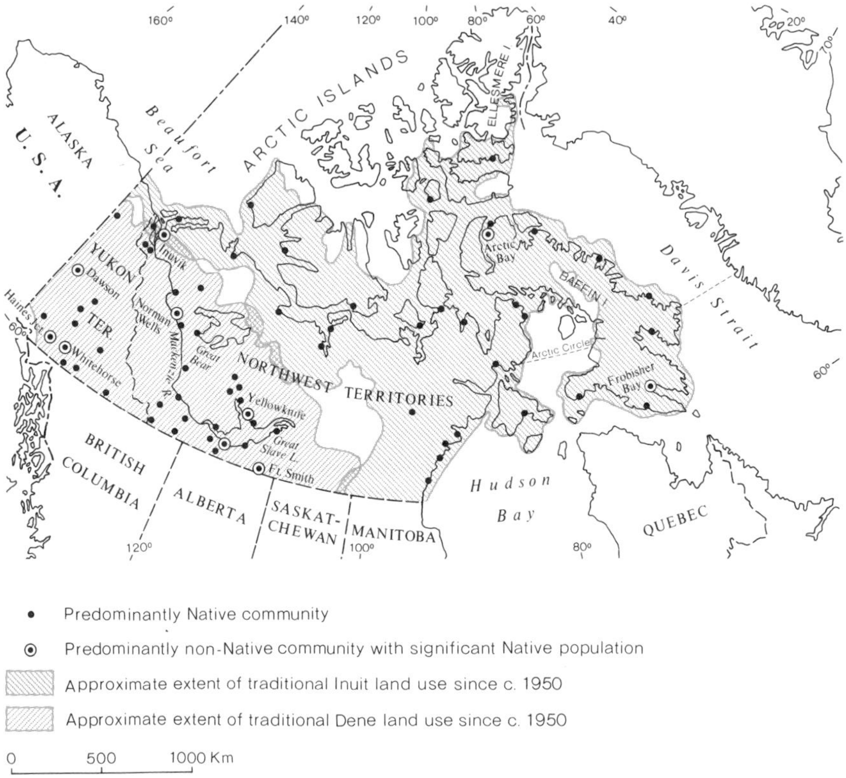

Figure 12.2 The Native economy: distribution of settlements and land use patterns.

The persistence and viability of the traditional mode of production explain why Native people have continued to assert both their present reliance on the land and their desire for the reliance to continue. These factors also explain why Native people do not always find it in their best interests to accept the full-time wage employment opportunities governments have sought to provide. The concern of Native people for the maintenance of their land and resource base, and for the way of life it sustains, has been echoed at major public hearings and inquiries across northern Canada since the early 1970s, and has been documented in numerous recent studies of Native northerners and northern development conflicts.

Figure 12.3 The industrial economy: distribution of settlements and land use patterns.

Native Claims

In the early 1970s, major new resource development proposals brought the conflict between the two modes of production into sharp focus. At the local level, Native northerners tended at first simply to oppose these developments.[15] The several northern Native political organizations founded at about this time, however, soon formulated a more comprehensive strategy. They sought first to establish a legal claim

TABLE 12.3 ETHNIC COMPOSITION OF POPULATED CENTRES BY FUNCTION AND SIZE, N.W.T., 1981

	Regional Administrative and Transport Centres	*Resource Towns*	*Major Native Communities* (≥250)	*Minor Native Communities* (≤250)	Total
Number of places	5	7	34	19	65
Total population	19 980	3 005	19 980	2 095	45 060*
Average population	3 996	429	588	110	693
Total non-Native population	14 170	2 535	2 070	115	18 890*
Total Native population	5 815	485	17 875	1 980	26 155*
Natives as % of total population	29.1	16.1	89.5	94.5	58.0
Percentage of total non-Native population residing in:	74.2	13.3	10.8	0.6	98.9*
Percentage of total Native population residing in:	22.0	1.9	67.7	7.5	99.1*

*Does not include 470 people (215 non-Native and 255 Native) residing outside of organized communities.
Source: Census of Canada, 1981.

to land based on aboriginal title and then to negotiate a settlement of the land question with the federal government. The claim of aboriginal title to northern lands is based on the fact that the Native people of the territorial North have never formally surrendered the lands they traditionally occupied.[16] (This was, as of the early 1970s, also the claim of Native people in northern British Columbia, northern Québec, and in Labrador.) According to European colonial precedent, Native lands in the Americas could not be seized without acknowledgment and compensation (however one-sided or inadequate the formal treaties and surrenders might actually be). Title must pass legally from the Native inhabitants to the European sovereign (with this legality to be defined and tested according to European law, however). Only then could the sovereign grant it in turn to his or her own subjects. Consequently, Native organizations have argued that there is an outstanding obligation on the part of the Government of Canada to settle the question of land rights.

In an historic statement of policy in August, 1973, the federal government acknowledged these outstanding obligations, pledging to negotiate the settlement of claims wherever a Native group could document its traditional use and occupancy of lands not previously surrendered by treaty or other legal means. Two important precedents led to this decision. One was the passage of the Alaska Native Claims Settlement Act by the United States Congress in 1971, and the other was the split decision by the Supreme Court of Canada on the Nishga land claim in northern British Columbia in early 1973.

While land and resource issues have been at the root of the Native claims movement in the North, both practically and legally, these claims have important political dimensions as well. The demands of the various Indian and Inuit groups have included regional or territorial government authority, specific resource management rights, jurisdiction over legislative and regulatory matters, and resource royalties in perpetuity. To date, however, they have gained few concessions in these areas.

The most contentious issues have been the Native proposals for self-determination as a people. Translated into political arrangements, these would mean the creation of large political units in which Indians and Inuit exercise substantial control over the course of economic and political development through their own political institutions. These units would differ from the traditional reserve system in southern Canada in that they would encompass enormous areas of land (hundreds of thousands of square kilometres), thereby placing the necessary lands and resources for a full range of economic activities, from hunting and trapping to industrial development, in control of Native peoples. Instead of being wards of the federal government, all residents, whether of Native ancestry or not, would exercise control over the instruments of government, although certain specified rights and benefits would rest only with the Native population. The success of such arrangements, from the Native point of view, would depend on the maintenance of a Native political majority, as well as on the devolution by Ottawa of critical elements of government power in the areas of resource management and economic development. Thus, Native people have consistently demanded the instruments of power that would allow them to maintain a separate and distinctive social, cultural, and economic identity in Canadian society.

The federal government, on the other hand, has taken a different view of the claims issue. The James Bay and Northern Québec Agreement, and the Western Arctic (Inuvialuit) Agreement (signed in 1975 and 1984 respectively), indicate the government perspective.[17] These agreements are similar in many respects to the Alaskan model. In exchange for the extinguishment of all aboriginal rights, they provide chiefly for varying degrees of ownership of up to about one-third of the original lands used;[18] for the payment of several tens or hundreds of millions of dollars as a once and for all compensation for lands lost; for the legal entrenchment of certain basic hunting, fishing, and trapping rights (without at the same time guaranteeing the supply or the quality of fish and wildlife resources); for the creation of certain government and economic institutions at the local or regional level, having structures and powers akin to municipal governments and development corporations; and for certain social and economic development programmes. The emphasis is on the property aspects of Native claims, rather than the jurisdictional ones. Governments have been unwilling to transfer significant legislative or regulatory powers over resources such as wildlife to Native political authority. Instead, they have offered advisory status at best.

It would appear that the negotiating objectives of the two sides remain far apart. The Native organizations seek to lay the basis for a distinctive indigenous society in the North. Government, on the other hand, seeks primarily to provide an economic and institutional basis for Native people to become effectively incorporated into the mainstream of Canadian society, and to remove any legal impediment from its authority to manage and allocate lands and resources in the national interest.

For these reasons, and because of the slackening pace of major resource development plans that lent urgency to the issue in the first place, progress in the negotiation of Native claims settlements has been slow. Since the process was formally initiated by the federal government in 1973, only the western Arctic claim has been settled in the territorial North. Claims submitted by other Inuit, Indian, and Métis organizations covering almost all of the territorial North except for the Beaufort Sea region, as well as a number of claims in northern B.C., Québec, and Labrador, remain under negotiation as of 1986. The constitutional status of aboriginal rights has also not be settled.

The demands of the settler population, on the other hand, which are for steady progress towards responsible government, provincial status, and resource and economic development, pose few obstacles to the extension of metropolitan control over the hinterland, or to the progress of industrialization there. The debate centres only on the rate of that progress, and the criteria for moving on to the next stage of political development. The debate between central and regional interests, however, should not be minimized. It focusses on such issues as the proper timing and appropriate threshold population for the establishment of responsible government institutions and devolution of powers, and the adequacy of the local tax base. In other words, the question is whether and when the territory will have the administrative and fiscal capacity to exercise certain constitutional powers, in line with the other provinces. The settler demands do not imply any substantially different political and economic institutions that would make the North unlike the other provinces.

However, just as participation in the Native and industrial modes of production does not break down strictly on ethnic lines, neither do the two visions of the North's future. Neither all southern Canadians nor all non-Native northerners favour all or even many of the consequences of an unchecked advance of the industrial mode. At the same time, neither do all Native northerners utterly reject that future. Both the evolution of Native organizations, and the development of local government in the North, have created in recent years a significant class of Native administrators and bureaucrats. To a more limited extent, there are now also Native people with small business interests. Indeed, the nature of the claims settlements will determine the rate at which this class grows, since the government model, which is heavily dependent on bureaucratic structures, will require extensive staffing.[19] It would therefore be incorrect to assume a unanimity of interest among Native northerners, any more than there is a unanimity among non-Native northerners.

THE FUTURE OF THE NORTH

The Canadian view of the North has incorporated both acquisitiveness and idealism. The North has been seen as empire and utopia. It is a place where the nation can enrich, enlarge, and improve itself; where the individual can realize his or her own dreams. Yet not all of these dreams, whether national or personal, can be fulfilled. The North cannot be rapidly developed as a treasure house of resource wealth and still remain an unspoiled wilderness. Nor can those who extol the North's virtues as a free and open frontier society, unsullied by urban conflicts and industrial pollution, also advocate the continued advance of metropolitan dominance and the industrial organization of production without sacrificing the very values they praise.

The incorporation of the northern hinterland into an expanding metropolitan orbit will inevitably continue. But what will be the outcome of our northward course of empire?[20] Internally, the industrial mode is challenged by hurdles of technology and economics. The ability of large corporate and government interests to solve these technological problems, and to accumulate adequate pools of capital in competition with other demands for capital, will strongly influence the rate of advance on the frontier.

There are also political and legal questions to be resolved. The present phase of internal national expansion, predicated on large-scale resource development, is hastening the allocation of lands and resources to specific uses and users. The settlement of native land claims is part of a larger process whereby lands are also being allocated for national parks, game sanctuaries, municipal expansion, resource extraction or, in some cases, for several of these uses at once. In the same way, rights of access to resources are also being more rigorously defined. The progress of northern development has in recent years required the implementation or revision of such diverse statutes and regulations as the Arctic Waters Pollution Prevention Act, the Territorial Land Use Regulations, the Canada Oil and Gas Act, and the N.W.T. Game Ordinance and Regulations. Where, until recently, northern lands and resources were used primarily by Native hunters and trappers, there are now many competing users. Their respective access to, and use of, land and resources must be regulated by the state.

The course of political development is most open to question at the regional level. In terms of the conventional model outlining the evolution of representative and responsible government, the Yukon Territory is the most advanced part of the North. It has a better established settler population (with a substantial numerical majority over the Native inhabitants), a more compact, accessible, and easily administered territory, and a less hostile physical environment. Resource development on a substantial scale has long been thought a more imminent prospect in the Yukon than in the N.W.T., and at relatively less cost to both the public and private sectors (although the recent downturn in the mining industry in the Yukon casts some doubt on this notion). The Yukon appears to be closer to achieving responsibilities typical of provinces, if not provincial status, than the N.W.T. There, only the Mackenzie Valley approximates the Yukon with respect to these criteria. There have been efforts to split that district off from the less developed Arctic regions, so that it could progress more rapidly towards provincial status.

Significantly, these moves have invariably been most strongly supported, if not indeed originated, by the resident small business sector (and often the mining industry) in the larger centres such as Yellowknife. They have received little attention and less support from the Native inhabitants of the smaller settlements of the Mackenzie District. In contrast, the proposals to create a separate territory in the Arctic have

The political future of the North: Traditionally, as this 1921 photograph of a federal government judicial party at Fort Providence, N.W.T., indicates, the North has been administered by external metropolitan centres. It is a matter of debate, therefore, whether or not the territories will ever be awarded complete autonomy over internal matters, and if so, the speed at which autonomy will advance. (*PA-18684/Public Archives of Canada*)

come from the Inuit, who see this move as a means to establish their own political institutions and authority in a territory where they presently far outnumber the non-Native residents. Whether the bureaucratic requirements of administering such a territory can be compatible with the maintenance, let alone the dominance, of the traditional mode of production remains to be seen.

How far and how fast political evolution along conventional lines will proceed, however, is not clear. The day when southern Canadians will permanently inhabit the Arctic, or even very much of the Subarctic, in great numbers is difficult to foresee. Native people will therefore continue to be a large, although perhaps declining, proportion of the northern population. The thesis of this chapter is that Natives and non-Natives are not "all northerners together," as the ideology promoted by non-Native institutions in the North suggests. The builders of empire have often been blind to the lives and needs of the people they displace. The continuing attempts to convert, modernize, and industrialize Native people, and the reluctance or outright refusal to accommodate their cultural, political, and economic systems, have seriously hindered the vitality and the future of the Native way of life.

The fundamental question in the North today is whether the Native mode of production must be entirely displaced, or whether it can be revitalized as the basis of a continuing and distinctive Native economic, social, and cultural identity. The settlement of Native claims remains critical. Yet to the extent that claims settlements are seen solely as a racial and cultural issue, they will not solve the problem of the Native economy. The government model, if it continues to be implemented unchanged, will likely further erode the basis of the Native economy and absorb the displaced population into the industrial mode.

The fact that the North is an internal colony, a domestic frontier of exploitation and settlement, cautions us against uncritically forcing our northern experience into centre-periphery models of development based on the relations between industrial and Third World countries. At the same time, this fact should not obscure the many analogies between those relations and the advance of the industrial mode of production in our own North.[21] Both the history of development and the current circumstances of the North suggest the possibility of growing racial discord, economic disparity, and social disorder, and of rising discontent among those who are displaced. Despite its mythical promise of national and personal renewal, the North has no intrinsic qualities that will prevent the repetition of old mistakes.

The Territorial North is clearly a distinctive hinterland within Canada. It is still the least touched by metropolitan influences, but perhaps also the most vulnerable to them. Yet, in part because public attention has become more sharply focussed on the North, there is more resistance to unwanted change. The challenge of the North for Canada is not simply to incorporate and develop it. It is also to recognize the North's distinctive peoples, cultures, and economy as the basis for its future contribution to Canada's richness in diversity.

NOTES

1. Dene is the term the Athapaskan Indians use to describe themselves (all Indians native to the territorial North are Athapaskans except those of the extreme southern Yukon). Inuit is the term that the people commonly known as Eskimos use to describe themselves. The terms Dene and Inuit are the ones now in general use in the North, and will be used throughout this chapter, except where the word Indian is, in the context, more inclusive

than Dene. There are also people in the territorial North who identify themselves as Métis. This identity is not simply a matter of mixed parentage, as there are many Native people in the North who consider themselves fully Dene or Inuit despite some non-Native ancestry. There are also many Dene who, although for one reason or another are legally classed as non-status with respect to the Indian Act, consider themselves fully Dene by heritage. The Métis by and large have a particular culture and history, dating from the early fur trade era, and have tended to play an intermediary economic and cultural role between whites and Indians.

2. Hence the title of the 1977 report of the Mackenzie Valley Pipeline Inquiry written by Justice T.R. Berger, *Northern Frontier, Northern Homeland.* This report provides a very useful, broad view of the environment and society of the western N.W.T. and northern Yukon, and of the major issues raised by large-scale resource development.
3. For a concise discussion of permafrost in northern Canada, and its implications for construction with special reference to pipelines, see P.J. Williams, *Pipelines and Permafrost* (London: Longmans, 1979).
4. This description of the aboriginal peoples of the North applies to the period of discovery from about 1600 to 1900. The prehistoric record of peoples in the North, as revealed by archeological research, is marked by successive cultures and migrations, but by and large there has been a clear difference between those who inhabited the Arctic and Subarctic environments.
5. L.-E. Hamelin has devised a complex scale of "Nordicity" based on ten criteria, of which six are environmental and four relate to human settlement and development (chiefly accessibility, density of population, and economic activity). On this basis, he has divided the North into three regions: the middle, far, and extreme Norths. (He also identified a region called the near North, which includes such agricultural fringe areas as the Peace River and the Clay Belt, and a number of the mining and forestry towns on or near the northernmost transcontinental railway.) These human criteria, however, relate to non-Native perceptions and objectives. Degrees of isolation and inaccessibility are entirely relative. Inuit would no more have thought of themselves as living in the far North, than Nova Scotians would think of themselves as living in the far northeast, although that would be an apt description from a Chinese or Australian perspective. See L.-E. Hamelin, *Canadian Nordicity: It's Your North, Too,* trans. William Barr (Montréal: Harvest House, 1978).
6. The reader unfamiliar with the concept of mode of production will find useful discussions in the following references: Samir Amin, *Unequal Development* (New York: Monthly Review Press, 1976), pp. 13-26; Michael Asch, "The Ecological-Evolutionary Model and the Concept of Mode of Production," in *Challenging Anthropology,* eds. D. Turner and G. Smith (Toronto: McGraw-Hill Ryerson, 1979), pp. 81-101; A. Foster-Carter, "The Modes of Production Controversy", *New Left Review,* 107 (Jan.-Feb. 1978), pp. 47-77; and Adrian Tanner, *Bringing Home Animals,* Social and Economic Studies No. 23, Institute of Social and Economic Research (St. John's: Memorial University of Newfoundland, 1979), pp. 1-13. The first three references are general, theoretical discussions, while the last discusses mode of production in the specific context of the Cree Indians of northern Québec.
7. Historically, all status Indians have been the direct responsibility of the federal government, and services to Indians are provided by federal government agencies in both the provinces and the territories. In the 1970s, however, there was a trend toward provincial agencies playing a greater role in providing government services to Indians, under a shared cost agreement with the federal government.
8. The term settler is used here in the conventional sense of colonial history: a resident, non-Native population that takes up Crown or public land resources after the military or political displacement of the Native population. Such colonization is normally encouraged by state policies and incentives. The term has a somewhat different and more specific meaning in the case of Labrador. There, settler refers to the fishermen and trappers of

Newfoundland origin who came to the Labrador coast in the 1800s and lived there in a style similar to that of the Inuit population, in contrast to those Newfoundlanders who fished the coast only seasonally and did not take up permanent residence. The Inuit and settler populations of Labrador have submitted a joint statement of claim to Northern Labrador on the grounds of traditional occupancy, in the face of more recent metropolitan incursions. See Carol Brice-Bennett, ed., *Our Footprints are Everywhere* (Nain: Labrador Inuit Association, 1977).

9. Cited in Morris Zaslow, *The Opening of the Canadian North, 1870-1914* (Toronto: McClelland and Stewart, 1971), p. 252.

10. See L.-E. Hamelin, *Canadian Nordicity,* pp. 157-193.

11. W. Smith, The Fur Trade and the Frontier: A Study On Inter-Culture Alliance," *Anthropoligica,* 15 (1973), 21-36.

12. Precise data are difficult to obtain, because Census of Canada occupation data are not broken down according to the sectors defined here.

13. Much of the research has been sponsored by Native organizations in support of their land claims, or in connection with public inquiries regarding major resource developments. The results of much of this work, particularly for the N.W.T., are summarized in Berger, *Northern Frontier, Northern Homeland.* See also Milton Freeman Research Limited, *Report: Inuit Land Use and Occupancy Project,* 3 vols. (Ottawa: Supply and Services Canada, 1977); and Mel Watkins, ed., *Dene Nation: The Colony Within* (Toronto: University of Toronto Press, 1977).

14. See, in particular, Berger, *Northern Frontier, Northern Homeland,* Vol. 2; Interdisciplinary Systems Ltd., *Effects of Exploration and Development in the Baker Lake Area* (unpublished report, Department of Indian Affairs and Northern Development, Winnipeg, 1978); P.J. Usher, "Evaluating Country Food in the Northern Native Community," *Arctic,* 29 (1976), pp. 105-20.

15. See, for example, P.J. Usher, *The Bankslanders: Economy and Ecology of a Frontier Trapping Community,* Vol. 3, NSRG-71-3, Northern Science Research Group (Ottawa: Department of Indian Affairs and Northern Development, 1971); P.J. Usher and G. Beakhust, *Land Regulation in the Canadian North* (Ottawa: Canadian Arctic Resources Committee, 1973); and D.H. Pimlott *et al., Arctic Alternatives* (Ottawa: Canadian Arctic Resources Committee, 1973).

16. In the Mackenzie Valley, Treaties Eight and Eleven were signed in 1898 and 1921 respectively. The former covers northern Alberta and British Columbia, with an extension to the south shore of Great Slave Lake; the latter covers the rest of the Mackenzie Valley. The Dene of the N.W.T., however, claim that their understanding of the treaty was one of peace with the white man, and that it did not involve the cession of lands. They presented evidence to this effect in court in 1973 which was by and large accepted. Partly as a consequence, the Dene of that region are seeking a settlement of a comprehensive claim similar to those of groups which had never signed a treaty.

17. Although Indians and Inuit are a federal responsibility, south of the sixtieth parallel the lands in question have already been transferred to the provinces, which must therefore also agree to any land transfers, and pass any necessary enabling provincial legislation, as a consequence of claims settlements. The territorial governments, in view of their anticipated eventual provincehood, are also involved in claims negotiations. To the extent that provincial governments have been willing to negotiate with Native representatives, they have taken a broadly similar stance to that of the federal government.

18. The land regimes effected or proposed under existing agreements involve several categories of land with varying degrees of ownership. For most lands, surface title only has been transferred, and consequently non-renewable resource development is not impeded by Native ownership. Only very small amounts of land have been transferred to Native ownership in fee simple, and even this form of title does not bestow the full range of land and resource rights Native people traditionally enjoyed under their own codes and practices.

19. For an excellent discussion of the political and labour effects of the implementation of the James Bay and Northern Québec settlement, see I. La Rusic, *Negotiating a Way of Life* (Montréal: Research Division, Policy, Research and Evaluation Group. Department of Indian and Northern Affairs, 1979).
20. The great northern explorer and publicist, Viljalmur Stefansson, wrote a book entitled *The Northward Course of Empire* (New York: Harcourt, Brace, 1922), in which he advanced the thesis that the successive imperial centres in world history had moved further and further northward, and would likely continue to do so. In that book he attempted to dispel some prevailing misconceptions about the North and discussed the prospects for northern development. (See also his autobiography, *Discovery* [New York: McGraw-Hill, 1964].) Although Stefansson and his theories were highly controversial, the theme of "our northward course" has persisted throughout Canadian history. Some more notable recent examples include Diefenbaker's "northern vision" electoral campaign of 1958, and author Richard Rohmer's advocacy of a Mid-Canada Development Corridor in the late 1960s. For examples of Canada's awakening sense of the North, and of our northern identity, see Canada, Parliament, Senate, Session 1888, *Report of the Select Committee of the Senate Appointed to Enquire into the Resources of the Great Mackenzie Basin* (Ottawa); and Carl Berger, "The True North Strong and Free," in *Nationalism in Canada,* ed. Peter Russell (Toronto: McGraw-Hill, 1966), pp. 3-26.
21. For a variety of interpretations of the historical development of the North, in addition to works already cited, see T. Armstrong, G. Rogers, and G. Rowley, *The Circumpolar North* (London: Methuen, 1978); Hugh Brody, *The People's Land* (Harmondsworth: Penguin, 1975); Canadian Arctic Resources Committee, *National and Regional Interests in the North, Third National Workshop on People, Resources, and the Environment North of 60* (Ottawa: 1984); Kenneth Coates, *Canada's Colonies* (Toronto: James Lorimer, 1985); G. Dacks, *A Choice of Futures* (Toronto: Methuen, 1981); Diamond Jenness, *Eskimo Administration: II, Canada* (Montréal: Arctic Institute of North America, 1964); R.F. Keith and J.B. Wright, eds., *Northern Transitions, Vol. II* (Ottawa: Canadian Arctic Resources Committee, 1978); K.J. Rea, *The Political Economy of the Canadian North* (Toronto: University of Toronto Press, 1968); W.C. Wonders, ed., *Canada's Changing North* (Toronto McClelland and Stewart, Carleton Library, 1971); and W.C. Wonders, ed., *The North* (Toronto: University of Toronto Press, 1972).

PART IV
Conclusion

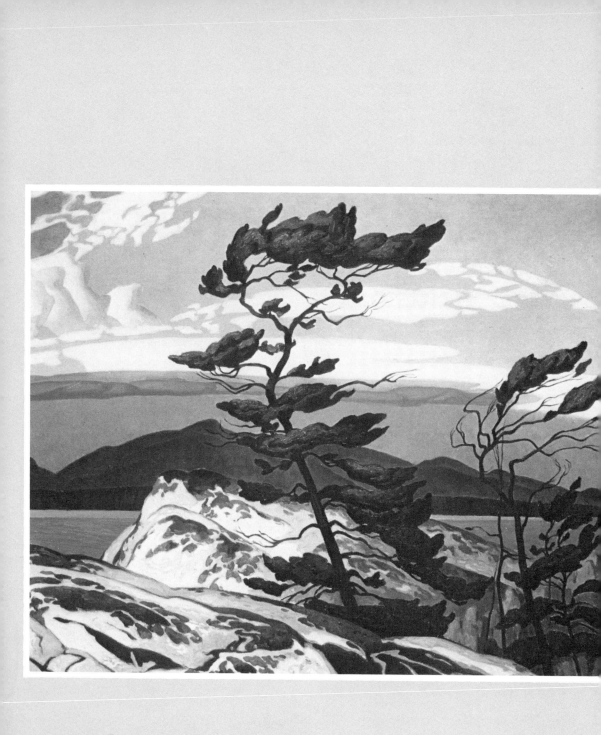

13

Regionalism and the Canadian Archipelago

R. Cole Harris

This chapter has three parts. It deals first with the underlying structure of the territory settled by Europeans which eventually was defined as Canada. This is done to establish the frame with which the conceptualization of this country has had to contend. The second part deals with sentiment and regionalism. It is, really, an inventory and perhaps, to some extent, an explanation of feelings about the parts and the whole of this country, including those between core and peripheral regions. Finally, the chapter deals with the relationship between these regional sentiments and the future course of Canadian development. Together, these parts stand in summary as a perspective on Canadian regionalism, and of some of the roles played by core and periphery in shaping Canada's evolving regional character.[1]

THE CANADIAN ARCHIPELAGO

The political map of North America sustains the illusion that Canada is a continental giant spanning 70° of longitude and some 40° of latitude; whereas on any long, clear-night flight, this Canada dissolves into an oceanic darkness spotted by occasional islands of light. These lights mark the lived-in Canada, the Canadian ecumene, an island archipelago spread over 7200 east-west kilometres. Between the islands in winter are snow and ice, and in summer are rock, muskeg, endless tangles of black spruce, and black flies — little possibility for the innumerable cabotage that over the centuries served the islands, peninsulas, and coastal plains of Braudel's Mediterranean.[2] There have been routes through the rock: first rivers navigated by canoes, then railways, and finally highways; but railways began to make connections just over a hundred years ago and highways

Pine Cleft Rocks, 1915, Tom Thomson. (*McMichael Canadian Collection*)

considerably more recently, while canoe routes, never followed by many people, preceded substantial white settlement. For the most part, the spaces between these islands have been hard to traverse and harder to use. Like Newfoundland outports, the islands back into rock.

The problem, if that is what it is, began to come into European focus in the sixteenth century. Verrazano, sailing off Carolina, thought he glimpsed Arcadia to the west; Cartier, along the shore of the Gulf of St. Lawrence, found himself face to face, as he said, with the land God gave as his portion to Cain. He had met the crystalline edge of the Canadian Shield. Over the years little enough would temper this stark, geographical reality. The Shield edge looms over Québec, is on the near horizon in Montréal, and is only just beyond it in Toronto and Winnipeg. On the plains its limiting place is taken by the short summer of a severe continental climate and, farther west, by the Cordillera. To the south, as time went by, a political boundary evolved, most of its length the negotiated balance, at different dates, between American perception of settlement opportunities and British interest in the fur trade. North and south, these were the confines of almost all the Canadian archipelago: together they defined its territory and constricted its possibilities.

Early European settlement of these northern islands had a particular inadvertency. On return voyages to Europe, fish were more profitable than fishermen, and men were left behind to struggle through bleak winters — the origin of Newfoundland's shifting, male population of the seventeenth and eighteenth centuries. Descended from a few immigrant families, a considerable Acadian population created cultivable niches out of tidal marshlands around the Bay of Fundy, lived in rude hamlets of close kin, and until its expulsion by the British early in the Seven Years' War, was little affected by the fluctuations of French and British jurisdiction to which its exposed location made it vulnerable. Along the lower St. Lawrence there was more bureaucracy and more of Europe. Québec City and Montréal approximately reflected the social gradients of French provincial towns, but most people lived in the countryside and depended on a primarily subsistence agriculture. They had little to do with the towns, with the fur trade for which the colony had been created but which could not employ its growing population, or with the larger world of the North Atlantic.[3] Overall, there was no master plan, no vision, as in New England, of Old World regeneration overseas, and next to no interaction among these somewhat adventitious French and British beginnings in the northwestern Atlantic.

In the early nineteenth century the islands received a massive British migration, principally Irish and Scottish, propelled by clearances, famine, and rural pauperization, and by the technological and demographic changes of early industrialization. Most of these immigrants passed through the seigneuries bordering the lower St. Lawrence to settle in southern Ontario and establish an English-speaking, largely Protestant population that viewed its Catholic, French-speaking neighbours with a large measure of contempt. Others stayed on the Atlantic islands to create the Irish and English shores of Newfoundland, the predominant Scottishness of northern Nova Scotia, and the pockets of Irish, English, and Scots that together with returned Acadians comprised the populations of New Brunswick and Prince Edward Island. All of these newcomers, save the Acadians, came to British colonies from a British hearth. Their nostalgia and, when they could write, their letters, returned to Britain. Other islands of the Canadian archipelago were by and large outside their experience.

Their descendants, together with those of the older French-speaking population along the lower St. Lawrence, soon faced a common predicament. The islands were small, their agricultural possibilities circumscribed, and as numbers multiplied in still rural, pre-industrial societies there was soon a shortage of land. The pioneer fringe ran into rock. There was no western safety valve; there were only the granite Shield and the other already settled British North American islands. The surplus young faced the choice of striking north into the land God had given to Cain or south into the United States.

Early in the nineteenth century the drain began from Québec to New England's first factory towns and then, later in the century, to the lumber camps of the American Midwest. Driven by demographic pressures, this was an annual migration first of hundreds, then of thousands. Worried nationalists could not stop it. With the blessing of priests, other young French Canadians, who would make the North serve for the West Québec did not have, went to the lumbercamps, sawmills, and podzols of the Canadian Shield — a brutal encounter of defenceless people with the devastating realities of an almost impossible agricultural land and of early industrial capitalism. In Ontario, population pressures built up a few years later. Government and manufacturers promoted northward expansion. Colonization roads were built into the Shield. By the 1850s there was official interest in the Red River, a thousand miles [1600 kilometres] away, but ordinary people had neither means nor desire to go there, and few would tackle the Shield. Rather, they slipped across the international border, creating by 1900 a plume of Ontarians and their descendants, as numerous as the Ontarians themselves, stretching westward through the United States to the High Plains. From the Atlantic islands, migration went to the "Boston States" as, vicariously, New England became their missing West. None of these migrations mixed the different populations of British North America. South of the border, immigrants were being absorbed into a larger America; north of it, island societies that now exported people bypassed the mixing effects of the migrations they had launched.

Then, about the time the American historian Frederick Jackson Turner lamented the closing of the American frontier,[4] a Canadian West finally opened for settlement. When the Canadian Pacific Railway (C.P.R.) reached Winnipeg in 1883, the fur trade was already gone from most of the prairies. Although a long way off, expensive to reach, and in a different physiographic realm of uncertain agricultural potential, a large new island, a possible counterpoise to the attraction of the United States, was available for settlement. In both Québec and Ontario, this West found dedicated promoters, although enthusiasm dwindled among French-speakers in Québec after the Protestant outburst over the Riel Rebellion and the collapse in Manitoba of French educational and linguistic guarantees. By 1900, leaders in Québec were almost unanimous that Québec should keep its young, or, failing that, should colonize a contiguous northern Ontario (or even, some felt, a contiguous New England); they turned deaf ears to western pleas for immigrants who might have stabilized the region's Catholic, French-speaking future.[5]

Prairie Landscape, 1877, Adrian Nelson.

As it turned out, neither Québec nor Ontario would be reproduced on the Canadian prairie. There would be more of the latter than of the former — some enclaves, such as southwestern Manitoba, were overwhelmingly Ontarian — but the Canadian prairie was settled over a short generation before World War I, when migrants from the eastern Canadian islands mixed with immigrants coming directly from the British Isles, with the northern fringe of the late nineteenth and early twentieth century peasant migration to North America from central Europe, and with a wave of American settlement that pushed northward along the eastern flank of the Rockies. Languages spoken in the new ethnic ghettoes in American cities appeared on the Canadian prairie, an element in a new mix of eastern Canadians, Britons, Americans, Germans, Scandinavians, Russians, Ukrainians, and Poles; of Lutherans, Eastern Orthodox, Mennonites, Doukhobors, and Mormons as well as Roman Catholics and Protestants of British origin. In British Columbia the mix was different again: much more of the British Isles, particularly of England, much less of continental Europe, a good deal of Ontario, something of the Atlantic islands, and, there on the Pacific Ocean, elements from the Orient.

Thus were settled the islands between an implacable north and the United States. There was no continuous, expansive Canadian experience with the land. What was common was the lack of continuity imparted by the close limits of confined lands. Settlement proceeded in patches, island by island. One island would fill up, then people would emigrate, south more often than north because the United States was more inviting than the Shield. Until the last hundred years, there was no settlers' West. The next Canadian island was inaccessible or occupied, and when a West finally opened, the eastern islands would be partially represented and much diluted there. The process of Canadian settlement has imparted striking discontinuities. Different islands were settled at different times with different technologies and economies by people from different backgrounds. Considered overall, the archipelago was settled island by island from Europe; it did not expand westward from an Atlantic beginning. Ranald Macdonald, Ralph Connor's *Man from Glengarry* who left his native Ontario to chop Douglas fir and extended a new Dominion in British Columbia, represents one strand of the Canadian settlement process; but Maria Chapdelaine, torn between the lure of the United States and the rock of Peribonka, represents its overriding dilemma.

This pattern of settlement sharply differentiated the Canadian experience from the American. In the United States, the land was perceived as a garden as readily as wilderness, and it attracted far more settlers, and focussed European dreams.[6] There, Eastern Seaboard beginnings could migrate westward across the piedmont plain, across the narrow and substantially inhabitable Appalachians, across the rich soils of the Mississippi basin to the desert margins, situated 3200 kilometres inland. These were the first major environmental obstacles to an expanding agrarian civilization. There the West — unoccupied land to the west suitable for cultivation — was a stimulant for three hundred years, to the point that the essence of the American experience could be plausibly interpreted as a succession of waves on a succession of westward-moving frontiers. There a Lockian liberalism, popularized by Thomas Paine and reinforced generation after generation by individual opportunities (for many if not for all) in a bounteous, on-going land, could become a pervasive ideology because the experience of so many seemed to attest to the rewards and the virtues of individual enterprise. And there, as different streams from the initial settlements along the colonial seaboard, augmented by newcomers from Europe, moved west across the Appalachians, different ways met and substantially merged. As it gathered momentum in the late eighteenth and nineteenth centuries, the American occupation of an essentially welcoming land had the capacity to mold different peoples into a relatively homogeneous culture as it spread them over an astonishing area. In Canada, all of this was checked by the land's ineluctable niggardliness.

In the United States there was also more North American time, more temporal as well as spatial continuity.[7] Behind the Republic lay almost two centuries of colonial America, ample time for English ways to evolve in different, New World directions that would be marked by the great nation-building events of revolution and independence. In Canada, only the French-speaking reach back like this in North America, and their early North American evolution was capped by the deportation of almost 10 000 Acadians, and by the conquest of Canada — by the imposition of limits rather than by the opening of autonomous beginnings. English Canada is a product of the nineteenth century, of the Victorian age. In the West some beginnings are still remembered. Such recency harbours lingering memories of homes elsewhere, and blurs new circumstances. Hence, of all Canadians it is the French Canadians who have recognized themselves most clearly as North American, and who have had fewest doubts about who and where they were.

However little they recognized what was going on, the different peoples on the British North American islands soon ceased to be European. Emigration undertaken with no radical intent by people who, for the most part, sought no more than a living, had unexpected implications for Europeans in non-European settings. Put briefly, these settings tended to accept some European ways and to reject others, and thereby to create societies that were selections reduced from the European social whole. Characteristically this selection pared back complex European hierarchies of honour, status, rank, and deference; and obliterated the fine spatial texture that in pre-industrial Europe was reflected in local cultures.[8]

For many years, land on these islands was relatively inexpensive, and because ordinarily people could substitute land for labour, labour was relatively dear. The development of new resources required strong backs, practical ingenuity and, in some cases, capital, but not social polish or refined learning. These circumstances provided opportunity for peasants, artisans, and a few of the middle class, but discouraged gentility. At the same time, new and often strikingly uniform work environments diminished European occupational labels and their implicit social sorting. European social hierarchies were being drastically simplified. Something of European gentility surfaced in the military, in civil bureaucracies, among the commercial elite and even, here and there, in the countryside – as with Susanna Moodie's incongruous presence in the Ontario bush and with orchardists who struggled to grow fruit and play polo on British Columbia's mountainsides. Something of the European occupational range survived in the towns. Overall, European gentility had been deprived of a landed base and of a context for its manners, and ordinary people had lost sight of most of the complex European hierarchy of status and deference.

On the other hand, a northwestern European sentiment of the family, a concept of private property, and the commercial values in the middle class, had found congenial settings. Where markets were poor and there was little to attract capital, as for years on the marshlands around the Bay of Fundy and on most seigneuries along the St. Lawrence, there emerged strikingly egalitarian rural societies of semi-subsistent families. Over the years, such societies developed dense networks of kin and local traditions that amalgamated elements of the different regional backgrounds of founding populations into distinctive folk cultures. Wherever commercial opportunities were greater, as they were in Newfoundland from the beginning, or as they became in *habitant* Québec early in the nineteenth century, the social gradient steepened, but this gradient was defined by the market rather than by custom. The same transformation, "the great transformation" Karl Polanyi called it,[9] was affecting European society, but here the pace of change was accelerated and the social dismemberment was more complete. The few deported Acadians who reached France and were settled on the Ile de Ré near the port of La Rochelle from which some of their ancestors had probably embarked, found themselves amid alien people. Like the other people on the Canadian islands, they were no longer Europeans, and most of them soon left for Louisiana.

While diverging socially from Europe, these North American islands all became British possessions. They were parts of the same empire, each connected by governors and colonial administrations to Westminster and the Crown, that is, to a European core. Each evolved political institutions derived from British models, and each depended on the presence of the British military. Whether a source of pride or of consternation, the British connection was a constant. In some expatriate minds, empire acquired a certain fanaticism, as it did on the 12th of July or, more gently, in the garden that Emily Carr's father molded into a patch of England overseas. But, as we shall see, the imperial fervour that led harmlessly back to Britain rasped across the grain of British North America. What was empire to some was colonialism to others. Islands that would rather have danced to different tunes were on strings held by the same puppeteer.

And finally, there were people on all the islands, particularly people of some eminence, who would not believe that the surrounding rock and climate were real. Settlement would have a larger outlet and some of the islands would merge. The mistake was easily made when there had been little scientific surveying, when climatology was more theoretical than empirical, when the air was full of the American West, and when one lived in the towns. Indeed, there was evidence that marginal environments could be settled. Irishmen from the bogs and rocks of Connemara, Highlanders from two- or three-acre crofts and a collapsing kelp industry, and French Canadians were all driven into the Shield where, given their prior experience and the unknown limits of untested land, long-term prospects could seem reasonably bright. The mirage of abundant agricultural land would persist into the twentieth century. Most spectacularly and most erroneously, it would accompany the National Transcontinental Railway (the Grand Trunk Pacific) across Canada from Moncton, New Brunswick, to a new town, Prince Rupert, hewn out of an Indian reserve at the mouth of the Skeena River, a railway created by visions of a northwest passage to the Orient and of a continuous band of agricultural settlement linking the islands of British North America.

Such was not to be. The geography of Canadian settlement remained disjointed and discontinuous. This is the underlying structure of Canada on which, as Braudel would have said, economic circumstances and political events would work their more ephemeral passage. Another Frenchman, the anarchist Elisée Reclus, surveyed the map of Canadian settlement and introduced the Canadian chapters of his *Géographie Universelle* (written c. 1890) in the following way. "The vast stretch of lands occupying all the northern section of North America and politically defined as the 'Dominion of Canada' constitutes no distinct geographical unit." Canada, he wrote, had a "fantastic frontier" with the United States. Only in the St. Lawrence-Great Lakes area was the population "dense enough to constitute really independent groups and autonomous centres of political and social life." Little political importance could be attached to a "precarious political frontier liable to be effaced by the least change of equilibrium."

THE GEOGRAPHY OF CANADIAN REGIONALISM

Elisée Reclus found no relationship between the political map of Canada and the pattern of Canadian settlement. The one was transcontinental, the other was local. The one was a geo-political vision, the other was the frame of ordinary lives. Indeed, as has been argued, Canada is a composition of islands. From island vantage points, outlooks have been bounded, local feelings intense, and ignorance of other circumstances considerable. Emotional lines of attachment often led back to distant homelands. But over and against this island Canada are the power, spatial range, and integrating capacity of modern technology; a transcontinental political territory that has survived far longer than Reclus thought it would; and on all the islands, if in varying intensity, a good deal of sentiment for Canada. Another level has been superimposed on the islands, and the mix has created a tangle of sentimental attachments. To deal with the components of this tangle, we shall start with the smallest units of regional feeling.

In our electronic age, it is worth remembering that local feeling in this country did not first develop with the province or, earlier, the colony, both

Village, Cape Breton, 1936, A.Y. Jackson. (*McMichael Canadian Collection*)

political abstractions well removed from daily life, but with the settlement, the place where people lived and whose horizons they knew. In Newfoundland and much of Nova Scotia these settlements were outports; in New Brunswick and on Prince Edward Island they were small towns or farm communities; in Québec they were the *rangs* and parishes that were the principal units of sociability beyond the family; in Ontario they were farmhouses along concession-line roads and a local service centre; on the prairie they were rural neighbourhoods, often strengthened by ethnicity, of farm families on quarter or half sections; in British Columbia they were fishing, logging, and mining camps. From Buckler's Annapolis Valley to Hodgins' Vancouver Island, this grain abounds in Canadian letters for it was the immediate horizon of everyday experience.[10] On this scale, nature and people were known. In the older settlements of the Maritimes, the rhythms of the land, the traditional ways that earned a living, and the people who lived nearby were the context of most experience. Even today, genealogical conversation is a Maritimes staple, a reflection of communities whose people have known each other through the generations. In the

West such conversation is rarer for the local texture has been different, having less of custom and the generations and more of movement, technology, markets, and memories of other places. In either case the settlement has been a tangible world, the home of one's people and of one's peoples' people or, at the other extreme, a place to boost because it was one's point of attachment in a new land and because its fortunes were substantially one's own. Beyond the settlement concept lay more amorphous scales of attachment, not so readily experienced or accepted, usually somewhat abstract and often threatening.

Cities provided the earliest and most direct connections beyond the local settlements. At first these ties were with a European core, but after a time some cities on the Canadian islands organized internal hinterlands of considerable size. Toronto's rise to metropolitan dominance as it displaced Kingston and other lakefront towns reflected the growing integration of the Ontario peninsula. Imported goods and services passed through Toronto's warehouses, insurance brokers, and merchants to be distributed throughout the province; politicians and bankers congregated there; secondary manufacturing concentrated in Toronto and in Hamilton nearby; and many an ambitious young man, with or without his cat, would go to Toronto as Dick Whittington had once gone to London. Broadly similar developments took place elsewhere. Early in the nineteenth century, fish merchants from Poole and Dartmouth, their operations disrupted by the Napoleonic Wars, joined by general trading partnerships from Greenock and Liverpool, moved to St. John's, the city that henceforth would dominate the Newfoundland fishery and the outport economy. In the West, the first transcontinental railway would dictate urban primacy. After the C.P.R. arrived in 1883, Winnipeg dominated the eastern prairie, and on the Pacific the railway created a western port that quickly displaced Victoria and soon would service most of the isolated settlements of the British Columbian coast and interior.

Regional metropolitan dominance brought about an increased circulation of goods, people, and ideas, thereby creating a framework for the emergence of regional awareness. The settlement acquired a context, an intermediate frame of reference between its own localness and a distant outside. The city might be visited now and then; its news, and perhaps its newspapers reached far afield; and it provided a channel for contact between the various places it served. On the other hand, urban dominance could easily appear as exploitation, as grandeur bought at local cost. As lesser towns in the urban system slipped into relative stagnation, as local enterprise was eclipsed and local economies became increasingly dependent, as lines of credit extended out from the city and perquisites seemed to be bestowed on it, this feeling was almost inescapable. The perception of injustice acquired a spatial dimension from which none of the regional metropolitan centres was immune. Halifax would not be popular on Cape Breton Island, nor Saint John along the Gulf Shore.

A Haida Village, c. 1930, Emily Carr. (*McMichael Canadian Collection*)

Provincial boundaries have corresponded poorly to the hinterlands of regional cities. In the West they were arbitrary lines drawn before substantial settlement. In the East they bore some relationship to colonial territories and to prior settlements; but with the exception of a small part of the southern boundary of Québec none of these political lines had been drawn to reflect cultural regions. They were lines of cartographic or administrative convenience suggested, usually, by the configuration of the land and the border with the United States. Still, local settlements developed within a province, and this meant, as time went on, that they were exposed to the same provincial politicians and laws; to the same provincial capital; and to an identifying name. Over time such exposure would foster a sense of provincial identity.

Provincial feeling would be strongest among French-speaking Quebecers. They lived where their ancestors had lived two hundred years before Confederation; were well aware that their civil law, language, and religion were unprotected outside the province; and were confronted by an alien population whose presence only reinforced their definition of themselves. If sometimes they have been tempted by larger visions, when the chips of survival were down, Québec has stood out as the largest political unit where a people were a majority and where institutions for collective defence were at hand. Inside Québec, therefore, French-speaking sentiment readily crystallized around the province. In Newfoundland, where separate Dominion status is well remembered, where after the Irish and southern English migrations of the early nineteenth century there has been little subsequent immigration, and where the elemental context of rock, settlement, and sea is everywhere apparent, the province corresponds to a strong sense of separate identity. Much the same is true of Prince Edward Island. Elsewhere, provincial feeling has been weaker. It has been diluted in New Brunswick and Nova Scotia by ethnicity, isolation, and the tension of local metropolis-hinterland relationships; in Ontario by a tendency to equate the centre with the whole — to think of English Canada rather than Ontario; and in the West by recency. British Columbians, for example, are recent immigrants from different backgrounds who have converged on a complex physiographic realm dominated by different, rapidly-changing local economies. Inevitably, their sense of themselves as British Columbians has been inchoate — a surrounding natural magnificence, a certain frontier optimism ("western spirit" some writers called it), and a certain unconventionality in a new and relatively benign setting, but nothing like the unconscious, generational identification of Prince Edward Islanders and Newfoundlanders with their islands, or of most Québécois with Québec.

Beyond the provinces are the larger regions; Central Canada, the Maritimes, the Prairies, the West, the East, the North. Clear enough from afar — Canadians apply these names to parts of the country where they do not live — these regions are less apparent from inside. They have not been reinforced by political organization, functional economic integration, or common settlement history. Yet the names locate blocks of the country in relation to each other and are part of the country's vocabulary of spatial ambition and resentment. In the Maritimes and on the Prairies, common landscapes, common experiences with land and economy, and common perceptions of an impinging outside give these regions additional meaning for those who live there. From time to time, as during the "Maritime Rights" movement of the early 1920s, there has been talk of regional political consolidation. Overall, however, such movements have been diffused by more local frames of reference, by the lack of functional economic integration at the regional scale, and by the growing visibility of the provinces. Of the other broad regions, the West, Central Canada, and the East have only fuzzy locational meanings. Although home of a three-centuries-old, tri-racial society created by the fur trade, the North sprawls across provincial boundaries; and until very recently its small, scattered settlements have been largely unknown to each other. As identity develops in the North, it probably will have more to do with race than with "northernness."

Finally, the terms French and English Canada are clear enough when used to indicate language, but are ambiguous foci of sentiment. French Canada comprises *Canadiens* and *Acadiens* — people with the same European roots but separated by more than three hundred different North American years — and French speakers in the West, most of whom are many generations from Québec. Accents and memories differ, although outside Québec there is a common sense of being part of a French-speaking minority in Canada. English-speaking Canada is more diffuse. From its long-established centre in Ontario and Montréal, it can look relatively firm, but from anywhere else English Canada looks like a collection of different English-speaking peoples with a common unease about the centre. Because neither French nor English Canada has a political base, the terms are unrepresented abstractions in Canadian political life.

Of singular importance, is the fact that, among all these different scales of Canadian sentiment, the provinces have become increasingly dominant. In effect, they are now the repositories of the country's fragmented structure. At Confederation the local settlement was still the predominant scale of Canadian life, but settlements that once provided definition and defence for traditional ways have been overridden by modern transportation and communications. Their isolation and stability have largely gone; they survive in some urban shadow of an urbanized and industrialized society. In such a society, horizons are broadened and the local defence of custom is superseded. The state assumes a growing symbolic and practical importance. In this situation, the Canadian province, with its constitutionally defined power, its growing political history, and a location that bears some relationship to the fragmented structure of the country, replaces both the local settlements that no longer support Canadian life, and the broader but amorphous regions that have no clear political definition. The provinces are crystal clear. Their territorial boundaries are precise. For all the arguments, their powers are explicit. Their scale is supportable within modern technology. As political territories that reflect something of the country's island structure, they enormously simplify Canadian reality, and it is this simplified and thereby politically more powerful regionalism that now confronts the concept and the sentiment of Canada.

In considering Canada as a whole we must begin, as George Grant has reminded us, with the relationship between technology and empire.[11]

There can be no doubt about this connection. The political boundary with the United States grew out of the transcontinental momentum of the fur trade as contained by the transcontinental momentum of the American settlement frontier, and was sustained by railways and factories: the Maritimes and the Intercolonial; the West and the C.P.R.; factories in central Canada and markets across a continent; eventually, airplanes, a highway, and the C.B.C. To say that Canadian confederation requires this technological arsenal is to understate the case. Confederation became conceivable within an industrial technology and, in good part, is one of its by-products.

Industrial technology has the capacity to integrate the bulky products of a large area within a single market. Associated with such spatial integration are metropolitan centres where there are clear economies of agglomeration and distribution, and extensive resource and market hinterlands. The railway and the factory would impose this structure on the Canadian archipelago. A continental market (no tariffs along the United States border) would impose a north-south economic orientation

A Northern Silver Mine, 1930, Frank Carmichael. (*McMichael Canadian Collection*)

and would strengthen primary and weaken secondary industry throughout the Canadian Islands. Market areas on the scale of the individual British North American colonies (tariffs between the colonies as well as along the United States border) would thwart grander entrepreneurial ambitions, undermine the scale economies of modern technology, and, in relation to any larger market area, depress average living standards. Implicit in Confederation and explicit in the National Policy that followed, was the decision to create a Canadian market, a decision that would shape the spatial structure of the Canadian economy for the next century. Protected from the United States by tariffs, the metropolitan centre — the core — would stabilize in the St. Lawrence-Great Lakes Lowlands where most of the market was located and where there was optimum overall access to the hinterlands — the peripheries — to east and west. The rest of the country would consume the manufactures of the core, and would supply it with some raw materials. This structure could be intensified by public or private policy (for example, by changing freight rates) but, given the pattern of Canadian settlement at Confederation and the spatial character of an industrial economy, it followed in all essentials from the one decision to create a Canadian market.

Such a spatial economy would have an obvious bearing on regional sentiment. Those at the core would tend to feel expansive about the country on which their economy relied and over which their institutions exerted much influence. Those on the peripheries would be suspicious of the core, their suspicion stemming from jealousy, from a sense that local circumstances were controlled by the uninformed from afar ("Ottawa," said a mayor of Vancouver in the 1930s, "is 2500 miles from Vancouver, but Vancouver is 25,000 miles from Ottawa"), and from the conviction that, by being forced "to sell cheap and buy dear," they are subsidizing the Industrial Heartland and absorbing the cost of Confederation. What was a "National Policy" in central Canada would easily be interpreted in the Maritimes as "Upper Canadian imperialism," and in the West as the dark manipulation of James and Bay Streets.

From a Prairie vantage point, Big Interests and Special Privilege lived in the Industrial Heartland. They were assumed to control the C.P.R. and hence freight rates, grain elevators, and box cars — the lifeline to the outside. They were assumed to control the insurance companies, the banks, the grain exchanges — the financial infrastructure of the wheat economy. Such talk often filled the prairie air. In a dependent primary resource economy, class conflict assumed a clear spatial direction. Eventually collective action would build grain elevators and, when goaded by depression and drought, would create radical political movements, but in an economy focussed on a distant core, power would not be transferred easily to the periphery. Neither capital nor votes was there. The lesson of the reciprocity election of 1911, when Ontario voted for protection, would echo through the West for the next seventy years. For a time, the relationship of the Maritimes with central Canada seemed less lopsided. In 1867 the Maritime economy was still vigorous, relying on fish, forests, agriculture, and a wooden merchant fleet largely locally built, that made the new Dominion the fourth largest shipping nation in the world. From this base and with abundant coal and iron and ice-free Atlantic ports, the Intercolonial Railway and the National Policy seemed to offer the Maritimes a continental market. During the 1880s, secondary industry — cotton mills, sugar refineries, rope works, iron and steel mills — developed rapidly in Nova Scotia and New Brunswick. Even so, trade from central Canada to the Maritimes was twice that in the other direction, and by the 1890s the Maritime provinces' vulnerability to their new continental connection was becoming apparent. The underpinning of the traditional regional economy — staple production — was threatened by American tariffs, by resource depletion, and by technological change, while the new industries scattered through the local maze of the Maritimes and remote from continental markets were not able to take up the slack. The railway had not imposed a primate city on the Maritimes as it had on British Columbia. Maritime enterprises were scattered and undercapitalized, and by 1895 many had been bought out by Montréal competitors. Control of the banks shifted west as well, and workshops and craftsmen, the life of many Maritime settlements, gradually succumbed to the competition of mass-produced goods from central Canada. With the creation of the British Empire Steel Corporation in 1920, Maritimers had lost control of every significant element of their secondary industry. Symbolizing the change all too clearly, the head office of the Intercolonial, the railway that once had brought a vision of industrial growth, was subsumed within the new Canadian National Railway and moved to Toronto. Even the Acadians, usually more interested in culture than in railways, felt that "la pacte de la confederation" had been broken. More gradually than Westerners, Maritimers, too, had come to perceive that the Big Cities and Big Interests were in the growing Industrial Heartland, a perception that circumstances would not alter.[12]

Not everyone in the core would feel expansive about a larger Canada. French Canadians, who worked in the factories but did not own them, would have no entrepreneurial enthusiasm for a transcontinental country and a good deal of cultural suspicion of it. The commercial empire of the St. Lawrence was not in their hands. Many clerics denounced a Protestant world of rationalism, individualism, and materialism, and some of them tended to reach out not to a Canada of railways and progress but, in an ecclesiastical dream that returned to the continental territory of the French fur trade, to the collapse of Protestantism and triumph of Roman Catholicism that Louisiana and Québec, as Spanish and French America, embraced on the banks of the Mississippi.[13] But for the English-speaking population in Montréal and Ontario, a British Dominion from sea to sea would do two very satisfactory things simultaneously: it would reinforce their traditions and it would expand their markets. For them, the West, as it came into focus in the second half of the nineteenth century, was to be settled. Sent from Canada in 1857 to report on the prairie environment, the geologist H.Y. Hind found both a northern extension of the Great American Desert that "is permanently sterile and unfit for the abode of civilized man," and also "a broad strip of fertile country" north of the desert. It was, he concluded, "a physical reality of the highest importance to the interests of British North America that this continuous belt can be settled and cultivated from a few miles west of the Lake of the Woods to the passes of the Rocky Mountains."[14] Twenty years later, John Macoun, botany teacher from Belleville, Ontario, asserted that Hind had found a desert only because "enormous herds of buffalo" had eaten the grass. According to Macoun, much of Hind's sterile area was arable and most of the rest was good pasture. Far more than a fertile belt, there was a vast tract of land, almost 250,000 square miles in Macoun's calculation, fit for agriculture. This was what Ontario and the C.P.R. wanted to hear. There was, after all, a British garden to the west. Canada could expand from sea to sea as a British Dominion, part of a British empire and of all that implied for cultural continuity and economic growth.

For most English speakers in the core, an image of a British Canada from sea to sea seemed authentic and just. It was rooted in a Loyalist tradition; in the trans-Atlantic migrations that had settled Ontario and the Maritimes; in a widely-felt sense of belonging to a British parliamentary tradition and empire; and in unease about the United States. It defined Canadians as separate in North America, made sense of the border, and held out a transcontinental vision of the Canadian future. A few argued for an imperial federation of Canada and Britain in which, they thought, power would shift from the Mother Country to her vigorous offspring. In such a Canada the crass pursuit of gain would be checked by men of breeding, leaders of a stable, conservative society that stood apart from the acquisitive, republican rabble to the south.[15] Far from this Tory vision, but equally British in sympathy, were the many thousands who knelt at their initiation into the Orange Lodge to swear "that I will be faithful and bear true allegiance to Her Majesty Queen Victoria and to her lawful heirs and successors . . . so long as she or they shall maintain the Protestant Religion," and who went on to declare that they had never been Papists, that they would never educate their children in the Roman Catholic faith, and that they would "steadily maintain the connection between the Colonies of British America and the Mother Country, and be ever ready to resist all attempts to weaken British influence or dismember the British Empire." "So help me God," they concluded, "and keep me steadfast in this my Orangeman's obligation."[16] The Lodge consistently advocated that Newfoundland enter Confederation, and worked vigorously to establish lodges in the West. Like other British imperialists, Orangemen had found the Canadian identity; their challenge was to impose it on Canada.

Such sentiments linger to the present, but as time went on English Canadians — especially those in central Canada — began to replace them with a vision of Canada's northern character and destiny. We were not so much British as northern, a people invigorated by arctic ozone in a bracing environment that generated freedom.[17] Decadence and slavery were southern. Such views reflected Darwinian strands in late nineteenth century thought, the contemporaneous American discovery of the wilderness, and the growing urbanization of Canada; and they were enormously convenient. They differentiated Canadians from Americans while placing Canadians on the side of virtue. They incorporated all Canadians, even Catholic, French-speaking ones. Who were French Canadians, after all, but Normans, and who were Normans but Vikings? Northern credentials could not be better. And, as Canada moved towards independence from Britain, they provided an autonomous vision that for two full generations — until sometime well beyond World War II — would give many English Canadians their most explicit sense of Canada.

The discovery of "northernness" could take many forms. Artists who eventually formed the Group of Seven were inspired by the fringe of the

Eclipse Sound and Bylot Island, 1930, Lawren Harris. (*McMichael Canadian Collection*)

Canadian Shield, and would leave their Toronto jobs as commercial artists for weekends in Algonquin Park and for vacations on the north shore of Lake Superior — the land settlers refused. Bold canvases depicted the wilderness; and their painters, and eventually many of their viewers, felt that they captured something at the heart of Canada. On the canvases of A.Y. Jackson, the farm buildings of the Laurentides merged into the geometry of a larger land, while Lawren Harris reworked the rocky headlands of Lake Superior and the glaciers of Baffin Island into a transcendentalist's vision of hope. Scholars, particularly Harold Adams Innis, emphasized the distinctiveness of an economy built on the northern staples of cod and beaver. Canada had grown out of the fur trade, out of its rivers and canoe routes, out of the Shield and the larger north where the best furs were to be had. Eventually the patterns of the fur trade would be reproduced in the grain trade. City and hinterland, civilization and wilderness, northern land and nation state — here was an encompassing theory of Canada, a Laurentian interpretation.

The problem with British and Laurentian visions was their fit with reality. Many of the polyglot settlers on the prairie and almost all French Canadians, who could readily equate Britishness with conquest, would not include themselves in an imperial and essentially Protestant conception of Canada. A British Canada from sea to sea implied the recasting of French Canadians in another cultural mold, a possibility intermittently envisaged but not so easily accomplished. The Laurentian vision had been culturally neutralized by shifting the Canadian focus from the islands of settlement to the rocks between. It was a dehumanized vision, expressed in beaver, maple leaves, and vibrant wilderness canvases, not in people. Academically, it moved the fur trade and transcontinental enterprise to centre stage, and island populations to the wings. This disembodied Canada could present an illusion of unity, for the country was certainly northern, wilderness was everywhere at hand, and the fur trade had left traces across the land. But to turn a part into the whole, which in their different ways both the British and Laurentian visions attempted, was either to impose a cultural tyranny or to ignore culture altogether. The price of Canadian definition was a severely distorted understanding of Canadian reality.

The fact was that a satisfying national definition would not be found. If some islands could be defined easily enough, the archipelago could not. Definitions that satisfied here, grated there. Symbols like the Union Jack or the *Fleur-de-lis* were island rallying points and national battle cries. More neutral symbols turned to nature, and no benign Uncle Sam pervaded the national mythology. But there could be, and there was, an accumulating national experience.

Confederation had launched a transcontinental state that, over the years, has become part of the consciousness of the people who live in it. For newcomers there have been immigration laws and immigration officers to deal with, and Canadian citizenship to obtain, a tangible definition of new circumstances. For French speakers, on whose North American past Confederation was grafted, there have been, at the very least, members of parliament to send to Ottawa and Canadian laws to obey. For imperialists there was prospect of empire. People connected to Canada in innumerable ways, but connections overlapped here and there, and cumulative experience grew. Politicians have become known, and the same political arguments have been joined, however differently, across the country. Federal legislation has been lived with and federal institutions — before radio, the post office was the most ubiquitous example — have reached into settlements across the land. The World Wars generated conscription crises, but also Canadian feeling as the magnitude of the national contribution became apparent. The country, Canadians knew, had become visible internationally. However badly and with whatever biases, something of Canada has been taught in Canadian schools. A host of private institutions from churches to corporations have been organized nationally. There were hockey games and Grey Cups, occasional Olympic successes, pensions and family allowance cheques, Crown corporations and Royal Commissions. A political space has been institutionalized across the archipelago, creating a web of experiences that are part of Canadian life and, much more on some islands than others but nowhere entirely absent, a sense of being Canadian.

Such experience has developed with the influence of modern communication. There have been many media and many messages with diverging implications for the geography of regionalism. The newspaper has probably reinforced provincialism for there has been no national press, while smalltown newspapers have been victims of regional metropolitan dominance. Magazines have been more nearly national, but do not cross the language divide. Electronic communication tends to organize space linguistically. On the English-speaking islands, particularly, north-south signals contend with and often obliterate east-west ones. The National Hockey League televises its all-star game in Los Angeles, and our children soak up hillbilly America in front of the "Dukes of Hazzard." The idea of Canada is squeezed between our long-standing localism and a continentalism reinforced by the electronic media. Yet these media also report the ongoing national experience, and regulation deflects part of the barrage from the south. The islands are better known to each other than ever before; considering their location, an astonishingly small number of Canadians would contemplate a continental political realignment.

Thus, an amalgam of sentiment attaches to Canada. For some there is a lingering sense of Britain, for others a northern vision, and for many more a sense of Canada that has grown out of the continuing experience of being here. Not everyone, of course, has appreciated the experience of Canada. As the Métis lad Jules Skinner told Morag in Margaret Laurence's *The Diviners*: "The Prophet and his guys and the Indians and their guys, they'd just beat the shit out of the Mounties at someplace, and everybody was feeling pretty fine." But, for all the current acrimony, it is likely that among English Canadians, national feeling outweighs provincial — except perhaps in Newfoundland. Western separatism still runs into a western wall of Canadian feeling. Among French speakers, Canada is approached more cautiously although, paradoxically, the viability of French outside Québec now depends on the federal defence of bilingualism. Provincial sentiment is predominant among French speakers in Québec but, as polls and a referendum have recently shown, Canadian sentiment is not absent. Of course, any concept of Canada must reckon with the profound structural localism of which this country is composed, with the regional tensions generated by a national economy, and with the provinces' growing visibility.

ON THE FUTURE OF CANADA

Given the location of the Canadian archipelago, the manner of its settlement, and the tensions inherent in a core-periphery economy, the overwhelmingly remarkable Canadian quality has been stability. On the face of it, Elisée Reclus should have been right. The country seems conceptually impossible. It is not remarkable that there have been and continue to be sharp regional tensions. They are built into the country's structure. It is remarkable that they have not been even stronger, that Canada has held together while generating a considerable reservoir of transcontinental feeling.

Such stability has much to do with isolation. Differences have not been perceived or, at least, have not had to be dealt with day by day because they were regionally compartmentalized. French speakers were conveniently tucked away on long-lot farms, in working-class Montréal, or in the Clay Belt. They did not obtrude nationally. Newfoundlanders kept to their fishing or went to Boston. This stability also has a good deal to do with standard of living. For all the trauma of relocation, most immigrants were better off here than in their homelands, and this bred satisfaction not only with personal circumstances but also with a new country. In the long run, economic oppression has been tempered by a resource base relatively abundant for a small population; by a productive industrial system and its associated institutions of working-class defence; and by the fact that Canada has managed to achieve a fair measure of regional and social redistribution of wealth — less than desirable but enough to diffuse a great deal of tension. Programmes for radical change encounter these muting realities. There is probably a relationship, too, between the rather quiet, undefined nature of Canadian nationalism and national stability. Clear cultural symbols are rallying points, but they are also targets. Canada is sustained by nationalism based on experience, and weakened by nationalism based on cultural belief. In sum, the country has been stable because most Canadians are not deeply angered by Canada as it is. Admitting the Conquest, the orange-green head-knocking in the Ottawa Valley, the Métis rebellions, the rabid anti-orientalism in British Columbia, and much raw exploitation in sweat shop and industrial camp, the country does not have a history of violence. Cultural conflict has been diffused by distance and ignorance and by the failure of national definition. Economic conflict has been diffused by relatively high standards of living, and by a tradition of government that has mitigated some of the more blatant inequities of unregulated industrial capitalism. Canada does not live with a festering memory of overwhelming injustice, as does Ireland, but rather with the all-too-smug satisfaction that accompanies the feeling that life here is fairly good. This satisfaction is widespread even in Québec, where the long pre-eminence of an English-speaking minority is fuel for anger; and it may even be fairly common among the Native people who would seem to be the clearest cultural victims of the events of the last several centuries.

This said, there is now more regional tension in Canada than there was a short generation ago. Even after the referendum in Québec, Canadians live with the possibility that Canada may disintegrate and, for all the fissionable tendencies built into the structure of this country, this is a relatively new apprehension. Earlier generations of Canadians wondered whether Canada had an identity apart from Britain or could withstand the continental pressure of the United States. We wonder whether the Canadian archipelago will hold together. Canada is a remarkably stable country, but it is not as stable as before. This change has only superficially to do with the combative personalities of our politicians. It reflects the challenge raised by the *Parti Québécois,* but that challenge itself is part of a structural change in the relationship between the various parts of this country. Heightened internal tension is the almost inevitable corollary of the growing role and visibility of the provinces and of provincial governments, especially when accompanied by the first major challenge in a century to the spatial character of the Canadian economy.

The consolidation of island sentiment in the provinces has taken place while governments were assuming a larger role in Canadian life and while the evolution of the Canadian economy was changing the significance of some of the terms of the British North America Act. In an age of water power and steam, control of natural resources did not mean what it does today. Provincial governments have been assuming a growing role in the economy, and the province a growing role in Canadian feeling. A host of activities that once were organized at many regional scales are now organized provincially. At the same time federal power has also increased, as Ottawa, too, has expanded its services and economic presence. In short, provincial and federal governments have grown simultaneously at the expense of a multitude of other levels of Canadian interaction. This is a recipe for conflict. It reduces a whole gamut of

St. Joseph, 1922, Albert H. Robinson. (*McMichael Canadian Collection*)

different relationships on different scales to a polarized struggle between the provinces and the federal government, and between the politically-defined hinterlands and the national heartland.

The effects of such reorganization are felt across the country, but are seen most clearly in Québec. There, the cultural defence of a French-speaking, Roman Catholic people once was mounted by the local community, by a variety of nationalistic societies, and, above all, by the Roman Catholic Church. For some, the clearest defence of culture was a rural life and a high birth rate, and from this perspective the provincial government could do little more than encourage colonization. The province was only one of the scales of cultural defence that ranged from the family and parish to French-speaking, Roman Catholic North America. The Church was not the church of Quebecers but of Roman Catholics, and it could never be altogether comfortable within provincial boundaries. In recent years, the defence of culture has shifted towards government. The effects are obvious. One level of cultural defence is mounted by a provincial government that is prepared, as the Roman

Catholic Church could never be, to write-off people outside Québec. The other level is mounted federally, and would provide more protection for French speakers outside Québec and less for those within. Two modes of cultural defence — both with long pedigrees — become the focus of rivalry between the provinces and the federal government. Elsewhere the issues have been different, having more to do with economics than culture, but across the country the tendency towards polarization has been essentially the same.

While this has been going on, the location of oil and gas fields, the spiralling world price of these commodities, and the rapidly growing economic importance of the Pacific basin have challenged the spatial economy that Canadians assumed for almost a hundred years. Core and peripheries seem to have come unstuck. Suddenly there is oil on the Grand Banks. In the West, the tar sands may have oil for two centuries, and there are already massive coal deals with the Japanese and the highest residential land prices in the country. In the centre, there is the strong possibility of de-industrialization in the face of competition from the very Japanese products that increasingly will be manufactured from western Canadian resources. Whether the Canadian spatial economy will be turned inside out is another question; in a country like Canada it takes only the possibility of spatial change to raise a clamour as the ghosts of the last hundred years of spatial conflict reappear.

Seen from the centre, the old peripheries of wheat farmers and fishermen would now seem to be infested with oil sheiks who wield the ominous power to turn off the tap. Seen from the peripheries, the centre is finally tasting some of its own medicine. Their turn would seem to have come — as long as the natural momentum of different circumstances is left to run its course. But if political power is in the centre, as the last federal election again demonstrated, and if the British North America Act leaves ample opportunity for federal influence on resource policy, then the economic advantages of the peripheries can be compromised by the protective instincts of the centre. Hence the Western provinces' and Newfoundland's paranoia over resource control. Hence the struggle between Alberta and Ottawa over the price of oil. As long as the federal government is elected in central Canada, as given the distribution of population it is likely to be, conflict over the spatial economy is immediately translated into conflict between the provincial hinterlands and the centre.

And so, in the foreseeable future Canadians will probably have to bear with a fractious, tense Canada but, hopefully, a Canada that we will appreciate for what it is. Three simple observations, if we can keep them in mind, would seem to bode well for our inevitably somewhat cantankerous future. First, however much we may recognize our debt to institutions and traditions from across the Atlantic, we are no longer British or French. A social change that is as old as Canadian settlement took care of that. But if North Americans, we are not Americans. The circumstances of Canadian and American life have always been different, and different societies are the result. We will not easily define this cultural divide between adjacent, New World peoples, but we experience it, and surely we can relax with that. Finally, we would do well to remember that in a society of islands the majority can be culturally destructive. For this reason minorities may need protection that majorities do not. This applies particularly to French-speaking Canadians, without whom this country would never have been, and who, through more than two hundred years, have held out against an anglicizing continent. The same could be said of the Native people. This country works when it displays understanding and humanity, and is not bottled up by dogma. "I never connected it with that," Jules told Morag, (in *The Diviners*), "because my dad's version was a whole lot different."

NOTES

1. A version of this essay was originally given as a Walter L. Gordon lecture at McGill University on March 17, 1981, and is published here with the kind permission of the Walter L. Gordon Lecture Series and the Canadian Studies Foundation.
2. Fernand Braudel, *The Mediterranean and the Mediterranean World in the Age of Philip II,* trans. Siân Reynolds (New York: Harper and Row, 1972).
3. Some of these points are discussed more fully in R. Cole Harris, "The Extension of France into Rural Canada," in *European Settlement and Development in North America: Essays on Geographical Change in Honour and Memory of Andrew Hill Clark,* ed. J.R. Gibson (Toronto: University of Toronto Press, 1978), pp. 27-45.
4. Frederick Jackson Turner, "The Significance of the Frontier in American History," first published in 1893 and reprinted in F.J. Turner, *The Frontier in American History* (New York: 1920).
5. A.-N. Lalonde, "L'intelligentsia de Québec et la migration des canadiens français vers l'ouest canadien, 1870-1930," *Revue d'histoire de l'amérique française,* 33 (1979), pp. 163-85.
6. See, for example, Henry Nash Smith, *Virgin Land: The American West as Symbol and Myth* (Cambridge, Mass.: Harvard University Press, 1950); and Leo Marx, *The Machine in the Garden: Technology and the Pastoral Ideal in America* (New York: Oxford University Press, 1964).
7. This point is made by Northrop Frye in a splendid essay that concludes *Literary History of Canada: Canadian Literature in English,* ed. C.F. Klinck (Toronto: University of Toronto Press, 1965), p. 826.
8. I have developed this argument in "The Simplification of Europe Overseas," *Annals of the Association of American Geographers,* 67 (1977), pp. 469-83.
9. Karl Polanyi, *The Great Transformation* (New York: Farrar and Rinehart, 1944).
10. Ernest Buckler, *The Mountain and the Valley* (New York: Holt, 1952); and Jack Hodgins, *The Invention of the World* (Toronto: Macmillan, 1977).
11. George Grant, "In Defense of North America," in *idem, Technology and Empire: Perspectives on North America* (Toronto: House of Anansi, 1969).

12. Ernest R. Forbes, *The Maritime Rights Movement, 1919-1927: A Study in Canadian Regionalism* (Montréal: McGill-Queen's University Press, 1979), especially chap. 2.
13. Christian Morissonneau, *La Terre Promise: le mythe du nord québécois* (Montréal: Hurtubise, 1978), especially chaps. 2 and 3.
14. The most relevant of Hind's and Macoun's writing, including the parts quoted here, are in John Warkentin, *The Western Interior of Canada: A Record of Geographical Discovery*, The Carleton Library, No. 15 (Toronto: McClelland and Stewart, 1964).
15. Carl Berger, *A Sense of Power: Studies in the Ideas of Canadian Imperialism, 1867-1914* (Toronto: University of Toronto Press, 1970).
16. Quoted in C.J. Houston and W.J. Smyth, *The Sash Canada Wore: A Historical Geography of the Orange Order in Canada* (Toronto: University of Toronto Press, 1980), p. 120.
17. Carl Berger, "The True North Strong and Free," in *Nationalism in Canada*, ed. Peter H. Russell (Toronto: McGraw-Hill, 1966), pp. 3-26.

14

Canada in Heartland-Hinterland Perspective

L.D. McCann

All countries have heartland and hinterland areas. Compare Megalopolis to the Great Plains in the United States; the Buenos Aires core to the Pampas periphery in Argentina; or southern Ontario to the Canadian Shield in Canada. Manufacturing and financial industries, large cities in densely settled areas, high personal wealth, and political power are characteristics of the heartland regions. Hinterlands differ in their geographic make-up: staple industries, populations scattered across vast areas, and limited political strength are common features.

Why is this so? Core and periphery, metropolis and hinterland, centre and margin, heartland and hinterland: these terms characterize not just geographies, but also society, politics, culture, and fundamentally — the economy. As sociologist Edward Shils argues, all societies have a centre and a periphery comprising elite and marginal classes, separated by status and power, even by custom and deference.[1] These social elements are thus associated with particular spatial contexts. People with status and power usually reside in core areas, perhaps in the metropolis itself. The metropolis certainly has its marginal classes, but the attributes of marginality — unemployment, low incomes, a weak political voice — are found more frequently in the hinterland. On the cultural and political level, it is characteristic that the centre creates, the periphery borrows; the centre determines policy, the periphery adopts policy. Finally, spatial distinctions are most obvious in the economic sphere. A diversified economy spread throughout an integrated urban system contrasts to the resource production of isolated, single-enterprise communities. Most particularly, the innovative power of the metropolis contrasts to the dependency of a resource town. As is true of the social order, political life, and culture, economic strength belongs to the centre. Concentration and profit are the centre's distinguishing traits; fragmentation and financial plight signal the periphery.

The reality, of course, is never so clearly defined. There are gradations of class from elite to marginal even in peripheral areas, just as peripheral areas can invent cultural traditions that the centre absorbs.[2] Sometimes a national political leader will emerge in a hinterland region. Similarly, a hinterland economy, buoyed by the development of staple industries that spawn linked manufacturing and financial services, may rise to claim heartland status. New geographies *can* be created. No system, least of all the spatial pattern of heartland and hinterland, is intractable. The product of these contexts and patterns, and of their changes, makes up the complex regional geography of a country.

With the structure of heartland and hinterland so pervasive in Canada, the heartland-hinterland paradigm is particularly useful for an interpretation of Canada's regional geography. Using this framework, the authors in this book have written about the economic and social development of Canada's regions, about the ways in which these regions were peopled and settled, and about urbanization and the rise of cities. They have also emphasized themes of regional interaction — the migration of capital and labour, the movement of staple commodities and manufactured goods, the transmission of social values and cultural features, the deployment of political policy. These processes of the heartland-hinterland model have shaped regional character in fundamental ways.

The book is therefore a synthesis that analyzes the shaping forces and evolution of Canada's regional geography. In each essay there are both fresh discoveries and familiar statements. Together the essays contribute to an interpretation of Canada that is both holistic and integrative. The structure of heartland and hinterland is an unmistakable, indeed enduring, feature of Canada's regional geography.

CANADA AND THE WORLD-SYSTEM

Canada is a developed country in the world-system, but its position in this system is paradoxical. It is neither metropolis nor hinterland. It fits more appropriately as a country of the semi-periphery, one of "the intermediate zones about the central pivot" — the heart of the world-economy.[3] As Robert Galois and Alan Mabin point out, Canada has many characteristics of a metropolitan economy: relative affluence, an international outreach in political matters, multinational corporations, and one of the highest standards of living in the world. But, paradoxically, Canada mirrors countries of the world periphery by its heavy reliance on foreign trade, the degree of foreign control of investment and technology, and the predominance of staple commodities in the mix of exports.

As an intermediate zone about a central pivot, Canada has close ties with the United States. Canada's regional geography has been shaped by

Canada and the world-system: Through its many ports, such as Montréal, Canada remains heavily dependent on exporting staple commodities to world markets. (*Gouvernement de Québec, Direction des Communications*)

relations with its southern neighbour. The impress of American capital, technology, entrepreneurship — even culture — is everywhere in evidence. American foreign and trade policies influence regional development: tariffs on British Columbia's red cedar shake and shingle industry force shutdowns of Lower Mainland mills; demands for natural gas alternatively spur or retard Alberta's economy; consolidation of factories in the manufacturing belt across Ohio, Illinois, and Michigan prompt closure of branch plants in adjoining Ontario; and fish and potato production in the Maritimes are reduced by American import restrictions. The result is a constantly changing geography of Canada. But true to Canada's paradoxical character, Canadian real estate companies are reshaping the business cores of such major American cities as New York, Houston, and Chicago. Similarly, the million or so ex-Canadians living in Los Angeles contribute to the cultural fabric of the United States.

There are shifting horizons for Canada in the ever-changing world-system as well. Links with Pacific Rim countries, notably Japan, suggest an option for future trade diversification. A more flexible immigration policy is redefining the cultural mosaic of Canada's largest cities. But in the final analysis, one pertinent fact is clear: Canada's regional geography, particularly its regional economic structure and associated settlement features, is shaped by the external forces of the world-system. Consider the declining single-industry communities of the Québec-Labrador iron mining belt,[4] or the demise of oil and natural gas exploration in Alberta in the face of falling world oil prices. For these regions in the late 1980s, dusk is on the horizon. Dawn awaits renewed demands for iron ore and petroleum products by the world's industrial core regions.

THE HEARTLAND REGIONS

Few students of Canada's geography would have difficulty identifying Canada's Industrial Heartland in southern Ontario and southern Québec. The rise to prominence of this region is well-outlined by Donald Kerr; its contemporary character is described by Maurice Yeates. Building on initial advantages of geographical situation centred on the Great Lakes-St. Lawrence River system, as well as a relatively rich resource base and access to markets for both staple commodities and manufactured goods, the Industrial Heartland became Canada's "central pivot" in the Confederation era. Cumulative forces added strength to strength: a large regional market, control of western Canadian development, strong financial institutions, and political dominance. By the mid-twentieth century — at the close of the *longue durée* — the region had changed from being a periphery on the margin of the British North Atlantic system, to become both the Canadian heartland and a hinterland for United States investment.[5] No region better symbolizes Canada's paradoxical position as both metropolis and hinterland.

Industrialization and urbanization spurred this course of development, creating the metropolitan centres of Montréal and Toronto and a surrounding system of integrated urban places — defined by Yeates as the Windsor-Québec City Axis. This is a richly textured landscape, at once united by the similarity of its economic structure and by its economic linkages, but also broken by a cultural divide separating Canada's "two solitudes." As Eric Waddell argues, nowhere in Canada are the tensions of regionalism at times more heightened.

Does economic unity mean that we are justified in defining the Industrial Heartland as a singular region? Viewed from the periphery and using economic criteria, there *seems* to be unity in the economic landscape. Maritimers abhor the collective strength of central Canadian cities because secondary manufacturing industries in New Brunswick and Nova Scotia towns must compete with their central Canadian counterparts. Western Canadians share similar sentiments. It is easy, when viewed from afar, to identify the centre of the Canadian space economy as rooted across the central Canadian landscape. Increasingly, however, all

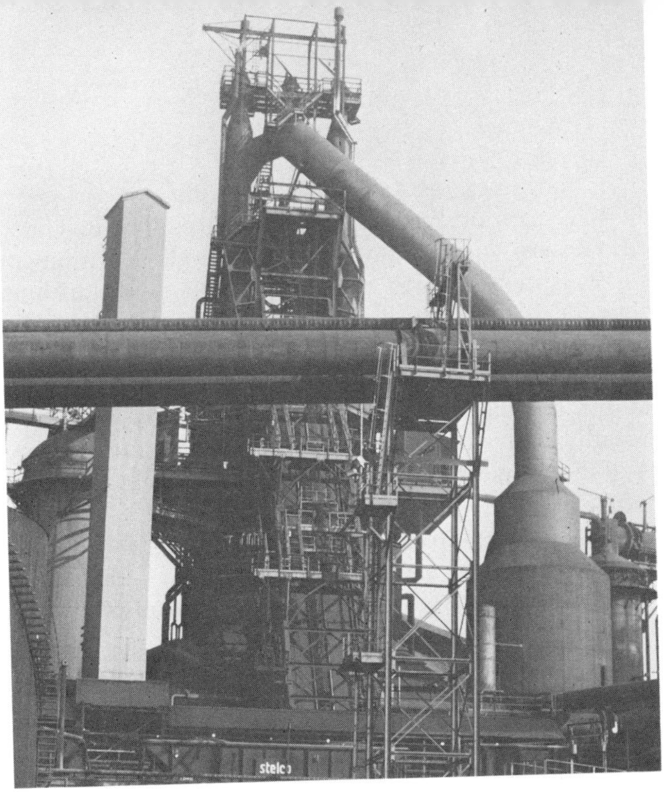

Manufacturing in the Industrial Heartland: Canada's steel industry, focussed on Hamilton, is employing the latest technologies to compete, quite successfully, in the world steel market. (*Larry McCann*)

Canadians are recognizing that Toronto is *the* national metropolis, not Montréal; and that southern Ontario, not southern Québec, is experiencing in the mid-1980s an economic growth spurt. These facts, when joined with measures of cultural differentiation such as language, religion, and ethnicity, suggest that the Industrial Heartland is a misconception. Rather, they support the idea that southern Ontario and southern Québec should stand as separate regions. Certainly the regional geography of the Industrial Heartland is in a state of transition. If the trend towards economic bifurcation continues, at what point will the prevailing view of a singular region, a unified Industrial Heartland, disappear? There is indeed much to consider and debate in our interpretation of Canada's geography.

THE HINTERLAND REGIONS

Canada's regional geography has been shaped by centuries o economic and social development. Different people have settled ac Canada at different times in response to specific economic opportu Canadian regions are, as a consequence, distinct in characte distinctiveness is particularly true of the hinterland regions.

The Maritimes, as Graeme Wynn illustrates, bear the imprint of nearly 400 years of French and British settlement. Unlike the recently settled Western Interior, there is no polyglot of immigrants here. The Maritimes is more akin to British Columbia, but Maritimers stem mostly from a rural Irish, Scottish, and English background, whereas the similar mix of British Columbians is urban-industrial in character. People of the Maritimes experienced a degree of prosperity during the era of mercantile capitalism, but the region's response to the new industrialism of the late nineteenth century did not result in sustained growth, nor in benefits for many of the people. The loss of manufacturing firms still overshadows the economy of many regional towns and cities. However, the staple industries — fish, pulp and paper, some minerals — continue to sustain other places and a rural way of life for many Maritimers. Such patterns reinforce the long-standing spatial fragmentation of the region, which has been further entrenched by the urbanization process. This is one of the least urbanized regions of Canada. Halifax is the major urban centre, but it anchors a poorly defined pattern of core and periphery. There is no strongly integrated settlement system like that of Alberta in the Maritimes.

Residences and factory in Saint John, New Brunswick: The Irving Oil Refinery across Courtney Bay is the largest in eastern Canada. But despite some manufacturing, the standard of living and quality of life in Saint John is less than that in the industrial cities of southern Ontario. (*Larry McCann*)

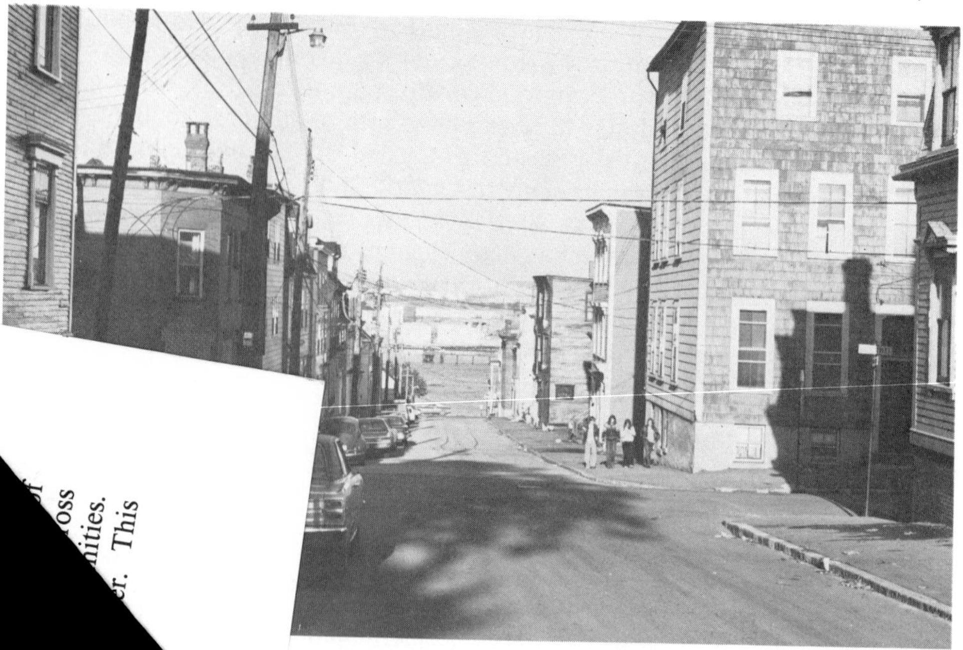

This weakness contributes as much as other factors — a limited resource endowment, physical fragmentation, small local markets, and long distances to external customers — to the region's marginal position within the Canadian economy. Regional disparities are relative measures, however, especially when the situation of the Maritimes is compared to the plight of many Third World countries.

Newfoundland, of all the Canadian regions, is closest in character to the Maritimes. Geographical and economic marginality, reliance on the sea for livelihood, and eighteenth and nineteenth century settlement by the Irish, Scots, and English are features that link the regions. Newfoundland is a distinctive place, however, set apart from the Maritimes in the North Atlantic realm by its political history, its almost singular dependence on the cod fishery, and its inability to create sustained growth and development. Marginality and dependency are quite pronounced in Newfoundland. The collapse of world oil prices in the mid-1980s was a telling blow against provincial aspirations for greater equality in the Canadian economy. In response to a difficult environment, Newfoundlanders have relied on traditional ways — shifting work from sea to land-based activities in different seasons, for example — to sustain a hinterland existence. They have also tried new techniques to develop tourism and expand the use of existing resources. They are breaking away from the accommodation — the acceptance of the *status quo* — which seems to have marked previous generations.[6] Development efforts have been partially successful, for the economy has become stronger since the region entered Confederation.

What roles have time, place, and circumstance played? Would the regions of the western and northern peripheries be different in character if they had been settled *before* the Maritimes and Newfoundland? It seems entirely likely that if the Maritimes had been developed late in the nineteenth century when different technologies prevailed and when knowledge of environmental limitations was more secure, then the region would bear a quite different character. The Maritimes would still be a hinterland, but one less populated and therefore potentially better off, where the sense of individualism that now prevails, particularly in one's response to work and making-do, would surely be subsumed by large-scale business enterprise, that is, by corporatism. It is unlikely, for example, that most of New Brunswick's forests would be owned as they are by thousands of small woodlot owners, or that Nova Scotia's inshore fishery would comprise similar thousands.

A basis of comparison is the regional geographic character of Britis Columbia. British Columbia was established in an era of indus capitalism. A geography was created, dominated by the patte metropolis and hinterland in microcosm, in which entrepreneurs u latest technologies and abundant capital exploited a variety of and sought the greatest productivity from labour. In this corporatism prevails over individualism. As John Bradbury further argues, the pace of development and therefore the degree of regional prosperity depended ultimately on the integration of British Columbia within the modern world-economy. Of all the Canadian regions, British Columbia has the ability to succeed on its own, for its markets are overwhelmingly external and its dependence on transfer payments from the federal government is slight. Viewed in this way, the factors of time, place, and circumstance are significant forces in the heartland-hinterland process shaping Canada's regional geography.

The case of Alberta points to another aspect of the heartland-hinterland model, that is, the ability of a region or province to challenge its traditional role in the Canadian space economy. Peter Smith uses the concept of the settlement system to examine the evolving character of Alberta's regional geography. Not only does this concept demonstrate how Alberta has become differentiated from Saskatchewan and Manitoba within the Western Interior's physical mold, but it also gives credence to the theoretical premise that regional economic viability is coincidental with the development of a core-periphery settlement system. The Edmonton-Calgary corridor has most of the traits and therefore the status of a mature and diversified core region: innovative entrepreneurship, access to capital and technology, and a skilled labour force. But the economic base of Alberta's drive to maturity is still vulnerable to the uncertainty of all those regions dependent upon natural resources. The decline in world oil prices in the mid-1980s has forced Albertans to consider more carefully how regional development can take place. The centre of the Canadian economy is unlikely to shift west from central Canada as some commentators once posited,[7] but neither is it likely that Alberta will revert to its once more limited hinterland status. In a post-industrial age, Alberta has developed a solid base of technological and business acumen evident in Canada and throughout the world-economy, particularly in areas where the management of energy resources is central to social and economic development.

It is the degree of cohesive internal development — that is, the presence of an integrated settlement system organized around the
principles of the heartland-hinterland process — that sets Alberta apart
katchewan and Manitoba. All three provinces share certain
istics: the environment of prairie, parkland, and
n of the Great Plains and the Shield; an initial
for organizing the space economy; and a mixture of
es such as Russia, Poland, Germany, Holland,
l France. Traditional geographical interpretations of
d these and other similarities as reasons enough to
egion — the Western Interior. Many Canadians share
Certainly it has historical merit — "the idea of the
Owran has argued in *Promise of Eden*.[8] Brent Barr and

John Lehr take this regional unity to its logical conclusion through their interpretation of the region's spatial and historical development. They nevertheless concede that in the future, when the heartland-hinterland process further unfolds, provincial autonomy may be a more pervasive factor in the regionalization process.

Clearly, as this book has demonstrated, provinces are assuming greater control over larger territorial blocks and are becoming meaningful regions in an interpretation of Canada's geography. This is particularly true when assessing the identity and the consciousness of regional societies. For some, western Canadian alienation is being replaced by the unique claims of Alberta, Saskatchewan, and Manitoba. However, particularly when the historical evolution of different parts of Canada is emphasized, larger territorial blocks such as the Western Interior and the Maritimes have merit for geographical interpretation.

Nowhere in Canada is the hinterland experience more pronounced than in the Canadian Shield and in the North. The metropolitan influence here is profound. The tapping of resource wealth across the northern reaches of Québec, Ontario, or Manitoba in the Canadian Shield is overwhelmingly dependent upon external demands emanating from the United States and countries in Europe. Development is typically handled through Canadian subsidiaries of multinationals located in Toronto and Montréal. This is not to deny the presence of world-scale Canadian corporations such as INCO, Noranda, or Canadian Pacific, all of which play an active role in exploiting the Shield's mineral and forest wealth. It illustrates instead the overriding trait of this region — separation from the core of the Canadian space economy and unremitting dependence on the broader world-economy. As Iain Wallace has revealed, the result is a region unified by its physical environment, resource-based economy, and single-enterprise settlement features.

The North shares many of these traits, but in the late 1980s it appears that the relationship between the federal government and the Yukon and the Northwest Territories is the critical shaping force in the heartland-hinterland process. True, the North has always provided Canadians with resources and the potential for economic salvation. The world oil crisis of the 1970s, for example, sparked an awareness of the rich Arctic oil and gas reserves, which in turn stimulated considerable debate about the future development of this vast and little-understood region. Canadians became aware as never before of the impact wrought by external forces upon the culture and livelihood of the region's Inuit and Dene peoples. In one land, two ways of life are on a collision course, and it is the responsibility of th federal government to mediate the opposing views towards change. Peter Usher argues, to the North lies not only Canada's economic de but also our country's moral and spiritual renewal. It is worth s that the context for interpreting the future course of northern dev falls clearly within the realm of the heartland-hinterland pa

CONCLUSION

There are other paradigms, of course, that could be used to interpret Canada's regional geography. One based on a rich description of places could tell us a great deal about the vast differences that exist within the country. Such an approach might lack the analytical rigour and integrative force of the heartland-hinterland model, but regardless of the approach geographers decide to use, there is need for on-going debate and discussion about the changing geographic character of Canada. This is the challenge for future generations of Canadian geographers. How can regional geography as a discipline offer as clear a statement as possible about the character of Canada? Those who contribute something towards this synthesis will have met the challenge and will have enhanced our understanding of Canada. The same challenge has guided the writers of this book.

NOTES

1. Edward Shils, *Center and Periphery: Essays in Macrosociology* (Chicago: University of Chicago Press, 1975), esp. pp. 17-47.
2. Eric Hobsbawm and Terrence Ranger, eds., *The Invention of Tradition* (Cambridge: Cambridge University Press, 1983) pp. 1-14; and Edward Shils, *Tradition* (Chicago: University of Chicago Press, 1981).
3. Fernand Braudel, *Afterthoughts on Material Civilization and Capitalism,* trans. P.M. Ranom (Baltimore: The Johns Hopkins University Press, 1977), p. 82.
4. John H. Bradbury, "Declining Single-Industry Communities in Québec-Labrador, 1979-1983," *Journal of Canadian Studies,* 19 (1984), 125-139.
5. For a discussion of the differences in meaning of periphery and frontier in the context of Old and New World settlement, see Bernard Bailyn, "New England and a Wider World," in *Seventeenth Century New England,* eds. David Hall and David Grayson Allan (Boston: The Colonial Society of Massachusetts, 1984), pp. 323-28.
6. The notion of accommodation is the central thesis explaining poverty and underdevelopment in John Kenneth Galbraith, *The Nature of Mass Poverty* (Cambridge, Mass.: Harvard University Press, 1979), esp. pp. 61-91.

...example, John Richards and Larry Pratt, *Prairie Capitalism: Power and Influence* ... (Toronto: McClelland and Stewart, 1979).

...*den: The Canadian Expansionist Movement and the Idea of* ... nto: University of Toronto Press, 1980).

Index

D

E

F

J

K

L

N

S

T

Additional Photo Credits

Page 2: Energy, Mines and Resources Canada
Page 38: Environment Canada, Atmospheric Environment Service
Page 70: Public Archives of Canada/C2642
Page 108: Ministry of Industry and Tourism
Page 148: Larry McCann
Page 246: Paul J. Dwyer
Page 286: Public Archives of Canada/C-21677
Page 350: Environment Canada, Parks
Page 442: Environment Canada, Parks
Page 482: National Film Board Canada
Page 532: McMichael Canadian Collection
Page 560: Environment Canada, Parks